JOHN LOCKE

AND THE EIGHTEENTH-CENTURY DIVINES

JOHN LOCKE
AND THE EIGHTEENTH-CENTURY DIVINES

Alan P. F. Sell

Wipf & Stock
PUBLISHERS
Eugene, Oregon

Wipf and Stock Publishers
199 W 8th Ave, Suite 3
Eugene, OR 97401

John Locke and the Eighteenth-Century Divines
By Sell, Alan P. F.

ISBN: 1-59752-871-4
Publication date 8/11/2006
Previously published by University of Wales Press, 1997

This edition of John Lock and the Eighteenth-Century Divines
is published by arrangement with University of Wales Press.

Another for
Karen

Contents

Preface		ix
1.	Introduction: An Intellectual Minefield	1
2.	Ideas, Knowledge and Truth	16
3.	Reason, Revelation, Faith and Scripture	62
4.	Morality and Liberty	109
5.	Toleration and Government	151
6.	Christian Doctrine	185
7.	Conclusion	268
Notes		278
Bibliography		368
Index of Persons		431
Select Index of Subjects		441

I very much question, whether any thing can give bad Men greater advantage in their endeavouring to promote *Scepticism*, and in their opposing and talking against the *Articles of the Christian Faith*, than Christians, and especially Divines, or Clergymens detracting any way from *the Credibility of Divine Testimony*, and making an Ostentation of knowing Things which God hath placed perfectly out of Humane reach; And treating others scurrilously, who are more modest, and more inquisitive then themselves, because they will not acknowledge that the Truth of certain Propositions can be demonstrated, meerly because they say, They can, tho' they will not be prevailed with, to be at pains to demonstrate their Truth.

(Samuel Bold, *Some Considerations On the Principal Objections and Arguments ... against Mr. Lock's Essay of Human Understanding*, 1699, 60)

Preface

This book is the immediate successor to my *Philosophical Idealism and Christian Belief*, though its theme concerns an earlier period. While each book may stand as a study in its own right, together they represent soundings taken in two prominent areas of Enlightenment and post-Enlightenment thought with a view to raising the question, How far do or can these modes of thought serve as adequate vehicles for the articulation of Christian truth? If it should transpire that Locke-influenced eighteenth-century thought is not entirely satisfactory in this regard, and having already shown that post-Hegelian idealism fails us at certain points, I shall, in a projected third volume, inquire what other methodological options there might be as Christianity prepares to greet its third millennium.

In the introductory chapter I discuss my objectives, and the pitfalls confronting me, in writing this book. It remains now to thank those bodies and individuals who have rendered willing assistance in a variety of ways. I began seriously to gather materials for this study on assuming the Chair of Christian Thought at the University of Calgary at the beginning of 1988. I was awarded a starter grant by the University's Research Services, and I am most grateful to Dr Emlyn Jessop and his colleagues for their good offices in this matter. I then successfully competed for a three-year grant from the Social Sciences and Humanities Research Council of Canada. Without the support of this body I should not have been able to undertake the extensive travel needed in order to see scarce books and pamphlets *in situ.* I warmly thank the Council's officers and the members of the relevant committee for their confidence and generosity.

I am much indebted to the librarians and staffs of the following institutions: The American Antiquarian Society, Worcester, Massachussetts; The American Philosophical Society, Philadelphia; Andover Newton Theological School; Newton Centre, Massachussetts; Boston College, Massachussetts; Bristol Baptist College; The British Library, London; The Bodleian Library, Oxford; The Department of History, Presbyterian Church USA, Philadelphia; Friends' Library, London; Lancaster Theological Seminary, Lancaster, Pennsylvania; Harris Manchester College, Oxford; The National Library of Wales; Princeton Theological Seminary; The United Theological College, Aberystwyth; and the following universities: Aberdeen; Birmingham; Boston; Calgary; Harvard; London; McGill, Montreal; Manchester (The John Rylands Library); Toronto; St Paul's Ottawa; and Wales at Aberystwyth and Lampeter.

In February 1995 I presented a version of part of chapter III as a lecture to the University of Calgary Eighteenth-Century Studies Group. This was a most happy return visit to an organization of which I was a founder-member. The responses to my paper were stimulating, and I look back with much pleasure upon my association with such former colleagues as Shadia Drury (Political Science), Glen Campbell (French), Robert Carnie (English), John Stephen Martin (English), Hugo Meynell and Terence Penelhum (Religious Studies) and Martin Staum (History). In 1996 I presented an extract from chapter 6 at Vanderbilt University Divinity School. I am grateful to Professor Dale A. Johnson for his kind invitation and hospitality. I learned much from Professor J. van den Berg, who warmly welcomed me to his home in Leiden, and the unfailing encouragement of Geoffrey F. Nuttall and John Heywood Thomas over many years has been a constant spur.

As before, and with some trepidation, I invited Dr D. O. Thomas to bring his formidable knowledge of eighteenth-century thought to bear upon my complete manuscript, and once again he has more than fulfilled the obligations of friendship. In particular, he has stimulated me with wise comments and paid close editorial attention to my text. I cordially thank him.

I should like to thank Ned Thomas, Director of the University of Wales Press, for his willingness to publish another of my books. It has been a pleasure to work once again with Ceinwen Jones, than whom no editor could be more obliging or efficient. I am most grateful to all of the Press's staff who have been, or will be, associated with this venture.

John Locke and the eighteenth-century divines have taken me away from home on numerous occasions, and turned me into a hermit on my return. Through it all Karen, my wife, has offered every support and maintained her customary faintly amused tolerance. She knows that I could not do the work without her, but I place the fact on record all the same.

Alan P. F. Sell
Aberystwyth

1

Introduction: An Intellectual Minefield

On the death of the high Calvinist Baptist John Gill, to whose name the adjective 'redoubtable' is frequently attached, Benjamin Francis composed 'An Elegy.' This literary gem informs us that the 'transparent breast' of 'heav'n-taught Gill' shone 'With light divine, imbib'd from the sole fount/Of evangelic and celestial truth ...'[1] Whatever else may remain obscure at the end of our study, it will at least become clear that the light derived from the sole fount was, in the eighteenth century (and not only then, of course) refracted in such varied ways as to yield not only a Gill, but also his opponents, among them the evangelical Arminian John Wesley, and the Arian Presbyterian John Taylor. In fact, none of them read off the truth from the biblical text neat; in their several ways they engaged in acts of interpretation, and in these they were influenced by the rationalism of their age: a rationalism which took deductive-dogmatic form in Gill, a more sensationalist form in Wesley, and a more rationalist form in Taylor.[2] All of which sufficed to place the question of the relative authority of Scripture, reason and revelation firmly among the agenda of the eighteenth century.

John Taylor will serve to introduce a further theme which will pervade this book: that concerning permissible degrees of tolerance in society and Church alike. What are the appropriate checks and balances in thought, doctrine, morals and government, against licence leading respectively to solipsism, heresy, subjectivism, relativism and anarchy? In 1742 Taylor reflected upon the period prior to the Glorious Revolution of 1688 – a period characterized, he thought, by intellectual absurdities branded 'mysteries', and by the popery of Rome which was succeeded by the Protestant popery of theological systems. Then, in 1688,

> LIBERTY at the Revolution, O bright, auspicious Day! reared up her heavenly Form, and smiled upon our happy Land. Delivered from the fears of Tyranny and Persecution, Men began freely to use their Understandings; the Scriptures were examined with more Attention and Care, and their true Sense, setting aside human Comments, and especially the Jargon and Sophistry of School-Divinity, was sought after.[3]

The accession of William and Mary was followed, in 1689, by the so-called Toleration Act – 'so-called' because the term 'toleration' appears neither in its official title, nor anywhere in its text. The Act accorded freedom of worship to orthodox Protestant Dissenters (not to Unitarians, Roman Catholics and Jews), though it did this not by rescinding earlier adverse legislation, but by declaring that penalties would no longer be applied to the newly favoured groups.[4] In the wake of the Act, men like Taylor began to claim not only their freedom to worship, but their freedom to think. They set their faces against authoritarianisms, whether theological or ecclesiastical, and were equally opposed to the vagaries of mysticism and the excitements of 'enthusiasm' (which Samuel Johnson defined as 'a vain confidence of divine favour or communication') in matters religious. They remembered only too well the apocalyptic zeal leading to civil unrest which, in the seventeenth century, had ensued from claims to privileged access to the divine mind. If the priest no longer had proprietary rights over biblical interpretation, and if the magistrate could no longer enforce religious conformity, it was all the more important that Locke's ideal of the reasonableness of Christianity (however construed) be upheld.[5] If, in his celebrated paper of 1860 Mark Pattison went too far in claiming that 'The title of Locke's treatise, *The Reasonableness of Christianity,* may be said to have been the solitary thesis of Christian theology in England for the greater part of a century',[6] he was not, in view of the pre-1688 situation, altogether without justification.

The reiteration of the year 1688 prompts me to point out that I have a slightly elongated eighteenth century in mind in this book. Locke's major works were first published from 1689 onwards, and reaction to them was swift. It would have been foolish to exclude these early responses simply because they appeared during the decade prior to the beginning of the eighteenth century. Similarly, although the Priestley Riots of 1791 suggest a possible terminus for our reflections, I shall on occasion stray into the nineteenth century, because some who began to comment upon Locke's work during our century did not cease from their labours with its turn. It would have been an artificial and arbitrary decision to arrest them before they had laid down their pens.

But how far did Locke influence the eighteenth-century divines? It is a major part of our purpose to address this difficult question. That Locke's influence was considerable is a commonplace of eighteenth-century scholarship, and it is not difficult to produce a random list of reputable authors who, over the past century, have joined in this chorus. Thus, Alexander Gordon delares that Locke's 'simplification of the Christian basis ... was accepted with avidity by liberal Dissenters; its central thesis retained with them, up to a very recent period, the position of an undisputed axiom.'[7] The evidence for this observation is not supplied. According to E. C. Moore, 'In the closing years of the eighteenth century in England ... Men sought to combine faith in revealed religion with the empirical philosophy of Locke.'[8] How did they do this, and with what degree of success? And what is the analysis of 'empirical'? These questions are not pursued. Again, we are expected simply to take the word of G. W. Richards that 'In the formative period of life in America, Locke was probably the strongest single intellectual influence in politics, philosophy, and even theology.'[9] In view of the selective way in which many divines responded to Locke, we cannot but modify Henry F. May's claim that 'Though at first many English divines were shocked by Locke's theories ... by mid [eighteenth] century the clergy had accepted his teachings as cordially as they had Newton's.'[10] Finally, when M. R. Watts declares that 'In so far as Dissenters were now looking to Locke rather than to Calvin for intellectual support for their faith, in proportion to their readiness to seek inspiration from the spirit of reason rather than the Spirit of God, their zeal flagged and their congregations dwindled',[11] we cannot but suspect the fallacy of the false cause – or at least that of incomplete enumeration.[12]

It is not difficult to see why there has been a certain reluctance on the part of scholars to pursue the question of Locke's influence in detail. First, there is the practical difficulty posed by the vast amount of relevant materials, many of which are scarce and widely dispersed. Whole books have been written on (a) the provenance of Locke's ideas; (b) the philosophical criticism of Locke's arguments; and (c) the intellectual indebtedness and subsequent influence of numerous eighteenth-century divines taken individually. Work continues in all of these areas. I have attempted to take stock of as many of these contributions as was feasible, and I shall allude to them as appropriate. But my Ockham's razor throughout has been the discussion of Locke by contemporary and successor divines. This has implications not only for my text, but also for my bibliography. The emphasis in the latter is upon post-1688 divines who in books, sermons and pamphlets discussed or at least referred to Locke by name. I estimate that the listed works represent about one-fifth only of the printed materials I have combed in pursuit of Locke's 'influence'. I may perhaps forestall any undue sympathy which might otherwise flow in my direction on account of the hours spent in wasted effort by confessing that when there are so many items to be analysed and discussed there is a certain comfort in drawing blanks. Concerning secondary literature there are bibliographical constraints too. Simply to mention the names of Berkeley, Butler, Jonathan Edwards, Wesley, Price, Priestley – not to mention Locke himself and dozens of other divines, many of them prominent – is to conjure up a vision of vast bodies of literature. A process of selection has been inevitable, and I have included only works referred to in my text and notes, together with others which, out of hundreds of volumes, I have found most helpful. I have also found it necessary to impose a geographical limitation upon my endeavours. While by no means denying that Locke was studied and discussed in Holland, France, Germany, Poland, Hungary and elsewhere,[13] my focus is upon the British religious and intellectual context, though with sidelong glances at America as appropriate.

Secondly, there is the slipperiness of the term 'influence'. In the texts we find everything from deferential passing references to 'the great Mr. Locke' (with or without an 'e'), through detailed discussion of aspects of his thought, to rampant plagiarism. We also find Locke-like ideas which may or may not have come from Locke himself. For example, a divine could sound Locke-like on reason or toleration, but actually have been influenced by Richard Baxter and John Owen respectively.[14] Again, the presence of Locke's works in a divine's library in no way guarantees that the books were approved of, or even read, by their owner;[15] and the fact that Locke's works appear on the curriculum of Dissenting academies[16] similarly provides no guarantee that those who studied him understood him, or agreed with him, or even remembered him once their examinations were passed. Indeed, where academic curricula are concerned we need to exercise special care in view of the widespread belief that Locke found a readier home among the Dissenting academies than elsewhere. This is broadly true, but the picture is complicated. True, the grand jury of Middlesex banned *The Reasonableness of Christianity* in 1697, claiming that it was an anti-trinitarian work. Certainly the Oxford University authorities, many of whom were politically opposed to the erstwhile exile, proscribed the reading of Locke's *Essay* in 1703; but this did not mean that it went entirely unread amidst the dreaming spires; while at Cambridge the writings of Locke, Newton and Samuel Clarke became for a number of years the staple intellectual fare of ordinands and others alike.[17] Again, Locke's political writings made an early impact in Dublin.[18] In America, the Congregationalist-turned-Anglican, Samuel Johnson, when a student at Yale, was cautioned not to read '*Descartes, Boyle, Locke* and *Newton*' on the ground that the new philosophy 'would soon bring in a new divinity and corrupt the pure religion of the country'[19] – though when he did turn to Locke he was converted to his epistemology, and during his tutorship at Yale he introduced Locke's works into the library there. Among the English Dissenters Locke's reception was equally mixed. The Independent tutor at Newington Green, Thomas Rowe, pioneered the study of Locke among his students, one of whom was the Presbyterian Henry Grove, subsequently tutor at Taunton, where Locke was read, though not formally studied.[20] Among other Independents who made considerable reference to Locke in their lectures were the tutors John Jennings of Kibworth/Hinckley, in his *Logica in usum Juventutis Academicae* (1721), and his pupil Philip Doddridge, who opened his academy at Market Harborough in 1729, removing with it to

Northampton in December of that year, and whose *An Abstract of the References in our Lectures of LOGICK* contains numerous references to Locke.[21] The Presbyterian Noah Jones, confessed that his Locke studies under the Independent Samuel Thomas at Carmarthen had taught him to think freely.[22] Presbyterian tutors who made use of Locke included Joshua Oldfield of Coventry and London, Thomas Dixon of Whitehaven,[23] Samuel Jones of Tewkesbury (whose most famous philosopher-student was Joseph Butler) and Ebenezer Latham of Findern.[24] On the other hand, the staunch Calvinist Independent Abraham Taylor delivered his *Lectures on Natural and Revealed Theology* (1739) without referring to Locke, and William Parry, though a pupil of Doddridge, gave his *Lectures on the Being and Natural Perfection of God* at Wymondley between 1799 and 1818 without discussing Locke at all: this notwithstanding the fact that his lectures were based upon Doddridge's.[25] For his part John Newton, the evangelical Anglican 'midwife' of the Independent academy at Newport Pagnell – a product of the Revival – proscribed philosophy altogether in favour of more godly pursuits.[26]

Yet again, when Locke is discussed by name we need to ensure that in that nicknaming age he is being handled fairly. But this, in turn, presupposes that we have as good an idea of his real intentions as possible – and those intentions are the subject of lively debate to this day. Was he an empiricist? A deist? A Socinian? Was he even a Christian? To the high Calvinist Anglican, John Edwards, Locke, in his *The Reasonableness of Christianity,* set out to frame a new Christianity, and in so doing he 'took Hobbes' Leviathan for the New Testament, and the Philosopher of Malmesbury for our Saviour and the Apostles'.[27] Some present-day scholars likewise question Locke's Christian credentials, arguing that Locke was more than a Socinian, he was an epistemological sceptic;[28] or at least that 'Whatever his day-to-day beliefs, Locke was anti-Christian in the impact his work made on eighteenth-century thought.'[29] We shall meet such views again as we proceed, and we shall need to weigh them against others which suggest that 'Locke was essentially and always a deeply religious man';[30] that his 'primary commitment was to certain principles of the Christian faith';[31] that he was 'deeply committed to the Christian faith which he understood in moral and experiential more than in dogmatic terms but which he believed rested on historic revelation';[32] and that 'Locke is, first and last, a *Christian* philosopher. We everywhere mistake him if we do not discern that this is so.'[33] As we go we shall do well to avoid stereotypes and to seek evidence at every point. This is not the least important in connection with the labelling of Locke as an empiricist. Owing not a little to the 'cops and robbers' nature of many university philosophy syllabi, wherein opposing camps are set up, so that a year of rationalists (Descartes, Spinoza, Leibniz) is followed by a year of empiricists (Locke, Berkeley, Hume), even the well-versed may overlook the fact that, as Gilbert Ryle pointed out, 'most of the doctrines which an Empiricist (as ordinarily defined) should hold are strenuously denied by Locke.'[34]

Caution is required in other directions, too. In attempting to discern the impact of Locke's thought upon later divines, we must be alive to the fact that some of the latter who drew most deeply from Locke, had no compunction about leaving behind what they did not find serviceable: for example, his view, inherited from Calvinism, that all government, civil as well as ecclesiastical, is under the law of God – a position which did not appeal to those who came to advocate a purely secular society. In this connection Herbert D. Foster's remark is to the point:

> Locke cites authorities sparingly; but in his *Two Treatises on Government,* his citations are almost entirely Calvinistic: Scripture occurs seventy-nine times; seven Calvinists (Hooker, Bilson, James I, Milton, Hunton, Ainsworth, Selden); one ex-Calvinist, the Dutch Remonstrant Grotius; and only one reference uninfected by Calvinism, the Scottish Catholic Barclay.[35]

This is not to say that Locke himself affirmed every Calvinist or Puritan doctrine. Again, although indebted to the Puritan understanding of total depravity,[36] and aware of biblical and other claims concerning the noetic effects of sin, he did not, for example, make capital out of the latter after the fashion of Robert Traill, who argued that it is not surprising that 'Gospel Truth makes little progress in the world,' for 'Natural reason is very fertile in its objections and cavils against the doctrine of the grace of God. And especially when this corrupt reason is polished by learning and strong natural parts.'[37] Yet again, and despite Locke's generally anti-scholastic mood, he could not altogether shrug off his scholastic inheritance, as witness, for example, the rationalism of Book IV of his *Essay concerning Human Understanding*, which includes, among other things, Locke's cosmological argument for God's existence.

Yet another complication resides in the possibility that on occasion Locke diplomatically toned down his real meaning on contentious points in order to retain his audience – even his freedom. Certainly the charge that Locke did not always fully disclose his hand is venerable indeed. Thomas Becconsall, for example, levelled it in 1698: 'I must confess, the *Author of the Essay of Humane Understanding*, discovers such a *reserved* Way of Writing in all his Performances, that, I'm perswaded, he *Designs* more than he as yet thinks it seasonable to *Express.*'[38] A clear example of this tactic is the excision of Book I of the *Essay*, with its attack upon innate ideas, from the *Abregé* in LeClerc's *Bibliothèque Universelle* (1688). Although Locke's Arminian friend, Limborch, had written against innate ideas in his *Theologia Christiana ad praxin pietatis ac promotionem pacis unice directa* (Amsterdam, 1686), Locke's similar views, if promulgated by one being given sanctuary by hated Arminians, would probably have aroused the ire of Dutch Cartesian theologians to fever pitch, and thereby have threatened the safety of Locke and his abettors.[39] Moreover, as Norman Fiering has pointed out, Locke found it in his interest to suppress the influence upon him not only of scholastic and Cartesian philosophy, but also of Malebranche, the French Roman Catholic whose views of English heretics were less than flattering, and who was perceived by many as legitimating enthusiasm.[40] For all that, such present-day scholars as Bluhm, Wintfeld and Teger, who have suggested that Locke deliberately set out to argue cases – for the existence of God, for example – which he knew would not succeed, so that those in the know would see the point, do strain our credulity a little. What is clear is that Locke's thought was ever on the move – hence the drafts and revisions of his more important works. It is equally clear that he is not offering a rounded system of thought; hence his habit of not spelling out his presuppositions on every occasion – a habit which has tempted some modern critics to overlook balancing considerations when expounding his arguments.

It may perhaps be desirable at this point briefly to indicate my own position, reached after an attempt to read and weigh all the relevant primary and secondary texts I have been able to find. It seems to me that Locke wished to discover both what we may reasonably hold, and what it is tolerable for us to hold in society. Indeed, on his own admission, he and five or six friends, meeting in his chambers during the winter of 1670–71, wished to determine the principles of morality and revealed religion.[41] It soon became evident, however, that first they must embark upon the epistemological quest in order to determine which objects the understanding was competent to deal with.[42] It is important to understand the quest of Locke and his friends not as a timid seeking of reassurance lest religion and morality should fail, but rather as a quest prompted by the danger of claiming to know more than could properly be known by the human understanding. Locke lamented the way in which 'Men, extending their Enquiries beyond their Capacities,' could not fail to 'raise Questions, and multiply Disputes, which never coming to any clear Resolution, are proper only to continue and increase their Doubts, and to confirm them at last in perfect Scepticism'.[43] Although in the event Locke could not bring himself to produce a thoroughly worked-out system of ethics (though he was urged to do so), his interest lay above all in discovering how best we might live. But this discovery was one which each of us must make for ourselves. As he wrote to Samuel Bold, rector of Steeple, Dorset, one of his defenders against the doughty John Edwards, 'how a rational Man, that should enquire and know for himself, can content himself with a Faith or Religion taken upon trust, or with such a servile Submission of his Understanding, as to admit all and nothing else but what Fashion makes passable amongst some Men, is to me astonishing.'[44] This is the later Locke, by now convinced that religious toleration (at least for some) is legitimate, and is indeed required if a person is duly to exercise reason in face of untoward authorities whether in the guise of tradition or current fashion. In the preface to *A Second Vindication of The Reasonableness of Christianity* (1697), Locke incorporated a further complimentary letter to Bold. He here explains that he resorted directly and seriously to Scripture in order to master the concept of faith as being that which justifies. He hopes that his results will be of use 'especially to those, who thought either that there was no need of revelation at all, or that the revelation of our Saviour required the belief of such articles for salvation, which the settled notions, and their way of reasoning in some, and want of understanding in others, made impossible to them. Upon these two topics the objections seemed to turn, which were with most assurance made by deists against christianity; but against christianity misunderstood.'[45] I shall suggest that Locke's motivation is fundamentally religious, and that we must take with the utmost seriousness his conviction that 'all Religion and genuine Morality depend' upon the truth that 'the invisible Things of GOD are clearly seen from the Creation of the World, being understood by the Things that are made, even his Eternal Power, and God-head.'[46] Like D. G. James before him, John Dunn has correctly pointed to 'the intimate dependence of an extremely high proportion of Locke's arguments for their very intelligibility, let alone plausibility, on a series of theological commitments';[47] and Nicholas Wolterstorff has properly reminded us that 'a striking feature of Locke's thought is that religious considerations enter into all parts of his thought ...'[48] In Locke's case it certainly seems that Santayana was right: besides Locke's fundamental naturalism, there was 'his Christian faith, which was not only confident and sincere, but prompted him at times to high speculation'. However, when Santayana proceeds to say that 'if we consider Locke's philosophical position in the abstract, his Christianity almost disappears,'[49] he begs the question of the viability of so considering it. It is my conclusion that Locke's presuppositions, though not everywhere stated, are intimately bound up with his Christian faith, and that they are never far below the surface of his writing. Accordingly, to leave them on one side is not to take Locke's philosophy whole. As Locke himself succinctly put it, 'The taking away of God, though but even in thought, dissolves all.'[50]

My objectives in undertaking this intricate task are twofold. First, as already announced, I wish to ascertain the 'influence' of John Locke upon the eighteenth-century divines. Because of the slipperiness of the term 'influence', and the difficulties inherent in any attempt to isolate and attribute strands of thought from a general intellectual climate, I shall for the most part concentrate upon texts in which Locke is at least mentioned by name, and preferably discussed in some detail. I shall not confine my attention to formal philosophical or theological treatises, because in any attempt to gauge the reception of a thinker, the response of the hinterland people cannot be overlooked. For this reason tracts, sermons, memoirs and other materials will be perused. We shall then be in a better position to see how Locke was received – by which I mean both 'What of Locke was received (and left behind)?' and 'How was what was received interpreted by subsequent writers?'[51]

Secondly, I examine this major theme (namely, Locke and his 'influence') which permeates what has somewhat inappropriately been branded the 'Age of Reason' (much of which was characterised rather by 'enthusiasm,' and, to a lesser degree by the mysticism of a William Law or of the pietistic Ephrata community of Pennsylvania),[52] with a view to articulating some questions posed by Locke's intellectual legacy which need to be addressed by any who are concerned with Christian apologetic method. I wish this reference to 'articulating some questions' to be strictly construed. I shall neither plunder the eighteenth-century divines for useful content which might be employed in the construction of an apologetic for the early years of Christianity's third millennium, nor shall I set out to demonstrate that the divines of the Enlightenment have nothing to offer in this respect. For example, although we shall see that in the eighteenth century the cosmological argument for God's existence was in the ascendant and was appealed to in a wide variety of literature ranging from the strictly philosophical to personal confessions of faith delivered by Dissenting ordinands, I am not here concerned to inquire what may be salvaged from this argument (though as it happens I suspect that any rounded Christian apologetic will need somehow to accommodate what might loosely be termed the religious-cosmological intuition to which expression is given in Psalm 19:1, 'The heavens tell out the glory of God, heaven's vault makes known his handiwork,' which words inspired Joseph Addison's majestic lines,

> The spacious firmament on high,
> With all the blue ethereal sky,
> And spangled heavens, a shining frame,
> Their great Original proclaim ...).[53]

Similarly, I shall not here inquire how far the views of Locke and his successors on the evidential value of miracles may nowadays assist us – and survive Hume's critique. Rather, my investigation will show that such questions as the place of reason, faith and experience in religion, the viability of natural theology, and the problem of authority are thrust to the fore when Locke's influence upon the eighteenth-century divines is scrutinized. I shall not claim that these questions arise exclusively from the study of *Locke's* influence upon his theologico-philosophical successors; my point is the more modest (and accurate) one that as a matter of fact these questions are posed when Locke's intellectual legacy is under review. It will emerge that the supremely important 'cliff-hanger' question bequeathed by Locke to Christian apologetics – the question to be resumed in the final volume of this trilogy – is, 'Can the epistemological starting-point be redeemed for Christian apologetic use, or is it not viable at all – in which event, is there a more satisfactory point of departure, or combination of approaches, which will permit Christians to give a reasoned testimony to and defence of the faith over against those who in our time declare that the apologetic enterprise is doomed?' Especially with reference to this question, this book, though able to stand on its own as a study of Locke's influence on the eighteenth-century divines, is to be set alongside my *Philosophical Idealism and Christian Belief* (1995). Taken together, the two works represent soundings in the history of modern Christian thought which suggest that in different ways both incautiously adopted Lockean and post-Hegelian immanentist models are less than fully efficient as starting-points for the articulation and defence of a Christian view of the world. The question, 'What other way is there?' is thus clamantly posed. I hope to address this question in my third volume.

I shall now cease from the articulation of aspirations and explanations and, as a prelude to an examination of Lockean themes of interest to eighteenth-century divines, and by way of alerting us to some of the tendencies of thought for which we must be prepared, I shall offer a brief sketch of the prevailing intellectual climate in which the latter worked and to which they contributed.

Since ideas know no geographical or temporal boundaries, we shall not be surprised to find that in the eighteenth century the legacy of Puritanism is still strong in some quarters. Tempering

Calvinism, both theologically and attitudinally, we find continuing Latitudinarianism and Arminianism, the latter increasingly tending in an Arian direction, the former often, and generally scurrilously, being branded 'Socinian', notwithstanding the opposition to Socinianism of the Latitudinarians Stillingfleet and Tillotson. As already noted, Locke's roots in Calvinism are important, but so too is his appreciation of *The Practice of Christian Graces, or the Whole Duty of Man* (1659) by the Arminian Richard Allestree, his friendship with a number of prominent Latitudinarians, and his appreciation of the sermons of Whichcote, Tillotson and Barrow.[54]

In the wake of Hobbesian mechanism, some feared that the emphasis upon the human being's capacity for making might so exalt persons as to threaten God's position as creator.[55] With this, in a number of writers, went a deep-seated fear of atheism. This tendency was opposed by the Cambridge Platonists (or Plotinists), and John Norris propagated a spiritualized Cartesianism in opposition to what he was convinced were the atheistic implications of Locke's anti-innate-ideas epistemology.[56] For his part, John Edwards, though equally opposed to Locke, found no solace in Descartes, whom he brands mechanistic: '*Des Cartes's* denial of *Final Causes* falls to the Ground ... Mr. *Boyl* hath observed well ... that this *French Wit,* by his throwing aside *Final Causes,* hath thereby deprived his Disciples of the chief End of Natural Philosophy, which is to set forth the Praises of God, and to admire his Goodness and Wisdom in the Fabrick of the Universe.'[57] Not indeed that Edwards was averse to spirits as such. On the contrary, he elsewhere argues that the fashionable denial of the existence of witches and demons was a step on the way to the denial of the existence of the Deity.[58] William Carroll, in more than one tract, found Locke to be an atheist after the style of Spinoza: 'This *Atheistical Shopkeeper* is the First that ever reduced *Atheism* into a *System,* and Mr. *Locke* is the Second; with this Difference, that the latter has only copied the former as to the main, *Spinoza* having, as he imagined, established the Existence of his One single Substance and cut off the Means of perceiving or proving, that there are more than One ...'[59]

Following the publication of John Toland's *Christianity Not Mysterious* in 1696, a running battle with deism commenced;

there were increasingly pointed discussions between Trinitarians and Arians (in which the question of subscription was also – even, on occasion, pre-eminently, at issue); there was the Puritan-influenced idealism of Jonathan Edwards of New England; the psychological idealism of Berkeley and his American disciple, Samuel Johnson; the alleged scepticism of Hume and its response in the Scottish common-sense philosophy of Reid and others; and Priestley's monism and more overt unitarianism. As a foil to all of this we find the Evangelical Revival in its Calvinist and Arminian varieties, and lingering antinomianism.[60]

In 1744, the very year in which, as we saw at the outset, John Taylor reflected upon the freedoms which had accrued from the Glorious Revolution, Gilbert Tennent, that revivalist 'son of thunder,'[61] whose theology and manner could scarcely be at a further remove from his English Presbyterian (albeit Arian) counterpart, appraised a number of the available intellectual options thus:

> *Reason* [cannot] be our *Rule,* as the *Deists* and *Socinians* dream; because it is obscure and imperfect, (I Cor. 2:14). And the absurd and contrary Sentiments of those who had no other Guide, is a sufficient Confirmation of this. Besides, some Things in Religion are Sublime and Mysterious, and so transcend the reach of Reason; yet they are not contrary to it: But tho' on the one Hand, we disclaim the *Socinian* Opinion, in making Reason the suppream Rule of Faith and Practice; yet on the other we equally detest the Foolry of *Enthusiasts,* who reject it altogether in the Affairs of Religion. Surely Religion *is a reasonable service;* Reason may and ought to be humbly us'd, in order to understand the meaning of the Rule God has given us. The *Quakers* notion, of the *Spirit* without the Word to be our Rule is a dangerous *ignis fatuus,* which may lead men any where. Neither is the pretended *New Nature* and *Love* of the *Antinomians* and *Moravians,* while they reject the Blessed Law of God and slight the Old Testament, a whit safer Guide then *will with the Wisp!* Christ *has not come to destroy the Law* as these Men pretend; *neither does Faith make void the Law!* [62]

Towards the end of our period Joseph Barber, tutor at the evangelical Independent academy at Hoxton from 1778 to 1791, expressed his view that a number of the intellectual bogeymen to whom I have already referred were not yet dormant: 'We live in shaking times, wherein many are departing from the faith; some professors running into arminianism, some into arianism or socinianism, and others into antinomianism; yea, some have gone into very wild enthusiastic notions, and others into avowed infidelity.'[63] It is not impossible that, humanly speaking, the intellectual health of Christianity in every age turns upon the adjudicating of the concerns of the 'conservative' and the 'liberal'.

2

Ideas, Knowledge and Truth

> It is an established Opinion amongst some Men, That there are in the Understanding certain *innate Principles*; some primary Notions, κοιναὶ ἔννοιαι, as it were stamped upon the Mind of Man, which the Soul receives in its very first Being; and brings into the World with it.[1]

In a number of other places in the *Essay*,[2] as well as in his early *Essays on the Law of Nature*,[3] Locke adversely criticizes this view – a view which, as John Yolton has amply demonstrated, was widely held by writers in seventeenth-century England,[4] and which, as Locke surely knew, was seriously entertained by the more Cartesian theologians of Holland, as well as by Herbert of Cherbury, his one named opponent. Locke declares,

> It would be sufficient to convince unprejudiced Readers of the falseness of this Supposition, if I should only shew ... how Men, barely by the Use of their natural Faculties, may attain to all the Knowledge they have, without the help of any innate Impressions; and may arrive at Certainty, without any such Original Notions or Principles.[5]

He does more than this, however, arguing that even if there were universal agreement on the principles deemed to be innate, we could not infer their innateness from the fact of that agreement; but as it happens there is no such common consent.

Locke makes it clear that the innate principles he rejects are those moral or practical principles which are alleged to instruct us as to our actions – within which are included the ideas of God, good and evil, and 'those magnified Principles of Demonstration, *Whatsoever is, is*; and *'Tis impossible for the same thing to be, and not to be* ...'[6] He does not deny that nature has bestowed upon people in every society the innate 'desire of Happiness, and an aversion to Misery ... But this makes nothing for innate Characters on the Mind, which are to be the Principles of Knowledge, regulating our Practice.'[7] On the contrary, if these 'were left to their full swing, they would carry Men to the over-turning of all Morality'.[8]

It is not germane to our purpose to delay over the ambiguous ways in which Locke uses the term 'idea'. Gilbert Ryle has discussed some of the main uses to which Locke puts 'this Pandora's box of a word'.[9] It will suffice for our present purpose to note Locke's guiding definition, which he shares with Malebranche and a number of others, namely, that 'idea' being

> that Term, which, I think, serves best to stand for whatsoever is the Object of the Understanding when a Man thinks, I have used it to express whatever is meant by *Phantasm, Notion, Species,* or whatever it is, which the Mind can be employ'd about in thinking.[10]

Why was Locke, who by no means denied that our minds can grasp religious and moral truths, so intent upon repudiating the view that we have innate knowledge of such truths? The answer is twofold. First, Locke was motivated by hostility to authoritarianisms (whether the Roman magisterium or the enthusiast's 'immediate Communication of the Divine Spirit')[11] which not only rested upon innate principles, but, capitalizing upon the intellectual laziness of others, specified them and demanded allegiance to them (though we must not overlook his own appeals to biblical authority at crucial points):

> When Men have found some general Propositions that could not be doubted of, as soon as understood, it was, I know, *a short and easy way to conclude them innate.* This being once received, it eased the lazy from the pains of search, and stopp'd the enquiry of the doubtful, concerning all that was once stiled innate: and it was of no small advantage to those who affected to be Masters and Teachers, to make this the Principle of *Principles,* That Principles must not be questioned: For having once established this Tenet, That there are innate Principles, it put their Followers upon a necessity of receiving some Doctrines as such; which was to take them off from the use of their own Reason and Judgment, and put them upon believing and taking them upon trust, without farther examination: In which posture of blind Credulity, they might be more easily governed by, and made useful to some sort of Men, who had the skill and office to principle and guide them.[12]

Secondly and positively, Locke genuinely believed that what mattered in knowledge and certainty was established upon surer foundations than those provided by innate principles: 'I perswade my self, at least, that the way I have pursued, being conformable to Truth, lays those foundations surer.'[13]

According to one tradition of Locke commentary, Locke went overboard in his attack upon innate principles: he was attacking a view to which nobody – least of all Descartes – had ever subscribed. Edward Caird, for example, declares that 'Des Cartes did not hold that doctrine in the coarse form in which it was attributed to him by Locke.'[14] Caird's older contemporary, A. Campbell Fraser, concurred.[15] Indeed, this criticism was made by William King as early as 1692,[16] and by Henry Lee in his *Anti-Scepticism* (1702).[17] Certainly Lord Herbert is the only author whom Locke cites on the matter – and he finds him wanting.[18] But John Yolton's case that the notion of innate ideas was much in the air through sermons, tracts and pamphlets is unanswerable; and that Locke was fully aware of this is clear from his rejoinder to the attacks upon him, as we shall see. Moreover, even in its weaker form, namely, that the innate idea of God, for example, was not fully developed until sense experience prompted reflection upon it, the doctrine was under increasing strain, for as John Spurr has pointed out, 'if our knowledge of God is innate but unknown until we reflect upon the experience of our senses, how can it be separated from our senses and be shown to be innate?'[19] Samuel Parker was but one of a number who, before Locke, queried the notion of innateness – in his case *contra* the Cambridge Platonists.[20]

Turning now to Locke's critics on this matter, we must understand that to them the dismissal of innate principles was far more than an epistemological quibble. In the absence of innate principles, held to be divinely imprinted on the soul, they could envisage only atheism, immorality, Hobbes-inspired materialism, and hence the shaking of prevailing social values. It is not without significance that, as Yolton has remarked, 'The principles which are listed as innate are always formulations of the existing values of society.'[21] While some, like Richard Burthogge, were intent upon challenging the epistemology on which those values were based, others, among them Locke's friend the historian James Tyrrell, were puzzled rather than fully persuaded by Locke's position. Thus, in his *Organum Vetus & Novum* (1678) Burthogge argues that knowledge is derived from sense experience, and sardonically declares that upholders of innate principles have no need to observe the world and experience: all they need to do is to contemplate their own minds and spin out 'all their notions of their own Bowels'. Such contemplation should have made them 'the wisest and most fruitful of men,' but, for all their subtlety and acuteness, their discourses are 'empty and barren'.[22] Tyrrell, however, confessed the puzzlement which he and others of Locke's sympathizers felt when, by denying innate principles, Locke appeared to rest morality on nothing more than custom and the praise and blame apportioned in the light of it.[23]

Among those who took Locke to task in the 1690s were writers of very different temperaments. John Norris and Locke held each other in mutual esteem, though the latter felt that the former's confidence in Malebranche's philosophy was misplaced.[24] Norris does not so much set out to defend innate principles as such, as to insist that Locke's sensationalism deflects our understanding of the source of knowledge from its true locus in the mind of God, to the phenomenal world. 'I,' says Norris, 'account for the Mode of *Human Understanding* after a very different way, namely, by the Presentialness of the Divine λόγος or Ideal World to our Souls, wherein we see and perceive all things.'[25] If ideas were derived from sensible objects, he argues, they would be material objects, since from the material comes only matter. In fact, ideas are spiritual realities. This is not to deny that God may exhibit some particular truths of the ideal world earlier, more clearly, and more constantly to the soul than others, and this might be 'something of near Analogy with' the 'grey-headed venerable Doctrin of Innate or Common Principles'.[26]

James Lowde is blunter. We gain knowledge from two sources: natural notions which are imprinted upon the soul, and revelation. God's ability to imprint such notions on our minds cannot reasonably be denied, he declares. He does grant, however, that education and the outward senses may excite these ideas – he is not a recollectionist after the Platonist fashion;[27] but Locke's argument against innate ideas on the ground that children and fools do not seem to have them wrongly presupposes that

> a thing could not be thus natural or innate to the Soul, unless it did so immediately and necessarily stare Children and Fools in the Face; that they must necessarily assent thereto, even before, by the common course of nature, they are capable of assenting to anything.

In fact defenders of innate ideas have no difficulty in making them depend 'upon the Concurrence of several other circumstances, in order to the Souls exerting of 'em'.[28] If innate ideas are denied we have no bulwark against scepticism and atheism: 'Next to a Sceptick, who grants no Principles at all, it is the greatest difficulty to convince an Atheist, who asserts such absurd and unreasonable ones.'[29]

John Edwards, the Calvinist divine who is more inclined than most to look for doctrinal skeletons in Locke's cupboard, makes a point of observing in his *The Socinian Creed* (1697) that Socinus had denied innate knowledge. He also argues that the 'natural impressions [which are] in all men's minds are the foundation of religion, and the standard of truth as well as of morality.'[30] Edwards elsewhere repeats his point that human beings, made in God's image, have in their minds fixed and indelible notions of truth and falsehood; these ideas originate in God's mind and have been copied out in us by him.[31] These notions include such epistemological ideas as that 'What is not cannot be known,' and such moral ideas as the certainty of rewards and punishments. Edwards grants that we do not have immediate use of the notions, 'But it is ridiculous to say that they are not there because they are not actually exerted.'[32]

Moral considerations are to the fore in Thomas Burnet's critique of Locke. He contends that in opposing innate ideas, Locke unintentionally builds upon principles which undermine morality, revealed religion and belief in the immortality of the soul. He cannot agree that the five senses yield the distinction between good and evil, virtue and vice, nor from the senses can it be concluded that moral distinctions are relative to the pleasure or pain or convenience or inconvenience which result from actions. He grants that Locke holds that moral good and evil are so antecedently to all human laws, and because of the divine law. 'But what is the Reason or Ground of that Divine Law? Whether the arbitrary Will of God, The Good of Men, or the intrinsick Nature of the Things themselves?'[33] Burnet cannot see how, on Locke's principles, the veracity of the author of revelation can be proved, for neither sensation nor reflection are competent here.[34]

Locke replied to the author of the anonymous *Remarks* in rather ill-tempered fashion thus:

> I cannot much blame him … for concealing his name: for, I think, any one who appears among christians, may well be ashamed of his name, when he raises such a doubt as this, viz. whether an infinitely powerful and wise being be veracious or no; unless falsehood be in such reputation with this gentleman, that he concludes lying to be no mark of weakness and folly. Besides, this author might, if he had pleased, have taken notice, that, in more places than one, I speak of the goodness of God; another evidence, as I take it, of his veracity.[35]

Burnet was not confounded, however, and returned to his charge later in the same year: 'The Question there is not, *Whether God be Veracious?* but, Whether, according to your Principles, he can be prov'd to be so?'[36]

John Milner was puzzled by Locke's insistence on the importance of the natural law, given his resolute opposition to innate principles: 'according to him, the Law of Nature is not innate; but he tells us, that the *knowledge of it is attain'd by the light of Nature, or by our natural Faculties from natural Principles*'.[37] This, to Milner, is a self-contradictory position. He is clearly not persuaded by the distinction which Locke had drawn between an innate law imprinted upon our minds from the outset, and our ability to attain knowledge of matters concerning which we were hitherto ignorant, by the use and due application of our natural faculties.[38] Locke's point seems to have been that to regard *dispositions* as innate was, while acceptable, not particularly informative; but against content-full innate ideas his protest was unyielding.

Henry Lee, a stalwart defender of the view that from birth human beings possess certain dispositions in common, was among those who claimed that Locke's denial of innate ideas opened the way to materialism in the wake of Hobbes;[39] but undoubtedly the most eminent of Locke's early critics was William Sherlock, dean of St Paul's, who had already rebuked Locke from the pulpit in the Temple; on which event Locke remarked, that Sherlock, 'a man of no small name … has been pleased to declare against my doctrine of no innate ideas … and as I have been told, charged it with little less than atheism.'[40] In his 'Digression concerning connate ideas' he argued that the 'great and profound Philosophers of our Age; who will allow no Innate Knowledge, but assert the Soul to be a *Rasa Tabula*, White Paper, whereon nothing is written, but is capable of any Impressions,' are simply reviving 'the Old Atheistick Hypothesis, which banishes Original Mind and Wisdom out of the World, makes Mind younger than Matter, later than the making of the World, and therefore not the Maker of it'.[41] Sherlock holds that to be a rational nature is to possess innate principles of reason. If the soul has no such innate knowledge, it cannot know external objects, for all ideas come by reflection, 'that is, by turning our Eyes and Thoughts inward upon our selves'.[42] Is it reasonable, he asks (echoing Milner's complaint), to suppose that God has 'implanted in us Natural Passions, which have Good and Evil for their Objects, but has implanted no Natural Ideas in us of Good and Evil?'[43] Locke supposes that innate ideas must be known without being taught, without the use of reason, experience or observation. Sherlock is the first to agree that there are no innate ideas of that kind! He can agree that our actual knowledge is acquired, and charges Locke with having mistaken the process of bringing innate ideas into view with the invention of ideas. In Sherlock's opinion, all eternal verities are innate. He concludes by returning to the hay the atheists will make with Locke's help:

> For if all the knowledge we have of God, and of Good and Evil, be made by our selves, Atheists will easily conclude, that it is only the effect of Education, and Superstitious Fears; and satisfie themselves, that they can make other Notions, more for the Ease and Security of Life ... [T]he general Reason why Men are so zealous against these Ideas being Innate, is to deliver themselves from the necessity of believing any thing of God or Religion.[44]

William Carroll concurs, albeit in more hysterical tones, and in his *Spinoza Reviv'd* (1709) he accuses Locke of endorsing Spinoza's atheistical hypothesis that the universe comprises one material substance only. Le Clerc is tarred with the same brush. The charges are repeated in 'Part the Second' (1711): 'In a word, Human Malice cannot invent a System more injurious to God, or fatal to Mankind, than that Hypothesis is.'[45]

Criticisms of Locke's position on innate ideas continued to appear from time to time, though no longer as frequently as in the first decade of the eighteenth century. There was, for example, an anonymous work, *A Dissertation on Deistical and Arian Corruption* (1742); this was followed by John Ellis's *Some Brief Considerations upon Mr. Locke's Hypothesis, That the Knowledge of God Is Attainable by Ideas of Reflexion* (1743), in which he welcomes Locke's demolition of innate ideas, but goes on to argue that on Locke's own principles the idea of God cannot be reached by reflection, but is given in revelation; and after a further lapse of years James Oswald published a rebuttal of Locke after the manner of the Scottish common-sense philosophy:

> If, as this author represents, we can have no ideas besides those arising immediately from impressions made on our organs of sense, or our own reflection upon these, then the authority of common sense must go for nothing, and a free scope is given to scepticism with respect to all truths that are not the immediate objects of sense.[46]

If all our knowledge of religion and virtue is 'gathered from abstractions made by ourselves,' such knowledge is precarious indeed; our memories may be at fault; we may overlook something of importance; and our need to have recourse to the ideas of others will make us susceptible to their errors too. Far from being shut up to our own self-produced evidence, we have the resource of the common sense of humanity. The primary truths of religion are founded upon simple perception and the judgement of the rational mind and, in framing his hypothesis, Locke overlooked this fact.[47] He thereby 'opened the door to universal scepticism'.[48]

Locke had his defenders on the question of innate ideas, however – some of them perhaps more embarrassing than others. In 1697 there appeared the Roman Catholic John Sergeant's, *Solid Philosophy asserted against the Fancies of the Ideaists.* Sergeant concurs with Locke in opposing innate ideas, but he is stoutly opposed to Locke's sensationalism. His objective is to restore the syllogistic procedures of Aristotelian philosophy, to secure rational deductions from first principles which would have demonstrative force, and to defend his view that those who espouse ideaism, whether Cartesian or sensationalist, are dealing in fancies only and, moreover, are ill-advisedly opening the door to enthusiasm. In his Epistle Dedicatory he laments that Cartesius and 'our Ingenious Countryman Mr. *Locke*' have set up in opposition to 'that Miracle of Nature,' Aristotle,

> these two Gentlemen, being better vers'd in the Mathematicks than in Metaphysicks; and, thence, not apprehending how Corporeal Natures could *get into* the Mind, or *be there*; nor reflecting that in a *Spiritual* Nature, being incomparably *Superior* in the Rank of *Beings* to that of *Corporeal* Things, must, consequently, have naturally and necessarily a Power to *comprehend*, after its manner, (or by way of Knowledge) that *Inferiour* one; they were forc'd, thro' want of Higher Principles, to build all Knowledge, not upon the *Things themselves* in their Knowing Power, but upon *Ideas* or *Similitudes* of them; tho' neither of them set themselves to make out or demonstrate how we could possibly have our *Notions*, or *First Notices* of the Things by them.[49]

Sergeant does not charge Descartes and Locke with intentional unkindness to Christianity, and he admits that school philosophy also can be inadequately grounded. Nevertheless,

> *I allow* Ideas or Resemblances *in the* Fancy *or* Imagination; *but, I absolutely deny there are any* Spiritual Ideas *or* Similitudes *in the* Mind *on which we* ground *any* Truth, *or which are the* Material of Knowledge; *but* NOTIONS *only, or the* Things *abstractedly or inadequately* conceiv'd *by the Understanding.*[50]

Sergeant wholeheartedly endorses Locke's view that there are no innate ideas, but firmly holds that the object of knowledge and the thing known are the same.[51] This enables him, towards the end of his book, to declare his certainty concerning some truths which, to Locke, are only probable – for example, that Julius Caesar existed. He does not stay to tease this out, but with an integrity which characterizes his whole work confesses, 'But I am weary, and hasten to an End.'[52]

Great support for Locke came from the anonymous author of *A Defence of the Essay of Human Understanding* (1702), who proved to be Catharine Cockburn. She agrees with Locke that there are no innate ideas, pointing out to his critics that

> Mr. Lock only contends against those who say there are Principles of Metaphysical or Moral Truths originally imprinted on the mind; by which, if they only mean that there is an *Innate* Power or Capacity in the Soul of knowing these Truths, they mean nothing different from Mr. *Lock*, who denies *Innate Principles*; for he does not deny that there is a Power of the Soul of perceiving, and assenting to those Truths; or of distinguishing Good and Evil ...[53]

That Locke welcomed this intervention is clear from his letter to Catharine Cockburn of 30 December 1702, in which he declares that she has 'not only vanquished my adversary, but reduced me also absolutely under your power ...'[54]

Locke's friend, the deist Anthony Collins, wrote to Locke in support of his opposition to innate ideas, contending that Locke's antagonists, Lee and Lowde, while intending to refute Locke, in fact through the improper use of terms concur with him.[55] On this John Yolton has rightly pointed out that Collins

> failed to see the very real antithesis which existed between Locke and his critics on this issue. The conviction held by Lowde, Burnet, and others was that there exists in the mind a disposition which, independent of experience, leads man towards good and away from evil. Locke was no more willing to subscribe to this dictum than he was to the naïve form of the theory of innate knowledge.[56]

In 1705 Samuel Bold published *A Discourse concerning the Resurrection of the Same Body,* in which he rebuts Milner's charges against Locke, and defends the latter's position on innate ideas. In 1722 there appeared William Wollaston's *The Religion of Nature Delineated,* in which he argues that those who seek to

> deduce the difference between good and evil from the *common sense* of mankind, and certain *Principles* that are born in us, put the matter upon a very *infirm* foot. For it is much to be expected that there are no such *innate* maxims as they pretend, but that the impressions of education are mistaken for them: and besides that, the sentiments of mankind are not so *uniform* and *constant,* as that we may safely trust such an important distinction upon them.[57]

It goes without saying that the support of deists such as Collins and Wollaston did little to enhance Locke's reputation in the eyes of more conservative divines, as we shall see later.

Isaac Watts, however, was highly regarded and trusted by many, and his position on innate ideas is therefore of particular interest. While denying with Locke that we are born with innate ideas imprinted on our minds, he does not wish to hold that the mind is an absolutely blank sheet of paper awaiting the impressions of experience.[58] Our minds, being gifts of God, are created – not, indeed, replete with ready-made propositions to be afterwards brought before our consciousness – but with the capacity for judging ideas true or false.[59] In support of his view he cites Locke's conviction concerning our 'innate' desire for happiness and aversion to misery.[60] He further suggests – and does not think that Locke would deny – that we have another set of ideas, which may be designated abstract ideas:

> Now, though Mr. Locke supposes *sensation* and *reflection* to be the only two springs of all ideas, and that these two are sufficient to furnish our minds with all that rich variety of ideas which we have; yet *abstraction* is certainly a different act of the mind, whence these abstracted ideas have their original; though perhaps sensation or reflection may furnish us with all the first objects and occasions whence these abstracted ideas are excited and derived. Nor in this sense and view of things, can I think Mr. Locke himself would deny any representation of the original of abstracted ideas, nor forbid them to stand for a distinct *species.*[61]

As the eighteenth century progressed, fewer found it necessary either to attack or to defend Locke on innate ideas. Among exceptions are Thomas Ludlam, who, as late as 1790, deemed it 'a common duty to humanity' to defend Locke against his critics – in this case Milner, Horne, Kett and Napleton;[62] but when Edward Oliver published *An Analysis of Mr. Locke's Essay concerning Human Understanding* at the end of our period, in 1810, he passed over Book One on the ground that Locke's victory over innate ideas was complete, and the doctrine generally given up.[63]

From our discussion of innate ideas we see clearly that Locke's views on the matter were by no means swallowed uncritically. He had his defenders, his stout opponents, together with some, like Watts, who judiciously attempted to balance the pros and cons of the case. It will be interesting to see how far, and in connection with which issues, this kind of conclusion will apply as we proceed. Having begun where Locke's epistemology begins – with the question of the demolition of innate ideas – we must now turn to his more positive epistemological positions.

I

Locke believes that 'the way I have pursued, being conformable to Truth,' offers the most secure foundation for knowledge and certainty.[64] His way, as we have seen, is the way of ideas. In building what he understands to be a firm epistemological foundation, Locke is at the same time eschewing other approaches, of which I note four. First, he makes it clear that the physicalist path is not for him. His concerns are psychological (what are the limits of our mental capacities?) and epistemological (what grounds have we for claiming to know?):

> This, therefore, being my *Purpose* to enquire into the Original, Certainty, and Extent of humane Knowledge; together, with the Grounds and Degrees of Belief, Opinion, and Assent; I shall not at present meddle with the Physical Consideration of the Mind; or trouble my self to examine wherein its Essence consists, or by what Motions of our Spirits, or Alteration of our Bodies, we come to have any Sensations by our organs, or any *Ideas* in our Understandings; and whether those *Ideas* do in their Formation, any, or all of them, depend on Matter, or no. These are Speculations, which, however curious and entertaining, I shall decline, as lying out of my Way, in the Design I am now upon.[65]

Secondly, Locke sets his face against the scholastic method which had come down via Thomas Aquinas from Aristotle (hence the concern of John Sergeant, to whom I have already referred). As Lady Masham learned from Locke's Oxford friend, James Tyrrell, 'Mr. Locke never loved the trade of disputing in public in the schools but was always wont to declaim against it as being rather invented for wrangling or ostentation than to discover truth.'[66] However, as we shall see in the next chapter, Locke's demonstration of God's existence owes more than a little to the scholastic inheritance.[67] Thirdly, Locke is disinclined to authoritarianism in thought and life. This, indeed, is an aspect of his anti-Thomist stance, for among his complaints against Sergeant was that the latter 'speaks every where as if *Truth & Science* had personally apeared to him & by word of mouth actually commissioned him to be their sole Defender & Propagator'.[68] But, more generally, he wishes individuals to utilize their rational powers over against authoritarian claims (though, as we shall see later, he is not above appealing to the authority of Scripture and of the teaching and example of Jesus where ethical issues are concerned). After all, 'It is an idle and useless thing to make it our business to study what have been other men's sentiments in things where reason only is the judge.'[69] The concept of toleration is clearly linked to this conviction, since we can understand and believe for ourselves (and others cannot do these things for us) only if we are free to think for ourselves.[70] Fourthly, Locke wishes to develop an epistemology in opposition to that of such a neo-Platonist follower of Malebranche as his critic John Norris, in which a strong emphasis upon faith in propositions believed to have been divinely revealed appeared to make the appeal to evidence redundant.

With what does Locke replace the doctrine of innate ideas? He has no interest in denying the real existence of phenomena external to the mind; his concern is with the way in which we acquire knowledge of them. The mind is a *tabula rasa,* and on it external objects leave impressions, or 'ideas of sensation'.[71] As he puts it, the senses 'furnish the yet empty Cabinet'.[72] The mind does not know external objects immediately, and our knowledge consists in 'the view the Mind has of its own *Ideas*'.[73] An object's quality is its 'Power to produce any *Idea* in my mind'.[74] Qualities are of two kinds. Primary qualities – solidity, extension, figure, mobility – are accurately replicated in the idea, while secondary qualities – colour, taste, sound, for example – do not inhere in the objects, but are sensations (which vary from person to person) produced in us by the objects.[75] From sensation or by reflection we observe that some simple ideas 'go constantly together'. Since we cannot imagine 'how these simple *Ideas* can subsist by themselves, we accustom our selves, to suppose some *Substratum,* wherein they do subsist, and from which they do result, which therefore we call *Substance*'.[76] Here is an Achilles' heel in Locke's philosophy. He admits that the idea of substance is not given either by sensation or by reflection,[77] whilst at the same time holding that knowledge is given by those routes alone.

By 'reflection' Locke means

> the *Perception of the Operations of our own Minds* within us, as it is employ'd about the *Ideas* it has got; which Operations, when the Soul comes to reflect on, and consider, do furnish the Understanding with another set of *Ideas,* which could not be had from things without: and such are, *Perception, Thinking, Doubting, Believing, Reasoning, Knowing, Willing,* and all the different actings of our own Minds.'[78]

Moreover, ''Tis the contemplation of our own abstract *Ideas,* that alone is able to afford us *general Knowledge.*'[79] Indeed, '*Knowledge* . . . seems to me to be nothing but *the perception of the connexion and agreement, or disagreement and repugnancy of any of our Ideas.* In this alone it consists.'[80]

Two questions immediately arise. First, does the object which occasions the idea subsist for only as long as we contemplate that idea? It may appear that Locke should, on his own principles, answer in the affirmative. But throughout, in his down-to-earth fashion, he presupposes the existence of the external world, and consequently he allows himself the licence of complex ideas such as '*Beauty, Gratitude, a Man, an Army, the Universe*; which though complicated of various simple *Ideas,* or *complex Ideas* made up of simple ones, yet are, when the Mind pleases, considered each by itself, as one entire thing, and signified by one name.'[81] Secondly, if the mind can contemplate only ideas, what grounds have we for believing that these ideas actually reflect external phenomena? Locke was aware of this difficulty, and he was willing to have recourse to a *deus ex machina*: since the mind cannot make simple ideas itself, he says, such ideas 'must necessarily be the product of Things operating on the Mind in a natural way, and producing therein those Perceptions which by the Wisdom and Will of our Maker they are ordained and adapted to'.[82] As we shall see, Reid, among others, was not impressed by this response.

Locke further presupposes that we have knowledge of our own existence by intuition: 'we perceive it so plainly, and so certainly, that it neither needs, nor is capable of any proof. For nothing can be more evident to us, than our own Existence.'[83] Moreover, intuition yields a degree of certainty which cannot be exceeded.[84] This instance, together with the possibility of the demonstration of God's existence apart, '*general Certainty* is never to be found but in our *Ideas.*'[85] Not indeed that Locke thinks we can proceed through life in absolute certainty on all epistemological matters. Against Aristotelian certainty respecting the real essences of phenomena, Locke holds that for much of the time we must be content with probability, declaring in homely fashion that 'He that will not eat, till he has Demonstration that it will nourish him; he that will not stir, till he infallibly knows the Business he goes about will succeed, will have little else to do, but sit still and perish.'[86]

Before providing an account of the responses of the divines to Locke's view of knowledge and its acquisition, we may return to a question of labelling which I announced in the first chapter. Was Locke an out-and-out empiricist?[87] It may perhaps be clear from the exposition so far that he was certainly not a died-in-the-wool sensationalist. It is not merely that he has a place for reflection, though this is important. It is also that he presupposes the existence of the material world; he contends that we can adduce demonstrative proofs of the existence of God and of the principles of morality; and he is an intuitionist in respect of the existence of our own selves – a prime example of rationalist *a priorism.* These are significant qualifications, which lend support to G. A. J. Rogers's view that 'Locke is a very conservative sort of empiricist, quite definitely committed to the existence of entities not empirically observable. The primary-secondary quality distinction patently rests upon this fact.'[88] Again, the problem posed by Locke's ideism, namely, that of guaranteeing the existence of the external world if all that we know are ideas, further removes him from the observational and experimental orbit of empiricism, and prompted Andrew Seth's remark that 'Locke's philosophy is ... peculiarly interesting, because in it "the theory of ideas" is seen just detaching itself, as it were, from the groundwork of common-sense and ordinary belief.'[89] As Seth later remarks, 'our ideas, instead of bringing us into connection with things, really shut us off from them.'[90]

This last consideration prompted a number of Locke's contemporaries and successors to charge him with scepticism. Before setting out the charge we shall do well to distinguish carefully between what might be called the limited scepticism of agnosticism, and dogmatic scepticism. Whereas the latter position announces our inability to know anything outside of our minds, the former is sceptical of our ability to know certain things – for example, the internal working of the persons of the Trinity.[91] Locke declares that 'the *Comprehension* of our Understandings, comes exceeding short of the vast Extent of Things.'[92] He confesses ignorance concerning 'the internal Constitution, and true Nature of things, being destitute of Faculties to attain it';[93] 'we may justly look on our certain *general Knowledge of Substances*, as almost none at all';[94] and

> If we are at [a] loss in respect of the Powers, and Operations of Bodies, I think it is easy to conclude, *we are much more in the dark in reference to Spirits*; whereof we naturally have no *Ideas*, but what we

> draw from that of our own, by reflecting on the Operations of our own Souls within us, as far as they can come within our Observation. But how inconsiderable a rank the Spirits that inhabit our Bodies hold amongst those various, and possibly innumerable, kinds of nobler Beings ...[95]

All of which is a long way from dogmatic scepticism.

Nevertheless in 1697 Edward Stillingfleet, bishop of Worcester, complained that Locke had, by his theory that we perceive only our ideas, 'almost discarded substance out of the reasonable part of the world,'[96] thereby landing in scepticism. Locke was well aware of the problem – indeed, he posed it himself: '*Our Knowledge* ... is *real*, only so far as there is a conformity between our *Ideas* and the reality of Things. But what shall be here the Criterion? How shall the Mind, when it perceives nothing but its own *Ideas*, know that they agree with Things in themselves?'[97] He answers that simple ideas and all complex ideas except those of substances, are caused by things, and of this we may be infallibly certain.[98] He reiterates this reply to Stillingworth, with the challenge: 'And what other certainty your lordship has by your senses of the existing of anything without you, but the perceived connection of those two ideas [namely, the sensation and the existence of the external object which causes the sensation], I would gladly know.'[99]

It would seem that Locke and the bishop talk past each other to the extent that Locke is rebaptizing the term 'substance'. Impressed as he was by the scientific achievements of a Newton, and of a common-sense turn of mind himself, he was not likely to deny that the modern scientists were investigating genuine material objects. His point against the bishop is that we have no access to a substance which undergirds all things – indeed, there is no such substance, and that our knowledge that we are dealing with genuine phenomena derives from our habit of supposing a substratum in which simple ideas subsist.[100] As he says, 'Whatever therefore be the secret and abstract Nature of *Substance* in general, all *the* Ideas *we have of particular distinct sorts of Substances,* are nothing but several Combinations of simple *Ideas*, co-existing in such, though unknown, Cause of their Union, as makes the whole subsist of itself.'[101] Locke's linguistic recommendation came to Stillingfleet as an unwelcome novelty and, along the line of a scholastic such as Sergeant, he sighs,

> Your Way of *Certainty by Ideas* is so wholly New, that here we have no *general Principles*; no *Criterion,* no *Antecedents* and Consequents; no *Syllogistical Methods* of *Demonstration*; and yet we are told of a better Way of Certainty to be attained, meerly by the help of *Ideas*. But how comes there to be such a *Way of Certainty by Ideas*, and yet the *Ideas* themselves are so *uncertain* and obscure?[102]

His own view is that the idea of substance is gained 'not by *meer comparing those Ideas* [the mind] *has got by Sense or Reflection*; but by forming distinct general Notions of things from particular *Ideas*'.[103] Ironically, this is how Locke himself gleaned the idea of substance, as John Yolton has pointed out: 'Locke's idea of substance as an addition to the sensible qualities, as the locus of the real essence, is not derivable from simple ideas of sense but is an hypothesis of reason.'[104] On this basis Locke turns the charge of scepticism around upon those *he* deems to be sceptics: 'If we will disbelieve every thing, because we cannot certainly know all things; we shall do much-what as wisely as he, who would not use his Legs, but sit still and perish, because he had no Wings to fly.'[105] As he later put it, 'I think no body can, in earnest, be so sceptical, as to be uncertain of the Existence of those Things which he sees and feels.'[106]

In his Preface to *Anti-Scepticism* (1702), Henry Lee repeated the charge:

> The Idea of one thing being no more an evidence of its real Existence, than its real Existence is of a person's having the Idea of it. – And this is one reason why I conceive those Ideal Principles must involve us in an endless Scepticism; namely because they will neither allow us to suppose, nor can prove the real Existence of Things without us.

The nub of Lee's case is that if all knowledge comes by sensation and reflection, 'there can be no *certain* Knowledge of the Truth of any *general* Proposition whatever; because our Senses can reach but to *particulars*, and Reflexion no further.'[107] Lee's concern is with the epistemological atomism to which Locke's position leads. His conviction is that truth is the 'Conjunction or Disjunction of things according to the real Relation those things have to each other'.[108] In other words, the innate, common principles of reason which do not so much produce knowledge as enable us to judge the deliverances of our senses, cannot be so easily dispensed with as Locke appears to think (though it must be admitted that Lee spends little time on Locke's understanding of reflection – to him Locke is very largely a sensationalist).

The charge of scepticism was reiterated by William Carroll[109] and John Witty, who argued that if knowledge is confined to sensation and reflection, we must forgo certainty concerning all matters of fact, persons and things, which we have not ourselves experienced.[110] Twenty-one years on Peter Browne published *The Procedure, Extent and Limits of Human Understanding.* This was an expansion of his *A Letter in Answer to a Book Entituled Christianity Not Mysterious* (1697). As before, his objective was to refute Locke's sensationalism. In 1743 there followed John Ellis's critique of Locke's epistemology. While appreciating that 'It is undoubtedly a task of utmost danger, to dissent from Mr. Locke's Essay,'[111] Ellis nevertheless regrets the way in which, when speaking of our knowledge of spiritual beings, Locke settles for probability only; he disapproves of Locke's advocacy of the rational demonstration of God's existence, deeming this to be a matter of revelation only – especially given the fallibility of human reason; and he charges Locke with failing to show how 'ideas of reflection are to connect our minds with the divine nature.'[112] His main point is that 'by the rules of Mr. Locke's philosophy, it is not possible for the human intellect to come at the knowledge of God, by a contemplation of those two principal mediums, the soul of man, or the works of creation.'[113] Revelation alone will suffice, and this may be seen 'from considering the true state of man at his first entrance into the world,'[114] which was probationary, and such as to require the promulgation of a perfect law, with covenantal obligations attached.

With Lee's assertion of the place of revelation, and his excursion into biblical teaching, we come to a miscellany of objections to Locke's position on the genesis of knowledge which take us wider than the charge of scepticism. In the light of his neo-Platonist commitment (Philip Doddridge warned his students that Norris 'is in general too abstruse and metaphysical')[115] John Norris contended that since ideas are not material beings they cannot be derived from sensible objects. More particularly, how could we attain the idea of God, for nothing in the material world resembles him? Not even God could make an idea of himself, for such an idea would be a creature, and no creature can represent God. The only possible idea of God is 'his Son, the

Divine λογος, or Ideal World ... 'Tis he that is the Idea of God, and of the whole Creation, that both *is*, and *represents* all things.'[116] Despite his reservations, Norris 'would not part with [Locke's] Book for half a *Vatican*'.

That Norris continued to reflect upon these matters is clear from his subsequent publications. In 1701 there appeared his *An Essay towards the Theory of the Ideal or Intelligible World*, in which he surmises that he may have misunderstood Locke. He sets out from his belief that an idea is 'that whereby we perceive any Being, as by its *Intelligible Representative*,' and that we have such ideas only of material beings.[117] As for angels and human souls, we do not perceive these at all, unless 'by their own immediate selves'.[118] Now,

> if by our having Ideas from our Senses, [Locke's] meaning be, that sensible Objects do send or convey Ideas from themselves to our minds by the mediation of the Senses ... it appears by the whole Tenour of this Discourse, that he has derived our Ideas from a false Original. But if his meaning be, as perhaps it may (for indeed his way of expressing himself upon this occasion is not so clear, but that one may pardonably mistake him) that sensible Objects do by the Impression which they make upon our outward Senses serve to excite Ideas in our Minds, so that we are beholding them as the occasions of our having such Ideas ... I think there is nothing either so dangerous, or so extraordinary in it, but that we may, without scruple, in great measure, allow it to him.[119]

For Edmund Elys, the question is whether the idea of God and of the infinite was bestowed upon us when we are created in God's image, or whether it can arise only through the senses. He is persuaded that the eclipse of the idea of God is the result of sin: '*We are now* Condemned, *as to the* Mines, *in Attaining Knowledge, and to work by Sense first.*'[120] To Elys, 'The First Act of the Rational Soul is the Perception, or Apprehension of Being Absolute or Universal.'[121] Were this not the case, we could not apprehend particular existents. The idea of God implies the idea of all things, for he is 'the Fountain of all Being'.[122] Where Locke argues that our ignorance of, and slowness to grasp, many practical principles shows such principles not to be innate, Elys retorts that what this shows is that our wills are perverse. His insistence throughout is that we have 'a kind of INTUITIVE Knowledge' of God.[123]

Less temperate is the anonymous F.B., an MA of Cambridge, who, in 1698, in his *A Free but Modest Censure,* endorses Stillingfleet's criticisms of Locke, brands Locke a materialist, and, in welcoming the rumbustious, satirical, style of John Edwards, opines that 'this sort of Medicaments hath cured [Locke's] Pen of the *Diarrhea* ...'[124]

For a final early adverse critic we may turn to George Cheyne's blast. His is the religious – indeed, the Calvinist – complaint that Locke has signally failed

> to consider Man as he really is, a *fallen, depraved, vitiated* Creature, (in which State his *lower,* his rational Faculties are impaired; his *higher* Faculties in some measure obliterated, at least buried and oppressed by the Load of present Corruption and Sensuality; and all of them in a State of *Anarchy,* Rebellion, and contrariety one to another).

Small wonder, then, that Locke's account of our faculties is '*lame* and *imperfect*'.[125]

Locke did not have to wait long for a number of divines and others to spring to his defence. In 1699 Samuel Bold published *Some Considerations on the Principal Objections and Arguments which have been Publish'd Against Mr. Lock's Essay of Humane Understanding.* He opens with a flourish: 'That Essay is a Book the best Adapted of any I know, to serve the Interest of Truth, Natural, Moral, and Divine ... [I]t is the most worthy, most Noble, and best Book I ever read, excepting those which were writ by Persons Divinely inspir'd.'[126] He supports Locke's view that knowledge is a matter of the agreement or disagreement of ideas rather than of deductions from self-evident rational principles by saying that we cannot know the truth of such principles, or properly apply them, except by the way of Ideas.[127]

Bold seeks to counter two charges which are levelled against Locke's view that '*Certainty of Knowledge is, to perceive the Agreement or Disagreement of Ideas, as expressed in any Proposition. This* (saith Mr. Locke) *we usually call knowing, or being certain of the Truth of any Proposition.*'[128] First, Locke's contention is denied, and it is argued that the way to certainty or knowledge is by drawing inferences from maxims; secondly, it is said that Locke's proposition is 'inconsistent with, and of dangerous consequence to the *Articles of the Christian Faith*'.[129] Bold replies that self-evident propositions are in no different case from any other type of proposition in respect of their need to be judged according as to whether 'the Ideas, signified by the words of which the Proposition doth consist, have such a connection or agreement, or repugnancy, or disagreement, as the Proposition doth express ...'[130] We can be certain of the truth of self-evident propositions only by comparing the ideas which comprise them. As for truths of divine revelation: the route by which propositions come is not to the point. However they are received, we become persuaded of their truth by analysing and judging the ideas of which they are composed: 'the way how a Proposition is brought to us, doth not alter its nature, consider'd as a Proposition, nor the nature of Certainty, or Knowledge, which are fixed, and unchangeable, and always the same ...'[131] But what of claims made in articles of faith which go beyond our powers of comprehension? They, declares Bold, will continue to be what they are, namely, 'Divine and Incomprehensible Truths' which are 'not proposed to us, by Divine Revelation, to be *Objects of Knowledge*, but only of *our Faith*'.[132] If someone should then ask whether this implies that faith is not a reasonable act, Bold replies,

> all reasonable Assent is not Certainty or Knowledge. My assent to the truth of a Proposition, or my believing it to be true, is a Reasonable Act, not because I am certain, or do know that it is true, but because my Assent is founded on such Evidence that it is true, as is in every way sufficient to justify my Assenting to it.[133]

Accordingly, if the evidence is that proposition *x* is divinely revealed by the God who cannot lie, we need have no qualms about assenting to its truth. (This, of course, begs important questions concerning the nature and reliability of the evidence in question.) He concludes, 'If Mr. *Lock's* Proposition can concern, or affect any *Christian Articles*, they must be *Articles of Christian Knowledge*, not of *Christian Faith.*'[134]

Other supporters included Mrs Cockburn, who sought to persuade Locke's adverse critic, Burnet, that he had been misled by the fact that when we assent to truths which we have been taught, we tend not to inquire into their origins. She further charged him with overlooking Locke's other principle of knowledge: reflection.[135] In 1736 and 1738 Vincent Perronet published *Vindications* in defence of Locke against Browne's charge of scepticism, arguing that Locke has proved that God is immaterial, and that we have certain knowledge of his existence.[136] For this Perronet earned the gratitude of Isaac Watts,[137] who himself, reservations concerning innate ideas notwithstanding, thought much of Locke's *Essay* 'worthy of Letters of Gold'.[138] He feared that Locke went too far, however, concerning substance. He agrees that 'Substance is another of those mysteries wherein we bewilder and lose ourselves by attempting to make something out of nothing'; and he applauds Locke because he has 'happily refuted that unreasonable notion of *substance* in general, which makes it out to be some real thing in nature, different from all the united qualities'.[139] He sees no reason, however, to depart from the scholastic definition, according to which substance is that which supports accidents in being, and exists in itself without dependence upon any created being. Indeed, he suggests that this in fact is what Locke holds. But that there is a separate being, substance in general, supporting all the properties of things, he stoutly denies, for this would enable it to be said that 'God and the creature, that body and mind, are the same in substance ... But this is a most palpable falsehood.'[140]

As he reflected from his vantage point at the end of our period, the Unitarian Thomas Belsham defined the principle of association as it had come to be received, acknowledging Locke as the fountain-head of this intellectual development: 'The doctrine of Association, opened by Locke, improved by Gay, matured by Hartley, and illustrated by the luminous disquisitions of Dr. Priestly, the author regards as established beyond the possibility of controversy, in the judgment of those philosophers who have studied, and who understand it.'[141] He defines 'association' as 'that LAW of the mind by which two or more sensations, ideas, or muscular motions are so united, that any one of them impressed alone shall introduce all the ideas or motions connected with it'; and he notes that although Locke first introduced this law, 'he applies it to the solution of very few phenomena.'[142]

But much water had flowed between Watts and Belsham. In particular, renewed and significant charges of scepticism against Locke were levelled by Richard Price, and from Scotland, by Reid and the common-sense philosophers. They were, of course, writing especially in response to Humean scepticism, but Locke did not emerge unscathed. Price's particular concern is with morals, and I shall have more to say about this later. For the present it will suffice us to note his view that the ethical theories of Hutcheson and Hume, which Price is intent upon countering, derive from their empiricist epistemologies; and of these Locke is the fountain-head:

> SENSATION and REFLECTION have been commonly reckoned the source of all our ideas: and Mr. *Locke* has taken no small pains to prove this. How much soever, on the whole, I admire his excellent *Essay,* I cannot think him sufficiently clear or explicit on this subject. It is hard to determine exactly what he meant by *sensation* and *reflection* ... If by the former we understand, the effects arising from the impressions made on our minds by external objects; and by the latter, the notice the mind takes of its own operations; it will be impossible to derive some of the most important of our ideas from them.[143]

Price thinks it probable that Locke meant that all our ideas are either 'derived *immediately* from these two sources, or ultimately *grounded* upon ideas so derived'.[144] But this would not entitle us to regard these ways as the sources of all our ideas. His own conviction is that 'The power ... that *understands*; or the faculty within us that discerns *truth,* and that compares all the objects of thought, and *judges* of them, is a spring of new [simple] ideas.'[145] He proceeds to argue that we have ideas other than from sensation, and that such ideas derive from the understanding. The latter he regards as an active power, whereas to him as to the empiricists, sensation is passive, and hence incapable of judgement.[146] At this point we may agree with Henri Laboucheix, who suggests that Price's interpretation of Locke's 'reflection' is too restricted, 'and misunderstands profoundly the fourth book of *An essay concerning human understanding,* in which Locke, very clearly, refers to intuitive knowledge by that name and considers it as the only certain form of knowledge, superior to any other kind'.[147]

If, to Price, Locke was too sensationalist in his epistemology, to one of his earlier critics, Peter Browne, he was not sufficiently consistent in his sensationalism. To Browne, 'the laying down the Ideas of *Sensation* and *Reflection* to be *Alike* the *Original* Sources and Foundation of all our Knowledge, is one great and fundamental Error which runs thro' most of the Discourses and

Essays of our modern Writers of Logicks and Metaphysics'.[148]

The burden of the complaint of Reid and his colleagues was not from the side of scholasticism (though their concern was analogous to that of Sergeant), or neo-Platonism, or Calvinism (though they were ministers of a Reformed Church); rather they elevated the common sense of humanity that the material world exists independently of the knowing mind, and contended that Locke's view that knowledge depends exclusively upon ideas ran disastrously counter to this, and that it had paved the way for Hume's theoretical scepticism. In a letter of 18 March 1763 Reid testifies to Hume that

> I have learned more from your writings in this kind, than from all others put together. Your system appears to me not only coherent in all its parts, but likewise justly deduced from principles commonly received among philosophers; principles which I never thought of calling in question, until the conclusions you draw from them in the Treatise of Human Nature made me suspect them.[149]

Thus inspired, Reid sets his face against the line of philosophers from Plato to Hume who have held that the immediate object of perception is a mental image. He judges that Hume's scepticism

> is built upon principles which were very generally maintained by philosophers, though they did not see that they led to scepticism. Mr. Hume, by tracing, with great acuteness and ingenuity, the consequences of principles commonly received, has shewn that they overturn all knowledge, and at last overturn themselves, and leave the mind in perfect suspense.[150]

In his *An Inquiry into the Human Mind,* Reid considers those who have probed the first principles of human nature, and names more names:

> Des Cartes no sooner began to dig in this mine, than scepticism was ready to break in upon him. He did what he could to shut it out. Malebranche and Locke, who dig deeper, found the difficulty of keeping out this enemy still to increase; but they laboured honestly in the design. Then Berkeley, who carried on the work, despairing of securing all, bethought himself of an expedient: – By giving up the material world, which he thought might be spared without loss, and even with advantage, he hoped, by an impregnable partition, to secure the world of spirits. But, alas! the 'Treatise of Human Nature' wantonly sapped the foundation of this partition, and drowned all in one universal deluge.[151]

Hume thus stands at the bottom of a very slippery slope. Among his immediate predecessors Locke, with his doctrine of ideas had deprived us of knowledge of the phenomenal realm; and Berkeley, though he did well to declare against Locke that 'from the existence of images, we can never, by any just reasoning, infer the existence of anything else, unless perhaps the existence of an intelligent Author of them,'[152] sadly demolished the material realm (a view which at the very least requires to be qualified, as we shall see), and devised a system which, 'although it leaves us sufficient evidence of a supreme intelligent mind ... seems to take away all the evidence we have of other intelligent beings like ourselves'.[153] Then, according to Reid, it remained only for Hume to query the realm of spirit, and ideaism's game was up.

Reid's alternative view was well summarized by Campbell Fraser thus:

> Reid's Common Sense is the final perception of a being who can know the universe of reality only in part, and is therefore needed by man in that intermediate position in which an absolute beginning or end of things must be to him incomprehensible. It is an appeal to that which must in reason be final, in an intelligence that only partly shares in divine omniscient reason. Although its judgments are not evolved from premises, they are nevertheless what all men, except infants and lunatics, more or less distinctly acknowledge in their individual actions, although they may misconstrue them in their uneducated opinions, or spoil them by indulgence in purely speculative systems. The divine inspiration of the common sense is therefore man's final support, amidst the so-called 'contingencies' of temporal change in himself and his surroundings.[154]

Thus, in welcoming Hume's candour in admitting that despite all he had done to discredit his senses, he still had to trust them in daily life, Reid declares in homely fashion, 'I never heard that any sceptic run his head against a post, or stepped into a kennel, because he did not believe his eyes.'[155]

Alexander Broadie has succinctly summed matters up thus:

> Locke is insisting that there are three elements to be considered, viz. (i) a cognitive act, (ii) an idea which is the direct object of that cognitive act, and (iii) what it is that the idea is an idea of, in contrast with Reid, Mair and the latter's associates, all of whom rejected the second of these elements.[156]

As Reid himself wrote to James Gregory, 'The merit of what you are pleased to call *my philosophy* lies, I think, chiefly in having called in question the common theory of ideas, or images of things in the mind, being the only objects of thought.'[157]

Positively, Reid and his sympathizers uphold observation and consciousness as the bases of knowledge, the latter being held to contain principles independent of experience which can order the deliverances of experience. These principles include the axioms of mathematics and the deliverances of common sense. By contrast, the systems of Reid's philosophical predecessors lead to scepticism,[158] and Reid rebukes them sternly:

> Let scholastic sophisters entangle themselves in their own cobwebs; I am resolved to take my own existence, and the existence of other things, upon trust; and to believe that the snow is cold, and honey sweet, whatever they may say to the contrary. He must either be a fool, or want to make a fool of me, that would reason me out of my reason and senses.
>
> I confess that I know not what a sceptic can answer to this, nor by what good argument he can plead even for a hearing; for either his reasoning is sophistry, and so deserves contempt; or there is no truth in human faculties – and then why should we reason?[159]

James Beattie, who held the chair of moral philosophy and logic at Marischal College, Aberdeen, displayed considerable sympathy with his neighbour Reid. While granting that 'Nothing was further from the intention of Locke, than to encourage verbal controversy, or advance doctrines favourable to scepticism,'[160] some of his tenets have prompted scepticism. His zeal against innate ideas and principles caused him to 'allow too little to instinct, for fear of allowing too much'.[161] Beattie argues that if truth be permanent,

> those perceptions or impulses of understanding by which we become conscious of it, must be equally permanent; which they could not be if they depended on education, and if there were not a law of nature, independent on [*sic*] man, which determines the understanding in some cases to believe, in others to disbelieve.[162]

Beattie is convinced that there are universal, instinctive judgements which are impressed upon our minds by the Creator.[163] To all of which an ideaist might reply (and some of them did reply) that Reid and Beattie's common sense amounts to no more than a prejudice lacking the rigour of a philosophical theory. Even such a materialist as the rational Dissenter Joseph Priestley sprang to Locke's defence:

> As to Dr. Reid's *Inquiry into the Human Mind on the Principles of Common Sense,* I frankly declare, that, excepting a few incidental things, foreign to his general object, I do not find in it a single observation that is *new,* and at the same time *just.* The only effect of all the pains that both this ingenious writer, Dr. Beattie, and Dr. Oswald have taken with the subject, appears to me to have terminated in nothing, besides beclouding and puzzling a business which, in the main, Mr. Locke left very clear and far advanced.[164]

As he elsewhere declared, 'so loose and incoherent a system as [Reid] would substitute in the place of Mr. Locke's, ought not to be adopted without the most urgent necessity; since it wants the recommendation of that agreeable *simplicity,* which is so apparent in other parts of the constitution of nature.'[165]

The common-sense philosophy of Reid and his colleagues made a considerable impact in America, though not all regions were equally open to it. The idealism of Cudworth, Norris and Berkeley was still prominent in New England, while the South was imbued with 'Anglican indifference' and 'Gallic scepticism'. This left the Middle States for Reid,[166] and there the Presbyterian, John Witherspoon, who emigrated from Scotland to become president of the College of New Jersey at Princeton, was instrumental in securing a hearing for Reid.[167] Reid began to replace Locke in the prescribed reading lists of many American students – this to the regret of some;[168] and some Unitarians at the beginning of the nineteenth century construed Reid's approach as a *return* to Locke in face of the devastating scepticism of Hume.[169] Meanwhile, in England in 1790, W. and T. Ludlam vindicated Locke against Mr Kett, Fellow of Trinity College, Oxford, who accused Locke of landing in scepticism, and proposed common sense as the way out.[170]

Having considered those who were decidedly opposed to Locke's way of ideas on the ground that it led to scepticism, and those who were ready to endorse and defend his views, we must now turn to those who, while they gave qualified approval to some of his views, were significantly influenced by other intellectual approaches.

II

We shall do well to turn first to George Berkeley, bishop of Cloyne.[171] He is the senior of those to be considered, and it is possible to link him in different ways with some of those to be noted subsequently: Johnson, Edwards, Butler and Wesley.

As distrustful of scholastic metaphysics as was Locke, Berkeley was much impressed by Locke's account of the way of ideas. He opposes innate ideas. He agrees that the mind is conscious only of ideas, but whereas Locke believes that ideas are generated by awareness in general, Berkeley holds that ideas originate in sensory experience of concrete objects which are always particulars, and in reflection. Concerning the latter he writes,

> We comprehend our own existence by inward feeling or reflexion, and that of other spirits by reason. We may be said to have some knowledge or notion of our own minds, of spirits and active beings, whereof in a strict sense we have not ideas. In like manner we know and have a notion of relations between things or ideas, which relations are distinct from the ideas or things related, inasmuch as the latter may be perceived by us without our perceiving the former.[172]

At first Berkeley repudiated 'the opinion that the mind hath a power of framing *abstract ideas* or notions of things'[173] (a view which was excised from later editions of *Alciphron*); and because of this he could not accept what he took to be Locke's view of material substance as being a distinct entity in which objects inhere (though, as we have seen, Locke was more cautious than this),[174] for substance is not perceivable, and *esse est percipi.* He sees Locke's view as tending towards materialism. Thus, although in the opening paragraph of Part I of the *Principles of Human Knowledge* (which, like Locke's *Essay,* was dedicated to the Earl of Pembroke) Berkeley can speak of ideas as being 'objects of knowledge', in the next paragraph he refers to the perceiving self which is distinct yet inseparable from them:

> [B]esides all that endless variety of ideas or objects of knowledge, there is likewise something which knows or perceives them, and exercises divers operations, as willing, imagining, remembering about them. This perceiving, active being is what I call *mind, spirit, soul,* or *my self.* By which words I do not denote any one of my ideas, but a thing entirely distinct from them, wherein they exist, or, which is the

> same thing, whereby they are perceived; for the existence of an idea consists in being perceived.[175]

Campbell Fraser was thus right to rebuke Reid, Stewart, Brown, Hamilton and Mansel for accusing Berkeley of positing ideas as independently existing entities, and of overlooking the simple fact that the mind can make its own operations its object.[176] T. E. Jessop neatly pronounced thus: '"*Esse* is *percipi*" has to be read in two ways, in order to keep in view a double emphasis – the corporeal can only be an *object* to mind, and it can *only* be an object to mind.'[177]

Equally, Berkeley cannot accept Locke's distinction between primary and secondary qualities, for this, he thinks (as others did), lands one in scepticism:

> I desire any one to reflect and try, whether he can by any abstraction of thought, conceive the extension and motion of a body, without all other sensible qualities. For my own part, I see evidently that it is not in my power to frame an idea of a body extended and moved, but I must withal give it some colour or other sensible quality which is acknowledged to exist only in the mind. In short, extension, figure, and motion, abstracted from all other qualities, are inconceivable. Where therefore the other sensible qualities are, there must these be also, to wit, in the mind and no where else.[178]

Berkeley's objective, over against mechanistic theories flowing down from Galileo, Kepler and Newton which, as construed by a Hobbes, admitted atheism, is to defend what has been branded immaterialism, and psychological idealism, but is perhaps best regarded (following Campbell Fraser) as spiritual realism: 'realism', because of Berkeley's concern to take objects in the phenomenal world at their face value: 'I question not the existence of anything that we perceive by our senses,' he wrote to Sir John Percival;[179] and 'spiritual' because of his contention that all things are eternally perceived and hence sustained in being by the sovereign God of providence:

> I do not deny the existence of any of those sensible things which Moses says were created by God. They existed from all eternity in the Divine Intellect, and they became perceptible (i.e. were created) in the same manner and order as is described in Genesis. For I take creation to belong to things only as they respect finite spirits, there being nothing new to God. Hence it follows that the act of creation

> consists in God's willing that those things should be perceptible to other spirits which before were known only to Himself.[180]

Hence Campbell Fraser's stern reply to Reid: '[W]hile Berkeley was in reality to be identified with Plato, with Cudworth, and with Clarke, [Reid] identified him with Gassendi, Hobbes, and Condillac.'[181]

As is plain from the third of the *Dialogues between Hylas and Philonous*, Berkeley's immaterialism does not reside in his denial of the reality of sensory objects, but in his view that these phenomena exist only as they are perceived by the mind – ours or God's: a view prompted by his conviction that the existence of matter (in itself a problematic term) cannot be demonstrated by inference or intuition.[182] Accordingly, such objects do not somehow exist both in the external world and in the mind. In this way (*pace* Reid, who concluded in connection with immaterialism that 'It is no more than justice to Father Malebranche, to acknowledge that Bishop Berkeley's arguments are to be found in him in their whole force'),[183] Berkeley pits himself against Locke's epistemological agnosticism, and against the conclusion of Malebranche who, 'after an arduously sustained philosophical effort, in the end fell back on a mystical intuition of God and a merely pious acceptance of a material world which he had shown to be theoretically dubitable and superfluous'.[184]

Berkeley's objective, however inadequately realised (and to pursue this question would take us too far from Locke) is summarized in the Preface to his *Three Dialogues* thus:

> Though it seems the general opinion of the world, no less than the design of Nature and Providence, that the end of speculation be practice, or the improvement and regulation of our lives and actions; yet those, who are most addicted to speculative studies, seem as generally of another mind ... Upon the common principles of philosophers, we are not assured of the existence of things from their being perceived. And we are taught to distinguish their real nature from that which falls under our senses ... Hence arise *scepticism* and *paradoxes* ... [I]t seemed necessary to ... rescue [the busy mind of man] from those endless pursuits it is engaged in. Which, with a plain demonstration of the immediate Providence of an all-seeing God, and the natural immortality of the soul, should seem the readiest preparation, as well as the strongest motive, to the study and practice of virtue ... If the principles, which I here endeavour to propagate, are admitted for

> true; the consequences which, I think, evidently flow from thence, are, that *atheism* and *scepticism* will be utterly destroyed ... and men reduced from paradoxes to common sense.[185]

Underlying all was Berkeley's conviction that 'we have at least as clear, full, and immediate certainty of the being of this infinitely wise and powerful Spirit, as of any one human soul whatsoever besides our own.'[186] This, we might almost say, is, for Berkeley, the fundamental insight of *common sense*: his God is not conceived as an underlying independent metaphysical substance of the kind variously attacked by Locke and Reid alike.[187]

To none did Berkeley's thought make a greater appeal than to Samuel Johnson, the New England Congregationalist turned Anglican, who became the first president of King's College (now Columbia University), New York. Whilst a student at Yale he had, as we saw, been warned off 'the new philosophy of *Descartes, Boyle, Locke* and *Newton*' on the ground that it would soon 'bring in a new divinity and corrupt the pure religion of the country'.[188] He gradually made good the omission, however, and became especially impressed by Locke's sensationalist epistemology, except that, like others, he feared its sceptical result, namely, that we can know only the ideas in our minds, not the realities in the phenomenal world which the ideas represent. From this predicament, and also from entanglement with Lockean abstract ideas,[189] Berkeley saved him. Johnson had met Berkeley during the latter's sojourn at Newport, Rhode Island (1729–31), and later, in 1752, he dedicated his *Elementa Philosophica* to his mentor. As Johnson understood him, Berkeley, though his denial of matter 'at first seemed shocking,' was concerned only to dispute 'the unintelligible scholastic notion of matter, and not anything either sensible, imaginable or intelligible'.[190] Like his contemporary, Reid, Johnson faulted Berkeley for not safeguarding the existence of selves other than our own, but unlike Reid he, as if echoing Malebranche and the Cambridge Platonists, resorted to 'a kind of intellectual light' of which 'we are immediately conscious'. This light is not self-originated, but comes from God.[191] He argues that

> Truth always consists in the agreement or conformity of anything with its standard. And this must be viewed (1) in the eternal mind which is truth itself and the standard of all truth ... (2) In the

> creatures, which is called *Veritas Rei* which consists in their conformity with the ideas of God which are their archetypes ... (3) In our minds, and this is called *Veritas Mentis,* which consists in the conformity of our minds with the things themselves ... (4) In our speech, and this is called *Veritas Sermonis,* which consists in the conformity of our words and speech to our minds and sentiments ... So that all the world streams forth from the divine Mind which is the original fountain of light and verity, the true ideal world, the archetype and standard of truth and goodness wherever we behold the emanations of them.[192]

Alive to the spectre of enthusiasm, Johnson cautions: 'Nor must this manner of thinking be suspected to savour of enthusiasm, it being the settled course or law of nature, according to which the great parent mind enlighteneth us ...'[193]

If Johnson's intellectual debts are clear, those of Jonathan Edwards, whose contact with Johnson at Yale appears to have been slight at best,[194] have been the subject of intense inquiry, speculation and argument. In 1716 Edwards entered Yale at the age of thirteen, and generations of students have been reared on Samuel Hopkins's report[195] that at fourteen he was eagerly reading Locke's *Essay* – a view which modern scholarship has seen fit to question,[196] and which need detain us no further. What is more important from our point of view is the insistence on the part of a number of twentieth-century scholars that Edwards's intellectual inheritance was diverse, and that the influence of Locke was more than tempered by that of other authors. Thus, for example, Berkeley, Malebranche, Norris, Cudworth, Clarke, Wollaston, Collier and the Cambridge Platonists have all been nominated as positive influences upon Edwards;[197] while William Sparkes Morris has served us well by adducing detailed evidence of the methodological importance of such antecedents of Edwards as the Dutch Calvinist scholastic logicians Burgersdyck and Heereboord (who were also staples on the syllabi of a number of English Dissenting academies),[198] and the experimental significance of such Puritans as Thomas Shepard.[199] The truth would seem to be that Edwards was a philosopher whose genius was so thoroughly theologically controlled by such notions as sin, providence and grace, that we cannot make him an out-and-out disciple of any single thinker to the exclusion of all others. He was eclectic in the most organized sense of that word, all of his sources being processed by a devout mind of unusual originality.

A considerable body of scholarship thus supports the view that Edwards was not as thoroughly committed to Lockean empiricism as some have claimed,[200] but this conclusion itself needs to be qualified by the realization that Locke himself, as we shall see in the next chapter, was much more the rationalist than he has sometimes been painted; and we do have to reckon with Edwards's death-bed testimony of indebtedness to Locke. It seems to me[201] that Edwards was stimulated by Locke (though not by him alone) at a number of critical points, and that he worked out his own positions in relation to the methods and stances of others, some of them very different in thought and style from Locke, whom he had already studied, or was concurrently studying. For the purposes of this epistemological chapter it will suffice to offer two examples in support of this contention.

First, Edwards accepts Locke's distinction between sensation and reflection, but differs from him in arguing that both presuppose the experiencing mind.[202] In this way he seeks to avoid the pitfall of scepticism which many felt loomed before Locke, and he also makes way for his metaphysical assumption of the supernatural divine spirit who holds all things in being. In other words, he qualifies and then relocates Locke's epistemological point within an ontological setting in a way quite foreign to Locke himself. Or, as James Hoopes has it, Edwards 'mainly attacked the metaphysical assumptions underlying empiricism in order to make *it* consistent with the old view of religious experience'.[203] One of the ways in which he does this is by contending that apart from knowledge of divine faith which is imparted by the Bible and the sacraments,

> the faculty of reason in [human beings] will be wholly vain ... [D]ivine subjects are the things, to know which we had the faculty of reason given us ... Therefore a man cannot have use of his faculty of understanding to any good purpose, further than he hath knowledge of divine truth.[204]

Moreover, as Edwards is careful to observe, 'This spiritual light is not the suggesting of any new truths or propositions not contained in the word of God.'[205]

Secondly, Edwards sets his face against Locke's critique of innate ideas and also his view that knowledge originates in sensory experience; but at the same time he wishes to allow due place to sensory experience when it is, as one might say, transposed into a new key. It is now the sensation of the divine presence; it is the experimentalism of the Puritans used to expand and relocate the sensation of the empiricists; it is the evidence of the heart rather than the impression in the mind.[206] At this point (although their epistemological approaches are not identical, and their theological positions are divergent in important ways) the link between the American revivalist, Edwards, and the English revivalist, Wesley, becomes clear. At least we may suggest that the 'strangely-warmed heart' is analogous to the 'sense-impressed mind'. It cannot be denied that the resulting position is significantly different from that of Locke, but that Locke was a factor in the epistemological adjustments which Edwards made is equally hard to deny. As Paul Helm has written, 'Edwards used Lockean terminology in an attempt to highlight the peculiar character of religious experience. What he emphasized was that true religious experience involved the possession of another sense altogether different in character from the natural senses.'[207] This other sense (for which he was indebted to such Calvinists as William Ames and Thomas Hooker)[208] is Edwards's 'new spiritual sense,' which is experienced by true believers, whereas the 'sense of the heart' is, though still an experimental matter, open to believers and nonbelievers alike.

On the new 'sense of the heart' as being a matter of supernaturally conveyed understanding Edwards writes at length:

> Truly spiritual and gracious affections ... arise from the enlightening of the understanding, to understand the things taught of God and Christ, in a new manner ... Such enlightenings of the understanding ... are entirely different in their nature, from strong ideas of shapes and colours, outward brightness and glory, or sounds and voices.

Spiritual understanding 'consists in the sensations of a new spiritual sense, which the souls of natural men have not,' and it is given to the saints in regeneration.[209] This 'new spiritual sense', then, is supernaturally given to believers only – a point reinforced in Edwards's *Treatise on Grace* :

> *Those that are not true saints, and in a state of salvation, not only have not so much of that holy nature and Divine principle that is in the hearts of the saints, but they do not partake of it,* because being '*partakers of the divine*

> *nature*' is spoken of as the peculiar privilege of true saints, (2 Pet. i. 4) ... Hence it will follow, that the sense of things of religion that a natural man has, is not only not to the same degree, but nothing of the same nature with that which a true saint has.[210]

Here we see clearly the way in which Edwards transposes Lockean sensationalism into an experimental key, with the underlying metaphysical motif played out in terms of saving grace conceived in particularist terms.

What, then, of human reason? Edwards insists that the saint's persuasion be reasonable. He grants that 'Men may have a *strong* persuasion that the christian religion is true, when their persuasion is not at all built on evidence, but altogether on education, and the opinion of others'; but 'By a reasonable conviction, I mean a conviction founded on *real evidence*, or upon that which is a good reason, or just ground of conviction.' The evidence is the saint's '*spiritual* conviction of the truth'.[211] Thus both the acquisition and the justification of spiritual truth are supernatural matters.

Living in revival times as he did, Edwards takes pains to insist that an individual's possession of this new sense may not be inferred from the individual's strong affections,[212] for while 'they greatly err, who condemn persons as enthusiasts, merely because their affections are very high. On the other hand, it is no evidence that religious affections are of a spiritual and gracious nature, because they are great.'[213] A 'godly walk' might provide better evidence of it (and the moral bearing of Edwards's epistemology should not be overlooked, though it is not our present concern), for the regenerate heart is acquainted with holiness. But still there is an analogy between this work of supernatural grace and Locke's epistemology, for the latter's 'simple idea' is, like the 'new spiritual sense' a matter of immediate apprehension. However, there are positive and negative analogies and, negatively, the unlikeness between the 'simple idea' and the 'new spiritual sense' is that the latter conveys *saving* knowledge.[214] The unregenerate are denied this knowledge, for

> saving grace in the heart, can't be produced in man by mere exercise of what perfections he has in him already, though never so much assisted by moral suasion, and never so much assisted in the exercise of his natural principles, unless there be something more than all this, viz., an immediate infusion or operation of the divine Being upon the

soul. Grace must be the immediate work of God, and properly a production of His almighty power on the soul.[215]

The unregenerate person is a stranger to this divine truth, 'so that he does not know what the talk of such things means; they are words without meaning to him; he knows nothing of the matter any more than a blind man of colours.'[216] Here is yet another echo of Locke's epistemology, albeit one now transposed as before; for the underlying idea here is that an unregenerate person would be using words without having corresponding ideas in the mind, and this would be in breach of Lockean epistemological propriety, for 'The use then of Words, is to be sensible Marks of *Ideas*; and the *Ideas* they stand for, are their proper and immediate Signification.'[217]

It might now be thought appropriate to exploit the link we have detected between Edwards and Wesley. But before turning to the latter we must retrace our steps to Joseph Butler, for his epistemological caution is greater even than Locke's, and his emphasis upon probability was a significant element in the air Wesley breathed.[218] Negatively, Butler eschews Berkeley's immaterialism and Edwards's supernaturalist epistemology. He is highly suspicious of metaphysical systems which purport to yield knowledge greater than is truly open to human beings, and he shuns the *a priori* road. As Terence Penelhum has pointed out, Butler follows Locke in suggesting that 'genuine knowledge of the physical world would be knowledge of the interrelationships of the primary qualities of things, and would consist of necessary, and therefore a priori truths.'[219] Such knowledge is denied to us – yet, as Penelhum also points out, 'Butler follows Locke in another key respect ...: whatever the limits in our understanding the system of the world, we are capable of understanding the fact that it is indeed a created system – that God exists and governs it.'[220] Whereas, as we shall see in the next chapter, Locke, in *scholastic* fashion, essayed a theistic proof, Butler did not; but the theistic assumption itself sits uneasily with proclaimed empiricism. As so often, philosophers are at their most revealing and vulnerable when they knowingly break their own ground rules.

Positively, Butler's thought moves in the line of Newtonian empiricism, and he is much indebted to Locke for his notion of probability. Moreover, as with Locke, so with Butler, his overriding concern is with morality, with the practical, though Butler deals more centrally with this than Locke ever did. To put Butler's theme in a crudely concise way, we may say that for him the fact that there is much that we do not know may have the advantage of directing our attention to what we do know – namely, our duty humbly to obey God. All of this becomes clear in the Introduction to *The Analogy of Religion*, and in the last of Butler's *Fifteen Sermons.*

Butler wastes no time. 'Probable evidence,' he writes in the first sentence of the *Analogy*, 'is essentially distinguished from demonstrative by this, that it admits of degrees, and of all variety of them, from the highest moral certainty to the very lowest presumption.'[221] He grants that 'Probable evidence, in its very nature, affords but an imperfect kind of information,' but 'to us probability is the very guide of life.' Moreover, it is far more prudent to content ourselves with this than to speculate upon the basis of unfounded assumptions, or to ask 'how the world might have been framed otherwise than it is,' because 'we have not faculties for this kind of speculation.' The appropriate procedure is to 'compare the known constitution and course of things with what is said to be the moral system of nature'.[222] A corollary of Butler's strict evidentialism is his anti-intuitionalism: 'religion is not intuitively true, but a matter of deduction and inference.'[223]

In the fifteenth Sermon, 'Upon the ignorance of man' (Eccles. 8:16–17), Butler allows that

> we may know somewhat concerning the designs of Providence in the government of the world, enough to enforce upon us religion and the practice of virtue : yet, since the monarchy of the universe is a dominion unlimited in extent, and everlasting in duration; the general system of it must necessarily be quite beyond our comprehension.[224]

It follows that 'If to acquire knowledge were our proper end, we should indeed be but poorly provided.' In fact, however, 'Knowledge is not our proper happiness'; rather, we are exhorted to 'Fear God, and keep his commandments; for this is the whole concern of man.'[225]

Like Locke and Butler, Wesley is well aware of the limits of human knowledge. There are mysteries which the human mind shall never fathom. But Wesley's response to this aspect of the human condition marks him off from both his forebears, and aligns him more closely with Edwards, whose *Affections* he had abridged. Whereas for Locke (as we shall see more fully in the next chapter), faith is intellectual assent to a proposition revealed by God by way of supplying the deficiencies of our reason;[226] while for Butler our remedy when we can see no further is to get on with what we can see; for Wesley 'A full conviction of our own ignorance may teach us a full trust in his wisdom. It may teach us (what is not always so easy as one would conceive it to be) to trust the invisible God, farther than we can see him.'[227] From the human side, then, faith, for Wesley, is trust: it is at the heart of experimental religion. But this faith is a response to God's revelation, and to the divine address to human beings by the Spirit – concerning which, in their famous exchange of August 1739, Butler declared to Wesley that 'the pretending to extraordinary revelations and gifts of the Holy Spirit was a horrid thing – a very horrid thing.'[228]

But however much Wesley may have filled out the idea of faith – even to the extent of fixing a gulf between his understanding of it and Locke's, he never ceased to praise Locke, whose *Essay* 'contains many excellent truths, proposed in a clear and strong manner by a great master both of reasoning and language'.[229] In particular, Wesley – at least on a number of occasions – welcomes Locke's demolition of innate ideas. He argues that if God had stamped an idea of himself upon every human soul, we could not but be aware of his attributes, 'but the truth is, no man ever did, or does now, find any such idea stamped on his soul.'[230] But it is important not to make Wesley too Lockean[231] for, on the other hand, Wesley has an important place for Edwards-like spiritual senses which are graciously stimulated by the Holy Spirit, and which enable the direct apprehension of God; though, to take up my point that Edwards and Wesley are not epistemologically identical, I have some sympathy with J. Steven O'Malley's remark that 'Whereas Wesley suggested the operation of two parallel systems of sense faculties, one for the natural and the other for the supernatural "worlds" Edwards sought to demonstrate the ontological unity between the two realms.'[232] Be that as it may, in his first *Appeal to Men of Reason and Religion*, Wesley announces the necessity of 'a new class of [spiritual] senses opened in your soul, not depending on organs of flesh and blood ... to furnish you with ideas of what the outward "eye hath not seen, neither the ear heard."'[233] This is so radical a rebaptism of Locke's sensationalism that Gerald Cragg's comment on these words, namely, that 'Wesley's interpretation of the senses is a part of the epistemology he derived from Locke'[234] is somewhat misleading; though, as Cragg says, Wesley did agree with Locke in rejecting innate ideas, as we have seen. The sentiments expressed by Wesley are much more akin (in interestingly different ways) to the Puritan and Platonist inheritance he shared with his American counterpart.[235] Furthermore, his position on the 'new class of senses' distanced him from Peter Browne (whose book *The Procedure, Extent and Limits of Human Understanding* Wesley abridged in 1730), who, disallowing Locke's ideas of reflection, held that knowledge is derived from sensation alone, and that knowledge of God could be gained indirectly only, from reasoning about experience.

Henry D. Rack has justly declared that

> Wesley, though he kept the capacity for the older kind of point-scoring and clever syllogisms which annoyed more than they convinced, was also much influenced by Lockeian empiricism. The way in which he combined this with a more traditional supernaturalism is important for any estimate of his outlook and character.[236]

I have suggested that it is the proposition contained in Dr Rack's second sentence which yields the clue to his distance from Locke, for all his undoubted indebtedness to him. This distance, in Wesley's case as in Edwards's, was occasioned by the recalling, in an intellectual context of deism, scepticism and encroaching materialism, of an older experimentalism now rebaptized in terms *analogous* (positively and negatively) *to* Locke's sensationalism, rather than by a radical new departure from it or a linear development of it. Locke's sensationalism provided a significant part of the stimulus to Wesley's thought (though other intellectual debts are not to be overlooked), but the supernatural, pneumatic and experimental elements in the thought of both Wesley and Edwards would almost certainly have aroused in Locke's mind – and they did in Butler's – the suspicion of enthusiasm.

III

It remains to introduce Locke's understanding of truth, and to investigate the responses of the eighteenth-century divines to it. Of the Presbyterian divine, Noah Jones (1725–85) it was written that when at Carmarthen academy under Samuel Thomas,

> One of the first books which Mr. Thomas put into his hands was Dr. Watts' Logick, which he read with great pleasure twice over. This treatise together with Mr. Locke's Essay on the Understanding taught him to think freely, and put him upon the right scent in his enquiries after truth.[237]

Many other eighteenth-century divines could have said the same, and many did. But what is interesting is the fact that Locke does not expatiate unduly on truth as such. Not surprisingly, therefore, the eighteenth-century divines do not have a great deal to say, positively or negatively, concerning Locke on truth. Locke bequeathed a method of inquiry, rather than a detailed theory of truth technically construed; and he advocated truth-telling as a moral duty – something which, in the climate of intellectual liberty following the Toleration Act of 1689 the divines had little excuse for declining. Moreover, Locke's view that truths received by long tradition grow more suspect the farther they are from their source fertilized a climate of thought in which more intellectually adventurous divines could flourish.[238]

There can be little doubt that Locke would have been gratified by Noah Jones's determination to go in quest of truth. In the 'Epistle to the Reader' prefixed to his *Essay*, Locke declares that he who has raised himself above the Alms-Basket, and not content to live lazily on scraps of begg'd Opinions, sets his own Thoughts on work, to find and follow Truth, will ... not miss the Hunter's Satisfaction ... Taking his own advice, and while open to the possibility that his *Essay* contained errors of which he was unaware, he declared, 'there is nothing in this Treatise of the Truth whereof I am not fully persuaded'.[239] In a letter to Anthony Collins he testified, 'to love truth, for truth's sake, is the principal part of human perfection in this world, and the seed-plot of all other virtues.'[240]

Over eighty years later Abraham Rees, Dissenting tutor at the liberal Hackney College (1786–96) noted Locke's words in a published address delivered in 1788 to supporters of the infant academy. The burden of his message was that students 'should be led to cultivate a prevailing love of [religious truth], to pursue it with integrity, to embrace it upon conviction, and to retain it against all opposing prejudices and interests, till farther information and new evidence constrain them to alter their opinion'.[241] That Rees practised what he preached is clear, though the manner in which he did it was not confrontational: 'The area of controversy he seldom entered. When he wished to destroy error, his plan was to inculcate the opposite truth. He aimed rather to sap than to storm the fortifications of the adversary.'[242]

Locke was under no illusions concerning the unscrupulous – or even well-intentioned – disfigurement of truth. He opens his celebrated chapter 'Of Enthusiasm,' which he added to the fourth edition of the *Essay* (1700), in very deliberate manner:

> He that would seriously set upon the search of Truth, ought in the first Place to prepare his Mind with a Love of it. For he that Loves it not, will not take much Pains to get it; nor be much concerned when he misses it. There is no Body in the Commonwealth of Learning, who does not profess himself a lover of Truth: and there is not a rational Creature that would not take it amiss to be thought otherwise of. And yet for all this one may truly say, there are very few lovers of Truth for Truths sake, even amongst those, who perswade themselves that they are so. How a Man may know whether he be so in earnest is worth enquiry: And I think there is this one unerring mark of it, *viz*, The not entertaining any Proposition with greater assurance than the Proofs it is built upon will warrant. For the evidence that any Proposition is true (except such as are self-evident) lying only in the Proofs a Man has of it, whatsoever degrees of Assent he affords it beyond the degrees of that Evidence, 'tis plain all that surplusage of assurance is owing to some other Affection, and not to the Love of Truth ...[243]

In an address to the British Academy delivered on 28 October 1904, Alexander Campbell Fraser quoted the above words and remarked,

> Perhaps exclusive regard for the *lumen siccum* made [Locke] apt unduly to disparage emotion and imagination, faith and will, as factors in the final interpretation of human existence, and to forget that all that is highest in man must be in response to all that is highest in existence, in order to a true insight of the realities.[244]

In Fraser's words lie the seeds of an apologetic method, as well as a reminder that when reviewing the work of philosophers we do well to consider what they overlook, as well as what they write. But my immediate purpose in quoting Campbell Fraser is to suggest that between Locke's time and his, Jonathan Edwards had already in practice, if not by way of overt criticism of Locke, filled out Locke's account of truth. In the context of epistemology, Locke's view is that truth has to do not with ideas, but with propositions derived from the judgements made regarding the relations of ideas:

> *Truth* then seems to me, in the proper import of the Word, to signify nothing but *the joining or separating of Signs, as the Things signified by them, do agree or disagree one with another.* The *joining* or *separating* of signs here meant is what by another name, we call Proposition. So that Truth properly belongs only to Propositions: whereof there are two sorts, *viz.*, Mental and Verbal; as there are two sorts of Signs commonly made use of, *viz.*, *Ideas* and Words.[245]

Edwards sets out from the very Locke-like definition that 'TRUTH is *The perception of the relations there are between ideas*'; proceeds to the definition: 'TRUTH, in the general, may be defined, after the most strict and metaphysical manner. *The consistency and agreement of our ideas, with the ideas of God*'; thence to this: 'TRUTH. After all that has been said and done, the only adequate definition of Truth is, The agreement of our ideas with existence'; and finally he defines knowledge thus: 'KNOWLEDGE is not the perception of the *agreement, or disagreement*, of ideas, but rather the perception of the *union*, or *disunion*, of ideas – or the perceiving whether two or more ideas belong to one another.' For these quotations I am indebted to the fuller account of William Sparkes Morris,[246] who concludes that on the question of truth, Edwards

> thinks through Locke's early view of truth as logical consistency of ideas, where coherence is both the nature and criterion of truth; through the later conception of truth as correspondence with fact, i.e., with existence; back to the Suáresian conception of truth as a transcendental attribute of God considered as ultimate being.[247]

How far this last position accords with Locke's view that the affirmation of God as true is an article of faith,[248] we need not stay to inquire.

Epistemology apart, 'truth' for Locke has serious moral

connotations. Thus, in his down-to-earth way, Locke writes on the 'management of children,' and laments the fact that 'Lying and equivocations ... are put into the mouths of young people, and commended in apprentices and children, whilst they are for their master's or parent's advantage.'[249] With reference to the child, he recommends that

> Having laid the foundations of virtue in a true notion of a God, such as the creed wisely teaches, as far as his age is capable, and by accustoming him to pray to him; the next thing to be taken care of, is to keep him exactly to speaking of truth, and by all the ways imaginable inclining him to be good-natured.[250]

It is equally important that children be given truthful answers to their queries.[251]

In a word, truth is a matter of practice. As Maurice Cranston has said, 'Locke believed that a life of action was a necessary part of the life of reason and that a man could not discover truth by sitting still and thinking, but only by personal experience of life.'[252] A number of divines concurred, especially when the experience of life was deemed to include the experience of God's grace. In part the divines were echoing the Puritan emphasis upon a 'godly walk' as evidence of a person's being 'in the truth';[253] and the Quaker ambition of 'truthing it in love' (Ephesians 4:15). But just as Jonathan Edwards went beyond Locke's epistemology in his metaphysical way, so the evangelical divines of the later eighteenth century went beyond Locke in their emphasis upon the claim that the truth is seen in Jesus Christ, and that this truth, though it presupposes truth claims concerning who Christ is, is fundamentally a matter of intimate acquaintance with Christ, the Truth. Such a view was propounded by the Baptist Robert Hall, Sr, in his *Help to Zion's Travellers*, (1781).[254] For his part, the pioneer and first secretary (the 'rope holder') of the Baptist Missionary Society (1792), Andrew Fuller, wrote an 'Essay on Truth' in which he declared,

> There is an importance in truth, as it relates to philosophy, history, politics, or any other branch of science, inasmuch as it affects the present happiness of mankind: but what is this when compared with that which involves their everlasting salvation? To be furnished with an answer to the question, 'What shall I do to be saved?' is of infinitely greater acount than to be able to decide whether the Ptolemaic or Copernican system be that of nature.[255]

The revealed truth of which Fuller speaks is 'the model and standard of true religion in the mind'; it 'furnishes the motive for every exercise of true holiness'; it is that for the sake of which we love other Christians, and it is 'the only solid foundation of peace and happiness'.[256]

It is not surprising that more missionary-minded Baptists should wish to make a 'credible profession,' and to avoid hypocrisy, for those to whom missionaries went would see their actions before they could understand their words. But their counterpart, the Independent David Bogue, a founder of the London Missionary Society (1795), applied lessons drawn from truthful living to doctrinal questions nearer to home. Contrasting the evangelical believer with the rational Christian he declared that while the former is assiduous concerning private devotions, the latter is not; the former delight more than the latter in public worship; the former rejoice in Christ at the approach of death, while the latter 'have not the same ground of hope'; while the evangelicals are found 'most anxiously thirsting after the salvation of their fellow-creatures,' the rational Christians have no such zeal; the views of the evangelicals are 'rejected and accounted foolishness by the self-righteous, and the children of human wisdom,' while 'We meet with nothing of this kind in the other system.'[257]

We may allow the rational Dissenter and Unitarian, Thomas Belsham, the right of reply:

> If a man does not believe the christian religion to be true, how can he teach it to others? If he does not believe the doctrine to be important, what inducement can he have to study the scriptures? If error is attended with no practical disadvantage, why should he take any pains to avoid it? If the knowledge of truth is of so little use as some seem to apprehend, why was Jesus divinely authorised to make it known?[258]

And the tribute to the evangelical Calvinist Caleb Evans, principal of Bristol Baptist College, by his friend Samuel Stennett makes it clear that some were able to walk the middle way:

> [A]midst the zeal he felt for the truth, he knew how to exercise charity towards those from whom he differed. He was no bigot, he could not be such, for he well understood the rights of private judgment [a phrase beloved of *liberal* Dissenters], was sensible of the weakness of the human intellect, and felt the difficulties of truly upright minds on points wherein he and they could not agree.[259]

The criteria of truth specified by Hall, Fuller and Bogue are far from what Locke had in mind (though he did think that the best way to find truth was by a good life).[260] He was concerned, however, with true religion, and deeply resented the contention of the high-church anti-Latitudinarian, Jonas Proast, that Locke's plea for toleration entailed the view that he sat loose to truth in religion. On the contrary, says Locke: 'To you and me the christian religion is the true, and that is built, to mention no other articles of it, on this, that Jesus Christ was put to death at Jerusalem, and rose again from the dead.'[261] He does, however, proceed immediately to grant that

> whatever is not capable of demonstration, as such remote matters of fact are not, is not, unless it be self-evident, capable to produce knowledge, how well grounded and great soever the assurance of faith may be wherewith it is received; but faith it is still, and not knowledge; persuasion, and not certainty.[262]

This (though, as we shall see, it sits uneasily with some of his remarks on revelation, faith and Scripture) is consistent with his general epistemological doctrine that

> the *Names of Substances*, when made use of as they should be, for the *Ideas* Men have in their Minds, though they carry a clear and determinate signification with them, *will not* yet *serve us to make many universal Propositions, of whose Truth we can be certain.* Not because in this use of them we are uncertain what Things are signified by them, but because the complex *Ideas* they stand for, are such Combinations of simple ones, as carry not with them any discoverable connexion or repugnancy, but with a very few other *Ideas.*[263]

In the next chapter we shall see that there is a certain ambivalence in Locke regarding the epistemological status of faith; in the fifth chapter we shall address in more detail his view on toleration; and in the sixth, his understanding of some prominent Christian doctrines.

IV

We set out from a consideration of Locke's critique of innate ideas, noting that while some eighteenth-century divines welcomed this, others rebuked Locke for, as they thought, opening the door to scepticism, atheism and materialism. We then turned to Locke's 'way of ideas', and discovered that here too there were cordial receptions and blanket condemnations on the part of the divines. But there were also more discerning analyses by those who, while far from willing to denounce Locke out of hand, nevertheless built upon, or supplemented his views in directions as diverse as Berkeley's immaterialism and Edwards's and Wesley's 'new spiritual sense'. Overall, there was relatively little slavish following of Locke, least of all on the part of the most notable thinkers. That he did, however, introduce many to a fresh quest of truth there can be no doubt. We shall have to see whether similar conclusions will follow our study of the divines' responses to Locke on reason, revelation, faith and Scripture.

Before proceeding, a word of caution is in order concerning the pitfall of anachronism. We shall see that Locke and the majority of the eighteenth-century divines were caught up in the cosmological approach which characterized the intellectual life of the eighteenth century. It is therefore all the more important to remember that the recovery by Edwards, Wesley and others of 'sense' and 'experience' in their Puritan and experimental connotations was not with a view to mounting novel theistic arguments. Not until after the Humean and Kantian devastation of the traditional theistic arguments, and the new departure in theology represented by Schleiermacher, were such arguments – with all the attendant charges of psychologism – devised. We must also be prepared for distinctly different understandings of the epistemic significance of 'faith' as between Locke and some of the divines, albeit Locke verges upon *fiducia* in his *Paraphrases.*

3

Reason, Revelation, Faith and Scripture

I now proceed to a discussion of reason; reason and revelation; reason, faith and the Spirit; and Scripture. In each case we shall see that Locke and those confessedly indebted to him were no 'mere' rationalists; while others, in adversely criticizing his views, were attempting to maintain the direct access of the human mind to God, and/or to commend a less intellectualist, or (to speak anachronistically) a more 'existentialist' view of faith.

I

> *The Word Reason* [says Locke] in the *English* Language has different *Significations*: sometimes it is taken for true, and clear Principles: Sometimes for clear, and fair deductions from those Principles: and sometimes for the Cause, and particularly the final Cause. But the Consideration I shall have of it here, is in a Signification different from all these; and that is, as it stands for a Faculty in Man, That Faculty, whereby Man is supposed to be distinguished from Beasts, and wherein it is evident he much surpasses them.[1]

Locke is here consciously departing from scholastic understandings of reason as logic, and from the syllogism as the supreme form of argumentation. In his view those skilled in syllogistic inference may not be as adept in perceiving a weakness in argumentation as those who are not so skilled; and scholastic reasoners are no less liable to fallacious reasoning than others. Moreover syllogistic reasoning is incompetent where the quest of probability is in view, and, far from enabling us to discover new proofs, its brief is but that of 'marshalling, and ranging the old ones we have already'.[2] Later, when distinguishing reason from faith (to which latter concept we shall come in due course), Locke explains that reason is 'the discovery of the Certainty or Probability of such Propositions or Truths, which the Mind arrives at by Deductions made from such *Ideas,* which it has got by the use of its natural Faculties, *viz.* by Sensation or Reflection'.[3] Reason is thus the faculty of ratiocination, of discursive reasoning. By it we enlarge our knowledge and regulate our assent; and, insofar as reason contains sagacity and illation, it enables us to discover, and to perceive the connection between, our ideas.[4] As he famously said, '*Reason* must be our last Judge and Guide in every Thing.'[5]

Nor is this all. As Roland Hall reminds us, 'Locke is very serious in laying emphasis on the God-given nature of Reason';[6] and he refers to the fact that, after the fashion of the Cambridge Platonist, Benjamin Whichcote, for whom 'The spirit of a Man is the Candle of the Lord; Lighted by God, and Lighting us to God',[7] 'candle' occurs nine times in Locke's *Essay.* Human beings thus 'have Light enough to lead them to Knowledge of their Maker, and the sight of their own Duties ... The Candle, that is set up in us, shines bright enough for all our Purposes.'[8] Not surprisingly, perhaps, the deliverances of this reason cannot be gainsaid.[9] In a word, we are now in the realm of 'natural *Revelation*, whereby the Eternal Father of Light, and Fountain of all Knowledge, communicates to Mankind that portion of Truth, which he has laid within the reach of their natural Faculties'.[10] With none of this would such Anglicans as Hooker, Chillingworth, William Sherlock, Stillingfleet and Warburton have disagreed.[11]

On this foundation natural theology can proceed. God's existence can be certainly known: indeed, of God's existence alone may we have knowledge otherwise than from sense experience: 'No existence of any thing without us, but only of GOD, can certainly be known farther than our Senses inform us.'[12] In the case of God, Locke maintains that we may, by a process of reflection upon the order and beauty of the world, conclude to the existence of God – such a conclusion having the force of a reasoned demonstration.[13] God has, after all, 'left so many footsteps of himself, so many proofs of His being.'[14] Thus far Locke is in the line of the classical cosmological-*cum*-teleological arguments. In the *Essay* he proceeds from our intuitive knowledge of our own existence to ourselves as knowers; and thence to God as the one alone who can produce knowing beings.[15] It is not that we have innate ideas of God (hence his disdain of the ontological argument),[16] but rather, that by a process of inference utilizing the faculties of sense, perception and reason we conclude to God with a certainty 'equal to mathematical Certainty,' and by going 'no farther than our selves' – that is, than the faculties with which we are endowed.[17] In framing our idea of the supreme being, we enlarge to infinity such ideas as those of existence, duration, knowledge, power, pleasure and happiness, which ideas we have gained from reflection upon our experience, 'and so putting them together, make our complex *Idea of God*'.[18] Like his Puritan forebears and contemporaries, Locke by no means thinks that we can have complete knowledge of God. He would have agreed with John Mason (?1646–94) that 'We may truly conceive of God, though we cannot fully conceive of Him. We may have right apprehensions of Him, though not an exact comprehension of Him.'[19]

A careful examination of Locke's theism leaves us in no doubt that for him, as, indeed, for most eighteenth-century divines, the cosmological argument is central. Indeed, it is 'so fundamental a Truth ... that all Religion and genuine Morality depend thereon'.[20] In this claim resides the final recurrent strand in Locke's understanding of 'reason' – 'right reason'. From right reason flow 'certain definite principles of action from which spring all virtues and whatever is necessary for the proper moulding of morals'.[21] On this I shall have more to say in the chapter on morality. For the present we may note that Locke's theism is largely in the tradition of Thomist scholasticism, whose deficiencies it shares;[22] and that while there are echoes of Puritan thought in his writing, these stop short of any serious recognition of the possible epistemological implications of the noetic effects of sin. In this connection the remark of John Laird (who had no Puritan axe to grind) is instructive:

> From the disputable principle that a cognitive principle implies a cognitive cause, Locke inferred that there must be a single cognitive First Cause which must have produced all the 'order, harmony and beauty which are to be found in nature.' All that his reasoning entitled

> him to infer, however, was that, since he existed, there must have been a sequence of cause-factors sufficient to produce all the order, harmony and beauty, as well as all the disorder, ugliness and discord, that were to be found in *him.*[23]

Our task now is not so much to attack or defend Locke's position on reason, but to see what the eighteenth-century divines made of it. It will make for clarity if we classify our findings according to the themes thus far exhibited: reason as a faculty and the activity of reasoning; and reason as enabling a viable natural theology. It will further assist if we think in terms of a continuum between two poles of thought. That the eighteenth century provides examples at either extreme is clear from the briefest glance at William Law and Ethan Allen (no divine he!).

In his book, *The Case of Reason, Or Natural Religion Fairly and Fully Stated* (1731), the English spiritual writer William Law inveighed against Latitudinarianism in general and the deist Matthew Tindal in particular. In his view, the present infidelity looks for its support to the 'absolute perfection of reason or Natural Religion'.[24] In fact, reason offers no support to Christianity, nor is it capable of refuting it. It is utterly distinct from revelation, and can in no sense judge its deliverances. It has nothing to say where matters of faith or morals are concerned. E. C. Mossner concluded, Law's book 'presages, on the destructive side, the universal skepticism of Hume, and on the constructive, Methodism or the renewal of enthusiasm foreshadowing the later idealistic theology of Coleridge'.[25] However, this verdict should be qualified by the realization that Wesley himself came to feel that 'Tauler, Behmen and an whole army of Mystic authors are with me nothing to St. Paul,'[26] while the question how far Hume was an unqualified sceptic is being debated to this day.[27] For his own part, Wesley may be placed somewhere between Locke and Law (though somewhat closer to the former) on our 'anti-reason/reason is all' continuum. To the 'Men of Reason and Religion' he says, 'We join with you … in desiring a religion founded on reason, and every way agreeable thereto.' He contends that the faculty of reason is that whereby we draw inferences from one thing to another; but the material on which reason works does not comprise Cartesian innate ideas, but the deliverances of experience – not least of religious experience, the latter issuing in a faith ('the eye of the new-born soul') which both knows and feels.[28] We are here verging upon an understanding of experience as 'experimental' – even, to speak anachronistically, as existential; and we must pay due heed to the distance, signalled in the preceding chapter, between Locke's sensationalism whereby representations of external objects are perceived by the mind, and Wesley's, whereby the heart is 'strangely warmed'. That Wesley himself appreciated the distinction is clear from his declaration in his *Earnest Appeal to Men of Reason and Religion* (1743) that 'the ideas of faith differ *toto genere* from those of external sensation,' and that 'the deep things of God are revealed by the Holy Spirit.'[29] But that Wesley's position was open to misunderstanding (whether intentional or otherwise) is clear from the assertion of Thomas Rutherford, professor of divinity at Cambridge, that the renunciation of reason was a 'fundamental principle' of Methodism – to which 'gross untruth' Wesley replied, 'It is a fundamental principle with us that to renounce reason is to renounce religion, that reason and religion go hand in hand, and that all irrational religion is false religion.'[30]

At the other pole stands the idiosyncratic war hero and self-taught rationalist, Ethan Allen, the title of whose work, *Reason the only Oracle of Man* (1784) is sufficiently indicative of his general stance. Allen was not sure whether he was a deist, but he was utterly persuaded that he was no Calvinist.[31] Allen's book is a homespun invective against the Puritan tradition which had nurtured his land and spawned scholastic systems of Calvinist theology which he proceeded to dismantle. Whereas the English Dissenting divine, Abraham Taylor, had underscored the noetic effects of sin, and held that 'If we consider matters justly and impartially, we must conclude; that Adam our common parent, impair'd his intellectuals greatly by his fall ...'[32] Allen expostulated, 'for depraved creatures to receive and give credit to a depraved doctrine, started and taught by depraved creatures, is the greatest weakness and folly imaginable, and comes nearer a proof of the doctrine of a total depravity, than any arguments which have ever been advanced in support of it.'[33] According to President Dwight of Yale, Allen's 'was the first formal publication in the United States openly directed against the Christian religion'.[34] With his theory of emanations Allen verged upon pantheism, but then, fearful of immanentism, he posited two causes: one first, one eternal, thereby bequeathing a God–nature dualism which Emerson subsequently sought to resolve by appealing to the absolute.[35]

The poles exemplified, we find Locke somewhat to the rationalist side of our continuum. Locke would have endorsed the words of his contemporary, Richard Baxter: 'What more can be done to the Disgrace and Ruin of Christianity than to make the world believe that we have no reason for it.'[36] However, Baxter was more favourably disposed towards the doctrine of innate ideas: 'Whatsoever the soul of man doth entertain must make its first entrance at the understanding.'[37] On the other hand, for all his suspicion of 'enthusiasm', we find Baxter writing towards the end of his life: 'Reason is a sleepy half-useless thing, till some Passion excite it.'[38]

Among those who were in broad sympathy with Locke's view of reason was Joshua Oldfield, a Presbyterian divine who conducted Dissenting academies successively at Coventry, Southwark and Hoxton Square, London, and who published *An Essay Towards the Improvement of Reason* in 1707.[39] Convinced, as was Locke, that reason is a moral and intellectual faculty, and willing to defend Locke against unjust accusations, the Anglican Arian Samuel Clarke was not a sensationalist in epistemology, and although he utilized a version of the cosmological argument for the existence of God, his thought took a decidedly *a priori* tilt, and assumed, in the words of James Martineau, 'some of the harder features of what is called Rationalism'.[40] But if Clarke the Arian veered in the direction of rationalism, so did those champions of orthodoxy, the Particular Baptists John Gill and John Brine.[41] Though not devoid of religious experimentalism, as we shall see, their systems of doctrine issued deductively from the controlling axiom of the sovereign God ('I shall begin with the Being of God,' declared Gill),[42] whose existence could, they thought, be proved by the arguments of natural theology,[43] but whose nature and purpose could be known only from authoritative Scripture.[44] The aforementioned Abraham Taylor, tutor at the Clerkenwell-Deptford Independent Academy, which was conducted under the auspices of the King's Head Society, was a staunch Calvinist (notwithstanding a dispute with John Gill, who in 1732 managed to find a tinge of Arminianism in Taylor). He charged Locke with being nothing more than a Socinian in principle, of being 'no great friend of revelation', and of having a low view of divine mysteries. Locke's literary knowledge 'was but very superficial'.[45]

We may observe in passing that not the least importance of the Gills, Brines, Taylors and their ilk is their reminder to the incautious that rationalism in theology does not necessarily lead to a reduction or paring down of Christian doctrines to suit the mind of the reasoner. Indeed, one might almost say that on occasion a rational approach to doctrine seems to tell us more than we have any right to know, or can know, concerning God's *inscrutable* will! Undeniably, however, rationalistic doctrinal reductionism did come more to the fore as the century progressed, and it was nowhere more in evidence than in the writings of Joseph Priestley. But even then the rationalism was selective. In Priestley's case there was what passed in him for a biblical control. This permitted him to dispense with the Virgin Birth, the sinlessness of Jesus, whilst retaining (even after Hume) his belief in the evidential value of miracles.

Among the excitements of 1741 was the publication of Henry Dodwell's *Christianity not founded on Argument.* Some on the evangelical wing of Christianity were persuaded that the author's intention was to make room for faith. To Philip Doddridge, however, the book was redolent of deism, and it provoked a rare piece of polemics in his *Answer to a Late Pamphlet* (1743). Doddridge, for all the warmth of his hymns and his pioneering yet temperate evangelical zeal, stood with Locke in maintaining the reasonableness of Christianity, and he construed Dodwell as maintaining that Christianity, being irrational, was inferior to the rational way.[46] Three years later, John Leland rebuked Dodwell thus:

> It certainly argues a very peculiar degree of Assurance in this Writer, in the same Pamphlet in which he takes occasion to mention the illustrious Names of Lord Bacon, Mr. Boyle, Mr. Locke, and Sir Isaac Newton, the greatest Philosophers of this, or perhaps any Age, to take upon him to pronounce with so much Confidence, that there is an irreconcilable Opposition between the Christian Religion and Philosophy, and that no Man can be a good Christian and Philosopher at once.[47]

John Wesley was among others who were far from having the wool pulled over their eyes. By presenting Christianity as irrational, Dodwell's 'great design,' he declared, 'was, to render the whole of the Christian Institution both odious and contemptible'.[48]

A different criticism of Locke's view of reason issued from Scotland in 1768. It took the form of a protest in favour of common sense from James Oswald, a member of that Scottish philosophical tradition. 'That Mr. Locke seriously believed the great truths of religion,' declares this parish minister, 'and was sincerely attached to them, will not be doubted: but the evidence he offers for the belief of those truths is not sufficient to give satisfaction to the bulk of mankind.'[49] We are not shut up to self-produced evidence: there is the common sense of humanity, and this Locke overlooks. He does not utilize 'that evidence which belongs to the primary truths of religion'.[50] More particularly, he does not distinguish between reason and reasoning. Had he done so, many cavils which beset philosophy would never have been articulated. As it is, according to Locke every kind of truth must be traced by a chain of reasoning either to the testimony of our senses or to the axioms of the schools. But the truths of religion are self-evident.[51]

With the increasing impact of the Great Awakening in the New World and the Evangelical Revival in the Old, some resorted to reason as a brake upon the excesses of enthusiasm which the revivals could engender. To take two random examples: Charles Chauncy, who had been a moderate Calvinist, was urged in a more liberal direction in part by his concern that

> there have not been wanting Instances, even in our own Day, of those, who under the vain Notion of being extraordinarily sent of God, have gone about venting their own wild Imaginations for divine Truths, to the great Reproach of CHRIST, and Scandal of Religion.'[52]

In 1747, now in connection with his view that civil government originates in reason, Chauncy declared that 'the voice of reason is the voice of God.'[53] For his part, John Taylor, in his posthumously published work, *The Scripture Account of Prayer*, qualified his general dislike of read prayers which cannot match the needs of the worshippers by saying that such prayers are nevertheless preferable to those of a man 'who fills his Prayers with fantastical, conceited Expressions, private Notions, senseless Sounds, tedious Babblings, and affected Heats'.[54]

Not that the evangelicals altogether repudiated the offerings of reason. On the contrary, Baptists commonly expected that candidates for believers' baptism would exercise reason and conscience; while those Independent Walsall seceders from Arianism, who adopted and signed their Confession of Faith on 21 September 1763, declared, 'We learn from both reason and Scripture that a Church of Christ has a Right to require satisfactory Evidence of Repentance towards God and Faith in our Lord Jesus Christ, of every one who desires admission to it ...'[55] Here reason precedes Scripture. It cannot, however, be denied that there is a change of tone in William Enfield's funeral oration for John Aikin, sometime professor of divinity at the Dissenting academy in the 'Athens of the North' – Warrington:

> Whilst he readily acknowledged the existence, and the powerful operation, of original principles in human nature, he was no advocate for that indolent philosophy (so well adapted to the spirit and manners of the present age) which has raised an unnatural contest between *Reason* and *Common Sense,* and instructed men to trust to their feelings rather than to their understandings. He thought it the duty of every rational being to employ his powers of reasoning and judging in the search of truth, and to endeavour to deduce the practical rules of life and manners from such theoretical propositions as have been established by conclusive argumentation. Accordingly, he employed his most serious thoughts in framing a consistent and connected system of belief, which, though not wholly free from difficulties, might however have the support of probable evidence from reason or testimony.[56]

But whether liberal or evangelical, Calvinist or Arminian, the majority of eighteenth-century divines were united in the belief that reason could and should supply theistic arguments as grounds of belief, and as supplements to the biblical revelation. Many eighteenth-century divines of various theological hues would have agreed with Thomas Amory, himself the successor of Henry Grove at Taunton Academy and a liberal, Clarkean Presbyterian, when he declared:

> As to the great Doctrines therefore of *Natural Religion,* which the *Gospel* takes for granted, and which are the foundations of our Faith in any Divine Revelation, because these can only be proved by reasonings on the nature of things, the frame of the world, and the like; we must, by arguments of this sort, addressed to the Reason of

> Men, endeavour to establish in them the belief of the Being, Perfections, and moral Providence of God; of the moral and essential differences of characters and actions, and of a future state of recompense ... As all men therefore are obliged to receive these Truths, and are *capable* of discerning the evidences of them; all they, whom we would confirm in the faith of these, have a right to demand from us *rational* grounds for their faith. To require that they should believe, without good reasons, what we affirm on these heads, is to exalt ourselves into *Lords of Faith*, and degrade them to a level with *brutes.*[57]

This is not to say that every divine produced a set of theistic arguments – Butler, for example, did not. Neither is it the case that all those who adduced arguments for God's existence took Locke's cosmological-*cum*-teleological course. But an impressive number did – even in their ordination statements. Many of these read like affirmations of natural theology supplemented by revealed; and this is so whether those concerned were more liberal or more evangelical.[58] The words of John Notcutt are typical of many. His confession of faith begins thus:

> When I take a Survey of this visible Creation, and seriously reflect on the several Objects which therein do continually offer themselves to our View, I cannot suppose this World, and the Things therein contained, to be independent; since nothing can cause itself to exist. I must therefore conclude, that there is one Supreme Being, who is independent, and upon whom all Things do depend for their Existence: And this great Being is God.[59]

Some, however, took Locke directly to task, and maintained that his principles vitiated theistic argumentation. Henry Lee, for example, the Rector of Tichmarsh, Northamptonshire, published his *Anti-Scepticism* in 1702, with the objective of demonstrating that Locke's doctrine of ideas actually precluded his theism, for from ideas in the mind we cannot conclude to real existents outside ourselves. Locke's position is thus inherently sceptical. Moreover, Lee contends that neither Locke's simple ideas nor his abstract ideas can be in the mind, and thus the rational comparisons of them which Locke advocates cannot take place.

Into his *A Discourse concerning the Happiness of Good Men, and the Punishment of the Wicked in the Next World* (1704) William Sherlock, dean of St Paul's, introduces 'A Digression concerning Connate Ideas, or Inbred Knowledge'. He here contends that the 'great and profound' philosophers who repudiate innate ideas are simply reviving 'the old Atheistical Hypothesis, which banished Original Mind and Wisdom out of the World, makes Mind younger than Matter, later than the making of the World, and therefore not the Maker of it'.[60] Locke grants that God made the world, but from this properly follow conclusions that Locke does not draw, namely, that 'Knowledge is before the things known, and is maker of them,' that ideal knowledge is found only in the divine mind, that all truths and ideas are eternal, and that ideas are not in 'the Things whose Ideas they are, but in the Mind that conceives and apprehends them'.[61] For his part, Sherlock is convinced that to be a rational creature is, *pace* Locke, to possess innate principles of reason.[62]

In a publication of 1741 John Ellis repeats the charge that Locke's view of our natural faculties 'must disable him from coming at the Knowledge of God by any Operation of the Mind'.[63] Ellis insists that if revelation alone can provide us with information concerning other spirits (as Locke holds), *a fortiori*, by revelation alone can we acquire knowledge of God. 'How,' after all, 'by the Help of a very few superficial Ideas we shall pass the vast Chasm between the human Soul and God?'[64] Locke's method is doomed to failure, and Ellis places his entire confidence in revelation by the Spirit.

Other writers objected to Locke's dismissal of the argument for God's existence from universal consent.[65] James Lowde, for example, was firmly in support of the argument, and felt that those who repudiated it

> might do well to consider whether they do not too much oblige the Atheist, and go too far towards the betraying the Cause of God, and Religion in the World, who willingly quit and give up that Argument which hath hitherto been managed with such good success by the best and wisest of men in all Ages: willingly, I say, to give it up *gratis*: for I verily believe, it can never be forc'd and wrested out of the hand of a Christian Philosopher, who rightly understands it.[66]

Thomas Becconsall, too, opposed Locke on the ground that the same argument which he deployed against universal consent could be turned against the law of nature.[67] Furthermore, we do not deny rationality to humanity 'because there are some Fools and Ideots'.[68] While agreeing that universal consent does not establish innate ideas, 'it's certainly a considerable Argument of a Law of Nature.'[69] For his part, John Milner, though he thought Locke wrong to oppose the argument from universal consent – and also the *a priori* argument for God's existence – nevertheless cautioned that 'we should not judge charitably, if we concluded from thence, that he doth not believe in a God.'[70]

Locke had a number of defenders, however. Prominent among them, and early in our period, was Catharine Cockburn. She is in entire accord with Locke in thinking that his principles yield genuine knowledge of ourselves, and from thence we may, by a process of reflection, come to knowledge of that being who is the creator of all other beings.[71] Towards the end of our period support for Locke's cosmological argument was still forthcoming, not least, albeit a little cautiously, from Timothy Dwight:

> This argument is, in my view, perfectly conclusive: nor has it been, or will it ever be, answered, except with sophistry, or sneers. I will not insist, that every step of it is attended with what logicians call intuitive evidence : nor, that it amounts to what is, in the logical sense, an absolute demonstration. But it is, in every step, attended with such evidence, as excludes all reasonable doubt; and approaches so near to the character of demonstration as to leave the mind completely satisfied. At the same time, it is opposed by no counter evidence.[72]

Among the most interesting and discriminating responses to Locke's theism was that of Peter Browne, who agreed with Locke as to innate ideas, who advanced a cosmological argument for God's existence, but who, as we saw, disagreed with Locke that ideas of reflection, as distinct from ideas originating in sensation, are a source of knowledge. We do not derive our idea of God, says Browne, simply by reflecting upon, and extending to infinity, human attributes and faculties. For this is not, as Locke thinks, a direct process, but an analogical one, for God is utterly distinct from us in kind, and not only in degree. Browne's conclusion is not, however, that natural religion will and must suffice, but rather, that revelation is needed.[73] This Locke did not at all deny, as I shall now proceed to show, pausing only to note Mark Pattison's sepulchral verdict on the theistic arguments which, for all its one-sidedness, makes an important point concerning the nature of religious faith and commitment: 'Evidences are not edged tools; they stir no feeling; they were the proper theology of an age, whose literature consisted in writing Latin hexameters.'[74]

II

We have already noted Locke's view that reason is natural revelation: it is the instrument by which God communicates to humanity that truth which is within the scope of our natural faculties. '*Revelation*', 'he immediately proceeds to say, 'is natural *Reason* enlarged by a new set of Discoveries communicated by GOD immediately, which *Reason* vouches the Truth of, by the Testimony and Proofs it gives, that they come from GOD. So that he that takes away *Reason*, to make way for *Revelation*, puts out the Light of both ...'[75]

Again, 'When [God] illuminates the Mind with supernatural Light, he does not extinguish that which is natural.'[76]

Among the significant points here are the following: Locke is not so much in the scholastic tradition in holding that revelation supplements the discoveries of natural reason; rather, he is in the line of those Reformed scholars who held that 'The truths of natural theology are not excluded from supernatural theology – they are included in the body of revealed doctrine – *not* because natural theology is the rational foundation of the system but because its truths belong to the higher truth ...'[77] For this reason the supernatural does not extinguish the natural; by revelation God conveys information otherwise inaccessible to us[78] (this is revelation as propositional, not the post-Romantic 'revelation as encounter'); reason pronounces genuine revelations as divine; apart from this activity of reason faith is on shaky ground. If some should argue, as they were soon to do, that Locke makes reason the arbiter of revelation (and the wild claims of some enthusiasts to deliverances from on high provoked him more than a little), thereby asserting its primacy over all, Locke would first deny that

> we must consult Reason and examine whether a Proposition revealed from God can be made out by natural Principles, and if it cannot, that then we may reject it: But consult it we must, and by it examine, whether it be a *Revelation* from God or no.[79]

There is a problem here, to which I shall allude further in the following section on faith, namely: since such a use of our limited powers of reasoning can, on Locke's own terms, yield probable truth only, we cannot know beyond peradventure – which, for him means we cannot *know* at all whether or not *x* is a revealed proposition. Logic apart, Locke clearly wishes to guard against enthusiasm. Indeed, he has just cautioned those who believe something to be a revelation 'only because they strongly believe it to be a Revelation, which is a very unsafe ground to proceed on, either in our Tenets, or Actions'.[80]

Secondly, Locke would insist that apart from revelation we should know nothing at all concerning matters of faith which are above, but not against reason – a theme to be echoed by many others. For example, Richard Watson, bishop of Llandaff, in *A Defence of Revealed Religion*, declared that 'There may be doctrines above reason; but nothing, which is evidently contrary to reason, can ever be justly considered as a part of the christian dispensation.'[81] With matters of faith, said Locke, '*Reason* has, directly, nothing to do.'[82]

In particular, apart from revelation we should know nothing of the role of Christ as Saviour of the world. Echoing Paul in Romans 1, Calvin in the opening paragraph of the *Institute*, and the Westminster Confession – repeated in the Savoy Declaration of Faith and Order – Locke declares that

> Though the works of nature, in every part of them, sufficiently evidence a Deity; yet the world made so little use of their reason, that they saw him not, where, even by the impressions of himself, he was easy to be found. Sense and lust blinded their minds in some, and a careless inadvertency in others ..[83]

True, 'The rational and thinking part of mankind' found God, 'but if they acknowledged and worshipped him, it was only in their own minds.'[84] Into this general state of darkness came the Saviour: 'the clear revelation he brought with him, dissipated this darkness; [and] made the "one invisible true God" known to the world ...'[85] That this divine revelation is authenticated by miracles is clear from his paraphrase of I Cor. 2:4–5. Paul there writes: 'And my speech, and my preaching was not with enticing words of man's wisdom, but in demonstration of the Spirit, and of power: That your faith should not stand in the wisdom of men, but in the power of God.' Locke paraphrases thus:

> Neither did I in my discourses, or preaching make use of any humane art of perswasion to inveagle you: But the doctrin of the gospel which I proposed I confirmed and inforced by what the spirit had revealed and demonstrated of it in the old testament, and by the power of god accompanying it with miraculous operations, that your faith might have its foundation not in the wisdome and endowments of men but in the power of god.[86]

For Locke a miracle is 'a sensible operation, which, being above the comprehension of the spectator, and in his opinion contrary to the established course of nature, is taken by him to be divine'.[87] It is important to note that for Locke the fulfilment of prophecy is classed as miraculous.[88] Indeed, James E. Force finds evidence in Locke that 'the miracles of Jesus are only significant because they were prophesied.'[89]

We should note that not all eighteenth-century divines were convinced by Locke's definition of 'miracle' or by his appeal to miracles as confirming revelation (not as evidence of God's existence). Thus Doddridge, prior to Hume's devastating critique of miracles, advised caution:

> Mr. Locke defines a miracle to be 'a sensible operation, which being above the comprehension of the spectator', *is in his opinion* contrary to the course of nature, and taken by him to be divine.
>
> But on this account of the matter, every juggling trick, which I cannot understand, will, while my ignorance continues, be a miracle to me. In answer to this, Locke urges, that if this definition be not taken, we can never know what a miracle is; because no man is acquainted with the whole course of nature. But though we acknowledge that great part of it is unknown, yet so much may be known, as that some instances may plainly appear to be above it: v.g. recovering the sight of the blind, or the life of the dead by a word speaking, or multiplying bread ... Besides this, the extraordinary works apprehended to be done by evil agents, would be miracles on this definition.[90]

As if in anticipation of Doddridge's last claim, Locke asserts that 'All other miracles that are done in the world, how many or great soever, revelation is not concerned in.'[91] This would seem to suggest that revelation occurs only in connection with those non-explicable events which Christians take to be miracles – a view which bristles with problems which need not detain us now. We ought, however, to note, as an indication of the apologetic hold of miracles upon the eighteenth-century mind, that even after Hume's critique the rational divine Joseph Priestley can write:

> The historical evidence that we now have of the miracles, the death, and resurrection of Christ, is of itself sufficient to produce christian faith , or a firm belief of the great facts on which christianity rests; and this faith, or belief, is sufficient to induce men to reform their conduct, and to fit them, by a life of virtue here, for a state of happiness hereafter.[92]

Be all this as it may, Locke is persuaded that revelation cannot invalidate reason: '[S]ince no evidence of our Faculties, by which we receive ... *Revelations*, can exceed, if equal, the certainty of our intuitive Knowledge, we can never receive for a Truth any thing, that is directly contrary to our clear and distinct Knowledge.'[93] He is, however, ambivalent concerning the degree of certainty to which we are entitled in respect of revealed truths. We may properly speak of the assurance of faith, even though the evidence supplied by the principles of reason yields probable proof only; and our faith 'as absolutely determines our Minds, and as perfectly excludes all wavering as our Knowledge itself'.'[94] His final appeal, which we shall discuss later, is to the authority of reason and Scripture.[95] For the present we must investigate what those divines who were his contemporaries and successors made of his view of the relations of reason and revelation.

Not surprisingly, the eighteenth-century divines had a vested interest in revelation, and many of them were in general agreement with Locke concerning the relations between reason and revelation. A few, like John Ellis, came to feel that reason was redundant, but this was always a minority view. Some, however, doubted whether Locke's principles really left room for revelation at all. This was the charge levelled against him in 1696 by the bishop of Worcester, Edward Stillingfleet. Stillingfleet had read John Toland's *Christianity Not Mysterious* (1695), in which the deist author had affirmed that true Christianity contained nothing above reason, and that we could not be obliged to believe anything that did exceed our rational grasp. If we once allowed supra-rational mysteries, he argued, what nonsense might not be foisted upon us?[96] Toland's invocation (in my view unjustly) of the support of Locke provoked the training of the episcopal guns upon the latter. Stillingfleet was especially concerned by the materialistic implications of what he took to be Locke's denial of revelation, and by the way in which Locke, as wrongly construed, appeared to vitiate such doctrines as the Trinity.[97] In 1706 William Carroll, convinced that Locke was a materialistic atheist in Spinoza's line, lamented that Locke so exalted reason as to deny the place of revelation and faith.[98] The deist Anthony Collins countered Carroll, claiming that he was building upon an unintelligible distinction, for while 'we can have Ideas to the words *contrary to Human Reason*, yet we can have none to the words *contrary to Divine Reason*'.[99] Meanwhile, in 1697 Thomas Burnet had queried whether Locke's understanding of God's perfections was defensible on his own principles. He conceded that Locke had demonstrated the existence of an eternal, omnipotent, omniscient God, but questioned whether God's moral attributes – notably veracity – were discoverable by Locke's sensationalist method.[100] In the same year, however, support for Locke was forthcoming from Richard Willis, who found that Locke 'discourses excellently well of the *insufficiency* of Human Reason, and the necessity the World lay under, of the assistance of Divine *Revelation*, to teach Mankind even *Moral* Duties and their *Obligation.*'[101]

In his posthumous work, *Natural Religion Insufficient; and Reveal'd Necessary to Man's Happiness in his present State* (1714), the Scottish theologian and professor at St Andrews, Thomas Halyburton, gave with one hand and took with the other. He welcomed the way in which the '*ingenious Mr. Lock'* had demonstrated the insufficiency of natural religion, adding that 'If he had done as well in other Points as on this, he had deserv'd the Thanks of all that wish well to Christianity: But so far as he follows the *Truth*, we shall take his Assistance ...'[102] He is in agreement with Locke that natural religion does not teach us the full scope of our obligations, and he welcomes his resort to the Bible. He regrets, however, Locke's suggestion that reason, the 'candle of the Lord,' suffices to point the way to reconciliation with God, and his opinion that the inspired prophets of the Old Testament sought confirmation of what was revealed to them from sources extrinsic to the revelation itself.[103] The upshot is that for all his recognition of the insufficiency of natural religion,

Locke's rationalism exerts a drag on his understanding of the scope of revelation. John Leland was later to welcome Halyburton's case against the deist Lord Herbert, but noted that 'the narrowness of his notions in some points hath prejudiced some persons against his work.'[104]

Yet Locke insisted, in a passage quoted with approval by Isaac Watts, that 'it is too hard a thing for unassisted reason to establish morality in all its parts upon its true foundations with a clear and convincing light.' This, says Watts, from Locke, 'whom all the world admires as a master of reason, and who allowed as much power to human reason as one could well desire ...'[105] But morality was not the only point at issue. In 1739 Archibald Campbell, professor of church history at St Andrews, quoted Locke in support of his own view that apart from revelation we should have no assurance of the immortality of the soul.[106] Meanwhile in North America, John Wise the Independent, in his *Vindication of the Government of the New England Churches* (1717), had argued that whether ecclesiastical polity be attributed to reason or revelation, it derives ultimately from God, for reason and revelation are 'equally an emanation of His wisdom'.[107] In 1736 Jared Eliot countered those who repudiated reason in the interest of revelation, and those who did the reverse, on the ground, 'Let not these which God hath joined together, be by any man under any pretence put asunder.'[108]

That the ideas I have been collating were by no means confined to authors and pamphleteers may be illustrated by reference to the confession of faith which Thomas Hadfield made at his ordination at Peckham in 1726. He does not refer to Locke by name, but he exemplifies the dissemination of Locke-like ideas from the pulpit – not surprisingly, perhaps, since this Independent minister had been trained under Ebenezer Latham at Findern Academy, where Locke's *Essay* was prescribed for study:

> The same Natural Light which thus evinces the Being and Perfections of One GOD, does I believe moreover and with equal Clearness evince, that universal Obedience and Conformity to his Holy Nature and Will is a Debt which the whole rational, intelligent Creation owe to this GOD, so long as their Existence and necessary Relation to Him is suppos'd; that is, so long as there are two such infinitely different Beings as GOD and our selves ...

> The Knowledge of the Divine Will to Man being in many Things above the highest Improvements of unassisted Reason to attain; 'tis evident, Mankind stands in need of a Supernatural Revelation: And whereas it implies no Contradiction to suppose GOD to make such a Discovery as this to his Moral Subjects, concerning what He would have us to understand, believe and do, in order to our real Perfection and Happiness, necessarily and invincibly desir'd by us; But whereas, on the contrary, the Wisdom, Goodness, Mercy, nay, and even the Governing Justice of God, added to the Consideration of the Necessities of Men, do afford many very probable Arguments that this GOD would some time or other, for the mention'd Ends, make Himself known to such Subjects of his Power and Providence: Consonant to this Scheme of Reasoning, I do believe, that the Everblessed GOD has evidently revealed Himself to us in all Things, necessary to our grand Spiritual and Everlasting Welfare, in those Writings known amongst us by the Names of the Old and New Testaments.[109]

The 1740s furnish us with a contrast. Bernard Foskett of Bristol Baptist College was teaching the standard line, namely, that since reason cannot yield full knowledge of God despite its best efforts,

> We should receive what Revelation discovers of the divine Being, the Trinity and hypostatic Union, and not with all the Socinians and others object their Repugnancy to Natural Reason – for there are as great seeming Absurdities in our Notions of God's Eternity, Immensity &c. which are universally own'd.[110]

The polar opposite point of view was expressed in 1743 by John Ellis, who (as our earlier encounter with him might lead us to expect) set out to show 'from Mr. Locke's own principles and argumentation, that the human mind cannot, by any ideas of reflection, or other internal operations, come to the knowledge of God, the great and fundamental article whereon all other spiritual truths depend.'[111] He gives no weight to Locke's admission that even natural knowledge of God is a matter of revelation. This is because of his conviction that 'the condition of man's nature and faculties, as represented by Mr. Locke, must disable him from coming at the knowledge of God by any operation of the mind.'[112] Ellis's positive assertion is that 'The deep things of God, and all notices we have of spiritual and immaterial objects of divine knowledge, "God hath revealed them unto us by his divine spirit".'[113]

In his pursuit of the deists, John Leland welcomed Locke's aid, declaring that in his *Reasonableness*, Locke

> hath, without formally mentioning Lord Herbert, furnished a proper antidote against his scheme, by showing, with great clearness and force, the usefulness of divine revelation, for setting the great principles of the law of nature, and the important duties of religion and morality in a strong and convincing light, and enforcing them with the most powerful motives; and that the mere unassisted light of reason was, as things were circumstanced, insufficient and ineffectual for that purpose.[114]

Leland subsequently praised Locke for pointing out that even if ancient moralists enunciated worthy moral principles, their hearers would not necessarily feel under obligation to take the right path: they might even reject it 'as suited their interests, passions, inclinations, or humours, if they were under no obligation'.[115] What is required is 'a Divine Revelation, clearly ascertaining and determining our duty in those instances, in plain and express terms, and enforcing it by a Divine Authority, and by sanctions of rewards and punishments ...'[116] Such a revelation, he believes, we have.

The Arian Presbyterian divine, John Taylor, concurs. In 1762 he writes:

> Nature and Reason, in their pure and most perfect State, may be sufficient to direct in the Way of Duty, yet when Nature is corrupted, and Reason obscured, or almost quite extinguished, they are by no means sufficient to restore and recover themselves to Knowledge and Obedience of the Truth ... [I]t was the primary Intention of Revelation to restore and preserve the Knowledge of God and of his Will in a corrupt and degenerate World ... So far therefore I see no Objection to Revelation, but it may be both very needful, and a very great Blessing to Mankind.[117]

At this point Taylor seems aware of what some of our Calvinistic contemporaries would call the noetic effects of sin (of which I shall have more to say in the next chapter); like Leland he underscores the necessity of revelation as making plain our moral duty – to which notion Leland adds the notions of authority, rewards and punishments. In all of this they are true sons of Locke, but it is worth pointing out that 'revelation' is a conveniently elastic term. In Leland, Taylor and others, it brings home to us our moral duty, which we may even perceive but refuse; in other writers the emphasis is rather upon its epistemological benefits, namely, that it yields knowledge which we would not otherwise have had. To exemplify the latter we may refer to Thomas Amory, Taylor's co-religionist, who was partly trained under, and later succeeded, Henry Grove at Taunton Dissenting academy. He calls Locke in support of his view that revelation assures us of the existence of angels, though reason corroborates this, for 'We may observe a *gradual rise* in the creatures of God.'[118] To all of which John Horsey, Independent tutor at Northampton academy from 1789 to 1798, added the consideration that the authenticity of revelation is attested by miracles. To him miracles are 'deviations from the law and course of nature,' they 'are not performed without an immediate divine imposition,' and 'in certain circumstances they are proper proofs of the divine original of any doctrine attested by them.'[119]

Meanwhile in New England, Gad Hitchcock was found arguing that since Locke has despaired of innate ideas (in us as in Adam), we are left in our quest of knowledge with the time-consuming tasks of receiving, comparing, compounding and reflecting. In this trying circumstance, revelation has the beneficial effect of speeding up the process of gaining moral knowledge which, if left to reason alone would, in Adam's descendants, 'undoubtedly have been very slow'.[120]

Towards the end of our period, also from North America, polar opposite opinions of Locke were still being expressed. If Uzal Ogden, in his two-volume work against Paine's *The Age of Reason*, enlists Locke's aid against deists, and praises him for his strong defence of revelation, to the deist Elihu Palmer, 'Locke has, perhaps, done more than Newton, to subvert the credit of *divine Revelation.*'[121]

Among points which some found neuralgic was Locke's insistence that reason, though requiring to be supplemented by revelation, is nevertheless in a position to determine whether what purports to be revealed is a genuine revelation: whether a particular revelation 'be a divine Revelation, or no, *Reason* must judge; which can never permit the Mind to reject a greater Evidence to embrace what is less evident, nor allow it to entertain Probability in opposition to Knowledge and Certainty'.[122] We recall his determination to exclude wayward and fantastic claims to revelation on the part of enthusiasts. Enthusiasm, he declares, 'laying by Reason would set up Revelation without it. Whereby in effect it takes away both Reason and Revelation, and substitutes in the room of it, the ungrounded Fancies of a Man's own Brain, and assumes them for a Foundation both of Opinion and Conduct.'[123] On this matter many were in accord with Locke. Thus, to Toland's claim that the orthodox unquestioningly accept what they take to be revealed truths, Peter Browne retorted, 'all the Revelations of God admit of the strictest enquiry, and severest search of our reason : and it is this that enables us to distinguish them from the wild extravagances of Enthusiasts, and the delusions of the Devil.'[124] In defence of Locke, Mrs Cockburn said that 'In matters of revelation, [Locke] used his reason indeed to discover *what* the Holy Spirit has declared,' and (here begging the question) if the Holy Spirit has revealed the truth of a doctrine, Locke 'has nothing to say against it'.[125]

Bishop Butler follows Locke in distinguishing between truths of reason and truths of revelation and, also like Locke, maintains that 'reason is the only faculty wherewith we have to judge anything, even revelation itself.'[126] He considers that 'objections against Christianity, as distinguished from objections against its evidence, are frivolous', and bids sceptics consider the evidence of Scripture which 'informs us of a scheme of divine Providence additional to' our knowledge of the known course of nature from reason and experience. From Scripture we learn that 'God has, by revelation, instructed men in things concerning his government, which they could not otherwise have known ...'[127] We cannot say that reason is impotent to judge revelation, for this would be to say that 'we are unable to judge of anything, because we are unable to judge of all things.' In fact, reason can judge the meaning, morality and evidence of revelation. This last is his particular concern, for he does not think there can be any objections to Christianity's morality, but only to its evidence.[128] Now by applying our reason to the puzzles and imponderables of Christianity we detect an analogy between such deficiencies and irregularities and those of nature; and we understand that it is not incredible if, on the assumption that a revelation has been given, it should contain 'many things different from what we should have expected, and such as appear open to great objections' – just as the natural order does.[129]

We breathe a significantly different air when we turn to Jonathan Edwards who, consistently with his view of the noetic effects of sin and the supernaturally given 'new spiritual sense', holds that God's revelation, attested by Scripture (for 'This spiritual light is not the suggesting of any new truths or propositions not contained in the word of God'),[130] is likewise *given* to the believer, who gratefully receives it, using sanctified reason to expand and defend it, but not, in Locke and Butler's sense, to judge it. Indeed, where Butler thinks that we may accept as revelation those things which are probably divinely given, and that even if we cannot adequately probe the mysteries we should accept them unless significant evidence against them emerges, Edwards would say that the believer (that is, one in whom the 'new spiritual sense' is operative) would be acting 'against reason' to doubt its divinely revealed deliverances. Hence, for example, he argues that Tindal's position that reason, apart from, or undirected by, revelation is competent to judge the validity of the propositions allegedly revealed, rests upon 'an unreasonable way of arguing,' because we cannot judge particular revealed propositions if we doubt the possibility of revelation as such. 'For this is certain,' he continues, 'that a proposition may be evidently true, or we may have good reason to receive it as true, though the particular propositions that depend upon it, and follow from it, may be such, that our reason, independent of it, cannot see the truth, or can see it to be true only by other means, than by first establishing that other truth on which it depends.'[131]

It would be tedious to supply further examples of those who echo the refrain that reason is competent to judge revelation. I ought, however, to note the ambivalence which occurs in such a writer as John Taylor. As we saw, he has some appreciation of the noetic effects of sin, which require the operations of revelation to clear our minds and harness our wills. But he also wishes to agree that reason must adjudicate upon proposed revelations – and, after all, 'testing the spirits' is a biblical principle; but what now of the noetic effects of sin? Is what was incompetent prior to revelation now competent to judge revelation? As I have elsewhere said,

> If [Taylor] were to forsake the former conviction his argument for revelation would fall; if he were to forsake the latter, he would be replacing blind allegiance to the Pope with equally blind allegiance to

> Scripture, and he would have no check upon the 'enthusiasm' of which he was so highly suspicious.[132]

It remains only to add that very few wished to take the line of the 'miscellaneous writer' Soame Jenyns, who declared that 'To prove the reasonableness of revelation is in fact to destroy it; because a revelation implies information of something which reason cannot discover, and therefore must be different from its deductions, or it would be no revelation.'[133] The majority of divines were, despite the pitfalls, inclined to agree with Locke's contemporary, Richard Baxter, that reason is the porter which may admit revelation to the understanding; and the porter must not be negligent.[134] As yet we are light-years away from such an idea as was to be so forcibly propounded in the twentieth century by P. T. Forsyth: 'Revelation means far more than information. It means more than manifestation. It is in the same act Redemption, new Creation.'[135]

III

We turn now to Locke's view, and the views of his successors, concerning the place of faith and the Spirit in relation to reason and revelation. Let us at once be cautioned that 'faith' is yet another slippery term. Richard Ashcraft is not alone in reminding us that whereas 'Locke generally identifies faith with opinion, and contrasts both with knowledge' – as when he declares, that faith or opinion 'mean that Assent, which we give to any Proposition as true, of whose Truth yet we have no certain Knowledge'[136] – in Book IV of the *Essay* he thinks not so much of the degree of certainty pertaining to the idea claimed as knowledge, as of the means to the acquisition of knowledge.[137] When Locke has revelation in mind, faith becomes the epistemological tool by which we come to assent to a proposition which is not a deliverance of reason, but is above (though not against) reason.[138] Faith is 'the Assent to any Proposition, not thus made out by the Deductions of Reason; but upon the Credit of the Proposer, as coming from GOD, in some extraordinary way of Communication. This way of discovering Truths to Men we call *Revelation*.[139]

As John Milner observed,[140] there is here, as elsewhere, a certain ambivalence in Locke's thought. On the one hand he wishes to say that faith in a divine revelation 'excludes all wavering' and 'carries with it Assurance beyond Doubt, Evidence beyond Exception'.[141] This is because the testimony in question comes directly from God himself, who neither deceives nor can be deceived.[142] On the other hand, although 'whatever GOD hath revealed, is certainly true; no Doubt can be made of it,'[143] we cannot be absolutely certain that any particular revelation is from God. The knowledge (or conviction) that such and such a revelation is divine 'can never be so sure, as the Knowledge we have from the clear and distinct Perception of the Agreement, or Disagreement of our own *Ideas*'.[144] Again: 'herein lies the *difference between Probability and Certainty, Faith and Knowledge*, that in all the parts of Knowledge, there is intuition; each immediate *Idea*, each step has its visible and certain connexion; in belief not so.'[145] In what appears to be a further ambivalence similar to that noted by Milner, Locke states that in matters of faith, 'a persuasion of our own minds, short of knowledge, is the last result that determines us in such truths.'[146] This is to exclude faith from knowledge.[147] But when Locke speaks of the *knowledge* we have that a revelation is from God as being *less sure* than 'the Knowledge we have from the clear and distinct Perception of the Agreement, or Disagreement of our own *Ideas*',[148] he appears to admit of degrees of epistemological certitude.

As Roland H. Bainton pointed out long ago, Locke is in the Erasmus–Castellio tradition in affirming that 'faith and reason are not antithetical,' and that unless 'religion can be understood it is of no practical consequence'.[149] Indeed, in the absence of understanding there can be no obligation to believe.[150] But, as with revelation, so with faith: it cannot go against reason. Among truths which are matters of faith is that concerning the resurrection to eternal life[151] and that concerning the Messiahship of Jesus.[152]

Thus far Locke's claims regarding faith have sounded an intellectualist note: faith yields knowledge which is above, though not contrary to, reason; and apart from faith's appropriation of them we should be ignorant of the deliverances of divine revelation. But there is also in Locke, and for all his dislike of enthusiasm, an increasing tendency to allow for direct spiritual communications from God to the human mind. In an important paragraph in which he laments the way in which some resort to revelation rather than take the harder way of reasoning, he has to grant that 'GOD I own cannot be denied to be able to enlighten the Understanding by a Ray darted into the Mind immediately from the Fountain of Light'[153] – though in the context the attendant enthusiastic dangers are so agonizingly adverted to that one almost feels that Locke would prefer God not to do anything of the sort.

Again, Locke can speak of the law of faith, by which means 'faith is allowed to supply the defect of full obedience: and so the believers are admitted to life and immortality, as if they were righteous.'[154] Their own obedience is, nevertheless, required for salvation. The 'Pelagian' overtones of this apparent denial of the sole sufficiency of faith, and Locke's stopping short of the doctrine of imputed righteousness, will not escape those of a Calvinistic turn of mind. But all such will breathe again when, in the same work, Locke designates repentance as, together with faith, an absolute condition of the covenant of grace,[155] though they will look in vain in Locke for much on humanity's being enabled by the Spirit.

It remains only to add that in *The Reasonableness of Christianity* Locke, having spoken of the law of Moses, proceeds to say that

> [C]hristian believers have the privilege to be under the law of faith too; which is that law, whereby God justifies a man for believing, though by his works he be not just or righteous, i.e. though he come short of perfect obedience to the law of works. God alone does or can justify, or make just, those who by their works are not so: which he doth, by counting their faith for righteousness, i.e. for a complete performance of the law.[156]

He further distinguishes between faith as 'bare assent' and 'justifying faith,' according a place to both.[157]

But it is in the posthumously published *Paraphrase* that Locke comes closer to faith as *fiducia* (as contrasted with *assensus*) than anywhere else. As J. R. Milton has written of the *Paraphrase*:

> It shows, much more clearly than *The Reasonableness of Christianity*, that the Christian vocabulary of Locke's earlier works cannot be interpreted either as a pious facade or (less implausibly) as a mere residue

> in a mind already fundamentally secular but either reluctant or unable to acknowledge itself as such.[158]

Under the influence of Paul, Locke thinks of faith in terms of trust and declares that the faithful are those 'who relye upon god and his promises of grace and not upon their own performances, they are the children who shall inherit and this is plain in the Sacred Scripture.'[159] It is as tempting as it is strictly fruitless to speculate what might have been the result had Locke reached clear convictions on *fiducia* earlier in his intellectual pilgrimage. Would his repugnance of enthusiasm have allowed him to make epistemological capital out of this more existential understanding of faith? What is clear is that Peter Browne, among others, followed the clues – and he in turn influenced John Wesley[160] and, through him, many in the evangelical succession.

Taking his cue from Locke's admission that God may speak directly to an individual, Browne first echoes such Puritan contemporaries of Locke as Baxter and John Owen in utilizing, to a degree which Locke did not, the notion of the inner witness of the Spirit. Just as our senses conduct external experience to us, so the Spirit addresses us internally, as it were. Baxter went so far as to declare that 'Reason sufficeth not without the spirit, being dark and asleep,' while Owen argued that apart from the Spirit's work we could not come to faith.[161] Whereas Locke upheld the place of the authority of God and the testimony of the Bible, Browne, as Richard Brantley has shown, extends the concept of testimony to the realm of faith, and 'suggests that religious attestation participates in, as well as corresponds to, revealed truth'.[162] Indeed, Browne defines evangelical faith as 'an Assent to a revealed and express Proposition upon the Testimony of God'.[163]

All of which proved congenial to John Wesley, who abridged Browne's *The Procedure*, and who, in his *Appeal* and *Farther Appeal to Men of Reason and Religion*[164] (the conjunction is significant), drew an analogy between the knowledge derived from our senses and the assurance derived from faith. While the young Wesley could sound very Locke-like in averring that there can be no belief, and hence no faith, without rational grounds,[165] and while he never departed from this base,[166] his modifications of it in a Pauline, 'existentialist' direction came to assume precedence; and just as he went further than Locke in understanding belief to be a ground of faith, so he outdid Browne in his emphasis upon the immediate inner witness of the Holy Spirit. Apart from the latter, and its experienced concomitants of peace, joy and love, Wesley did not see how a person could be a true Christian.[167] Moreover, reason is impotent where the acquisition of faith is concerned: 'Can *you* give yourself this faith? ... The more you labour so to do, the more you will be convinced, "it is the gift of God".[168] Not without cause has Brantley found in Wesley an Enlightenment-grounded harbinger of Romanticism. Similarly, John Hoyles's claim that 'Wesley's success in imposing his classical vocabulary on an essentially romantic movement, was the final death blow to any absolutist integrity the English Enlightenment may previously have claimed'[169] is understandable, though I should prefer to say that while some Enlightenment thinkers may have aspired to absolutist integrity, on the evidence already adduced they could not honestly have claimed it, since all the key terms 'reason,' 'revelation,' 'faith', were ambiguously used, and epistemological methods varied considerably, the appeal to reason notwithstanding.

Lest it be thought that evangelical Arminians alone embraced the notion of faith as *fiducia,* we may note the clear declarations of the staunch Calvinist John Gill on the matter:

> Faith is an assent to Christ as a Saviour, not upon a human, but a divine testimony, upon the record which God has given of his Son, and of eternal life in him ... Knowledge of Christ as a Saviour, and assent unto him as such, is attended by love and affection to him; faith works by love, love always accompanies faith, at least follows it ... The efficient cause is God ... [T]he good work of grace ... is begun, carried on, and performed by the Spirit of Christ; and from it the whole is denominated, the *work of faith* which is wrought and finished with the power of God.[170]

Contemporary with Browne were other divines who were not so inclined to invoke faith as an epistemological aid, or to follow Locke. To Edward Stillingfleet faith was a matter of intellectual assent on reasonable grounds, and he confidently declared that if God requires us to believe something, he provides evidence as to its truth.[171] Robert South did not hesitate to draw the rationalist conclusion when he said that whereas

> the Ultimate Object of Faith is Divine Revelation, that is, I believe

> such a Thing to *be true*, because it is revealed by God ... my Reason must prove to me, that it is revealed; so that, this Way, Reason is that, into which all Religion is at last resolved.[172]

At the opposite pole stood the critic of Locke's *Essay*, John Norris, rector of Bemerton and neo-Platonist follower of Malebranche. It was Norris's deep and constantly reiterated conviction that revelation is all: faith as faith, he declared, has no regard to evidence, and faith as divine has no need of it.[173] We detect quite a different tone in the Anglican Henry Felton's Lady Moyer lectures delivered at St Paul's Cathedral in 1728–9. He here rebukes the deists and others, and also turns upon Locke. He disagrees that all our knowledge is derived from sensible experience; indeed, he argues that sensible evidence and demonstration are inconsistent with faith, and that it is absurd to require them in relation to articles of faith.[174]

In a somewhat different key Metternich, staunchly upholding a faculty psychology with the several faculty functions uniquely apportioned, argued that since faith and reason proceed from two 'different and distinct Principles in Man,' they can neither coincide nor conflict. Metternich is not opposed to reason as such, but considers that Locke has been unduly influenced by 'Crafty Reason, the most Pestilential Offspring of the Serpent'.[175]

Standing between Browne and Wesley on the one hand, and Norris and Metternich on the other, is the Calvinist Anglican, John Edwards, a constant opponent of Locke. In 1708 we find him reviewing the arguments for the existence of God, and asserting that if people do not place faith in rational arguments when they are proposed, the fault lies with those concerned, not with the arguments themselves. At the same time, we must also rely upon 'the Divine Testimony, the Word of God in the Inspired Writings, because these cannot fail us, they being endited by him who is Truth itself'.[176] Hence, on the one hand we must repudiate the view of Toland that 'Divine Revelation is not a motive of Assent, not a ground of our Persuasion, or a reason we have to believe a thing,'[177] while on the other hand we must demolish Locke's view that faith yields probability only. He further rebukes Locke for holding that 'None are Sentenc'd or Punish'd for Unbelief, but only for their own misdeeds.' Edwards contends that this is directly contrary to Mark 16:16 and John 12:48, which he quotes, and that 'If our Faith be amiss, our Lives will be irregular; and if they be so, the sentence at the Last Day will pass upon us accordingly.'[178] Against the presumed 'Pelagianism' of Locke's assertion that 'the Law of Faith, is that whereby God justifies a Man for Believing, or for Faith,' Edwards is dismissive: anyone who could write in such a way 'was not acquainted with the Language of the New Testament'.[179]

Locke's early defender, Samuel Bold, was quite content to construe faith (in the sense of articles to be assented to) as being in some way above knowledge, and as yielded by revelation. He first utters a paean of praise for Locke's *Essay* as being 'the most Worthy, most Noble, and best Book I ever read, excepting those which were writ by Persons Divinely inspir'd,'[180] and laments the fact that its author, the 'Incomparable Gentleman,' has been attacked for his views. The attack has been upon two grounds: first, Locke's claim that 'Certainty of Knowledge is, to perceive the Agreement or Disagreement of Ideas, as expressed in any Proposition,' has been deemed false by those who contend that the only way to certain knowledge is by inferences drawn from maxims; and secondly, Locke's claim has been declared 'inconsistent with, and of dangerous consequence to the *Articles of the Christian Faith*'.[181] Concerning the first objection, Bold agrees that maxims are self-evident propositions, but this simply means that the ideas signified by their terms do agree or disagree as Locke's proposition asserts. As to the second objection, he insists that since some propositions are deliverances of divine revelation, we cannot compare the ideas therein, and hence we cannot perceive agreement or disagreement. This is no disadvantage to revealed propositions, however, for their truth does not turn upon our certainty of them.[182] Bold magisterially concludes:

> The greatest service that can be done to Truth and Godliness, is to preserve our *Reason* within its proper Bounds, and to let Faith have its just scope. I very much question, whether any thing can give bad Men greater advantage in their endeavouring to promote *Scepticism*, and in their opposing and taking against the *Articles of the Christian Faith*, than Christians, and especially Divines, and Clergymens detracting any way from the *Credibility of Divine Testimony*, and making an Ostentation of knowing Things which God hath placed perfectly out of Humane reach ...[183]

There you have that begging of questions (the proper bounds of reason; faith's just scope) combined with proper agnosticism concerning the mysteries of God which was so characteristic of early-eighteenth-century divines of all ecclesiastical stripes, when 'faith' was taken to mean intellectual assent to truths deemed to be revealed. That so much of this spirit lingered in the Brownes and the Wesleys of the age enabled them to hold aloof from the dreaded enthusiasm, though the grounds on which they did this seemed flimsy indeed both to their contemporaries who wished to maintain a strong disjunction between faith and reason, and to deists and early nineteenth-century rationalists who were content with reason alone.

Among American contemporaries who endeavoured to hold the middle ground was Charles Chauncy:

> There is no Doctrine of Faith, but it perfectly accords with the Principles of true Reason: Nor otherwise might it be received as an Article of Faith. We should never therefore oppose Faith and Reason; but rather consider them as Helps and Spurs to each other; for so they really are: Nor can there be Faith without Reason.[184]

As a harbinger of later rational divines I summon 'A Rational Christian' (Francis Webb), who objects to Locke's invocation of the 'law of faith' as a substitute for perfect obedience, on the ground that belief in the law of faith and perfect obedience may be equally impossible to human beings, whose dilemma is thus presented:

> They must either pay a *perfect* obedience to the law of nature, which, [Locke] says, no man ever *did* , and St. Paul says, 'no man ever *could*;' or else they must believe Jesus *to be the Messiah*, or Son of God, in what our churchmen call the Gospel sense. Now this is what *many* may never be able to do, even though menaced with the punishment of eternal death.[185]

IV

It remains to consider Locke's convictions concerning the place of Scripture. It will conduce to orderly exposition if we consider first Locke's understanding of the relation of Scripture to reason and revelation,[186] and then turn to his contribution to the study of the Bible. In each case we shall note the responses of some eighteenth-century divines to his views and practice.

Writing in the context of faith and reason, Locke declares,

> [S]ince GOD in giving us the light of *Reason* has not thereby tied up his own Hands from affording us, when he thinks fit, the light of *Revelation* in any of those Matters, wherein our natural Faculties are able to give a probable Determination, *Revelation*, where God has been pleased to give it, *must carry it, against the probable Conjectures of Reason.*[187]

It must be admitted that this does not sit altogether comfortably with what he has elsewhere said concerning knowledge and probability – and least of all with his statement in the added chapter following that '*Reason* must be our last Judge and Guide in every Thing';[188] but it does indicate the route by which he is able to assent to Scripture, even when its deliverances are of a kind concerning which certain knowledge cannot be had in this life. Consider, for example, his paraphrase of I Corinthians 13:12: 'For now we see through a glass darkly; but then face to face: now I know in part, but then I shall know even as also I am known' (AV). Locke writes:

> Now we see but by reflection the dimn and as it were enigmatical representation of things: but then we shall see, things directly as they are in themselves as a man sees another when they are face to face. Now I have but a superficial partial knowledg of things, but then I shall have an intuitive comprehensive knowledg of them, as I my self am known and lie open to the view of superior seraphick beings, not by the obscure and imperfect way of deductions and reasoning.[189]

Here we see a hint of representationalism, an anticipated efficient and comprehensive intuitionalism, and the implication that there is a route to knowledge superior to those of deductive method and reasoning. We may also infer Locke's willing endorsement of Paul's testimony to the partial nature of human knowledge, for this is in keeping with his general epistemological humility, to which I drew attention in the first chapter, and which he reaffirms in the Preface to his *Paraphrase*:

> I am far from pretending Infallibility in the Sense I have any where given in my Paraphrase or Notes; That would be to erect my self into an Apostle, a Presumption of the highest Nature in any one that cannot confirm what he says by Miracles.[190]

What, then, of Scripture? Locke's reply is that in cases where knowledge is attained either by revelation or not at all – and not only in such cases, we may properly resort to the Bible. As he wrote, movingly and honestly, to Stillingfleet:

> The holy scripture is to me, and always will be, the constant guide of my assent; and I shall always hearken to it, as containing infallible truth, relating to things of the highest concernment. And I wish I could say, there were no mysteries in it: I acknowledge there are to me, and I fear always will be. But where I want the evidence of things, there is yet ground enough for me to believe, because God has said it: and I shall presently condemn and quit any opinion of mine, as soon as I am shown that it is contrary to any revelation in the holy scripture.[191]

Placing all the evidence together, the general truth (for the remark applies to some who were not Presbyterians) of J. J. Tayler's comment is evident:

> The Presbyterian theology of this period may indeed be described as the offspring of an alliance between the new philosophy of Locke and the Scripturalism of the old Puritans. Scripture was accepted as a Divine record – an ultimate fact in the researches of the theologian ... but upon that record, reason was to be exercised with the greatest freedom and impartiality, not only in eliciting its contents, but also in establishing their coincidence with those natural truths which the same reason as clearly affirmed.[192]

Not the least importance of Scripture, in Locke's view, is that it, together with reason, serves to check untoward claims to the immediate guidance of the Holy Spirit, and spurious claims to interpretative authority. Concerning the former he declares,

> I am far from denying, that GOD can, or doth sometimes enlighten Mens Minds in the apprehending of certain Truths, or excite them to Good Actions by the immediate influence and assistance of the Holy Spirit, without any extraordinary Signs accompanying it. But in such Cases too we have Reason and Scripture, unerring Rules to know whether it be from GOD or no ... Where Reason or Scripture is express for any Opinion or Action, we may receive it as of divine Authority.[193]

Concerning the latter, Locke has stern things to say against those 'learned Disputants, these all-knowing Doctors' who rest their authority on their power to utter '*learned Gibberish*,' and to entangle their auditors in an 'endless Labyrinth'[194] – in other words, to blind them with 'science'.

We thus have the position that despite his suspicion of authorities in other contexts, Locke determines to uphold the authority of Scripture as a revelation from God against all false authoritarian claims; he urges the appeal to it and to reason over against enthusiasm; but, further, he is alive to the fact that Bible readers may not only find in its pages what they wish to find, but may proceed to turn their discoveries into badges of sectarianism and principles of exclusion from church fellowship:

> If the reading and study of the scripture were more pressed than it is, and men were fairly sent to the bible to find their religion; and not the bible put into their hands, only to find the opinions of their peculiar sect or party; Christendom would have more christians, and those that are, would be more knowing, and more in the right, than they now are. That which hinders this, is that select bundle of doctrines, which it has pleased every sect to draw out of the scriptures, or their own inventions, with an omission … of all the rest … For how else can they turn men of as unblameable lives as others of their members out of the church of Christ (for so they count their communion) for opinions, unless those opinions were concluded inconsistent with Christianity? Thus systems, the invention of men, are turned into so many opposite gospels; and nothing is truth in each sect, but what suits with them. So that the scripture serves but, like a nose of wax, to be turned and bent, just as may fit the contrary orthodoxies of different societies.[195]

Similar claims to authoritative interpretations may issue from those charged with the government of the realm; indeed, they may be promulgated with a view to the subjugation of others. As Locke wrote in answer to Robert Filmer, 'learning and religion shall be found out to justify all, that [an absolute prince] shall do to his subjects, and the sword presently silence those that dare question it.'[196] The fact that the few who have 'much leisure, improved understandings, and were used to abstract reasonings' are at an advantage over everyone else (all others being unskilled in reasoning, and under the necessity of taking things on trust) might be said to load the dice in favour of would-be tyrants.[197]

The upshot is that, recognizing that people will differ in their interpretations of Scripture, Locke is concerned with the manner in which such differences are appealed to and used. His own view is that

> a great many of the truths revealed in the gospel, every one does, and must confess, a man may be ignorant of; nay, disbelieve, without danger to his salvation: as is evident in those, who, allowing the authority, differ in the interpretation and meaning of several texts of scripture, not thought fundamental ...[198]

That the question begged in the phrase 'not thought fundamental' was sharply to be raised we shall discover in our penultimate chapter in connection with the indispensable minimum of belief.

Be that as it may, Locke, consistently with his denial of infallibility in interpretation, declares that

> God when he makes the Prophet does not unmake the Man. He leaves all his Faculties in their natural State, to enable him to judge of his Inspirations, whether they be of divine Original or no. When he illuminates the Mind with supernatural Light, he does not extinguish that which is natural. If he would have us assent to the Truth of any Proposition, he either evidences that Truth by the usual Methods of natural Reason, or else makes it known to be a Truth, which he would have us assent to, by his Authority, and convinces us that it is from him, by some Marks which *Reason* cannot be mistaken in. *Reason* must be our last judge and Guide in every Thing.[199]

The implications of this affirmation reverberate (or should do so) to this day in connection with biblical hermeneutics on the one hand, and positivistic theological embargoes against apologetics on the other. But my main point now is that underlying his approach to Scripture is Locke's conviction, derived from Descartes, that God addresses people by means of clear and distinct ideas which, though expressed through prophets and apostles, are nevertheless attainable without supernatural illumination.[200] This is not to deny that the Spirit of God 'dictated these Sacred Writings,'[201] but it is, once again, to rule out enthusiasm. We shall see that as the eighteenth century proceeds the epistemological role of the Holy Spirit – namely, that he takes the things of Christ and shows them to us – comes increasingly to the fore in evangelical circles, where it is concomitant with the emphasis upon the noetic effects of sin. In this last connection, Romans 1:28 is the *locus classicus*, referring as it does to those who wilfully suppress the knowledge of God and are given over to a reprobate mind – a term softened by Locke to an 'unsearching and unjudicious mind'.[202] While Locke does not deny the illuminating work of the Holy Spirit (indeed, in his early *Essay on Infallibility* he affirmed it more strongly than he was later to do),[203] he is cautious regarding it: 'It will be idle for us, who know not how our own spirits move and act us, to ask in what manner the Spirit of God shall work upon us.'[204]

It is hardly surprising that, given Locke's oscillation between the view that reason judges Scripture and is therefore in some sense above Scripture, and his less frequently expressed opinion that God can give a revelation which goes 'against the probable conjectures of reason,' some divines should emphasize the former position and others the latter. What did contemporary and subsequent divines make of Locke's position on Scripture, reason and revelation?

Isaac Watts (like Henry Grove) was educated under the Independent Thomas Rowe at the Dissenting academy at Newington Green, London, which had been established possibly in 1666 and was closed in 1706.[205] Of Rowe it was said that he

> was the first to desert the traditional text-books, introducing his pupils, about 1680, to what was known as 'free philosophy.' Rowe was a Cartesian at a time when the Aristotelic philosophy was dominant in the older schools of learning; and while in physics he adhered to Descartes against the rising influence of Newton, in mental science he became one of the earliest exponents of Locke.[206]

While still a student, Watts wrote in a letter of 1696 that 'In matters of the christian faith, I would make the scripture my guide.' He went on,

> My reason should be used as a necessary instrument to compare the several parts of revelation together, to discover their mutual explication, as well as to judge whether they run counter to any dictates of natural light. But if an inquisitive mind overleap the bounds of faith, and give the reins to all our reasonings upon divine themes in so wide and open a field as that of possibilities and probables, it is no easy matter to guess where they will stop their career. I have made experiment of this in my own meditations; when I have given my thoughts a loose, and let them rove without confinement, sometimes I seem to have carried reason with me even to the camp of *Socinus* ; but then *St. John* gives my soul a twitch, and St. Paul bears me back again (if I mistake not his meaning) almost to the tents of John Calvin.[207]

In the field of morality, Watts was particularly keen to affirm, against the deists, 'The Necessity of Divine Revelation, both to Clear up the Rules of Virtue, and to Strengthen the Obligations'. To this extent he echoes Locke's sentiments as expressed in many places including *The Reasonableness of Christianity*:

> he that shall collect all the moral rules of the philosophers, and compare them with those contained in the New Testament, will find them to come short of the morality delivered by our Saviour, and taught by his apostles; a college made up, for the most part, of ignorant, but inspired fishermen.[208]

However, while not denying that if people rightly employ their reasoning powers they may discover their duty, Watts pays more attention than Locke to the noetic effects of sin: 'man, by nature, in his present corrupted state, is born in the midst of so much darkness, that he hardly knows how to find the rules of his duty in a thousand instances, without some further revelation or assistance.'[209] Happily,

> God, by the revelation of his will in scripture, has given so bright a discovery of these general boundaries between vice and virtue, and made plain a multitude of these particular duties both by express commands, and prohibitions, and various parallel examples, both of vice and virtue, that even the common people may learn what they are to believe, and what they are to practice, or avoid, by a far more easy and ready way of instruction. Milk-maids and plowmen, and the meanest offices or capacities in the world may learn their duty here. All the rules of virtue given us by the heathen philosophers, from their supposed fitness of things, fall vastly short of what Moses and the prophets, Christ and his apostles, have done in clearing up the common rules of virtue to mankind.[210]

In the same year that Watts wrote the letter from which I have quoted, William Whiston published his *A New Theory of the Earth.* On hearing Newton lecture, he turned from 'the fictitious hypotheses of the Cartesian philosophy,' read Newton's *Principia*, and wrote his own work which Locke, in a letter to Molyneaux, cordially welcomed. Whiston insisted that our present knowledge should not be elevated into the criterion of all truth and, in particular, that it should not 'be oppos'd to the Accounts receiv'd from profane Antiquity much less to the inspir'd writings'.[211] Whiston's Independent contemporary, the ardent Calvinist Thomas 'bold' Bradbury, who was said to have preached on the text 'God now, see to this accursed woman, and bury her, for she was a king's daughter' (II Kings 9:34) on the death of Queen Anne, and who suspected Isaac Watts's position on the Trinity and would not have his *Psalms* sung in his presence, was much more inclined to oppose reason to Scripture – this as an antidote to rational*ism*.[212] He was trained for the ministry under Timothy Jollie at Attercliffe academy (*c*.1690–1714), of which institution it was said, 'only the old philosophy of the schools was taught there, and that neither ably nor diligently,' and from which Jollie 'forbad the Mathematicks, as tending to scepticism & infidelity'.[213] Near the beginning of the thirty-six-page confession of faith which he delivered at his ordination in 1707 Bradbury declared of the Bible, 'To this Law and Testimony *I profess to bring every opinion.*'[214] Consciously or otherwise in the wake of Tertullian's 'It is certain because it is impossible,' Bradley held that 'The Doctrines of the Gospel are unaccountable. The Words of Scripture, which set them forth are absurdities to the reason of man.'[215] Not surprisingly, the deist Anthony Collins, stood at the opposite pole in contending that variant readings within the biblical text, together with widely differing interpretative options, necessitated the application of reason over against revelation and all assumed religious authorities.[216] Contemporaneously, the pendulum swung back again when from America Cotton Mather identified Scripture with right reason:

> Many hearers do much admire *that* which they call *Rational Preaching*; but when they have oppos'd it unto *Scriptural Preaching*, they have but betray'd a sufficient want of *Reason* . The most shallow *Divines*, and the most empty *Harangues*, have been sometimes distinguish'd by the Name of *Rational*. Whereas, the more of the *Gospel* there is in our *Preaching*, the more of Reason there is in it. *Scripture* is *Reason*, in its highest Elevation.[217]

In the following year the diametrically opposed view was propounded in Scotland by Thomas Halyburton:

> [W]e cannot go along with Mr. *Lock* in what he Means by this Expression, *That our Belief of* Scripture Propositions, is an Act of Reason, that is, an *Assent* not built upon *Divine Testimony*, but on such other Arguing and Reasonings, as we can find out for proving

God reveal'd it. Because we say ... That the Scriptures do evidence themselves to be from God ... [Accordingly] there is no Reason for ranking all the Truths therein delivered amongst those conjectural Things that lean only on Probabilities and Reasonings from them, which Mr. *Lock* evidently does, while he sinks *traditional Revelation* as to the Point of Certainty below our *intuitive, rational* and *sensible Knowledge;* and banishes all *Faith,* properly so call'd, out of the World, leaving no Room for it, and substituting in its place an *Act of Reason,* proceeding upon *Probabilities,* that is, on *historical Proofs,* which he reckons only among *Probabilities* ...[218]

Though not a tub-thumper of the Bradbury sort, Daniel Waterland, canon of Windsor and archdeacon of Middlesex, was no less concerned to counter Arianism and deism. In the latter connection he invoked Locke against Matthew Tindal's *Christianity as Old as the Creation* (1730). He supposes that Tindal will regard himself as testing revelation by reason, for 'reason is the name he gives all his *conceits* . Which puts me in mind of a pleasant saying of Mr. Locke's, in one of his private letters: To be rational is so glorious a thing, that two-legged creatures generally content themselves with the *title*.'[219] We need not follow Waterland in his detailed critique of deist errors, though we may note his concluding testimony to Locke's worth:

Mr. Locke, I may observe, was no *priest* , nor a *bigot* to priests: but he understood the high worth and excellency of our Bible ... Mr. Locke was a person of excellent sense, and good learning, and had a fine *taste*. But what he so much prized and admired, our writer has so slight a notion of, that he is for throwing it off as *rubbish*: which is his mannerly expression for all *external* revelation.[220]

Waterland's fellow Anglican, Humphrey Prideaux, dean of Norwich, also addressed a *Letter to the Deists* (1748), in which he advised,

Let what is written [in all the books of the New Testament] be tried by that which is the Touchstone of all *Religions*, I mean that *Religion* of Nature and Reason which *God* hath written in the hearts of every one of us from the first Creation; and if it varies from it in any one particular ... I will then acknowledge this to be an argument against us, strong enough to overthrow the whole Cause, and make all things else that can be said for it, totally ineffectual to its support.[221]

Samuel Bourn, the Presbyterian minister of New Meeting, Birmingham, had no doubt of the importance of reason in relation to Scripture. He posed a question expecting the answer 'No' in these terms, 'Can we prove the Scriptures to be from God, find out the Meaning of them, or pay a wise and acceptable Obedience to them, without the Exercise of *Reason*?'[222] The like-minded John Taylor charged his students at Warrington academy

> that in all your Studies and Inquiries of a religious Nature ... you do constantly, carefully, impartially, and conscientiously attend to Evidence, as it lies in the holy Scriptures, or in the Nature of things, and the Dictates of Reason; cautiously guarding against the Sallies of Imagination, and the Fallacy of ill-grounded Conjecture.[223]

George Benson was more concise, 'by our reason we are to make trial of what is offered to us as a revelation from God. Otherwise how could we distinguish between the Koran of Mahomet and the Bible?'[224] The corollary was temperately stated with reference to II Timothy 2:24, by Thomas Amory, among others:

> If Persons do not immediately yield to your Arguments, we must not pronounce them dishonest or stupid, but carefully examine, whether we ourselves are not mistaken. And if after a review we see good reason to conclude, that we have Truth of our side, we should try whether placing our Arguments in other Lights, or offering new, taken from Reason and Scripture; whether continued kindness and candor, joined with a good Example, may not prevail over their Prejudices ... Where we cannot by good Arguments convince others, to pronounce them Enemies to Truth and Goodness, is to exalt ourselves into *Lords* indeed.[225]

One might almost have attributed the 'wish to be in every point, great and small, a scriptural, rational Christian' to one or other of these Arian divines. In fact the wish was expressed by John Wesley.[226] As we might expect, many of the more evangelical divines increasingly came to emphasize the sufficiency of Scripture as the rule of faith and order. At the end of our period, for example, Thomas Craig completed his studies at the evangelical Calvinistic Homerton College (1730–1820). In his ordination confession of 1802 he declared, 'I believe that the scriptures of the Old and New Testament were written under the inspiration of God ...'; and he proceeded through the several Christian doctrines in moderate Calvinist fashion, with no specific use of the term 'predestination' or of language concerning the covenants of works and of grace.[227] At the opposite theological pole, Alexander Christie, one of the founders of Scottish Unitarianism had meanwhile, in 1790, published *The Holy Scriptures the Only Rule of Faith, and Religious Liberty Asserted and Maintained in Sundry Letters to the Kirk Session of Montrose, with Extracts in Defence Thereof from the Writings of Eminent and Rational Christians, Laymen as well as Divines.*[228] As if this were not enough, we find the evangelical Arminian Baptist, Dan Taylor, founder of the New Connexion of General Baptists (1770), invoking Locke's *Essay* IV.xvi in support of his view that the empirical claims made in the Bible should be substantiated by a sufficient number of competent witnesses of integrity, and by applying the tests of consistency and coherence.[229] His contemporary, the evangelical Calvinist Baptist, Andrew Fuller, came to the opposite conclusion in 1799:

> I conceive these sacred writings may contain such *internal* evidence of their being what they profess to be as that it might, with equal reason, be doubted whether the world was created by the power of God, as whether they were written by the inspiration of his Spirit: and, if so, our dependence is not upon mere tradition.[230]

Finally, also during the 1790s, both an anonymous London clergyman and Richard Watson, bishop of Llandaff, quoted Locke's *Posthumous Works* with approval – the latter against Gibbon's rationalistic scepticism: 'Study the holy scripture, especially the new Testament: Therein are contained the words of eternal life. It has God for its author; Salvation for its end; and Truth without any mixture of error, for its Matter.'[231] It also allows plenty of scope to theologically disparate interpreters, all of whom may be committed to belief in its sufficiency.

With Locke's testimony ringing in our ears we turn to our second question: how was Locke's biblical work received by the eighteenth-century divines? Here I can be relatively brief, for the history of biblical exegesis is not our primary concern. Were it so we should, for example, have to dwell upon the debate between the Quakers Benjamin Coole and Josiah Martin, the former of whom concluded that Locke's interpretation of I Corinthians 11:3 could not be used in support of women preachers, while the latter took the opposite view;[232] and upon the criticism of James Fraser of Alness to the effect that in the case of Romans 5:1–7:8,

Locke had not been faithful to his own principles of interpretation.[233] Many other divines welcomed Locke's general approach, but did not feel bound to agree with him on all points of detail. Of these, Philip Doddridge is typical:

> I own I cannot fall in with his exposition of many particular texts; but I have very little to except against his general scheme, and his division of the matter, which seems to me to throw an additional light upon the whole.[234]

In his helpful Introduction to his edition of Locke's *Paraphrase and Notes*, Arthur W. Wainwright reminds us that Locke was not a pioneer in the production of biblical paraphrases,[235] and adduces evidence to support the following two claims, which I recapitulate in my own words. First, it is by no means the case that Locke waited until near the end of his life before turning his attention to the Bible.[236] On the contrary, from his early *Two Tracts on Government* (1660–1), from his letters, journals, controversies, as well as from his major writings, not excluding the *Essay*, Locke emerges as a person saturated with biblical thought, adept at marshalling biblical evidence, and more than willing to draw illustrations from the Bible to underline his points.

Secondly, as far as biblical scholarship was concerned, Locke's mind was by no means *tabula rasa.* We should not forget that, as John Marshall has well said,

> There is an important sense in which Locke's entire religious career can be described in terms of a succession of 'sincere' friendships, starting with various Anglican Oxford fellows in the early 1660s, next with Shaftesbury and various Latitudinarians in the later 1660s and 1670s, then with Arminians in Holland in the 1680s,[237] and ending with Arminians and Unitarians in England in the 1690s.[238]

Thus Wainwright is able to list a considerable number of authorities on whom Locke drew when writing his *Paraphrase*;[239] and this despite his paper of 1677, in which he declared that 'It is an idle and useless thing to make it our business to study what have been other men's sentiments in things where reason is the only judge.'[240] In fact, by the time he introduced his *Paraphrase,* he had come to the conclusion that

> if the Comments and Expositions of pious and learned Men cannot be depended on, whether shall we go for Help? To which I answer, I

would not be mistaken, as if I thought the Labours of the Learned in this Case wholly lost, and fruitless.[241]

We do, however, need a means of determining which interpretation best yields Paul's meaning. Hence Locke's method of reading the epistles through in one sitting – and more than once if need be:

> I continued to read the same Epistle over and over, and over again, till I came to discover, as appeared to me, what was the Drift and Aim of it, and by what Steps and Arguments *St. Paul* prosecuted his Purpose.'[242]

That Locke did not originate this method of reading the Bible is emphasized by the master of St John's College, Cambridge, Robert Jenkin, in the Introduction to his *Remarks on Some Books Lately Publish'd* (1709).[243] Later, while not denying Locke's religious sensitivity, he opines, 'Few men perhaps ever wrote upon St. Paul's Epistles, who took less pains to understand them, than Mr. Locke seems to have done.'[244]

We have seen that on other matters Locke could not do much to please the high Calvinist, John Edwards, and the same applies regarding biblical interpretation:

> And whereas, not only Mr. Whiston, but his Admirer Mr. Lock, think that they sufficiently disparage the Apostolical Epistles by saying they were Occasional, we are to know that this is part of their just condemnation. For by these Occasions and Emergencies in the Christian Churches, the Vertue and Usefulness of the Apostles Rules and Laws are discovered, and their Efficacy is known and confirm'd by Tryal and Experience; which wonderfully brightens them, and sets them off, and renders them serviceable and practicable in all future Ages.[245]

Even Isaac Watts found Locke's doctrinal expositions inadequate and, in lyrical vein, wrote 'On Mr. Locke's Annotations upon several Parts of the New Testament, left behind him at his Death' in the following terms:

> Reason could scarce sustain to see
> Th' Almighty One, th'eternal Three,
> Or bear the infant deity ...

Then come Locke's words from heaven itself:

> 'Forgive,' he cries, 'ye Saints below
> The wavering and the cold Assent

I gave to Themes divinely true;
Can you admit the Blessed to repent?
Eternal Darkness veil the Lines
Of that unhappy Book,
Where glimmering Reason with false Lustre shines,
Where the mere mortal Pen mistook
What the celestial meant.'[246]

Watts's charges against Locke are the more interesting given the accusation of Socinianizing to which he was himself subjected later in life.

No one could have doubted the ardent Calvinism of the president of Yale, Ezra Stiles, who, in his diary entry of 18 May 1775, took exception to what he calls Locke's 'new *Mode* of Scripture Commentary, by *Paraphrase & Notes.*' He continues:

> This *Mode* received great Applause ever since even from those who differed from Mr. Lock as to Doctrines & religious principles: but as his Arian & Arminian principles have had a general spread & Reception among the Chh of Engld & Dissenters the half Century past, so Mr. Lockes Reputation as a Scripture Commentator has been exceeding high with the public ... But a *continued Paraphrase* is as absurd as a *continued Notation or Comment*, because it implies that, the whole Hebrew & Greek Language is Idiom; whereas it is certain that by far the greater Part of all the Oriental Languages & the English Tongue is not Idiom, but common familiar & intelligible in a litteral Translation ... [The English Bible] is too intelligible to need the Paraphrase of even a Locke ... I wish ... to have the pure word of Gd by itself.[247]

But, imitation being the sincerest form of flattery, Stiles had to concede that 'The Dissenting Divines were captivated with Locks Manner. Hence the Paraphrases & Notes by Benson, Peirce, Hallet, Lowman, Taylor, Guyse & Doddridge ...'[248] Of these, the first three were Presbyterian divines who were tending in an Arian direction – indeed, James Peirce's Exeter congregation ejected him for Arianism in 1717.[249] He tackled Colossians (1725), Philippians (1725) and Hebrews (its concluding three chapters, completed after Pierce's death by his colleague Joseph Hallett, appeared with the first two in a composite volume in 1727);[250] while George Benson, who regretted that Locke on occasion went against his own conviction that each text has a literal meaning only by finding a spiritual sense also,[251] attended to the remainder of Paul's letters and the catholic epistles. Doddridge included Peirce, Hallett and Benson

> in the number of the most ingenious commentators I have ever read ... They plainly thought very closely ... But they all err in too great a fondness for new interpretations ... It must be allowed that BENSON illustrates the spirit of Paul sometimes in an admirable manner, even beyond any former writer.[252]

The Presbyterian minister Moses Lowman, who like Peirce had studied in Utrecht, produced a *Paraphrase and Notes upon the Revelation of St. John* (1737),[253] which was also highly commended by Doddridge.[254] Doddridge was not so happy with the Arian John Taylor's *Key to the Apostolical Writings*, which he prefixed to his *Paraphrase with Notes on ... Romans* (1745). On 19 April 1745 he confided to Samuel Wood, 'The pure uncorrupted Scriptural Gospel – without the Aid or Incumbrance of humane Schemes – is becoming dearer than ever to my Soul. Nor the less so for a certain *Key* which *inter nos* ... seems broke in the Lock.'[255] Doddridge welcomed his fellow Independent John Guyse's rebuttal of Taylor in the preface to his paraphrase of Romans, which appeared as part of his *Practical Exposition*, 1739–52.[256]

Among others who gave a generally cordial welcome to Locke's *Paraphrase* were William Whiston, Nathanael Lardner and Joseph Priestley.[257] Of these the last cited Locke on Galatians 3:27 in support of his contention that 'all Christians are the sons of God, as our Lord Jesus Christ was.'[258] Towards the end of our period the Anglican divine and educational reformer, John Napleton, published some guidance to a university student contemplating holy orders. With reference to the study of the New Testament epistles he wrote,

> You may take the joint assistance of Dr. Hammond, Dr. Whitby, Mr. Locke, and Poole's Synopsis. Mr. Locke has considerable discernment in tracing the occasion and circumstances of St. Paul's Epistles. He may be read with advantage after one caution. In translating and explaining passages which have reference to the Divinity of our Lord and the Assistance of the Holy Spirit, his mind seems to be under a bias; and his opinion ought not to have weight with you.[259]

At the turn of the century, the Unitarian Thomas Belsham was under no such inhibitions:

> What learning may do to illustrate and confirm the evidences of revealed religion, to interpret prophecy, to solve difficulties, to correct errors in the received text, to expunge interpolations, to clear up the true sense and spirit of the sacred writers, and to repel the attacks of uninformed or unprincipled unbelievers, the inestimable writings of Leland and Lardner, of Clarke and Chandler, of Lowth and Kennicott, of Locke and Taylor, of Farmer, Newcome, and Wakefield, and of many living authors abundantly testify.[260]

This comment, uttered about a century after Locke was writing his *Paraphrase*, should give pause to any who may be tempted to think that Locke's continuing influence was confined to the fields of epistemology and government. Who can say how many were treated to his biblical interpretations through sermons, lectures and addresses during the hundred years after his death? Belsham himself, in his biblical expositions, adopted Locke's method, thereby giving it a further lease of life.

V

This account of 'reason,' 'revelation,' 'faith' and 'Scripture' has to a considerable degree been a tale of ambiguous terms, many of the ambiguities turning upon whether usage is more sensationalist, more intellectualist or more 'existential'. We have seen that few divines wished to dispense with reason altogether, and that some of the more rationalistic divines were far removed from that paring down of doctrines to suit the modern mind which so preoccupied their nineteenth-century successors. Locke was variously extolled and excoriated but, taking the divines as a whole, there was no slavish following of him either in theory or in biblical exegesis (though his method of Bible study was highly influential, not only upon liberal Anglicans and Dissenters, but also upon such a moderate Calvinist as Philip Doddridge); and some of those most indebted to his epistemology thought it proper to make more theoretical capital than he had done from faith *qua fiducia* – to which definition Locke's *Paraphrases* of Paul, posthumously published, had finally brought him, and which could not fail, in the end, to prompt an understanding of revelation as more than merely a supplement to reason and a supplier of additional truths expressed in propositions. But, to recapitulate the point made at the end of the previous chapter, we are still some way from faith/experience *qua* apologetic devices.[261] Furthermore, Locke's ambivalence on the relative authority of reason and Scripture could not but play into the hands of those who wished to focus exclusively upon one or other aspect of the implicit bifurcation: they could select what appealed, and leave, or repudiate, the rest.

Three huge themes now await our attention: Locke's concern for *right reason* – that is, for morality; the implications of morality for toleration and government; and Locke's convictions regarding Christian doctrine. Since we have already investigated Locke on Scripture, which has often been understood as a depository of doctrine, it might have seemed appropriate to proceed straight to doctrine. But I have elected not to do this, because the eighteenth-century divines were thinking doctrinal thoughts in an atmosphere of moral freedom engendered by the degree of toleration accorded to them by law; and because many of them came to apply a moral test to doctrine itself. Accordingly, we shall first step gingerly into the quagmire of eighteenth-century ethics.

4

Morality and Liberty

I

> Rationalism can object to the old sacramental system that it degrades a spiritual influence into a physical effect. But rationalism itself, in order to make the proof of revelation universal, is obliged to resolve religion into the moral government of God by rewards and punishments, and especially the latter.[1]

Thus Mark Pattison who, for good measure, quotes A. J. Vaughan in support: 'To degrade religion to the position of a mere purveyor of motive to morality is not more dishonourable to the ethics which must ask, than to the religion which will render such assistance.'[2]

We may find grounds for thinking that Pattison has correctly observed a tendency in eighteenth-century thought, and that Vaughan's remark has much to be said for it. But I shall seek to show that any blame for the lamented condition would be inappropriately apportioned if it were to be laid exclusively at the door of Locke. For as in epistemology, so in ethics, Locke seeks to hold a number of considerations together – hedonism, natural law and Scripture among them. Not surprisingly, therefore, in ethics as elsewhere, subsequent divines were able to construe him in significantly different ways and, in some cases, to draw from him what suited their own purposes whilst leaving the remainder on one side.

There can be no question that Locke was in earnest concerning morality. Although 'our Faculties are not fitted to penetrate into the internal Fabrick and real Essences of Bodies,' they can yield 'the Being of GOD, and the Knowledge of our selves, enough to lead us into a full and clear discovery of our Duty'. Indeed, '*Morality* is *the proper Science, and Business of Mankind in general*'.[3] How do we know what our duty is? Locke has no more place for innate ideas in ethics than in epistemology. This is because '*practical Principles ... come short of an universal Reception*,' and because 'moral Principles require Reasoning and Discourse, and some Exercise of the Mind, to discover the certainty of their Truth.'[4] Instead, Locke appeals variously to intuitive principles, to reasoning on the basis of sense experience, and to hedonistic considerations; but in every case the final arbiter is Scripture. Let us consider each of these in turn.

First, Locke holds that there are intuitive ethical principles which have the demonstrable certainty of mathematics:

> The *Idea* of a supreme Being, infinite in Power, Goodness, and Wisdom, whose Workmanship we are, and on whom we depend; and the *Idea* of our selves, as understanding, rational Beings, being such as are clear in us, would, I suppose, if duly considered, and pursued, afford such Foundations of our Duty and Rules of Action, as might place *Morality amongst the Sciences capable of Demonstration*: wherein I doubt not, but from self-evident Propositions, by necessary Consequences, as incontestable as those in Mathematicks, the measures of right and wrong might be made out, to any one that will apply himself with the same Indifferency and Attention to the one, as he does to the other of these Sciences.[5]

Prior to the publication of the *Essay*, Locke's friend the philosopher William Molyneaux had invited him to

> think of obliging the world with 'A Treatise of Morals,' drawn up according to the hints you frequently give in your essay, of being demonstrable according to the mathematical method. This is most certainly true. But then the task must be undertaken, only by so clear and distinct a thinker as you are.[6]

Succumbing neither to the flattery nor acceding to the request Locke had replied, 'whether I am able so to make it out, is another matter.'[7] When Molyneaux reiterated the request on the appearance of the *Essay*, Locke, in mitigation, pleaded his age and the state of his health, and declared that in any case 'the gospel contains so perfect a body of ethics, that reason may be excused from that enquiry, since she may find man's duty clearer and easier in revelation, than in herself.'[8] Mrs. Catharine Cockburn was another who urged Locke to give the world a treatise on ethics. 'Who is there so capable of pursuing to a demonstration those Reflections on the grounds of Morality which you have already made?' she asked 'the excellent Mr. Lock' in the dedicatory epistle to her work of 1702, *A Defence of the Essay of Human Understanding.*

Apart from the question of demonstrability, it is interesting in passing to reflect, with Morton White, that while Locke did not think that natural philosophy could become a 'science' by yielding 'truths that would be perceived by intuitive reason, axioms from which theorems would be deduced by discursive reason,' he did think this possible in the field of moral science.[9] However, when he returned to the possibility in *The Reasonableness of Christianity*, Locke pointed out that before Christ came, 'philosophy seemed to have spent its strength and done its utmost,' but it had failed to produce 'from undeniable principles ... ethics in a science like mathematics, in every part demonstrable'. Even if it had done this, the result 'would not have been so effectual to man in this imperfect state, nor proper for the cure'. For the fact is that 'The greatest part of mankind want leisure or capacity for demonstration ... And you may as soon hope to have all the day-labourers and tradesmen, the spinsters and dairy-maids, perfect mathematicians, as to have them perfect in ethics in this way.' Happily,

> To one who is once persuaded that Jesus Christ was sent by God to be a King, and a Saviour of those who do believe in him; all his commands become principles; there needs no other proof for the truth of what he says, but that he said it.[10]

Not surprisingly, in view of this appeal to authority, Locke advocates Bible teaching for the young; indeed, he doubts whether children 'should read any other discourses of morality, but what he finds in the bible' – until, that is, they can read and assimilate Tully's *Offices.*[11] Again, it is not surprising, in view of his obvious discomfort with the mathematics–morality analogy, that the possibility that the latter may be capable of demonstration is not reiterated in Locke's *Paraphrase*, the work of his declining years.

Secondly, Locke invokes reason which, by reflecting upon sense experience, ascertains moral truths. It is by this process that we become aware of the deliverances of the natural law – a matter on which Locke drew from Hugo Grotius, Samuel Pufendorf, Nathanael Culverwel, Richard Hooker and Robert Sanderson.[12] As compared with intuiting truths of reason, it would seem that natural law is a great leveller: mastery of Latin is not required; its deliverances are plain to all rational people;[13] and it 'stands as an eternal rule to all men, legislators as well as others,' for the natural law is a declaration of the will of God.[14] The law of nature is 'the Will and Law of a God'.[15] More fully, it is 'the decree of the divine will discernible by the light of nature and indicating what is and what is not in conformity with rational nature, and for this very reason commanding or prohibiting'.[16] The link between morals and theology here is cosmological. God has made and ordered all things, and we are his workmanship, over whom he rules and to whom he gives his divine law.[17] At the same time, speaking now as he often does in rationalistic terms, Locke declares that the natural law is 'that rule of rectitude which god has given to man kind in giveing them reason,' and he suggests that Paul's phrase 'the judgement of God' (under which the wilfully wicked stand) might be translated, 'the rectitude of God'.[18] Believing as he does that the will of God and the rational order of things are in complete accord, Locke experiences no tension between his voluntaristic and more rationalistic modes of speech.[19] In either case, the natural law may be promulgated either by 'the light of Nature, or the voice of Revelation,'[20] the latter being delivered to us by Jesus Christ himself.[21] In him 'morality has a sure standard, that revelation vouches, and reason cannot gainsay, nor question; but both together witness to come from God the great law-maker.'[22] It follows, thinks Locke, that 'Those are not at all to be tolerated who deny the being of God. Promises, covenants, and oaths, which are the bonds of human society, can have no hold upon an atheist. The taking away of God, though but even in thought, dissolves all.'[23] Here is reiterated the Psalmist's conviction that it is the fool – that is, the *immoral* person – who says in his heart there is no God.[24] In a word, both natural law and positive divine law are binding because 'the basis of obligation is in both cases the same, i.e., the will of a supreme Godhead.'[25]

The decision of immoral atheists in refusing to honour the God on whom the natural law rests is not the only reason Locke offers for the adoption by some of principles which flout the natural law. He also attributes this lamentable situation to the fact that people are

> either carried off by inveterate habit and traditional examples or led aside by their passions, thus yielding to the morality of others; also they follow the herd in the manner of brute beasts, since they do not allow themselves the use of their reason, but give way to appetite.[26]

What is interesting here is the omission. In view of Locke's frequent theistic grounding of the natural law, and of his ready appeal to the New Testament, it is somewhat surprising in view of his later remarks in *The Reasonableness of Christianity*[27] and in his *Paraphrase* of Romans 1, that he does not here allude to the noetic effects of sin, on which subject many a Puritan divine was waxing eloquent all around him.[28] As it is, he seems rather to give the cue to those eighteenth-century divines who asserted the need to control the passions and to elevate them,[29] and who could say with Samuel Clarke that passions and affections are 'not in themselves evil, as some of the ancient philosophers vainly imagined,' and that sinful passions are those which are not subject to reason.[30]

Now, since 'natural religion, in its full extent, was no-where, that I know, taken care of, by the force of natural reason,'[31] the teaching given in the New Testament and summed up by the Saviour was required. Hence, 'such a body of ethics, proved to be the law of nature, from principles of reason, and teaching all the duties of life; I think nobody will say the world had before our Saviour's time.'[32] It is not my purpose to defend or to attack Locke's reasoning here, but simply to point out that he is laying rationalist, empiricist and theological considerations alongside one another in such a way that the joins show; he is making an appeal to authority which, elsewhere, he would view askance as entailing the derogation of one's rational duty; and, whether he sets out from intuitive principles or from sense experience, he ends with Scripture. This is consistent with his view that notwithstanding the insights of ancient and modern philosophers, 'the morality of the gospel doth so exceed them all, that, to give a man full knowledge of true morality, I shall send him to no other book, but the New Testament.'[33]

Thirdly, we must note the hedonistic aspect of Locke's ethical thought which is epitomized in the following quotation:

> Things then are Good or Evil, only in reference to Pleasure or Pain. That we call *Good*, which *is apt to cause or increase Pleasure, or diminish Pain in us; or else to procure, or preserve us the possession of any other Good, or absence of any Evil.* And on the contrary we name that *Evil*, which *is apt to produce or increase any Pain, or diminish any Pleasure in us; or else to procure us any Evil, or deprive us of any Good.*[34]

The words 'in reference to' in the first line of the quotation indicate Locke's view that while reason may inform us of what is right or wrong, considerations of pain and pleasure will commend the right course to our affections and prompt our desire of it. As he elsewhere wrote, with reference to 'the rod' on the one hand and 'little encouragements' on the other, 'good and evil, reward and punishment, are the only motives to a rational creature; these are the spur and reins whereby all mankind are set on work and guided ...'[35] In stronger theistic vein he writes of God that 'He has Goodness and Wisdom to direct our Actions to that which is best: and he has Power to enforce it by Rewards and Punishments, of infinite weight and duration, in another Life ...'[36] When we come to *The Reasonableness of Christianity* we find that the prospect of eternal felicity, unknown to ancient philosophers, is held before the virtuous:

> The philosophers, indeed, showed the beauty of virtue; they set her off so, as drew men's eyes and approbation to her; but leaving her unendowed, very few were willing to espouse her ... The view of heaven and hell will cast a slight upon the short pleasures and pains of this present state, and give attractions and encouragements to virtue which reason and interest, and the care of ourselves, cannot but allow and prefer. Upon this foundation, and upon this only, morality stands firm, and may defy all competition. This makes it more than a name; a substantial good, worth all our aims and endeavours; and thus the gospel of Jesus Christ has delivered it to us.[37]

In the *Paraphrase*, too, the concept of reward is present, as we should expect. In I Corinthians 3:8 Paul writes of preachers and tenders of the Gospel, 'Now he that planteth, and he that watereth, are one: and every man shall receive his own reward, according to his own labour.' Locke paraphrases thus:

> We the preachers of the Gospel are but labourers imploid by god, about that which is his work. and from him shall receive reward hereafter every one according to his own labour, and not from men here,

> who are liable to make a wrong estimate of the labours of their teachers, prefering those who doe not labour togeather with god, who doe not cary on the designe or worke of god in the gospel, or perhaps doe not cary it on equally with others, who are undervalued by them.[38]

As far as the Christian is concerned, he or she 'has the view of Happiness and Misery in another Life ...'[39] On the other hand, those who do not weigh prudential matters with care are sub-rational: 'he that will not be so far a rational creature, as to reflect seriously upon infinite Happiness and Misery, must needs condemn himself, as not making that use of his Understanding he should.'[40] God, declares Locke elsewhere, 'has in his Hand Rewards and Punishments, and Power enough to call to account the Proudest Offender.'[41]

Locke's sayings on the quest of happiness might further be multiplied, but the pressing question of his stance *vis-à-vis* utilitarianism arises. When Locke's moderate, reasonable hedonism is seen in the context of his ethical teaching as a whole – with its emphasis upon intuitive principles and sense experience, and with its constant resort to the Bible, I submit that he is far from 'neat' utilitarianism. Rather, his view is that it is a function of the natural law, whose author is God, that happiness or punishment shall be apportioned to actors as appropriate. Similarly, utility is not the criterion of virtuous action, the will of God is.[42] As David Gauthier has pointed out, Locke shares individualism, an emphasis upon self-preservation, and a subjectivist hedonic value theory with Hobbes; 'And if these are all, then morality fails.'[43] For then we should have removed God and dissolved all. But with God we have, in Christ, encouragement and assistance.[44]

I

As might be expected, those divines who were most in favour of innate ideas regarded Locke's denial of them as undermining morality. Early in the lists was the clergyman James Lowde. We recall his critique of Locke's epistemology from the standpoint of a believer in natural inscriptions on the human mind (which are brought to consciousness by sensation or education), and revelation. Although the argument of his book *A Discourse concerning the Nature of Man* (1694) is largely directed against Hobbes, the preface contains an implicit rebuke of Locke. Lowde clearly has in mind Locke's words, '*Vertue* is every-where that which is thought Praise-worthy; and nothing else but that which has the allowance of publick Esteem, is called *vertue*.'[45] Horrified, he declares that, with English dictionaries and ancient philosophers alike, he understands vice and virtue as grounded in 'something more fixt and certain than the Custom of Countries, or the Mode and Fashion of those with whom we do converse'.[46] To this criticism Locke responded in the preface to the second edition of his *Essay* (1694). He sought to mollify Lowde by amending the last phrase to 'is called vertue'. This, he hoped, would make it clearer that he was 'not laying down moral Rules, but showing the original and nature of moral *Ideas*, and enumerating the Rules Men make use of in moral Relations, whether those Rules were true or false ...' Locke proceeds to refer Lowde to passages in which he asserts the eternal nature of right and wrong.[47] Lowde was not convinced, however, that Locke had successfully rebutted his charge, though it was not until his *Moral Essays* of 1695 that he returned to the matter in print. The nub of his position remained that while 'what ever is truly vertuous, is generally counted laudable ... it is not therefore vertuous, because laudable, but therefore laudable because vertuous.'[48] He further challenged Locke to explain how the intuitionist position advanced in the fourth book of the *Essay* was compatible with Locke's earlier claim that knowledge was by sensation and reflection alone. He remained convinced that the soul is competent to frame propositions 'the truth, or knowledge whereof no way depends upon the evidence of sense, or observation'.[49]

Somewhat similar concerns exercised Thomas Burnet, who published three sets of *Remarks* on Locke's *Essay*, in the third of which he challenged Locke to explain how, apart from revelation, and since conscience as an innate practical principle is denied, people can know which moral laws they ought to obey. Burnet makes it clear that he does not advocate innate moral propositions, but rather an innate capacity to judge between good and evil, which is developed and refined through experience.[50] For this reason, those who are not skilled in making deductions from first moral principles, are not disadvantaged; for they have natural conscience, which is 'a Natural Sagacity to distinguish Moral Good and Evil, or a different perception and sense of them, with a different affection of the Mind arising from it; and this so immediate as to prevent and anticipate all External Laws, and all Ratiocination.'[51] What Locke perceived in this affirmation was not simply disagreement with his own view that conscience is a person's moral *self*-judgement,[52] but an inlet to enthusiasm.[53]

Mrs Catharine Cockburn sprang to Locke's defence, insisting in her prefatory letter to 'the excellent Mr. Lock' that

> the Great Mr. *Lock* was reserv'd for a Curious and Learned Age, to *break in upon this Sancuary of Vanity and Ignorance*, and by setting Man on considering first the *Bounds of Human Understanding*, to help them in a close Pursuit of True and Useful Knowledge.

No one, she insists, has set morality on so firm a ground as Locke, and she regrets that Burnet has so sadly misunderstood him. Locke does not deny the reality of moral good and evil, and he grounds morality in the existence of God (though James Oswald was later to regret that Locke did not advise us of the source of the idea of a governing mind, which could not have come either from sensation or from reflection as understood by Locke).[54] Whereas Burnet seems able to conceive of virtues in abstraction from a subject, 'the Nature of Man and the Good of Society, are *to us* the Reason and Rule of Moral Good and Evil; and there is no danger of their being less immutable on this Foundation than any other, whilst *Man continues a Rational and Sociable creature*.'[55] This being Locke's foundation, Burnet is wrong to claim that Locke's ethics rest entirely upon future rewards and punishments. In answer to Burnet's query concerning Locke's method of deriving perfection (including veracity) from the senses, Mrs Cockburn charges Burnet with having overlooked Locke's other principle of knowledge, reflection.[56] Yet again, Locke does not say that universal consent is necessary for a principle to be natural; he

> only contends against those who say there are Principles of Metaphysical or Moral Truths originally imprinted on the mind; by which, if they only mean that there is an *Innate* Power or Capacity in the Soul of knowing these Truths, they mean nothing different from Mr. *Lock*, who denies *Innate Principles*; for he does not deny that there is a Power in the Soul of perceiving, and assenting to those Truths; or of distinguishing Good and Evil ...[57]

On discovering the identity of his defender, Locke was grateful – even glutinous:

> You have ... not only vanquished my adversary, but reduced me also absolutely under your power, and left no desires more strong in me than those of meeting with some opportunity to assure you with what respect and submission I am, Madam, Your most humble and most obedient servant, J. Locke.[58]

In 1700 John Milner was puzzled by Locke's claim that, without recourse to revelation, we can attain knowledge of the law of nature by exercising our natural faculties upon natural principles; for if innate ideas are ruled out, whence come the natural principles?[59] A similar point was made in the year of Mrs Cockburn's defence of Locke by Henry Lee who, as we might by now expect, rebuked him on ethics as we have already seen he did on epistemology. The charge now, as with that of Lowde and Burnet, is that Locke, having discarded innate ideas has rejected immutable moral principles with them. Lee does not argue that such principles yield direct moral guidance or imperatives – and he accuses Locke of wrongly supposing that this view is held by supporters of innate principles; rather, by means of such principles we classify and justify such knowledge as we have – not least that which comes from sensation. Indeed, it is our ability to do this which distinguishes us from brutes.[60]

In 1732 John Conybeare, later to become bishop of Bristol, published *A Defence of Revealed Religion* in answer to the deist Matthew Tindal's *Christianity as Old as the Creation* (1730). He has nothing but praise for Locke:

> In the last century there arose a very extraordinary genius for philosophical speculations; I mean Mr. Locke; the glory of that age, and the instructor of the present. This gentleman had examined into the nature and extent of human understanding beyond any person before him, and made such discoveries as have highly obliged the curious. In the course of his enquiries it occurred to him, from considering the nature of moral ideas; that Ethics was capable of strict demonstration, as well as mathematics ... [H]e doth not ... maintain, that every man is capable, by his own force, of demonstrating whatsoever is really capable of being demonstrated in morality; but only, that if a right method were taken, a great part of morality might be made out with that clearness that could leave to a considering man no more reason to doubt ...[61]

In the event, Conybeare continues, Locke was not sure whether he could produce such a demonstration, 'and therefore it must be vain for others, so much inferior to this great man, to attempt it after him.'[62] Locke is applauded for his resort to the Gospel for 'a perfect body of Ethics,' thereby testifying that

> reason may be excused from the enquiry, since she may find man's duty clearer, and easier in revelation, than in herself. And this [Locke] affirms, though he knew well at the same time, that the proof of a traditional revelation was not of that kind which is strictly and properly demonstrative.[63]

Conybeare manifestly had no intention of taking up the challenge which Locke had declined.

In his Boyle Lectures William Worthington, a Welsh divine, added a theological postscript to Locke's point (and made capital out of the ambiguity of 'demonstration' = 'logically coercive proof' and 'demonstration' = 'confirmation in experience'):

> A great master of reason was persuaded, that morality is capable of demonstration; and, if so, the internal evidence of christianity is certainly capable of it likewise, because morality is included in it – the purest and most excellent morality ... And the christian morality is, moreover, attended with *the demonstration of the Spirit.*[64]

On the next page he appears to retract a little:

> [W]hether the great truths of christianity are strictly demonstrable, or not, from their own natures, this I doubt not to affirm, that, being founded on facts, or reducible to fact, the evidence of them is so great, that, when placed in a proper light, it must be allowed to be morally certain: And what demonstration is, with regard to mathematical truths, moral certainty is, with regard to moral and religious truths; for the demonstration, or proof, must be of the same kind with the principles on which it is founded: And the moral proof may be no less depended upon, if not more so, than even the mathematical; as our gross and limited understandings are not so subject to err in palpable matters of fact, and objects of sense, as in idea matters and abstract reasonings.[65]

Meanwhile Abraham Tucker, who turned his hand to most professions except divinity, had published his good-humoured work, *The Light of Nature Pursued* (1768), in which he applauds Locke for 'clearing away that incumbrance of innate ideas, real essences, and such like rubbish'.[66] He begs to differ on certain points, however. For example, where Locke says that both acting and forbearing to act are the result of willing, he cannot see that the latter requires the exercise of any active power at all.[67] Again, whereas Locke finds desire a cause of uneasiness (and Tucker agrees that in some cases it may be), it is not always or necessarily so – as he explains in a eulogy on courtship and marriage, the point of which is that desire can be quite enjoyable![68]

A decade later, Jackson Barwis was found censuring Locke for denying that conscience is an innate principle, and for claiming that our ethical opinions are formed by 'education, company and customs of our country'.[69] On this basis, he thought, monstrous crimes could be committed with a clear conscience – 'What strange errors do the greatest men sometimes run into!'[70] Barwis does not contend for innate ideas, but for innate principles from which ideas arise. He welcomes Locke's view that knowledge derives from sensation and reflection, but cannot understand why Locke did not recognize the existence of a moral sense. Were it not for this sense – an innate principle common to all – we could not discourse intelligibly about morals.[71]

In America in particular, a lively debate followed the eruption of the Awakening on the one hand and the determination of more liberal theologians to elevate humanity's nobler aspects on the other. Claude Newlin has paid detailed attention to this matter,[72] and I content myself with two examples. First, the prominent Boston liberal minister, Jonathan Mayhew, invoked Locke in support of his view that human knowledge is certain and sufficient, and that the senses may be trusted.[73] He maintains

1. That there is a natural difference betwixt truth and falsehood, right and wrong.
2. That men are naturally endowed with faculties proper for discerning these differences.
3. *And lastly*, That men are under obligation to exert these faculties; and to judge for themselves in things of a religious concern.[74]

Mayhew proceeds to counter two species of sceptics, 'one of which exploded the whole notion of truth and right, as opposed to falsehood and wrong conduct; and another which seemingly allowed such differences to have an existence in nature; but held it impossible for *us* to *discern* them'.[75] Along these lines Mayhew dismisses the doctrine of total depravity with some contempt.[76]

From the Calvinist side came the opposition of Peter Clark, in his Dudleian Lecture of 1763. His title, *Man's Dignity and Duty as a Reasonable Creature; and his Insufficiency as a Fallen Creature*, leaves us in little doubt of the line to be taken. We are under obligations which we cannot fulfil by reason of our sinful state. One such obligation is that of repentance. Although both natural and revealed religion require this duty of sinners, the former cannot supply the necessary aids and inducements. Supernatural influence must intervene, for 'The light and power of reason is too much darkened and debilitated ... to be able to throw off vicious customs and also to root out evil inclinations and reform the heart, which is the work of true repentance.'[77] Into the discussion of such implications of his general stance Locke, as we have seen, did not enter.

II

We must now turn to those divines who paid attention to the empiricist strand in Locke's ethical thought. Of those most indebted to Locke at this point, Butler stands supreme. Like Locke he is an intuitionalist in ethics, holding that we have 'a moral nature, and moral faculties of perception and of action,' together with 'a capacity of reflecting upon actions and characters, and making them an object to our thought,' and a faculty of approving and disapproving;[78] but, also like Locke, he pays due heed to the facts in the ethical situation, not least to the analysis of human nature. This is by no means to suggest that Butler – any more than Locke – is a latter-day positivist, believing that those propositions only are meaningful which are either analytic or – in principle at least – empirically testable. For one thing, as Anders Jeffner has pointed out, 'We know immediately, [Butler] says, both the meaning and the fact of personal identity. An immediate knowledge of personal identity seems to be the same kind of cognizance as moral knowledge given through conscience.'[79] Butler is in further agreement with Locke in believing that religion both fertilizes, and is the final guarantor of, morality:

> The happiness of the world is the concern of him who is the Lord and the Proprietor of it; nor do we know what we are about, when we endeavour to promote the good of mankind in any ways but those which he has directed; that is, indeed, in all ways not contrary to veracity and justice.[80]

Other writers were not so generally content with Locke as was Butler. Thomas Burnet, for example, argued that since Locke's epistemology allows us no scope for *knowing* God's attributes, it makes no sense to say that we ought to obey his will. He further queried Locke's position on the divine law undergirding all. He wondered what, in Locke's opinion, was the ground of that law – was it 'the arbitrary will of God, the good of men, or the intrinsic nature of the things themselves'?[81] To this latter point Locke replied,

> Whoever sincerely acknowledges any law to be the law of God, cannot fail to acknowledge also, that it hath all that reason and ground that a just and wise law can or ought to have; and will easily persuade himself to forbear raising such questions and scruples about it.[82]

After such a 'put down' it is scarcely surprising that two further sets of *Remarks* followed, but Burnet did not take the measure of Locke's frequently reiterated declaration that 'The [divine] law is the eternal, immutable standard of right.'[83]

Archibald Campbell, Regius professor of divinity and ecclesiastical history at St Andrews, was not so remiss. Defending the necessity of revelation, he argued that a revelation from heaven, namely, Jesus Christ, was more likely to enlighten the bulk of humanity than ethical arguments drawn from reason; and that without knowledge of a law-maker (and this comes by revelation), ethical practice is not adequately grounded. In both connections he appealed for support to Locke's *Reasonableness.*[84] Later in the century, Campbell's compatriot, James Oswald, welcomed the fact that Locke 'resolves the source of moral obligation into the will of God,' but regretted that, revelation apart, he 'left us no criterion to be depended on for discovering the divine will'. He further lamented the fact that Locke 'seems to have known nothing of the inherent beauty of good, and ugliness of bad actions'.[85]

While some were accusing Locke of disregarding the divine law, others, including his pupil Shaftesbury, complained that he resolved ethics into the arbitrary will of God:

> THUS virtue, according to Mr. LOCKE, has no other Measure, Law, or Rule, than *Fashion* and *Custom*: Morality, Justice, Equity, depend only on *Law* and *Will*: And GOD indeed is a perfect *Free Agent* in this Sense, that is, *free to anything, that is however Ill*: For if he wills it, it will be made Good; Virtue may be Vice, and Vice Virtue in its Turn, if he pleases. And thus neither *Right* nor *Wrong, Virtue* nor *Vice* are any thing in themselves; nor is there any Trace or Idea of them *naturally imprinted* on Human Minds.[86]

What concerned Thomas Becconsall (among other things) was Locke's definition of conscience, namely, that it is 'our own Opinion or Judgment of the Moral Rectitude or Pravity of our own Actions'.[87] Becconsall does not deny that a vitiated conscience may still be called a conscience, but if we follow it we enhance our guilt rather than our merit. But what Locke will not admit is that 'the Foundation of Conscience ... arises from the Conformity of our Actions to the proper Rule, or Law of Conscience, the Law of God'.[88] Above all, he is concerned that, by undermining the argument from universal consent, Locke has severely damaged the idea of natural law. After all, we do not deny rationality to man 'because there are some Fools and Ideots'.[89]

I shall shortly refer to others who pitted a more thoroughly rationalistic understanding of law and obligation against Locke's more eclectic 'rational empiricism with a dash of hedonism and an appeal to Scripture as the final authority'. But chronology demands that I first introduce Francis Hutcheson, who was professor of moral philosophy at Glasgow in succession to his teacher, Gersom Carmichael, from 1729 until his death in 1746. Influenced by the altruism (against Hobbes's self-interest) of Shaftesbury's *Characteristics of Men, Manners, Opinions, and Times* (1711),[90] though repudiating Shaftesbury's identification of the aesthetic with the moral sense in favour of their distinctness from each other, Hutcheson's position was concisely compared with that of 'the judicious Mr. Locke' by his pupil Adam Smith: the moral sense

> which Mr. Locke calls reflection, and from which he derived the simple ideas of the different passions and emotions of the human mind, was, according to Dr. Hutcheson, a direct internal sense. That faculty again by which we perceived the beauty or deformity, the virtue or vice of those different passions and emotions, was a reflex, internal sense.[91]

In Hutcheson's own words which, in view of their importance, I quote at length,

> THESE *Determinations* to be pleas'd with any Forms, or Ideas which occur to our Observation, the Author chooses to call SENSES; distinguishing them from the Powers which commonly go by that Name, by calling our Power of perceiving the *Beauty* of *Regularity, Order, Harmony*, an INTERNAL SENSE; and *that Determination* to approve *Affections, Actions*, or *Characters* of *rational Agents*, which we call *virtuous*, he marks by the Name of a MORAL SENSE.
>
> HIS principal Design is to shew, 'That *Human Nature* was not left quite indifferent in the Affair of *Virtue*, to form to itself Observations concerning the Advantage, or Disadvantage of Actions, and accordingly to regulate its Conduct.' The Weakness of our Reason, and the Avocations arising from the Infirmities and Necessitys of our Nature, are so great, that very few Men could ever have form'd those long Deductions of Reason, which shew some Actions to be in the whole advantageous to the *Agent*, and their Contrarys pernicious. The AUTHOR of Nature has much better furnish'd us for a virtuous Conduct, than our *Moralists* seem to imagine, by almost as quick and powerful Instructions, as we have for the Preservation of our Bodys. He has given us strong *Affections* to be the Springs of each virtuous Action; and made Virtue a lovely Form, that we might easily distinguish it from its Contrary, and be made happy by the Pursuit of it.92

Hutcheson has variously been placed by some scholars in the line of Locke, and by others in decided opposition to him. Careful examination would seem, for example, to show that equally concerned as they are to reject innate ideas (in his student days Hutcheson had found Clarke's *a priorism* wanting) and empirically to examine human consciousness, as between Locke's and Hutcheson's sensationalism there is a wide gulf fixed, for Hutcheson's moral sense is neither an idea of sensation or reflection, nor a combination of both.[93]

As to innate ideas, Hutcheson writes,

> We are not to imagine, that this *moral Sense*, more than the other Senses, supposes any *innate Ideas, Knowledge, or practical Proposition*: We mean by it only *a Determination of our Minds to receive the simple Ideas of Approbation or Condemnation, from Actions observ'd, antecedent to any Opinions of Advantage or Loss to redound to ourselves from them;* even as we are pleas'd with a *regular Form*, or an *harmonious Composition*, without having any Knowledge of *Mathematicks*, or

> feeling any *Advantage* in that Form or Composition, different from the immediate Pleasure.[94]

Scarcely concealed by this definition are Hutcheson's abhorrence of the egoistical hedonism of Hobbes and Mandeville[95] whom he is intent on rebutting, his distance from Lockeian representationalism, and his inclination towards 'the Berkeleyan doctrine of sensations, as signs of causal power'.[96] He further removes the activity of the moral sense from selfish calculations thus:

> This *moral Sense*, either of our *own* Actions, or of those of *others*, has this in common with our other Senses, that however our Desire of *Virtue* may be counterbalanc'd by Interest, our Sentiment or Perception of its *Beauty* cannot; as it certainly might be, if the only Ground of our Approbation were Views of *Advantage*.[97]

From this it is clear that whereas Locke had work for deductive reason to do on the basis of sense impressions – albeit a few only had the leisure and competence for this activity[98] – Hutcheson has none. Our moral sense is immediately informative, so to speak, without any inferences requiring to be drawn. As compared with Locke's somewhat aristocratic rationalism it is therefore a societal leveller. Further, the pleasure which accompanies approbation of a virtuous act – one's own, or that of another – is quite distinct from the perception of the act as such, the latter being the deliverance of the moral sense.[99] Along these lines Hutcheson hoped to shun the inadequate ethical foundations upon which many who had followed Locke in rejecting innate ideas were now building:

> Nothing is more ordinary among those, who after Mr. LOCKE have rejected *innate Ideas*, than to alledge, 'That all our Relish for *Beauty* and *Order*, is either from prospect of *Advantage, Custom*, or *Education*,' for no other Reason but the *Variety* of *Fancys* in the World: and from this they conclude, 'That our *Fancys* do not arise from any *natural Power of Perception*, or *Sense*.'[100]

In his early writings, such as those from which I have just quoted,[101] Hutcheson proceeds as if, on the basis of this non-cognitive sensing we may make true moral statements. This practice was queried by Gilbert Burnet, prebendary of Salisbury, in 1725. He requested 'some further test, some more certain rule, whereby I could judge whether my sense (my moral sense, as the author calls it), my taste of things, was right and agreeable to the truth of things or not'.[102] In reply Hutcheson refers Burnet to passages in the *Inquiry* in which he

> recommends the most serious application of our reason to inquire into the natural tendencies of our actions as the means to attain this end [i.e. the public good] that we may not be led by every slight appearance to do actions which may have prepollent evil consequences ... Our moral sense and affections determine our end, but reason must find out the means.[103]

From this it is clear that reason is invoked not with intuitive or deductive intent, but by way of ascertaining whether or not desirable consequences will ensue from the enactment of a particular deliverance of the moral sense. We may therefore agree with David Fate Norton that 'Hutcheson builds on a foundation very different from that of Locke, a foundation that allows him to present his moral ideas as ectypal – as being patterned after a substantial reality – and not as merely arbitrary constructions of our own minds.'[104]

Although John Witherspoon was not willing to join Hutcheson in criticism of those who made

> reason the principle of virtuous conduct, yet I think it must be admitted, that a sense of moral good and evil, is as really a principle of our nature, as either the gross external or reflex senses, and as truly distinct from both, as they are from each other.[105]

In his view, 'This moral sense is precisely the same thing with what, in scripture and common language, we call conscience. It is the law which our Maker has written upon our hearts, and both intimates and enforces duty, previous to all reasoning.'[106] Those of a more thoroughgoing rationalist turn of mind were not persuaded. To them Hutcheson had reduced the basis of morals to feelings, while Locke failed to ground morality in immutable truths ascertainable by reason. Chief among these was the Dissenting divine, Richard Price:

> I do not at all care what follows from Mr. *Hume*'s assertion, that all our ideas are either *impressions, or copies of impressions*; or from Mr. *Locke*'s assertion that they are all *deducible from* SENSATION *and* REFLEXION. – The first of these assertions is, I think, destitute of all proof; supposes, when applied in this as well as many other cases,

> the point in question; and, when pursued to its consequences, ends in the destruction of all truth and the subversion of our intellectual faculties. – The other wants much explication to render it consistent with any tolerable account of the original of our moral ideas: Nor does there seem to be any thing necessary to convince a person, that all our ideas are not deducible from sensation and reflexion, except taken in a very large and comprehensive sense, besides considering how Mr. *Locke* derives from them our *moral ideas.* He places them among our ideas of relations, and represents *rectitude* as signifying the conformity of actions to some rules or laws; which rules or laws, he says, are either *the will of God, the decrees of the magistrate, or the fashion of the country*: From whence it follows, that it is an absurdity to apply *rectitude* to rules and laws by themselves; to suppose the *divine* will to be directed by it; or to consider it as *itself* a rule and law. But, it is undoubted, that this great man would have detested these consequences; and, indeed, it is sufficiently evident, that he was strangely embarrassed in his notions on this, as well as some other subjects.[107]

Price develops his own theory in such a way as to avoid both the Scylla of innate ideas (as espoused, for example, by Cudworth, to whom he was otherwise indebted), and the Charybdis of empiricism. He does not think the latter can yield universals (here resides a debt to Plato's *Theaetetus*), as this would conduce to a relativism devastating for morality; while the doctrine of innate ideas would imprison us in non-generalizable independent ideas.[108] His remedy is to expound an intuitionist view of moral judgement. As D. D. Raphael has put it, 'He is simply saying that the Cartesian intuition of self-evident truths is to be found in our awareness of moral principles, and that morals is in this respect (and not in respect of any deduction) like mathematics and ... physics.'[109] To which may be added C. B. Cone's remark,

> The moral faculty Price lodges in the understanding. Because it furnished the mind a priori with general ideas or universals, the understanding was the faculty that apprehended objective truth. Price thus held that moral ideas were simple – derived from the understanding – though in Locke's view simple ideas came immediately from sense perception.[110]

Price's position was cordially received by many. The Arian Presbyterian John Taylor, while a tutor at Warrington academy found, to his dismay, that Hutcheson's position in ethics was preferred to his own, and published *An Examination of the Scheme of Morality, advanced by Dr. Hutcheson* (1759) in which he espoused the general line taken by Price in his *Review*, which had been published in the preceding year.[111] In his address delivered at Price's interment Andrew Kippis, Presbyterian minister at Princes Street, Westminster for forty-three years, said,

> By his moral writings he has laboured, with distinguished ability, to build the science of Ethics on an immutable basis ... For myself I scruple not to say, that I regard the treatise referred to as a rich treasure of valuable information, and as deserving to be ranked among the first productions of its kind. With respect to the other ethical works of our friend, every one must admire the zeal, and earnestness, and strength with which he endeavours to lead men into pious views of God, of Providence and of Prayer, and to promote the exercise of devout and amiable dispositions.[112]

For a third testimony we may turn to America, and to William Ellery Channing's retrospective remark that during his Harvard days (1794–8) 'Price saved me from Locke's Philosophy. He gave me the doctrine of ideas, and during my life I have written the words Love, Right,&c., with a capital.'[113]

III

What did Locke's theological contemporaries and successors make of the hedonistic strand in his ethics? In his first *Remarks* on Locke's *Essay*, Thomas Burnet refers to the following definitions:

> Good and Evil ... are nothing but Pleasure and Pain, or that which occasions, or procures Pleasure or Pain to us. *Morally Good and Evil*, then, is only the Conformity or Disagreement of our voluntary Actions to some Law, whereby Good or Evil is drawn on us, from the Will and Power of the Law-maker; which Good and Evil, Pleasure or Pain, attending our observance, or breach of the Law, by the Decree of the Law-maker, is that we call *Reward* and *Punishment*.[114]

We have already noted Burnet's concern that Locke did not, in his opinion, adduce the ground of the moral law with sufficient clarity; but our concern now is with the hedonist flavour of the above words. Burnet cannot see how Locke can reach his conclusion here on the basis of his own epistemology:

> As to Morality, we think the great Foundation of it is, the Distinction of Good and Evil, Virtue and Vice, Turpis & Honesti, as they are usually call'd : And I do not find that my Eyes, Ears, Nostrils, or any other outward Senses, make any Distinction of these Things, as they do of Sounds, Colours, Scents, or other outward Objects; nor from any Idea's taken in from them, or from their Reports, am I conscious that I do conclude, or can conclude, that there is such a Distinction in the Nature of Things; or that it consists only in Pleasure and Pain, Conveniency and Inconveniency.[115]

Burnet returned to the charge in his *Second Remarks*, this time relating his ethical query to his conviction that Locke's view of the limitations of the light of nature and of revelation as far as certain knowledge are concerned leaves immortality in a very insecure position; and if that is the case, the supposition of future rewards and punishments is very uncertain indeed. Taking a broad sweep, but wasting no words, Burnet declares, 'If Morality stands upon Future Punishments and Rewards, and Future Punishments and Rewards stand upon the Immortality of the Soul, and the Immortality of the Soul be only Probable, then Morality cannot be Mathematically demonstrable.'[116]

As if to answer Burnet, Thomas Halyburton, professor of divinity at St Andrews, linked the idea of the moral law with that of rewards and punishments in the course of arguing that a system of morality cannot be produced by the light of nature alone, and invoked '*the ingenious Mr Locke*' in support:

> It is not enough to recommend Duty, that is useful to us, or the Societies we live in. When we act only on such grounds, we shew some Regard to ourselves and the Societies whereof we are Members; but none to GOD. Where are these clear'd to be the *Laws* of GOD? Who is he that presses *Obedience* upon the Consciences of Men, from the Consideration of *GOD's Authority* stampt upon these Laws he prescribes? And yet without this, you may call it what you will: *Obedience* you cannot call it. It is well observ'd by Mr. *Lock*, 'Those just Measures of *Right* and *Wrong*, which Necessity had any where introduc'd, the *Civil Laws* prescib'd or *Philosophers* recommended, stood not on their true Foundations. They were look'd on as Bonds of Society, and Conveniencies of common Life, and laudable Practices: But where was it that their Obligation was thoroughly known, and allow'd, and they receiv'd as precepts of a *Law*, of the *highest Law*, the *Law of Nature*? That could not be without the clear Knowledge of the *Law-giver*, and the *great Rewards* or *Punishments* for those that would not, or would obey . . .[117]

John Leland heartily concurred.[118]

William Carroll, in his anxiety to demonstrate that the deist Anthony Collins derives his ethical libertarianism from Locke and Spinoza, fastens upon two paragraphs in which Locke argues that 'the *Idea* of *Liberty*, is the *Idea* of a Power in any Agent to do or forbear any particular Action, according to the determination or thought of the mind, whereby either of them is preferr'd to the other ...'[119] Construing this as a recipe for anarchy in society, Carroll deems Locke to have rendered all laws, human and divine, absurd, and hence all talk of rewards and punishments unreasonable. Such partisan conclusions are easily reached by any who extract from an admittedly eclectic position that which suits their purpose, whilst overlooking counterbalancing factors.

Locke's friend and former pupil, Shaftesbury, deeply regretted that, with his attack upon innate ideas, Locke 'struck at all Fundamentals, threw all *Order* and *Virtue* out of the World, and made the very *Ideas* of these (which are the same as those of GOD) *unnatural*, and without Foundation in our Minds'.[120] What especially exercised him was that this seemed to rule out the inner moral sense, to which he was deeply committed, and which, to him, was the means whereby we apprehend that some actions are intrinsically good, others intrinsically bad:

> [T]he incentive to well-doing and the deterrents from evil doing are to be sought not solely, or even mainly, in the opinion of mankind, or in the rewards and punishments of the magistrate, or in the hopes and terrors of a future world, but in the answer of a good conscience, approving virtue and disapproving vice, and in the love of a God who, in His infinite wisdom and His all-embracing beneficence, is worthy of the love and admiration of His creatures.[121]

By contrast,

> If ... there be a Belief or Conception of a Deity, who is consider'd only as *powerful* over his Creature, and inforcing Obedience to his *absolute Will* by particular Rewards and Punishments; and if on this account, thro' Hope merely of *Reward*, or fear of *Punishment*, the Creature be incited to the Good he hates, or restrain'd from doing the Ill to which he is not otherwise in the least degree averse; there is in this case ... no Virtue or Goodness whatsoever.[122]

Lying behind Shaftesbury's critique of Locke was his fear of the ethical relativism to which he was convinced Hobbes's hedonism led. By overlooking the total context of Locke's religiously grounded hedonism, he too easily equated his teacher's position with that of his arch-opponent.[123]

Jackson Barwis, alleging that Locke's view is that things are good or evil 'only in reference to pleasure or pain,' argued that this would mean that to say that a thing is good means that it is pleasant. But if by 'good' we mean 'morally right, just, or reasonable,' then many good things are not pleasant, while some bad things are.[124]

For our final reference to considerations of self-interest – the acquisition of pleasure, the avoidance of pain, the pursuit of happiness – we may note the observations of two rational Dissenters. They were not, indeed, referring directly to Locke, but their remarks indicate the enthusiasm with which this approach was adopted by some. Priestley declared, 'it is most adviseable to leave every man at perfect liberty to serve himself, till some actual inconvenience be found to result from it';[125] while Belsham defined virtue as 'the tendency of an action, affection, habit, or character, to the ultimate happiness of the agent'.[126]

Having set out from Locke's eclectic ethics, it is appropriate that I end with two policy statements which are equally eclectic, and typify the attitude of many more liberal divines. In the first third of the century Henry Grove declared:

> Upon the whole, this notion which resolves all obligation into the *promises* and *threatenings* annexed to the law of God, or, which is the same thing, into the hopes and fears of men's minds raised by them, tho' it presupposes the will of God which hath enacted the law, and fixed the sanction, yet, under pretence of doing more honour to God and his law, hath in reality no respect to them at all, but terminates wholly in self-interest; whilst the other notion which asserts obligations antecedent in nature to the will of God, carries in it a tacit acknowledgement of the necessary and immutable perfections of God, and of his unmerited favour which hath bestowed *being* with all the privileges belonging to it: forasmuch as among these antecedent obligations, the obligations to the love of God, and a cheerful obedience to his will, is one of the principal ... [W]hen God and nature, reason and scripture have joined the love of God with the hope of a reward, it is but presumption in any man to put them asunder.[127]

In the last third of the century we find an eclectic credo and methodological affirmation which occurs in Institutes of Moral Philosophy, a set of manuscript lectures probably used by John Horsey, who was the Homerton-educated successor to Thomas Belsham at the second Northampton academy from 1789:

> We profess ourselves christian philosophers and the criteria to which we shall appeal in the following lectures to prove that the rules laid down in them are the precepts of virtue will sometimes be the dictates of the moral sense, and sometimes the authority of the best heathen or Christian moralists – but the principle standard and test of judgment will be the apparent tendency of the rule to promote the happiness of individuals and societies, and above all the express dictates and decisions of divine revelation, as the only compleat and infallible guide [the last clause is added in another hand].[128]

With this I conclude my account of the responses of a number of divines (and a few others – Shaftesbury could not be excluded, and Tucker deserved a mention) to Locke's general position on morality. Before passing to two specific ethical issues – liberty and government – I would only observe that most of the divines whose moral views I have reviewed, and certainly the most distinguished ethicists among them, appeal much less frequently in their ethical treatises to the authority of Scripture and the deliverances of the New Testament and the teaching and example of Christ than did Locke. I attribute this to the increasing 'professionalization' or at least specialization of ethics, and its increasing divorce, even in the Christian mind, from dogmatics.[129] By contrast, in doctrinal matters, as we shall see in the next chapter, there was a constant appeal by conservative and liberal theologians alike to the principle of the sufficiency of Scripture.

IV

Locke's works on liberty and government have spawned a vast literature, and I must at the outset utter the reminder that mine is not a work of political theory. I am concerned with the responses of eighteenth-century divines to Locke's philosophy, and, not surprisingly, in connection with the two topics now to be broached their practical interest was much more in liberty of thought, freedom of worship – in a word, in toleration – than in the libertarianism *versus* determinism debate. I shall, however, set out from the last-mentioned debate by way of providing a context for the others. The socio-political concerns of many divines – for the liberty of slaves, for example – important though it was as representing the outworking of their convictions, will not concern us here. As for questions of government, their interest in the role of the magistrate was inextricably interwoven with their diverse views of the right relations of Church and state. This emphasis will, accordingly, be mine, notwithstanding the fact that some divines also sounded forth on particular points of policy – as when Welsey thought that it was legitimate to tax American colonists even though they had no representation in Parliament, while the Baptist Caleb Evans took the opposing view.[130]

John Locke had a centuries-long debate behind him over the roles of the intellect and the will when he proposed that our minds have the faculties, or powers, of understanding (intellection) and volition:

> we find in our selves a *Power* to begin or forbear, continue or end several actions of our minds, and motions of our Bodies, barely by a thought or preference of the mind ordering, or as it were commanding the doing or not doing such or such particular action.[131]

Underlying this conviction was a theology according to which God thinks and wills, and we, after our fashion, do likewise. It is *we* who do these things. By this emphasis I mean that Locke is generally hostile to the multiplication, or hypostasization, of faculties, though it must be admitted that on occasion he drops his guard, as when he declares, of our volitional powers, that it is 'the Mind that operates and exerts these Powers; it is the Man that does the Action; it is the Agent that has this power.'[132] In the very next paragraph, however, he reminds himself that 'the fault has been, that Faculties have been spoken of, and represented, as so many distinct Agents.'[133] This is what he objects to, and his objection means, for example, that in his opinion we cannot be controlled by our will, as if our will were somehow a distinct agent apart from our selves. Moreover, our ability to understand and to will are key *differentia* as between ourselves and animals. Hence, when we transgress the known law of nature, we become a danger to others, and 'trespass against the whole species'.[134]

In Locke's time one of the questions at issue was whether freedom is a matter of the intellect, or of the will, or of both together.[135] Another concerned the distinction which some drew between freedom and volition. Locke's view was that a willed act was free only if one had the power to perform it, and could freely have chosen to do something else or nothing at all. Throughout, Locke's focus is upon what we are able to do, rather than upon the nature of the will – as free or determined – as such. Indeed, he does not think it proper to ask whether the will is free, for the will is a power we have, and which we use; it is not an agent which could be determined or at liberty. On the other hand, he can speak of desire as determinative of the will, as when he speaks of the reasoned consideration we must give to the question which course of action will be most likely to lead us towards perfection or happiness:

> That in this state of Ignorance we short-sighted Creatures might not mistake true felicity, we are endowed with a power to suspend any particular desire, and keep it from determining the *will*, and engaging us in action. This is *standing still*, where we are not sufficiently assured of the way: Examination is *consulting a guide*. The determination of the *will* upon enquiry is *following the direction of that Guide*: And he that has a power to act, or not to act according as such determination directs, is a *free Agent*; such determination abridges not that Power wherein Liberty consists. He that has his Chains knocked off, and the Prison-doors set open to him, is perfectly at *liberty*, because he may either go or stay, as best he likes; though his preference be determined to stay, by the darkness of the Night, or illness of the Weather, or want of other Lodging. He ceases not to be free; though the desire of some convenience to be had there, absolutely determines his preference, and makes him stay in his Prison.[136]

In all of which there is an uneasy alliance of libertarian and deterministic elements. This feeling is confirmed when we examine Locke's account of what it is which prompts a person to choose between two alternative courses of action. In such cases, he says, a person will continue in his or her current line if no uneasiness motivates a change of direction; but urgent or pressing desires may provoke a contrary choice.[137] On the other hand, the rational weighing of the rightness or wrongness of a possible action, and a consideration of its likely consequences, coupled with a judgement as to their desirability or otherwise – these factors also influence our choice of actions:

> For the mind having in most cases, as is evident in Experience, a power to *suspend* the execution and satisfaction of any of its desires, and so all, one after another, is at liberty to consider the objects of them; examine them on all sides, and weigh them with others. In this lies the liberty Man has; and from the not using of it right comes all that variety of mistakes, errors, and faults which we run into, in the conduct of our lives, and our endeavours after happiness; whilst we precipitate the determination of our *wills*, and engage too soon before due *Examination.* To prevent this we have a power to *suspend* the prosecution of this or that desire, as every one daily may Experiment in himself. This seems to me the source of all liberty; in this seems to consist that, which is (as I think improperly) call'd *Free will.*[138]

Whether suspending or acting, Locke's sights are always set upon our eternal happiness – a point on which G. A. J. Rogers has compared Locke with Henry More: 'Teleology, then, fills Locke's view of things no less than that of More';[139] but it is a teleology rooted in the idea of natural law.

Most of our quotations from Locke on liberty have come from his long chapter in the *Essay*, 'Of power'. References to this chapter recur in the writings of the divines throughout our period, as I shall now show. Isaac Watts, for example, finds 'many excellent thoughts on morality' in the chapter;[140] but in a fuller discussion of the chapter he dissents from Locke's view that we cannot properly ask whether or not the will is free (because it is the person who is free):

> But in answer to this I would say, That perhaps in strict and philosophic speech it may be better to say, *The man, or the soul is free*, yet since this is the common language of men, and the usual way of speaking on this subject, and since this way of speaking, *viz.* ascribing *liberty to the will*, has not such tendency to lead one to mistaken ideas, (if the powers of the soul be but a little explained, and the powers of it proved not to be two distinct beings or substances) I can see no necessity that a philosopher should change the common forms of speech: And notwithstanding all that Mr. Locke has said, I see no impropriety in asking, *Whether the will be free or no*, or in attributing liberty to the will, since it signifies no more than if we enquired, *Whether the mind in its volitions is free to will or not? And to will this not*

that? Common forms of speech should not be renounced and abandoned without evident necessity, and Mr. Locke owns this is the meaning of the question in the latter end of section 22.[141]

For his part, Samuel Strutt of the Inner Temple regrets that Locke ('in whom a great many as implicitly believe, as *Roman* Catholicks do in Transubstantiation')[142] dissociates freedom and volition, and contends that where volition is concerned we are under necessity. His own view is that 'the Power of *Willing* or *Resolving*, without being necessitated so to will or resolve, is essential to Liberty; and without it, 'tis impossible, as far as we can conceive, that any Being in the Universe should be free.'[143] This is a response typical of those who take part of Locke's fluctuating position and represent it as if it were the whole.
The Baptist theological tutor at Bristol, Bernard Foskett, challenged Locke in the following terms:

> Mr. Lock & L'Clerk define the Will as a Power or faculty of the Mind whereby solely by a Thought the Mind endeavours to give Rise continuation or Stop to any Action which it takes to be in its Power. But this definition unreasonably limits the Objects of the Will for it restrains it to our Actions whereas our own Actions are only the mediate Objects of the Will. It first moves towards Pleasure or Happiness which gives Rise to a Thought of the Mind or an Action of the Body as a Means to this End & therefore cald the Will while in the latter it is stiled Election or Choice & this gives Occasion to multiply Faculties without Cause. 2dly This Definition allows the Will to have to do with those only of our own Actions which are supposed to be in our Power ... In my Definition of the Will Desire is included ... But Mr. Lock censures confounding the Will with several of the Affections & especially Desire & says not distinguishing between desire & Will has occasion'd much mistake. A man whom I cant deny may oblige me to perswade another whom at the Time I am speaking of I don't desire to prevail upon. But with Mr. Locks leave I may will both the Action & the persons not being perswaded by it for these are not counter Acts about the same Object the Action & the Effect of Action being 2 different things. Nor 2dly is here an Act at the same instant exercised about contrary Objects. I will this perswading him not as a Means of working upon him but as that which will oblige my friend whom I cant deny.[144]

Another Dissenting academy tutor, the temperate Independent Philip Doddridge, reached a conclusion with which many would have agreed, and which is, indeed, difficult to fault:

> What Mr. Locke's view of liberty on the whole was, is much debated. The truth of the matter seems to be, that he changes his idea of it; sometimes meaning external liberty ... sometimes philosophical ... and sometimes he seems to recur to the notion of natural liberty again, especially when he says in so many words, that freedom consists in not being under a necessary determination of our will in any particular action, and in a power of suspension: by which last matter of stating it he seems not to throw any light upon the question; since all the difficulty attending a possibility of determining to act in one way of another, will attend a possibility of determining to act or not at all.[145]

Much more thoroughgoing opposition to some of the libertarian aspects of Locke's thought came from the American Jonathan Edwards, though in saying this, certain important similarities between the two must not be overlooked. Thus, while propounding a deterministic ethic, Edwards nevertheless wishes to prove that '*necessity is not inconsistent with liberty.*'[146] Again, he adopts, with acknowledgements, Locke's definition of liberty:

> The plain and obvious meaning of the words freedom and liberty, in common speech, is *the power, opportunity, or advantage that any one has, to do as he pleases.* Or in other words, his being free from hindrance or impediment in the way of doing, or conducting in any respect as he wills.[147]

But the significant difference arises where Edwards argues that while (as with Locke) our choices are free, and while (again, as with Locke) our motives determine our actions, this determination has directly to do with our standing before God. Those who are saved by grace are enabled to will actions which please God, while others cannot:

> Men's natural faculties and principles may be assisted by the operation of the Spirit of God on their minds, to enable them to exert those acts which to a greater or lesser degree, they exert naturally. But the Spirit don't at all communicate Himself in it in His own nature, which is Divine love, any more than when He moved upon the face of the waters ... 'Tis the Spirit itself that is the only principle of true virtue in the heart, So that to be truly virtuous is the same as to be spiritual.[148]

Although the context of Edwards's thought is the allegation that Calvinist ideas of God's sovereignty deprive human beings of genuine freedom, Edwards's reply echoes Luther's response to Erasmus on the bondage of the will. For Edwards, people are morally free if they are *able* (at least in principle, for they may be externally constrained) to act in accordance with their choices. Because of God's 'common grace,' which restrains the worst excesses of the sinful nature and accounts for the good which the unregenerate may do, all people may perform some good actions and make some worthy choices. In the wake of Shaftesbury and Hutcheson, he posits an internal moral sense of which all are possessed, albeit the outcome of reliance upon it by the unregenerate would be selfish. For those only who are the beneficiaries of saving grace have pure motives and perform God-pleasing acts. The actions of all are determined by God as cause of all, who provides that each shall act in accordance with his or her nature. This, of course, gave rise to the charge that God is thus made the author of sin. We need not risk being stung in this hornet's nest; like Locke, we may skirt it.

The American Baptist, Isaac Backus, was influenced by both Edwards and Locke. Like the former he was concerned to maintain the Calvinist insistence upon God's sovereignty, and he agreed with both that motives determine actions. The human tragedy is that

> evil imaginations have usurped the place of reason and a well informed judgment and hold them in such bondage that instead of being governed by those noble faculties, they are put to the horrid drudgery of *seeking out inventions for the gratification of fleshly lusts which war against the soul*, and to guard against having these worst of all enemies detected and subdued.[149]

Where Locke held that we can reason our way through the consideration of means, desirable ends and possible untoward consequences, Backus argued that because of the 'evil imaginations,' reason is incompetent to conduct such an examination unless divine influence intervenes.[150]

Charles Chauncy was not prepared to concede so much as Edwards and Backus to the devastations of original sin. Of human beings he wrote in Lockeian terms,

> As intelligent moral beings, they are endowed not only with perceptive powers, rendering them capable of admitting ideas into their minds, the original materials of all knowledge; they are endowed not only with the faculty of retaining these ideas there, of attending to

> them, of comparing them one with another, of judging their agreement or disagreement, and, in these ways, of discovering a great variety of truths: I say, not only are they endowed with these capacities, but with liberty of choice, and a power, in consequence hereof, of acting this way or that, without hindrance or restraint.

Sinners are not precluded from employing these abilities, he continues, their guilt and depravity notwithstanding; indeed, if they cannot act on the basis of justifying faith, they may nevertheless 'do a great deal from other principles planted in their nature'.[151] To the strict Calvinists, Chauncy had planted his feet on a slippery slope indeed, for, to them, the more human ability was exalted, the less God's enabling grace was seen to be necessary.

Augustus Montague Toplady, evangelical Calvinist minister of the Church of England, writer of hymns, and opponent of Wesley's Arminianism, was in no danger of minimising the importance and necessity of grace. But what is especially interesting from our point of view is the way in which he invokes Locke to support his claim that

> Calvinism disclaims all compulsion, properly so called. It pleads only for that victorious conciliating efficacy, which is inseparable from the grace of divine attraction: and acknowledges no other energy, but that to which the apostle sets his comprobatum est, where he says, the love of Christ constraineth us.[152]

He quotes Locke's claim that compulsion takes place 'When the beginning or continuation of any action is contrary to the preference of the mind',[153] and turns this to the advantage of his own theological position by contending that 'in the supernatural agency of grace on the heart, compulsion is quite excluded,' because the more effectually grace operates, the more certainly it engages the 'preference of the mind'. And when the mind's preference is secured compulsion is not in question.[154] He further welcomes Locke's remark that 'voluntary is not opposed to necessary, but to involuntary. For a man may prefer what he can do, to what he cannot do';[155] and his conviction that to ask whether or not a person's will is free is to pose 'an unreasonable, because unintelligible question ... Liberty being as little applicable to the will, as swiftness of motion is to sleep, or squareness to virtue'.[156] There is, however, a slight sting in the tail, for

Toplady muses, 'How far such concessions, as these, are reconcileable with some parts of that great man's theological system; or even with some of his own favourite metaphysical principles; I leave to the determination of more competent readers.'[157]

Lest any should think that rational Dissenters are necessarily bound to approve of Locke and all his works, we may observe that Priestley is much less impressed with the chapter on power than his theological polar opposite, Toplady. Indeed, he gives it short shrift. The chapter, Priestley declares, is 'remarkably confused,' because while Locke's general maxims imply, and are consistent with, necessity, they are inconsistent with the liberty he also wishes to attribute to human beings. Collins, says Priestley, removed the confusion in his *Philosophical Inquiry concerning Human Liberty,* 1715.[158]

Stephen West, pastor at Stockbridge, Massachusetts, was similarly puzzled by the chapter on power:

> Even the accurate Mr. *Locke* speaketh of a *power to begin actions in the mind, by a preference of the mind.* As if the *action* and *preference* of the mind, were so different from each other, as that they might properly be treated of, as *cause* and *effect*! Or, as if the mind was not always *in action*, when it *prefers* any thing![159]

The Ludlams may represent those who, in the early nineteenth century, continued to find Locke's chapter on power puzzling, and thought it worthwhile to say so at some length.[160]

Less liberal than Chauncy, more moderately Calvinist than Toplady, the American Congregationalist divine, Nathanael Emmons, published a sermon on Philippians 2:12, 13: 'Work out your own salvation with fear and trembling. For it is God which worketh in you, both to will and to do of his good pleasure.' The sermon is entitled, 'Man's activity and dependence illustrated and reconciled,' and in it Emmons rebukes those who become confused from reasoning too much on this subject. His remedy is to prescribe distinct territories in which the activities of reason and common sense respectively are properly conducted:

> Many complain that they have often attempted to reconcile dependence with activity, but after all their efforts, have been obliged to give up the subject, as surpassing the reach of their comprehension. And to keep themselves in countenance, they bring in Mr. Locke, that oracle of reason, who ingenuously owns that he could never reconcile

> prescience in the Deity with human liberty; or, in other words, man's dependence with moral freedom. This however will not appear strange, if we consider that it belongs not to the office of reason to reconcile these two points. Though activity and dependence are perfectly consistent, yet they are totally distinct; and of course fall under the notice of distinct faculties of the mind. Dependence falls under the cognizance of reason; but activity falls under the cognizance of common sense. It is the part of reason to demonstrate our dependence upon God ... But it is the part of common sense to afford us an intuitive knowledge of our activity and moral freedom.[161]

We may be forgiven for thinking that Emmons's reconciliation was achieved only by drawing lines of demarcation which are most difficult to maintain. As Emmons notes, Locke himself took an even shorter way in his letter of 20 January 1692/3 to Molyneaux:

> I own freely to you the weakness of my understanding, that though it be unquestionable, that there is omnipotence and omniscience in God, our maker, and I cannot have a clearer perception of any thing, than that I am free; yet I cannot make freedom in man consistent with omnipotence and omniscience in God, though I am as fully as persuaded of both, as of any truths I most firmly assent to. And, therefore, I have long since given off the consideration of that question, resolving all into this short conclusion, that if it be possible for God to make a free agent, then man is free, though I see not the way of it.[162]

V

With that suitably agnostic note ringing in our ears, we may turn to consider Locke's position on liberty of thought or, as it was frequently construed, the right of private judgement.[163] However he may have been understood by some of the more doctrinally free-wheeling divines who came after him, Locke very carefully distinguished between intellectual liberty and licence. We recall his deep suspicion of enthusiasm and his view that atheists were not to be tolerated, both of which positions entailed the imposition of restrictions on absolute freedom of thought.[164] Neither should we overlook Locke's emphasis upon that natural law the deliverances of which, he maintains, reason can discern. Freedom of thought is relative to this law which can curb it; to flout the law is to go against reason, and to demonstrate one's departure from the path of virtue. Hence the need for rewards and punishments as appropriate.[165]

These significant cautions apart, Locke certainly advocated the use of reason – not least as a bulwark against the unwarranted impositions of would-be dictators. Indeed, one of the reasons for his opposition to innate ideas was his conviction that if belief in them was adopted, lazy mental habits might ensue, for why take the trouble to reason things out if knowledge is available *a priori*? But such laziness would merely play into the hands of what we might nowadays call the 'thought police', political or religious, who insist that the (allegedly) innate principles to which they appeal, being imprinted upon our minds by God, may not be questioned: 'if it be the privilege of innate Principles, to be received upon their own Authority, without examination, I know not what may be believed ...'[166]

We may thus say that Locke's thought exhibits the tension between the right of individual liberty of thought on the one hand and the demands of public order on the other. This tension is exhibited to varying degrees throughout the eighteenth century, though increasingly freedom of thought was perceived as less of a threat to civic life, until not only atheists but even Roman Catholics became tolerated. None did more to advance the cause of free thought in Christian circles than intellectually open Dissenting divines. Of such as these Richard Ashcraft has rightly said, '"rational theology" meant a great deal more to nonconformists than simply a general exhortation in favor of a positive role for reason in religion. It meant a willingness to *rely* upon the judgment of the individual as a rational free agent.'[167]

As we have seen, Locke was read in a number of the Dissenting academies, and the methodological testimonies which have come down from some of the academy tutors clearly echo the ideals of Locke, even though they do not mention him by name. Thus, of Henry Grove of Taunton academy it was said that 'To his pupils he allowed the most enlarged freedom of enquiry, and it is well known that some of them followed a path in controversy very different to that of the tutor.'[168] Grove's pupil and successor, Thomas Amory, delivered the sermon at the Young Men's Lecture at Exeter on 11 September 1735. His theme was Christ, the light of the world, and his text, John 8:12.

In the Preface to the published version of the sermon, Amory, himself an Arian, reflects upon those whom he addressed in the following terms:

> *Let me be allowed ... to declare my great Satisfaction in the Readiness of the young Gentlemen, to encourage a rational and amiable Representation of the Christian Doctrines; and exhort them to push their Inquiries in Religion, and lay the Foundation firm, in a rational Assurance of its Truth. Whatever some may imagine, an* implicit Faith *which rests only on the* Authority *of* Parents, *or* Ministers; *or an* Enthusiastick *one which is resolvable only into some warm* Emotions, *and* unaccountable Impulses *on the Mind, are, for real Excellency and valuable Effects, no way comparable to that Truth* [surely Faith?], *which is produced by an honest and impartial* Study *of the* Proofs *of* Christianity, *and a* clear *Discernment of its Evidences.*[169]

Enthusiasts, he continues, risk having their faith shaken and overturned by unbelievers, and even by their own thoughts, succumbing to '*absurd Party Notions*', and having their morality undermined. By contrast, '*the Believer, whose Faith is built on a clear and full Conviction of the Excellency and Evidences of true Religion, like a House founded on a Rock, will triumph over the Assaults of Infidelity and the Shocks of Temptation.*'[170]

Sixteen years on Amory, now in Grove's chair, preached at Lewin's Mead, Bristol, on the occasion of the ordination of William Richards. On this occasion his text was II Corinthians 1:24: 'Not for that we have dominion over your faith, but are helpers of your joy' – which words he applied to the role of ministers of the Gospel. He reminded his hearers that the great doctrines of natural religion, which the Gospel takes for granted, may be discerned by all people. Indeed,

> As all men ... are obliged to receive these Truths, and are *capable* of discerning the evidences of them; all they, whom we would confirm in the faith of these, have a right to demand from us *rational* grounds for their faith. To require that they should believe, without good reasons, what we affirm on these heads, is to exalt ourselves into *Lords of Faith*, and degrade them to a level with *brutes*.[171]

Amory also returned to his familiar theme regarding those who would seek to exercise dominion over the minds of believers

> Under pretence that the Scriptures have not sufficiently guarded against *Heresies* in certain matters, to contrive and impose *unscriptural*

Creeds as *Tests* of *Orthodoxy* , and *Terms* of *Communion,* and to *ruin* in their *Credit* and *Interests* all such, who receiving the *Scriptures* will not submit to our additional explications; this is not only to *lord* it unjustly over our Brethren, but to reflect also on the Wisdom and Goodness of our great *Master*; as if he either could not, or would not, reveal important Truths in a clear and satisfactory manner, but left his Gospel in want of our improvements to render it a perfect rule of Faith.[172]

We may note in passing that the young Priestley refused to attend the Plasterers' Hall academy under Zephaniah Marryatt, where he would have had to subscribe to 'ten printed articles of the strictest Calvinist faith'.[173] Instead he went to Daventry where he found 'Dr. Ashworth taking the orthodox side of every question, and Mr. [Samuel] Clark, the sub-tutor, that of heresy, though always with the greatest modesty'.[174]

Returning to Amory's sermon we find that what particularly repels him is the fact that the law is invoked in support of would-be mind-controlling behaviour:

[W]ithout first convincing the Judgment, and ingaging the Conscience, to require and exact *implicit* Faith and Obedience, to urge men to profess what they do not believe, or practise what they do not approve, by the *temptations* of worldly Profits or Honours; or to *terrify* them from the contrary by Disgrace, Fines, Imprisonments, and corporal Punishments – this is not only usurping *Dominion* in the kingdom of Christ, but directly counteracting the great designs of it.[175]

Six years later the Arian Presbyterian Richard Price was to underline the point, though with more attention to the underlying morality of the matter:

How absurd ... are all claims to dominion over conscience? Such dominion is little to the purpose of those who have pleaded for it, if it does not mean a power or right to oblige persons to act against their private judgment, that is, a *right* to oblige persons to *do wrong.* Every man ought to be left to follow his conscience because then only he acts virtuously.[176]

In 1759 Amory removed to London, where he was among those who campaigned for the abolition of the laws enjoining subscription to the doctrinal articles of the Church of England on the part of Dissenters. With his departure the academy removed from Taunton to Exeter, where, until 1771 when the academy ceased, Micaijah Towgood taught biblical exegesis. Yet another Arian Presbyterian, Towgood continued in the tradition of his predecessors, encouraging his students 'to think freely and impartially on every subject of natural and revealed religion, which the study of the scriptures would necessarily bring under their consideration ... His lectures were rather the open information of a friend, than the dictates of a master.'[177] Meanwhile, in 1752, Caleb Rotheram the elder, founder and president of the Dissenting academy at Kendal (1733–53) had died. His pupil James Daye of Lancaster paid tribute to his teacher in these terms: 'As a *protestant dissenter* he was a credit to his *profession*: For he was a *friend*, a *faithful friend* to *liberty*, the *distinguishing principle* of that *profession*.'[178]

John Aikin, trained at Northampton academy under Doddridge, was an Arian Presbyterian tutor at Warrington academy from 1758 to 1780. Of him it was said that

> he was always open to conviction himself, and always disposed to allow the utmost scope for freedom of enquiry to others ... Perceiving that freedom of discourse, as well as of thinking, is necessary to the discovery of truth, he listened with a candid ear to every argument which was proposed with ingenuity and modesty.[179]

Towards the end of our period Thomas Belsham zealously, and with increasing concern, endorsed the points made by his liberal predecessors. He regarded it as

> the indispensable duty of all who profess faith in the christian religion, to exert their best endeavours to acquire a distinct and correct conception of revealed truth, to separate it as accurately as possible from the corruptions with which it has been debased, to avow their faith with meekness and candour, but at the same time with zeal and courage, and by all fair and honourable means to communicate to others the light which they have discovered and enjoy.[180]

Four years later, in the course of a benefit sermon preached on behalf of the third Exeter academy (1799–1805) which had fallen upon hard times, he urged the importance of such institutions:

> It is incumbent upon those, who are the friends of pure unadulterated christianity, and of freedom of investigation, which is its best support, to give their sanction to those Institutions, which are conducted by

> able instructors, upon enlarged principles, and upon the success of which the rising ministry chiefly depends ...'[181]

Elsewhere, in a sermon in which he compared 'the preceding with the present age with respect to theological inquiry,' he struck a sombre note: 'The fact is but too evident. Rational Christianity is out of fashion with the learned and the great. Much more so than it was a century ago.'[182] He proceeded to take some heart from the fact that the cause of religious liberty was advancing – for example, 'A cruel statute which, if it had been put in force, would have banished Locke from his country, would have deprived Clarke of his ecclesiastical preferment, and would have consigned Newton to a dungeon,' had recently been repealed;[183] and from the fact that the middle classes, 'who have a spirit to *think as they please, and to speak as they think*' are becoming increasingly interested in religious matters.[184]

At the very end of our period, and in the approach to Catholic emancipation, John Horsey introduced a new note. He, we recall, had been a pupil at the evangelical academy at Homerton. When Belsham resigned on conscientious grounds from the Daventry academy, the cause was restarted at Northampton (1789–98) under Horsey. In his Inaugural Address he was very clear concerning what he was not going to do:

> It is not the design of this institution, and it is very far from my inclination, to usurp any authority over Conscience, or to cherish Bigotry or party zeal ... My object is not to stamp infallibility on any human system of Religion, not to require your subscription to articles of faith before you have examined into the truth of them – not to bias your minds during the process of examination – not to encourage a severe and illiberal disposition toward any class of your fellow-Christians, but the highest object of my ambition is to promote a Scriptural Christianity ...[185]

So anxious was Horsey 'not to give an undue bias to his youthful auditors, that it was very difficult to ascertain in the lecture-room his own precise views in the more controverted subjects'.[186] On the other hand, in lectures to young people published in his memory, he expressed the hope that his young hearers would always honour the principle of investigation and enquiry exemplified by Luther, Calvin and others, 'which emancipated the Protestant world from the shackles of ignorance, superstition, and cruelty, in the church of Rome; and it must be by reason and argument, not by force, that the unhallowed claims of dominion over conscience must still be subverted, wherever they exist.'[187]

It was not, of course, only the academy tutors who asserted the right and duty of freedom of thought. Many ministers in pastoral charge were to the fore on the matter, and this on both sides of the Atlantic. Thus, to take a few random examples, in Birmingham in 1747 the Arian Presbyterian minister Samuel Bourn, declared that

> If a Man only professes to believe what another dictates, or acts only as another requires, without using his own Reason, or attending to the Dictates of his Conscience, he has nothing like a divine Faith, but substitutes a blind Obedience to Man instead of a Regard to God and Truth.[188]

When Priestley later reflected upon the New Meeting congregation, to which he had himself ministered from 1780 to 1791, he described it as 'the most liberal, I believe of any in England; and to this freedom the unwearied labours of Mr. Bourn had eminently contributed'.[189]

The year 1747 also saw Jonathan Mayhew's ordination in Boston, Massachusetts. At Harvard he had come under the influence of Locke and Clarke, and had turned his back upon Calvinism. The Boston ministers – even including Charles Chauncy – boycotted his ordination, not so much because of his heterodox beliefs as because of his apparent reduction of religion to a private matter: 'God and nature and the gospel of Christ injoin it upon us as a duty to maintain the right of private judgment.'[190] A quarter of a century later we find Simeon Howard, in *A Sermon Preached to the Ancient and Honourable Artillery-Company, in Boston* (1773), declaring that

> A man cannot ... give up the liberty of private judgment in matters of religion, or convey to others a right to determine of what religion he shall be, and in what way he shall worship God. A grant of this nature would destroy the foundation of all religion in the man who made it, and must therefore be a violation of the law of nature.'[191]

The overriding impression gleaned from the writings of the more liberal divines is that they had much more to say about the right and the duty to exercise free thought than Locke did about the dangers which might result from such practice. But some sounded cautionary notes. Preaching at the ordination of William Field in the revolutionary days of 1790, Priestley made it clear that not any beliefs, and not any behaviour, would suffice:

> We who profess what we wish to be considered as *rational christianity*, have least of all any just excuse for a deficiency in that temper, and a want of those good works, which our religion requires. We, depending on the free mercy of God to the penitent, reject the idea of being saved by any righteousness that is not our own. We believe that no man can obey the laws of God for another, or suffer the punishment due to the crimes of another; and we disclaim the belief of any thing whatever standing in the place of moral virtue. We believe the gospel both to contain a sufficient rule of life, and also sufficient motives to the observance of it.[192]

Such was Priestley's confidence in free thought that he did not think that the differing conclusions people reached would lead to anarchy. On the contrary, the controversial diversity of opinions is 'a necessary' but 'only a temporary inconvenience. It is the only way to arrive at a permanent and useful uniformity, which it is sure to bring about at last.'[193]

It would be a serious mistake to suppose that avowedly liberal (and Presbyterian) divines alone trod in the footsteps of Locke on the question of freedom of thought. On the death of Isaac Watts, Caleb Ashworth observed,

> He was a true Friend of Liberty, though he would never give up the cause of Truth, or sacrifice any part of the Gospel, to make a comprehension with Infidels. He knew how to *contend earnestly* [Jude 3], and yet in the Spirit of Peace, for the *Faith once delivered to the Saints*: and had explained and defended what appeared to him, according to the Scripture standard, to be *Orthodoxy*, at the same time presenting it in the closest connection with *Charity*.[194]

Again, Philip Furneaux, Independent minister and one of the (Calvinistic) Coward Trustees, addressed some *Letters to the Hon. Mr. Justice Blackstone* (1770). Against Blackstone, who had argued that Nonconformity was a crime, Furneaux signalled his intention of promoting 'amongst my readers in general just conceptions of the right of private judgment, and of impartial liberty in matters of conscience; which of all human rights seems to me to be one of the most sacred and unalienable'.[195] In the same year, however, his fellow Independent, the evangelical Joseph Barber, tutor at the second Hoxton academy, insisted that we are not free to believe as we please, and that Christian love does not entail indifference to religious principles. Some say,

> we are to have charity for all sorts of Heretics; to have charity for Jews, Deists, Atheists, &c. i.e. we are to believe, they may be very good men, and may be saved, notwithstanding any erroneous principles they have imbibed. But the Gospel knows nothing of this sort of charity.[196]

It was left to John Bruce, the Independent evangelical, to answer his ordination question of 1808 in splendidly eighteenth-century order. Asked why he opted for Dissent rather than for the Church of England, he listed his reasons as follows: 'the right of private judgment and liberty of conscience with regard to religious sentiment and duty; the supremacy of Christ as the only Head of his church; and the sufficiency of the Holy Scriptures as the rules of faith and practice.'[197]

The Baptists, too, had their friends of liberty. Against Edmund Burke, Robert Robinson upheld the right of private judgement, declaring that to deny it was to destroy Christianity itself.[198] And of their Bristol tutor, Caleb Evans, it was said,

> amidst the zeal he felt for the truth, he knew how to exercise charity towards those from whom he differed. He was no bigot, he could not be such, for he well understood the rights of private judgment, was sensible of the weakness of the human intellect, and felt the difficulties of truly upright minds on points wherein he and they could not agree.[199]

The upshot would seem to be that whether liberal or evangelical, whether Presbyterian, Independent or Baptist, many eighteenth-century Dissenting divines would have affirmed the first answer in Samuel Palmer's *Protestant Dissenter's Catechism* of 1773 (though many would have refused formal subscription to it!):

> Q: What are the grand principles on which the Protestant Nonconformists ground their separation from the Church by law established.
>
> A: The right of private judgment and liberty of conscience, in opposition to all human authority in matters of religion; the supremacy of Christ as the only Head of His Church, and the sufficiency of the Holy Scriptures as the only rule of faith and practice.[200]

With this we come to the third consideration, liberty of worship – toleration. This was Locke's primary interest in all his discussions of freedom and determinism and freedom of thought, as I shall now hope to show.

5

Toleration and Government

In the opinion of Roland H. Bainton, Locke's 'ideas on religious liberty were not original ... But the case did need to be restated in terms pertinent to the immediate situation.'[1] Since the thrust of my work is in the direction of the eighteenth-century divines I must not delay unduly over the scholarly interpretation of Locke in his historical context. It will suffice if I briefly endorse the two main points made by Bainton, namely, that in this as in other fields of intellectual inquiry, Locke was a debtor; and that his position on the question of toleration underwent development (some would say, suffered a sea-change) during his writing life.

Locke's intellectual indebtedness was many-sided. Raised in the home of one of Cromwell's captains, schooled at Westminster and then at Oxford, where his tutor was the Independent Thomas Cole[2] and his professor of history the Huguenot scholar Lewis Du Moulin, who published works on liberty of conscience and toleration,[3] Locke had the Calvinist-Puritan tradition within his sights from his youth onwards. He was familiar with the views of the dean of his college, Christ Church, John Owen, who in his more open phases would have accorded freedom of worship to non-licentious trinitarians, and these views were represented not only in his writings,[4] but in the Independents' modification of the Westminster Confession, the Savoy Declaration of Faith and Order (1658), of which Owen was the principal architect:

> God alone is Lord of the Conscience, and hath left it free from the Doctrines and Commandments of men which are in anything contrary to his Word, *or not contained in it*;[5] so that to believe such

> Doctrines, or to obey such commands out of Conscience, is to betray true Liberty of Conscience; and the requiring of an implicit faith, and an absolute and blinde obedience, is to destroy Liberty of Conscience, and Reason also.[6]

It is much to our purpose to note the significant revision by the Savoy divines of Westminster's paragraph on the civil magistrate. Whereas the latter accorded to the magistrate the right to suppress heresies and abuses in worship, together with the power to call and attend synods and to ensure that 'whatsoever is transacted in them be according to the mind of God,' the Savoy revision reads:

> Although the Magistrate is bound to incourage, promote, and protect professors and profession of the Gospel, and to manage and order civil administrations in a due subserviency to the interest of Christ in the world, and to that end to take care that men of corrupt mindes and conversations do not licentiously publish and divulge Blasphemy and Errors in their own nature, subverting the faith, and inevitably destroying the souls of them that receive them: Yet in such differences about the Doctrines of the Gospel, or ways of the worship of God, as may befall men exercising a good conscience, manifesting it in their conversation, and holding the foundation, not disturbing others in their ways of worship that differ from them; there is no warrant for the Magistrate under the Gospel to abridge them of their Liberty.[7]

The Savoy divines proceeded to omit the fourth section of the Westminster Confession, XX, which warns that

> they who, upon pretence of Christian liberty, shall oppose any lawful power, or the lawful exercise of it, whether it be civil or ecclesiastical, resist the ordinance of God And for their publishing such opinions, or maintaining such practices, as are contract to the light of nature, or to the known principles of Christianity ... they may lawfully be called to account, and proceeded against by the censure of the church, and by the power of the Civil Magistrate.

I by no means suggest that Locke was a crypto-Independent. Indeed the young Locke could not accept Owen's view that all should be permitted to believe and worship freely provided that they did not disturb the public peace.[8] Locke was and remained a loyal member of the Church of England, receiving the sacrament according to the rites of the Church by law established on his death-bed; and if he denounced his own Church for undue reliance upon the civil magistrate, this, he realized, was only what the Presbyterians had done when they had had the opportunity.[9] Any toleration of sectaries which he advocated was, to him, second best to the comprehension he coveted but increasingly saw no likelihood of witnessing.

Again, the tolerance advocated by William Chillingworth, Jeremy Taylor[10] and others was 'in the air', while Locke was impressed by such Latitudinarians as Tillotson, and was on friendly terms with such a non-Independent Dissenter as Baxter. As to his reading, Herbert D. Foster has reminded us of Locke's citations from Calvinistic authors.[11]

Some of Locke's reading was designed to provoke a negative response in him. For example, in 1670 the Erastian bishop of Oxford, Samuel Parker, published a work whose thesis is aptly indicated by its title: *A Discourse of Ecclesiastical Politie, wherein the authority of the Civil Magistrate over the Consciences of Subjects in matters of Religion is asserted; the Mischiefs and Inconveniences of Toleration are represented, and all Pretenses pleaded in behalf of Liberty of Conscience are fully answered.*[12] Stillingfleet's tract on *The Unreasonableness of Separation* (1680) similarly accorded the magistrate more power in religious matters than Locke came to think appropriate. But not all Anglicans were of one mind. Gilbert Burnet was among those who advocated the restriction of the powers of the civil magistrate to societal matters, for 'our Thoughts, with relation to God ... are God's immediate province.' Consequently, 'a Magistrate by encroaching upon them, breaks in upon God's Propriety, and upon the Essential Right of Human Nature of worshipping God according to our conviction, which is in us Antecedent to all Humane Government, and can never be subject to it.'[13] If Parker and Stillingfleet appealed to Augustine,[14] and Thomas Long, prebendary of Exeter, in *The History of the Donatists* (1677) likened the troublesome Donatists to the equally troublesome Dissenters of his own day, Burnet's words are found in the introduction to his translation of *De mortibus persecutorum* by the more amenable Lactantius. For some Anglican divines there was a thin line drawn between constraint and educative seriousness. As the archbishop of Canterbury, Thomas Tenison, wrote in 1683, 'Good Governours do not use Severity to force Men to dissemble their Minds, and to make them Hypocrites, but to move them, after a Tryal of fair means, to greater *consideration.*'[15]

In a different vein, Locke knew the writings of Herbert of Cherbury, in whose *De Veritate* (1624) is to be found an epistemologically based argument for religious toleration of the kind Locke was to find very congenial, namely, that in view of the limitations of human knowledge and the consequent impossibility of attaining absolute certainty, the toleration of differing views is right and necessary.[16] One way of construing the doctrinal implication of this position had been voiced even earlier by Erasmus: 'The sum of our religion is peace and unanimity and these can scarcely stand unless we define as little as possible and in many things leave each one free to follow his own judgment.'[17]

In addition to these literary influences there was Locke's experience of life. There was his conviction that 'I no sooner perceived myself in the world but I found myself in a storm' of sectarian schism and struggle;[18] there was his experience of toleration in the Duchy of Cleves, and his conversations with Shaftesbury; above all there was his period of exile in Holland, 1683–8, during which time he became acquainted with Remonstrant Arminianism, and with its principal theologian Philip Limborch, to whom he dedicated his *Epistola de tolerantia* (1689). Whilst he was in Holland the Edict of Nantes was revoked in 1685, and in the same year the Duke of Monmouth's abortive rebellion against James II led to the execution of many Dissenters.[19]

All of the factors I have mentioned all too briefly went into the development of Locke's views on toleration, and the general consensus among scholars is that that development was considerable. Locke could not support the tolerationist line of Henry Stubbe during the 1650s, both because Stubbe would have extended toleration to Roman Catholics – a possibility which Locke feared throughout his life on the ground that Roman Catholics owed allegiance to a foreign power;[20] and because the wars of religion had raised the question of the practicability of toleration.[21] That Locke heartily welcomed the Restoration of the Monarchy in 1660 is clear from his remark that 'I find that a general freedom is but a general bondage, that the popular asserters of public liberty are the greatest ingrossers of it too.'[22] He viewed the return of the King as a stabilizing influence, and wrote *Two Tracts* in answer to Edward Bagshaw's pro-toleration pamphlets of 1660 and 1661.[23] In these he urged every person to delegate his powers, including those over things indifferent, to the absolute monarch, Charles II, who would then introduce such regulations as would make for peace and stability in the land. By 1667, when he wrote four drafts of *An Essay concerning Toleration,* Locke had had experience of toleration in the Duchy of Cleves,[24] Clarendon, the mastermind of the oppressive legislation against Nonconformists, was no longer in office,[25] and the ideas of the tolerationist Anthony Ashley Cooper,[26] whose private secretary Locke now was, gained increasing sway over his mind. These influences combined seriously to moderate Locke's commitment to absolute monarchy. Indeed, he now urged Charles II to take the path of toleration, and to return rights not so much to Parliament, as to the people themselves. For individuals have a *right* to act in accordance with their conscientious beliefs; to do otherwise, even at the behest of the magistrate, is to sin. It is not simply that, as sectaries and more orthodox Dissenters had shown, they will not yield to coercion in matters of religion; there is also the epistemological consideration that where religious beliefs are concerned we cannot know with absolute certainty which, if any, of them is true, for we lack appropriate criteria of verification; and further, that on Locke's view if we had knowledge, faith would be redundant, 'for where vision, knowledge, and certainty is, there faith is done away.'[27] A harbinger of Locke's final position, that people not only have a right to their convictions, but a right and *duty* to uphold and defend them – even by force if necessary – is found in his *A Letter from a Person of Quality to his Friend in the Country* (1675),[28] and is fully worked out in the *Two Treatises on Government* and *A Letter concerning Toleration,* both of which were published in 1689, the year of the so-called Toleration Act (by which time Locke had lived among the Dutch Remonstrants, and was enjoying increasing contact with English Dissenters).[29]

At first sight we have here a development in Locke's thinking from deference to the absolute monarch, via the assertion of the people's rights in matters of religious belief, to their duties in this respect. It does not seem to me that this development, fostered as it was by changing circumstances and continuous thought over many years, can be gainsaid. But before we abstract Locke altogether from his world, we should recall first his consistent conviction that Roman Catholics should not be tolerated while they owed allegiance to a foreign power, and that atheists should not be tolerated because they cannot be trusted; and secondly, his equally consistent views that liberty and licence are not identical; that the horrors of enthusiasm and sectarianism are to be avoided; and that a significant part of the magistrate's role is to ensure this, provided only that it is remembered that 'Whatsoever is lawful in the commonwealth, cannot be prohibited by the magistrate in the church.'[30] Locke, we may say, is ever the man of affairs, and the expression and application of his ethical desiderata are intimately entwined with his perception of the political realities of the day.[31] To say this is not to agree totally with P. J. Kelly's statement that 'Despite his Puritan commitment to liberty of conscience, at least in respect of belief, Locke attached greater importance in all of his writings to the peace and stability of the social order,'[32] for the comparison 'greater' cannot be made with absolute confidence, since Locke never weighed peace and stability against liberty of conscience in quite the way implied here. That he placed a high premium upon social peace and stability is clear; but his respect for those who stood by their consciences in turbulent times and in face of unjust powers is equally clear, and suggests that his ideal world would be characterized by peace, stability and liberty of conscience – not least by peace between those who differ over doctrine. From Cleves he had, in December 1665, written to Robert Boyle of the mutual tolerance of Calvinists, Lutherans and Roman Catholics in these approving terms:

> They quietly permit one another to choose their way to heaven; for I cannot observe any quarrels or animosities amongst them upon the account of religion. This good correspondence is owing partly to the power of the magistrate, and partly to the prudence and good nature of the people, who (as I find by enquiry) entertain different opinions, without any secret hatred or rancour.[33]

Locke's endorsement of this harmonious spirit never waned: for example, he later declared that if a person 'be destitute of charity, meekness, and goodwill in general towards all mankind, even to those that are not christians, he is certainly yet short of being a true christian himself.'[34] What changed, as David C.

Snyder has pointed out, is that whereas in the *Two Tracts* Locke had allowed that religion has to do with personal beliefs deemed to be private, he subsequently deemed religious practice an equally private matter.[35] Indeed, as early as 1667 Locke added the following remarks to the final draft of *An Essay concerning Toleration*:

> 'Twill be said that if a toleration shall be allowed as due to all the parts of religious worship it will shut out the magistrate's power from making laws about those things over which it is acknowledged on all hands that he has a power, viz. things indifferent, as many things made use of in religious worship are, viz. wearing a white or a black garment, kneeling or not kneeling, etc. To which I answer that in religious worship nothing is indifferent, for it being the using of those habits, gestures, etc. which I think acceptable to God in my worshipping of him, however they may be in their own nature perfectly indifferent, yet when I am worshipping my God in a way I think he has prescribed and will approve of, I cannot alter, omit, or add any circumstance in that which I think the true way of worship.[36]

This has ecclesiological implications, as we shall see shortly.

I

I now wish to underline the importance of the epistemological, moral and religious underpinnings of Locke's view of toleration. The epistemological-cum-moral key is found in Locke's remarks upon assent, to which I have already referred, but to which I must now briefly revert.[37] Locke writes,

> Since therefore it is unavoidable to the greatest part of Men, if not all, to have several *Opinions*, without certain and indubitable Proofs of their Truths; and it carries too great an imputation of ignorance, lightness, or folly, for Men to quit and renounce their former Tenets, presently upon the offer of an Argument, which they cannot imediately answer, and shew the insufficiency of: It would, methinks, become all Men to maintain *Peace*, and the common Offices of Humanity, and *Friendship, in the diversity of Opinions*, since we cannot reasonably expect, that any one should readily and obsequiously quit his own Opinion, and embrace ours with a blind resignation to an Authority, which the Understanding of Man acknowledges not ... Those who have fairly and truly examined, and are thereby got past doubt in all the Doctrines they profess, and govern themselves by,

would have a juster pretence to require others to follow them: But these are so few in number, and find so little reason to be magisterial in their Opinions, that nothing insolent and imperious is to be expected from them: And there is reason to think, if men were better instructed themselves, they would be less imposing on others.[38]

With this we are reminded of Locke's ever-present consciousness of the limitations of human reason, and of that epistemological scepticism with which it was the objective of the *Essay* to deal. We might even say that while the candle of the Lord does illuminate, it is a candle, not a floodlight. At the same time there is the running implication that it would be immoral for individuals to yield unthinkingly to the opinions of another, or to seek to impose their views upon others, for faith is non-coercible, and if we were to allow Christian magistrates to impose their faith upon others on which grounds could we prohibit civil authorities elsewhere in the world (where they are the orthodox believers) from doing likewise in respect of their non-Christian faiths?[39] This being so, the toleration of views other than one's own is sensible, right, and makes for peace in society. All of which, thinks Locke, is not only consonant with the Gospel, but is an implication of that law which orders the state of nature in which all find themselves (which law, since it is objective and discernible by all, and not private, constitutes a bulwark against subjective 'enthusiasm'):

> The state of nature has a law of nature to govern it, which obliges every one: and reason, which is that law, teaches all mankind, who will but consult it, that being all equal and independent, no one ought to harm another in his life, health, liberty, or possessions: for men being all the workmanship of one omnipotent and infinitely wise Maker ... they are his property ... And that all men may be restrained from invading others rights, and from doing hurt to one another, and the law of nature be observed, which willeth the peace and preservation of all mankind, the execution of the law of nature is, in that state, put into every man's hands ...[240]

It follows that

> The toleration of those that differ from others in matters of religion, is so agreeable to the gospel of Jesus Christ, and to the genuine reason of mankind, that it seems monstrous for men to be so blind, as not to perceive the necessity and advantage of it, in so clear a light ... No private person has any right in any manner to prejudice another

> person in his civil enjoyments, because he is of another church or religion. All the rights and franchises that belong to him as a man, or as a denison, are inviolably to be preserved to him. These are not the business of religion. No violence or injury is to be offered him, whether he be christian or pagan. Nay, we must not content ourselves with the narrow measures of bare justice: charity, bounty, and liberality must be added to it. This the Gospel enjoins, this reason directs, and this *that natural fellowship we are born into requires of us.*[41]

In thus arguing that intolerance defies both the law of nature and the Gospel, Locke is in accord not only with much Latitudinarian thought, but also with the view of such Dissenting divines as John Owen and others.[42]

The religious aspects of the matter are frequently expressed by Locke with reference to the functions of the civil magistrate. At the root of his mature thought is the conviction that there is a distinction of supreme importance between Church and state, which is grounded in the fact that whereas under the old dispensation there was a unified and absolute theocracy, with the coming of Christ, who inaugurated no commonwealth, there are two realms, the churchly and the civic, both under God (Locke is no modern secularist), but distinct.[43] Thus Locke, in *The Reasonableness of Christianity*, notes that Jesus resisted those who would have construed his Messiahship in temporal terms, as if he had come to rescue the Jews from the shackles of Rome;[44] and in his discussion of Romans 10:9 he further explains that

> The expectation of the Jews was that the Messiah who was promised them was to be their deliverer, and so far they were in the right. But that which they expected to be delivered from at his appearing was the power and dominion of Strangers. When our Saviour came their reckoning was up.[45]

Because of the new dispensation inaugurated by Christ, under which Christians now live, the power of the magistrate requires to be carefully delimited.

Not surprisingly, Locke's developing view of toleration went hand in hand with his changing understanding of the magistrate's role. Whereas in the *Two Tracts* Locke had contended that the magistrate had 'absolute and arbitrary' power over all indifferent matters,[46] by the time he came to write his four drafts of the *Essay on Toleration* (1667/8) he was ready to place religious and moral matters outside the magistrate's terms of reference except where public order or the public good were threatened by actions expressing moral or religious convictions. The Roman Catholics were among the exceptions, for reasons already stated. The exceptions apart, Locke's final view is that

> It is the duty of the civil magistrate, by the impartial execution of equal laws, to secure unto all the people in general, and to every one of his subjects in particular, the just possession of these things belonging to this life ... [T]he magistrate [is] armed with the force and strength of all his subjects, in order to the punishment of those that violate any other man's rights. Now that the whole jurisdiction of the magistrate reaches only to these civil concernments ... it neither can nor ought in any manner to be extended to the salvation of souls.[47]

Consequently (echoing a principle articulated centuries before by Tertullian),[48] 'the magistrate has no power to enforce by law either in his own church, or much less in another, the use of any rites or ceremonies whatsoever in the worship of God.'[49] This not only because of the division of realms and because inner conviction cannot so be forced (though people can be silenced by force), but also because

> no man can so far abandon the care of his own salvation, as blindly to leave it to the choice of any other, whether prince or subject, to prescribe to him what faith or worship he shall embrace. For no man can, if he would, conform his faith to the dictates of another. All the life and power of true religion consists in the inward and full persuasion of the mind; and faith is not faith without believing.[50]

As for the churches, 'the business of these assemblies of the people is nothing but what is lawful for every man in particular to take care of; I mean the salvation of their souls.'[51] Locke goes further: he asserts the right of Jews and Muslims to freedom of worship:

> neither pagan, nor mahometan, nor jew, ought to be excluded from the civil rights of the commonwealth, because of his religion. The gospel commands no such thing ... Shall we suffer a pagan to deal and trade with us, and shall we not suffer him to pray unto and worship God?[52]

In view of this Susan Mendus's remark that 'the *Letter* contains no general argument for a right to freedom of worship at all'[53] requires qualification. The *Letter* does contain a general argument for such a right, and the argument is reinforced in the *Third*

Letter[54] where the law of nature is invoked as the ground of such freedom. But, in view of his convictions concerning Roman Catholics and atheists, Locke, unlike the Socinian William Popple who, in his preface to his translation of Locke's *Letter*, appealed for 'Absolute liberty, just and true liberty, equal and impartial liberty,' does not wish to translate theory into practice under the currently prevailing conditions.[55]

Further evidence of this practical inconsistency emerges in connection with Locke's reception of the Toleration Act. On 6 June he wrote to Limborch in the following terms:

> No doubt you will have heard before this that Toleration has now at last been established by law in our country. Not perhaps so wide in scope as might be wished for by you and those like you who are true Christians and free from ambition or envy. Still, it is something to have progressed so far. I hope that with these beginnings the foundations have been laid of that liberty and peace in which the church of Christ is one day to be established. None is entirely debarred from his own form of worship or made liable to penalties except the Romans, provided only that he is willing to take the oath of allegiance and to renounce transubstantiation and certain dogmas of the Roman Church. In the case of the Quakers the oath has been dispensed with.[56]

In one respect, as is clear from his letters on toleration, Locke was far ahead of those of his Dissenting friends who coveted comprehension (and on whose Bill of 1680 the Toleration Act was based) – not to mention his Anglican co-religionists. His distinction between Church and commonwealth prompted his advocacy of disestablishment, and of the mutual tolerance of the several churches.[57] A harbinger of this view was the Baptist Roger Williams who, in the 1630s, had argued for the separation of Church and state and for government by consent of the people. Further, he contended against John Cotton of the First Church, Boston, that the godly had no divine right to rule.[58] On the other hand, Locke's contemporary, the Presbyterian Richard Baxter, staunchly upheld the principle of theocratic government: 'The more Theocratical, or truly Divine any Government is, the better it is'; and he accorded to the civil magistrate the right to prevent the propagation of 'intolerable Errors'.[59] How subsequent divines responded to Locke's view of Church–state relations we shall shortly discover; but first we must attend to his adverse and favourable critics on the question of toleration in general.

II

In his *Anti-Scepticism* (1702) Henry Lee, whom we have met before, evinced his decided aversion to universal toleration, insisting that such toleration is to matters of practice and morality as anarchy is to government and scepticism is to faith. He failed to mention, however, that Locke's appeal was not for universal toleration. Equally partisan is the anonymous author of *An Essay upon Government, Wherein the Republican Schemes reviv'd by Mr. Lock, Dr. Blackal &c. are fairly consider'd and refuted* (1705), who contends that atheists, deists, fanatics and the 'spawn of Jesuits' are united in advocating toleration only with a view to subverting the state by ruining the Church. The author declares that monarchy is the only true form of government established by God; that God has determined the right of inheritance; and that the English constitution is founded on God's law.[60] We need not follow his arguments against Locke in connection with Adam's headship of the human race.[61]

It would seem that it became increasingly unfashionable to mount wholesale attacks upon the idea of toleration as such as the eighteenth century progressed. Certainly adverse criticisms of Locke's view decrease in number quite rapidly. One of the most powerful voices heard against him in the declining years of the century is that of Priestley. But his opposition is quite different in kind from that of Lee and others. In Priestley's opinion Locke's failure was that he did not advocate a sufficiently wide toleration. Concerning the Toleration Act of 1689 he writes, 'Mr. Locke strangely complimented this act, or forgot the *Unitarians*, when he said of it, *Nulli à cultu suo penitùs excludun-tur, – nisi Romani.* See his Letter to *Limborch*, June 6, 1689.'[62] He elsewhere regrets that 'Mr. Locke was staggered at the thought of tolerating *Atheism*,'[63] and he himself staggered so temperate a rational Dissenter as Andrew Kippis by his advocacy of toleration for Roman Catholics. Priestley concedes that two centuries ago there may have been a case for proscribing Roman Catholicism, but 'persecution by Protestants, in this enlightened age, appears so utterly repugnant to the great principle of their cause,' and the threat to liberty from Roman Catholics is now so unlikely, that a more mature approach may properly be adopted.[64] Indeed, he considers that Locke's excepting of Roman Catholics and atheists from toleration by the state has 'an obvious tendency to multiply hypocrites in a state, while the magistrate, instead of devoting himself to his arduous duty of controlling actions by established law, must become a vexatious inquisitor of opinions.'[65] Because of such views – and not only because of his unitarianism, and certainly not only because of mob-inciting socio-economic factors – Priestley had to flee the country following the Birmingham Riots of 1791.[66] As Martin Fitzpatrick has rightly said, 'By 1790 it was quite clear that the Dissenters had taken over the Catholics' role as the major threat to the constitution.'[67]

Priestley apart, the vast majority of eighteenth-century Dissenters, as well as a number of English Churchmen and many American divines, looked back with gratitude to Locke (often to the disregard of his pro-toleration forebears and contemporaries) as the exemplar of tolerationist views.[68] For his part, Edmund Calamy welcomed Locke's endorsement, shortly before he died, of Calamy's *Defence of Moderate Nonconformity* (1703–5):

> I had also a message from the ingenious Mr. Locke, letting me know that he had read this Introduction, and thought it such a defence of Nonconformity as could not be answered; and that standing to the principles there laid down, I had no occasion to be afraid of any antagonist.[69]

Locke's 'admirable' *Letter* did more than instruct Isaac Watts, it transported him: it

> led me as it were into a new region of thought, wherein I found myself surprised and charmed with truth. There was no room to doubt in the midst of sun-beams. These leaves triumphed over all the remnant of my prejudices on the side of bigotry, and taught me to allow all men the same freedom to choose their religion, as I claim to choose my own.[70]

Watts's friend and co-religionist Philip Doddridge was equally in sympathy with Locke's position, though, in his sermon of 1735 on the iniquity of persecution, he confined reference to Locke to a footnote thus:

They who are for a toleration limited, as good Mr. Baxter used unhappily to express it, 'to errors which are not quite intolerable;' and would have such punished at least with fines and imprisonments, if not with greater severities, seem not to be aware of the consequences of their own scheme: and, as Dr. Owen very forcibly speaks, in his excellent Treatise of Toleration,* 'They had need to examine their light; for their tenet must lead down to the chambers of blood.'
* Which, by the way, goes on as large principles, as Mr. Locke's afterwards did, and contains what is most essential in the controversy.[71]

Four years later, from across the Atlantic, Charles Chauncy argued that to use force in matters of religion and conscience was to act in opposition both to Christ's example and Gospel precepts and to natural law.[72] To William Warburton, bishop of Gloucester, writing in 1763, the law of toleration is 'certainly of *divine original*';[73] while John Henry Livingston, the 'father of the Reformed Dutch Church in America,' who founded New Brunswick Seminary and was concurrently president of Queen's College (now Rutgers University) explicitly acknowledged the debt he owed to Locke for leading him to the same conclusion.[74] Such was the diversity and geographical spread of Locke's ministerial supporters on the issue of toleration. Not to be outdone, Scotland produced a number of defenders of at least qualified toleration. Hutcheson had briefly, but significantly, advocated toleration in *A Short Introduction to Moral Philosophy* (1747) – a translation of his *Philosophiae Moralis* (1742), and in his posthumous *A System of Moral Philosophy* (1755); but he stopped short of a detailed discussion of toleration *vis-à-vis* a national Church such as that of Scotland. Reid was more alive to this issue, and to the practical implications of it:

So various, nay so absurd and capricious are often the opinions of Men, especially in more enlightened ages that a Legislator might almost as soon hope to make one coat fit all his Subjects as one Religion. Therefore it is necessary in every State, that there be a Tolleration for those whose sentiments do not allow them to joyn in the National Religion, while at the same time they may have no notions of Religion that are inconsistent with their being good Subjects and good members of the Society.[75]

A number of divines enlisted Locke's aid in the cause of toleration during the last thirty years of the eighteenth century. Nor were these Dissenters only. In 1772 the Nonconformists received support from Richard Watson, who went on to become bishop of Llandaff. He agreed with Locke that each person must employ reason in the determination of belief, and that there was a core of doctrine to be adhered to, and much that was peripheral. Loyal to the Establishment (unlike Priestley and, to a lesser degree, Price) he nevertheless believed that people should be able to worship in accordance with their convictions. He further held that the supreme Christian virtue is charity towards others.

> Are the Gates of Heaven open only to us, the Athanasians and Calvinists of the Age? Is yours the only intelligible Interpretation of Scripture; Yours the only saving Faith? Away with such unlearned Arrogance, such an uncharitable Judgement! ... The Question will not be at the last Day, Are You of the Church of Jerusalem or of Antioch, of Rome or England ... ? ... But, what hungry have you fed? What Naked have you clothed? What Sick have you visited? What Souls have you saved? Not, what barren metaphysical Creeds have you repeated? But, What Fruits of your Faith have you brought forth?[76]

The Anglican Bible commentator, Thomas Scott, who was among others who coveted a greater degree of toleration, acknowledged 'the vast obligation' under which Locke's letters on the subject had placed supporters of the cause.[77]

The Feathers Tavern Petition of 1772, the objective of which was to secure Dissenters relief from the necessity of subscription to the Thirty-nine Articles of the Church of England, found the Independent divine Philip Furneaux among its supporters. Among other things he invited Mr Justice Blackstone to view matters in historical perspective. Where once Rome had initiated persecutions against dissenters, in Stuart times especially Protestants had done the same thing until

> At length, the great Mr. Locke pleaded, with a clearness and strength peculiar to himself, the cause of universal [the overstatement again] and impartial liberty of conscience, in his celebrated Letters on Toleration. Sensible and enlarged minds quickly felt the force of his argument. But it required time for the most perspicuous and cogent reasonings, to eradicate general prejudices, and to alter the sentiments and complexion of the publick.[78]

Following the defeat in the Commons of the Petition (in which defeat a speech by Burke was instrumental), Furneaux returned to the fray in 1773, opening his plea for the amending of the Toleration Act with the testimony that 'The reasoning of that great man Mr. Locke in defense of Toleration, in his celebrated Letters on that subject, must, I think, to every attentive mind, carry irresistible conviction.'[79] The Baptist Caleb Evans spoke for many Dissenters when he declared that in Furneaux's book '*every objection* to this most reasonable and important privilege [i.e. that of toleration] is ANNIHILATED.'[80] Andrew Kippis also took up his pen in 1773 in order to explain that

> We dissent, because we deny the right of any body of men, whether civil or ecclesiastical, to impose human tests, creeds, or articles ... Independently, therefore, of the truth of the Thirty-nine Articles, the generality of Dissenting Ministers object to the imposition of these Articles. Persuaded as they are of the sufficiency of Scripture, and of the liberty which every one ought to have of following the guidance of his own conscience in religious concerns, they will not subscribe to human formularies, which they themselves believe, when such formularies are pressed upon them by an incompetent and usurped authority.[81]

In the course of his argument Kippis invokes Locke on the magistrate's incompetence in matters concerning 'the eternal interests of mankind,' and refers to 'the immortal writings of Locke, Hoadly, and other friends to civil and religious liberty' with much appreciation.[82] Nor were 'advanced' Anglicans alone appealed to. In the course of his case for a renewed application to Parliament of 1773 the Independent Samuel Wilton does statutory obeisance to 'the celebrated Letters of the great Mr. *Locke*,' and proceeds to invoke the support of that staunch Calvinist Toplady:

> It is with peculiar satisfaction, that I can produce so unexceptionable an Evidence, as the Reverend Mr. *Toplady*, in favour of my Assertion. It is impossible that either the Orthodoxy of that Gentleman, or his Zeal for the Articles of the Church can be called in question, after the many proofs his Writings afford, that he is to be numbered among the most ingenious, and learned Champions for the Doctrines of the Church of *England*. And yet notwithstanding his firm Belief, both of the Truth, and Importance of the Articles, and his zealous opposition to the Petitioning Clergy; he has said some of the strongest things, on the reasonableness and propriety of an Enlargement of the Toleration.

> 'The Toleration of Protestants (says he,) should, by every Law both of God, of Nature, and of Civil Policy, be absolutely unlimited ... As far as the *Protestant Dissenters* are concerned, I should, as a Well-wisher to Mankind, rejoice to see *Subscription*, I will not say *relaxed*, but intirely *taken out of the way.*'[83]

The prosecution of the case was not left to individual Dissenters alone. In 1787 the General Meeting of the Deputies of the Three Denominations meeting at Dr Williams's Library, Red Cross Street, London, on 5 January agreed to publish *The Right of Protestant Dissenters to a Compleat Toleration, Asserted.* The Deputies cite Locke's case against persecution in his *Second Letter*. Locke's point is that if persecution were really designed to secure conformity, it would be accompanied by inquiries to determine whether persons were conforming on reasoned grounds and out of conviction; and this does not happen.

> If persecution, as is pretended, were for the salvation of men's souls, this would be done; and men not driven to take the sacrament to keep their places, or to obtain licenses to sell ale, for so low have these holy things been prostituted; who perhaps knew nothing of its institution, and considered no other use of it but the securing some poor secular advantage, which without taking of it they should have lost. [84]

From his vantage point in 1812, Thomas Belsham looked back to early protagonists in the toleration debate:

> Mr. Baxter himself, pious and charitable as he was, and even persecuted as he himself had been, was only for *tolerating* all that were *tolerable*, from which pale Antinomians were excluded. Mr. Locke, as might be expected from that truly great man, held sentiments far more liberal: and in a letter to Mr. Limborch, he thus expresses his regret that the Toleration Act then lately passed had been framed ... 'not with the latitude which you, and such as you who are genuine Christians, void of all ambitious or party views would wish. It is something, however, to advance thus far.'[85]

Belsham himself was with Limborch, as he made plain in a book published as the eighteenth century turned: '[W]e admit in the most unrestrained sense the right of every man to think for himself in matters of religion, and apprehend that this right extends to judging the importance of opinions as well as the truth of them.'[86]

III

As Alexander Gordon observed a century ago, 'Toleration is not reached until, to the right of worshipping God in one's own way, is joined the right of forsaking the established forms.'[87] We have already had cause to refer to the role of the civil magistrate *vis-à-vis* toleration, but now the question of church government comes into view. What is the nature of the Church, and what is its proper relation to the state? This is the question which especially concerned many eighteenth-century divines, some of whom had recourse to Locke on the matter, as we shall see. I must emphasize that the issue of the bearing of government on the nature and ordering of the Church alone will concern us here. I exclude from consideration, for example, the indebtedness to Locke of the framers of the American Constitution, on which much has been written.[88] I also leave on one side the indebtedness of eighteenth-century British politics to Locke – an indebtedness which, according to some, has been exaggerated.[89] My concern is ecclesiological, and this section might well have been included in the next, doctrinal, chapter (and it will in any case constitute a bridge to that chapter). But since most of what Locke had to say about the Church is found in his political writings, there is a natural link between that subject and his views on liberty and toleration which I have just reviewed.

As with other themes, so with government: Locke's intellectual indebtedness is manifold. Discerning ears can readily hear echoes in his writings of the natural-law writings of Pufendorf; of Grotius, Limborch and the Dutch Arminians (in observing that Locke's *Two Treatises* are 'saturated with Christian assumptions – and those of a Christianity in which the new Testament counted very much more than the Old'[90] John Dunn fastens upon a characteristic Anabaptist-Mennonite emphasis); of Latitudinarianism; of the Reformed heritage in general,[91] and of its Dissenting representatives in particular. In connection with the diversity – both theological and ecclesiological – of the mid-seventeenth-century Nonconformists, Richard L. Greaves has rightly pointed out that 'Locke ... was linked to an intellectual circle that included the Calvinists John Owen and Robert Ferguson as well as the Quaker Benjamin Furley.'[92] Locke had an ecclesiological bran tub in which to dip.

In the light of our earlier discussion we may further agree with Dunn, who writes elsewhere,

> It was *not* Locke's theory that all human political duties were necessarily exclusively derived from consent; and it indisputably was his theory that all valid human political duties were rationally to be interpreted as specifications of God's purposes for man. Political duty was a theoretical derivative of natural theology.[93]

This comes out clearly in Locke's paraphrase of Romans 13:1: 'Let every one of you none excepted be subject to the overruleing powers of the government he lives in. There is noe power but what is from God'; and in his preamble to the paraphrase: 'St. Paul in this direction to the Romans does not soe much describe the magistrates that then were in Rome, as tels whence they and all magistrates every where have their authority; and for what end they have it, and should use it.'[94] It follows that those responsible for governing assume their duties as a trust donated under natural law:

> Since the purpose of governing is quite precisely given by the law of nature as Locke understands it, the problem of ruling in civil society is not how to unite a multitude of diverse wills, or how, given the variety of opinion and wants, to determine what the public good requires. It is the much simpler problem of how to achieve what everyone knows ought to be done. The legislature is entrusted with power so that it may pursue a known end.[95]

For Locke the end is the public good. Whereas in the 'state of nature' individualism prevails, for human society ('God having made man such a creature, that in his own judgment, it was not good for him to be alone')[96] 'the consent of any number of freemen capable of a majority, to unite and incorporate into such a society'[97] is required; for only so can certain benefits (supremely the preservation of property)[98] be guaranteed:

> Political power, then, I take to be a right of making laws with penalties of death, and consequently all less penalities for the regulating and preserving of property, and of employing the force of the community, in the execution of such laws, and in the defence of the commonwealth from foreign injury; and all this only for the public good.[99]

In a word, the governed comprise 'a society of rational creatures, entered into a community for their mutual good'.[100] This anti-absolutist social compact theory Locke defends against Sir Robert Filmer's view that absolute monarchy is derived from Adam's headship of the human race.[101]

The state, for Locke, then, originates in the natural law which itself is promulgated by God. Human beings are in society and are governed: this is the way of things, and over this they have no choice. By contrast, membership of the Church is voluntary, and over the Church's beliefs and (law-abiding) activities the state has no powers, not least because the end of the Christian faith is not a terrestrial good, but eternal life. Further, while we may know that we are in violation of the civil law, neither we nor the civil magistrate can *know* that our conscientious religious worship and convictions are or are not flawed. Accordingly they are not amenable to legislation. Let us look at each of these aspects in turn. Locke defines a church as follows:

> A church ... I take to be a voluntary society of men, joining themselves together of their own accord, in order to the public worshipping of God, in such a manner as they judge acceptable to him, and effectual to the salvation of their souls.[102]

Locke's voluntarism implies that

> Nobody is born a member of any church; otherwise the religion of parents would descend unto children, by the same right of inheritance as their temporal estates ... No man by nature is bound unto any particular church or sect ... [I]f afterwards he discover any thing either erroneous in the doctrine, or incongruous in the worship of that society to which he has joined himself, why should it not be as free for him to go out as it was to enter?[103]

While churches may discipline erring members, and peaceably propagate their beliefs, they may not resort to force or destabilize civic society.[104]

It is of some importance that we understand Locke's ecclesiology, for in the declining years of the twentieth century there is in some Christian circles a campaign being fought against individualism and against what is called the privatization of religion. That there are signs of such phenomena cannot be denied, though this is not the place to adduce the evidence. Since these misfortunes are attributed, often in a 'blanket' way, to the Enlightenment, it is, however, necessary to exonerate the father of the English Enlightenment from the charge of unmitigated individualism. For while Locke was a voluntarist *vis-à-vis* church membership, he was, as we have just seen, equally clear that persons joined the Church as social beings entering into fellowship with others.[105] My review of the evidence leads me to concur with Shirley Letwin, who writes, 'Since Locke does not see human beings as intrinsically private personalities, his picture of the human world is far from individualistic.'[106] As for individual Christians, Locke thinks that they are free to leave a church if they conclude that its doctrine is erroneous or its worship is incongruous; but persons cannot as individuals opt out of a wayward state. When government (which depends upon consent and entails decisions and actions taken representatively on behalf of those who have ceded power to it) breaks down, the people resume the powers they had voluntarily surrendered to their representatives:

> whenever the legislators endeavour to take away and destroy the property of the people, or to reduce them to slavery under arbitrary power, they put themselves into a state of war with the people, who are thereupon absolved from any farther obedience, and are left to the common refuge, which God hath provided for all men, against force and violence ... What I have said here, concerning the legislative in general, holds true also concerning the supreme executor, who having a double trust put in him, both to have a part in the legislative, and the supreme execution of the law, acts against both, when he goes about to set up his own arbitrary will as the law of the society.[107]

For Locke, then, revolution must always be a last, reluctant, resort on the part of the *people.*[108]

At this point the Dissenting strand of Locke's inheritance becomes important. With pardonable exaggeration Winthrop S. Hudson has said that 'Locke did no more than restate the argument that had been fashioned by the Independents.'[109] In 1647 the Independent divine William Bartlett of Wapping expounded his preferred church polity in these terms:

> This visible church-state is a free society of visible Saints, embodied or knit together, by a voluntary consent, in holy fellowship, to worship God according to his word ... The godly are bound everywhere, to gather themselves into such a Church-state if they are of a competent number, or to join themselves to such Churches as are already gathered.[110]

From Hartford, Connecticut, the Independent Thomas Hooker published *A Survey of the Summe of Church Discipline* in 1648. He lays greater emphasis upon the priority of grace where the gathering of the saints is concerned:

> The mystical Body is the Church of true Believers, who being effectually called by his word and spirit, by faith yielding to the call, are spiritually united unto Christ ... Mutual covenanting and confederating of the Saints in the fellowship of the faith according to the order of the Gospel, is that which gives constitution and being to a visible Church.[111]

The constituents of divine vocation and voluntary human assent are brought together in the *Savoy Declaration of the Institution of Churches* (1658) thus:

> Those thus called (through then Ministery of the Word by his Spirit) [Christ] commandeth to walk together in particular Societies or Churches, for their mutual edification, and the due performance of that publique Worship, which he requireth of them in this world.[112]

Although Locke, ever hoping for religious comprehension, was and remained a loyal member of the Church of England, we can readily find traces of the congregational polity in his ecclesiological thought. For this reason, while I cannot dissent from the view of a latter-day Dissenter, H. F. Lovell Cocks, who quotes Locke's definition of the Church as a voluntary society, and finds it theologically wanting insofar as it might be applied to any social organization – a trade union or a tennis club, for example,[113] it must be said that Locke is not unaware of the divine initiative. This is clear from his paraphrase of I Corinthians 12:13:

> For by one spirit we are all baptised into one church and are thereby made one body ... And the bloud of Christ which we all partake of in the Lords supper makes us all have one life, one spirit, as the same blood diffused through the whole body communicates the same life and spirit to all the members.

As Roland Bainton remarked, 'despite the compact theory of government, Locke still held to the birth theory of the State, and, despite his Anglicanism, to the new birth theory of the Church.'[114] It is true, however, that as with 'faith", his maturest ecclesiological thoughts are not adequately represented in his earlier works. None of which is to say that Locke was a crypto-Dissenter; he was not. But in ecclesiology as elsewhere he drew eclectically upon a broad inheritance. Further, the ease with which the more strictly theological strand of Locke's ecclesiology could be overlooked by those who came after him is evidenced by Joseph Angus, a Baptist who, writing roughly half-way between Locke's death and Lovell Cocks's remark, upheld voluntarism as constitutive of the Church, but did not invoke the later Locke's grasp of the divine initiative. He thereby fuelled the secular understanding of the Church which became prevalent in some nineteenth-century circles.[115]

IV

It is not surprising, in view of Locke's ecclesiological convictions, that, though an Anglican, he cannot endorse the notion of church–state relations implied in Establishment theology. Positively,

> The commonwealth seems to me to be a society of men constituted only for the procuring, preserving, and advancing their own civil interests. Civil interest I call life, liberty, health, and indolency of body; and the possession of outward things, such as money, lands, houses, furniture, and the like.[116]

But the Church 'is a thing absolutely separate and distinct from the commonwealth. The boundaries on both sides are fixed and immovable,' and not to see this is to jumble heaven and earth together.[117] There need be no discord between church and state if only each will keep to its proper tasks, 'the one attending to the worldly welfare of the commonwealth, the other to the salvation of souls.'[118] Locke's strongly negative conclusion is that 'there is absolutely no such thing, under the gospel, as a christian commonwealth.'[119] A person does not become a church member by virtue of being born in a nation, but by God's call and the human voluntary response: 'Faith only, and inward sincerity, are the things that procure acceptance with God,'[120] and 'true and saving religion consists in the inward persuasion of the mind, without which nothing can be acceptable to God'.[121] Consistently with this Locke rebuts Proast's argument that the Church of England represents the only true faith. He does not deny

> that there are national religions that contain all things necessary to salvation, and nothing inconsistent with it, and so may be called true religions. But since they all of them join with what is necessary to salvation, a great deal that is not so, and make that as necessary to communion, as what is necessary to salvation, not suffering any one to be of their commmunion, without taking all together; nor to live amongst them free from punishment, out of their communion; will you affirm, that any of the national religions of the world, which are imposed by penal laws, and to which men are driven with force; can be said to be that one only true religion, which if men embrace, they shall be saved; and which, if they embrace not, they shall be damned?[122]

There is, further, the disconcerting circumstance that 'the church, if a convention of clergymen, making canons, must be called by that name, is for the most part more apt to be influenced by the court, than the court by the church.' For example, 'in the reigns of Henry VIII. Edward VI. Mary, and Elizabeth, how easily and smoothly the clergy changed their decrees, their articles of faith, their form of worship, every thing, according to the inclination of those kings and queens.' Monarchs favour those who agree with them, yet no 'sincere and upright worshipper of God could, with a safe conscience, obey their several [very different] decrees.'[123] In view of such considerations as these, Locke expostulates, 'how that can be called the church of Christ which is established upon laws that are not his, and which excludes from its communion persons whom Christ will one day receive into the kingdom of heaven, I understand not.'[124] Least of all, in his view, should such exclusions be based upon failure to approve of certain rites and ceremonies, to endorse the episcopalian polity, and to subscribe to less than central points of doctrine.[125] Thus, for example, Locke rebuts those who

> may object, that no such society can be said to be a true church, unless it have in it a bishop, or presbyter, with ruling authority derived from the very apostles, and continued down unto the present time by an uninterrupted succession.
>
> To these I answer. In the first place, Let them show me the edict by which Christ has imposed that law upon his church ... Next, pray observe how great have always been the divisions amongst even those who lay so much stress upon the divine institution, and continued succession of a certain order of rulers in the church ... And, in the last place, I consent that these men have a ruler of their church,

> established by such a long series of succession as they judge necessary, provided I may have the liberty at the same time to join myself to that society, in which I am persuaded those things are to be found which are necessary to the salvation of my soul. In this manner ecclesiastical liberty will be preserved on all sides, and no man will have a legislator imposed upon him, but whom himself has chosen.[126]

Consistently with this, and against Proast, who argued for the legitimacy of the use of force by the civil magistrate in religious matters, Locke declares,

> Our Saviour has promised that he will build his church on this fundamental truth, that he is 'Christ the Son of God; so that the gates of hell shall not prevail against it:' and this I believe, though you tell us the true religion is not able to subsist without the assistance of force, when miracles cease.[127]

Locke's opinions on the nature and polity of the Church, and on the establishment question found both support and opposition from Anglicans and Dissenters alike. Thomas Tenison of St Martin-in-the-fields, who was to become archbishop of Canterbury in 1695, may illustrate a popular line in anti-Nonconformist polemic. He opposes voluntarism on the ground that it makes for the multiplicity of sects, thereby rendering comprehension impossible. He cannot see how there can be communion between Arians, Anabaptists, Muggletonians, Sweet-Singers (I select from a long list), and ruefully declares,

> These may associate in a *Caravan*, but cannot joyn in the Communion of a Church. Such a Church would be like the *Family of Errour* and her Daughters, described in *Mr. Spencer's Fairy-Queen*, of which none were alike, unless in this, that they were all deform'd.[128]

Thomas Long, prebendary of Exeter Cathedral, was concerned to make the same point directly against Locke, and did so with reference to a still wider range of religious persuasions. He construes Locke's idea of the church as a 'voluntary Society of Men, joyning themselves together of their own accord, in order to the publick Worship of God' as opening the door to Turks, or Jews, for Locke does not specify Christians, nor refer to the Bible, the sacraments, bishops, pastors, nor to any rule of guidance.[129]

The nonjuror Charles Leslie objected to Locke's founding of

government on consent on the grounds that it was impractical, unwieldy and made for chaos whether in civic society or the Church. He contended that Tindal and Collins advocated Locke's view only in order to advance the cause of deists, Socinians and Libertines against the established ecclesiastical authorities.[130]

Samuel Johnson, the pastor of West Haven Congregational Church, agonized over the polity he was called to serve, and in 1722 became an Anglican. Writing of himself in the third person he says,

> He had ... an early dislike to the independent or congregational form of church government, in which every brother has a hand ... He was convinced that a way so entirely popular could but very poorly and he thought not long subsist, to answer any ends of government; but must from the nature of it crumble to pieces, as every individual seemed to think himself infallible.[131]

But Locke had his supporters too, among them the Latitudinarian Bishop Benjamin Hoadly of Bangor. His sermon preached before the King on 31 March 1717 launched the Bangorian controversy. Taking John 18:36 as his text ('Jesus answered, My kingdom is not of this world') Hoadly denied that Christ instituted a specific church order; rather, Christ alone is Lord of the heavenly kingdom, and every person is subject to his rule equally. His will is revealed in Scripture, and all must judge what they read there.[132] As John Walsh and Stephen Taylor have pointed out,

> Though the controversy produced much wearisome logomachy, it raised important questions. Was the Church of Christ a visible or an invisible body? Should a terrestrial Church be regarded as essentially a voluntary society (as Locke and some advanced Low Churchmen claimed) whose members had a God-given right of private judgement, to join it or leave it, and individually to assess the truth of its doctrines? Or was the Church (as High Churchmen insisted) a corporate, visible, universal society, which demanded dogmatic obedience by virtue of its apostolic commission. Were Christians to be judged for the 'sincerity' of their belief or for their allegiance to the dogmas of the Church?[133]

The Congregationalist John Wise of Ipswich, Connecticut, who had been one of the few ministers opposed to the Salem witchcraft trials, published *A Vindication of the Government of the New-England Churches* in 1717. In the wake of Pufendorf and Locke he argues that whereas aristocracy and theocracy might have sufficed had people made Scripture, and not their own wills, the rule, in the event they have proved unsatisfactory and the Church has been despoiled. He finds that Christ has instituted a democracy:

> [I]f Christ has settled any form of power in his church he has done it for his churches safety, and for the benefit of every member: Then he must needs be presumed to have made choice of that government as should least expose his people to hazard, either from the fraud, or arbitrary measures of particular men. And it is plain as day light, there is no species of Government like a Democracy to attain this End.[134]

We may note in passing that Wise here departs significantly from the balance represented by the Cambridge Platform of 1648, according to which

> This *Government* of the Church, is a mixt Government (& so hath been acknowledged long before the term of Independency was heard of:) In respect of *Christ*, the head & King of the church, & the Soveraigne power residing in him, & exercised by him, it is a *Monarchy*: In respect of the body, or *Brotherhood* of the church, & powr from Christ granted unto them, it resembles a *Democracy.* In respect of the *Presbytery* & powr committed to them, it is an Aristocracy.[135]

Wise, whose books were influential for many years so elevated democracy as to eschew consociation.[136]

Wise's English Independent contemporary, Isaac Watts, while recognizing that

> it is a fashionable and modish thing now-a-days, to represent the whole religion of Christ, whether personal or social, as little more than the mere religion of nature ... which opinion I can never assent to, so far as it regards the peculiar evangelical and glorious truths and duties, which relate more immediately to our personal religion, to our salvation and eternal life in the world to come. Yet, in matters relating to the constitution and government of christian churches ... I am not afraid to say, there is a most happy correspondency and similarity between the dictates of the light of nature, and the prescriptions of the New Testament almost all the way. In this affair revelation does

not add a great deal of new duty beyond what reason would teach us ...[137]

Thus, for example, 'Wheresoever public and social religion is to be maintained, the light of reason teaches us, that several persons, who profess the same religion, must sometimes meet together, to celebrate the solemnities, rites, and ordinances thereof, and to worship God according to the rules of it.' Again, 'The light of nature and reason teaches, that where persons join together for any religious service, they must be agreed in the main and most important points that relate to it.'[138] It would appear that at the points specified both Wise and Watts are in danger of minimizing the idea of the Church as primarily a divinely constituted society.

That towards the end of the eighteenth century Locke was still being invoked on the nature of the Church as a voluntary covenanted body is clear from the writings of the American Baptist Isaac Backus. He supports his view that the Church is a voluntary society of believers by quoting from Locke's *A Letter concerning Toleration*, and further explains that 'no person can be brought into [a church covenant] without his own consent'; neither can the covenant be used to 'bind any person or community to act any thing contrary to the revealed word of God, nor ever exempt any from their obligation to act agreeably thereto with their hearts.'[139] The need to achieve the pastorally appropriate balance between the right of private judgement and the responsibility of the covenant community to reach a common mind has ever been the supreme practical challenge to those who follow the congregational way – not only where questions of church discipline are concerned,[140] but also, for example, in the calling of ministers.

In the preamble to the confession of faith which he delivered at his ordination service in 1767, the Baptist Caleb Evans opened thus:

> The right of private judgment, especially in matters of religion, I apprehend is the undoubted and unalienable privilege of every rational intelligent creature. It is a privilege I claim myself, and for the use of which I am accountable only to God; and it is a privilege which I think every one *ought* to exercise, and has a right *fully* and *freely* to enjoy.[141]

At the same time he is conscious of the fact that ministers in his tradition are called by the will of the people. His case is that the church members and neighbouring ministers have a right to hear a public articulation of the newly arrived minister's confession of faith. While this requirement in no way adversely affects the minister's right of private judgement, his doctrinal judgements need to be sufficiently in accord with those amongst whom he will minister:

> [A]s it is not possible for a conscientious people to make a choice of a minister, without being satisfied in what they apprehend to be the soundness of his faith, as well as the purity of his morals, so it does not seem consistent for any conscientious ministers to join in the ordination of another minister without having the like satisfaction.[142]

The upshot would seem to be that a number of apologists for congregationalism in both its Baptist and Independent varieties invoked the support of Locke's voluntarism, albeit at the risk of underemphasizing the divine initiative in the constitution of the Church.

V

Locke's predilections towards disestablishment can only have been reinforced by the first two Anglican divines to enter the lists against him. Thomas Long countered Locke in *The Letter for Toleration Decipher'd and the Absurdity and Impiety of an Absolute Toleration Demonstrated, by the Judgment of Presbyterians, Independents, and by Mr. Calvin, Mr. Baxter, and their Parliament, 1662.* His case was that the objective of pro-tolerationists was the overthrow of the English Church and the restoration of Roman Catholicism as the religion of the land. The term 'absolute' in his title shows that, polemicist that he was, he was not unduly concerned to observe the qualifications *Locke* placed upon toleration. In fact, his attack is directed against Popple's prefatory remark to Locke's *Letter*, namely, that true liberty is absolute liberty. This sentiment Long regards as indicative of a Jesuitical plot.[143] He objects to Locke's restriction of the civil magistrate's role to civil matters, and brands Locke a locust from the bottomless pit.[144]

Far abler and more temperate was the high Tory Jonas Proast, chaplain successively at The Queen's College, and All Souls, Oxford,[145] who was encouraged to enter the lists against Locke by the *bon viveur,* Arthur Charlett, soon to become master of University College.[146] Proast finished *The Argument of the Letter concerning Toleration Briefly Consider'd and Answer'd* in March 1690, and that Locke took him seriously is evidenced by the swift appearance of *A Second Letter concerning Toleration,* completed two months later. Proast's *Third Letter concerning Toleration* and Locke's *Third Letter for Toleration* appeared in 1691 and 1692 respectively. Proast returned to the subject in 1704 with *A Second Letter to the Author of the Three Letters for Toleration,* and Locke's reply, his *Fourth Letter,* was posthumously published in 1706. The nub of Proast's case was that the civil magistrate does have the right and duty to enforce religious conformity in the interests of public order and security. That Proast was, as I have described him, temperate, is seen in his agreement with Locke that the use of force is of no avail in the implanting or changing of belief, and in his plea that moderate penalties only be imposed upon Nonconformists in order to counter negligence and prejudice.[147] 'What means is left', he asks, '(besides the Grace of God) to reduce those of them that are got in a wrong Way, but to lay Thorns and Briars in it?'[148] Certainly, the force must be 'duly proportioned to the Design of it,' but this, thought Locke, was easier said than done. It presupposed that one could readily determine who merited punishment and the degrees of punishment appropriate, and that one expression of religion only, the Established, was true and legitimately enforceable:

> I beseech you to tell me, are you not persuaded, nay fully assured, that the church of England is in the right, and all that dissent from her are in the wrong: Why else would you have force used to make them consider and conform? If then the religion of the church of England be, as you are fully assured, the only true religion, and the magistrate must ground his persuasion of the truth of his religion on such clear and solid proofs as the true religion alone has, and no false one can have; and by that persuasion the magistrate must be directed in the use of force ... what is this but covertly to say, that it is the duty of all magistrates to use force to bring men to embrace the religion of the church of England?[149]

Morally, then, Locke is anti-force in the matter of religious allegiance; epistemologically, and consistently with his view of faith which we have already considered, he denies that the magistrate can *know* that his religion is the true one, for none of us can have such *knowledge*:

> Knowledge, then, properly so called, not being to be had of the truths necessary to salvation, the magistrate must be content with faith and persuasion for the rule of that truth he will recommend and enforce upon others; as well as of that whereon he will venture his own eternal condition.[150]

Locke and Proast never reached agreement, and the latter never departed from his view that 'all who have sufficient means of Instruction provided for them, may justly be punish'd for not being of the *National Religion*, where the true, is the National Religion.'[151] As G. A. J. Rogers has said,

> The failure to grasp the force of Locke's case suggests that it was an argument not well understood by men of undoubted intelligence in his own day, and the most likely sources of their incomprehension lie partly in the novelty of the argument and partly, perhaps, in a strong inner resistance to the conclusion.[152]

Throughout the eighteenth century both Locke and Proast had their supporters on the establishment question. In 1705 an anonymous author branded both Locke and Bishop Blackall (not to mention atheists, deists, fanatics and the 'spawn of Jesuits') republicans, and insisted against them that Christ, not the people, is the fount of both civil and ecclesiastical authority. To deny this is to join the subverters of the state.[153] So wedded was Henry Sacheverell to the High Church position that as late as the end of the first decade of the eighteenth century he professed himself uncertain whether toleration had in fact been enacted.[154] At the opposite pole, Edmund Calamy lamented the disabilities which remained in force against Dissenters from the Church of England even after the Toleration Act of 1689: 'And are not Protestant Dissenters now cast out from all Places of Profit and Trust, unless they'll quit their Principles, and entirely fall in with the Publick Establishment?'[155] For his part, Isaac Watts exhorted his co-religionists to take special care of those whom the civil society neglects 'because they do not profess the established or national religion'.[156]

Disabilities apart, many Dissenters brought Scripture and

theology to bear upon the idea of church establishment. Among more significant contributions in this vein were those of the Presbyterian Micaijah Towgood, who was regarded as the Dissenters' 'ablest advocate in the points of controversy which occasion their separation from the Church of England'.[157] He did not, however, have great recourse to Locke, but he was trounced by Wesley. Against Towgood's argument that since Christ alone was head of the Church the concept of Church-state was untenable, Wesley claimed that civil authorities may properly determine 'things indifferent,' and that separation over such matters was not justifiable. As Henry Rack has pointed out, Wesley had his own reasons for adopting this stance and welcoming the fluidity of the then current establishment but, he drily remarks, 'Towgood might well feel aggrieved that men of principle and conscience should be condemned for not having such flexible notions of conformity as John Wesley.'[158]

From the context of the Scottish establishment (under which, be it remembered, the Church retained authority over spiritual matters and church polity) Thomas Reid suggested that the desirability or otherwise of an established religion could be determined only by experience. Such a religion should have its articles of belief and its modes of worship. However,

> The Articles of Belief in an Established Religion ought not to be matters of doubtfull disputation about which the best & wisest of the Subjects differ nor ought they to be matters of small importance to real Virtue and Piety. And all the Institutions of an established religion ought, as far as possible in a consistence with the End of that Establishment to be adapted [to] the main body of the Nation, even those who may differ in opinion from one another in many points. Were it possible to frame a Model of established Religion in which every good & pious Man in the Nation could joyn it were desireable. But this seems to be impossible.[159]

Reid's tempering of establishment theory, and his scepticism concerning the practical possibility of an established Church in which all in a nation could join, would not have satisfied Richard Price. To Price there were serious theoretical – even theological – arguments against the idea of an established Church. In his sermon of 1789, *A Discourse on the Love of Our Country*, he argued that religion should be regarded not as a matter of rites to be observed, but as a 'reasonable service' entailing the worship of

God with a pure heart and the living of a righteous life. Sadly, the civil authorities have come to support a religion whose motivation is fear of punishment; against such a religion Locke and others rightly protested. Price was convinced that the endorsement by the govenment of 'particular modes of faith' could only vitiate human improvement and perpetuate error;[160] and he was surprised that dean of Gloucester, Josiah Tucker, should construe Price to have meant that 'because a man cannot depute another to make a creed or to settle a mode of worshipping God for him, therefore he cannot depute another to defend his property or to settle any temporal concern for him.'[161] As we might expect, Priestley was even more forcefully opposed to the establishment idea than Price. Indeed, he was, at least metaphorically, inflammatory, for he believed that the Rational Dissenters were, by their silent witness to truth, 'laying gunpowder, grain by grain under the old building of error and superstition [the Anglican establishment], which a single spark may hereafter inflame ... in consequence of which the work of ages may be overturned in a moment'.[162]

In the same year, but now from the pen of Archdeacon William Paley of Carlisle, there came both general praise for Locke's arguments and partial dissent from his position on church establishments. Paley agreed that 'A religious establishment is no part of Christianity,'[163] but he felt that it had a utilitarian value in inculcating it. For his part Richard Watson fastened upon the fact that Locke accorded to the civil magistrate the duty of preserving the peace of society and preventing crime, and turned this into an argument for an established Church:

> [A]s the belief of the existence of a God governing the affairs of this present World and ordaining a future state of rewards and punishments, is amongst the most powerful means of such prevention [here is the approach abhorred by Price]; it seems to be his duty to provide, at the public expence, public Teachers of some Religion; and, in fact, every nation in the world has made such provision.[164]

That neither Paley's pragmatism nor Watson's 'carrot and stick' persuaded most Dissenters of the propriety of the Anglican (or any other) church establishment cannot be denied, and the aspiration which Limborch expressed in a letter to Locke remains unrealized to this day: 'God grant that by embracing all who by the rule of the Gospel are not manifestly shut out from Heaven, [the Church of England] may give us the spectacle of a truly Catholic and Christian Church.'[165]

Nowhere is the general feeling of eighteenth-century Dissenters to establishment theory more poignantly evoked than in Thomas Amory's Preface to Samuel Chandler's *Sermons*:

> [T]he high reputation which [Chandler] had gained, by his defences of the Christian religion, procured him from some of the governors of the established church, the offers of considerable preferments, which he nobly declined. He valued more than these the liberty and integrity of his conscience, and scorned for any worldly considerations to profess as divine truths, doctrines which he did not really believe, and to practice in religion, what he did not inwardly approve. An honourable sacrifice to truth and honesty, and well compensated by the affection and generosity of his people; as far as such sacrifices are recompenced on this side of the grave.[166]

It would seem that Chandler gave living testimony to the truth of Locke's words: 'All the life and power of true religion consists in the inward and full persuasion of the mind; and faith is not faith without believing.'[167] But are there any doctrines which ought to be believed? Not the least of Locke's reasons for distinguishing sharply between Church and state was his conviction that neither the endorsement of particular church polities nor doctrinal rectitude qualify a person for heaven. On the other hand, he insists that 'those who have one and the same rule of faith and worship, are of the same religion, and those who have not the same rule of faith and worship, are of different religions.'[168] What, then, is the rule of faith? With this we come to Christian doctrine – a subject at least as vexed as any other with which we have had so far to deal.

6

Christian Doctrine

> A christian I am sure I am, because I believe 'Jesus to be the Messiah,' the King and Saviour promised and sent by God: and, as a subject of his kingdom, I take the rule of my faith and life from his will, declared and left upon record in the inspired writings of the apostles and evangelists in the New Testament; which I endeavoured to the utmost of my power, as is my duty, to understand in their true sense and meaning. To lead me into their true meaning, I know ... no infallible guide, but ... the Holy Spirit, from whom these writings at first came.[1]

I place Locke's testimony, cast in terms which are at least informally trinitarian, prominently at the head of this chapter, partly because of its clarity, but mostly because, unless we are to accuse Locke of deliberate deception, it constitutes the standing challenge to those who, from his day to our own, have questioned whether he was a trinitarian or even a Christian.

When considering Locke's position *vis-à-vis* Christian doctrine we must first pay heed to the poles between which he was operating. On the one side is his desire not for utter licence, but for freedom of conscience; on the other is his quest of ecclesiastical comprehension, which implies a principle of cohesion. Locke is by no means opposed to 'purity of doctrine, holiness of life, and decent form of worship' in the Church:[2] on the contrary, these things are to be striven for. His difficulty is with those who require too much in the way of essential belief, and who adopt a disruptive sectarian stance towards those who disagree with them. This concern parallels his denial, which we noted in the previous chapter, that specific polities, whether episcopal or presbyterial, are necessary to the being of the Church.

Locke was by no means alone in seeking an indispensable minimum of belief. Benjamin Whichcote, for example, declared that 'vitals in religion are few.'[3] Among other respondents to Stillingfleet's 'Sermon of schism' was John Howe, who roundly declared, 'without all controversy the main inlet of all the distractions, confusions and divisions of the Christian world, hath been by adding other conditions of Church communion than Christ hath done.'[4] In similar vein Richard Baxter exhorted his contemporaries not to 'make a larger creed or more necessaries than God hath done'.[5] When Locke's friend, Limborch, was writing his *Theologia Christiana* in 1685, Locke offered comments on this work in which commitment to the belief that Jesus was the Christ was deemed to be the credal minimum. The translator of his *Letter concerning Toleration*, William Popple, adopted the same stance in his *A Rational Catechism* (1687).[6]

Locke's most sustained plea for a minimum of qualifying belief is found in *The Reasonableness of Christianity* (1695), a work published as the Happy Union of Presbyterians and Independents of 1690, for which Baxter had worked so hard, was breaking down because of Presbyterian suspicions that the Independents were reviving the antinomianism of Tobias Crisp.[7] He was appalled by the attitude of the Anglican John Edwards, who will 'boldly affirm, you have no christianity, if you will not swallow it just as it is of his cooking. You must take it just as he has been pleased to dose it; no more, nor no less, than what is in his system.'[8] In thus prescribing correct belief Edwards usurps the throne of Christ.[9] Nor are individuals alone guilty of doing this: the Christian traditions excel in such divisive 'heresy':

> [H]owever clearly we may think this or the other doctrine to be deduced from scripture, we ought not therefore to impose it upon others, as a necessary article of faith, because we believe it to be agreeable to the rule of faith; unless we would be content also that other doctrines should be imposed upon us in the same manner; and that we should be compelled to receive and profess all the different and contradictory opinions of lutherans, calvinists, remonstrants, anabaptists, and other sects which the contrivers of symbols, systems, and confessions, are accustomed to deliver unto their followers as genuine and necessary deductions from the Holy Scripture. I cannot but wonder at the extravagant arrogance of those men who think that

> they themselves can explain things necessary to salvation more clearly than the Holy Ghost, the eternal and infinite wisdom of God.[10]

The 'extravagant arrogance' which Locke abhorred was, in his opinion, of little practical consequence, as the following words demonstrate:

> The dissenting congregation are supposed by their teachers to be more accurately instructed in matters of faith, and better to understand the christian religion, than the vulgar conformists, who are charged with great ignorance; how truly, I will not here determine. But I ask them to tell me seriously, 'Whether half their people have leisure to study? Nay, Whether one in ten, of those who come to their meetings in the country, if they had time to study them, do or can understand the controversies of this time so warmly managed amongst them, about "justification," the subject of the present treatise?'[11]

As Locke had earlier observed, the most irrational principles can be sacred to some, and 'Men even of Good Understanding in other matters, will sooner part with their Lives ... than suffer themselves to doubt, or others to question, the truth of them.'[12]

Locke's quest of an indispensable minimum of belief was, then, prompted by his hatred of sectarianism, and by his conviction that toleration (not to mention his epistemology, according to which we cannot have knowledge and certainty of doctrinal matters) requires tolerance where such matters are concerned. Indeed, he writes, 'I esteem [the mutual toleration of Christians] to be the chief characteristical mark of the true church.'[13] If there were an article of faith which Christ and the Spirit had proclaimed as essential, that was the one to be subscribed to in the interests of Christian unity and peace; and such an article there is. In contrast to the theological hair-splitting of the theologians, 'the all-merciful God' has delivered a 'plain intelligible proposition' which 'the labouring and illiterate man may comprehend.'[14] Locke's candidate doctrine is, on the face of it, the doctrine that Jesus is the Messiah. I say, 'on the face of it,' because while Locke does affirm this, for him the connotation of 'Messiah' is wide-ranging, and he also posits other essential considerations respecting our eternal salvation, as we shall see.

First, however, it cannot be denied that Locke nominates the Messiahship of Jesus as the indispensable minimum of belief.

That the 'fundamental article' of belief is that Jesus is 'the Messiah, our King,'[15] he is at great pains to demonstrate. In *The Reasonableness of Christianity* and its sequels he adduces scriptural evidence to show that this was at the heart of the apostles' preaching, that Christ's Messiahship fulfils Old Testament prophecy, and that it is proved by miracles. Belief in this doctrine is what makes a person a Christian, notwithstanding that the Saviour, through the apostles, 'taught a great many other truths, for the explaining this fundamental article of the law of faith'.[16] In view of these other truths, Locke denies Edwards's charge that 'nothing is required to be believed by any christian man, but this, that Jesus is the Messiah,'[17] later remarking that Edwards 'does not observe the difference there is between what is necessary to be believed by every man to make him a christian, and what is required to be believed by every christian'.[18]

In all of this, to repeat, Locke's motive is the establishment of a common doctrinal platform with a view to unity and peace in the Church. Quite different was the motive of some late-nineteenth-century liberal theologians, of whom P. T. Forsyth complained that they were paring down the Gospel so that it would accord with what enlightened modern human beings had always thought: '[T]oo many are occupied in throwing over precious cargo; they are lightening the ship even of its fuel.'[19]

It is important to observe that for Locke – at least on occasion – the term 'Messiah' carries a good deal of freight. It implies a range of doctrines concerning Christ, namely,

> that he had a kingdom, that he should be put to death, and rise again, and ascend into heaven to his Father, and come again in glory to judge the world; this he had told [the disciples in the upper room]: and so had acquainted them with the great counsel of God, in sending him the Messiah.[20]

Thus, when Locke declares a few pages later that the Messiahship of Christ is 'the sole doctrine pressed and required to be believed in the whole tenour of our Saviour's and his apostles preaching,'[21] we must take him to have in mind the full connotation of the doctrine. The importance of this is that many of his critics, as we shall see, take him to be advocating a 'bare minimum' doctrine rather than a multifaceted indispensable one. Indeed, in defending himself against John Edwards, Locke declares that 'the article of the one only true God, was also necessary to be believed';[22] and that belief in the Apostles' Creed makes a person a Christian, to the contents of which Creed he assents.[23] Locke further contends that in addition to profession of Christ's Messiahship, persons should enter Christ's kingdom by baptism.[24]

We should next observe that contrary to what some commentators have supposed, Locke's *Reasonableness* is not primarily concerned to determine the indispensable minimum of belief which qualifies a person to be a Christian. In the midst of the antinomian controversy over the place of works in relation to justification by grace through faith, Locke regards his book as a treatment of justification. Belief that Jesus is the Messiah suffices to make a person a Christian (though this is not the only article to be believed),[25] but to Locke beliefs are secondary to morality, and his great concern is how people may be right with God and gain eternal life.[26] Hence his assertion that 'These two, faith and repentance, i.e. believing Jesus to be the Messiah, and a good life, are the indispensable conditions of the new covenant, to be performed by all those who would obtain eternal life.'[27] To these two he further adds obedience: righteousness, 'a complete obedience, and freedom from sin, are still sincerely to be endeavoured after.' Such obedience is, like faith, a condition of the new covenant, as Christ's Sermon on the Mount makes plain.[28] This is a considerable addition to Locke's earlier claim that 'all that was to be believed for justification, was no more but this single proposition, that "Jesus of Nazareth was the Christ, or the Messiah".'[29] Justification, for Locke, is a matter of intellectual assent and a fruit-bearing life.

We may permit Locke to summarize his own position thus:

> The preaching of our Saviour, and his apostles, has sufficiently taught us what is necessary to be proposed to every man, to make him a christian. He that believes him to be the promised Messiah, takes Jesus for his King, and repenting of his former sins, sincerely resolves to live, for the future, in obedience to his laws, is a subject of his kingdom, is a christian.[30]

None of which, as I have already hinted, was calculated to satisfy John Edwards. In 1695, the year of publication of Locke's

Reasonableness, Edwards rushed out *Some Thoughts concerning the several Causes and Occasions of Atheism, especially in the present Age. With some Brief Reflections on Socinianism: And on a late Book entituled The Reasonableness of Christianity as deliver'd in the Scriptures.* The title contains Edwards's main 'bogeyman' terms, 'atheist' and 'Socinian,' and he finds both applicable to Locke. He contends that in designating 'Jesus is the Messiah' the only doctrine required to be believed by Christians, Locke follows Socinian authors. Moreover he neglects the Pauline epistles 'because they are fraught with *Other Fundamental Doctrines* besides that One which he mentions'.[31] Interestingly, Locke later admitted that although he had known Paul's letters, he had not understood 'the doctrinal and discursive parts of them: Though the practical Directions ... appear'd to me very plain, intelligible, and instructive';[32] and Maurice Cranston suggests that Edwards's challenge may have 'stung' Locke into this realization.[33] Be that as it may, Edwards strongly accuses Locke of sacrificing all other articles and doctrines to 'the Darling Notion of the Antitrinitarians, namely, that Christ is not the True God, and coessential with his Father'.[34] For good measure, Edwards nominates Hobbes as Locke's divinity, and his writings as Locke's scriptures.[35]

Locke responded with his *Vindication of the Reasonableness of Christianity*, and this in turn prompted Edwards's *Socinianism Unmasked* (1696). In this rollicking tract Edwards labels Locke one of 'the right *Racovian* breed'.[36] As before, he construes Locke as teaching not that the sincere confession of Christ's Messiahship (a term whose broad connotation Edwards overlooks) makes a person a Christian, but that this is the only requisite belief 'in order to salvation'. He can then argue that 'if there be but One Point necessary to be believ'd, then the doctrines concerning the *Trinity,* concerning the *Incarnation* and *Divinity of Christ*, concerning his *Satisfaction,* &c. are rendered unnecessary as to the making us Christians.[37] All of which is nothing more than a '*Racovian* plot'.[38] Edwards's objective 'is to alert and defend the *Christian Faith* which this Author hath misrepresented, maim'd and abused'.[39]

I shall return to Edwards's charges that Locke is an anti-Trinitarian, and that he has a deficient doctrine of the atonement in due course. For the present I remain with his first complaint,

'That he unwarrantably crowded all the Necessary Articles of Faith into *One,* with a design of favouring *Socinianism*'.[40] Among the doctrines thus omitted are those concerning our rescue by Christ from evil, his nature as true God and true man, his satisfying divine justice on our behalf, our justification by faith and not by works, and the doctrines of the resurrection, final judgement and eternal glory.[41] These doctrines are the bases of the Christian faith, and hence 'a man cannot be a *Christian* without the knowledg and belief of these Truths ... Wherefore for any man to make up Christianity without the belief of these is a Ridiculous and absurd attempt.'[42] Nor is Edwards moved by Locke's appeal to the Apostles' Creed, for this, he replies, is but an abstract; it does not contain all that is to be believed, 'So if a man *believe* no more than is in *express* terms in the *Apostle's Creed,* his Faith will not be the *Faith* of a Christian.'[43] Had Locke contented himself with saying that belief in Jesus's Messiahship is 'one of the first and leading acts of Christian Faith,' nobody would have opposed him. But he goes no further than this article, and

> This is as if a *Breeder-up of Children and Youth* should carry them no further than the A B C. He is wholly for *reducing* of Christianity, whereas he should have given it in its Full and Ample Extent; especially he should not have kept back any thing of the *Foundation.*[44]

In short, Locke's one article is 'the direct Spawn and Product of *Socinianism.*'[45]

Why should some wish to proffer so reduced a Christianity? For several reasons, declares Edwards. First, a single article can embrace many who would be excluded by credal detail, and thus suits those who believe that all will be saved. Secondly, it keeps the promoters safe from civil and ecclesiastical censure, for if there is but one essential doctrine, nobody could justifiably punish them for not espousing others. Thirdly, their one article becomes the principle of exclusion which they employ to dispense with such doctrines as the Trinity and Christ's satisfaction, to which they are not committed.[46] No doubt not all necessary doctrines are mentioned in one place in Scripture, but they are all to be found somewhere.[47]

Intense provocations notwithstanding, Locke did not reply at once to *Socinianism Unmasked.* This served only to encourage

Edwards in the belief that his points were unanswerable, a point he hastened to make in *The Socinian Creed* (1697). He regarded it as 'an unquestionable verity' that his opponents are vanquished, 'and that they *have not Answered* because they *could not*'.[48] He describes Locke as a 'Well-willer to the *Racovian* way,'[49] and reminds his readers of the sceptical epistemology which underlies Locke's reductionist doctrinal stance. For from the denial of natural principles Locke proceeds to deny Christian principles.[50] Edwards repeats his charge that to claim 'Jesus is the Messiah' as the sole article of faith is to Socinianize, and he regrets that Locke 'unfortunately ingages in a Province above his capacity, and boldly attempting to correct and amend *Christianity,* overthrows it'.[51]

This time Locke did respond – in his *A Second Vindication of The Reasonableness of the Christian Religion*; but not even this silenced Edwards, who, having taken an unusually long breath, published *The Doctrin of Faith and Justification Set in a True Light* in 1708. Once again he rebukes Locke for his reduced creed, whilst being equally impatient with atheists who do not believe at all, and others who are much too credulous.[52] He also takes exception to Locke's assertion that '*none are Sentenc'd or Punishe'd for Unbelief, but only for their misdeeds*, which is directly contrary to what our Saviour saith, Mark 16. 16 ... Joh. 12. 48,'[53] whilst overlooking Locke's declaration that from those who would enter and receive the benefits of the new covenant, 'An explicit belief of [the fundamental articles of faith] is absolutely required of all those to whom the gospel of Jesus Christ is preached, and salvation through his name proposed.'[54]

Far from being alone in attacking his restricted understanding of Locke's position on the indispensable minimum of belief, Edwards was but the forerunner of a number of others. In 1697 there appeared, *Animadversions On a late Book Entituled The Reasonableness of Christianity as Delivered in the Scriptures*, which is sometimes attributed to Richard West.[55] It is this author's opinion that Locke's minimum belief is inadequate: 'there is something more required, as necessary to be Believed: As that this *Messiah* was *God*, as well as *Man*, and that through the Merits of his Satisfaction, he redeemed us from Eternal Misery, &c.'[56] It is, he thinks,

> most evident, that the End of Christ's Coming into the World, was for

> some other Design than to give us Title to Immortality: And that was to put us in a Condition of saving our selves from Everlasting Misery, which we should otherwise most unavoidably have suffered.[57]

The same year saw the publication of a number of *Occasional Papers,* possibly written by Richard Willis, bishop of Winchester. More temperate than Edwards, he is prepared to accept that Locke intended that more than one article should be believed, but wishes that the point had been made more clearly.[58] Though Locke did not reply to the *Animadversions*, he did respond to the author of the *Occasional Papers.* He denies the charge that he had taken any of his ideas from Hobbes's *Leviathan*,[59] and in the fifth *Paper* the author accepts this denial.[60] He also quotes Locke's own three propositions with approval, wishing only that Locke had taken greater pains earlier to make his meaning clear:

> 1. That there is a Faith that makes Men Christians.
> 2. That this Faith is the believing that Jesus of Nazareth is the Messiah.
> 3. That the believing Jesus to be the Messiah, includes in it a receiving of him for our Lord and King, promis'd and sent from God, and so lays upon all his Subjects an absolute and indispensable necessity of assenting to all that they can attain the Knowledge that he taught, and of a sincere Obedience to all that he commanded.[61]

In the following year F.B. of Cambridge is found endorsing Edwards's complaints, and declaring that while the *Reasonableness* and its *Vindication* 'sufficiently discover [Locke] to be one of a musing Head, and a thoughtful Brain ... at the same time they testify him to be either a great Stranger to the Christian Religion, or else a great Corrupter of it'.[62] As we saw, he looks forward to more from Edwards's pen, deeming satire to be quite in order in controversy, for 'this sort of Medicaments hath cured [Locke's] Pen of the *Diarrhea*, at least as to this present Cause for a time.'[63]

John Milner, the unnamed author of *Mr. Locke's Account of Religion* (1700), has no difficulty in finding more than one fundamental article in Locke: Jesus is the Messiah; Jesus is the Son of God, and so on; but far from being in Locke's favour this is evidence that Locke 'had shew'd how wavering and uncertain he himself is concerning them, assigning sometimes only one, sometimes two, sometimes more'.[64] Among other things, Milner is troubled by Locke's equation of 'Messiah' with 'Son of God,' for this is a Socinian indentification which permits a less than full-blooded doctrine of the person of Christ.[65]

Having become sated with the accusation that Locke does not believe enough, or that if he does he is insufficiently clear on the matter, it is something of a relief to jump to the year 1765, and to find 'A Rational Christian' – Francis Webb – distressed that Locke required far too much in the way of belief! Webb is arguing that the religion of nature is the foundation of the religion of Christ. Hence,

> If, in any system, instead of piety towards God, of justice, charity, and universal benevolence to mankind, (which is the religion of nature,) the *belief* of certain propositions is substituted; such a religion cannot be *reasonable*, nor fit to be embraced by rational beings, whatever authorities from men or books may be brought to support it.[66]

In particular,

> If Mr. *Locke*, in order to shew the *Reasonableness of Christianity, as contained in the Scriptures*, had made choice of only the *moral* doctrines of Christ and his Apostles; no rational Christian could have differed from him:– But to bring the *mysterious* doctrines of the New Testament to prove the *reasonableness* of Christianity, when *reason* can have no comprehension of such doctrines, is indeed very extraordinary. The doctrines of *original sin*, the *incarnation* of Christ, the *redemption* through his blood, and his being the *Messiah* in the gospel sense, are certainly to be ranked among the *mysteries* of the *New Testament.* – To make then the *belief* of *all* these doctrines necessary to salvation, as the church does, or even the *last*, as Mr. *Locke* does, is extreamly surprising.[67]

Webb points out that to believe in Jesus as Messiah in 'the Scripture sense of the word' is to believe that he is '*Son of God, the King, the Lord and Saviour of the world*'. He laments that according to Locke's treatise, those who have heard and rejected this gospel 'after the best use of their faculties' and despite their sincerity and good works can expect only eternal death 'from their merciful Father'.[68] His verdict is, 'I reverence Mr. *Locke* as a great author; but am sorry to find among his writings, so unmerciful a proposition, whatever authority may be produced to support it.'[69]

The significance of Webb's case is not only that it constitutes a polar opposite way of disagreeing with Locke from that propounded by Edwards and his contemporaries; it also exemplifies a claim I made at the outset, namely, that in respect of some doctrines and general attitude of mind, Locke was closer to his Puritan contemporaries and forebears than he was to some of the rational Christians who succeeded him.

One way of taking our bearings on the doctrinal question is to take a random example from the many criticisms of rational Christianity made by Webb's evangelical Calvinist contemporaries. I select some words of David Bogue of Gosport, Independent minister and one of the founders of the London Missionary Society (1795). On 29 July 1788 Bogue addressed an Association of Ministers at Ringwood on *The Great Importance of Having Right Sentiments in Religion.* In this sermon he contrasts rational believers unfavourably with evangelical ones. The former, he says, do not worship with as much delight, or maintain family worship, or face death with as much joy, or manifest so much zeal for the salvation of others, as do evangelical Christians. And

> What are the doctrines that these men cannot brook and bear? Are they not those which evangelical Christians hold? Namely, that God was manifest in the flesh in the person of Christ; that, by the atonement and righteousness of Christ alone, we obtain pardon and justification; that our natures, which are wholly depraved, must be renewed by the Holy Ghost; and that as we are all condemned by God's righteous law, we must all be saved by an act of grace.[70]

Having regard to the fact that among his other duties Bogue conducted a ministerial academy in Gosport, the remarks at the end of our period of the Unitarian Thomas Belsham, when he was preaching a fund-raising sermon in aid of the Exeter academy, are interesting:

> [T]hose christians who are of opinion that the doctrines of the trinity, of original sin, of unconditional election, of atonement and satisfaction, of imputed righteousness, of irresistible grace, and of final perseverance, are the grand peculiarities of the gospel, the belief of which is essential to salvation, act very consistently, and upon their own principles very justly, in the zealous and liberal support which they are known to give to Academical Institutions for the education of ministers for the promulgation of those principles which they so highly revere.

> We, my christian friends, have we trust been better instructed in the doctrines of christianity, and are satisfied with the simplicity of the apostles' creed; not indeed with that which is commonly so called, and which contains many articles of which the apostles never thought, but with that which is truly such, namely, 'that there is ONE God even the Father, and one mediator between God and man, the MAN Christ Jesus.' And it surely becomes us to be as zealous in the propagation of truth as others in that of error.[71]

In addition to shaming liberal Christians into opening their purses in the cause of truth, Belsham here is clearer than Locke on the doctrines he rejects, and closer than Locke to meriting the charge of 'Socinian' as levelled by Edwards and others. Elsewhere he construed the essentials of religion in moral terms:

> The essentials of religion may be expressed in very few terms. Fear God and keep his commandments, for this is the whole duty of man. Thou shalt love the Lord thy God with all thy heart, and thy neighbour as thyself. But these propositions, simple as they may appear, comprehend a variety of articles, concerning which mankind are more or less prone to fall into error.
>
> The christian doctrine is so simple and intelligible in itself, and so plainly taught in the New Testament, that if we could read the scriptures with unprejudiced minds, and with a little attention to its peculiar phraseology, it seems next to impossible to mistake the meaning of the sacred writers. [As it is], genuine christianity is almost lost amidst the vast multitude of adventitious principles.[72]

In his parting message on resigning his pastorate at Hackney in 1805, Belsham returned to the theme:

> Nor was the plain unsophisticated doctrine of the apostles either perplexing to the understanding or burthensome to the memory of their hearers. Christianity had not yet become an abstruse system of metaphysical dogmas at which *reason stands aghast, and faith herself is half confounded.*[73]

As we proceed with our doctrinal investigation, we shall do well to entertain the possibility that although Edwards and Locke's other orthodox (Calvinist) critics did not hear their favoured 'language of Canaan' sufficiently clearly from the lips of Locke, and granted that he did not systematically expound Christian doctrines, still less propose a specific *ordo salutis*, he nevertheless gave his assent to Bogue's list of 'evangelical' doctrines and expected Christians to believe them. If he was thereby inconsistent in the eyes of a later rational Christian such as Webb, his stance was in keeping with his practice of oscillating between the place and claims of reason, the fact of revelation, and the assent of faith.

However, before launching further into doctrinal waters it is only proper to advert to those who sprang to Locke's defence over the question of the indispensable minimum of belief. In 1695 an anonymous author (possibly Stephen Nye, rector of Little Hormead, Hertfordshire) published a work the title of which sufficiently indicates its contents: *The Exceptions of Mr. Edwards, in his Causes of Atheism, against The Reasonableness of Christianity, as deliver'd in the Scriptures, examin'd, and found unreasonable, unscriptural, and injurious. Also it's clearly proved by many Testimonies of Holy Scripture, that the God and Father of our Lord Jesus Christ, is the only God and Father of Christians.* Against the '*Systematical Men*' he welcomes Locke's reduction of Christianity's essentials to one article, and considers that if asked, atheists and deists would tell John Edwards that 'obscure and contradictious Fundamentals' had turned them away from Christianity.[74] How, he asks, 'Will Mr. *Edwards* say, His Fundamentals are such irrefragable and indubitable Truths, about which there are among Protestants such hot and irreconcilable Contentions?'[75] By denying that the systematizers' doctrines are essential,

> the Unitarians take the direct Course to prevent Atheism and Deism, by letting the World see, that those Fundamentals are no Doctrines of Christ; but that the necessary Faith of Christ is a plain and short Doctrine, easy to be understood by the Poor, and clearly exprest in Scripture, most reasonable in itself, and most agreeable to the Unity and Goodness of God, and the other Divine attributes.[76]

The excess of fundamentals has driven the Quakers to their 'Light that lighteth every Man,' concerning which each one is as infallible as the Papists declare the Pope to be; while 'The Obscurity, Uncertainty, and Multiplicity of Fundamentals, is that which has given an Argument to Popish Priests and Jesuits, wherewith to seduce Protestants to Popery.'[77]

More regular support came from the indefatigable Samuel Bold, Locke's defender on other matters, who in 1697 published his *Discourse on the True Knowledge of Christ Jesus*, in which he defended Locke's view that it sufficed for Jesus and the apostles that Jesus be believed to be the Messiah, and opposed the views expressed in Edwards's *Socinianism Unmasked*. For this he was favoured with some *Brief Animadversions* from John Edwards, who claims that Bold, like the author of *Christianity Not Mysterious*, denies that revelation is a ground or motive of assent, with the consequence that Christianity becomes merely a 'Notional Speculative thing'; denies the authority of Scripture which exhorts us to believe revealed doctrines; and destroys his own one favoured article and with it all revealed religion, for revelation cannot be held to be efficient here and not elsewhere.[78] This drew forth Bold's *A Short Discourse of the True Knowledge of Christ Jesus. To which are added, Some Passages in The Reasonableness of Christianity, &c. and its Vindication. With some Animadversions on Mr. Edwards's Reflections on the Reasonableness of Christianity, and on his Book, entituled, Socinianism Unmasked* (1697). The burden of his message is that Locke proves 'That Jesus, and his Apostles did not teach anything as necessary to be believed, *to make a Man a Christian*, but only this Proposition, *That Jesus of* Nazareth was the Christ, or the Messiah';[79] and that Edwards fails both to make it clear what he considers the fundamentals of the faith to be, and to demonstrate the necessity of their being believed.[80] In a postscript to his *The Socinian Creed* (1697), Edwards retaliated with some *Animadversions* on Bold's tract in which he finds it odd that, in respect of the one article, Bold, a Churchman, 'should accept the Office of an Under-Puller for *Racovianism*', and surmises that the next step will be to dispense with even the one article. If this happens, Bold will then write 'rather like a *Turkish Spy* than a *Christian Preacher*'.[81] Edwards counters Bold's view that while other articles of faith are necessary to be believed they do not make a person a Christian, by retorting that in that case they are not necessary;[82] and he brands Locke's *Reasonableness* 'one of the Worst [books] that hath appear'd in the world since the date of Christianity'.[83]

In the following year Bold published *Observations on the Animadversions … on a Late Book, entituled, The Reasonableness of Christianity, As delivered in the Scriptures*. He here repeats his defence of Locke, and his charges against Edwards. To

Edwards's claim that Locke has introduced a new scheme of belief in opposition to 'the anciently received Doctrine of the Church,' Bold retorts that Locke in fact stands by the same principle which Jesus introduced, and which his Apostles invoked when admitting unbelievers into the Church.[84] He adds his own testimony: 'The Reason of my believing any Doctrine as I am a Christian, is, Divine Revelation, and not the Nature of the Doctrine, that is of the Matter taught.'[85] As to Edwards's charge of Hobbism against Locke, Bold remarks that whereas Hobbes argued that a Christian cannot be obliged to believe more than the minimum article, Locke holds that 'one who is a Christian, is necessarily obliged to believe as many Articles, as he can attain to know are taught in the Holy Scriptures.'[86] For his pains, Bold was rewarded with a commendatory letter from Locke himself, and by the latter's point-by-point defence of Bold against Edwards.[87]

In the early decades of the eighteenth century the question of the indispensable minimum of belief featured strongly in the subscription controversies of the time. With some, in both the Church of England and Dissent, tending in an Arian direction the question of doctrinal latitude could not but be raised. Among the Anglicans, Samuel Clarke's *The Scripture Doctrine of the Trinity* (1712) was viewed askance by many in whom the spirit of Puritanism lingered, while to others, and also to a number of Dissenters, it came as a ray of light. While some weighed Clarke against the Thirty-Nine Articles and found him wanting, others could point to such a bishop as Burnet, who acknowledged that articles might have a more than literal and grammatical sense – a circumstance which facilitated subscription.[88] The question of the Son's relation to the Father was the ostensible subject of the Dissenters' gathering at the Salters' Hall in 1719, though the underlying issue was that of the propriety of subscription to 'man-made' unbiblical formulae.[89] In the wake of these discussions Edmund Calamy spoke for many when he said,

> [I]t appears to me a very pardonable Thing, for Persons to be the less inclin'd to regard or value Subscriptions, when they observe how awkwardly they are manag'd by the Arian Subscribers to Trinitarian Articles, and the Arminian Subscribers to Calvinistical Articles, of both which Sorts I doubt there are great Numbers in the church of England.[90]

Burnet's latitude and Locke's plea for doctrinal essentials could only encourage those who shared Calamy's position.

In 1735, the year in which he moved from Bridgnorth to Walsall, the Presbyterian minister Josiah Owen sounded a distinctly Lockean note:

> The Almighty can take no Pleasure in puzzling his Creatures or bewildering their weak Understandings: the Truth is, whatever the Bigoted, the Interested, or the Designing, may advance to the Contrary; the Fundamentals of Christianity are few and Obvious. That there is a God, that Jesus is the Messiah promis'd; that Salvation is to be attain'd in the way he has appointed, are Truths adapted to the Capacities of All but such as stubbornly resist Conviction. The Man who believes these Things and discovers the Sincerity of his Belief by a suitable Conduct, stands as fair for Happiness as those who rack their Brains with School Sophistry, and Ecclesiastical Jargon.[91]

In her works published posthumously in 1751, Catherine Cockburn defends Locke by name. Against the charges of Dr Holdsworth, she declares that for Locke the terms 'Son of God' and 'Messiah' have the same signification. As to the 'one article,' Holdsworth admits that Locke believes in the one eternal God; but Locke also believes in Christ as Son of God; and how could we believe that Jesus was the Messiah without believing that his miracles were wrought in the power of the Spirit? So Locke's 'one article' in fact contains all the trinitarian claims.[92]

In his *Course of Lectures* to his Northampton students Philip Doddridge gave a more accurate interpretation of the surface meaning of Locke's one article:

> Mr. *Locke* and many othrs with him, maintain, that the only fundamental of christianity is, that Christ is the Messiah: but here a question arises concerning the extent of these words: perhaps it may be sufficient to answer it by saying, that wherever there appeared to be such a persuasion of the dignity of Christ's person and the extent of his power, as should encourage men to commit their souls to his care, and to subject them to his government, those who professed such a persuasion were admitted to baptism by the apostles, and ought to be owned as *Christians.*[93]

Among others to echo (and refer to) Locke's *Reasonableness* was the Scottish Presbyterian divine, William McGill. In 1786 –

under the influence, so some said, of Priestley – he published *A Practical Essay on the Death of Jesus Christ*, in which he writes, 'The foundation of the christian character is faith, or believing that Jesus is the Son of God; which by a necessary consequence, leads to a belief of all the doctrines and promises of God, delivered by him, and to the diligent performance of all good works.'[94] A number of divines scented Socinianism in this work, but what really incensed his opponents was his slight upon the Westminster Confession, whose non-scriptural phrases had been elevated by some into objects of reverence and worship. A heresy trial ensued in 1789. Eventually McGill offered an apology, but the dispute rumbled on for some time thereafter.[95] Many Scots felt that the Church had been too lenient with a heretic. His friend Robert Burns immortalized McGill in 'The Kirk's Alarm'. Not surprisingly, Thomas Belsham suggested that McGill had been intimidated by a Church as persecuting as the Roman.[96]

In an appendix to his sermon on the occasion of Belsham's death John Kentish summed matters up from the rational Christian perspective. He reaffirmed Locke's one article as the common ground upon which all Christians might stand, though not all will as yet.

> Meanwhile, the well-informed Unitarian Christian, reposes with humble confidence on the stability of the basis, which Locke has so clearly illustrated; and amidst reproaches, denunciations and invectives, which are little honourable to an age and country professing to be enlightened, he hence gains his persuasion, that 'he, too, is of Christ.[97]

As I leave the one article I would only remark that both Locke's Calvinist opponents and his later rational Christian supporters found it convenient, for their disparate reasons, to treat 'Jesus is the Messiah' in as univocal manner as possible, and that Locke's supporters as cited were, with the notable exception of Philip Doddridge, more liberal Anglicans and Presbyterians rather than Independents and Baptists.

I

Before proceeding to investigate specific areas of doctrine some cautionary words are appropriate. First, although Christian reflection is at the heart of Locke's thought, he by no means paid equal attention to every Christian doctrine. For the most part his doctrinal references are occasional; they arise in passing, not least when he is defending himself against attack. On a number of aspects of doctrine he has little or nothing to say. This is not surprising for if Locke had an abhorrence of the rounded (scholastic) philosophical system, he was no systematic theologian either. In philosophy and theology alike he worried at the problems which engaged him in a systematic enough way, but neither in philosophy nor theology did he proffer a unified intellectual conspectus. Again, we should pay Locke the courtesy of heeding his objectives. For example, *The Reasonableness of Christianity according to the Scriptures* was, as Locke points out to John Edwards, designed 'chiefly for those who were not yet thoroughly, or firmly, christians, proposing to work on those, who either wholly disbelieved, or doubted of the truth of the christian religion'.[98] To set enquirers and doubters thinking positively about the faith was his goal; he did not set out to produce a compendium of doctrine. Accordingly, those of his critics who accused him of silence on specific doctrines (in some cases couched in linguistic formulations of which they approved) to which they were themselves wedded, may be doing him less than justice. As for Edwards, he does grasp Locke's intention, but only to repudiate it:

> [H]e would make us believe that he intended his Piece for *Atheists, Turks, Jews* and *Pagans,* and a few Weak Christians; for these he must mean by those that *wholly disbelieve,* and those that are *not firmly Christians.* And he would bring in his Title to speak for him, but it saith not a word in his behalf; for how those that wholly disregard and *disbelieve the Scriptures* of the New Testament, (as Gentiles, Jews, Mahometans and all Atheists do) are like to attend to the *Reasonableness of Christianity as deliver'd in the Scripture* is not to be conceived, and therefore we look upon all this as mere Sham and Sophistry.[99]

As well as tilting at Locke, Edwards seems here to eschew the apologetic task altogether.

Though he does not affect Edwards's swashbuckling style, so careful a twentieth-century writer as Gerald R. Cragg can say of Locke's *Reasonableness*, that 'even the most casual reader is aware that what he propounded is far removed from the historic formulations of the Christian faith. The familiar phrases of theological discussion have been eliminated because Locke felt no need for the concepts to which they refer.'[100] I should be inclined to say that *only* the most casual reader could conclude thus, for such a verdict overlooks Locke's stated aim in writing *Reasonableness*; it disregards, for example, the multifaceted connotation of 'Messiah' which we have found in Locke's writings; and the assertion that Locke had no need of the concepts to which the familiar doctrinal phrases refer overlooks Locke's resolve not to exclude 'the belief of any of those many other truths contained in the scriptures of the Old and New Testaments, which it is the duty of every christian to study, and thereby build himself up in our most holy faith'.[101]

Where Locke is concerned the argument from silence is notoriously perilous. Edwards and others too easily concluded that because Locke does not mention a particular doctrine, he does not believe it. No doubt he did find some doctrines beyond his comprehension, but he did not attack them. Was he being prudent, timid (concerning the Trinity, for example, which it was illegal to deny), or a prevaricator? We shall never know for certain; but what is clear is that Locke was a devout, studious layman who, just at the time of his most urgent doctrinal and biblical enquiries, lost his chief mentor. On Tillotson's death he lamented, 'I have scarcely anyone whom I can freely consult about theological uncertainties.'[102]

It is further the case that while some of the eighteenth-century divines applaud or rebuke Locke on particular points of doctrine, many of them are preoccupied with matters which were not within his purview – for example, the debate between evangelical Arminians and high and evangelical Calvinists over the respective roles of God's grace and the human response in the matter of salvation.[103]

Secondly, we shall do well to recall the pejorative way in which such terms as 'Socinian,' 'Arian' and 'deist' were bandied about during the eighteenth century. Certainly where the more polemical writers are concerned we must not automatically assume that these terms are being used with technical precision; and even where the usage rises above mere pugilism, 'Socinian,' for example is ambiguous, and may not in every case denote all or even most of the views of Socinus himself. In the interests of clarity, though without any intention of making a smooth plain out of a furrowed field, I shall take the risk of characterizing (rather than strictly defining) the positions denoted by the terms in question. By a rationalistic Arminianism I understand a broad conviction that the place of reason is to be honoured in matters of religious belief and biblical interpretation.[104] Such Arminians wished to present Christ's religion 'in its original simplicity and native beauty, free from adulteration and mixture'.[105] More narrowly, in Holland rationalistic Arminianism denotes the Remonstrant opposition to Calvinism (especially to the doctrines of predestination and election), while in general 'toleration' and 'liberty of conscience' are rationalistic Arminian watchwords. A Latitudinarian is one who, having settled on a basic core of doctrine (including original sin, on which topic the Latitudinarians were united against the Socinians), adopts a relaxed attitude towards 'non-essential' doctrines. More inclined to Arminianism than to Calvinism, the liberty of the Latitudinarian is tempered in Church of England circles by the concern to maintain establishment theology and to accord to the civil magistrate the right to enforce the 'true' (that is, the national) religion.[106] An evangelical Arminian, such as Wesley, couches the Arminian protest against Calvinist predestination and election in the context of the quest for holiness and the imperative of mission, and emphasizes the free response to the Gospel which all (and not only the elect) are able to make. Thus, to describe Wesley as an evangelical Arminian is to say (a) that he is not a rationalistic Arminian; and (b) to say that he is not, like George Whitefield, Howel Harris, Andrew Fuller and others, an evangelical Calvinist. An Arian has a particular interest in the person of Christ, which is construed in a subordinationist manner. Arianism, the high version of which favours the worship of Christ, is frequently seen to be, and is in fact, a rather unstable half-way house between Trinitarianism and Unitarianism. A Socinian in the earlier decades of the eighteenth century would characteristically deny Christ's pre-existence and essential divinity, and would be reductionist concerning Christ's 'satisfaction'.[107] In the later part of the century the term might denote an advocate of the exemplary humanity of Christ, and an upholder of the sole supremacy of the one God. As early as 1680 the term 'deist' was being applied to those who settled for natural rather than for revealed religion, and held the Scriptures in low esteem.[108] The deists sought to construe Christianity as a non-mysterious republication of the religion of nature. Deism was a mood rather than a coherent movement, and Samuel Clarke was able to detect the following varieties of it: (a) those who, while believing in the supreme creator, regarded him as an absentee; (b) those who believed in the being and providence of God but did not find him involved in the affairs of humanity; (c) those who believed in God's existence, providence and concern for morality, but denied immortality; and (d) those who held correct views of God but claimed to have derived them solely from natural religion, not from revelation.[109] Those in the first two categories in particular felt that God's transcendent unchangeableness was not to be compromised by post-creation interventions in the world. In the words of S. C. Carpenter, 'Genesis relates that God rested on the seventh day from all His work. The deists may be said to have extended this week-end indefinitely.'[110] As a whole deism was anti-miracle and anti-supernatural, and its natural (mark the word!) heirs were those nineteenth-century thinkers for whom the idea of God was redundant. It should, however, be noted that

> Deism in America, during the first half of the eighteenth century, was of the constructive, not the destructive sort. Its earliest colonial representatives, like the father of English deism [Herbert of Cherbury], argued from natural reason for the existence of God, the immortality of the soul, the certainty of rewards and punishments, and the life to come. The system was at first hardly distinguishable from theism; it was more akin to Butler's *Analogy* than to Hume's *Enquiry*; it took two generations to develop into the revolutionary systems of the doubting Thomases, Paine and Jefferson[111]

– not to mention the reductionist Cadwallader Colden. Colden somewhat grudgingly allowed an intelligent creator of matter, but on no account would brook any interference from him in the world's affairs: 'The intelligent agent never acts in opposition or contradiction to the material agents.'[112]

That a number of the brands of thought I have epitomized were still disturbing the faithful towards the end of our period is clear from the warning from Joseph Barber, the Independent evangelical Calvinist, which is embedded in the sermon he preached in 1793 on the occasion of the death of Nathaniel

Trotman: 'We live in shaking times, wherein many are departing from the faith; some professors running into arminianism, some into arianism or socinianism, and others into antinomianism; yea, some have gone into very wild enthusiastic notions, and others into avowed infidelity.'[113] From the polar opposite theological camp, we might spare a thought for Thomas Belsham, who bemoaned the fact that true Unitarians 'have heard nothing from the Arians for the last twenty years but lugubrious complaints against the Unitarians for appropriating to themselves that honourable name'.[114] Assuredly, the path of the labeller is perilous!

Against the background thus sketched I may have some hope of probing Locke's position upon the doctrines of God and Christ in relation to the complaints lodged against it. I turn first to the accusation that Locke was a deist.[115] We have already seen that in relation to his ideas of substance, morality, government and, more specifically in connection with the theism which he thought was rationally defensible, Locke invoked the concept of God. What now of God's attributes?

That Locke thinks of God as a perfect, omniscient spiritual being who has existed from eternity is clear from the *Essay* IV.x. God has created all things *ex nihilo* – on which point Locke invokes Paul in support: 'I judge it as certain and clear a Truth, as can be anywhere delivered, That *the invisible Things of GOD are clearly seen from the Creation of the World, being understood by the Things that are made, even his Eternal Power and God-head.*'[116] The eternal mind exists necessarily, and other knowing beings depend upon him for their knowledge, while inanimate objects witness to his omniscience, power, providence, and all his other attributes.[117] I am not here concerned with the strength or weakness of Locke's argumentation, though I may hint that in the wake of the criticisms of traditional theism levelled by Hume and Kant it is, to put it mildly, difficult to endorse. Rather, in the convictions just stated, which are located in the midst of his epistemology, Locke's God is seen to possess the traditional attributes assigned to him, none of which are denied, and of which God's providence is explicitly affirmed. This, together with the anti-materialistic thrust of the chapter, already places Locke at a distance from some varieties of deism at least (Bolingbroke's, for example). On the other hand, Locke's view that the attributes listed above could be known by reason without recourse to revelation, was taken by some deists to favour their view that natural religion sufficed.[118] But it is Locke's insistence on the place of revelation, to which, he declares, 'many are beholden' though 'they do not acknowledge it,'[119] which places him at a distance from all who contended that Christianity was simply a republication of the religion of nature. Indeed, Locke insisted that those who 'made Jesus Christ nothing but the restorer and preacher of pure natural religion' did 'violence to the whole tenour of the New Testament';[120] and he wrote of his *Reasonableness*,

> I was flattered to think it might be of some use in the world; especially to those, who thought either that there was no need of revelation at all, or that the revelation of our Saviour required the belief of such articles of salvation, which the settled notions, and their way of reasoning in some, and want of understanding in others, made impossible to them.[121]

In this latter connection, it must be said that Locke welcomes the deists' determination to consign systematic doctrinal obfuscation to the flames, and this, as we might expect, was turned against him by some who felt that their favoured doctrinal essentials were being minimized. For his part, Locke declared himself against 'all systems ... so far as they are set up by particular men, or parties, as the just measure of every man's faith,'[122] and vowed that he would take his doctrine exclusively from the plain teaching of Scripture. Locke's principle is exemplified when, against Edwards's elevation of a certain number (unspecified) of fundamental articles of belief, he writes,

> As men, we have God for our King, and are under the law of reason: as christians, we have Jesus the Messiah for our King, and are under the law revealed by him in the gospel. And though every christian, both as a deist and a christian, be obliged to study both the law of nature and the revealed law, that in them he may know the will of God, and of Jesus Christ, whom he hath sent; yet, in neither of these laws, is there to be found a select set of fundamentals, distinct from the rest, which are to make him a deist, or a christian. But he that believes one eternal, invisible God, his Lord and King, ceases thereby to be an atheist; and he that believes Jesus to be the Messiah, his king, ordained by God, thereby becomes a christian, is delivered from the power of darkness, and is translated into the kingdom of the Son of

> God; is actually within the covenant of grace, and has that faith, which shall be imputed to him for righteousness; and, if he continues in his allegiance to this his King, shall receive the reward, eternal life.[123]

Those possessed of doctrinally sensitive antennae will observe Locke's use of the Calvinist terminology concerning the covenant of grace and imputed righteousness against the Calvinist Edwards; though in the concluding clauses he does not similarly invoke 'the perseverence of the saints,' but rather suggests, in rationalistic Arminian fashion, that our eternal security depends upon our present fidelity. It is interesting to speculate upon the possibility that Locke, writing in the midst of the antinomian debate, was wishing to counter any suggestion that the reception of sovereign grace permitted licentious practice. As he later explained, by taking Christ to be our King 'is meant not a bare idle speculation, a bare notional persuasion of any truth whatsoever, floating in our brains; but an active principle of life, a faith working by love and obedience'.[124] Certainly, at no point was Locke at a further remove from the deists than in connection with morality which, as we saw in chapter IV, he grounded not exclusively in the natural law, as did the deists, but in the gospel. For 'it is too hard a task for unassisted reason to establish morality in all its parts, upon a true foundation, with a clear and convincing light.'[125] In the light of the evidence thus briefly adduced, I have no difficulty in accepting Locke's words in a letter to Limborch of 29 October 1697, to the effect that he wrote the *Reasonableness of the Christian Religion* in the hope of dissolving the deists' prejudices against Christianity.[126]

The fact remains, however, that some deists and some orthodox divines were inclined to designate Locke a deist. Though he did not openly acknowledge any indebtedness to Locke (though he twice refers obliquely to 'an excellent modern Philosopher'),[127] and while it appears that he was working on his book prior to the publication of Locke's *Reasonableness*, John Toland, in his *Christianity Not Mysterious* (1696), gives every sign of having imbibed the epistemology of Locke's *Essay*. He agrees with Locke that knowledge is intuitive and rational, and is derived from the comparison of clear and distinct ideas; he agrees that revelation can yield information which must be tested by reason; he does not deny that '*Reason* is not less from God than *Revelation*; 'tis the Candle, the Guide, the Judge he had lodg'd within every Man that cometh into this World';[128] but, unlike Locke, he denies that there can be any truths of revelation which are above reason.[129] Such alleged truths he brands 'mysteries,' and he will have none of them. What is more, he utilizes Locke's distinction between the nominal and the real essence of a thing in order to make out his case. Since (according to Locke) we are ignorant of the essence of things, 'nothing can be said to be a Mystery, because we are ignorant of its real Essence, since it is not more knowable in one thing than another, and is never conceiv'd or included in the Ideas we have of things, or the Names we give 'em.'[130] The deist Matthew Tindal followed suit in 1730 in his *Christianity as old as the Creation: or, the Gospel A Republication of the Religion of Nature.* The title is his thesis, and despite acknowledgements to Locke at many points, he parts company with him on the question of revelation – to Tindal a redundant concept.

Anthony Collins had no inhibitions about referring to Locke by name. He had visited the elderly Locke at Oates, and Locke had corresponded with him in 1703–4.[131] In a letter written on 23 August 1704, to be delivered to Collins after Locke's death, Locke writes, 'I know you loved me living, and will preserve my memory now I am dead.'[132] These words were subsequently seized upon by William Warburton, 'the rather knock-kneed giant of theology, whose swashing blows, if too apt to fall upon his allies, represented at least a rough intellectual vigour,'[133] in the course of an attack upon Collins for his churlishness in dishonouring the memory of his erstwhile friend.[134] What Collins had done was to publish his deistic work, *A Discourse of Free Thinking* (1713), in which he reveals a significant difference between Locke and himself. Unlike Locke who, as we saw, appealed to the fulfilment of Old Testament prophecy as a central proof of Christianity, Collins denies that the prophecies were literally fulfilled by Christ, and rejects typological and allegorical interpretations of the prophecies as simply inventions of their several propounders.[135]

The main problem posed to Locke by the deists was that of guilt by association. Stillingfleet was perhaps the most prominent of those who found the use of Locke by the deists suspicious. As we have seen, he objected to Locke's position on substance, and in this he was inspired by Toland's endorsement of it. But to

Stillingfleet substance was the foundation card in the house of cards, and if it were removed, the other cards – the Trinity, personal identity and individual immortality – were bound to topple also. In reply, Locke rested upon his distinction between the certitude of knowledge and faith in the divine revelation, arguing that Stillingfleet's attempt to adduce rational grounds for the deliverances of revelation left no room for faith or for a distinct revelation either. Locke represents Stillingfleet as holding that 'a proposition divinely revealed, that cannot be proved by natural reason, is less credible than one that can.' This, he declares, is 'The direct contrary' to his own opinion, and he expostulates:

> If this be your lordship's way to promote religion, or defend its articles, I know not what argument the greatest enemies of it could use, more effectual for the subversion of those you have undertaken to defend; this being to resolve all revelation perfectly and purely into natural reason, to bound its credibility by that, and leave no room for faith in other things, than what can be accounted for by natural reason without revelation.[136]

Clearly, this is a *tu quoque* response to Stillingfleet's attempt to align Locke with the deists,[137] whereby Locke seeks to tar his episcopal opponent with the deists' brush.

Locke's protestations notwithstanding, the nonjuror George Hickes, titular bishop of Thetford, had no qualms about aligning Locke with Tindal in a preface he wrote to William Carroll's *Spinoza Reviv'd* (1709). He was not at all surprised that Locke and Tindal had an aversion to logic as taught in the universities, for logic would have enabled them to distinguish false arguments from true, and this they did not wish to do.[138]

A variety of witnesses appear on the other side, however. William Popple regretted that the deists had not sufficiently profited from reading Locke's *Reasonableness*, and wrote to Locke that many self-styled deists 'deny all Immaterial Beings,' yet constantly talk of God, laugh at both natural and revealed religion, and seek to erect morality on nothing more secure than 'the good-nature of particular persons' or the 'fear of the Magistrate's Rod'. Not surprisingly, he continued, 'I fear their Superstructure will be very tottering.'[139] Le Clerc likewise came to Locke's defence. He grants that Toland had used 'several Reasonings, that were very like to some Mr. *Locke* imploys in his

Treatise of *Humane Understanding*', but thinks Stillingfleet no match for Locke; indeed, 'I confess, I never read a Dispute managed in so cool Blood, or with so much Art and Exactness on the one side, nor on the other, so unjustly, confusedly, or so little to the Credit of the Author.'[140]

In 1731 an anonymous pamphleteer published *The Infidel Convicted: or, A Brief Defence of the Christian revelation. In which The Excellency of the Christian Morality is fully shewn, and the Consistency of Revelation with human Reason proved. Corroborated by Unanswerable Arguments from Mr. Locke, on whose Writings many persons causelessly profess to build their Sceptical Notions. And Addres'd to the Serious Consideration of the British Youth in general; and in particular of such of the Young Gentlemen of the Inns of Court, as are tainted with Atheistical or Deistical Principles, but are not wholly given up to a Reprobate Mind.* For good measure the author adds *A Pathetic Letter from a Father on the Degeneracy of his Son* ... The son in question had been a student of the Inns of Court, had been seduced into becoming a deist, had become ill, repented of his deism, returned home and died. Youngsters at the Inns of Court would, no doubt, draw the moral. The author rebukes Woolston for his position on miracles, chastises Collins for disturbing the faithful by the zealous propagation of his own doubts, and invokes Locke's view that reason unassisted by revelation is unable to establish morality on a true foundation against all 'who would separate *Reason* from *Revelation*, as *inconsistent* with each other, and so would use the *first* to destroy the *last*, which is the Scheme of the present *Deists* and *Sceptics*'.[141] He groups Locke, Addison, Boyle and Newton together as those who, though opposed to enthusiasm and superstition, aimed to 'increase their *Faith*, and strengthen their *Belief* of the *Mysteries* of Providence, and of the *Truth* of the *Christian Revelation*'. Moreover, since these were all laymen, they 'could not be suspected to be in a Plot to promote that *Priestcraft* which it is so much the Fashion of our present *Ridiculers* of the *Christian Faith*, to cry out upon'.[142]

In the following year Thomas Burnet defended Locke, Newton, Burnet, Clarke and Wollaston against accusations by deists that they disbelieved in the divine revelation;[143] while John Conybeare, rector of Exeter College, Oxford, and subsequently bishop of Bristol, extolled Locke as 'the Glory of that Age, and the Instructor of the present,' and replied to Tindal's *Christianity as Old as the Creation.* If Locke, who had believed that morality had the same demonstrative force as mathematics, could not produce a proof of this claim, how much less, he asks, could those, like Tindal, whose intellectual powers do not equal Locke's reason their religion from creation without recourse to revelation?[144]

John Leland's *A View of the Principal Deistical Writers* appeared in 1754. In the course of his review he adverts to Locke's *Reasonableness*, taking Locke's insistence upon the necessity of divine revelation as a rebuttal of the unnamed Lord Herbert;[145] and he cites Thomas Chubb's revision of *The Case of Deism fairly Stated* in which the claim is made that 'in order to render Christianity amiable,' Christian divines ornamented it with moral precepts which, far from originating in divine revelation, are drawn from deism. Leland endorses Benson's view that Locke had forestalled such a view with his conviction of the inadequacy of unaided human reason in moral affairs.[146]

There can be no doubt that some deists utilized Locke's epistemology to their own ends. Equally, there can be no doubt that he resented this, and sought to uphold the importance of revelation against the deists. While arguments from silence are never conclusive, the fact that not even the vociferous John Edwards branded Locke a deist is not without interest. Stillingfleet had his suspicions, but most eighteenth-century divines who pronounced upon the matter denied that Locke was a deist, and some of them regarded him as having been betrayed by Collins and abused by others in that broad category of advocates of reason and of the sufficiency of natural religion. More serious from the doctrinal point of view was the accusation of Socinianism, and to this I now turn.

II

The charge against Locke, in a nutshell, is that his understanding of the person of Christ and of the Trinity is deficient. Let us first hear him on these matters.

In the words of Arthur W. Wainwright, 'while Locke protested that he never denied the doctrine of the Trinity, he never took the trouble to affirm it.'[147] No exception can be taken to the first clause here. For example, when Stillingfleet published his *A Discourse in Vindication of the Doctrine of the Trinity* (1697) in answer to Toland's *Christianity Not Mysterious*, he classified Locke with Toland as 'the new men of ideas' and charged them with denying the Trinity. (We recall that in Stillingfleet's mind Locke's anti-scholastic views on substance, which we saw were ambivalent, were the underlying culprit in prompting his heterodoxy on the Trinity, the incarnation and the eucharist.) In reply Locke declared that 'in my whole Essay, I think there is not to be found any thing like an objection against the Trinity';[148] and one will look in vain for direct repudiations of the doctrine anywhere else in Locke's published writings. Wainwright's second clause requires qualification (a) because as the quotation at the beginning of this chapter shows, Locke could use what might be called a trinitarian pattern of speech without qualms; and (b) because of the likelihood that on occasion Locke took trouble not to affirm the Trinity not because he did not believe in it, but because, against the deists, for example, he did not wish to introduce hostages to fortune, and wished to rebut them on the precise ground of their denial of revelation; (c) because of Locke's strongly practical bent (over against wanton doctrinal scholasticism), which, in view of the imperfections of life prompted him to recommend the quest of happiness in 'the enjoyment of his, with whom there is fulness of joy, and at whose right hand are pleasures for evermore';[149] and (d) because of the seriousness with which Locke took the principle of the sufficiency of Scripture, in whose texts he could not find the term 'Trinity'.

This last point provides an excellent illustration of the difficulty of pinning Locke down on the issue. Locke writes to Stillingfleet with reference both to the Trinity and to the person of Christ:

> My lord, my Bible is faulty again; for I do not remember that I ever read in it either of these propositions, in these precise words, 'there are three persons in one nature, or, there are two natures and one person.' When your lordship shall show me a Bible wherein they are so set down, I shall then think them a good instance of propositions offered me out of scripture; till then, whoever shall say that they are propositions in the scripture, when there are no such words, so put

> together, to be found in holy writ, seems to me to make a new scripture in words and propositions, that the Holy Ghost dictated not. I do not here question their truth, nor deny that they may be drawn from the scripture: but I deny that these very propositions are in express words in my Bible. For that is the only thing I deny here; if your lordship can show them me in yours, I beg you to do it.[150]

If we take this statement at face value, it is clear that Locke is making a carefully restricted point, namely, that the precise doctrinal terms proposed by Stillingfleet are not written down in the bishop's way in Locke's Bible. He does not question the truth of the doctrines; he does not even 'deny that they may be drawn from scripture,' but they are not there as expressly dictated by the Holy Ghost. Leaving on one side the dictation theory of inspiration as not being germane to our present discussion, I should say that Locke grants, as we might nowadays say, that the doctrinal concepts are in the Bible, but the precise terms are not. This, no doubt, would be his answer to John Edwards, who associates Locke with the 'Gentlemen of Racovia' in denying mysteries, refusing to use the term 'Trinity' because it was not in the Bible, whilst inconsistently using 'sacrament' and 'Christianity' which are not there either.[151]

In view of the cumulative effect of points (a) to (d) above, I do not think we need concur in J. T. Moore's speculation that, while, as Moore points out, Locke undoubtedly crusaded against coined words which had 'scarce any clear and distinct *Ideas* which they are annexed to,' Locke's repeated request to Stillingfleet to show him where in Scripture 'Trinity' occurs 'may indicate his desire to characterize such a term as "empty".'[152] I am more inclined to take Locke's word that his motivation in replying to Stillingfleet was to distance himself from deists and Socinians alike lest, in view of the bishop's misrepresentations of his position, 'the world will be apt to think that I am the person who argue against the Trinity and deny mysteries, against whom your lordship directs these pages.'[153] There is no question that the Locke of 1662 affirmed both the doctrine of the Trinity and the human-divine nature of Christ, whilst recognizing that the human mind could not explain how these things could be so;[154] there is no question that especially from the 1690s onwards he was actively reviewing the matter; there is no hard evidence that he ever repudiated the doctrine; and there is no reason to doubt that his surprise was genuine when, in a letter to Molyneaux he wrote,

> My book crept into the world about six or seven year ago, without any opposition, and has since passed among some for useful, and, the least favourable, for innocent. But, as it seems to me, it is agreed by some men that it should no longer do so. Something, I know not what, is at last spied out in it, that is like to be troublesome, and therefore it must be an ill book, and be treated accordingly.[155]

On the assumption that Locke felt he could speak openly to his friend, we may affirm that at the very least these are not the words of one who deliberately set out to be a 'troubler of Israel' where doctrinal matters were concerned. He was not even, for example, in the mould of his contemporary the General Baptist Matthew Caffyn, whose avoidance of 'unrevealed sublimities' in his preaching made him suspect among his co-religionists who, nevertheless, in 1701 allowed a Latitudinarian interpretation of the disputed doctrinal points.[156] Finally, from the fact that in his letters to Limborch Locke argued strongly for the unity of God, we should not conclude to crypto-unitarianism on his part, for the unity of God was among the classical orthodox list of divine attributes.[157]

It must, however, be conceded that Locke's interpretation of relevant passages of Scripture were, to put it mildly, less than full-bloodedly pro-trinitarian. Indeed, some of them left the way open to Socinianizing interpretations. Since this matter has been fully discussed elsewhere[158] I need give two opposite examples only. Thus, Paul informs the Romans that he is writing 'Concerning [God's] son Jesus Christ our Lord, which was made of the seed of David according to the flesh, And declared to be the Son of God with power, according to the spirit of holiness, by the resurrection from the dead ...' In Locke's paraphrase, Paul writes

> concerning his son Jesus Christ our Lord (who according to the flesh, i.e. as to the body which he took in the womb of the blessed virgin his mother was of the posterity and lineage of David; according to the spirit of holyness i.e. as to that more pure and spiritual part which in him over ruled all and kept even his frail flesh holy and spotless from the least taint of sin, and was of another extraction, with most mighty power declared to be the son of god by his resurrection from the dead ...[159]

Clearly, Locke goes further than Paul here in characterizing the person of Christ; all the more significant, then, that he does not assert Christ's full humanity and divinity, and that he leaves open (as Paul does in the immediate context) the question whether an adoptionist Christology – that Christ was adopted as Son of God at some time during his earthly life prior to the resurrection – is appropriate. Although in a note Locke further defines 'the spirit of holyness' as 'that more pure and spiritual part in him which by divine extraction he had immediately from god', he does not make clear whether he had this part from eternity or from, or subsequent to, his birth, or whether, and if so to what degree, it differs from that bestowed upon everyone else. That the charge of Socinianizing is possible here cannot be denied.

On the other hand, Locke elsewhere remarks upon Ephesians 1:10, that prior to Satan's revolt, 'Christ at first had the Rule and Supremacy over all, and was Head over all.'[160] As Wainwright points out, this teaching, which is not found in *Reasonableness*, is 'inconsistent with Socinian teaching'.[161] But this readjusting of the balance towards orthodoxy may be deemed to be undermined if Locke were the author of 'Some General Reflections on the Beginning of St. John's Gospel,' where emphasis is placed upon the fact that the evangelist states his purpose to be that of persuading others to believe that Jesus is the Son of God, not of proving that Christ is eternally divine, or that the doctrine of the Trinity is viable. Rather, Jesus is Messiah, or Son of God, *ex officio*.[162]

More generally, we may note Locke's way of treating the claims of Christ and the work of the Holy Spirit. One appropriate starting-place is Locke's *A Discourse of Miracles* (1702), where 'miracle' is defined thus: 'A miracle then I take to be a sensible operation, which, being above the comprehension of the spectator, and in his opinion contrary to the established course of nature, is taken by him to be divine.'[163] He grants that on this definition an event 'should be a miracle to one, which is not so to another,' but this, he thinks, would apply to any definition of 'miracle'. To the objection that miracles may occur which are neither extraordinary nor supernatural, and hence have no value as attesting to divine revelation, he replies: 'To know that any revelation is from God, it is necessary to know that the messenger that delivers it is sent from God, and that cannot be known but by some credentials given him by God himself.'[164] He proceeds to argue that

> the number, variety, and greatness of the miracles wrought for the confirmation of the doctrine delivered by Jesus Christ, carry with them such strong marks of an extraordinary divine power, that the truth of his mission will stand firm and unquestionable, till any one rising up in opposition to him shall do greater miracles than he and his apostles did.[165]

In drawing to a conclusion he observes, with reference to Christ's miracles, that

> miracles being the basis on which divine mission is always established, and consequently that foundation on which the believers of any divine revelation must ultimately bottom their faith, this use of them would be lost ... if miracles be defined to be none but such divine operations as are in themselves beyond the power of all created beings, or at least operations contrary to the fixed and established laws of nature.[166]

In *The Reasonableness of Christianity* Locke discusses Jesus' miracles in some detail. Jesus announces that God's kingdom has come, but 'who the King was of this kingdom, he leaves to his miracles to point out.'[167] In his teaching Jesus first paves the way by explaining the nature of the kingdom of God in parables, and builds gradually towards his own messianic claim (not wishing to be mistaken for a revolutionary political leader),[168] for 'believing on, or in him ... signifies believing that he was the Messiah.'[169] The fact and meaning of Christ's Messiahship was not immediately grasped,

> And therefore, though his disciples believed him to be the Messiah, yet they neither understood it so well, nor were so well confirmed in the belief of it, as after that, he being crucified and risen again, they had received the Holy Ghost; and with the gifts of the Holy Spirit, a fuller and clearer evidence and knowledge that he was the Messiah. They then were enlightened to see how his kingdom was such as the scriptures foretold; though not such as they, till then, had expected. And now this knowledge and assurance, received from the Holy Ghost, was of use to them after his resurrection; when they could now boldly go about, and openly preach, as they did, that Jesus was the Messiah; confirming that doctrine by the miracles which the Holy Ghost empowered them to do.[170]

And yet, as at other points, so here. There is ambivalence in Locke's writing, for in 1684, for example, he observes to Edward Clarke that education (not the Holy Spirit) makes ninety-nine people out of a hundred what they are.[171] This prompts John Marshall to remark that

> from the date of this letter at the latest Locke's thought was very clearly focused not upon man's only possible hope of acting morally through regeneration by faith in Christ and the immediate operations of the Holy Spirit, but upon the natural means, particularly education, by which men could develop control of their desires by reason, and by which the development of the love of virtue would itself allow them to act morally.[172]

But this is not the whole story, for (to anticipate the next section of this chapter), *after* 1684 – indeed, in the very decade in which Locke was both reading Socinian works with interest and moving more firmly in the direction of 'faith' as *fiducia*, he can write, 'Christ's coming into the world was ... to reform the corrupt state of degenerate man; and out of those who would mend their lives, and bring forth fruit meet for repentance, erect a new kingdom.'[173] Granted that there is no specific reference to the Holy Spirit here, it is nevertheless clear that the amendment of life is not to be achieved by human effort or by education, but by the regenerative action of God in Christ.

The verdict of Marshall is just as far as it goes: 'Locke's intellectual commitment to eclecticism throughout his life invalidates any simple description of Locke as Socinian in a systematic, dogmatic sense.'[174] To this we may add his temperamental disinclination to speak boldly where the mysteries of the faith are concerned, his limited methodological objectives at certain points, and his genuine desire not to rock the theological boat or bring needless trouble upon himself – not least in view of the severe penalties which could be applied to those who denied the Trinity. Thus while agreeing with Alexander Gordon that where Locke and the Socinians were concerned, 'There was the same lay disengagement from scholasticism, the same purpose of toleration tempered by prudence, the same interest in minimising the essentials, and the same recurrence to Scripture, interpreted (that is to say rationalized) by common sense rather than by profound exegesis,' I should not, in view of the ambivalences noted, designate Locke in an absolute sense 'the Socinus of his age'.[175]

None of which, as we might by now expect, prevented some from seeing fire where others saw only the faintest wisp of smoke. Indeed, Stillingfleet and Edwards have already come before our view, and about each it is necessary to say a little more. Roused by Toland, Stillingfleet turned upon Locke, and in particular charged him and his friends of 'this new way of reasoning' with having 'almost discarded Substance out of the reasonable world'. This done, the doctrines of the Trinity, the Incarnation and the eucharist were undermined. Assuming that Locke embraces the Cartesian programme of clear and distinct ideas (something which Locke denied),[176] Stillingfleet takes Locke to mean that we can have no such idea of substance. Stillingfleet explains that he is so far in agreement with Locke, but his conclusion is that Locke's way of ideas from sensation and reflection yields insufficient ideas to our reason. The mind must in addition form some general ideas which do not derive from the comparison of ideas gained from sensation and reflection, but which are formed as distinct notions of things from particular ideas; 'And among these general Notions of things, or rational Ideas, Substance is one of the first.'[177] This is the epistemological crux of the matter. Locke has little place for general principles of reason, and teaches that certainty comes by intuited ideas, while Stillingfleet affirms that 'all the Certainty we can attain to, is from General Principles of Reason, and necessary Deductions made from them.'[178] The upshot for Stillingfleet is that Locke's epistemology prohibits our having any ideas of persons or objects as substances having modes and attributes; and if we cannot have such ideas concerning human beings, how much less can we have knowledge of God as one substance in three persons? When Locke went so far as to admit that '[S]ubstance is supposed always something, besides the extension, figure, solidity, motion, thinking, or other observable idea, though we know not what it is,'[179] Stillingfleet was not impressed. The bishop had good reason to feel exasperated by ploys of this kind, and his outburst is understandable: could not Locke easily have cleared up any misapprehensions and 'declared to the World, that you owned the *Doctrine of the Trinity*, as it hath been received in the Christian Church, and is by ours in the *Creeds and Articles of Religion*?'[180] But, as we saw, Locke did little more than reiterate the fact that he had never denied the doctrine and was not concerned to do so. What little more he did included his reiterated observation that the Apostles' Creed is the ground of baptism in the Church of England, and that that Creed is devoid of a trinitarian formula.[181]

The comment of Gerard Reedy on the Locke–Stillingfleet dispute is instructive:

> Alluding to St. John and early Christian heresies in a sermon on Christmas Day 1693, Bishop Stillingfleet asked: 'What could be more uneasie to so true a lover of Christ as *St. John* was, that he lived to see his Doctrine so perverted, and his Design in so great a measure rendered ineffectual?' In the midst of the Trinitarian controversy, the Bishop might as well have been speaking of himself and the other great divines who had been born in the 1630s: Isaac Barrow, South, and Tillotson. All Anglican rationalists, they all had stressed the perfect reasonableness of the doctrine and morality of Christianity. Barrow had died in 1677; the others lived to see their doctrine 'perverted.'
>
> Having praised the reasonableness of Christianity, in their old age they are forced to turn and argue with those who claim reasonableness not simply as a desirable quality of Christianity but as the only criterion for true doctrine ... The divines find themselves off balance in the Trinitarian controversy; they experience an attack from the theological left, towards which they had been moving their congregations for thirty years.[182]

Recalling the dispute with hindsight, William Whiston remarked that 'Dr. Bentley, Bp. *Stillingfleet's* Chaplain told me, that he believ'd Mr. *Lock's* thorough Confutation of the Bishop's Metaphysics about the Trinity, hastened his End.'[183]

More robust than Stillingfleet, if blunter in mind, John Edwards entered the lists against Locke in 1695, taking his cue from Locke's *Reasonableness*. We have already recorded his opposition to Locke's 'one article' of faith, Locke denies as indicative of Socinianizing tendencies: by advancing the statement 'Jesus is the Messiah' as the one indispensable article of faith, Locke denies the Trinity, and proclaims himself as 'all over Socinianized'.[184] Edwards even declared that, if not an atheist, a Socinian inclines to atheism.[185] This stung Locke into a prompt reply in the same year: *A Vindication of the Reasonableness of Christianity, &c. from Mr. Edwards's Reflections.* Locke quotes Edwards's charge against him thus:

> When [Locke] proceeds to mention the advantages and benefits of Christ's coming into the world, and appearing in the flesh, he hath not one syllable of his satisfying for us; or, by his death, purchasing life or salvation, or any thing that sounds like it. This, and several other things, show, that he is all over socinianized.[186]

Locke replies:

> [Edwards] might have taken notice of these words in my book, 'From this estate of death, JESUS CHRIST RESTORES all mankind to life.' And a little lower, 'The life which Jesus Christ restores to all men.' And p. 109, 'He that hath incurred death for his own transgression, cannot LAY DOWN HIS LIFE FOR ANOTHER, as our Saviour professes he did.' This, methinks, SOUNDS SOMETHING LIKE 'Christ's purchasing life for us by his death.' But this reverend gentleman has an answer ready; it was not in the place where he would have had it in, it was not where I mention the advantages and benefits of Christ's coming. And therefore, I not having there one syllable of Christ's purchasing life and salvation for us by his death, or anything that sounds like it: this, and several other things that might be offered, show that I am 'all over socinianized.' A very clear and ingenuous proof, and let him enjoy it.[187]

Locke further invites Edwards to consider his purpose in writing his book. It was written 'for those who were not yet thoroughly, or firmly, christians ... who either wholly disbelieved, or doubted of the truth of the christian religion'.[188] Hence his resolve to mention only those points in which all Christians agree. Locke ruefully observes that 'some men will not bear it, that any one should speak of religion, but according to the model that they themselves have made of it.'[189]

By all of this Edwards, one might say, was underwhelmed, and back he came in the following year with his rollicking tract, *Socinianism Unmask'd.* At one point, concerning the Trinity, he comes as close as he ever does to conceding a difficulty, but at once surmounts it:

> Indeed there is a *Difficulty* in this and several Other Truths of the Gospel as to the *Exact Manner* of the things themselves, which we shall never be able to comprehend, at least not this side of Heaven:

> but there is *no Difficulty* as to the Reality and Certainty of them, because we know they are Revealed to us by God in the Holy Scriptures. Nay, as to the thing it self, thus far we can apprehend that it is not impossible or absurd that the Three Distinct Persons in the Deity should be One God, for there may be a Plurality of Persons in the same Infinite Essence. Every Person doth not require a Single Particular Essence.[190]

Pulling out all the stops, Edwards bids us note the

> Affinity and Correspondence which hath been between the *Turks* and this Gentleman's Party. *Servetus* conferr'd notes with the *Alcoran*, when he undertook to fetch an Argument out of it to disprove the *Deity* of our Saviour. It is observable that those Countreys of *Europe* which border on the *Sultan's* dominions, as *Hungary, Transylvania,* &c. abound with *Socinians* and *Antitrinitarians.*[191]

Socinianism is not only wrong, but dangerous and pernicious; it is 'a Contrivance for the bringing in of *Darkness* and *Barbarism* into the Christian world'.[192] Edwards does not accuse Locke of intending such a result: he can even sound like a harbinger of the writ-avoiding technique of *Private Eye*: 'it would be quite wrong to suggest that ...', when he explains, 'I charge him not with any such thing as a formal designing of this. (No: I will not entertain such a thought) but I only take notice how serviceable his Papers and Opinions are to ths purpose.' He proceeds to repeat his charge that 'those Texts of Scripture which respect the Holy *Trinity* were either disregarded by him, or were interpreted by him after the *Anti-trinitarian* Mode.'[193] While in general I think it more appropriate to enjoy Edwards than to reply to him, I think it must be said here that Locke interprets no texts in an anti-trinitarian mode, but that he does not interpret them in a positively trinitarian way. On this point he had already replied to Edwards. He concedes that he has omitted many more pasages than those Edwards notices, but claims to have included those 'which contain what our Saviour and his apostles preached, and required assent to, to make men believers'.[194] We are here back at the position that while there may be many other doctrines that Christians ought to believe, there is one doctrine (albeit one with a broad connotation), belief in which suffices to make a person a Christian, namely, that Jesus is the Messiah.

Locke was not without his defenders, though some of them,

like Stephen Nye, who embraced a variety of Sabellianism, and wrote favourably of unitarians and others, were not such as to impress a high Calvinist like Edwards: indeed, Edwards opposed Nye's *The Exceptions of Mr. Edwards, in his Causes of Atheism* (1695) in an addendum to *Socinianism Unmask'd.* Against Edwards's assertion of the eternal generation of the Son, Nye asks, 'Does he not know that Jesus is the *only Son* of *God*, by reason of that Generation which befell him in Time?"[195] He upholds Locke's position on the unity of God as scriptural: '*God is a Person*, or a perfect intellectual Nature or Substance, and ... he is the *only one* such; ... to deny either of these Propositions, is to me to deny the Truth of Holy Scripture ... in the chief Fundamental of all Religion.'[196] He quotes texts of Scripture to show 'not only that God and the Father are the same Person, and that the same is plainly distinguished from our Lord Christ ... but that the Son is no more the same God that sent him, than he is the same Father that sent him.'[197]

From the orthodox side, and less sensationally than Edwards, Thomas Burnet also complained that Locke had played down if not completely overturned the idea of Christ's satisfaction and mediatorial work.[198] The nonjuror John Milner was similarly concerned by evidences of Socinianism which he detected in Locke's writings. He quotes Locke as saying that some Scripture mysteries will always be mysteries to him, suggesting that if Locke had omitted the last two words and allowed that some things are essentially mysterious, he might more easily have escaped the charge of unitarianism.[199] As it is, Milner finds Locke evasive:

> As to the Doctrines of the Trinity, the Incarnation of the Son of God, and his Satisfaction, it is so well known what the *Socinians* hold, that it is wholly needless to cite or set down the Words of any of them: And if Mr. *Lock* had been pleas'd to let the World know plainly what he held as to these weighty points, he would have done a great Kindness to others in freeing them from their jealousies of him, and certainly no small Kindness to himself.[200]

That Milner has a point cannot be gainsaid. We have found Locke to prevaricate upon texts which might have been interpreted, as they generally were, in a much more full-blooded trinitarian or high Christological sense than he allowed; and it is not impossible that clearer hints on the doctrines in question could have been given without Locke's tumbling into the scholastically systematic pitfalls which he deplored so much. Milner proceeds to examine biblical texts concerning which Locke says that they do 'not necessarily import the Deity of our Saviour, and the Doctrine of Eternal Generation'[201] (though, as we have seen, in his later *Paraphrase* he counters Socinianism on the latter point). Locke's is the unexceptionable point that 'Son of God' is an ambiguous term, and that on the lips of people so various as John the Baptist, Nathanael, Peter, Martha, the sanhedrin, the Roman centurion and others it should not be taken as always signifying the doctrine of the eternal generation of the Son. Again, as we saw in connection with the 'one article,' Milner suspects that Locke's advocacy of 'Jesus is the Messiah,' and his equating 'Messiah' with 'Son of God' is a way of not saying (if not, with the Socinians, of denying) that he is fully divine.[202] William Carroll made an analogous point in 1707, when he charged both Locke and Collins with making human and divine reason one and the same thing, thereby opening the door to Socinianism, deism and atheism'.[203]

By contrast, William Whiston rose to Locke's defence against the author of an anonymous pamphlet, *A Discourse of Free Thinking.* As if from a great height he regretted that such authors do not

> well consider what Ends they serve, when they unwarily stigmatize such men as the Archbishop [Tillotson], Mr. *Lock, &c.* with the Names of *Socinian*, *Deist*, or *Atheist*; It being certainly not the way to support the Credit of Religion, or any of its Doctrines in the World, to have it thought that the most considering, fair, and judicious Persons are dissatisfied or Unbelievers; and such Suspicions proving, generally, upon Enquiry, intirely contrary to Truth, and built on no Foundation in the World.[204]

In a Postscript Whiston presents himself as the vindicator of the wantonly abused:

> Since Mr. *Lock* is here and every where esteem'd an eminent *Free-Thinker*; and that not seldom in the irreligious sense of the Words; nay has been very often esteem'd not better than a *Deist*; I shall here, by way of Vindication of his Memory, and in Hopes that his Authority may make some Impression on all of us, and particularly on the real

> irreligious *Free Thinkers* themselves, produce unquestionable Evidence of his fixed and last Sentiments about such Matters, from his own Words in two Letters to two of his intimate Friends.[205]

He proceeds to quote from Locke's letters to two of his friends. In the first, Locke wishes the recipient 'the Everlasting Happiness of the World to come, God send us a happy meeting in the Resurrection of the Just'; in the second, his letter delivered posthumously to Collins, he refers to his 'Hopes of another life'.[206] In Whiston's opinion, 'The Expressions ... are so sensible, serious and christian; and come from a Person of such great Sagacity, Integrity, and Freedom, as to make them exceeding Remarkable.'[207] We may recall that Locke said of Whiston,

> He is one of those sort of writers, that I always fancy should be most esteemed and encouraged. I am always for the builders who bring some addition to our knowledge, or, at least some new thing to our thoughts. The finders of faults, the confuters and pullers down, do not only erect a barren and useless triumph upon human ignorance, but advance us nothing in the acquisition of truth.[208]

With hindsight Whiston reflected upon his own trinitarian teaching, and placed himself in a long line of distinguished servants of truth, including Locke:

> [T]he most Learned and Impartial, both Papists and Protestants, and those of our Church in particular, have in this last Age been forc'd to leave the vulgar Notions in that Matter, and to come still nearer and nearer, to that most Primitive and Rational Account which I plead for, as appears by *Erasmus*, *Grotius*, *Petavius*, *Huetius*, Dr. *Cudworth*, Bp. *Pearson*, Bp. *Bull*, the Bp. of *Gloucester*, Mr. *Locke*, and many others. So that my Notions are so far from New, that they are rather the proper and last Result of the Enquiries of the Learned since the Reformation.[209]

Further support for Locke came from Catharine Cockburn in 1726/7, who took up the cudgels against Winch Holdsworth, fellow of St John's College, Oxford. In 1720 Holdsworth had preached an Eastertide sermon before the University, in which he accused Locke of being a Socinian.[210] The emphasis of the sermon was upon the resurrection, and to this I shall come in due course. Mrs Cockburn addresses the general complaint thus:

> The great zeal Mr. *Locke* showed for the conversion of Deists, the serious veneration he expresses for the divine revelation, and (how little soever he was fond of particular systems) the care he took not to oppose any established articles of faith, make it a work worthy of a sincere Christian to support his character against the injudicious [*sic*] of those, who have reproached him as a *Socinian* heretic, an enemy, an underminer of religion.[211]

Since Holdsworth adduces no evidence for his claim that Locke is a Socinian, she feels her first task is to clear his name on that score. She insists that Locke does not deny the Trinity, and claims that the only reason why Stillingfleet raised the matter with him was that some enemies of the faith had taken some of Locke's expressions and used them to their own ends.[212] None of this satisfied Holdsworth, who nailed his colours to the mast in no uncertain terms:

> Mr. Lock hath Usurped in the Empire of Learning too Much, and too Long. It is Time He should be deposed from his Tyranny; And brought down to His Proper Sphere. It was not to be endured, that Religion should be Sacrificed in the Worship paid to Him. It is, as servile to follow Blindly the Tract of a Freethinker, as, the most Inveterate Imposition.[213]

He reminds Mrs Cockburn that there is more to Socinianism than the denial of the Trinity, and lists the following doctrines which Locke shares with Socinians: the notion of God is not naturally implanted in human minds; the soul sleeps between death and the resurrection; there is no original corruption deriving from Adam; Christ did not make a proper satisfaction to divine justice for human sin; the wicked will not suffer eternal torments hereafter; and the same bodies shall not be raised at the general resurrection.[214] Undeterred, Catharine Cockburn returned to the fray in manuscripts which were first published in her *Works* of 1751 under the title, *A Vindication of Mr. Locke's Christian Principles.* She reiterated her claim that Locke was no Socinian and paid particular attention to the resurrection question.

That we are here confronted by a bewildering variety of finely tuned perceptions may be illustrated by reference to Isaac Watts. On the one hand we recall that (in verse not his greatest) Watts has doubts as to whether he will see Locke in heaven because of Locke's indefinite attitude towards central Christian doctrines:

> Reason could scarce sustain to see
> Th'Almighty One, th'eternal Three,
> Or bear the infant deity;
> Scarce could her pride descend to own
> Her Maker stooping from his throne,
> And drest in glories so unknown,
> A ransom'd world, a bleeding God,
> And heav'n appeas'd with flowing blood,
> Were themes too painful to be understood.

The poem concludes with Watts's vision of Locke in heaven, asking forgiveness:

> Sister of faith, fair charity,
> Shew me the wondrous man on high,
> Tell how he sees the godhead Three in One;
> The bright conviction fills his eye,
> His noblest powers in deep prostration lie
> At the mysterious throne.
> 'Forgive, he cries, ye saints below,
> The wav'ring and the cold assent
> I gave to themes divinely true;
> Can you admit the blessed to repent?
> Eternal darkness veil the lines
> Of that unhappy book,
> Where glimmering reason with false lustre shines.
> Where the mere mortal pen mistook
> What the celestial meant.'[215]

In a footnote Watts explains that Locke's *Annotations* on Romans 3:25 and his *Paraphrase* on Romans 9:5

> inclined some readers to doubt whether he believed the deity and satisfaction of Christ. Therefore in the fourth stanza I invoke charity, that by her help I may find him out on heaven, since his Notes on 2 Cor. v, ult. and some other places, give me reason to believe he was no Socinian, though he has darkened the glory of the gospel, and debased christianity, in the book which he calls The Reasonableness of it, and in some of his other works.[216]

On the other hand, Watts himself can write on the same range of doctrines in such a way as to cause puzzlement. He proposes a dual Christ having a human soul, who dwells in God. This, he thinks, 'enables us to answer many inconveniences and appearing absurdities which the arians fling upon the common explications of the trinity'.[217] For this he was trounced from one side by the staunch Calvinist Independent, Abraham Taylor, who thought 'he ought to beg pardon of the Church of Christ,' for, among other things,

> obtruding upon us the Socinian scheme, in a new dress, and yet not knowing he does so: for making Christ to be, as to his Divinity, only a property of God, and for denying his true humanity, by making him to have a soul vastly above what is human[218]

while from the other side the Arian Presbyterian Caleb Fleming, using the same texts as Watts, advised that the only appropriate course for Watts was to agree that the Son was a created being.[219]

In his lectures to students, Taylor did not spare Locke himself:

> The Popish writers have run into great confusion in endeavouring to make free thinking consistent with implicit faith in the dictates of their church; and Mr. Locke, who let his admirers say what they will of him, was no better than a Socinian in principle, and but a mean Divine for that sort, and no great friends of revelation, has interlarded his work with a great many subtleties, which tend to bring persons to have a mean and low view of what is properly mysterious. These men were certainly persons of deep thought, and penetrating genius, but their learning was very inconsiderable, and their reading was not large. This, in a particular manner, was true of Mr. Locke. Those that knew him personally were satisfied, that, as to ancient literature he was but very superficial.[220]

With his last sentence Taylor puts Locke in his place in a peculiarly English manner![221]

As the century moved on, relatively fewer gave detailed attention to Locke's position on the Trinity and the person of Christ. Perhaps this is in part a function of Locke's elusiveness on these doctrines; it is certainly attributable to the fact that those who sought support in moving in an Arian direction, and those who rebuked them, variously found more positive solace or a bolder target in Samuel Clarke's influential work, *The Scripture Doctrine of the Trinity* (1712). But occasionally Locke was referred to in connection with these doctrines. Thus, although John Conder,

Independent tutor at the evangelical Homerton academy, happily classed Locke with the Arians Daniel Whitby and John Taylor, branding them all Socinians,[222] Joseph Priestley declared that 'Had all such men as *Locke*, *Clarke*, and *Newton*, acted with perfect uprightness and true wisdom, as well as thought with freedom, the Church of England would not now have been Trinitarian';[223] while the New England transcendentalists, to whom Locke was a 'symbol of commitments too diverse and too profoundly rooted to permit facile compromise,'[224] appealed to Locke for support in ways some of which would almost certainly have surprised him.

III

I now turn to the views of Locke and the divines on humanity, sin and salvation, though with the caution that the question of personal identity will be reserved to the concluding section of this chapter, where immortality, resurrection and eternal life will be under consideration.

We may take as our starting-point the following words from the fluent pen of Carl L. Becker:

> What Locke aimed at no doubt, what the eighteenth century acclaimed him for having demolished, was the Christian doctrine of total depravity, a black, spreading cloud which for centuries had depressed the human spirit. For if, as Locke maintained, the mind at birth was devoid of implanted and ineradicable ideas and dispositions, was in fact no more than a blank white sheet of paper upon which the outer world of nature and human association was to write whatever of good or ill repute might be found recorded there, why, then, the mind of man was a record made by that outer world: jazzed and discordant now that the outer world was so; a satisfying and ordered symphony when that outer world should become, as it might, what men had conceived it ought to be. This was Locke's great title to glory, that he made it possible for the eighteenth century to believe with a clear conscience what it wanted to believe, namely, that since man and the mind of man were shaped by that nature which God had created, it was possible for men, 'barely by the use of their natural faculties,' to bring their ideas and their conduct, and hence the institutions by which they lived, into harmony with the universal order. With what simple faith the age of enlightenment welcomed this doctrine![225]

While some in the eighteenth century may have lauded Locke for having dispelled the 'black, spreading cloud' of total depravity, Becker surely goes too far in saying that this was Locke's aim. On the contrary, as W. M. Spellman has shown,[226] there is a good deal of evidence to suggest that at this point Locke was much more in sympathy with his contemporary and predecessor Puritans, and with a line of Broad Churchmen from Jeremy Taylor to Tillotson, than with some of the rational divines who succeeded him. Moreover, Locke, though insisting on human rationality, never lost sight of the reality of actual and universal human moral weakness and sin.[227]

Proceeding step by step, and guided at this point by John Marshall, we may first note that in all probability the early Locke's view was realistic (even tending towards the pessimistic) in delineating the human condition as being in urgent need of God's grace for salvation. In this view he was confirmed by the Jansenist Pierre Nicole, whose view of human nature was Augustinian, and part of whose *Essais de morale* Locke translated in 1676.[228] Later, in the interests of his political theory, Locke needed to distance himself from Robert Filmer's view of absolute monarchical power as not only handed down from Adam, but as accruing to humanity because we are all represented in Adam. But if Locke wished to deny this in the interests of a non-absolutist political theory in which the people freely choose their representative leaders,[229] he must, by analogy, have difficulty with Paul, Augustine and Calvin construed as teaching that Adam's sin and guilt are imputed to all humanity because Adam is our representative. Locke concludes that sin is universal in that every person actually sins, and that each person's guilt is the consequence of freely willed sinful behaviour, and not the result of the imputation of Adam's guilt. Furthermore, in *Some Thoughts concerning Education* the individual's bias towards certain 'predominant passions, and prevailing inclinations' is attributed to human nature, not to the Fall.[230] Elsewhere he paraphrases Paul on 'the flesh' – that which deflects human beings from their proper course – thus:

> For the inclinations and desires of the flesh are contrary to those of the spirit: And the dictates and inclinations of the spirit are contrary to those of the flesh; so that under these contrary impulses you doe not doe the things that you propose to yourself. (Galatians 5:17).

In a note he explains that 'By *flesh* is meant all those vitious, and irregular appetites, inclinations, and habitudes whereby a man is turned from his obedience to that eternall law of right, the observance whereof god always requires and is pleased with.'[231]

Underlying all of this is Locke's conviction that a person cannot be punished for another's sin – even Adam's. In this, as on such other topics as toleration, he was not entirely original. As early as the 1660s, when he was a tutor at Christ Church. Oxford, Locke had set his students to read *The Practice of Christian Graces, or the Whole Duty of Man* (1659) and *The Gentleman's Calling* (1660) by the royalist anti-Presbyterian Richard Allestree, whose views on original sin were largely compatible with Locke's;[232] and his friend Limborch likewise moved in a similar direction.

Locke turns still more definitely against imputation (and this in such a way as to veer towards the Socinian authors whom he had been reading from 1679 onwards) in *The Reasonableness of Christianity*. Locke here sets out from the doctrine of the Fall. What Adam lost was immortality and the happiness of unsullied Eden. Locke's paraphrase of Romans 5:12 underlines the point:

> You must know, that as by the act of one man Adam the father of us all, sin entered into the world, and death, which was the punishment annexed to the offence of eating the forbidden fruit enterd by that sin for that Adams posterity thereby became mortal.[233]

Adam was punished for his own sin, and so, likewise, are we all. We 'all die in Adam, yet none are truly punished, but for their own deeds' – on which point Paul is invoked: 'God will render to every one.' How? 'According to his deeds' (Romans 2:6).[234] Locke values Paul's words not least because they can appear by analogy to endorse a central plank in his political platform, namely, that rulers rule only by the consent of the people (however limited a connotation that term may have had in his mind). That is to say, he objects to the notion that 'all Adam's posterity [is] doomed to eternal, infinite punishment, for the transgression of Adam, whom millions had never heard of, and no one had authorised to transact for him, or be his representative.'[235] This may be read both as an implication of Locke's view of individual responsibility – we cannot excuse our wrongdoing by reference to Adam's sin – and as an ethical protest against a

God who would countenance an arrangement whereby people necessitated to sin were then punished for sinning.[236]

Equally, Locke gives no credence to the polar opposite (deist) view, that (natural religion being all in all) 'there was no redemption necessary, and consequently, that there was none.'[237] Indeed, there is a strong hint in Locke's epistemology and ethics as propounded in the *Essay* that left to their own devices human beings are in an important sense impotent. He there concedes that although human beings have 'Light enough to lead them to the Knowledge of their Maker, and the sight of their own Duties,'[238] 'I am forced to conclude, that *good*, the *greater good*, though apprehended and acknowledged to be so, does not determine the *will*, until our desire, raised proportionally to it, makes us *uneasy* in the want of it.'[239] This very uneasiness, as Locke's *Paraphrase* of Paul makes clear at a number of points, is indicative of our inability, unaided, to do as we ought, and hence of the need of redemption.[240]

The nub of the matter is that for Locke the Fall has incapacitated us – not least our will – and thus Christ's saving work is necessary to salvation. But what has Christ done? Locke explains that 'Adams laps came barely for the satisfaction of his own appetite, and desire of good to him self: but the restauration was from the exuberant bounty and good will of Christ towards men, who, at the cost of his own painfull death, purchased life for them.'[241] There could scarcely be a more poignant testimony to the benefits of Christ than that uttered by Locke on his deathbed: 'I humbly thank God, for all his goodness and mercies to me, but above all for his redemption of me by Jesus Christ.'[242]

Ardent though the testimony is, as with the Trinity and the person of Christ, it would be claiming too much to say that Locke has a fully worked-out *theory* of the atonement to offer us. He does, however, as we have seen, express his understanding of the purpose of Christ's coming in terms which cannot easily be misconstrued: 'Christ's coming into the world was ... to reform the corrupt state of degenerate man; and out of those who would mend their lives, and bring forth fruit meet for repentance, erect a new kingdom.'[243] Such reformed persons live by the law of faith and, against John Edwards (and mixing the language of free grace beloved of Calvinists with the reiterated claim for the one article of faith which Edwards repudiated), Locke declares, 'I see no reason why every body, with me, should not magnify the goodness and condescension of the Almighty, who having, out of his free grace, proposed a new law of faith to sinful and lost man; hath, by that law, required no harder terms, nothing as absolutely necessary to be believed, but what is suited to vulgar capacities, and the comprehension of illiterate men.'[244] Further, against Edward's complaint that since he is a 'Disciple of *Socinus*'[245] Locke has no place for Christ's satisfaction, Locke reminds Edwards of passages 'where I say, that the design of Christ's coming was to be offered up, and speak of the work of redemption; which are expressions taken to imply our Saviour's satisfaction'.[246] Again, underscoring Bold's defence Locke avers, 'it is very hard for a christian, who reads the scripture with attention, and an unprejudiced mind, to deny the satisfaction of Christ'; though he at once grants that since the word is variously defined by those who use it, and since it is a stumbling-block to those (the deists) whom he was addressing, he left it on one side.[247] More positively, he reiterates his view that while there is 'no condemnation of any one, for what his fore-father Adam had done,' we have inherited death from Adam. From this death we are restored to life by Christ, and apart from it we should have been 'lost for ever'.[248] Moreover, as he elsewhere remarks on Ephesians 2:8:

> The Apostle, whose aim it is in this Epistle to give [Christians] an high Sense of God's extraordinary Grace and Favour to them, and to raise their Thoughts above the mean Observances of the Law, shews them that there was nothing in them; no Deeds or Works of theirs, nothing that they could do to prepare or recommend themselves, contributed ought to the bringing them into the Kingdom of God under the Gospel; that it was all purely the Work of Grace, for they were all dead in Trespasses and Sins, and could do nothing, not make one Step or the least Motion towards it. Faith, which alone gained them Admittance, and alone opened the Kingdom of Heaven to Believers, was the sole Gift of God; Men by their natural Faculties could not attain to it. 'Tis Faith which is the Sourse and Beginning of this new Life; and the Gentile World, who were without Sense, without Hope of any such thing, could no more help themselves, or do any thing to procure it themselves, than a dead Man can do anything to procure himself Life. 'Tis God here does all; by Revelation of what they could never discover by their own natural Faculties, he bestows on them the Knowledge of the *Messiah*, and the

> *Faith* of the Gospel; which, as soon as they have received, they are in the Kingdom of God, in a new State of Life; and being thus quicken'd by the Spirit, may as Men alive work if they will ... [E]ternal Life is the Gift of God, the Gift of Free Grace, since their Works of sincere Obedience afford no manner of Title to it ... and so they are still saved by Grace.[249]

Here Locke almost vehemently reiterates an anti-Pelagian stance. God's grace is prevenient; the very faith whereby people respond to grace is itself a gift; works should follow faith, but do not themselves justify; and (recalling his epistemology) revelation, communicated by the quickening Spirit, supplements the work of natural reason. All of this is thoroughly Pauline; so ardently is it expressed that it is difficult to believe that it is not Lockean too. Certainly Locke's realistic appreciation of the sinner's need causes one to query Maurice Cranston's unqualified assertion that

> Locke's biography is the story of a philosopher who squarely rejected the grim doctrine of the Fall of Man he learned in a Puritan childhood to develop a happy conception of the human race being born with natural rights to life, liberty and property and endowed with enough good sense to associate together for the peaceful enjoyment of those rights.[250]

It would seem that at most this is but one side of the coin.

On other related matters, however, Locke is not so clear. He does not think, with the Calvinists, that God predestined the elect to salvation, for this seems to him to obliterate human freedom and responsibility. But, as Marshall notes, it is not clear whether, with the Arminians, he thinks that God foreknew those who would freely respond to the call of the Gospel, or whether he holds that God simply saves those who as a matter of fact respond to the Gospel.[251] Moreover, if, according to Locke, Adam's guilt is not imputed to sinners, there is no clear suggestion in Locke's writings that human guilt is imputed to Christ. Locke construes Paul's claim in II Corinthians 5:12 that Christ was 'made to be sin' thus:

> For god hath made him subject to sufferings and death the punishment and consequence of sin as if he had been a sinner though he were guilty of noe sin, that we in and by him might be made righteous by a righteousness imputed to us by god.[252]

This might be taken as a Socinian interpretation; but lest we rush towards any over-hasty conclusions on this matter, A. W. Wainwright properly reminds us that Locke emphasized Christ's cross–resurrection victory over the devil to a degree that Socinians did not; and hence, 'In his understanding of the meaning of Christ's death, as in other aspects of his theology, Locke did not fit into the mould of any particular school.'[253]

As with the Trinity and the person of Christ, while a few, notably Edwards, hotly pursued Locke on the doctrines of humanity, sin and redemption, few positively embraced him in his entirety – possibly because of the difficulty in knowing exactly what was to be embraced; and some, who were frequently opposed to him on other matters, were ambivalent towards him on these points. Edwards apart, the poles of such discussion as there was may be represented by Richard West and Catharine Cockburn. West expresses his complaint thus: according to Locke, Christ came into the world

> to restore Mankind to that State, which was forfeited by the Sin of our *First Parents*. But as he makes Adam's Punishment to consist only in a Temporal Death, or a total ceasing to be; so does he confine the End and Design of our Saviour's coming into the World, to the freeing us from such a Death only, and restoring to us that Immortality, which our *First Parents* lost. Which overthrows the Notion of our Saviour's redeeming us from an Eternity of Torments, and makes the effect of Original Guilt no more than becoming subject to Death; and so destroys in a great measure the Doctrine of *Christ's Satisfaction.*[254]

In defence of Locke on this as on other matters, Catharine Cockburn argues that so far is Locke from Pelagianism and Socinianism, that he declares that 'death came upon all men by reason of *Adam's* sin.'[255] Locke further declares that Christ came to restore what was lost to us in Adam. Not, indeed, that Locke believed in hereditary guilt, 'which perhaps men would not have so readily received, or been so tenacious of, if it were not to excuse or attenuate their own guilt, by laying the blame on their forefather, or even on their Maker himself'.[256] Moreover, Locke certainly does not subscribe to Calvinist views of reprobation and '*unconditional decrees*'[257] – a point which reminds us that many orthodox divines had difficulty with Locke because of familiar and much-loved confessional language which they were *not* hearing from him, and which they regarded as a criterion of doctrinal soundness. Whitby had earlier agreed with Locke that Adam's guilt was not imputed to his descendants, and that guilt accrued too, and punishment was merited by, those who voluntarily flouted the law.[258]

Between the two poles of antagonism and support we find a number of divines who are puzzled by Locke's position, or ambivalent towards it. Milner, for example, is concerned at what Locke said, but is not as willing as others to equate his words with those of Socinus, the Racovian Catechism and Johannes Volkelius, which he cites:

> *Socinus* and his Followers deny Original Sin, and the Corruption of our Nature, because of *Adam's* Transgression ... Mr. Lock is not so positive as they are; but he says, that *the New Testament doth not any where take notice of the Corruption of Humane Nature in* Adam's *Posterity, nor tells us that Corruption seiz'd on all because of* Adam's *Transgression, as well as it tells us so of Death.*[259]

John Leland, in his temperate way, travelled with Locke as far as he could, but was forced to part company with him at a critical point. He first quotes Locke:

> 'God had by the light of Reason reveal'd to all Mankind, who wou'd make use of that Light, that he was good and merciful.' This is very true; but he had also revealed to them by the same Light, that he was just and wise and holy, a Hater and Punisher of Sin; and though they might know in general, that he is good and merciful, yet how far his Mercy wou'd extend, how far and in what Instances he wou'd pardon Sin, and when and how far he would think fit to punish it, they had nothing in the Light of Nature to give 'em certain Information.[260]

Locke-like objections to the imputation of Adam's sin to his descendants were prominently displayed in the work of a number of Arian Presbyterian divines, though few of them referred specifically to Locke, whose works, we recall, were read at the more liberal Dissenting academies. John Taylor of Norwich, in his work of 1740, *The Scripture-Doctrine of Original Sin* does not discuss Locke by name. He does, however, reject both imputed guilt – 'Imputed Guilt is imaginary Guilt'[261] – and, in his later work, *A Scheme of Scripture Divinity* (1762), original righteousness. The latter, he declares, could only have been produced in Adam without his knowledge or choice, and hence could only have been a natural instinct, not a moral quality.[262] That Taylor touched a raw nerve is clear from the fact that such prominent divines as John Wesley and Jonathan Edwards girded up their loins to rebuke him.[263]

Again, when the Presbyterian Arian Thomas Amory contributed the preface to the sermons of Samuel Chandler he felt it necessary to reassure his readers that a Lockean reading of Chandler was in order:

> Should any Readers be less pleased with some Sermons in the *fourth* volume, on a controverted subject, and think the account therein given of the *corruption* of *human nature* to be *aggravated* above fact and experience; we beg them to consider, – that the Doctor allows this *disorder* , as far as it is *natural* , to be in no sense our *fault*, or imputed to us as such by God our Creator; but to be merely a *trial* of our virtue, and obedience to our heavenly Father, who will, as becomes his equity and goodness, make every reasonable *allowance* for it, and grant answerable *assistance* to those who ask it, and who hath provided a suitable *remedy*. That the *honour* of God as our *Creator* and *moral Governor* is thus *vindicated*; and persons may amicably differ as to the *more* or *less* of this natural disorder and weakness, and be left to determine their sentiments by impartial observation and experience.[264]

By the time these words were published another pole of the discussion had come into view. It is not simply that Locke was opposed by high Calvinists and supported by Catharine Cockburn and, on a number of points at least, by the Arian divines; he also began to be opposed by some of the more decidedly rational divines. In a work of 1765 Francis Webb quotes Locke and then responds to him thus:

> '[T]hose who have lived in an *exact* conformity to the law of God, are out of the reach of death; but an exclusion from paradise, and loss of immortality, is the portion of sinners; of all those who have any way broke that law, and failed of a compleat obedience to it, by the guilt of any one transgression ... [B]ut Christian believers have the privilege to be under *the law of faith too*; which is that law, whereby God justifies a man for believing, though, by his works, he be not just or righteous; that is, though he comes short of perfect obedience to the law of works.' ... Is it reasonable to suppose, that a God of infinite goodness and mercy would require of his frail imperfect creature, man, a full, compleat, perfect and sinless obedience to his laws; or that he would punish the least breach of them with eternal death? – Surely there is something horrid in the supposition, and which

> appears to be inconsistent with all our rational ideas of infinite perfection.[265]

Webb grants that Locke supports his position by quoting such texts as 'Be ye perfect,' but these are not to be taken in a literal sense. Knowing frail humanity as he does, would God have expected perfection of us? Locke's reply to the effect that the purity of God's nature required the law of perfection does not satisfy Webb. He agrees with Locke that the law of reason must be the law for human beings, but he cannot agree that God would punish even the least breach of it with eternal death had he not found a way in Christ to justify some:

> To suppose that God would bring a creature into being, and give him a law for the rule of his conduct, enforced with the awful santions of eternal life and death, when, at the same time, he knew that this creature would not, or could not, comply with it; does, I confess, appear very extraordinary to me, and is quite inconsistent with my notions of the Supreme Being.[266]

Webb does not doubt that God's remedy for Adam's sin was 'the *best* that could be applied,'

> But surely Mr. Locke could not, with propriety, call this a *reasonable* doctrine. – Human reason cannot comprehend it – The mind of man, unassisted by a particular divine revelation, cannot conceive that the spilling the blood of an innocent creature, can possibly take away the sins of a guilty one, or be of any effect towards reconciling a sinful creature to God. There does not seem to be, in reason, any sort of correspondence or connection between the sufferings of an *innocent* being and the crimes of a *guilty* one.[267]

As to Locke's law of faith, Webb denies that it is consistent with infinite wisdom to require belief in any doctrine whatsoever as a substitute for that perfect obedience of which God found human beings were incapable:

> In how wretched a situation then are mankind left, upon Mr. *Locke's* plan! They must either pay a *perfect* obedience to the law of nature, which *he* says, no man ever *did*, and St. Paul says, 'no man ever *could*;' or they must believe Jesus *to be the Messiah*, or Son of God, in what our churchmen call the Gospel sense. Now this is what many may never be able to do, even though menaced with the punishment of *eternal death.*[268]

The upshot is that 'Mr. Locke's method of shewing the *reasonableness* of Christianity has certainly failed.'[269]

If Locke, Taylor, Webb and others based their objections against Calvinist views of imputation upon moral grounds, by the time the nineteenth century dawned, others were couching their objections in common-sense terms. Thus Nathaniel Taylor wrote to William Chauncy Fowler, 'We must have a sound, deep philosophy, and yet it must be common-sense philosophy, such as all the world can understand if we would defend orthodox theology. This can be done in my humble but very considerate opinion.'[270] Accordingly, moral depravity '*is man's own act consisting in a free choice of some object rather than God, as his chief good*'.[271]

But if relatively few supported or denounced Locke on humanity sin and salvation, the same cannot be said of personal identity, immortality and eternal life, to which themes I finally turn.

IV

A very considerable literature has been engendered by Locke's views on personal identity, substance and the possibility that matter might be accorded the power of thought. But it is not difficult to imagine that Locke *redivivus* would think that large tracts of this material, though interesting, miss his main point, which was practical *cum* moral. In *The Reasonableness of Christianity* he spells this out very clearly in a passage in which he reflects upon the significant advantage the Christian era has over preceding ages. Among the many blessings consequent upon the Saviour's coming

> is the great encouragement he brought to a virtuous and pious life; great enough to surmount the difficulties and obstacles that lie in the way to it, and reward the pains and hardships of those who stuck firm to their duties, and suffered for the testimony of a good conscience. The portion of the righteous has been in all ages taken notice of, to be pretty scanty in this world. Virtue and prosperity do not often accompany one another; and therefore virtue seldom had many followers.[272] ... Before our Saviour's time the doctrine of a future state, though it were not wholly hid, yet it was not clearly known in the world ... [I]t

> was no-where made an article of faith, and principle of religion, until Jesus Christ came; of whom it is truly said, that he, at his appearing, 'brought life and immortality to light.' ... How has this one truth changed the nature of things in the world, and given the advantage to piety over all that could tempt or deter men from it! ... The view of heaven and hell will cast a slight upon the short pleasures and pains of this present state, and give attractions and encouragements to virtue which reason and interest, and the care of ourselves, cannot but allow and prefer.[273]

Though cast in decidedly Christological terms, this confident assertion is consistent with Locke's view as expounded in the *Essay*. He there declares that people at large may give general approbation to the deliverances of the law of nature 'without either knowing, or admitting the true ground of Morality; which can only be the Will and Law of a God, who sees Men in the dark, has in his Hand Rewards and Punishments, and Power enough to call to account the Proudest Offender'. Indeed, while many will outwardly observe moral rules on grounds of self-interest, their 'Actions sufficiently prove, that they very little consider the Law-giver, that prescribed these Rules; nor the Hell he has ordain'd for the Punishment of those that transgress them'.[274] Again,

> All the great Ends of Morality and Religion, are well enough secured, without philosophical Proofs of the Soul's Immateriality; since it is evident, that he who made us at first begin to subsist here ... can and will restore us to the like state of Sensibility in another World, and make us capable there to receive the Retribution he has designed to Men, according to their doings in this Life.[275]

Which awesome thought should be a spur to virtuous living here below.[276]

Locke's conviction that the fact of the soul's immateriality was not crucial to resurrection and eternal life was radical indeed and, as we shall see, it prompted a considerable amount of discussion in his own time as well as subsequently. For the present, and in order to proceed one step at a time, I observe that Locke here rests upon an understanding of personal identity which he had begun to work out in 1683,[277] and which became the subject of a significant insertion in the second edition of the *Essay* (II.xxvii). In making this insertion Locke was responding to a suggestion of Molyneaux,[278] and, as Henry E. Allison has reminded us, he was also reviewing some of the implications of his empiricist rejection of Cartesian views of the indivisibility of the self. For if we do not have clear and distinct ideas of substance, as Locke says we do not, we cannot draw inferences therefrom concerning the human self.[279] His question therefore was, What, on the basis of my epistemology, can I say concerning personal identity? While not denying that 'man' is comprised of 'constantly fleeting Particles of Matter, in succession vitally united to the same organized body,' he denies that the 'person' is simply a material organism (thereby inviting entry to a Cartesian emphasis on the person as an incorporeal spirit which he elsewhere finds epistemologically inconvenient).[280] Conversely, he rejects the view that the locus of personal identity is in our soul, for it would be odd to use the word 'man' of an idea 'out of which Body and Shape is excluded'. Furthermore, it would follow that a particular soul might, by transmigration, enter a person from a preceding generation – or even a hog, and then the latter would be the man concerned, which is preposterous.[281]

By 'person' Locke understands

> a thinking intelligent Being, that has reason and reflection, and can consider it self as it self, the same thinking thing in different times and places; which it does only by that consciousness, which is inseparable from thinking, and as it seems to me essential to it.[282]

But what of continuing identity? This cannot be a matter of material continuity, says Locke, for if limbs were severed from a person, the person's identity would not be adversely affected.[283] Neither is it a question of continuity of normal thought processes, for in sleep, or when drunk, these are interrupted.[284] Contrary to the received tradition, then, Locke argues that personal identity 'consists, not in the Identity of Substance, but ... in the Identity of *consciousness*'.[285] As he further observes,

> Nothing but consciousness can unite remote Existences into the same Person, the Identity of Substance will not do it. For whatever Substance is there is, however framed, without consciousness, there is no Person: And a Carcass may be a Person, as well as any sort of Substance be so without consciousness.[286]

To return to our ethical starting-point: the crucially important element of consciousness for Locke is memory, for without this we are not able to accept responsibility for our past actions or our future aspirations. 'Person,' he writes,

> is a Forensick Term appropriating Actions and their Merit; and so belongs only to intelligent Agents capable of a Law, and Happiness and Misery. This personality extends it *self* beyond present Existence to what is past, only by consciousness, whereby it becomes concerned and accountable, owns and imputes to it *self* past Actions, just upon the same ground, and for the same reason, that it does the present.[287]

Locke is alive to the difficulties posed to his reliance upon memory by such phenomena as forgetfulness, experience-less sleep, and false memory. His general remedy is to appeal to 'the Goodness of God, who as far as the Happiness or Misery of any of his sensible Creatures is concerned in it, will not by a fatal Error of theirs transfer from one to another, that consciousness, which draws Reward or Punishment with it'.[288] By way of qualifying the unhelpful branding of Locke and Berkeley as alike 'empiricists', we may note that Berkeley's understanding of the person was quite different from that of Locke. Whereas Locke's 'person' has an adjudicating role over its past actions as agent, for example, in Berkeley's view the will and the understanding are distinct, the former having to do with our role as agent, the latter with our reception of ideas whose source is God.[289] Thus, as R. C. Tennant has pointed out,

> As an alternative to Locke, Berkeley's *esse est percipi* principle locates personal identity in the same theoretical structure as actual existence: both are created and sustained by the voluntary and attentive perception of God (the Father). A Person is not identified by its own consciousness (especially memory), nor by its creator's, but by the divine *act* of creation.[290]

Since the vast majority of Locke's contemporaries unquestioningly accepted the dualistic view that bodies are material substances while souls or minds are immaterial substances, Locke's refusal to ground on substance, coupled with his epistemological scepticism concerning our ability to know that a person is an immaterial substance, prompted intense debate. Not surprisingly, those divines who felt that the foundations of the faith were here being eroded were among the quickest to reply to Locke.[291]

In Cartesian fashion, Richard Bentley entered the lists with his contention that the soul is an immaterial substance or, as he calls it, a 'cogitative substance' and 'incorporeal inhabitant', essentially distinct from our bodies; accordingly, *pace* Locke, the idea of the transmigration of souls is not absurd.[292] For his part, Thomas Burnet queried Locke's view that the soul could be without thoughts during life, and could not understand what could cause a temporarily thoughtless soul to resume thinking again. It seemed clear to him that unless the soul is distinct from the body, 'when that is corrupted and dissolved, 'tis manifest she must be dissolved also.' Furthermore, if the soul could be without thoughts during life, why not after death? But, on Burnet's terms this would be tantamount to saying that the soul had no *life* after death. As his letter to Locke of 1697 shows, he cannot understand 'how far you allow us to be the *same Men*, and the *same Persons* then that we are now'.[293] He returns to the question later in the same year, expressing continuing puzzlement over Locke's positing of the thoughtless soul, and pressing him to consider whether the soul may not be a permanent substance distinct from the body.[294]

Burnet's *Second Remarks* were prompted by Locke's reply to his first letter, which was appended to Locke's second pamphlet against Stillingfleet, to whom I now turn. Stillingfleet was convinced that an individual's personhood derives from his or her own non-communicable substance: 'An *Individual, intelligent Substance*, is rather supposed to the making of a *Person*, than the proper *Definition* of it.'[295] That is to say,

> a *Person* is a compleat Intelligent Substance, with a peculiar manner of Subsistence; so that if it be part of another Substance, it is no Person; and on this account the Soul is no Person, because it makes up an entire Being by its Union with the Body.[296]

Locke's first *Reply* failed to satisfy Stillingfleet, who understands Locke as saying that 'nature' and 'person' are merely abstract complex ideas – a view which he deems a direct threat to the doctrine of the Trinity. He therefore contends for 'an Antecedent Foundation in the Nature of things upon which we form this Abstract idea' of common nature.[297] Locke's promptly written *Second Reply* to Stillingfleet, in which he insists that the soul's immateriality cannot be proved by natural reason but is known by revelation,[298] did not arrest the bishop's pen. He now fastens upon the adverse consequences of Locke's view of personal identity for the doctrine of the resurrection of the same body:

> The Dispute is not, how far *Personal Identity* in it self may consist in the very same Material Substance; for we allow the Notion of *Personal Identity* to belong to the same Man under several changes of Matter; but whether it doth not depend upon a *Vital Union* between the Soul and Body and the Life which is consequent upon it; and therefore in the *Resurrection* the same Material Substance must be reunited; or else it cannot be called a *Resurrection*, but a *Renovation*; i.e. it may be a *New Life*; but not *a raising the Body from the Dead.*[299]

Lamenting Locke's dismissal of substance in favour of consciousness, Stillingfleet shortly, and bluntly, asks, 'How comes *Person to stand for this* and nothing else?'[300] This is indicative of the novelty of Locke's proposal, and the degree to which not unintelligent people were flummoxed by it. The bishop in no way strays from the truth in claiming that in common parlance 'person' stands for a '*compleat intelligent Substance*'.[301] This was certainly Henry Lee's view, as is clear from his *Anti-Scepticism* (1702).[302] Such writers were not at all mollified by Locke's agreement that 'the more probable Opinion is, that this consciousness is annexed to, and the Affection of, one individual immaterial Substance,' for Locke (true to his epistemology) made no capital out of this, and was content to 'let Men according to their divers Hypotheses resolve of that as they please'.[303]

Locke's *Reply to the Right Reverend the Lord Bishop of Worcester's Answer to his Second Letter* was published in 1699, but it drew no further episcopal response; Stillingfleet died in the same year.

From his neo-Platonist perspective John Norris continued the debate by contending that the crucial constituent of personhood is not consciousness or memory, but the intuition of God. In him we know ourselves as persons.[304] In a different vein John Milner returns to Locke's denial that the immateriality of the soul could be proved; this, he thinks, weakens the proof of the soul's immortality, while Locke's agreement that 'there is a spiritual immaterial Substance' encourages Milner to hope that he thinks God is such, and that God is to be worshipped. If so, why does Locke baulk at the conclusion that such a one could be worshipped only by persons using their minds, 'which Minds are likewise spiritual immaterial Substances'?[305]

In 1702 the idea of the soul's necessary immateriality was refuted by one E.P. (said to be William Coward) in a pamphlet entitled, *Second Thoughts concerning Human Soul. Demonstrating the Notion of the Human soul, believ'd to be a Spiritual Immortal Substance, united to Human Body, to be a Plain Heathenish Invention, and not Consonant to the Principles of Philosophy, Reason, or Religion* ... A second edition followed in 1704. In 1703 John Broughton replied in his *Psychologia: Or, An Account of the Nature of the Rational Soul.* He opposes Locke's position on personal identity, especially the view that the immateriality of the soul is not the prerequisite of immortality.

A different slant was put upon the question of personal identity by Henry Felton of Oxford in 1725. He builds upon Norris's view that persons have their being in God, but develops it in relation to a functional view of human activity in the world. Far from being concerned (as in Locke, he declares) with the notion of intelligent beings abstracted from the body, 'person', 'In common Acceptation ... is very properly apply'd to the *characters* and *Offices* of Men in all their Transactions, *Sacred,* or *Civil, Public,* or *Private*'.[306]

Some more conventional *Remarks on some parts of Mr. Locke's Essay* were published by Isaac Watts in 1733. He quotes Locke to the effect that 'A *person* is a thinking intelligent being, which has reason and reflection, and can consider itself as itself... which it does only by that *consciousness,* which is inseparable from thinking.'[307] Watts finds this definition inadequate, and urges that 'the word *person* implies one thinking being, one intelligent substance, which is always the same whether it be or be not conscious and mindful of its own actions at different times and places.'[308] Watts grants that

> There is no need of debating the point about a man's being the same person with himself at the *present time,* because a man's own present consciousness will secure to him his own personal identity, though perhaps it will not continue it to himself alone. But the chief difficulty relates to his being the same with himself at *distant times.*[309]

Watts notes that Locke seems to allow that, by his definition of personal identity, two different people may be one and the same person. But this, he counters, would be false remembrance: 'It is only a delusive impression on the mind or fancy imitating the act of memory. And can such a frenzy be sufficient to turn two men into one person?'[310] Again, Locke 'seems to suppose, that real forgetfulness may make a distinct person as well as fancied memory may make the same'. But this turns upon Locke's distinction between 'man' and 'person' – a distinction Watts finds unacceptable.[311] Locke's way out of these difficulties, namely, his employment of 'person' in a forensic sense will not serve, not least because 'The word *person* is often used, if not most frequently, without any forensic sense.'[312] Watts acknowledges that in ordinary speech we may refer to a tall person, and that this phrase and others like it refer to qualities of the body. But the adequate and complete philosophical definition of the term is that a person is

> the same spirit united to the same body, that is, in short, *the same man*; person and man are here the same. Nor is this personal sameness altered or abolished, though the man should sometimes be so imposed upon by frenzy, as to suppose himself to have a conscious memory of actions which were not his own; or though he should be utterly forgetful of his own proper actions.[313]

His fellow Independent, Philip Doddridge, was in complete accord with Watts on this matter, adding that whether speaking of ourselves or of others, we do not make consciousness the only criterion of personhood. For 'no one is conscious on his having been born, nor of many other events and actions of his life, which nevertheless upon the evidence of reason and testimony, without consciousness, he would not at all scruple to apply to himself.'[314]

Joseph Butler was among others who queried Locke's reliance upon consciousness in his account of personal identity. He agrees with Locke that 'consciousness of what is past does ... ascertain our personal identity to ourselves,'

> yet to say that it makes personal identity, or is necessary to our being the same persons, is to say, that a person has not existed a single moment, nor done one action, but what he can remember; indeed none but what he reflects upon. And one should really think it self-evident, that consciousness of personal identity presupposes, and therefore cannot constitute personal identity any more than knowledge, in any other case, can constitute truth, which it presupposes.[315]

Butler finds Locke 'hasty' on this question, and urges that our consciousness that we are who we once were implies that

> this he, person, or self, must either be a substance, or the property of some substance. If he, in person, be a substance, then consciousness that he is the same person, is consciousness that he is the same substance. If the person, or he, be the property of a substance, still consciousness that he is the same property, is as certain a proof that his substance remains the same, as consciousness that he remain the same substance would be; since the same property cannot be transferred from one substance to another.[316]

But may we not be deceived in thinking that we are now the person that once we were? Here Butler calls a halt to argumentation and declares (echoing Berkeley),

> For it is ridiculous to attempt to prove the truth of those perceptions, whose truth we can no otherwise prove than by other perceptions of exactly the same kind with them, and which there is just the same ground to suspect; or to attempt to prove the truth of our faculties, which can no otherwise be proved than by the use or means of those very suspected faculties themselves.[317]

Austin Duncan-Jones aptly summarized Butler's position thus: '[W]e form or become aware of the idea of personal identity by the very same act in which we recognise instances of it.'[318] I resist the feeling that Butler's victory is too easily won, in that notwithstanding the problematic nature of Locke's position – which Locke himself fully recognized – Locke did at least have an acute appreciation of the difficulties attaching to the substance philosophy, the viability of which Butler was only too ready to presuppose. None of which prevented Reid from recasting Butler's position in his own mould. 'It may be observed,' he writes of Locke's doctrine, that 'not only is consciousness confounded with memory, but, which is still more strange, personal identity is confounded with the evidence which we have of our personal identity.'[319] With regard to Locke's forensic use of 'person', Reid further pointed out that since consciousness is transitory, and

> if personal identity consisted in consciousness, it would certainly follow that no man is the same person any two moments of his life; and, as the right and justice of reward and punishment is founded on personal identity, no man could be responsible for his actions.[320]

He immediately adds his conviction that Locke would have 'rejected with abhorrence' his doctrine had he foreseen such a consequence.

Locke was not altogether bereft of supporters, however. Among them was Vincent Perronet, who published *Vindications* of Locke in 1736 and 1738. In the former he leaves us in no doubt where he stands. He esteems 'Mr. *Locke* as one of the finest Genius's [*sic*] of the Age he lived in, a sincere Christian and an Honour to his Country'.[321] He especially trains his sights upon Peter Browne's *The Procedure, Extent and Limits of Human Understanding*, 1728. Locke is not the ultra-sensationalist Browne makes him out to be, and it is no argument against Locke to propose that we have knowledge of spiritual and immaterial things, for Locke has proved that God is immaterial and spiritual, and that we have knowledge of him.[322]

But it is in *A Second Vindication* that Perronet discusses personal identity in detail. He declares that if Butler had confined himself to demonstrating the soul's immateriality and the real but dependent existence of matter he would have done well. Unfortunately, however, he attacked Locke and for this he must be rebuked. Perronet sets out from Butler's view that consciousness presupposes personal identity, but is not identical with it, while Locke defined 'person' as a self-conscious rational being. Since Butler and Locke differ on the definition of 'person', 'It is no Wonder they disagree as to what constitutes the *Sameness* of That *Person.*'[323] He proceeds to belabour Watts for misinterpreting Locke, and against Watts's view that Locke errs in playing down substance, Perronet asks, '[D]oes not the Doctor's own *Hypothesis,* full as much as Mr. *Locke's,* require that the *same Substance* should be *unnecessary* to *Personal Identity*? I really think it does; since *Body* is one Part of the Doctor's *Idea* of *Person.*'[324] When Watts observes that '*the more probable Opinion is that this Consciousness* (in which he supposes Personal Identity to consist) *is annexed to one individual immaterial Substance,*' Perronet regrets that the author did not conclude that the idea of the immateriality of the soul and Locke's doctrine of personal identity were consistent with each other.[325] He reproves Watts for failing to appreciate the usefulness of Locke's distinction between 'man' and 'person', and laments that Locke's introduction of 'person' as a forensic concept did not carry more weight with Watts.[326]

Perronet's friend John Wesley was no less blunt on the other side of the argument. He construes Locke thus:

> 'consciousness makes personal identity;' that is, knowing I am the same person, makes me the same person. Was ever a more palpable absurdity? Does knowing I exist, make me exist? No; I am before I know I am; and I am the same, before I can possibly know I am the same. Observe, *before* here refers to the order of thinking, not to the order of time.[327]

Another, to whom Wesley was indebted and whose influence as a spiritual guide was considerable, was the nonjuror William Law. He denied that personal identity resides in consciousness or memory, but did not resort to the traditional view of substance. Rather, he thought in terms of the creation of human beings in the divine image. Persons are brought into being as distinct individuals, and human souls are made in the likeness of God: indeed, they are the divine in creaturely form.[328] They are held in being by the 'continual and immediate Inspiration of the Spirit'.[329] However, because our will and thoughts derive from the self-existent God they are self-moving, self-directing, and 'cannot be bounded and constrained'.[330] The natural man's objective, therefore, must be to redirect them to their source – which, in a sinful world entails regeneration by God's grace.

Edmund Law, bishop of Carlisle, adopted the opposing stance. In 1769 he published *A Defence of Mr. Locke's Opinion concerning Personal Identity.* He endorses Locke's position in general, but wishes that Locke had defined 'forensic' more closely; and where Locke says that a person is a thinking intelligent being, Law would have preferred him to say that 'person' 'stands for an attribute, or quality, or character of a thinking intelligent Being'.[331]

During the latter half of the eighteenth century a number of American divines, regarding themselves as in the line of Jonathan Edwards (I express myself in this way because Edwards's speculations on 'The Mind,' in which he rejected the idea of substance were not published until 1829) struggled with the problem, also inherent in William Law's position, of human agency in relation on the one hand to creation in the divine image, and on the other hand, to sin. The question, bluntly posed, is whether or not God is the author of sin. The options have been concisely presented by James Hoopes thus:

> The exercisers would hold that in the absence of any empirical knowledge of human soul substance it was reasonable to hold God's

> immediate agency responsible for all of the soul's acts or 'exercises', as they were called at the time, including sin. This was a strong view of the Creator, but it was also rigorously Calvinist. The tasters, on the other hand, would attempt to use a substantial view of the soul to create a human identity distinct from the immediate agency of God and thus relieve Him of responsibility for sin. Human behavior, they would assert, is based on a substantial bias, 'disposition', or 'taste of the heart' existing in the soul prior to even its first actions in infancy. Regeneration is then the acquisition of a new, holy taste resulting from a substantial or, as they often unphilosophically put it, a 'physical' change in the soul.[332]

Following these criteria Hoopes places Nathanael Emmons among the exercisers, and Timothy Dwight among the tasters.[333] Clearly this discussion took a turn which Locke had not himself envisaged.

Thomas Ludlam was among the last to defend Locke against sundry critics before the turn of the eighteenth century. This he did in his *Logical Tracts* (1790), though it must be said that as regards personal identity he could not forbear to remark, 'It is curious to see what sort of reasoning, even able men are given to employ, when they must needs inquire into what cannot be understood.'[334]

V

So far, my brief allusion to the later Americans apart, I have reviewed the positions of those divines who supported and opposed Locke's anthropology as such. Underlying the concerns of his opponents on this score, however, was deep disquiet that his view of personal identity directly threatened the doctrine of resurrection, a conviction which was only strengthened by Locke's speculation that God might, if he so chose, endow matter with thought. Let us examine each of these aspects in turn.

A major concern of Locke's critics *vis-à-vis* the implication of his views for the doctrine of resurrection was their inability to comprehend how, without recourse to the received understanding of an immaterial substance, and given his forensic understanding of 'person', Locke could maintain that the *same* body which had lived on earth would be raised after death. Stillingfleet, though distinguishing between 'substance' which could be raised, and particles of matter not all of which need be raised, was among a number who challenged Locke on this point.

It is important to observe in the first place that here, as elsewhere, Locke's thought was constantly developing. In the first three editions of the *Essay*, for example, he referred to the resurrection of 'bodies';[335] but in subsequent editions he spoke at the same points of the resurrection of 'the dead'. Secondly, Locke nowhere denied the doctrine of resurrection; on the contrary, he affirmed it. When Stillingfleet charged him with grounding his understanding of resurrection in 'the idea of identity,' Locke replied that 'the reason of believing any article of the christian faith ... to me and upon my grounds, is its being a part of divine revelation.'[336] He shortly repeats the point and comes to the nub of the matter: 'The resurrection of the dead, I acknowledge to be an article of the christian faith: but that the resurrection of the same body, in your lordship's sense of the same body, is an article of the christian faith, is what, I confess, I do not yet know.'[337] But, thirdly, Locke is content to be agnostic (the bishop thought he was being sceptical) concerning the nature of the resurrected body, and in this he is confident that he is in accord with Scripture, for, with respect to Pauline and other New Testament affirmations on the matter, Locke declares of bodies, in a paper probably written in 1699, 'They shall be raised: that is said over and over, But how they are raised or with what bodys they shall come the Scripture as far as I have observed is perfectly silent.'[338] Similarly, Locke paraphrases I Corinthians 15:49–50 thus:

> [A]s in the animal corruptible mortal state we were born in we have been like him that was earthy soe also shall we who at the resurrection partake of a spiritual life from Christ be made like him the Lord from heaven heavenly. i.e. live as the spirits in heaven doe without the need of food or nourishment to support it, and without infirmitys decay and death. injoying a fixed stable unfleeting life. This I say to you Brethren to satisfie those that aske with what bodys the dead shall come, that we shall not at the resurrection have such bodys as we have now For flesh and blood cannot enter into the kingdom which the saints shall inherit in heaven: Nor are such fleeting corruptible

things as our present bodys are fitted to that state of immutable incorruptibility.[339]

Locke's general view, therefore, is that the person shall be raised, though with which kind of body he cannot say, except that it will be a body appropriate to the resurrected state. Certainly he found Stillingfleet's view that provided that a certain number of bodily particles were united with the soul the same body would be raised incomprehensible, for how could a resurrected body with only a selection of its earthly particles be the same body which had lived on earth?[340] But there is some ambivalence in his writings. Earlier passages may be found in which he seems to have in mind the 'Greek' view of the immortality of the soul apart from the body. Thus he asserts that the immortality of the soul must be presupposed if the natural law is to exist;[341] and we recall his insistence that 'the care of souls does not belong to the magistrate,' and that 'In vain ... do princes compel their subjects to come into their church-communion, under pretence of saving their souls.'[342] He can even categorically affirm that 'Every man has an immortal soul, capable of eternal happiness or misery.'[343] But his adverse critics could not, or would not, grasp the novel distinction he was making in his mature thought between the man and the person, the physical components of the former becoming redundant at death.

John Milner was among those who not only repudiated Locke's general position, but invoked Paul against it by analysing 'It'. He refers to I Corinthians 15:42–4 on the body:

> *It is sown in Corruption, it is rais'd in Incorruption ... it is sown a natural Body, it is rais'd a spiritual Body.* Now I ask, What is it that is rais'd in Incorruption, in Glory, in Power, and a Spiritual Body? Mr. *Lock* will surely answer, that it is the Body. And if the Body be so necessarily understood, it is the same as if it was express'd. *The Body is rais'd Spiritual*; and so we have the express words, that the Body is raised.[344]

As on other issues, Samuel Bold and Catharine Cockburn were early in the lists in defence of Locke. Bold points out that

> Mr. *Lock* doth not say that the Soul is Material: He owns that we have the highest degree of probability that it is Immaterial, but that we cannot obtain to demonstrative Certainty or Knowledge, by comparing the Ideas of Matter and Thinking, that the Soul is an Immaterial

> Substance, tho' we may this way know that it is a Spiritual Substance.[345]

For her part Mrs Cockburn asks why it should be objected that Locke gives us no certainty of immortality apart from revelation, when there is no other way than revelation by which we may become certain of immortality, which is only probable by the light of nature. Certainly, the proof of immortality does not depend upon the assumption that the soul always thinks, so why should the possibility of its not always thinking disturb? Conversely, even if it were granted that souls always think, this would not suffice to demonstrate their immortality. Indeed, if our future state depended upon the soul's always thinking, then, since this cannot be proved, immortality would rest upon a very insecure foundation.[346] Similar points were later to be made by Archibald Campbell, Regius Professor of Divinity and Ecclesiastical History at the University of St Andrews, in which, against Tindal, he agreed with Locke that apart from revelation we have no secure knowledge of immortality.[347]

In 1703 Daniel Whitby published his *Paraphrase and Commentary on the New Testament*, a work which Locke was happy to recommend in a letter to Richard King.[348] While in considerable sympathy with Locke's view of original sin, Whitby could not agree with him as to the resurrection of the same body, and wrote to Locke to say so. Locke replied, 'I being fully perswaded of the resurrection and that we shall have bodys fitted to that state it is indifferent to me whether any one concludes that they shall be the same or not.'[349]

Locke's staunch ally, Samuel Bold, replied to Stillingfleet, Milner and Whitby in his *A Discourse concerning the Resurrection of the Same Body* (1705). '[T]he matter lies thus,' he declares:

> Mr. *Locke* hath been charged with Publishing in his *Essay concerning Humane Understanding*, something that was of dangerous Consequence to Articles of Christian Faith. And to make good this Charge, the Resurrection of the same Body, is produced as a necessary Article of Christian Faith; and it was pretended, there was something in Mr. *Locke's* Book, that was of dangerous Consequence to this necessary Article of Christian Faith. Mr. *Locke's* Replies vindicate the Christian Faith, and vindicate his own Book; discover a double Cheat, or mistake at the same time, and set Truth upon its own Basis. And this is that which has thrown some People into some disorder.[350]

Noting in passing that 'Affecting Dominion over the Faith of Christians, is an old Distemper' he proceeds to point out that the Bible is silent as to the nature of the resurrection body, claiming only that the dead shall be raised. Accordingly, speculations on the matter do not rise above 'meer Humane Opinions'.[351]

On Easter Monday, 2 April 1711, William Lupton, fellow of Lincoln College, preached before the University of Oxford in St Mary's Church. His theme was *The Resurrection of the Same Body*, and his sermon included a lengthy critique of Locke on this subject. Locke, indeed, is the 'Principal Abettor' of the opinion 'That the Reunion of the same Body to the Soul is not Necessary to constitute the same Man, and is no where taught in *Holy Scripture*',[352] and this claim Lupton sets out to refute. He dwells especially (at the Easter season) on the necessity that the Jesus who died is the same as the Jesus who was raised; he summons Tertullian on the same grain of wheat which dies in order to live; but he nowhere takes account of Locke's distinction between the man and the person.[353] On the same day in 1719, Winch Holdsworth, fellow of St John Baptist's College, resumed the theme,[354] admitting that the idea that the same bodies which are laid in graves are then resurrected is a contentious one, but rebutting Locke's view as a Socinian heresy. Some years later Holdsworth was answered on this latter point by Catharine Cockburn. She reminds her opponent that Locke nowhere denied belief in the resurrection of the same body, but simply refused to accept Stillingfleet's definition of the doctrine as an article of faith.[355] Appealing to the apostle, she declares that 'St. *Paul* plainly distinguishes between the dead that shall be raised, and the *bodies of the dead*; but that this implies no more than that persons *once dead shall live again*, Mr. Locke has nowhere said.'[356] Holdsworth's reply was more prompt, his *A Defence of the Doctrine of the Resurrection of the same Body* appearing in the following year, 1727. He here reasserts his belief that denial of the resurrection of the same body (a denial he attributes to Locke) is a Socinian doctrine. Mrs Cockburn's further reply was published in her *Works* under the title, *A Vindication of Mr. Locke's Christian Principles, from the injurious Imputations of Dr. Holdsworth.* She returns to Holdsworth's point that if the same body is not resurrected then the same man is not raised. This she deems 'a very bold affirmation, for the identity of a man is not dependent upon his material body'.[357] Here, implicitly, is the 'man–person' distinction which was so frequently overlooked by Locke's intellectual foes.

In his Easter Monday sermon of 1725, Henry Felton shows that he is not among those just referred to. He notes Locke's distinction between 'man' and 'person', but does not think it serves Locke well. On the contrary, Locke mistakenly advances his distinction 'not only as if each could, but as if each ought to be conceived without the other'.[358] Felton replies that we are able to draw the distinction in our thoughts only, but not in reality. He criticizes Locke for teaching that the identity of a person consists in consciousness only, and not in the thinking substance, arguing that 'Whatever makes *Identity* in other *Beings*, makes it in the Soul; and by the same Principle, the Body or any thing else is the *same*, that is the same also'.[359] Against Locke, Felton urges that it makes a huge difference which body is united with the soul at the resurrection, and sums up his case thus:

> The *Author* of the *Essay* has a Notion of the Resurrection of the Dead, without any Resurrection of the *Body*, whether the *same* or any *other*; But his Resurrection of the *Dead* is only a *Resurrection* of *Persons*, and as far as he holds the *Resurrection* of the *same Person*, 'tis no more than a *Resurrection* of the same *Consciousness*.[360]

To Felton, however, it is bodies that must be raised, and the same body at that. It is interesting that even as late as 1725 Felton does not consider Locke's posthumously published *Paraphrase*, with its claimed biblical endorsement of Locke's position.

Three years later, however, Robert D'Oyly did challenge Locke on biblical grounds. By the doctrine of the resurrection he understands 'the *re-union of the Body to the Soul separated from it by Death*'.[361] This doctrine, he laments, is currently under attack by heathens and heretics alike, and some 'even pretending to be Members of our own Communion,' appear to embrace the Article whilst actually undermining it – at which point he cites Locke's *Essay*, II.xxvii.15.[362] D'Oyly represents the offenders as teaching that 'in the *Resurrection* a Person can be said to be the same, tho' his Body consists of *foreign Substance*, and has not any Particles of the *same Matter* in it.'[363] He insists that if we take the Scriptures 'in their natural and *obvious Sense*' we shall have no need of such theories. Locke wrongly argues *a priori* from the nature of the thing, suggesting in his *Third Letter* to Stillingfleet that it would be hard to determine whether a raised soul united to its former particles was a more congruous idea than one united to particles of matter to which it was not previously joined. D'Oyly takes a short way with all such speculations, contending that in fact we must ground in scriptural revelation received as authoritative.[364] D'Oyly proceeds to observe that the Socinians wrongly interpret I Corinthians 15:35–45 as allowing what Locke suggests as a possibility; for Scripture as a whole points to 'the *Re-union of the Body separated by Death*.'[365] There follows a catena of citations from authorities Christian, Jewish and heathen in support of his position, and then D'Oyly declares that no new particles of matter will be needed for resurrection bodies, still less need we speculate that a man's bodily particles may hereafter be united with a different soul, for the omnipotent God is quite capable of restoring fully natural bodies which have died and perished.[366] We may therefore safely conclude that the resurrection body will be as artfully built as are our present bodies: not indeed that all of our present bodily particles will necessarily be utilized in the resurrected body, for the latter will be suitably adapted to the resurrection life, as Paul teaches in I Corinthians 15:43–4. This is the witness of divine revelation on the subject, and here we must rest, for our ignorance of the glorious state disables us from drawing comparisons between it and the state of nature, and hence we can specify no further.[367] We may, however, draw some practical lessons from all of this. If this body is to be the consort of the soul we should shun all sensual excess; be encouraged in face of the disadvantages of our present state; strive after piety and virtue; and be confident when confronted by the terrors of death.[368]

In his essay on 'The resurrection of the same body,' Isaac Watts first summarizes the arguments of Stillingfleet and others, finding 'some weight' in the view that

> Since body and soul united constitute the man, if it be not the same body that dies which is raised, then one essential part of man is lost. If it be another body, it is another man that is raised from the earth, and not the same man that died.

On the other hand, there are the scriptural references to the resurrection body *qua* spiritual, and Locke and those who agree with him that the resurrection of the original material body is needless refer to these.[369] Watts maintains that an individual's total number of material particles cannot be raised after death and reunited, not least because 'several of the particles that made one's man's body at the time of his death are very probably turned to grass ... and so become food for cattle, or other men, and are become part of the bodies of other men several times over.'[370] However, if Christ's resurrection and Paul's discourses on the subject are to stand, it must in some sense be the same body which is raised. Provided that there are sufficient of the material particles remaining – and even a few will serve – the need is met:

> For if the new-raised body has but as many essential atoms of the dead body in it, as the new stalk and ear of wheat has of the grain that was sowed, it is enough: And the union of the same conscious mind or spirit, makes it the same man.[371]

Watts concludes his essay with a 'short and plain remark':

> There are some of those who follow Mr. Locke and his way of thinking in many of these matters, who also go a step further, and suppose the spirit or conscious principle in man to lose all consciousness when the body dies, and that at the resurrection God shall give consciousness to the person again, or make a conscious principle to exist in the new-raised body. Now if this be the case, then it is neither the same body nor the same spirit that is raised from the dead, but a new spirit and a new body, which I think must necessarily be called *another person*, as well as Mr. Locke would call it *another man:* and I am sure such a new-made creature consisting of another mass of matter, and another conscious principle, can never be justly rewarded or punished for *personal* virtues or vices, good or evil actions done in the former life by a different body and spirit, i.e. by *another person.*[372]

In a footnote Watts observes that he has not here observed the distinction between 'same person' and 'same man' of which Locke makes so much, and he refers us to the end of his twelfth essay, where he remarks,

> *Personality* and *sameness of persons* either in this world or the other must not stand upon such a shifting and changeable principle, as may allow either one man to be two persons, or two men to be one person, or any one man to become another, or to be really any thing but himself.[373]

Here Watts, like Butler and others, repudiates Locke's suggestion in the *Essay*, II.xxvii.6 that 'if the Identity of Soul alone makes the same Man, and there be nothing in the Nature of Matter, why the same individual Spirit may not be united to different Bodies.' What is more, Watts and also, as we saw, Butler[374] – in other ways so greatly indebted to Locke – make their protest in the name of the ethical notion of eternal rewards and punishments – the very notion which Locke intended to endorse by introducing 'person' as a forensic term.

But if Locke caused concern among some divines because of the way in which his position on personal identity related to the doctrine of the resurrection of the dead, his remark (so 'scholastic' in character from one who was so overtly opposed to scholasticism) to the effect that God could, if he so chose, endow matter with the power of thought, caused something akin to panic. It spawned a large number of pamphlets, in which Locke's defenders were outnumbered roughly seven or eight to one.[375]

Locke's speculation concerning the possibility of thinking matter is prompted by his consideration of the extent and limitations of human knowledge. Since I have already discussed his epistemology in some detail, it will suffice here to say that Locke adduces considerations to support his conclusion that 'the *extent of our Knowledge* comes not only short of the reality of Things, but even of the extent of our own *Ideas*'.[376] He grants that the range of human knowledge is expandable, but even so we can 'be confident, that our Knowledge would never reach to all we might desire to know concerning those *Ideas* we have.'[377] Then comes the critical point:

> We have the *Ideas* of *Matter* and *Thinking*, but possibly shall never be able to know, whether any mere material Being thinks, or no; it being impossible for us, by the contemplation of our own *Ideas*, without revelation, to discover, whether Omnipotency has not given to some Systems of Matter fitly disposed, a power to perceive and think, or else joined and fixed to Matter so disposed, a thinking immaterial Substance: It being, in respect of our Notions, not much more remote from our Comprehension to conceive, that GOD can, if he pleases, superadd to Matter a Faculty of Thinking, than that he should superadd it to another Substance, with a Faculty of Thinking; since we know not wherein Thinking consists, nor to what sort of Substances the Almighty has been pleased to give that Power, which cannot be in

> any created Being, but merely by the good pleasure and Bounty of the Creator.[378]

As if to forestall possible objections, Locke proceeds at once to explain that his claim is that there is no contradiction in holding that God might so act as to endow matter with the power of thought; and he reminds his readers that he has already proved that 'it is no less than a contradiction to suppose matter (which is evidently in its own nature void of sense and thought) should be that Eternal first thinking Being.'[379]

It is not that Locke denies that there are properties pertaining to matter and different properties pertaining to mind – thus far he is Cartesian. But, unlike Descartes, his epistemology forbids him to affirm (and also categorically to deny) that there is a corresponding dualism of substances, and consequently that there could not be a transfer of properties from mind to matter. Moreover, his *quasi*-Calvinistic appeal to God's sovereignty in these matters is, I think, sincere. He does not think that God has, or will, endow matter with the power of thought, but rather that it is not contradictory to suppose that he could do so if he chose, and there is always the possibility that he may so choose to act.

From what has already been said, it is easy to predict how such a view would distress many of Locke's contemporary and successor divines. For first he defines 'person' out of relation to substance; he now contemplates the possibility that matter might think – but to them thinking is the business of the soul. If matter should think, does not this entail soul-destroying materialism? And if the soul *qua* thinking substance is not immaterial (because matter may think), is not the doctrine of immortality further undermined? Some did not need much encouragement to (mis)construe Locke as opting for a pantheistic monism in which God and the world were equated, and to brand him Spinoza *redivivus*. It has been well said of Locke that 'Coming as an apostle of peace to set an example of quiet thinking in an age of excitement, he suffered the ironic fate of exciting a religious controversy so intense that it might be considered a climax even for the turbulent Seventeenth Century.'[380]

As before, Locke's most prominent early opponent was Stillingfleet who, in *A Discourse in Vindication of the Doctrine of the Trinity* (1696), dissented from Locke's observations on thinking matter. Quite apart from the materialistic implications which he perceived in Locke's views, the bishop, as we have seen, quarrelled with what he regarded as the underlying sceptical epistemology which did not permit certainty in matters of faith. On the specific point which now concerns us he protests that along Locke's line, 'for all that we can know by our ideas of matter and thinking, matter may have a power of thinking: and if this hold, it is impossible to prove a spiritual substance in us, from the idea of thinking.'[381] Locke replies,

> [I]f your lordship means by a spiritual an immaterial substance, I grant I have not proved, nor upon my principles can it be proved, (your lordship meaning, as I think you do, demonstratively proved) that there is an immaterial substance in us that thinks. Though I presume, from what I have said about the supposition of a system of matter thinking (which there demonstrates that God is immaterial) will prove it in the highest degree probable, that the thinking substance in us is immaterial. But your lordship thinks not probability enough.[382]

The controversy rumbled on, each party refusing to allow the basic premisses of the other, and in his *Second Reply* to Stillingfleet we find Locke still contending that the bishop's opposition to the possibility of thinking matter leads him to threaten the omnipotence of God;[383] and this despite Stillingfleet's declaration in his answer to Locke's first *Letter*:

> We do not set bounds to *God's Omnipotency*: For he may if he please, change a Body into an *Immaterial Substance*; but we say, that while he continues the Essential Properties of Things, it is as impossible to Matter to think, as for a Body by Transubstantiation to be present after the manner of a Spirit; and we are as certain of one as we are of the other.[384]

It is interesting in passing to note Voltaire's verdict on the Locke–Stillingfleet exchange. He considers that Locke had the best of the debate, philosophically, and as to the substance of the matter he declares that while faith commands us to believe in the immortality of the soul, discussions of the nature of the soul have nothing to do with religion, 'which only requires the soul to be virtuous, whatever substance it may be made of'.[385]

Few English divines who considered the question were disposed to shelve it so swiftly, and many of them follow the general line of Stillingfleet.[386] Among these is Thomas Burnet, who finds Locke playing into the hands of materialists, for if the soul is not distinct from the body, will it not suffer dissolution when the body dies?[387] Again, if God may give matter the power of thought, how do we know that he has not done so and, hence, that our souls are not material?[388] Locke replied briefly to Burnet,[389] and a dissatisfied Burnet pressed him further in his *Second Remarks* (1697). When Locke did not reply, Burnet addressed some *Third Remarks* to him in which he concluded that Locke is a philosophical deist, for there is no reason on his principles why, particular spiritual substances being abolished, matter should not be all.[390]

Among early respondents to Locke for whom Spinoza was an omnipresent bogeyman was the author of *A Letter to a Clergy-man in the Country*, (1704) who was convinced that Locke's views on thinking matter were directly attributable to Spinoza;[391] and William Carroll.[392]

As we might by now expect, Locke had his defenders and, as we might also by now expect, most prominent among them were Samuel Bold, Catharine Cockburn and Vincent Perronet. On this occasion Bold was concerned to defend Locke against the charge of Robert Jenkin, master of St John's College, Cambridge, who found the idea of thinking matter unintelligible – unless God should change the nature of matter.[393] Where Jenkin makes capital out of the fact that 'it seems not intelligible how God should superadd' thought to matter, Bold replies that Locke's meaning is that while we cannot understand how this may be, the possibility of its happening cannot thereby be precluded, for 'God hath done, and does do many things, which we cannot understand the manner how he did, or does do them.'[394] Catharine Cockburn concurred;[395] so also (against Watts) did Perronet.[396]

At the half-way point in the century we find the physiologist Malcolm Flemyng monitoring the situation, and lamenting that free-thinkers such as Collins and Tindal, have, 'spider-like', converted into poison Locke's supposition that God might endow matter with the power of thought. Since Locke grants that on its own matter is 'void of all Sense and Thought ... To superadd to Matter a Property incompatible with its Nature, while its Nature remains the same as before that Property was bestowed upon it, seems to be making it both what it is, and what it is not, at the same time.'[397] He concludes that it is

> a fair Consequence, either that Matter and Motion must be acknowledged capable of producing Thought, which is directly contrary to Mr. *Locke's* Reasonings on that Subject; or, that whenever Thought is, as he expresses it, superadded to Matter, there a new cognitive Being or Substance is created.[398]

I shall mention one further criticism of Locke's position on thinking matter, and it is in quite a different key from those already noted. If Stillingfleet, Carroll and the rest felt that Locke strayed too far in the direction of materialism, Priestley, later in the century, declared that he had failed in not proceeding far enough in that direction. He cannot understand why Locke should suppose that

> the faculty of thinking may be a property of the body, and yet to think it more probable that this faculty inhered in a different substance, viz. an immaterial soul. A philosopher ought to have been apprised that we are to suppose no more *causes* than are necessary to produce the *effects*; and therefore, that we ought to conclude that the whole man is material, unless it should appear, that he has some powers or properties that are absolutely incompatible with matter.
>
> Since, then, Mr. Locke did not apprehend, that there was any real inconsistency between the known properties of body, and those that have generally been referred to mind, he ought, as became a philosopher, to have concluded, that the *whole substance of man*, that which supports all his powers and properties, was one uniform substance, and by no means that he consisted of *two substances*; and those so very different from one another as *body* and *spirit* are usually represented to be.[399]

VI

What, in conclusion, of the final destiny of the individual? As with other major Christian doctrines, so here: Locke does not offer a fully fledged eschatology but, as we shall see, he says enough to cause consternation in some theological quarters. First, Locke's epistemology requires him to deny that we can have natural knowledge of the soul's immortality:

> [S]ince we having but some few superficial *Ideas* of things, discovered to us only by the Senses from without, or by the Mind, reflecting on what it experiments in it self within, have no Knowledge beyond that, much less of the internal Constitution, and true Nature of things, being destitute of Faculties to attain it,[400]

such knowledge is 'above reason,' and is revealed to a faith not opposed to reason.[401] As we have seen, many divines found epistemological scepticism of this kind destructive of the Christian's confidence, Locke's conviction that in the afterlife the just shall know many things which are now hidden from them notwithstanding.[402]

Secondly, Locke relates his understanding of immortality closely to his concern for morality. Indeed, as a Christian – and especially as a paraphraser of a number of the New Testament epistles – he could hardly do otherwise, for the final destiny of the individual is in the Christian tradition closely related to – even in many authors determined by – the moral character of the life lived here below. In connection with immortality Locke's practical interest is once again apparent. But here as elsewhere it must be admitted that the articulation of his position is ambivalent.[403] There is, first, ambivalence concerning the fate of the wicked. As far as the righteous are concerned, Locke is consistent throughout his writings, and his paraphrase of I Corinthians 15:23–4 may be taken as summarizing his own view of the matter, namely, that at the resurrection people

> shall return to life again not all at once but in their proper order: Christ the first-fruits is already risen: Next after him shall rise those who are his people his church and this shall be at his second comeing. After that shall be the day of Judgment. which shall bring to a conclusion and finish the whole dispensation to the race and posterity of Adam in this world. when Christ shall have deliverd up the kingdome to god and the father, which he shall not doe till he hath destroid all empire power and authority that shall be in the world besides.[404]

But Locke is less consistent concerning the eternal punishment of the wicked. On the one hand, he can contemplate *post mortem* existence without referring at all to the punishment of wrongdoers:

> it seems the unalterable purpose of the divine justice, that no unrighteous person ... should be in paradise: but that the wages of sin

> should be to every man, as it was to Adam, an exclusion of him out of that happy state of immortality, and bring death upon him ...
>
> Immortality and bliss, belong to the righteous ... but an exclusion from paradise and loss of immortality is the portion of sinners.[405]

On the other hand, Locke has no qualms about listing Jesus' moral injunctions, which were delivered 'upon pain of hell-fire';[406] and he elsewhere speaks of the 'exquisite Misery' of a wrongdoer's 'immortal Soul hereafter'.[407] Catharine Cockburn was not slow to remind Winch Holdsworth of this when he accused Locke of Socinianism because of his denial that the wicked will be punished eternally; and she points out that Holdsworth himself has noted Locke's assertion that the wicked will suffer 'great and terrible, and everlasting punishments in a future state'.[408]

The question which presses (leaving on one side the philosophical problem concerning the propriety of speaking of temporal duration at all in connection with an eternal afterlife) is, does Locke think that 'punishment in eternity' is synonymous with 'never-ending eternal punishment'? It would seem that he does not, and that after a measure of *post mortem* punishment the wicked will simply die, or be annihilated. This is the conclusion of his paper, 'Resurrectio et quae sequuntur' of *c.* 1699,[409] in which he construes Matthew 25:41, 46, 12:42, 50 and 18:8; and Luke 33:36, Galatians 6:7–8 as teaching that while the wicked shall be cast into hell fire to be tormented ('there can be noe doubt about it'), they shall not live for ever: they shall die. However,

> Takeing it then for evident that the wi[c]ked shall die and be extinguished at last how long they shall be continued in that unexpressable torment is not that I know any where expressed, but that it shall be excessively terrible by its duration as well as sharpness the current of the Scripture seems to manifest.[410]

Secondly, there is ambivalence concerning the destiny of those who are in, and those who are out of, Christ. On the one hand Locke teaches that both those who believe in Christ shall be saved, as shall all the faithful of previous ages who have been faithful to the revelation they received;[411] on the other hand, in his notes to Ephesians 2:8, he adopts a more restricted stance: 'God in the Fulness of Time set up his Kingdom in this World under his Son; into which he admitted all those who believed on him, and received Jesus the Messiah for their Lord.' This, it should be noted, is said with specific reference to 'The Apostate Heathen World [who] were dead' until they received the Gospel.[412]

On the question, topical in Locke's day, whether between bodily death and the second coming of Christ the individual is conscious during an intermediate state, or enjoying the sleep of the soul, Locke, though less than fully clear seems in general sympathy with the latter option.[413] Further, he understands the resurrection of the just at Christ's second coming as following the ingathering of the Gentiles and the conversion of the Jews.[414]

It is important to observe that Locke's case against eternal punishment of the wicked is argued purely upon the ground that the possibility is not envisaged in the biblical revelation. That is to say, Locke implicitly appeals throughout to the principle of the sufficiency of Scripture. His objections are not of the same kind as those lodged during the past century and a half from the side of ethics against 'immoral' views of 'hell-fire and brimstone' eschatology;[415] against the penal substitutionary theory of the atonement; against the theology of church establishments; or against the theological justification of apartheid. They are not on all fours with those of William Whiston, who in 1740 published *The Eternity of Hell Torments Considered*, and introduced his work thus:

> [S]ince I think the common opinion for the *proper Eternity* of those torments to be no less absurd, nor less reproachful to christianity than the *Athanasian* Doctrine of the Trinity; the *Calvinist* Doctrine of Reprobation; or the Popish Doctrine of Transubstantiation; I think it high time for me to keep silence no longer.[416]

Charles Chauncy is among others who take the next, universalist, step:

> The salvation of the whole human kind is indeed the great thing aimed at, in the scheme, the bible has opened to our view, as now in prosecution, by the benevolent Deity, under the management of that glorious personage, Jesus Christ; who, we are there assured, will go on prosecuting this design, till all the individuals of the human race that ever had, have now, or ever will have, existence, shall be fixed in the possession of compleat and everlasting happiness.[417]

Not, indeed, that all earlier agreed with Locke's biblical interpretation on these matters. John Milner, for example, declares that 'I cannot reconcile the Immortality of the Soul with Mens *ceasing to be* when they die. Mr. *Lock*, who useth that Expression of *ceasing to be*, more than once ... must invent some unknown Sense of it, which may reconcile them.'[418] Later, having observed that the sleep of the soul and the denial of the eternity of punishment are Socinian notions to which Locke seems to subscribe, he ends on a puzzled note:

> On the other hand, How far his mentioning infinite Misery, exquisite Misery, unspeakable Punishments, perfect Misery, Tribulation and Anguish, Indignation and Wrath which shall be after this Life, and his transcribing the words of our Saviour in which he speaks of everlasting Fire and everlasting Punishment, may argue that he doth not hold with them [i.e. with the Socinians], I know not.[419]

Others were less puzzled, and were able to be more definite than I can be that Locke believed in the sleep of the soul until the resurrection. In a diatribe against Henry Grove, the conservative Presbyterian divine, John Ball of Honiton, accused Locke of blunting the edge of such biblical texts as 'thou shalt surely die' with his suggestion that after death the wicked have no sensation or being.[420] By no means theologically conservative, Caleb Fleming was no less concerned to deny the notion of the sleep of the believer's soul after death, contending against Locke for the believer's immediate felicity.[421] And Nathanael Emmons protested:

> It is indeed strange that Mr. Locke should suppose the soul sometimes sleeps in the body; but stranger still, that he should suppose that it continues sleeping from death till the resurrection. This, however, was his opinion, and is still the opinion of many others, but without any foundation in scripture or reason.[422]

The general impression left is that direct engagement with Locke on the question of the eternal destiny of the individual, and especially on the *post mortem* fate of the wicked is desultory, and certainly not as voluminous as that concerning the resurrection of the same body, or thinking matter. This is, no doubt, partly because Locke's disinclination to speculate beyond the epistemological boundaries he had set himself resulted in the measures of ambivalence to which I have drawn attention; and partly because subsequent divines had, on this subject, bolder fish to fry, so to speak, as, for example, when John Horsey of Northampton Dissenting academy advises his students that concerning the future state of humanity such 'modern infidels' as Bolingbroke maintain that the whole of man is dissolved at death; Collins maintains that the doctrine of a future state is the invention of the Egyptians; Chubb denies the doctrine, and Hume argues expressly against it; while Lord Shaftesbury represents the belief of a future state as unfavourable to real virtue.[423]

Above all, Locke's interest was, as we have seen throughout this study, practical. This is epitomized in a letter to Denis Grenville:

> [W]e are not born in heaven, but in this world, where our being is to be preserved with meat, drink and clothing and other necessarys that are not borne with us, but must be got and kept with forecast care and labour: and therefor we cannot be all Devotion, All Prayses and Halilujahs, and perpetually in the Vision of things above.

At the same time, we are not placed in this world to stay here for ever, so we must direct our thought to the author of our being, and to that 'other world' towards which we proceed.[424] Good advice is none the worse for being expressed in homely language.

7

Conclusion

My objectives in this study were twofold: to investigate the influence of John Locke upon the divines of the slightly extended eighteenth century with which I have been concerned; and to articulate some questions posed by the Locke-influenced strand of the overambitiously titled 'Age of Reason' to any who contemplate a Christian apologetic method as Christianity's third millennium advances upon us.

Granting that Locke, or at least Locke-like ideas, influenced many who never put pen to paper, I have shown that a considerable number of divines did refer to Locke's philosophical and theological ideas in print, and some discussed them in detail. As might have been expected, the bulk of responses on most topics were forthcoming during the years 1690–1720, but throughout the eighteenth century there was at least spasmodic interest on the part of divines in Locke's epistemology, his views on toleration, personal identity and thinking matter, and his biblical exegesis. A few, notably Samuel Bold and Catharine Cockburn, were content to swallow Locke more or less whole, and these were his stoutest defenders. Others, though not detailed in their defences of Locke, were nevertheless in no doubt as to the value of his intellectual contribution. To Timothy Dwight Locke is among other laymen who 'will be had in everlasting remembrance, as champions of truth and righteousness, illustrious supporters of Christianity, and glorious instruments of piety and salvation to mankind'.[1] In Thomas Belsham's eyes Locke is 'the first of metaphysicians, and the father of rational criticism'.[2] The prize for eulogy must, however, go to William Warburton:

> [T]he sage Locke supported himself by no system on the one hand; nor, on the other, did he dishonour himself by any whimsies; the consequence of which was, that, neither following the fashion nor striking the imagination, he at first had neither followers nor admirers: but being everywhere clear, and everywhere solid, he at length works his way; and afterwards was subject to no reverses. He was not affected by the new fashions in philosophy, who leaned upon none of the old: nor did he afford ground for the after-attacks of envy and folly by any fanciful hypothesis; which, when grown stale, are the most nauseous of all things.[3]

It may gently be suggested, in view of our analysis, that to say that Locke is 'everywhere clear, and everywhere solid' is to claim rather too much. At certain points he has been found ambivalent, elusive and at times possibly evasive, and this by friend and foe alike. While some endorsed his denial of innate principles, others viewed this as paving the way to atheism, materialism and scepticism. For the latter reason Locke's novel and ambivalent doctrine of substance caused concern to Stillingfleet, prompted something akin to apoplexy in John Edwards and stimulated the diverse responses of Berkeley's immaterialism and Jonathan Edwards's and Wesley's 'new spiritual sense'. The last-named were much more inclined than Locke himself to build upon the hints Locke had left concerning faith as trust. By leaving the appeal to reason's authority alongside the appeal to the authority of Scripture, thereby fostering, for example, ambivalence concerning the noetic effects of sin, Locke gave encouragement to later divines who wished to opt for one or the other but not both. Again, Locke shrank from producing a demonstration of ethical principles, but appealed to natural law, intuition, hedonism and Scripture in such a way that, once again, the joins showed and hostages to fortune were given. Nevertheless it cannot be denied that many more liberal divines found in Locke's writings much support for the convictions concerning the right of private judgement to which they were, in any case, predisposed. Locke's views on toleration and his defence of civil and religious liberty appealed to many – especially, of course, to Dissenters, some of whom, together with a few Anglicans, sought a wider toleration than Locke envisaged: one which would embrace Roman Catholics, unitarians and Jews. Dissenters were similarly to the fore, though not alone, in endorsing Locke's view (including its anthropocentrism as stated) that the Church is a voluntary society though, surprisingly, few adverted directly to his supportive sentiments when making out their own anti-establishment case. As to Christian doctrine, Locke's conviction concerning the indispensable minimum of belief, namely, that Jesus is the Messiah, his Christology, and the lacuna concerning Christ's satisfaction which may be detected in his soteriology, prompted charges (ill placed in my view) of deism and Socinianism, as did his anti-substance view of personal identity, his agnosticism concerning the resurrection of the same body, and his speculation concerning thinking matter.

In the course of reviewing Locke's favourable and adverse critics it has become clear that we may not draw a straight line between him and the later rational Dissenters. To put it otherwise, at a number of points Locke is much more a child of his own Puritan age than he is of the age of Priestley. Thus, for example, Priestley opposed Locke's view of power and his continuing immaterialism, while Francis Webb contended that Locke adhered to far too many mysterious doctrines which defied reason, and that he upheld a doctrine of the atonement which adversely reflected upon God's love and righteousness. On the other hand, while some later evangelicals – John Newton comes to mind – shunned philosophy, others even in their ordination statements revealed how wedded they were to the natural-theology-supplemented-by-revealed approach which was so characteristic of their century.

The conclusion thus far is that Locke encouraged many divines to set out from the starting-point of epistemology, and to seek a reason for their faith. In this he was pre-eminent though not alone; nor was he absolutely original for, as we have seen, he was intellectually indebted to Arminians, neo-Platonists, Latitudinarians and Puritans, as well as to Newton and other pioneers of modern scientific method. However, we have also seen that most divines had no compunction about utilizing what they found helpful in Locke's writings and discarding or opposing the rest.

The variety of Locke's intellectual debts may in part explain the ambivalence in his method. Though not uninfluenced by the heritage of thought to which he was heir, he was not a systematizer either in philosophy or in theology; on the contrary, he was highly suspicious of the systems of the schools. As if in acknowledgement of diverse influences upon him he appeals now to reason, now to the authority of Scripture, now to the example of Christ. It is thus not correct to say that for Locke reason is all; and it obscures more than it reveals to label him an 'empiricist'. Equally, we may query Hans Aarsleff's verdict that Locke's 'great message was to set us free from the burden of tradition and authority'.[4] From the dead hand of tradition, yes; and from untoward authorities whether scholastic, ecclesiastical or civic, yes; but not from all authority.

An important implication of the remarks just made is that those who in our own time wish to 'hammer' the Enlightenment for its elevation of reason above all else, cannot claim the entire support of the Enlightenment's English father, Locke. I have in mind those postmodernists who consider that imperialistic reason's hegemony having failed, we must seek strategies for dealing with atomized human existence; and those present-day theologians and preachers for whom the Enlightenment is the source of an individualism which has led to the privatization of religion and the removal of the Gospel from the arena of public truth. Locke (however inconsistently from the point of view of his epistemology) appeals to scriptural authority and not only to reason; and in his ecclesiology, for all its anthropocentrism, there is a socio-covenantal emphasis which might be held to relativize out-and-out individualism. To contradict the judgement of John Walsh and Stephen Taylor that 'Among the liberals of the Church of England [as also, I should add, among many Dissenters] there was a positive desire to Christianize the Enlightenment, rather than merely to anathemtize it, and leave it – as in France – to become subversive and overtly irreligious,'[5] is to overlook a good deal of evidence, much of which I have here presented.

None of which is to deny that Locke and the eighteenth-century divines have bequeathed a series of issues to which any late-twentieth-century apologist must pay heed, or that they proceed on the basis of certain assumptions which have subsequently been called into serious question, so that they cannot be our guides in all matters. There is first the matter of the place of reason in religion. Locke, as we have seen, has a place for the cosmological argument for the existence of God. In this connection I can only concur with Basil Mitchell, who has written, 'Too much ... has happened since [Locke's] time in the way of historical research in general and biblical criticism in particular for the Lockian pattern [of reason supplemented by revelation] to be at all plausible to the modern reader.'[6] What future, if any, is left to natural theology? And if there is no future, are we any the worse off? The very confidence of Locke and the eighteenth-century divines, when viewed with hindsight from our own vantage point leaves us with this question. However, there are, as we have seen, the seeds of another approach in Locke's writings, for he has a place for faith as assent; and there is more than a hint of *fiducia* in his work – a theme which Jonathan Edwards, Wesley and others were later to develop – frequently without any reference to Locke.

By the early years of the nineteenth century, when Belsham was lamenting that 'Rational Christianity is out of fashion with the learned and the great,'[7] others in increasing numbers were already insisting that 'dry' rationalism must be replaced. For them it was not sufficient that revelation should be invoked to supplement the deliverances of reason; moreover, the classical theistic arguments – not least the cosmological, so favoured by eighteenth-century divines of all stripes[8] – which were the foundation of the widely prevalent natural theology, had been weighed and found wanting by Hume and Kant. There developed a new emphasis upon the inward, upon feeling, upon experience – epitomized by the father of modern theology, Schleiermacher, and by the Romantic movement at large.[9] If, as Clement Webb averred, 'Rationalism is not really so much an excess of confidence in reason as a want of confidence in it; since it does not attempt to understand a great part of human experience,'[10] the question presses, with what is reason to be replaced or supplemented? Should we be guided by Channing, who declared, 'Locke's philosophy has quenched spirituality in modern thought,'[11] and redress the balance from that direction? Should we follow the lead Newman took from Keble? To him, 'It is faith and love which give to probability a force which it has not in itself.'[12] Should we eschew the Locke-like quest of evidences and become Reformed epistemologists, mystics, Wittgensteinians? Or ought we to realign ourselves with a long tradition which sets out from the conviction that the truly rational agent is not the human being, but God? Conversely, should we opt for postmodernism? And in ethics, should we endeavour to re-establish rationalism, sensationalism, hedonism, utilitarianism in Locke's uneasy combination, should we focus upon one of these, or should we have recourse to emotivism or to one of the many varieties of theological ethics? And on which grounds should our choice be made?

How is the underlying question of authority to be determined? Locke's sometimes uneasy alignment of the authority of reason with that of Scripture poses the question but does not exhaust the possibilities. What of the authority of tradition, of conscience, of the Gospel? And is an appeal to authority best made by individuals, or within a community of interpretation? In the mid-nineteenth century J. W. Nevin, a pioneer of the Mercersburg theology, was horrified by the proliferation of sects, all of them generated by the private biblical interpretation of a charismatic or otherwise prominent leader, without recourse to the catholic churchly tradition of the ages.[13] Locke did not consider in detail the question of the locus of authority in relation to the social ecclesiology which he espoused, neither could he foresee the degree to which the latter might be undermined in practice by his emphasis upon the conscientious rights of the individual. But these questions press the churches hard today.

What, then, of the classical Christian doctrines? I am prepared to take Locke at his word: he was not a deist or a Socinian, still less an atheist. He was a Christian. But the appropriate relation of the right of private judgement and liberty of thought to ecclesiology is not easy to determine, and this question is bequeathed to us also. Put otherwise, it is the question, 'What are the degrees of doctrinal tolerance within the Church?' Locke's quest of an indispensable minimum of belief is relevant at this point – indeed it might be said still to haunt late-twentieth-century ecumenical discussion. Even though, as I have suggested, Locke's assertion of the Messiahship of Christ may be construed as a portmanteau claim rather than as a minimalist one, he is not specially helpful on the doctrine of the Trinity, in which he believed, did not deny, but did not affirm with fervour or examine in detail; on the person of Christ; on the atonement; or on eschatology at large. Not indeed that we need fault a writer for not covering all the doctrinal terrain – and I (unlike John

Edwards) have taken him at his word that in *The Reasonableness of Christianity* his desire to avoid hostages to fortune when dealing with deists tied his doctrinal tongue. Nevertheless Locke's doctrinal silences are somewhat disconcerting; he cannot be our sole guide on Christian centralities; and while, as I have suggested, a number of those who opposed him on doctrinal grounds were at least partly perturbed by the fact that they were not hearing from him that approved 'language of Canaan' to which their ears had become so finely attuned, their concerns respecting Locke's doctrinal lacunae are not altogether to be dismissed.

The question is, Do Locke's Christology and soteriology keep pace with his developing understanding (*pace* George Cheyne) of the perilous state in which sinners are found, and of their need of salvation? I do not think that they do. I have no doubt that Locke sincerely believed that salvation is in Christ alone; but Locke's Christ remains a somewhat attenuated one, whose person is not clearly understood in trinitarian terms. There may be good reasons why this should be so, but the case needs to be made. The upshot is that just as Locke's epistemological method left him needing to invoke revelation, and just as his ethics required completion by the appeal to Scripture and to the teaching of Jesus, so his view of humanity *qua* sinful required a divine salvation. But for none of these is there an adequate, which is to say a seamless, theoretical basis. This is not altogether surprising, given Locke's suspicion of systems, but it does leave us with the impression that at crucial points his theoretical foundation, whose elements are laid side by side rather than fused together, is not strong enough to support his (sometimes weakly expressed but none the less sincere) Christian convictions.

The question, How (that is, on what basis and in which manner) may Christian views on the nature of humanity, sin, salvation and eternal life best be commended? has added urgency in our own time, for in the West at least the theistic assumption cannot as readily be made as it was in Locke's day, and the religious complexion of society is increasingly pluralistic (it was ever thus in the East). Locke's question mark over the state establishment of religion also presses in such a context. In this connection, partly because of his polarization of the personal (religious) and the public (civic), and partly because his ecclesiology insufficiently emphasized the divine initiative in calling out the Church, Locke could not find that middle ground which suggests that while Christ does not equal Caesar, the two cannot be utterly divorced from each other, and that both need room to move if there is to be creative and mutual interaction between them.[14] To put it otherwise, despite his view of the Church as social, Locke did not emphasize the role of the Church in society as leaven. I, of course, speak with hindsight. It is quite possible that Locke moved as far on this question as was psychologically (even legally) conceivable in his time.[15] At the present time we find that some, no longer constrained as he was, have yet to catch up with him.

From specific questions arising from our study I return finally to the matter of apologetic procedure. Locke had an all-pervading Christian vision, but he was not a systematizer. For this reason, and also because of his tendency to confine himself to particular questions while leaving on one side both presuppositions articulated elsewhere and matters which might distract the reader or endanger himself, he has played into the hands of adverse critics from his day to our own, as we have seen. He worried at specific problems – in some cases over many years – and was constantly revising his thoughts. In this he acted consistently with the belief he expressed in the posthumously published essay *On the Conduct of the Understanding*, that

> God has made the intellectual world harmonious and beautiful without us; but it will never come into our heads all at once; we must bring it home piece-meal, and there set it up by our own industry, or else we shall have nothing but darkness and a chaos within, whatever order and light there be in things without us.[16]

But on which principles are we to set to work? The question remains, to put it bluntly, Where Christian apologetics are concerned, is Locke to be endorsed, repaired, modified or forsaken? The diverse answers given to this question by the eighteenth-century divines suggests the complexity of the question; and the fact that the question can still meaningfully be raised nearly three centuries after Locke's death is a telling tribute to his importance. I think, however, that the overriding lesson of this study is that (his stimulus on many particular points notwithstanding) Locke's way of setting out from epistemology and then invoking revelation, Scripture, Christ as appropriate, may not be best suited to our needs now. This may, indeed, be to express the point too mildly. Can it be that Locke's elision of the question of the genesis of our ideas (the psychological interest) with the question of the truth of the claims we are able to make (the epistemological interest) imposes a straitjacket upon rational inquiry and faith alike? The way in which Locke reached out in the direction of divine authority, the teaching of Scripture and the example of Christ, suggests that he himself felt the strain imposed upon his deepest convictions by his epistemological stance which, while properly acknowledging the limitations of human knowledge imposed the restrictions of sensation and (ambiguously construed) reflection upon the human capacity to know, and was ignored by Locke himself at crucial points. If this is so, the problem bequeathed by Locke to modern thought is not so much that of the alleged illicit elevation of reason, as that of the illegitimate constriction of the sphere of human knowledge.

It is not, of course, a foregone conclusion that we shall solve all simply by starting somewhere else, as the Romantics and their heirs did. For example, from one point of view the story of the British post-Hegelian philosophical idealists is one of thinkers who were constitutionally ill at ease with loose ends of thought. If they viewed the Enlightenment with some concern because of the materialistic, naturalistic and agnostic turns taken by some of its heirs, their own temptation, in *quasi*-gnostic fashion, was that of understanding all mysteries. As I have attempted to show in *Philosophical Idealism and Christian Belief*, those Christian idealists who sought to propound Christian ideas in relation to, or in terms of, post-Hegelian idealism lived dangerously. For all their breadth of vision and their good intentions they (especially the absolutists among them) found it hard to accommodate the Creator–creature distinction; the historical rootedness of the Christian faith; the fact of evil as something more desperate than a stage on the way to a greater good; and the scandal of particularity which lies at Christianity's heart. It is not without significance that one of the idealists discussed, A. E. Taylor, who in his early professional life tended towards positivism, came eventually to feel the need to import into his idealism insights from Thomism and, to a lesser extent, from Scottish common-sense realism. It is not too much to claim that those post-Hegelian idealists who were most inclined towards orthodox Christianity bore a striking resemblance to Locke insofar as both they and he believed more than could be comfortably accommodated within the bounds of their preferred philosophical 'isms'.

The moral is that a change of starting-points is not necessarily a cure-all. But if Locke's methodology and that of the post-Hegelian idealists leave something to be desired, what other way forward may there be for the Christian apologist? Unless Christian thought is to be imprisoned within a circle of revelation the question must seriously be addressed as Christianity's third millennium approaches. Is it possible nowadays to delineate and defend a coherent view of the world which both articulates fundamental Christian claims (a huge begging-of-the-question this) and engages with the intellectual world as it is, undaunted by the embargoes of Barthians, Wittgensteinians, existentialists and postmodernists? Will a viable apologetic take the form of an eclectic reasoned testimony – that is, will it be a conjunctive 'both–and' dialogue with the intellectual environment, in which pros and cons are duly weighed, with the attendant risk that distinctively Christian claims may be watered down? Or will it set out from a given revelation in disjunctive, 'either–or' terms, with the attendant risk of an Olympian, even an imperialistic, failure to communicate? Or are there other possible ways forward?

My present inclination (and having quoted so many others I may be forgiven for quoting myself) is to think that 'Since the terrain to be traversed by Christian testimony is wide, involving a texture of historical, existential, theological, metaphysical, ethical, aesthetic, liturgical assertions, its method must be correspondingly hospitable.'[17]

The devising and pursuing of such method is a daunting task for another day. It is a task which I hope to pursue – however tremblingly, and with no advance confidence of success. I should, however, prefer to be labelled, if labelled at all, as one who over-reached himself, and not as an intellectual coward. And I shall strive to proceed in the spirit of Locke's dying words, namely, 'in perfect charity with all men and in sincere communion with the whole church of Christ, by whatever names Christ's followers call themselves'.[18]

Notes

Chapter 1: Introduction: An Intellectual Minefield

1 In J. Rippon, *A Brief Memoir of the Life and Writings of the Late Rev. John Gill, D.D.*, London, 1838, 121–57. I use short titles in the notes, and provide fuller titles in the bibliography.

2 Works on Wesley (1703–91) are legion. Among recent offerings Henry Rack, *Reasonable Enthusiast*, London: Epworth Press, may be noted. For Gill (1697–1771) see Alan P. F. Sell, *The Great Debate: Calvinism, Arminianism and Salvation:* Worthing: H. E. Walter, 1982, Grand Rapids: Baker Book House, 1983, and Seoul: Word of Life Press, 1989, ch.III. I find that on p.73 of the British and American editions, an undetected printer's error has increased Gill's life-span by eighteen years. For Taylor (1694–1761) see idem, *Dissenting Thought and the Life of the Churches: Studies in an English Tradition*, Lewiston, NY: Edwin Mellen Press, 1990, ch.VII. Gill, Taylor and Wesley are in *The Dictionary of National Biography* (hereinafter, DNB).

3 J. Taylor, *A Narrative of Mr. Joseph Rawson's Case,* 2nd edn, 1742, 9.

4 For the circumstances leading to, and resulting from, this Act see Alan P. F. Sell, *Commemorations: Studies in Christian Thought and History*, Cardiff: University of Wales Press, and Calgary: University of Calgary Press, 1993, ch.V. We should remember that 'Till 21st July 1813, the profession of Unitarianism was punishable in England by forfeiture of citizenship and by imprisonment, while in Scotland it was a capital crime.' So Alexander Gordon, *Heads of English Unitarian History,* London: Philip Green, 1895, 49.

5 For the pre-1688 impetus towards these convictions see John Spurr, '"Rational religion" in Restoration England', *Journal of the History of Ideas,* XLIX no. 4, October-December 1988, 563–85.

6 Mark Pattison, 'Tendencies of religious thought in England, 1688–1750', in *Essays and Reviews*, 3rd edn, 1860, 258.

7 Gordon, *Heads of English Unitarian History*, 32.

8 E. C. Moore, *An Outline of the History of Christian Thought since Kant*, London: Duckworth, 1912, 193.

9 G. W. Richards, *History of the Theological Seminary of the [German] Reformed Church in the United States 1825–1934, Evangelical and Reformed Church 1934–1952,* Lancaster, Pa: Theological Seminary of the Evangelical and Reformed Church, 1952, 292.

10 Henry F. May, *The Enlightenment in America,* New York: OUP, 1976, 10.

11 M. R. Watts, *The Dissenters,* Oxford: Clarendon Press, 1978, 392.

12 See further Sell, *Dissenting Thought and the Life of the Churches*, ch.V.

13 See, for example, John W. Yolton, *Locke and French Materialism,* Oxford: Clarendon Press, 1991; Jean S. Yolton and John W. Yolton, 'Locke's suggestion of thinking matter and some eighteenth-century Portuguese reactions', *Journal of the History of Ideas*, XLV, 1984, 303–7; Janina Rosika, 'John Locke and the Polish Enlightenment', in G. A. J. Rogers (ed.), *Locke's Philosophy: Content and Context,* Oxford: Clarendon Press, 1994, ch.X; B. Toth, 'The influence of John Locke's philosophy in Debrecen', *Hungarian Studies in English,* XVIII, 1985, 49–57.

14 For the Presbyterian divine, Baxter (1615–91), and the Independent divine, Owen (1616–83) see DNB.

15 Cf. Daniel Boorstin, *America and the Image of Europe: Reflections on American Thought*, New York: Meridian Books, 1960, 73: 'One of the commonest and most misleading assumptions of intellectual historians is that in a period like the eighteenth century the content of a man's library was roughly the same as the content of his mind.'

16 See further Alan P. F. Sell, 'Philosophy in the eighteenth-century Dissenting academies of England and Wales', *History of Universities*, XI, 1992, 75–122.

17 See further J. Gascoigne, *Cambridge in the Age of the Enlightenment,* Cambridge: CUP, 1989. For varying attitudes towards Locke in one Oxford college see E. G. W. Bill, *Education at Christ Church, Oxford 1660–1800,* Oxford: Clarendon Press, 1988, 300. For Isaac Newton (1642–1727) and Samuel Clarke (1675–1729) see DNB.

18 See Patrick Kelly, 'Perceptions of Locke in eighteenth-century Ireland', *Proceedings of the Royal Irish Academy,* LXXXIXc, 1989, 17–35.

19 S. Johnson, 'Autobiography', in Herbert and Carol Schneider (eds.), *Samuel Johnson, His Career and Writings,* 4 vols., New York: Columbia University Press, 1929, I, 6. Cf. Merle Curti, 'The great

Mr. Locke: America's philosopher, 1783–1861', *Huntington Library Bulletin,* XI, 1937, 117. For Johnson (1696–1772) see *The Dictionary of American Biography* (hereinafter, DAB).

20 For Rowe (1657–1705) and Grove (1684–1738) see DNB; and for the latter, Sell, *Dissenting Thought and the Life of the Churches,* ch.VI.

21 For Jennings (d. 1723) and Doddridge (1702–51) see DNB. Doddridge's *Abstract* is at Dr Williams's Library, London, New College MSS. L95.

22 See Sell, *Dissenting Thought and the Life of the Churches,* 374, in a chapter on Noah Jones (1725–85). For Thomas (1692–1766) see *The Dictionary of Welsh Biography down to 1940,* London: Honourable Society of Cymmrodorion, 1959.

23 See the Note Books (1708–13) of his pupil, Henry Winder (1693–1752), Manchester College, Oxford, Winter MSS 1/1(i).

24 For Oldfield (1656–1729), Dixon (1680?–1729), and Jones (1680?–1719) see DNB. For Dixon and Latham (1688–1754) see H. McLachlan, *Essays and Addresses,* Manchester: Manchester University Press, 1950, 131–46 and 147–64, respectively. Thomas Secker (1693–1768), who became archbishop of Canterbury, was among Butler's contemporaries at the Tewkesbury academy. See DNB, 'Secker.'

25 For Taylor (fl. 1727–40) and Parry (1754–1819) see DNB. Taylor's *Lectures* are at the Congregational Library at Dr Williams's Library, London, MSS 1.d.34; Parry's are in the New College, London, collection at Dr Williams's Library, L.17.1.

26 See further Sell, 'Philosophy in the eighteenth-century Dissenting academies of England and Wales', 88–9; H. McLachlan, *English Education under the Test Acts,* Manchester: Manchester University Press, 1931.

27 J. Edwards, *A Brief Vindication of the Fundamental Articles of the Christian Faith,* 1697, Dedication. For Edwards (1637–1716) see DNB.

28 See William T. Bluhm, Neil Wintfeld and Stuart H. Teger, 'Locke's idea of God: rational truth or rational myth?', *The Journal of Politics,* LXII, 1980, 414–38.

29 R. C. Tennant, 'The Anglican response to Locke's theory of personal identity', reprinted from *Journal of the History of Ideas,* XLIII, 1982, in John W. Yolton (ed.), *Philosophy, Religion and Science in the Seventeenth and Eighteenth Centuries,* Rochester, NY: University of Rochester Press, 1990, 192.

30 Maurice Cranston, *John Locke: A Biography,* London: OUP, 1985, 124.

31 Richard Ashcraft, 'Faith and knowledge in Locke's philosophy', in

John W. Yolton, (ed.), *John Locke: Problems and Perspectives,* Cambridge: CUP, 1969, 194.

32 Samuel C. Pearson, 'The religion of John Locke and the character of his thought', *The Journal of Religion,* LVIII, 1978, 248.

33 D. G. James, *The Life of Reason: Hobbes, Locke, Bolingbroke,* London: Longmans, 1949, 98.

34 G. Ryle, 'John Locke on the human understanding', reprinted from J. L. Stocks (ed.), *Tercentenary Essays on John Locke,* London: OUP, 1933, in C. B. Martin and D. M. Armstrong (eds.), *Locke and Berkeley,* London: Macmillan, n.d., 25.

35 Herbert D. Foster, 'International Calvinism through Locke and the Revolution of 1688', *American Historical Review,* XXXII, no.3, April 1927, 476. Richard Hooker (1554?–1600) – whom Foster wrongly designates a 'secular writer', Thomas Bilson (1547?–1616), James I (1566–1625), John Milton (1608–74), Henry Ainsworth (1571–1622/3) and John Selden (1584–1654) are in DNB, as is William Barclay (1546/7–1608).

36 See William M. Spellman, *John Locke and the Problem of Depravity,* Oxford: Clarendon Press, 1988; and cf. my review of this book in *Enlightenment and Dissent,* IX, 1990, 134–7.

37 R. Traill, *A Vindication of the Protestant Doctrine concerning Justification* ... from the Unjust Charge of Antinomianism (1692), in Traill's *Works,* Edinburgh: The Banner of Truth Trust, 1975, I, 273. For Traill (1642–1716) see DNB.

38 T. Becconsall, *The Grounds and Foundation of Natural Religion Discover'd,* 1698, vii.

39 See further, Mario Montuori, *John Locke on Toleration and the Unity of God,* Amsterdam: J. C. Gieben, 1983, 195–6. Cf. John W. Yolton, *John Locke and the Way of Ideas,* Oxford: Clarendon Press, 1956, 51–2.

40 Norman Fiering, *Jonathan Edwards's Moral Thought and its British Context,* Chapel Hill: University of North Carolina Press, 1981, 40–1.

41 So a manuscript note on the copy of Locke's *Essay* which belonged to James Tyrrell, one of the friends who met with Locke. See J. Locke, *An Essay concerning Human Understanding,* abr. and ed. A. S. Pringle-Pattison, Oxford: Clarendon Press, 1924, 4 n. 1. Cf. H. R. Fox Bourne, *The Life of John Locke,* London: Henry S. King, 1876, I, 248–9.

42 J. Locke, *An Essay concerning Human Understanding,* ed. Peter H. Nidditch, Oxford: Clarendon Press, 1974, 7. Throughout this work I use this edition of the *Essay* unless otherwise stated. For other writings by Locke I use the eleventh edition of his *Works,* 1812, unless otherwise stated. Needless to say, Locke's proposal did not commend itself to the absolute idealist Edward Caird: '[W]e have

nothing to measure [our intellectual powers] with, except the very powers that are to be measured. To see round our knowledge and find its boundary, we must stand outside of it, and where is such a standing ground to be found?' See his *Essays on Literature and Philosophy,* Glasgow: Maclehose, 1892, II, 443.

43 Ibid., I.i.7. Not, indeed, that Locke wished only to provide a fresh account of the range of human consciousness. Although I am primarily concerned with the responses of others to Locke, and not with his responses to his predecessors, I should like to record my conviction that Locke is not simply a cartographer of sensation. He is also concerned to defend his empiricism against the Cartesians. G. A. J. Rogers has shown this *vis-à-vis* the concept of infinity. Locke's strategy, he says, is to proceed on the basis that 'We can account for the idea [of infinity] quite satisfactorily by appeal to simple ideas of extension and duration combined with the idea of repetition.' There is thus no need to invoke innate ideas. See G. A. J. Rogers, 'Innate ideas and the infinite: the case of Locke and Descartes', *The Locke Newsletter,* XXVI, 1995, 67.

44 J. Locke, letter to Bold of 16 May 1699. See E. S. de Beer (ed.), *The Correspondence of John Locke,* Oxford: Clarendon Press, VI, 1981, 627. Locke responds to Bold's defence, *Some Considerations on the Principal Objections and Arguments which have been Publish'd aginst Mr. Locke's Essay of Humane Understanding,* 1699. For Bold (1649–1737), rector of Steeple in the Isle of Purbeck for fifty-six years, see DNB.

45 J. Locke, *Works,* VII, 188.

46 Idem, *Essay,* IV.x.7, quoting Romans 1:20.

47 John Dunn, *The Political Thought of John Locke,* Cambridge: CUP, 1969, x–xi.

48 N. Wolterstorff, 'Locke's philosophy of religion', in Vere Chappell (ed.), *The Cambridge Companion to Locke,* Cambridge: CUP, 1994, 174.

49 G. Santayana, *Some Turns of Thought in Modern Philosophy,* Cambridge: CUP, 1933, 13.

50 J. Locke, *A Letter concerning Toleration,* in *Works,* VI, 47.

51 For a full discussion of the matters here alluded to see Steven M. Dworetz, *The Unvarnished Doctrine. Locke and the American Revolution,* Durham, NC: Duke University Press, 1990, chs.I and II.

52 Cf. the view of Lester G. Crocker: 'It could possibly be argued that the Enlightenment belonged to an age of sentimentalism, emotionalism and intuitionism: the claims made for them are apparent in all countries and they were displayed in literature and the arts. As the century grew old, anti-rationalism became more frequent. We see it

in such manifestations as mesmerism, the Gothic fad, the extravagant doctrines of leading figures of certain masonic lodges – men who in some ways were also tied to the Enlightenment's quest for new directions.' See his Introduction to John W. Yolton et al. (eds.), *The Blackwell Companion to the Enlightenment,* Oxford: Blackwell, 1991, 1–2.

53 The words were first published in the *Spectator,* no.465, 23 August 1712. For Addison (1672–1719), essayist, poet and statesman, see DNB.

54 For Edward Stillingfleet (1635–99), John Tillotson (1630–94), Richard Allestree (1619–81), Benjamin Whichcote (1609–83) and Isaac Barrow (1630–77) see DNB.

55 See further Amos Funkenstein, *Theology and the Scientific Imagination: From the Middle Ages to the Seventeenth Century,* Princeton: Princeton University Press, 1986.

56 For John Norris (1657–1711) see DNB.

57 John Edwards, *A Demonstration of the Existence and Providence of God,* London, 1696, 18.

58 Idem, *Some Thoughts concerning the Several Causes and Occasions of Atheism,* London, 1695, 100–1.

59 [William Carroll], *Remarks upon Mr. Clarke's Sermons, Preached at St. Paul's against Hobbs, Spinoza, and other Atheists,* London: Jonathan Robinson, 1705, 9. Cf. idem, *A Dissertation upon the Tenth Chapter of the Fourth Book of Mr. Locke's Essay,* London, 1706, *passim.*

60 For John Toland (1670–1722), George Berkeley (1685–1753), David Hume (1711–76), Thomas Reid (1710–96) and Joseph Priestley (1733–1804) see DNB. For Jonathan Edwards (1703–58) see DAB.

61 The description is George Whitefield's. See his *Journals,* 14 November 1739; London: The Banner of Truth Trust, 1960, 348.

62 G. Tennent, *Twenty-three Sermons upon the Chief End of Man,* Philadelphia: William Bradford, 1744, 82–3. For Tennent (1703–64) see DAB.

63 J. Barber, *A Sermon occasioned by the death of the Rev. Nathaniel Trotman,* London, 1793, 17. For Barber (1727–1810) see *Evangelical Magazine,* 1811, 161.

Chapter 2: Ideas, Knowledge and Truth

1 J. Locke, *Essay,* I.ii.1.

2 See I.iii.8; I.iii.13; I.iii.14; I.iv.14.

3 See Locke's *Essays on the Law of Nature,* ed. W. von Leyden, Oxford: Clarendon Press, 1954, 123, 125, 137, 143, 145.

4 See John W. Yolton, *John Locke and the Way of Ideas,* Oxford: Clarendon Press, 1968, 26–48.

5 J. Locke, *Essay,* I.ii.1.

6 Ibid., I.ii.4.

7 Ibid., I.iii.3.

8 Ibid., I.iii.13.

9 G. Ryle, 'John Locke on the human understanding', in C. B. Martin and D. M. Armstrong (eds.), *Locke and Berkeley,* London: Macmillan, n.d., 17–22.

10 J. Locke, *Essay,* I.i.8.

11 See J. Locke, *Essay,* I.iv.12; IV.xx.10.

12 Ibid., I.iv.24.

13 Ibid., I.iv.23.

14 E. Caird, *Essays on Literature and Philosophy,* Glasgow: Maclehose, 1892, II, 296. Cf. Alan P. F. Sell, 'Locke and Descartes through Victorian eyes [i.e. those of Henry Rogers]', in idem, *Dissenting Thought and the Life of the Churches: Studies in an English Tradition,* Lewiston, NY: Edwin Mellen Press, 1990, 512–13. For Rogers (1806–77) see ibid., ch.XVII, where I point out that in philosophical method Rogers was determinedly in the line of Butler and Reid – unlike the absolute idealist Caird, for example, for whom see idem, *Philosophical Idealism and Christian Belief,* Cardiff: University of Wales Press and New York: St Martin's Press, 1995.

15 See Alexander Campbell Fraser (ed.), *John Locke: An Essay concerning Human Understanding,* Oxford: Clarendon Press, 1894, 37 n. 2.

16 See E. S. de Beer (ed.), *The Correspondence of John Locke,* Oxford: Clarendon Press, IV, 1979, 534. For King (1663–1712) see DNB.

17 Henry Lee (matric. 1661; d. 1713), a former Fellow of Emmanuel College, Cambridge, was now rector of Tichmarsh, Northamptonshire. See *Alumni Cantabrigienses,* I.iii.62.

18 J. Locke, *Essay,* I.iii.15. For Edward Herbert (1583–1648) see DNB.

19 John Spurr, '"Rational religion" in Restoration England', *Journal of the History of Ideas,* XLIX, 1988, 573.

20 See Samuel Parker, *A Free and Impartial Censure of the Platonick Philosophie,* 1666; and the remarks upon it by G. A. J. Rogers, 'Locke, Newton and the Cambridge Platonists on innate ideas', *Journal of the History of Ideas,* XL, 1979, 193–4; reprinted in John W. Yolton (ed.), *Philosophy, Religion and Science in the Seventeenth and Eighteenth Centuries,* Rochester, NY: University of Rochester Press, 1990. For Parker (1640–88), bishop of Oxford, see DNB. For a modern argument against Locke on innate ideas, but not in favour of such ideas, see Peg O'Connor, 'Locke's challenge to innate practical principles revisited', *The Locke Newsletter,* XXV, 1994, 41–51.

21 Yolton, *John Locke and the Way of Ideas,* 29.

22 R. Burthogge, *Organum Vetus & Novum. Or, A Discourse of Reason and Truth,* (1678), in Margaret W. Landes (ed.), *The Philosophical Writings of Richard Burthogge,* Chicago: The Open Court, 1921, 38. For Burthogge (1638?–94?) see DNB. Not that Burthogge agreed with Locke in all particulars. As M. W. Landes points out, he did not hold Locke's view that sense impressions enter the mind unaccompanied; rather, notions dormant in the mind are rendered operative on the occasion of sense experience. Op. cit., xxii.

23 James Tyrrell to Locke, 30 June 1690; see de Beer (ed.), *The Correspondence of John Locke,* IV, 101. For Tyrrell (1642–1718) see DNB.

24 See Charlotte Johnston, 'Locke's *Examination of Malebranche* and John Norris', *Journal of the History of Ideas,* XIX, 1958, 551–8.

25 John Norris, *Cursory Reflections upon a Book call'd, an Essay concerning Human Understanding,* 1692, 20. This work was originally incorporated within Norris's *Christian Blessedness; or, Discourses upon the Beatitudes of Our Lord and Saviour Jesus Christ,* London, 1690.

26 Ibid., 21.

27 James Lowde, *A Discourse concerning the Nature of Man,* 1694, 52–3. Lowde notes that although Norris 'agrees with Dr. *Lock* in denying all natural and innate Notions in the Mind of Man; yet it is for other Reasons than those which Dr. *Lock* goes upon, and upon a far different *Hypothesis.*' (ibid., 81). Among his charges against Norris is one to the effect that the latter does not sufficiently distinguish divine revelation from human knowledge (p.85). For Lowde (matric. 1656, d. 1699, aged 59) see *Alumni Cantabrigienses.*

28 Ibid., 78–9.

29 Ibid., 136.

30 J. Edwards, *The Socinian Creed,* 1697, 122.

31 J. Edwards, *A Free Discourse concerning Truth and Error,* London: Jonathan Robinson, et al., 1701, 27–8.

32 Ibid., 28–9; 38. Cf. idem, *The Eternal and Intrinsick Reasons of Good and Evil,* Cambridge, 1699, 26.

33 [Thomas Burnet], *Remarks upon an Essay concerning Humane Understanding,* 1697, 6. For Burnet (1635?–1715), master of the Charterhouse, see DNB.

34 Ibid., 6.

35 J. Locke, *An Answer to Remarks upon an Essay concerning Human Understanding,* in *Works,* IV, 187.

36 [T. Burnet], *Second Remarks upon an Essay concerning Humane Understanding,* 1697, 3.

37 John Milner, *An Account of Mr. Lock's Religion,* 1700, 60. For Milner

(1628–1702) the nonjuror, see DNB.

38 J. Locke, *Essay,* I.iii.13. See S. G. Hefelbower, *The Relation of John Locke to English Deism,* Chicago: University of Chicago Press, 1918, 55–9.

39 See H. Lee, *Anti-Scepticism,* 1702. As we shall see, Lee's quest is for certainty, and he denies that Locke's comparison of ideas yields this.

40 J. Locke, *Works,* IX, 396; letter to William Molyneux of 22 February 1696/7.

41 William Sherlock, *A Discourse concerning the Happiness of Good Men,* 1704, 124. For Sherlock (1641?–1707) see DNB.

42 Ibid., 132.

43 Ibid., 133.

44 Ibid., 161–2.

45 W. Carroll, *Spinoza Reviv'd. Part the Second,* 1711, 3.

46 J. Oswald, *An Appeal to Common Sense in behalf of Religion,* London: J. Hughes, 2nd edn, 1768, I, 70–1. For Oswald (1703–93) see *Fasti Ecclesiae Scoticanae,* ed. Hew Scott et al., Edinburgh, 1866, etc., IV, 223; G. Ardley, *The Common Sense Philosophy of James Oswald,* Aberdeen: Aberdeen University Press, 1980; S. A. Grave, *The Scottish Philosophy of Common Sense,* Oxford: Clarendon Press, 1960.

47 Ibid., 77.

48 Ibid., 109.

49 J[ohn] S[ergeant], *Solid Philosophy Asserted against the Fancies of the Ideists,* London, 1697, The Epistle Dedicatory (unpaginated), 5–6.

50 Ibid., Preface (unpaginated), final sentence.

51 Ibid., 119–26.

52 Ibid., 453.

53 [Catharine Cockburn], *A Defence of the Essay of Human Understanding,* London, 1702, 62. For Catharine Cockburn (1679–1749) see DNB.

54 J. Locke to Catharine Cockburn, 30 December 1702; see de Beer, (ed.), *The Correspondence of John Locke,* VII, 1982, 731.

55 Ibid., 243–4, Collins to Locke; letter of 15 March 1703/4. For Collins (1676–1729) see DNB.

56 Yolton, *John Locke and the Way of Ideas,* 57.

57 W. Wollaston, *The Religion of Nature Delineated,* London, 1722, 17. For Wollaston (1660–1724) see DNB.

58 I. Watts, *The Works of the Rev. Isaac Watts, D.D.,* Leeds: Edward Baines VI, 525. Watts's essay, 'Of innate ideas' was first published in 1733. For Watts (1674–1748) see DNB.

59 Ibid., VI, 522–3.

60 Ibid., 527.

61 Ibid., 21.

62 T. Ludlam, *Logical Tracts,* Cambridge, 1790, 5. For Ludlam (1727–1811); George Horne (1730–92), bishop of Norwich; Henry Kett (1761–1825), incumbent of Elsfield, Oxfordshire; and John Napleton (1738?–1817), prebendary of Hereford, see DNB.

63 E. Oliver, *An Analysis of Mr. Locke's Essay concerning Human Understanding,* London, 1810, 1. For Oliver (1736–1818), rector of Swanscombe, Kent, see *Alumni Cantabrigienses,* II.iv.588.

64 J. Locke, *Essay,* I.iv.23.

65 Ibid., I.i.2. It is, however, evident that on occasion Locke confuses the question of the genesis of our ideas with that of their truth value.

66 Remonstrants' MSS J. 27a, in the University Library, Amsterdam. Cited by Maurice Cranston, *John Locke: A Biography,* Oxford: OUP (1957), 1985, 38.

67 For an analogous qualification in another field see Catherine Wilson, 'Visual surface and visual symbol: the microscope and the occult in early modern science,' reprinted in Yolton (ed.), *Philosophy, Religion and Science in the 17th and 18th Centuries,* 104:

> Though a number of writers have seen in Locke's crusade against Aristotelian 'essences' the origins of a distinctively modern conception of natural science aiming at the regular correlation of phenomena, it is important to recognize that there is a reactionary aspect to it as well. Writing in the prime period of disillusionment with the microscope, Locke continually measures microscopical science against angelic science and finds it wanting.

68 Locke's *Note,* no.39, 239, in his copy of J. Sergeant, *Solid Philosophy Asserted,* 1697, which is in the library of St John's College, Cambridge.

69 Quoted by Joel C. Weinsheimer (from A. Campbell Fraser, *Locke,* Edinburgh: Blackwood, 1890, 47), *Eighteenth-Century Hermeneutics: Philosophy of Interpretation in England from Locke to Burke,* New Haven: Yale University Press, 1993, 27. Weinsheimer's purpose, however, is to fault Locke for what he regards as his 'Crusoe-like self-reliance' in intellectual and moral matters. Cf. Steven M. Dworetz, *The Unvarnished Doctrine: Locke, Liberalism and the American Revolution,* Durham, NC: Duke University Press, 1990, 174–5.

70 See J. Locke, *Essay,* I.iv.23; cf. idem, 'An Essay for the Understanding of St. Paul's Epistles,' prefixed to his *A Paraphrase and Notes on the Epistles of St. Paul,* ed. Arthur W. Wainwright, Oxford: Clarendon Press, 1987, I, 115.

71 J. Locke, *Essay,* II.i.2.

72 Ibid., I.ii.15.

73 Ibid., IV.ii.1; cf. IV.iv.3.

74 Ibid., II.viii.8.

75 Ibid., II.viii.15; II.viii.10.

76 Ibid., II.xxiii.1. See Edwin McCann's exposition in Vere Chappell (ed.), *The Cambridge Companion to Locke,* Cambridge: CUP, 1994, ch.III; M. R. Ayers, in G. A. J. Rogers, (ed.), *Locke's Philosophy: Content and Context,* Oxford: Clarendon Press, 1994, ch.II.
77 Ibid., I.iv.18.
78 Ibid., II.i.4.
79 Ibid., IV.vi.16.
80 Ibid., IV.1.2.
81 Ibid., II.xii.1.
82 Ibid., IV.iv.4.
83 Ibid., IV.ix.3.
84 Ibid., IV.ii.1.
85 Ibid., IV.vi.16.
86 Ibid., IV.xiv.1.
87 See further Louis E. Loeb, *From Descartes to Hume: Continental Metaphysics and the Development of Modern Philosophy,* Ithaca, NY: Cornell University Press, 1981, 34ff. Among older writers, it served T. H. Green well to present Locke as highly empiricist – a position which James Gibson sought to temper. See Green's *Works,* ed. R. L. Nettleship, London: Longmans, 1885, I, 5–132; James Gibson, *Locke's Theory of Knowledge and its Historical Relations,* Cambridge: CUP, 1917.
88 G. A. J. Rogers, 'Boyle, Locke, and reason', reprinted in Yolton (ed.), *Philosophy, Religion and Science in the Seventeenth and Eighteenth Centuries,* 342.
89 A. Seth, *Scottish Philosophy,* Edinburgh: Blackwood, 2nd edn, 1890, 15.
90 Ibid., 150. In the context, Seth makes this remark by way of indicating a similarity between Kant and Locke. Cf. Edward Caird, *A Critical Account of the Philosophy of Kant,* Glasgow: Maclehose, 1877, 58.
91 See the interesting paper by Jonathan Barnes, 'Scepticism and relativity', *Philosophical Studies,* XXXII, 1988–90, 1–31.
92 J. Locke, *Essay* , I.i.5.
93 Ibid., II.xxiii.32.
94 Ibid., IV.vi.15.
95 Ibid., IV.iii.17.
96 Cited by Locke, *Letter to the Bishop of Worcester,* in *Works,* IV, 5; cf. E. Stillingfleet, *A Discourse in Vindication of the Doctrine of the Trinity,* 1697, 233–5.
97 J. Locke, *Essay* , IV.iv.3.
98 Ibid., IV.iv.4–5.
99 Idem, *Third Letter* to Stillingfleet in J. Locke, *Works,* IV, 360.
100 Idem, *Essay* , II.xxiii.1.

[101] Ibid., II.xxiii.6. Cf. ibid., I.iv.18, where Locke says that 'we signify nothing by the word *Substance*, but only an uncertain supposition of we know not what.'

[102] E. Stillingfleet, *The Bishop of Worcester's Answer to Mr. Locke's Second Letter*, London: J.H. for Henry Mortlock, 1698, 120–1.

[103] Idem, *A Discourse in Vindication of the Doctrine of the Trinity*, 2nd edn, 1697, 235.

[104] Yolton, *John Locke and the Way of Ideas*, 134. Henry Home (Lord Kames) thought that Locke had made a pitfall for himself by attempting an idea of substance in general, abstracted from all properties. Equally, we cannot think of properties abstracted from a substance. See his *Essays on the Principles of Morality and Natural Religion*, Edinburgh: R. Fleming, 1751, 248–51. For Home (1696–1782), a Scottish judge, see DNB.

[105] J. Locke, *Essay* , I.i.5.

[106] Ibid., IV.xi.3.

[107] H. Lee, *Anti-Scepticism*, 67.

[108] Ibid., 264.

[109] W. Carroll, *A Dissertation upon the Tenth Chapter of the Fourth Book of Mr. Locke's Essay*, London, 1706, 44–5.

[110] J. Witty, *The First Principles of Modern Deism Confuted*, London, 1707, 23–4. For Witty (matric. 1667; d. 1726) see *Alumni Cantabrigienses*, I.iv.445.

[111] John Ellis, *The Knowledge of Divine Things from Revelation* (1743), 1837 edn., 434. Ellis was vicar of St Catharine's, Dublin.

[112] Ibid., 127.

[113] Ibid., 133.

[114] Ibid., 399.

[115] Philip Doddridge, *Works*, V, 436.

[116] J. Norris, *Cursory Reflections upon a Book call'd, an Essay concerning Human Understanding*, London, 1692, 30. For a discussion of Norris and others see John Hoyles, *The Waning of the Renaissance 1640–1740: Studies in the Thought and Poetry of Henry More, John Norris and Isaac Watts*, The Hague: Martinus Nijhoff, 1971.

[117] Idem, *An Essay towards the Theory of the Ideal or Intelligible World*, London, 1701, 370.

[118] Ibid., 371.

[119] Ibid., 371–2. Cf. idem, *An Essay towards the Theory of the Ideal or Intelligible World*, London, 2 vols., 1701–4, II, 516–17.

[120] E. Elys, *A Refutation of Some of the False Conceits in Mr. Locke's Essay concerning Humane Understanding*, London, 1697, 7. For Elys (fl. 1707) see DNB.

[121] Ibid., 10.

122 Ibid.

123 Ibid., 25.

124 F.B., *A Free but Modest Censure,* London, 1698, 15.

125 G. Cheyne, *Philosophical Principles of Religion,* London (1715), 4th edn, 1734, 114.

126 S. Bold, *Some Considerations on the Principal Objections,* London, 1699, 1.

127 Ibid., 10.

128 Ibid., 2, citing Locke's *Essay* , IV.vi.iii.

129 Ibid., 4.

130 Ibid., 6.

131 Ibid., 11. Cf. my earlier remark concerning the epistemology/psychology distinction.

132 Ibid., 12–13.

133 Ibid., 13–14.

134 Ibid., 16.

135 [C. Cockburn], *A Defence of the Essay of Human Understanding,* 13, 25.

136 See V. Perronet, *A Vindication of Mr. Locke from the Charge of giving Encouragement to Scepticism and Infidelity,* 1736, 54.

137 See V. Perronet, 'Memoirs of the Rev. Mr. Vincent Perronet, A.M.', *The Methodist Magazine,* XXII, 1799, 54. The ailing Watts's letter is dated 26 February 1741–2. For Perronet (1693–1785) see DNB.

138 I. Watts, *Works,* VI, 483.

139 Ibid., 502.

140 Ibid., 503; cf. ibid., VI, 12n. For Perronet's criticism of Watts see his *A Second Vindication of Mr. Locke,* 1738, 106–10.

141 T. Belsham, *Elements of the Philosophy of the Mind,* London: J. Johnson, 1801, iii.

142 Ibid., 22–3.

143 R. Price, *A Review of the Principal Questions of Morals,* ed. D. D. Raphael, Oxford: Clarendon Press, 1974, 17–18. For Price (1723–91), the Presbyterian divine, see DNB.

144 Ibid., 18.

145 Ibid.

146 For a fuller discussion of Price's position see D. O. Thomas, *The Honest Mind: The Thought and Work of Richard Price,* Oxford: Clarendon Press, 1977, ch.III; John Stephens, 'The epistemological strategy of Price's *Review of Morals*', *Enlightenment and Dissent,* V, 1986, 39–50.

147 Henri Laboucheix, *Richard Price as Moral Philosopher and Political Theorist,* trans. Sylvia and David Raphael, Oxford: The Voltaire Foundation at the Taylor Institution, 1982, 45.

[148] P. Browne, *The Procedure, Extent and Limits of Human Understanding*, London: William Innys, 1728, 64.
[149] T. Reid, *Works*, ed. W. Hamilton, Edinburgh: Maclachlan and Stewart, 1863, I, 91.
[150] Ibid., 438.
[151] Ibid., 103.
[152] Ibid., 374.
[153] Ibid., 285.
[154] A. Campbell Fraser, *Thomas Reid*, Edinburgh: Oliphant Anderson & Ferrier, 1898, 135.
[155] T. Reid, *Works*, I, 234. He refers to Hume's *A Treatise of Human Nature*, I.iv.2.
[156] A. Broadie, 'Thomas Reid and his pre-Reformation Scottish precursors', in Peter Jones (ed.), *Philosophy and Science in the Scottish Enlightenment*, Edinburgh: John Donald, 1988, 17.
[157] T. Reid, *Works*, ed. William Hamilton, Edinburgh: MacLachlan and Stewart, 1863, I, 88. For Reid (1710–96) see DNB; Melvin T. Dalgarno and Eric Matthews (eds.), *The Philosophy of Thomas Reid*, Dordrecht: Kluwer Academic Publishers, 1989; K. Lehrer, *Thomas Reid*, London, 1989; S. A. Grave, *The Scottish Philosophy of Common Sense*.
[158] Ibid., 103.
[159] Ibid., 104.
[160] J. Beattie, *An Essay on the Nature and Immutability of Truth*, Edinburgh: A. Kincaid & J. Bell, 1770, 244. For Beattie (1735–1803) see DNB.
[161] Ibid., 245.
[162] Ibid., 246.
[163] Ibid., 247.
[164] J. Priestley, *Works*, II, 257.
[165] Ibid., III, 27.
[166] So I. Woodbridge Riley, *American Philosophy: The Early Schools*, New York: Russell & Russell, 1957, 18.
[167] See Sydney E. Ahlstrom, 'The Scottish philosophy and American theology', *Church History*, XXIV, 1955, 257–72. For Witherspoon see DAB; V. S. Collins, *President Witherspoon: A Biography*, Princeton: Princeton University Press, 2 vols., 1925; G. E. Rich, 'John Witherspoon: His Scottish Intellectual Background', unpublished dissertation, University of Syracuse, 1964; A. Green, *The Life of the Reverend John Witherspoon*, Princeton: Princeton University Press, 1973; Jack Scott (ed.), *An Annotated Edition of Lectures on Moral Philosophy by John Witherspoon*, Newark: University of Delaware Press, 1982, esp. 31–4; G. L. Tait, 'John Witherspoon, American

intellectual leader', *Journal of Religious Studies,* XII, 1986, 1–13.

168 See Cameron Thompson, 'John Locke and New England transcendentalism', *New England Quarterly,* XXXV, 1962, 437–8; Bruce Kuklick, *Churchmen and Philosophers from Jonathan Edwards to John Dewey,* New Haven: Yale University Press, 1985, ch.V.

169 See Daniel Walker Howe, *The Unitarian Conscience: Harvard Moral Philosophy, 1805–1861,* Middletown, Conn.: Wesleyan University Press, 1988, 37. For descriptions by transcendentalists of Locke's philosophy as narrow, wooden and the like see C. Thompson, 'John Locke and New England transcendentalism', 445–8.

170 W. and T. Ludlam, *Essays, Scriptural, Moral, and Logical,* London: J. G. Barnard, 1807 edn, II, 458–67.

171 For Berkeley (1685–1753) see DNB, and a vast literature.

172 G. Berkeley, A *Treatise concerning the Principles of Human Knowledge,* (1710), ed. T. E. Jessop (vol.II of *The Works of George Berkeley Bishop of Cloyne,* eds. A. A. Luce and T. E. Jessop), London: Nelson, 1949, 80; cf. ibid., 106.

173 Ibid., 27, 30–3; idem, *An Essay towards a New Theory of Vision* (1709), ed. A. A. Luce (in vol.I of Berkeley's *Works,* London: Nelson, 1948), 221–2; idem, *A Defence of Free-thinking in Mathematics,* in *Works,* IV, 133–6. See further, E. J. Craig, 'Berkeley's attack on abstract ideas', *The Philosophical Review,* LXXVII, 1968, 425–37.

174 Cf. Loeb, *Continental Metaphysics and the Development of Modern Philosophy,* 349.

175 G. Berkeley, *Works,* II, 41–2.

176 A. Campbell Fraser in *The North British Review,* XXXIV, no.LXVIII, May 1861, Art. VII, 462–5.

177 T. E. Jessop 'Introduction' to Berkeley's *Works,* II, 10.

178 G. Berkeley, *Works,* II, 45.

179 Berkeley to Percival, 6 September 1710; in *Works,* VIII, 37.

180 Ibid. See further, A. A. Luce, *Berkeley and Malebranche,* Oxford: Clarendon Press, 1967; idem, *The Dialectic of Immaterialism: An Account of the Making of Berkeley's Principles,* London: Hodder and Stoughton, 1963; I. C. Tipton, *Berkeley: The Philosophy of Immaterialism,* London: Methuen, 1974.

181 A. Campbell Fraser in *The North British Review,* May 1861, 456.

182 G. Berkeley, *Works,* II, 229ff.

183 T. Reid, *Works,* I, 266.

184 T. E. Jessop, 'Great thinkers (XI), Bishop Berkeley', *Philosophy,* XII, 1937, 281.

185 G. Berkeley, *Works,* II, 167–8. See further, Jonathan Bennett, *Locke, Berkeley, Hume: Central Themes,* Oxford: Clarendon Press, 1971, ch.VII.

186 Ibid., III, 147; cf. ibid., II, 108. In this connection Isaac Watts's

regret at not having read Berkeley in his 'Philosophical age of Life' on the ground that Berkeley was at that time considered too 'whimsicall and chimerick' is interesting. See Arthur Paul Davis, *Isaac Watts,* London: Independent Press, 1943, 262 n. 63, where the reference is to an unpublished letter of 13 May 1735 discovered in the Pennsylvania Historical Society's collection.

187 See further A. Campbell Fraser, 'The real world of Berkeley', *Macmillan's Magazine,* 1862, 192–202. A. S. Pringle-Pattison writes of his teacher that when Fraser

> suggests the practical agreement of Berkeley and Reid as 'immediate' Realists in common opposition to the hypothetical or mediate Realism – the representative perception – of the majority of philosophers, he can easily be shown to ignore the ultimately more important speculative difference between the two positions; for 'the ideal theory' of the representationists – the doctrine that we immediately know only our own states – is the very foundation of Berkeley's immaterialism.

See his 'Alexander Campbell Fraser 1819–1914', *Mind,* NS XXIV, 1915, 311. But a careful reading of Fraser's paper, especially pp. 198–201, reveals that this cannot be shown as easily as Pringle-Pattison supposes – and the latter himself (ad loc.) admits that Fraser was aware of the issues his pupil raises. See also R. M. Adams, 'Berkeley's "notion" of spiritual substance', *Archiv für Geschichte der Philosophie,* LV, 1973, 47–69.

188 S. Johnson, 'Autobiography', in Herbert and Carol Schneider, *Samuel Johnson, His Career and Writings,* New York: Columbia University Press, 4 vols., 1929, I, 6.

189 See Berkeley's letter to Johnson of 24 March 1730, in Berkeley's *Works,* II, 293.

190 *Samuel Johnson, His Career and Writings,* I, 25–6.

191 Ibid., II, 379–80.

192 Ibid., II, 248–9.

193 Ibid., II, 380.

194 See Norman Fiering, *Jonathan Edwards's Moral Thought and Its British Context,* Durham, NC: University of North Carolina Press, 1981, 32. For Edwards (1703–58) see DAB.

195 Samuel Hopkins, *The Life and Character of the late Reverend Mr. Jonathan Edwards* (1765), in David Levin (ed.), *Jonathan Edwards: A Profile,* New York: Hill and Wang, 1969, 5.

196 See, for example, Wallace E. Anderson, 'Editor's Introduction' to *The Works of Jonathan Edwards,* vol.VI, *Scientific and Philosophical Writings,* New Haven: Yale University Press, 1980.

197 See William Sparkes Morris, *The Young Jonathan Edwards: A Reconstruction,* New York: Carlson, 1991, 6–7; N. Fiering, *Jonathan*

Edwards's Moral Thought and Its British Context.

198 See Alan P. F. Sell, 'Philosophy in the eighteenth-century Dissenting academies of England and Wales', *History of Universities,* XI, 1992, 75–122.

199 William Sparkes Morris, *The Young Jonathan Edwards,* chs.II, VI.

200 For example, Perry Miller, *Jonathan Edwards* (1949), New York: Meridian Books, 1959, 52–68.

201 And the implication of what I am about to suggest is that perhaps Norman Fiering's disjunction is too strong when he asserts that 'Edwards belongs not with Locke, but with Locke's rivals, with Norris and Bishop Berkeley and Malebranche ... a sub-branch of the so-called Continental school.' See his 'The rationalist foundations of Edwards' metaphysics', in Nathan O. Hatch and Harry S. Stout (eds.), *Jonathan Edwards and the American Experience,* New York: Oxford University Press, 1988, 77.

202 The point is elaborated by Bruce Kuklick, *Churchmen and Philosophers from Jonathan Edwards to John Dewey,* New Haven: Yale University Press, 1985, 30.

203 James Hoopes, 'Jonathan Edwards's religious psychology', *The Journal of American History,* LXIX, 1983, 851.

204 Jonathan Edwards, *Christian Knowledge: or, the Importance and Advantage of a Thorough Knowledge of Divine Truth,* in his *Works* (1834), reprinted Edinburgh: The Banner of Truth Trust, 1974, II, 159.

205 Idem, Sermon on Matt. 16:17, in *Works,* II, 13.

206 I am pleased to find confirmation of this in W. S. Morris, *The Young Jonathan Edwards,* e.g., 249–50 and 434, which came into my hands after I had reached the conclusion myself.

207 Paul Helm, 'John Locke and Jonathan Edwards: a reconsideration', *Journal of the History of Philosophy,* VII, 1969, 58.

208 For Ames (1576–1633) see DNB. For Hooker (1586?–1647) see DAB.

209 J. Edwards, *On Religous Affections,* in *Works,* I, 282–3.

210 Idem, *Treatise on Grace,* ed. Paul Helm, Cambridge: James Clarke, 1971, 28–9.

211 Idem, *Works,* I, 289–90.

212 Cf. James Hoopes, 'Jonathan Edwards's religious psychology', 857–8, 862.

213 J. Edwards, *Works,* I, 246.

214 On the 'new spiritual sense' and Edwards's Puritan inheritance, see Terence Erdt, *Jonathan Edwards: Art and the Sense of the Heart,* Amherst: University of Massachusetts Press, 1980, especially xii–xiii, 1–4, 18–20, 41–2. See further, John Stephen Martin, 'The rhetoric of

grace in Jonathan Edwards' *Personal Narrative*', *Man and Nature. Proceedings of the Canadian Society for Eighteenth-Century Studies,* IV, 1985, 112. That positive and negative analogies may also be drawn between Edwards's 'new spiritual sense' and the 'moral sense' of Shaftesbury, Hutcheson and others, need not be denied.

215 J. Edwards, *Treatise on Grace,* 39.

216 Ibid., 29.

217 J. Locke, *Essay,* III.ii.1.

218 For Butler (1692–1752) see DNB.

219 Terence Penelhum, in *Joseph Butler's Moral and Religious Thought,* ed. Christopher Cunliffe, Oxford: Clarendon Press, 1992, 121. He cites Locke's *Essay,* IV.iii.25–6. Cf. J. Butler, 'Sermon XV – Upon the ignorance of man', in W. R. Matthews (ed.), *Butler's Fifteen Sermons* (1914), London: G. Bell, 1953.

220 Ibid., 122. See also Terence Penelhum's fine study, *Butler,* London: Routledge & Kegan Paul, 1985, especially ch.IV.

221 Joseph Butler, *The Analogy of Religion,* Introduction, para. 1.

222 Ibid., paras. 1–5.

223 Ibid., II.vi.6

224 Idem, *Butler's Fifteen Sermons,* London: Bell, 1953, 234.

225 Ibid., 237, 240, 242.

226 See J. Locke, *Essay,* IV.xviii.2.

227 J. Wesley, *The Works of the Rev. John Wesley, A.M.,* ed. Thomas Jackson, London: John Mason, 14 vols., 1829–31, VI, 349.

228 Norman Sargent, 'John Wesley's meetings with Bishop Butler 1739', *Report of the Friends of Bristol Cathedral,* 1981, 23–7; Frank Baker, 'John Wesley and Bishop Joseph Butler', *Proceedings of the Wesley Historical Society,* XLII, May 1980, 3–10.

229 J. Wesley, *Works,* XIII, 424.

230 Ibid., VI, 339; cf. ibid., VII, 231.

231 Richard E. Brantley is strongly tempted in this direction, and on occasion succumbs, in his *Locke, Wesley and the Method of English Romanticism,* Gainesville, Fla.: University of Florida Press, 1984. Among reviews of this book see Henry D. Rack, in *Proceedings of the Wesley Historical Society,* XLV, September 1985, 63–5; Alan P. F. Sell, in *Enlightenment and Dissent,* VIII, 1989, 140–4. See further, John C. English, 'The Cambridge Platonists in John Wesley's "Christian Library"', *Proceedings of the Wesley Historical Society,* XXXVI, October 1968, 161–8; idem, 'John Norris and John Wesley on the "Conduct of the Understanding"', ibid., XXXVII, February 1970, 101–4.

232 J. Steven O'Malley, 'Recovering the vision of holiness: Wesley's epistemic basis', *The Asbury Theological Journal,* XLI, no.1, Spring 1986, 11.

[233] John Wesley, *The Appeals to Men of Reason and Religion,* ed. Gerald R. Cragg, vol. XI of *The Works of John Wesley,* ed. Frank Baker, Oxford: Clarendon Press, 1975, 57. Cf. idem, *Sermons on Several Occasions,* London: Epworth Press, 1944, 177–8; idem, *Works* (Jackson edn), VII, 351–2.

[234] Ibid., n.

[235] We should not overlook the even older heritage of which Bernard of Clairvaux was representative, nor the sensory language of the medieval mystics. I think especially of their use of 'taste' and 'tasting,' in connection with their experiences of God. Edwards and Wesley use the same words and, no doubt, the usage has its roots in such an injunction as, 'Taste and see that the Lord is good. Happy are they who find refuge in him!' (Psalm 34:8). At the same time, we must not overlook the differences between the intellectual climate of the medieval mystics, some of whom were in stout opposition to the rationalism of their day, and that of the eighteenth-century divines, many of whom were happy to be on the rationalist continuum over against enthusiasm and ultra-subjectivism.

[236] Henry D. Rack, *Reasonable Enthusiast: John Wesley and the Rise of Methodism,* London: Epworth Press, 1989, 65.

[237] Jones wrote his Memoir shortly before his death, and James Scott supplemented it with comments and independent information. The Scott MS is held by Messrs Haward and Evers, Solicitors, of Stourbridge, who kindly allowed me to take extracts for publication. For Noah Jones see further Sell, *Dissenting Thought and the Life of the Churches,* ch.XII.

[238] J. Locke, *Essay* , IV.xvi.10. Not, indeed, that all of the more liberal divines endorsed Locke's view. For example, Caleb Rotheram (1694–1752), Presbyterian minister and Dissenting academy tutor at Kendal, successfully defended the contrary thesis and was awarded the Degree of Doctor of Divinity (Edinburgh) in 1743. See *The Monthly Repository*, V, 1810, 219. Cf. DNB; Francis Nicholson and Ernest Axon, *The Older Nonconformity of Kendal*, Kendal: Titus Wilson, 1915, ch.xxv; Alan P. F. Sell, *Church Planting: A Study of Westmorland Nonconformity*, Worthing: H. E. Walter, 1986, 39–41.

[239] Ibid., 6–7.

[240] J. Locke to A. Collins, letter of 29 October 1703, *Works,* X, 271.

[241] Abraham Rees, *The Advantages of Knowledge, Illustrated and Recommended,* London: H. Goldney, 1788, 30 and n. For Rees (1743–1825) see DNB.

[242] Thomas Rees, *Address delivered at the Old Jewry Chapel in Jewin Street, on Saturday, the 19th day of June, 1825, over the body of the late Rev. Abraham Rees, D.D., F.R.S., &c., &c., previously to his*

interment in Bunhill Fields, London: Longman, 1825, 49. Abraham and Thomas Rees were not related.

243 J. Locke, *Essay,* IV.xix.1.

244 A. Campbell Fraser, 'John Locke as a factor in modern thought', *Proceedings of the British Academy,* I, 1903–4, 235.

245 J. Locke, *Essay* , IV.v.2.

246 See William Sparkes Morris, *The Young Jonathan Edwards,* 418–22. He, in turn, quotes J. Edwards, *Works* (1829–30), I, 688, 697–8, 690.

247 Ibid., 433.

248 J. Locke, *The Reasonableness of Christianity,* in *Works,* VII, 156: '[T]o acknowledge any proposition to be of divine revelation and authority; and yet to deny, or disbelieve it; is to offend against this fundamental article and ground of faith, that God is true.'

249 J. Locke, *Some Thoughts concerning Education,* in *Works,* IX, 30.

250 Ibid., 131.

251 Ibid., 116–18.

252 Maurice Cranston, *John Locke. A Biography* (1957), Oxford: OUP, 1985, 419.

253 Cf., for example, John Owen's account of the requirements laid upon, and the obligations undertaken by, those who are church members in his *The True Nature of a Gospel Church and its Government,* in his *Works* , ed. William H. Goold (1850–3), reprinted London: The Banner of Truth Trust, 1968, XVI, ch.I. For Owen (1616–83) see DNB.

254 Robert Hall, Sr, *Help to Zion's Travellers,* Halifax, 1781, 48 ff. For Hall (1728–91) see under his son Robert's entry in DNB.

255 Andrew Fuller, *Works,* London: Holdsworth and Ball, 5 vols., 1831–2, V, 329. For Fuller (1754–1815) see DNB.

256 Ibid., 330–5. Cf. his dialogue between Crispus and Gaius 'On the importance of truth', ibid., II, 458–61. For the Baptists see further, Frank Louis Maudlin, 'Truth, heritage, and eighteenth-century Baptists', *The Baptist Quarterly,* XXXV, no.5, January 1994, 211–28.

257 David Bogue, *The Great Importance of having Right Sentiments in Religion,* London, 1788, 34–41. For Bogue (1750–1825) see DNB.

258 Thomas Belsham, *The Character of the Christian Teacher Delineated, and the Means of Forming it Represented,* London, 1804, 5. For Belsham (1750–1829) see DNB.

259 Samuel Stennett, *The Mortality of Ministers contrasted with the Unchangeableness of Christ: In a Sermon, Occasioned by the Decease of The Rev. Caleb Evans, D.D., Who departed this Life Aug. 9, 1791, In the 54th Year of his Age,* London, 1791, 29. Evans was born in 1731. See Norman Moon, *Education for Ministry: Bristol Baptist College*

1679–1979, Bristol: Bristol Baptist College, 1979, 114–15 and *passim.*

260 J. Locke, *A Second Letter concerning Toleration,* in *Works*, VI, 66.

261 Idem, *A Third Letter for Toleration,* ibid., 144; cf. ch.VII below. Locke here replies to J. Proast's 1791 *Reply* to Locke's *Second Letter on Toleration.* For Proast (*c.*1642–1710) see DNB *Missing Persons.*

262 Ibid., 144.

263 Idem, *Essay* , IV.vi.6.

Chapter 3: Reason, Revelation, Faith and Scripture

1 J. Locke, *Essay,* IV.xvii.1. See Roland Hall, 'The place of reason in Locke's *Essay', The Locke Newsletter,* XXIII, 1992, 11–23.

2 Ibid., IV.xvii.6.

3 Ibid., IV.xviii.2.

4 Ibid., IV.xvii.2. G. A. J. Rogers finds Locke in agreement with Boyle at this point among others. See his, 'Boyle, Locke, and reason', *Journal of the History of Ideas,* XXVII, no.2, 1966, 213.

5 Ibid., IV.xix.14.

6 R. Hall, op. cit., 14. Cf. Nicholas Wolterstorff, 'John Locke's epistemological piety: reason is the candle of the Lord', *Faith and Philosophy,* XI, no.4, October 1994, 572–91.

7 B. Whichcote, *Moral and Religious Aphorisms,* F. Burges, Norwich for A. J. Churchill, London, 1703, no. 916. The biblical basis is *Proverbs* 20:27. Dr Hall notes that Lady Masham volunteers the information that Whichcote was Locke's favourite preacher.

8 J. Locke, *Essay,* I.i.5.

9 See further Peter A. Schouls, 'Locke and the dogma of infallible reason', *Revue Internationale de Philosophie,* XLII, no.165, 1988, 115–32.

10 J. Locke, *Essay,* IV.xix.4.

11 See S. G. Hefelbower, *The Relation of John Locke to English Deism,* Chicago: University of Chicago Press, 1918, 64–7.

12 J. Locke, *Essay,* IV.xi.13; cf. IV.xvii.2.

13 J. Locke, *Essays on the Law of Nature,* ed. W. von Leyden, Oxford: Clarendon Press, 1954, 153ff.

14 Idem, *Journal,* 8 February 1677, MS f.2.

15 Idem., *Essay,* IV.x.10.

16 Ibid., IV.x.7.

17 Ibid., IV.x.1 and *passim.*

18 Ibid., II.xxiii.33.

19 John Mason, *Select Remains,* reprinted as *Mason's Sayings,* Sheffield: Zoar Publications, *c.*1974, 2. For Mason (1646?–94) see *Alumni*

Cantabrigienses. For an example of Locke's proper agnosticism concerning the full being of God see his *Essay,* IV.x.13.

20 J. Locke, *Essay,* IV.x.7.

21 Idem, *Essays on the Law of Nature,* 111. That Locke regards the inculcation of such principles as a major motive in education is clear from his writings on that subject. See his *Some Thoughts concerning Education,* eds. John and Jean Yolton, Oxford: Clarendon Press, 1989, *passim.*

22 These deficiencies have widely been rehearsed in the extensive literature on the arguments for the existence of God. They include the following considerations: Why a first cause and not an infinite regress of causes? Why but one designer and not a team of designers? What price a divine designer who admits nature's 'red-in-tooth-and-claw-ness'? Cf. the first three and the fifth of Aquinas' 'five ways', in *Summa Theologica,* Q 2 Art. 3. For a sceptical view of Locke's sincerity in advancing theistic 'proofs' see William T. Bluhm, Neil Wintfeld and Stuart H. Teger, 'Locke's idea of God: rational truth or political myth?', *The Journal of Politics,* XLII, no.2, May 1980, 414–38. For Michael S. Rabieh's argument that 'The reasonableness of Christianity for Locke … consists in the political effectiveness of a properly interpreted Christianity, and in nothing more than this', see *The Journal of Politics,* LIII, no.4, November 1991, 933–57.

23 John Laird, *Theism and Cosmology,* London: Allen and Unwin, 1940, 88–9.

24 W. Law, *The Case of Reason, Or Natural Religion Fairly and Fully Stated,* 1731, i. For Law (1686–1761) see DNB.

25 E. C. Mossner, *Bishop Butler and the Age of Reason,* New York: Macmillan, 1936, 128.

26 See J. Wesley to William Law, 6 January 1756, in *The Letters of the Rev. John Wesley, A.M.,* ed. John Telford, London: Epworth Press, 1931, III, 332.

27 For example, by Terence Penelhum in his 'Scepticism, sentiment and common sense in Hume', *Dialogue,* XXIV, 1988, 515–21; idem, 'Human nature and belief: Hume and Pascal', *Lumen,* XII, 1993, 45–64.

28 J. Wesley, *The Appeals to Men of Reason and Religion and Certain Related Open Letters,* ed. Gerald R. Cragg, being *The Works of John Wesley,* ed. Frank Baker, Oxford: Clarendon Press, 1975, XI, 46–7, 55.

29 Idem, *Works,* Jackson's edn, VIII, 14.

30 J. Wesley, *The Letters of the Rev. John Wesley,* V, 364. See further, Arthur Skevington Wood, *Revelation and Reason: Wesleyan Responses*

to Eighteenth-century Rationalism, Glaston, Leics.: The Wesley Fellowship, 1992.

31 Among those influenced by Allen's anti-Calvinism was the Universalist Hosea Ballou, a former Calvinistic Baptist.

32 Abraham Taylor, *An Introduction to Logick, with a few Lectures on Perception, the first part of that Science,* 1739, 12, Dr Williams's Library, London, MSS 69. 24. For Taylor, an Independent of Calvinist persuasion (fl. 1727–40), see DNB.

33 E. Allen, *Reason the Only Oracle of Man,* 185. For Allen (1737–89) see DAB; Darline Shapiro, 'Ethan Allen, philosopher-theologican to a generation of American Revolutionaries', *The William and Mary Quarterly,* 3rd series, XXI, no.2, April 1964, 236–55.

34 T. Dwight, *Travels in New England and New York,* (1821–2), ed. Barbara Miller Solomon with the assistance of Patricia M. King, Cambridge, Mass.: The Belknap Press of Harvard University, 1969, II, 283.

35 For a fuller discussion of the points here summarized see I. Woodbridge Riley, *American Philosophy: The Early Schools,* New York: Henry Holt, 1915, ch.II. It is not without significance that, as so often, extremes meet: in this case the excesses of Law on the one hand and Allen on the other were eventually tempered by Romanticism whether Coleridgeian or Emersonian.

36 R. Baxter, *The Saint's Everlasting Rest,* 1650, II, Preface.

37 Ibid., III, i.

38 Idem, Epistle to *Poetical Fragments,* 3rd edn, 1699, A2.

39 For Joshua Oldfield (1656–1729) see DNB. For the influence of Locke upon Dissenting academies and tutors see Alan P. F. Sell, 'Philosophy in the eighteenth-century Dissenting academies of England and Wales', *History of Universities,* XI, 1992, 75–122.

40 James Martineau, *Types of Ethical Theory,* Oxford: Clarendon Press, 1885, II 549. See further, Alan P. F. Sell, 'Samuel Clarke on the existence of God', in idem, *Dissenting Thought and the Life of the Churches,* ch.IV. For Clarke (1675–1729) see DNB.

41 For John Brine (1703–65) see DNB.

42 John Gill, *Complete Body of Doctrinal and Practical Divinity: Or, A System of Evangelical Truths Deduced from the Sacred Scriptures* (1767, 1770), reprinted (from the 1839 edn) Grand Rapids: Baker Book House, 1978, I, 1.

43 In his first chapter Gill argues from general consent; the law and light of nature; the works of creation; the sustentation and government of the world; works done in the world which are inexplicable save on the supposition of a superior divine influence; prophecies; guilty torments and the fear of a future state; such divine judgements

as famine and pestilence, as well as those which have befallen the wicked.

44 See further Frank Louis Maudlin, 'Truth, heritage, and eighteenth-century English Baptists', *The Baptist Quarterly,* XXXV, no.5, January 1994, 211–28.

45 Ibid., 44.

46 For Dodwell (d. 1784) see DNB.

47 John Leland, *A Second Letter, Containing Remarks On a Late Pamphlet, entitled, Christianity not founded on Argument,* 1744, 88–9. For Leland (1691–1766) see DNB.

48 John Wesley, *Works,* ed. T. Jackson, 14 vols., 1829–31, VIII, 14.

49 James Oswald, *An Appeal to Common Sense in behalf of Religion,* (1766), 2nd edn, London: J. Hughes, 1768, I, 74.

50 Ibid., 77.

51 Ibid., 77–81.

52 Charles Chauncy, *Ministers Exhorted, etc.,* 1744, 24. For Chauncy (1705–87) see DAB; R. C. Whittemore, *Makers of the American Mind,* New York: William Morrow, 1964, ch.III.

53 Idem, *Election Sermon,* Massachusetts, 1747, 9. For others who made the same point see Steven M. Dworetz, *The Unvarnished Doctrine: Locke, Liberalism and the American Revolution,* Durham, NC: Duke University Press, 1990, 140.

54 John Taylor, *The Scripture Account of Prayer,* 1761, 5.

55 Quoted by Sell in *Dissenting Thought and the Life of the Churches,* 349.

56 William Enfield, *A Funeral Sermon, Occasioned by the Death of the Late Rev. John Aikin, D.D., Professor of Divinity at the Academy in Warrington,* Warrington: W. Eyres, 1781, 8–9. For Aikin (1713–80) and Enfield (1741–97) see DNB.

57 Thomas Amory, *Ministers not Lords over the Faith of Christians, but Helpers of their Joy: A Sermon Preached at Lewin's-Mead, Bristol, at the Ordination Of the Reverend Mr. William Richards, May the 22d. 1751,* London: J. Waugh, [1751], 12. For Amory (1701–74) see DNB.

58 Though later in the century, under the influence of the Evangelical Revival, those more evangelically inclined set out from a thoroughly biblical basis. See, for example, *An Introductory Discourse by Mr. John Angus, Mr. Fell's Confession of Faith; a charge by Thomas Davidson; and a Sermon by Thomas Towle, B.D., all delivered at the Ordination of the Rev. Mr. John Fell. In Thaxted, Essex, October 24th 1770.* After an introductory paragraph John Fell continues, 'I believe the scriptures of the Old and New Testament to be the inspired and holy word of God.' For Fell (1735–97), an Independent, see DNB. For further examples of ordination statements of faith see Sell, *Dissenting Thought and the Life of the Churches,* 34–47.

59 See *A Sermon Preached at the Ordination of the Reverend Mr. John Notcutt, at the Meeting-House in Green-Street, Cambridge, on July 22, 1735, by William Ford. With the Charge then given him by the Revd. Mr. Tobias Wildboar; and Mr. Notcutt's Confession of his FAITH*, 1735. Notcutt, who began as an Independent, became a Socinian, left the ministry for business in Ipswich, and died in 1778.

60 William Sherlock, *A Discourse concerning the Happiness of Good Men*, 1704, 124.

61 Ibid., 125–6.

62 Ibid., 130.

63 John Ellis, *Some Brief Considerations upon Mr. Locke's Hypothesis, That Knowledge of God is attainable by Ideas of Reflexion. Wherein it is Demonstrated, Upon his own Principles, That the Knowledge of God is not attainable by Ideas of Reflexion*, London, 1743, 34.

64 Ibid., 43.

65 See J. Locke, *Essay* , I.iv.9.

66 J. Lowde, *A Discourse concerning the Nature of Man*, 1694, 133.

67 T. Becconsall, *The Grounds and Foundation of Natural Religion Discover'd*, 1698, 46.

68 Ibid., 51.

69 Ibid., 72.

70 [J. Milner], *An Account of Mr. Lock's Religion*, 1700, 9.

71 Catharine Cockburn, *A Defence of the Essay of Human Understanding, written by Mr. Lock*, London, 1702, Epistle Dedicatory. For Mrs Cockburn (1679–1749) see DNB.

72 See Timothy Dwight, *Theology; Explained and Defended, in a Series of Sermons ... with a Memoir of the Life of the Authors* (1818–19), Glasgow: Blackie, 1835, I, 9. For Dwight (1752–1817) see DAB; Robert C. Whittemore, *The Transformation of the New England Theology*, New York: Peter Lang, 1987, 203–39.

73 For Peter Browne (d. 1735) see DNB; Arthur Robert Winnett, *Peter Browne, Provost, Bishop, Metaphysician*, London: SPCK, 1974, especially, 124–6. Winnett proceeds to note the criticisms of Browne levelled by Vincent Perronet and Edmund Law, ibid., 127–8.

74 M. Pattison, 'Tendencies of religious thought in England', 261.

75 J. Locke, *Essay*, IV.xix.4. The consideration announced in the last sentence, did not, as we saw, occur to those Christians who received Dodwell's argument as being in their favour. It is not without significance that Locke's words appear in the chapter entitled 'Of enthusiasm'.

76 Ibid., IV.xix.14.

77 Richard A. Muller, *Post-Reformation Reformed Dogmatics*, Grand Rapids: Baker Book House, 1987, I, 193. The evidence is clearly set

out in the chapter from which my quotation is drawn. David C. Snyder is not without excuse in interpreting Locke as saying, 'not only can we know some propositions without consulting faith and revelation, but none of our ideas can be received from revelation', for he can quote Locke's view that our ideas 'are the Foundation, and sole Matter of all our Notions, and Knowledge' (*Essay,* IV.xviii.3). He does, however, seem to overlook what Locke elsewhere says concerning reason as natural *revelation.* See David C. Snyder, 'Faith and reason in Locke's *Essay', Journal of the History of Ideas,* XLVII, no.2, April–June 1986, 201. Mr Snyder follows Nicholas Wolterstorff in thinking of Locke as in the train of Aquinas' complementarist view of the relation between reason and revelation. See N. Wolterstorff, *Reason within the Bounds of Religion,* Grand Rapids: Eerdmans, 1976, 24–9; and, more recently, idem, 'The assurance of faith', *Faith and Philosophy,* VII, no.4, October 1990, 396–417.

78 Cf. Locke's comment in n.17(h) on Ephesians 1:17 in his *A Paraphrase and Notes on the Epistles of St. Paul,* ed. Arthur W. Wainwright, Oxford: Clarendon Press, 1987, II, 623.

79 J. Locke, *Essay,* IV.xix.14.

80 Ibid., IV.xix.11. See further Paul Helm, 'Locke on faith and knowledge,' *The Philosophical Quarterly,* XXIII, 1973, 52–66; cf. T. H. Green, *Works,* ed. R. L. Nettleship, London: Longmans, 1885–8, I, 125.

81 R. Watson, *A Defence of Revealed Religion, in Two Sermons preached in the Cathedral Church of Llandaff; and a charge delivered to the Clergy of that Diocese, in June 1795,* London: T. Evans et al., 1795, 68.

82 J. Locke, *Essay,* IV.xviii.7. Cf. Locke's *Paraphrase,* I Cor. 2:6, 15, commentary.

83 Idem, *The Reasonableness of Christianity,* in *Works,* VII, 135.

84 Ibid.

85 Ibid., 137.

86 Idem, *A Paraphrase,* I, 172. Cf. idem, *A Discourse of Miracles,* in *Works* , IX, 262–4.

87 Idem, *Works* , IX, 256.

88 For further discussions of Locke *vis-à-vis* the points made in this paragraph see, for example, J. T. Moore, 'Locke's concept of religious assent', *Southwestern Journal of Philosophy,* VIII, no.2, Summer 1977, 5–30; Samuel C. Pearson, 'The religion of John Locke and the character of his thought', *The Journal of Religion,* LVIII, July 1978, 244–62.

89 See James E. Force, 'Hume and Johnson on prophecy and miracles: historical context', *Journal of the History of Ideas,* XLIII, 1982, 465, reprinted in John W. Yolton (ed.), *Philosophy, Religion and Science in the Seventeenth and Eighteenth Centuries,* Rochester, NY: University

of Rochester Press, 1990, ch.IX, 129. See further, J. J. MacIntosh, 'Locke and Boyle on miracles and God's existence', in Michael Hunter (ed.), *Robert Boyle Reconsidered,* Cambridge: CUP, 1994, ch.XII.

90 P. Doddridge, *The Works of the Rev. P. Doddridge, D.D.,* Leeds: Edward Baines, IV, 543.

91 J. Locke, *A Discourse of Miracles,* in *Works,* IX, 257.

92 J. Priestley, Preface to *A View of Revealed Religion; A Sermon preached at the Ordination of The Rev. William Field of Warwick, July 12, 1790 by Joseph Priestley LL.D., F.R.S. With a Charge Delievered at the same Time by the Rev. Thomas Belsham,* Birmingham, 1790, 30.

93 J. Locke, *Essay,* IV.xviii.5.

94 Ibid., IV.xvi.14.

95 Idem, *Essay,* IV.xix.16.

96 J. Toland, *Christianity Not Mysterious,* (1695), Stuttgart-Bad Cannstatt: Friedrich Frommann Verlag, 1964, 147–8.

97 E. Stillingfleet, *Discourse in Vindication of the Doctrine of the Trinity,* (1696), London: J.H. for H. Mortlock, 2nd edn, 1697, ch.X.

98 William Carroll, *A Dissertation upon the Tenth Chapter of the Fourth Book of Mr. Locke's 'Essay,'* London, 1706.

99 [Anthony Collins], *An Essay concerning the Use of Reason in Propositions, The Evidence whereof depends upon Human Testimony,* London, 1707, 40–1.

100 T. Burnet, *Remarks upon a Essay concerning Humane Understanding,* London (1697), reprinted in George Watson (ed.), *Remarks on John Locke by Thomas Burnet,* Gringley-on-the-Hill, Doncaster: The Brynmill Press, 1989, 26.

101 [Richard Willis], *The Occasional Paper, no. 1,* London, 1697, 18. For Willis (bapt. 1613/14; d. 1690) see *Alumni Cantabrigienses,* I.iv.422.

102 T. Halyburton, *Natural Religion Insufficient,* Edinburgh, 1714, 83–4. For Halyburton (1674–1712) see DNB.

103 Ibid., I, 134; II, 115 citing Locke's *Reasonableness,* 255–6 and *Essay* IV.xix.15 respectively.

104 J. Leland, *A View of the Principal Deistical Writers* (1745–6), London: T. Tegg, 1837, 18. For Leland (1691–1766) see DNB.

105 I. Watts, *The Strength and Weakness of Human Reason,* in Watts's *Works,* Leeds, 1810, III, 18. Watts quotes *Reasonableness,* 268.

106 A. Campbell, *The Necessity of Revelation,* London, 1739, 174; he quotes Locke's *Essay,* IV.iii.140. The work is a reply to Tindal. For Campbell (1691–1756) see DNB.

107 Quoted by Steven M. Dworetz, *The Unvarnished Doctrine,* 139.

108 Ibid., quoting Eliot's *Election Sermon,* Connecticut, 1738, 27, where Eliot refers to Locke.

[109] *Ordination to the Ministry, an entrusting Men with the Gospel. A Sermon Preach'd at the Ordination of Thomas Hadfield, M.D. At Peckham in the County of Surrey, October xix, MDCCXXVI. By Joseph Hill. With Dr. Hadfield's Confession of Faith, and his Answers to the Questions then propos'd to him by the Reverend Mr. John Beaumont. To which is Added The Charge given by the Reverend Mr. Thomas Reynolds,* London, 1727, 44–45. Hadfield was baptized at Chesterfield on 9 October 1701; he died on 21 February 1741. See *The Congregational Magazine,* 1824, 611; John Waddington, *Surrey Congregational History,* London: Jackson, Walford, and Hodder, 1866, 264; Edward E. Cleal, *The Story of Congregationalism in Surrey,* London: James Clarke, 1908, 20. For Latham (1688–1754) see H. McLachlan, *Essays and Addresses,* Manchester: Manchester University Press, 1950, ch.IX; for Findern Academy see idem, *English Education under the Test Acts, Being the History of the Nonconformist Academies 1662–1820,* Manchester: Manchester University Press, 1931, 131–4.

[110] Bernard Foskett, Lecture notes, *Pneumatology,* MSS Z.e.39 at Bristol Baptist College, 4. I am grateful to the former principal of the College, J. E. Morgan-Wynne, and to the librarian, Stella Reed, for granting me access to the College's manuscript collection. For Foskett see Caleb Evans, *Elisha's Exclamation,* Bristol: W. Pine, 1781, 22–7; Norman Moon, *Education for Ministry: Bristol Baptist College 1679–1979,* Bristol: Bristol Baptist College, 1979, passim.

[111] [John Ellis], *Some Brief Considerations upon Mr. Locke's Hypothesis, That the Knowledge of God Is Attainable by Ideas of Reflexion,* (1743), London, 1837, 29.

[112] Ibid., 129.

[113] Ibid., 142.

[114] J. Leland, *A View of the Principal Deistical Writers,* 18. He cites the 4th edn of Locke's *Works,* II, 574ff.

[115] Leland's citation of Locke's *Reasonableness,* ibid., 533, in his *The Advantage and Necessity of the Christian Revelation,* 2 vols., London, 1764, II, 88.

[116] J. Leland, ibid., 89.

[117] John Taylor, *A Scheme of Scripture Divinity,* 1762, 2, 405.

[118] Thomas Amory, *Twenty-Two Sermons,* 1766, 65. He cites Locke's *Essay,* III.vi.2 and IV.xvi. For Amory (1701–74) see DNB.

[119] John Horsey, *Evidences of Christianity,* MS 69.1, 107, 97, 83–5. For Horsey (1754?–1827) and his academy see H. McLachlan, *English Education under the Test Acts,* 165–9.

[120] G. Hitchcock, *Natural Religion aided by Revelation and Perfected in Christianity,* 1779, 20, 16.

[121] See Uzal Ogden, *Antidote to Deism,* 2 vols., Newark: John Woods, 1795, I, 289–301; and Elihu Palmer, *Principles of Nature,* London, 1819, 95. For Ogden (1744–1822) and Palmer (1764–1806) see DAB.

[122] J. Locke, *Essay,* IV.xviii.10.

[123] Ibid., IV.xix.3; cf. ibid., paras. 6, 7.

[124] P. Browne, *A Letter in Answer to a Book Entituled, Christianity Not Mysterious,* 1697, 29.

[125] Catharine T. Cockburn, *A Letter to Dr. Holdsworth,* London, 1726, in her *Works,* 2 vols: London: J. and P. Knapton, 1751, I, 152. These seem to be over-confident assertions.

[126] Joseph Butler, *The Analogy of Religion,* II.iii.1.

[127] Ibid., II.iii.1,2.

[128] Ibid., II.iii.12–13.

[129] Ibid., II.iv.

[130] Jonathan Edwards in a sermon on Matt. 16:17, in his *Works* (1834), reprinted Edinburgh: The Banner of Truth Trust, 1974, II, 13.

[131] Ibid., 479.

[132] Sell, *Dissenting Thought and the Life of the Churches,* 210.

[133] Soame Jenyns, *Works,* London: T. Cadell, III, 249. For Jenyns (1704–87) see DNB.

[134] R. Baxter, *The Saint's Everlasting Rest,* 1650, III.i.1.

[135] P. T. Forsyth, *The Principle of Authority* (1913), London: Independent Press, 1952, 156.

[136] J. Locke, *Essay,* I.i.3.

[137] Richard Ashcraft, 'Faith and knowledge in Locke's philosophy', in John W. Yolton (ed.), *John Locke: Problems and Perspectives,* Cambridge: CUP, 1969, 215. Ashcraft finds Locke wanting at certain points, but at least coherent on faith and reason. Paul Helm, however, finds 'manifold inconsistencies' in Locke; see his 'Locke on faith and knowledge', *Philosophical Quarterly,* XXIII, 1973, 52–66.

[138] See further the careful discussion by Stephen Nantlais Williams, 'John Locke on the status of faith', *Scottish Journal of Theology,* XL, no.4, 1987, 591–606.

[139] J. Locke, *Essay,* IV.xviii.2.

[140] [J. Milner], *An Account of Mr. Lock's Religion,* 1700, 77, 78.

[141] J. Locke, *Essay,* IV.xvi.14.

[142] Ibid. See further, J. T. Moore, 'Locke's analysis of language and the assent to Scripture', *Journal of the History of Ideas,* XXXVII, no.4, October–December 1976, 707–14.

[143] J. Locke, *Essay,* IV.xviii.10.

[144] Ibid., IV.xviii.4.

[145] Ibid., IV.xv.2. Cf. M. Jamie Ferreira, 'Locke's "constructive skepticism" – a reappraisal', *Journal of the History of Philosophy,* XXIV,

1986, 211–22. Beware that on p.219 he wrongly cites p.665 for p.655 for the quotation here given.

146 Idem, *A Third Letter concerning Toleration,* in *Works,* VI, 144.

147 David C. Snyder takes this as in fact Locke's final position on the matter. See his 'Faith and reason in Locke's *Essay*', 213.

148 J. Locke, *Essay,* IV.xviii.4. I have italicized *knowledge.*

149 Roland H. Bainton, *The Travail of Religious Liberty. Nine Biographical Studies,* Philadelphia: Westminster Press, 1951, 248.

150 J. Locke, *A Second Vindication of The Reasonableness of Christianity,* in *Works,* VII, 408;

151 Idem, *Essay,* IV.xviii.7. See further, J. T. Moore, 'Locke on the moral need for Christianity', *Southwestern Journal of Philosophy,* XI, no.1, Spring 1980, 61–8.

152 J. Locke, *The Reasonableness of Christianity,* in *Works,* VII, 101–2, 112.

153 J. Locke, *Essay,* IV.xix.5.

154 Idem, *The Reasonableness of Christianity, Works,* VII, 14.

155 Ibid., 121.

156 Ibid., 15.

157 See ibid, 129ff.; *A Second Vindication,* ibid., 285–6, 414.

158 J. R. Milton, 'Locke's life and times', in Vere Chappell (ed.), *The Cambridge Companion to Locke,* Cambridge: CUP, 1994, 24.

159 J. Locke, *A Paraphrase and Notes on the Epistles of St Paul to the Galatians, 1 and 2 Corinthians, Romans, and Ephesians,* I, 136, on Galatians 3:7.

160 On which matter see Richard E. Brantley, *Locke, Wesley, and the Method of English Romanticism,* Gainesville, Fla.: University Presses of Florida, 1984, ch.I.

161 See R. Baxter, *The Unreasonableness of Infidelity,* 1655, 157; J. Owen, *Works,* ed. W. H. Goold, (1850–3), reprinted London: The Banner of Truth Trust, 1965ff., IV, 1–115.

162 R. Brantley, *Locke, Wesley, and the Method of English Romanticism,* 41.

163 P. Browne, *The Procedure, Extent and Limits of Human Understanding,* 2nd edn, 1729, 335.

164 See J. Wesley, *The Appeals to Men of Reason and Religion and Certain Related Open Letters,* ed. Gerald R. Cragg, being vol.XI of *The Works of John Wesley,* ed. Frank Baker, Oxford: Clarendon Press, 1975.

165 See the quotations from R. Brantley's transcription of Wesley's letter to Susanna of 29 July 1725, in the John Rylands University Library of Manchester, which corrects Telford by removing quotation marks from Wesley's definition of belief as 'Assent to a Proposition upon Rational Grounds'. See Brantley, *Locke, Wesley and the Method of English Romanticism,* 238, n.3.

166 E. C. Mossner's comparison of Butler with Wesley is thus inaccurate as far as Wesley is concerned: 'The two might speak alike of religious *faith,* but to Butler faith meant intellectual conviction [as it did to Wesley, A.S.], while to Wesley it meant an inward sentiment of instinctive feeling [this is not all it meant to Wesley, A.S.].' See his *Bishop Butler and the Age of Reason,* New York: Macmillan, 1936, 166.

167 *The Letters of the Rev. John Wesley, A.M.*, ed. John Telford, London: Epworth Press, 1931, II, 64.

168 J. Wesley, *Works,* Baker edn, XI, 48; cf. Jackson edn, VI, 360.

169 John Hoyles, *The Waning of the Renaissance,* The Hague: Martinus Nijhof, 1971, 155.

170 See John Gill, *A Body of Practical Divinity,* II, 395, 404.

171 See Edward Stillingfleet, *A Rational Account of the Grounds of Protestant Religion* (1664), Oxford, 1844, I, 219, 323. Maurice Cranston suggests that Stillingfleet 'missed a trick,' so to speak: 'He might have shown that Locke's distinction between faith and knowledge implied not the rationality of Christianity but an absolute fideism; as it was, the Bishop took another and less effective line.' See M. Cranston, *John Locke: A Biography* (1957), Oxford: OUP, 1985, 414.

172 Robert South, *Sermons Preached on Several Occasions* (1679), London, 3 vols., 1692, II, 486–7. For South (1634–1716) see DNB.

173 John Norris, *An Account of Reason and Faith, in Relation to the Mysteries of Christianity* (1697), II, sect. 23.

174 Henry Felton. *The Christian Faith Asserted against Deists, Arians, and Socinians,* Oxford, 1731, 10 (where he cites Locke's *Essay,* IV.iii.i), 28. For Felton (1679–1740) see DNB.

175 Wolf von Metternich, *Faith and Reason compared; Showing that Divine Faith and Natural Reason proceed from Two different and distinct Principles in Man. Against the Notions and Errors of the Modern Rationalists,* (Amsterdam, 1708, Latin), London, 1713, 12.

176 John Edwards, *The Doctrin* [*sic*] *of Faith and Justification Set in a True Light,* 1708, 62.

177 Ibid.

178 Ibid., 63.

179 Ibid., 318.

180 Samuel Bold, *Some Considerations on the Principal Objections and Arguments Which have been Published against Mr. Lock's Essay of Humane Understanding,* London, 1699, 1.

181 Ibid., 2–4.

182 Ibid., 10–12.

183 Ibid., 59–60.

[184] C. Chauncy, *Ministers exhorted and encouraged to take heed to themselves, and to their Doctrine,* Boston: Rogers and Fowle, 1744, 17.

[185] [Francis Webb], *The Morality of the New Testament,* 1765, 309. For Webb (1735–1815), who was educated under Doddridge at Northampton and Caleb Ashworth at Daventry, and served as a General Baptist minister from 1758 to 1766, see DNB. A number of General Baptists underwent doctrinal change in a Unitarian direction during the eighteenth century. See Raymond Brown, *The English Baptists of the Eighteenth Century,* London: The Baptist Historical Society, 1986, 103–9; Ian Sellers, 'The Old General Baptists 1811–1915', *The Baptist Quarterly,* XXIV, nos.1 and 2, 1971, 30–41; 74–88.

[186] On which matter see further Peter A. Schouls, *The Imposition of Method: A Study of Descartes and Locke,* Oxford: Clarendon Press, 1980, ch.VIII.

[187] J. Locke, *Essay,* IV.xviii.8.

[188] Ibid., IV.xix.14.

[189] Idem, *A Paraphrase and Notes on the Epistles of St Paul,* ed. Arthur W. Wainwright, Oxford: Clarendon Press, 1987, I, 238. I use this edition exclusively for references to the *Paraphrases.*

[190] Ibid., I, 115. Cf. idem, *Essay,* III.ix.23.

[191] Idem, Postscript to *A Letter to the Right Rev. Edward Lord Bishop of Worcester,* in *Works,* IV, 96.

[192] J. J. Tayler, *Retrospect of Religious Life in England,* London: John Chapman, 1845, 372. For Presbyterian doctrine in eighteenth-century England see Sell, *Dissenting Thought and the Life of the Churches,* ch.V.

[193] J. Locke, *Essay* , IV.xix.16.

[194] Ibid., III.x.9; cf. III.x.12.

[195] Idem, *A Second Vindication of the Reasonableness of Christianity,* in *Works,* VII, 294–5.

[196] Idem, *Two Treatises on Government,* in *Works,* V, II, 391.

[197] Idem, *The Reasonableness of Christianity,* in *Works,* VII, 146–7.

[198] Ibid., 156.

[199] Idem, *Essay,* IV.xix.14.

[200] See further, Peter A. Schouls, 'John Locke and the rise of Western fundamentalism: a hypothesis', *Religious Studies and Theology,* X, nos.2 and 3, May, September 1990, 9–22.

[201] J. Locke, Preface to his *Paraphrase,* 111.

[202] Ibid., II, 496.

[203] See J. C. Biddle (ed.), 'John Locke's "Essay on Infallibility": introduction, text and translation', *Journal of Church and State,* XIX, 1977, 326–7.

[204] J. Locke, *The Reasonableness of Christianity,* in *Works,* VII, 151.

205 See H. McLachlan, *English Education under the Test Acts,* Manchester: Manchester University Press, 1931, 49–52. For Rowe (1657–1705) see DNB.

206 Alexander Gordon, *Addresses Biographical and Historical,* London: The Lindsey Press, 1922, 203–4.

207 I. Watts, *Works* , 1753, IV, 532; quoted by Arthur Paul Davis, *Isaac Watts,* London: Independent Press, 1948, 14. The question how far John's twitching and Paul's bearing sufficed towards the end of Watts's career need not here detain us.

208 J. Locke, *Works,* VII, 140.

209 I. Watts, *Works,* 1800, II, 367.

210 Ibid.

211 William Whiston, *A New Theory of the Earth,* London, 1696, 379. For Whiston (1667–1752) see DNB; James E. Force, *William Whiston: Honest Newtonian,* Cambridge: CUP, 1985. For Locke's letter of 22 February 1696 see E. S. de Beer (ed)., *The Correspondence of John Locke,* Oxford: Clarendon Press, VI, 1981, 6.

212 For the continuation of this variety of Calvinism into the nineteenth century – albeit now in a context in which the bogeymen are not deists, Socinians and Arians, but evolutionary thinkers and biblical 'higher critics,' see my account of Robert Watts in *Dissenting Thought and the Life of the Churches,* especially p. 522.

213 'An account of the Dissenting Academies from the Restoration of Charles the Second,' Dr Williams's Library, London, MS 24.59.25., 33. See further, Sell, 'Philosophy in the eighteenth-century Dissenting academies of England and Wales', 75–122.

214 *A Confession of Faith at the Publick Ordination of Thomas Bradbury, London, July the Tenth,* 1707, 4. For Bradbury (1677–1759) see DNB; Sell, *Dissenting Thought and the Life of the Churches,* 36–7, 401–3.

215 Quoted by F. J. Powicke in Albert Peel (ed.), *Essays Congregational and Catholic,* London: Congregational Union of England and Wales (1931), 306. Powicke disapproves of Bradbury's stance, though Bernard Lord Manning was more charitable:

> With affectionate respect I cannot be sure that Dr. Powicke is right. At a time when an exaggerated estimate of reason was to eat into the very heart of faith, it was not an unhappy thing that Congregatonalists asserted with violence the independence of faith and its superiority to reason. To say that faith was contrary to reason was indeed to go too far, but it was at that moment an error in the right direction.

See his essay in *Congregationalism through the Centuries,* London: Independent Press, 1937, 79–80.

216 Anthony Collins, *A Discourse of Freethinking,* London, 1713, 32–99.

[217] Cotton Mather, *Reasonable Religion: Or, the Truths of the Christian Religion Demonstrated,* London, 1713, 37.

[218] T. Halyburton, *Natural Religion Insufficient; and Revealed Necessary to Man's Happiness in his present State,* Edinburgh: Andrew Anderson, 1714, 135.

[219] Daniel Waterland, *Works* , VI, 108. For Waterland (1683–1740) see DNB.

[220] Ibid., VI, 164–5, referring to *Christianity as Old as the Creation,* 421.

[221] Humphrey Prideaux, *Letter to the Deists,* 1748, 59. For Prideaux (1648–1724) see DNB.

[222] Samuel Bourn, *A Dialogue between a Baptist and a Churchman,* 1739, 6. For Bourn (1689–1754) see DNB; Sell, *Dissenting Thought and the Life of the Churches,* ch.VII.

[223] John Taylor, in the Dedication of *A Paraphrase, with Notes on the Epistle to the Romans,* 1745.

[224] George Benson, *The Reasonableness of the Christian Religion,* I and II, 1759, 158. For Benson (1699–1762) see DNB.

[225] Thomas Amory, *Ministers not Lords over the Faith of Christians,* 13–14.

[226] J. Wesley, *The Letters of the Rev. John Wesley,* VIII, 112; letter of 24 January 1789 to Freeborn Garrettson.

[227] See *An Introductory Discourse by Samuel Newton, an address to the minister, By Robert Stevenson, and a Sermon to the People, By William Parry; Delivered on the Solemn Separation of The Rev. Thomas Craig to the Pastoral Office In the Congregational Church at Bocking in Essex, October 12, 1802. To which is prefixed a Discourse, delivered on the preceding evening by John Pye Smith,* 1802, 39.

[228] For Craig (1780–1865) see S. Clarkson's 'Sketch of his Life and Character', at Dr Williams's Library, London. For Christie (1728–95) see L. Baker Short, *Pioneers of Scottish Unitarianism* privately printed (1963), ch.6.

[229] Dan Taylor, *An Essay on the Truth and Inspiration of the Holy Scriptures,* London: T. Knott et al., 1790, 48–9. Taylor describes Locke as 'one of the fairest and ablest reasoners of the last age', ibid., 47. For Taylor (1738–1816) see DNB.

[230] Andrew Fuller, *The Gospel its Own Witness,* in his *Works,* I, 5.

[231] See Anon., *Remarks on the Religious Sentiments of Learned and Eminent Laymen ...,* London, 1790, 41; Richard Watson, *An Apology for Christianity in a Series of Letters addressed to Edward Gibbon, Esq.,* Cambridge: J. Archdeacon, 1796, 268.

[232] See Benjamin Coole, *Some Brief Observations on the Paraphrase and Notes of the Judicious John Locke relating to Women's Exercising their Spiritual Gifts in the Church,* London, 1716; Josiah Martin, *A Letter to*

the Author of Some Brief Observations, London, 1716; B. Coole, *Reflections on a Letter to the Author of Some Brief Observations*, London, 1717; J. Martin, *A Vindication of Women's Preaching*, London, 1717. See also the exchange between H.B., and William Notcutt: H.B., *A Vindication of Robert Barclay's Apology for the Principles of the People call'd Quakers*, 1732, 86–7; W. Notcutt, *A Reply to H.B's Vindication of Robert Barclay's Apology*, 1733, 134–6 ('the famous Mr. *John Locke* ... speaks directly *against* their [i.e. the Quakers'] Practice of Women's speaking in the Church; unless there should arise an *Extraordinary* Prophetess; one immediately inspired of God,' 135); H.B., *An Examination of William Notcutt's Reply to H.B.'s Vindication of R. Barclay's Apology*, 1735, 154. That the matter was not entirely dormant throughout our period is evidenced by the publication in 1801 of William Rawes Jr's pamphlet, *The Gospel Ministry of Women, under the Christian Dispensation, Defended from Scripture, and from the writings of John Locke, Josiah Martin, etc.* He notes (p.27) that the Methodists have lately 'occasionally permitted women both to preach and pray in their religious assemblies'.

233 See Sell, *Dissenting Thought and the Life of the Churches*, ch.VIII. Fraser's critique is to be found in his posthumous work, *The Scripture Doctrine of Sanctification*, Edinburgh, 1774. For Fraser (1700–69) see DNB.

234 Philip Doddridge, *The Correspondence and Diary of Philip Doddridge, D.D.*, ed. J. D. Humphreys, London: Henry Colburn and Richard Bentley, 5 vols., 1829–31, I, 428.

235 A. W. Wainwright, Introduction to Locke's *Paraphrase*, 22.

236 Ibid, 1–3.

237 In which connection Damaris Cudworth's remark in a letter to Locke of 8 October 1684 is instructive:

> I cannot but Fancie by your Letter that you have learnt more Scripture there than ever you Knew in your whole life before, whom I little thought once would ever have writt me a letter not to be understood without turning to St. Paul, and St. Peters Epistles.

See de Beer (ed.), *The Correspondence of John Locke*, II, 1976, 640.

238 John Marshall, 'John Locke's religious, educational, and moral thought' (a review article), *The Historical Journal*, XXXIII, no.4, 1990, 997; cf. idem, *John Locke: Resistance, Religion and Responsibility*, Cambridge: CUP, 1994, 78 n. 7.

239 See A. Wainwright, Introduction, 11–16.

240 Quoted by A. Campbell Fraser, *Locke*, Edinburgh: Blackwood, 1891, 47.

241 J. Locke, Preface, *Paraphrase*, 108.

[242] Ibid., 110.

[243] For Jenkin (1656–1727) see DNB.

[244] R. Jenkin, *Remarks on Some Books Lately Publish'd,* London, 1709, 123; cf. 173.

[245] John Edwards, *Some Brief Observations and Reflections on Mr. Whiston's late Writings, Falsely Entitle'd Primitive Christianity Reviv'd,* London, 1712, 20–1.

[246] Isaac Watts, *Works* , VII, 261–2.

[247] Ezra Stiles, *The Literary Diary of Ezra Stiles, D.D.,* 3 vols., New York: Scribners, 1901, I, 556–8. For Stiles (1727–95) see DAB.

[248] Ibid., 557–8.

[249] We must, however, be a little more cautious than A. W. Wainwright, who writes that Peirce, Hallett and Benson

> were known as Non-subscribers because of their refusal to subscribe to the doctrine of the Trinity as defined in the Thirty-Nine Articles and the Westminster Confession ... [They] were known to be unwilling to accept the traditional statements of the doctrine of the Trinity. (Introduction to Locke's *Paraphrase*, 66).

But of the forty-seven non-subscribing Presbyterians at the Salters' Hall conference of 1719, Benjamin Avery and Nathanael Lardner only were convinced Arians. Moreover, the non-subscribers subsequently published *An Authentick Account of Several Things Done and agreed upon by the Dissenting Ministers lately assembled at Salters-Hall*, 1719, in which they declared, 'we utterly disown the Arian Doctrine, and sincerely believe the Doctrine of the Blessed Trinity ...' (ibid., 15). Accordingly, I follow those who suggest that at Salters' Hall, while the question concerned the Trinity, the issue was subscription. See Sell, *Dissenting Thought and the Life of the Churches,* 128–47.

[250] For Peirce (1674?–1726) and Hallett (1691?–1744) see DNB

[251] G. Benson, *A Paraphrase and Notes on Six of the Epistles of St. Paul ... Attempted in Imitation of Mr. Locke's Manner,* 1752, xvi–xvii.

[252] P. Doddridge, *Works,* V, 473.

[253] For Lowman (1680–1752) see DNB.

[254] See P. Doddridge, *Works,* II, 37.

[255] Geoffrey F. Nuttall (ed.), *Calendar of the Correspondence of Philip Doddridge DD (1702–51),* London: Her Majesty's Stationery Office, 1979, no.1055. Wood (d. 1767), a former student at Doddridge's Northampton academy, ministered at Rendham and at Norwich.

[256] See P. Doddridge, *The Family Expositor* (1739–56), at Romans 5:1. For Guyse (1680–1761) see DNB.

[257] See W. Whiston, *Sermons and Essays upon Several Subjects,* London: Benjamin Took, 1709, 254–5; N. Lardner, *The Works of Nathaniel*

Lardner, D.D., London: William Ball, 10 vols. 1835–8, X, 110, 146, 152, 154; J. Priestley, *Works*, 25 vols., VII, 377, 411. For Lardner (1684–1768) see DNB.

258 J. Priestley, *Works*, VII, 411.

259 John Napleton, *Advice to a Student in the University concerning the Qualifications and Duties of a Minister of the Gospel in the Church of England*, Oxford, 1795, 34. For Napleton (1738?–1817) see DNB.

260 Thomas Belsham, *The Character of the Christian Teacher Delineated*, London, 1804, 15–16.

261 This is not to dispute Norman Fiering's claim that there have been able supporters of 'head' against 'heart' and *vice versa* in every age. As far as American divines are concerned my findings support his contention that '[T]he direct influence of Locke's *Essay Concerning Human Understanding* on the American mind in the first half of the eighteenth century has been almost as much exaggerated as the influence of his *Treatises on Government.*' See his 'Will and intellect in the New England mind,' *The William and Mary Quarterly*, 3rd series, XXIX, 1972, 558.

Chapter 4: Morality and Liberty

1 Mark Pattison, 'Tendencies of religious thought in England 1688–1750,' *Essays and Reviews*, London: John W. Parker, 1860, 293.

2 Ibid.

3 J. Locke, *Essay*, IV.xii.11. Cf. Peter King, *The Life of John Locke* (1829), London: Henry Colburn and Richard Bentley, new edn, 1830, II, 123, where Locke declares that morality is 'the great business and concernment of mankind'.

4 Ibid., I.iii.1; cf. I.iii.13.

5 Ibid., IV.iii.18.

6 Molyneaux to Locke, in Locke's *Works*, IX, 291. For Molyneaux (1656–98) see DNB.

7 Locke to Molyneux, 20 September 1692, in *Works*, IX, 294.

8 Locke to Molyneaux, 30 March 1696, ibid., 377.

9 Morton White, *The Philosophy of the American Revolution*, New York: OUP, 1978, 158.

10 J. Locke, *The Reasonableness of Christianity*, in *Works*, VII, 146–7.

11 Idem, *Some Thoughts concerning Education*, in *Works*, IX, 176.

12 See W. von Leyden, *John Locke: Essays on the Law of Nature*, Oxford: Clarendon Press, 1954, 43–60. Culverwell (d. 1651?), the Cambridge Platonist, Hooker (1544?–1600, the apologist of the Elizabethan Settlement, and Sanderson (1587–1663), bishop of

Lincoln, are in DNB. Grotius (1583–1645) was a Dutch jurist and theologian, while Pufendorf (1632–94) was a German professor of natural and international law. I do not suggest that Locke's position simply duplicates that of the others mentioned. It hardly could, given their differences from each other. To draw an example from James Tully, *A Discourse on Property: John Locke and his Adversaries,* Cambridge: CUP, 1980, 41: whereas Grotius argued that natural laws are binding independently of God's existence,

> Locke agrees with the voluntarist that God's will is the source of obligation, but rejects the inference that the test of the validity of natural law cannot be reason. He accepts the rationalist tenet that natural laws are discovered by reason, are wise and good by independent criteria, but he denies the inference that this is the source of their binding force.

A. W. Wainwright finds evidence of Locke's voluntarist–rationalist oscillation in Locke's *Paraphrase* of Romans. See his Introduction, 47–8. See also W. Randall Ward, 'Divine will, natural law and the voluntarism/intellectualism debate in Locke', *History of Political Thought,* XVI, no.2, Summer 1995, 208–18.

13 See J. Locke, *Essays on the Law of Nature,* 201.

14 Idem, *Of Civil Government,* in *Works,* V, 418.

15 Idem, *Essay,* I.iii.6. In 'John Locke: liberalism and natural law', in Knud Haakonssen (ed.), *Traditions of Liberalism,* Canberra : Center for Independent Studies, 1988, 5, Shirley Robin Letwin notes that Locke's view of natural law is, as one might say, blunter than that of those medieval authors whose 'highly refined categories ... allowed for a distinction between different sorts of ends or purposes'.

16 Idem, *Essays on the Law of Nature,* 111.

17 Ibid., 133, etc. Cf. *Essay,* IV.iii.18. In view of this, and of the two preceding quotations, I must query J. B. Schneewind's comparison of Locke with Richard Hooker to the effect that Locke rejected both Hooker's view that 'the laws of nature can be known through reason because they are written in everyone's conscience', and his view that the *consensus gentium* provides evidence of their divine origin. Locke seems in fact to have maintained the former of these views and to have rejected the latter. See J. B. Schneewind, 'Locke's moral philosophy', in Vere Chappell (ed.), *The Cambridge Companion to Locke,* Cambridge: CUP, 1994, 209.

18 J. Locke, *A Paraphrase,* II, 496.

19 Cf. John W. Yolton, *Locke and the Compass of Human Understanding,* Cambridge: CUP, 1970, 172; John C. Biddle, *John Locke on Christianity: His Context and Text,* doctoral dissertation, Stanford University, 1972, 86.

20 J. Locke, *Essay,* II.xxviii.8.

21 Idem, *The Reasonableness of Christianity,* in *Works,* VII, 147.

22 Ibid., VII, 143.

23 Idem, *A Letter concerning Toleration,* in *Works,* VI, 47.

24 Psalm 14:1 and 53:1.

25 J. Locke, *Essays on the Law of Nature,* 189. See further, Thomas L. Pangle, *The Spirit of Modern Republicanism: The Moral Vision of the American Founders and the Philosophy of Locke,* Chicago: University of Chicago Press, 1988, ch.XVII.

26 Ibid., 203.

27 See J. Locke, *The Reasonableness of Christianity,* in *Works* , VII, 135–7.

28 David Wootton has claimed that whereas Locke had, in his *Essays on the Law of Nature,* recorded his conviction that there is a law of nature knowable by all reasonable persons, he 'really did not' believe this by the end of his life:

> for in the posthumous *A Paraphrase and Notes on the Epistles of St Paul* he maintained that there was no clearly established moral law aside from the revealed law; the Jew before Moses, the Gentiles until the crucifixion had been 'laws unto themselves' ... because they had been governed by no known, absolute moral law.

See David Wootton, 'John Locke: Socinian or natural law theorist?' in James E. Crimmins (ed.), *Religion, Secularization and Political Thought,* London: Routledge, 1989, 42–3. He refers (p.64 n.16) to Romans 2:14 which, Locke says, may be translated thus: 'For when the Gentiles who have not a law doe by nature the things conteined in the law, these not haveing a law are a law to themselves ...' See J. Locke, *A Paraphrase,* II, 499 n. 14. This seems to be an affirmation of natural law, rather than a denial of it. So with Locke's paraphrases of the other verses Wootton cites: Romans 1:32 and 5:13. The plain reading of these texts is that the Gentiles were aware of the natural law, but did not recognize its divine origin, or the confirmatory revelation which was to come (or had now come). Later in his paper Wootton grants that after 1689 Locke 'may well in good faith have believed that [the law of nature] ought to be rationally demonstrable' (54). This is, of course, a more stringent requirement (into which Paul does not probe) than that such a law simply be known by all. The main point is that I am not persuaded that Locke ever abandoned 'the idea of a divinely ordained moral law, accessible to all men' (56).

29 See Alan Brinton, 'The passions as subject matter in early eighteenth-century sermons', *Rhetorica,* X, no.1, Winter 1992, 49–66.

30 Ibid., 52–3.

31 J. Locke, *Works,* VII, 139.

32 Ibid., 141.

33 Idem, 'Some thoughts concerning reading and study for a gentleman', in *Works,* III, 271.1.

34 Idem, *Essay,* II.xx.2. Cf. ibid., II.xxi.42; II.xx.3, etc.

35 Idem, *Some Thoughts concerning Education,* in *Works,* IX, 40. J. D. Mabbott suggests that Locke substituted his concern for rewards and punishments for his early reliance upon conscience (as in his *Essays*) because of the ease with which fanatics and enthusiasts and others could persuade themselves that their consciences were God's voice; and he notes concerning rewards and punishments that 'Locke devotes greater space to hammering this point home than he does to any other single argument in the *Essay.*' See his *John Locke,* London: Macmillan, 1973, 125–6.

36 J. Locke, *Essay,* II.xxviii.8.

37 Idem, *The Reasonableness of Christianity,* in *Works,* VII, 150–1.

38 Idem, *Paraphrase,* I, 183. A. W. Wainwright (Introduction, 49) suggests that 'the hedonistic element is not totally absent from the *Paraphrase.*' John Marshall proposes grounds for thinking that this is an understatement. See his 'John Locke's religious, educational and moral thought,' 998–9.

39 J. Locke, *Essay,* I.iii.5.

40 Ibid., II.xxi.70.

41 Ibid., I.iii.6.

42 Ibid., II.xxviii.5; cf. I.iv.8. Though there is a distinction to be drawn between the virtue of the action and the virtue of the agent. See further, David Gauthier, 'Why ought one to obey God? Reflections on Hobbes and Locke', *Canadian Journal of Philosophy,* VII, 1977, 425–46; Morton White, *The Philosophy of the American Revolution,* 44, 230–1.

43 Ibid., 427.

44 J. Locke, *The Reasonableness of Christianity,* in *Works,* VII, 148–51.

45 Idem, *Essay,* II.xxviii. 11.

46 James Lowde, *A Discourse concerning the Nature of Man,* London: T. Warren, 1694, unpaginated preface, xv–xvi.

47 J. Locke, *Essay* , II.xxviii.11, n.

48 James Lowde, *Moral Essays,* 1699, 8.

49 Ibid., 32.

50 [T. Burnet], *Third Remarks upon an Essay concerning Humane Understanding,* 1699, 5–7.

51 Ibid., 7–8.

52 Cf. J. Locke, *Essay,* I.iii.8

53 See his 'Marginalia Locke-a-na', 38. Quoted by S. A. Grave, *Locke and Burnet,* Perth: Philosophy Society of WA and Department of Philosophy, University of Western Australia (1981), 10. Ch.II of this

work is an illuminating account of Locke and Burnet on 'Moral good and evil'. See further, J. B. Schneewind in *The Cambridge Companion to Locke,* 206–7, 220.

54 James Oswald, *An Appeal to Common Sense in behalf of Religion,* 1768, I, 107.

55 [Catharine Cockburn], *A Defence of the Essay of Human Understanding,* 1702, 10.

56 Ibid., 25.

57 Ibid., 62.

58 Locke to Catharine Cockburn, 30 December 1702, in *Works,* X, 315.

59 [J. Milner], *An Account of Mr. Lock's Religion,* 1700, 60.

60 Henry Lee, *Anti-Scepticism,* 1702, 67.

61 John Conybeare, *A Defence of Revealed Religion* (1732), 4th edn, 1788, 167–8. For Conybeare (1692–1755) see DNB.

62 Ibid., 169.

63 Ibid., 214.

64 William Worthington, *The Evidence of Christianity,* 1769, 94. For Worthington (1703–78) see DNB, and *The Dictionary of Welsh Biography,* where his year of birth is given as 1704.

65 Ibid., 95.

66 Abraham Tucker, *The Light of Nature Pursued,* 1768. I quote from the second edn, 1802. For Tucker (1705–74) see DNB.

67 Ibid., 41.

68 Ibid., 122–5, 138. Tucker, a generous husband and a good father, transcribed his letters to his wife under the title, 'Pictures of an artless love'. Though garrulous and diffuse, he was no buffoon. William Paley, in the preface to his *Moral and Political Philosophy,* said he owed more to him than to any other writer. In 1771 he went blind, and was cared for by his daughter, Judith, who went to the lengths of learning sufficient Greek to read her father's favourite authors to him.

69 [Jackson Barwis], *Dialogues concerning Innate Principles,* 1779. For Barwis, 'Lately a wholesale-grocer on Snow-hill, and a frequent *speechifier* at the India-house', see *A New Catalogue of Living English Authors,* London, 1799.

70 Ibid., 5.

71 Ibid., 67, 23, 80.

72 See Claude M. Newlin, *Philosophy and Religion in Colonial America* (1962), New York: Greenwood Press, 1968, 194–212.

73 Jonathan Mayhew, *Seven Sermons,* 1749, 37. For Mayhew (1720–66), pastor of the West Church, Boston, see DAB.

74 Ibid., 5.

75 Ibid., 6.

76 See, for example, his second sermon, ibid., 22–40.

77 Peter Clark, *Man's Dignity and Duty,* Boston: Richard and Samuel Draper, 1763, 31. Clark was pastor of the First Church, Danvers.

78 Joseph Butler, *Dissertation II. Of the Nature of Virtue,* appended to idem, *The Analogy of Religion,* ed. F. A. Malleson, London: Ward Lock, n.d., 209.

79 Anders Jeffner, 'Our knowledge of ourselves', in Christopher Cunliffe (ed.), *Joseph Butler's Moral and Religious Thought,* Oxford: Clarendon Press, 1992, 191.

80 Ibid., 215.

81 [T. Burnet], *Remarks upon an Essay concerning Humane Understanding,* 6.

82 J. Locke, *An Answer to Remarks upon an Essay concerning Human Understanding,* in *Works,* IV, 188.

83 Idem, *The Reasonableness of Christianity,* in *Works,* VII, 133.

84 Archibald Campbell, *The Necessity of Revelation,* London: William Bowyer, 1739, 377n., 382.

85 James Oswald, *An Appeal to Common Sense in behalf of Religion,* London: J. Hughes, 2nd edn, 2 vols., 1768, I, 89.

86 Shaftesbury, *Several Letters Written by a Noble Lord to a Young Man at the University,* 1716, 40–1. Catharine Cockburn was later to defend Locke on this point. See her *Works,* 1751, II, 242–3.

87 J. Locke, *Essay,* I.iii.8.

88 Thomas Becconsall, *The Grounds and Foundation of Natural Religion Discover'd,* 1698, 219.

89 Ibid., 51.

90 Thomas Hobbes (1588–1679) and Anthony Ashley Cooper, third Earl of Shaftesbury (1671–1713) are in DNB.

91 Adam Smith, *The Theory of Moral Sentiments,* eds. D. D. Raphael and A. L. Macfie, Oxford: Clarendon Press, 1976, 322. For Smith (1723–90) see DNB. For a modern study see William Blackstone, *Francis Hutcheson and Contemporary Ethical Theory,* Athens, Ga.: University of Georgia Press, 1965.

92 Francis Hutcheson, *An Inquiry into the Original of our Ideas of Beauty and Virtue; in Two Treatises* (1725), London, 4th corrected edn, 1738, I, Preface, xiii–xiv. Later in the *Inquiry concerning Moral Good and Evil* he defines 'sense' as 'a Determination of the Mind, to receive any Idea from the Preference of an Object which occurs to us, independent of our Will' (I.i.). The Presbyterian, Thomas Amory, cited this work to prove his contention that God's goodness is, *inter alia,* shown from the moral sense he has planted in us. See his *Twenty-two Sermons,* 1766, 39. That Amory's fellow Presbyterian, John Taylor, did not agree we shall shortly see. For Hutcheson (1694–1746) see DNB.

93 W. Bernard Peach, Introduction to F. Hutcheson, *Illustrations of the Moral Sense,* Cambridge, Mass.: The Belknap Press of Harvard University Press, 1971, 37.

94 F. Hutcheson, *An Inquiry concerning Moral Good and Evil* (1725) (i.e. the second of the *Two Treatises* at n. 92 above), section I.vii.

95 For Bernard Mandeville (1670–1733) see DNB.

96 John Veitch, 'Philosophy in the Scottish Universities,' *Mind,* II, 1877, 211.

97 F. Hutcheson, *An Inquiry concerning Moral Good and Evil,* I.iv.

98 J. Locke, *The Reasonableness of Christianity,* in *Works,* VII, 146–7.

99 F. Hutcheson, *An Inquiry,* I.viii.

100 Idem, *An Inquiry into the Original of our Ideas of Beauty and Virtue in Two Treatises,* I, 78.

101 The question of the early and the later Hutcheson continues to intrigue scholars. James Moore, for example, finds that Hutcheson's early works are coherent, whereas his expositions of the Glasgow syllabus, to which he was tied, while they led him into areas incompatible with it, did not undermine his continued adherence to his moral sense theory as at first propounded. Knud Haaknonssen has queried Moore's 'two systems' theory, and Moore has replied. The sequence of papers is: James Moore, 'The two systems of Francis Hutcheson: On the origins of the Scottish Enlightenment', in M. A. Stewart (ed.), *Studies in the Philosophy of the Scottish Enlightenment,* Oxford: Clarendon Press, 1990; Knud Haakonssen, 'Natural law and moral realism: the Scottish synthesis', in ibid.; James Moore, 'Theological politics: a study of the reception of Locke's *Two Treatises of Government* in England and Scotland in the early eighteenth century', in Martyn P. Thompson (ed.), *John Locke und/and Immanuel Kant,* Berlin: Duncker & Humblot, 1991; idem, 'Civic virtue and the law of nature: the eclectic "systems" of George Turnbull and Francis Hutcheson', forthcoming.

102 *Letters between the Late Mr. Gilbert Burnet, and Mr. Hutchinson,* appended to F. Hutcheson, *Illustrations of the Moral Sense,* ed. W. Bernard Peach, 204. For Burnet (1690–1726) see DNB. His father, Gilbert (1643–1715) was bishop of Salisbury.

103 Ibid., 214–15.

104 David Fate Norton, 'Hutcheson's moral realism', *Journal of the History of Philosophy,* XXIII, 1985, 404.

105 Jack Scott, *An Annotated Edition of Lectures on Moral Philosophy by John Witherspoon,* Newark: University of Delaware Press, 1982, 78.

106 Ibid.

107 Richard Price, *A Review of the Principal Questions in Morals,* ed. D. D. Raphael, Oxford: Clarendon Press, 1974, 42–3.

[108] Ibid., 30–1.

[109] Ibid., Introduction, xix.

[110] Carl B. Cone, *Torchbearer of Freedom: The Influence of Richard Price on Eighteenth Century Thought,* Lexington: University of Kentucky Press, 1952, 22.

[111] See Alan P. F. Sell, *Dissenting Thought and the Life of the Churches: Studies in an English Tradition,* Lewiston, NY: Edwin Mellen Press, 1990, 198, 214–20.

[112] Andrew Kippis, *An Address delivered at the Interment of the late Rev. Dr. Richard Price on the twenty-sixth of April 1791,* 1791, 8–9. For Kippis (1725–95) see DNB.

[113] William Henry Channing, *Memoirs of William Ellery Channing* (1848), Boston: American Unitarian Association, 1880, 34. For Channing (1780–1842) see DAB.

[114] J. Locke, *Essay,* II.xxviii.5. It would seem that a number of factors are here inadequately distinguished by Locke: (a) the criterion of right action, namely, conformity to the moral law; (b) the criterion of virtue in the agent, namely, the desire to act in conformity with the law; (c) the consequence of (b), namely, pleasure, to the agent. Burnet's puzzlement is not without excuse. A conversation with Dr D. O. Thomas greatly assisted my exposition of this point.

[115] [T. Burnet], *Remarks upon an Essay concerning Humane Understanding,* 1697, 4–5.

[116] Idem, *Second Remarks upon an Essay concerning Humane Understanding,* 1697, 20.

[117] Thomas Halyburton, *Natural Religion Insufficient; and Reveal'd Necessary to Man's Happiness in his Present State,* Edinburgh: Andrew Anderson, 1714, 85–6. Halyburton quotes Locke's *The Reasonableness of Christianity, Works,* VII, 144.

[118] See John Leland, *The Advantage and Necessity of the Christian Revelation,* 1764, II, 87–9, 251–2.

[119] J. Locke, *Essay,* II.xxi.8. Carroll refers to this paragraph and to the preceding one. See his *A Letter to the Reverend Dr. Benjamin Prat,* 1707, 8–9.

[120] Shaftesbury, *Several Letters,* 39.

[121] Idem, *Works,* Birmingham, 1773, I, 102.

[122] Ibid., 55.

[123] See further, W. M. Spellman, *John Locke and the Problem of Depravity,* Oxford: Clarendon Press, 1988, ch.VII. Dr. Spellman properly notes the many points of agreement between Locke and Shaftesbury.

[124] [J. Barwis], *Dialogues concerning Innate Principles,* 95–9.

[125] Joseph Priestley, *Lectures on History,* Dublin: Luke White, 2 vols.,

1788, 230. The context of Priestley's remark is a discussion of the principle that the general good, *qua* the interests of the majority, should prevail.

126 Thomas Belsham, quoted in *On the Character and Writings of the Rev. Thomas Belsham,* 1830, 31.

127 H. Grove, *A Sermon Preach'd at the Ordination of the Rev. Mr. Thomas Amory, and Mr. William Cornish, at Taunton, Somerset, Oct. 7, 1730 . . .,* 1731, xiv–xv.

128 *Institutes of Moral Philosophy,* Dr Williams's Library, London, MS 69.5, 107. For Horsey (1754–1827) see *Congregational Magazine,* III, 1827, 344; *Evangelical Magazine,* 1827, 264; *The Monthly Repository,* I, 1827, 448, 609–10; H. McLachlan, *English Education under the Test Acts,* Manchester: University of Manchester Press, 1931, *passim.*

129 See further, Sell, *Dissenting Thought and the Life of the Churches,* ch.VI.

130 See J. Wesley, *Calm Address to our American Colonies,* London: R. Hawes, 1755, and C. Evans, *A Letter to The Rev. Mr. Wesley, Occasioned by his Calm Address to the American Colonies,* London: Edward and Charles Dilly, 1775. See further, Norman S. Moon, 'Caleb Evans, Founder of the Bristol Education Society', *Baptist Quarterly,* XXIV, 1971–2, 175–190.

131 J. Locke, *Essay,* II.xxi.5. See further Vere Chappell, 'Locke on the freedom of the will', in G. A. J. Rogers (ed.), *Locke's Philosophy: Content and Context,* Oxford: Clarendon Press, 1994, ch.IV.

132 Ibid., II.xxi.19.

133 Ibid., II.xxi.20.

134 Idem, *Of Civil Government,* in *Works,* V, 342.

135 See further, Norman S. Fiering, 'Will and intellect in the New England mind', *The William and Mary Quarterly,* 3rd series, XXIX, 1972, 513–58.

136 J. Locke, *Essay,* II.xxi.50.

137 Ibid., II.xxi.29,31, etc.

138 Ibid., II.xxi.47.

139 G. A. J. Rogers, 'More, Locke and the issue of liberty', in S. Hutton (ed.), *Henry More (1614–1687),* Dordrecht: Kluwer Academic Publishers, 1990, 195.

140 Isaac Watts, *Works* , III, 558.

141 Ibid., VI, 595–6.

142 S. Strutt, *A Defence of the late Learned Dr. Clarke's Notion of Natural Liberty . . . Together With some Remarks on Mr. Locke's Chapter of Power,* 1730, 31.

143 Ibid., 33.

144 Bernard Foskett, *Pneumatology,* 43–44; MS Z.e.39 at Bristol Baptist

College. The following inscription is inside the cover: 'This manuscript written by the Revd. Bernard Foskett then Pastor of the Church in Broadmead & Tutor of the Baptist Academy was given to the Baptist Library belonging to the Education Society by the Revd. Benj. Beddome of Bourton on the Water. 1794.' I quote fully because of the relative inaccessibility of this text. For Beddome (1717–95), pastor at Bourton for fifty-five years, see DNB. His sons, Benjamin and Foskett, died in their twenties.

145 The late Reverend Philip Doddridge, DD, *A Course of Lectures on the Principal Subjects of Pneumatology, Ethics, and Divinity: with reference to the most considerable Authors on each Subject,* ed. Samuel Clark, Birmingham, 1763, 39. Doddridge refers to Locke's *Essay,* I.xxi.49,51,52. For a slightly different version see idem, *Works,* IV, 341.

146 Jonathan Edwards, *Works,* I, 9.

147 Ibid., I, 11.

148 Idem, *Treatise on Grace,* ed. Paul Helm, Cambridge: James Clarke, 1971, 70, 75.

149 See William G. McLoughlin, *Isaac Backus on Church, State, and Calvinism: Pamphlets, 1754–1789,* Cambridge, Mass.: Harvard University Press, 1968, 311. The quotation is from *An Appeal to the Public for Religious Liberty,* Boston: John Boyle, 1773. For Backus (1724–1806) see DAB.

150 Isaac Backus, *The Doctrine of Sovereign Grace Opened and Vindicated,* Providence, RI: John Carter, 1771, 62.

151 Charles Chauncy, *Twelve Sermons,* Boston: D. and J. Kneeland, 1765, 203, 204.

152 A. M. Toplady, *Historic Truth of the Doctrinal Calvinism of the Church of England,* in his *Works* , 1828, I, 304. For Toplady (1740–78) see DNB.

153 J. Locke, *Essay,* II.xxi.13.

154 A. M. Toplady, *Works,* I, 304, n.

155 He quotes Locke's *Essay,* II.xxi.11.

156 He quotes ibid., II.xxi.14.

157 Idem, *Works* , 304, n.

158 Joseph Priestley, *The Doctrine of Philosophical Necessity Illustrated,* in his *Works,* ed. J. T. Rutt, 25 vols., 1817–31, III, 457.

159 Stephen West, *An Essay on Moral Agency,* New Haven: Thomas and Samuel Green (1772), 36.

160 W. and T. Ludlam, *Essays, Scriptural, Moral, and Logical,* London: J. G. Barnard, 2 vols., 1807, II, 518–22. They are equally concerned on other matters to vindicate Locke against his opponents.

161 Nathanael Emmons, *Works,* 1842, IV, 348. For Emmons

(1745–1840) see DAB; Robert C. Whittemore, *The Transformation of the New England Theology*, New York: Peter Lang, 1987, ch.VI.

162 J. Locke, *Works*, IX, 305.

163 See further John Dunn, 'The claim to freedom of conscience, freedom of speech, freedom of thought, freedom of worship?', in Ole Peter Grell, Jonathan I. Israel and Nicholas Tyacke (eds.), *From Persecution to Toleration: The Glorious Revolution and Religion in England*, Oxford: Clarendon Press, 1991, ch.VII.

164 See J. A. Passmore, 'Locke and the ethics of belief', *Proceedings of the British Academy*, LXIV, 1978, 185–208; J. Tully, 'Governing conduct', in E. Leites et al.(ed.), *Conscience and Casuistry in Early Modern Europe*, Cambridge: 1988, 12–71.

165 J. Locke, *Essay*, II.xxviii.6.

166 Ibid., I.iii.27.

167 R. Ashcraft, 'Latitudinarianism and toleration: historical myth versus political history', in Richard Kroll (ed.), *Philosophy, Science, and Religion in England 1640–1700*, Cambridge: CUP, 1992, 167. I take Ashcraft to mean that an individual would rely upon his own judgement as a rational free agent. That a given individual did not always rely upon the judgements of other rational free agents is demonstrated by the disputations which it is part of my purpose to record.

168 Walter Wilson, *History and Antiquities of Dissenting Churches and Meeting-houses in London, Westminster and Southwark*, III, 1808, 171.

169 Thomas Amory, *Christ the Light of the World; Or, The Principal Improvements made in Religion by Christianity*, 1735, vi.

170 Ibid., vii.

171 Idem, *Ministers not Lords over the Faith of Christians, but Helpers of their Joy* (1751), 12.

172 Ibid., 17.

173 J. Priestley, *Works*, I, 21. For Marryatt (1685–1754) see Thomas Hall's funeral sermon and Thomas Towle's funeral oration, 1754; H. McLachlan, *English Education under the Test Acts*, 176–9.

174 Ibid., 23.

175 T. Amory, *Ministers not Lords*, 18–19.

176 Richard Price, *A Review of the Principal Questions of Morals*, 180n.

177 James Manning, *A Sketch of the Life and Writings of the Rev. Micaijah Towgood*, 1792 (abbreviated in *The Protestant Dissenter's Magazine*, October 1794, 385–93, and November 1794, 425–32), 65. For Towgood (1700–92) see in addition DNB; Sell, *Dissenting Thought and the Life of the Churches*, ch.VII.

178 James Daye, *The Christian's Service, compleated with Honour. A Sermon Occasioned by the Death of the Reverend Caleb Rotheram, D.D.* (1752), 20.

[179] William Enfield, *A Funeral Sermon occasioned by the Death of the Late Rev. John Aikin, D.D.*, Warrington, 1781, 14, 15. For Aiken (1713–80) see P. O'Brien, *Warrington Academy 1757–86. Its Predecessors and Successors,* Wigan: Owl Books, 1989. For Enfield (1714–97), a pupil of Caleb Ashworth at Daventry, who taught at Warrington from 1770 to 1783, see DNB.

[180] Thomas Belsham, *Freedom of Enquiry, and Zeal in the Diffusion of Christian Truth,* London: G. Woodfall, 1800, 2–3.

[181] Idem, *The Character of the Christian Teacher Delineated,* 1804, 30–1.

[182] Idem, *Discourses Doctrinal and Practical,* London: R. Hunter, 1826, 478.

[183] Ibid., 479. He refers to the Nonconformist Relief Act of 1779, which modified the doctrinal affirmation required of Nonconformists.

[184] Ibid., 482.

[185] Quoted by H. McLachlan, *English Education under the Test Acts,* 166.

[186] *Monthly Repository,* NS, I, 1827, 610.

[187] John Horsey, *Lectures to Young Persons on the Intellectual and Moral Powers of Man,* London: Samuel Leigh, 1828, 253.

[188] Samuel Bourn, *A Vindication of the Principles and Practice of the Protestant Dissenters,* 1748, 130–1. For Bourn (1689–1754) see DNB; Sell, *Dissenting Thought and the Life of the Churches,* ch.VII.

[189] Joseph Priestley, *Memoirs of the Rev. Dr. Joseph Priestley to the year 1795,* London: Joseph Johnson, 1809, I, 87.

[190] Jonathan Mayhew, *Seven Sermons,* Boston, 1749, 86.

[191] Simeon Howard, *A Sermon Preached To the Ancient and Honourable Artillery-Company, in Boston, New-England, June 7th, 1773. Being the Anniversary of their Election of Officers,* Boston: John Boyles, 1773, 10. Howard was pastor of the West Church, Boston.

[192] Joseph Priestley, *A View of Revealed Religion,* in his *Works,* XV, 361.

[193] Idem, *The Importance and Extent of Free Enquiry,* Birmingham, 1785; in his *Works,* XVIII, 550. See further, Margaret Canovan, 'Two concepts of liberty – eighteenth-century style', *The Price–Priestley Newsletter,* II, 1978, 27–43.

[194] Caleb Ashworth, *Reflections on the fall of a great man,* 2nd. edn, 1749, 32–3.

[195] P. Furneaux, *Letters to the Hon. Mr. Justice Blackstone,* Preface to 2nd edn, London: T. Cadell, 1771, iii. For Furneaux (1726–83) see DNB.

[196] Joseph Barber, *Sermons on Regeneration,* London: Joseph Buckland, 1770, 16. For Barber (1727–1810), tutor at Hoxton Independent academy 1778–91, see Walter Wilson, *History and Antiquities,* II, 95, 555; *Evangelical Magazine,* XIX, 1811, 161–6.

[197] *Discourses delivered at the Solemn Separation of the Rev. John Bruce to the Pastoral Office over The Congregational Church assembling in St. James's-Street, Newport, Isle of Wight,* 1808, 10.

[198] Robert Robinson, *Arcana, or the Principles of the late Petitioners to Parliament for Relief in matter of Subscription,* Cambridge: Fletcher & Hodson, 1774. See further, Raymond Brown, *The English Baptists of the Eighteenth Century,* London: The Baptist Historical Society, 1986, 132–6.

[199] Samuel Stennett, *The Mortality of Ministers contrasted with the Unchangeableness of Christ,* Bristol, 1791, 29.

[200] For Palmer (1741–1813) see DNB. He was educated under Caleb Ashworth at Daventry.

Chapter 5: Toleration and Government

1 Roland H. Bainton, *The Travail of Religious Liberty: Nine Biographical Studies,* Philadelphia: Westminster, 1951, 237.

2 Thomas Cole (1627?-1697), for whom see DNB, was ejected at the Restoration and subsequently opened a Dissenting academy at Nettlebed, where Samuel Wesley was among his students.

3 See, for example, L. Du Moulin, *The Power of Christian Magistrate,* 1650; *Right of Churches,* 1658; *Les Désmarches de l'Angleterre vers Rome,* 1679; *An Appeal of all the Nonconformists in England,* 1681. For Du Moulin (1606–80) see DNB.

4 See, for example, John Owen, *Indulgence and Toleration Considered,* in *Works* (1850–3), ed. W. H. Goold, London: Banner of Truth Trust, 1968, XIII, 517–40.

5 The Westminster Confession reads, 'or beside it in matters of faith or worship'.

6 *The Savoy Declaration of Faith and Order,* ed. A. G. Matthews, London: Independent Press, 1959, 103 (= XXI.ii.)

7 Ibid., 108–9 (= XXIV.iii). The divines at Boston in 1680 and at Saybrook in 1708 rejected the Savoy statement in favour of a less radical revision of Westminster. See Williston Walker, *The Creeds and Platforms of Congregationalism* (1893), Boston: The Pilgrim Press, 1960, 393–4n.

8 See further Maurice Cranston, *John Locke: A Biography* (1957), Oxford: OUP, 1985, 43; and P. Abrams's remarks on Locke's early conservatism in his edition of Locke's *Two Tracts on Government,* Cambridge: CUP, 1967, 6–10.

9 J. Locke, MS c34, *passim.* Robert S. Paul has demonstrated that the Independent divines at the Westminster Assembly did not begin to make out a case for toleration until it appeared that they were shortly

to be in a minority under Presbyterian rule. See his *The Assembly of the Lord: Politics and Religion in the Westminster Assembly and 'The Grand Debate'*, Edinburgh: T. & T. Clark, 1985, 122–3, 206–9, 439–40, 487–91 and *passim*. Cf. John Owen, *Works*, XIII, 461. As Waldo Beach has noted in another context, '[T]he political question of power is interlocked with the doctrinal question of truth.' See his 'Sectarianism and skepticism: the strange allies of religious liberty', in Franklin H. Littell (ed.), *Reformation Studies: Sixteen Essays in Honor of Roland H. Bainton*, Richmond, Va.: John Knox Press, 1962, 200.

10 For Chillingworth (1602–44) and Taylor (1613–67) see DNB. Taylor's *A Discourse of the Liberty of Prophesying* (1646) was particularly influential – and heartily disliked by Charlės I.

11 See above, ch.I, n. 35.

12 For Parker (1640–88) see DNB.

13 G. B., *The Case of Compulsion in Matters of Religion*, 1688, 1, 4. See further Johannes van den Berg, *The Idea of Tolerance and the Act of Toleration*, London: Dr Williams's Trust, 1989; Richard Ashcraft, 'Latitudinarianism and toleration: historical myth versus political history', 159–60.

14 See Mark Goldie, 'The theory of religious intolerance in Restoration England', in Ole Peter Grell, J. Israel and Nicholas Tyacke (eds.), *From Persecution to Toleration: The Glorious Revolution and Religion in England*, Oxford: Clarendon Press, 1991.

15 Thomas Tenison, *An Argument for Union*, London: Thomas Basset et al., 1683, 40. For Tenison (1636–1715) see DNB.

16 R. H. Bainton notes that during the struggle for religious liberty, Locke and Sébastien Castellio alone wrote treatises on both liberty and the problem of knowledge. See his *The Travail of Religious Liberty: Nine Biographical Studies* (1951), Hamden, Conn.: The Shoe String Press, 1971, 247.

17 Quoted ibid., 58.

18 J. Locke, *Two Tracts on Government*, ed. Philip Abrams, Cambridge: CUP, 1967, 119.

19 For an account of the circumstances from the 1662 Act of Uniformity to the Toleration Act of 1689 see Alan P. F. Sell, *Commemorations: Studies in Christian Thought and History*, Calgary: University of Calgary Press and Cardiff: University of Wales Press, 1993, ch.V.

20 Maurice Cranston refers to the translation by Locke's friend, William Popple, of Locke's *Epistola de Tolerantia*, and says that there is one especially striking phrase in Popple's preface: '"Absolute liberty, just and true liberty, equal and impartial liberty, is the thing we stand in

need of." This was Popple's demand. It was not Locke's. Locke wanted toleration, not "absolute liberty".' See his 'John Locke and the case for toleration', in John Horton and Susan Mendus (eds.), *John Locke: A Letter Concerning Toleration in Focus,* London: Routledge, 1991, 85. Mark Goldie has pointed out that Locke's

> exclusion of Catholics was not unmitigated ... Catholics were reputed to hold two subversive doctrines: the Jesuitical notion that promises need not be kept with heretics, and the doctrine of the Pope's deposing power. Both were incessantly repudiated in English Catholic polemic, which was almost wholly anti-Papal, anti-Jesuit, and tinged with Jansenism.

See M. Goldie, 'Locke and Anglican Royalism', *Political Studies,* XXXI, 1983, 84. He cites E. Duffy, 'A Rubb-up for Old Sores: Jesuits, Jansenists, and the English secular clergy, 1705–15', *Journal of Ecclesiastical History,* XXVIII, 1977, 291–317, in support of his second sentence. We recall that Locke had experienced harmonious relations between Roman Catholics and Protestants in Cleves. Locke went so far as to draw up a list of doctrines which Roman Catholics should renounce if they were to be tolerated. See Locke MS c.27, fo.30. Short of such renunciation they were not to be tolerated. At the same time, the later Locke had no difficulty, for example, with the notion that Roman Catholics might 'believe that to be really the body of Christ, which another man calls bread', or with the use of Latin in church, for in neither case was injury caused to neighbours. See his *A Letter concerning Toleration,* in *Works,* VI, 40, 51.

21 As to the former, he wrote to Henry Stubbe in 1659: 'The only scruple I have is how the liberty you grant the Papists can consist with the security of the Nation (the end of government).' See E. S. de Beer (ed.), *The Correspondence of John Locke,* Oxford: Clarendon Press, 1976, I, 111. For Stubbe (1632–76), author and physician, see DNB. See also J. Locke, *A Letter concerning Toleration,* in *Works* , VI, 46; John Dunn, *The Political Thought of John Locke,* Cambridge: CUP, 1969, 37–40; Richard Ashcraft, *Revolutionary Politics and Locke's Two Treatises of Government,* Princeton: Princeton University Press, 1986. As J. D. Mabbott reminds us, such defenders of toleration as Milton and Marvell also excluded Roman Catholics from consideration. See his *John Locke,* London: Macmillan, 1973, 179. Jeremiah Burroughes, a Savoy divine, observed that 'They who are for a Congregationall way, doe not hold absolute liberty for all Religions.' See his *Irenicum, to the Lovers of Truth and Peace,* London: Robert Dawlman, 1646, 41. For the extent to which, during the eighteenth century, Dissenters – rational and otherwise – adopted an anti-Roman stance see Martin Fitzpatrick, 'Joseph Priestley and the cause of universal toleration,' *The Price–Priestley Newsletter,* I, 1977,

3–30. For an extended, careful account of the matters here baldly summarized see John Marshall, *John Locke. Resistance, Religion and Responsibility,* Cambridge: CUP, 1994, Part I.

22 J. Locke, BL MSS Locke, c.28, f.2a.

23 See E. Bagshaw, *The Great Question concerning Things Indifferent in Religious Worship,* 1660; *The Second Part of the Great Question,* etc., 1661. For Bagshawe (1629–71) see DNB.

24 See de Beer (ed.), *The Correspondence of John Locke,* I, 227–9 : 'Locke to the Hon., Robert Boyle, 12/22 December 1665'.

25 For this legislation and its consequences see Sell, *Commemorations,* ch.V. Laura Brace regrets David Wootton's omission of what she calls 'the sectarian context' in his Introduction to *John Locke: Political Writings,* Harmondsworth: Penguin, 1993. See her review of this work in *The Locke Newsletter,* XXVI, 1995, 190.

26 He became the first Earl of Shaftesbury in 1672.

27 J. Locke, *A Third Letter for Toleration,* in *Works,* VI, 143.

28 See J. Locke, *Works,* X.

29 'So called' because the term 'toleration' appears neither in the title nor the text of the Act. The Puritan Arminian Independent John Goodwin (1594?–1665) and the Baptists Thomas Helwys (1550?–1616?) and Roger Williams (1604?–83) were early advocates of the individual's duty to abide by his or her convictions. For these see DNB. For a fuller – yet still concise – account of the matters briefly touched upon in this paragraph see James H. Tully's 'Introduction' to Locke's *A Letter concerning Toleration,* Indianapolis: Hackett Publishing Company, 1983. For considerably more detail see John Marshall, *John Locke.*

30 J. Locke, *A Letter concerning Toleration,* in *Works,* VI, 34.

31 On the question how far Locke's views changed see the contrasting positions of J. W. Gough, 'The development of Locke's belief in toleration', Maurice Cranston, 'John Locke and the case for toleration' and P. J. Kelly, 'John Locke: authority, conscience and religious toleration', reprinted in John Horton and Susan Mendus (eds), *John Locke: A Letter concerning Toleration in Focus,* London: Routledge, 1991. Cf. David Wootton's 'Introduction' to *John Locke: Political Writings,* 36.

32 P. J. Kelly, 'Authority, conscience and religious toleration', 132.

33 John Locke to Robert Boyle, 12/22 December 1665; see de Beer (ed.), *The Correspondence of John Locke,* I, 1976, 228.

34 J. Locke, *A Letter concerning Toleration,* in *Works,* VI, 6.

35 David C. Snyder, 'John Locke and the freedom of belief', 231. Cf. J. D. Mabbott, *John Locke,* 174–5; J. W. Gough, 'The development of Locke's belief in toleration', in John Horton and Susan Mendus (eds),

John Locke: A Letter concerning Toleration in Focus, 70–1. John Marshall associates this change with Locke's increasingly elevated view of human beings who, in the *Two Tracts* were 'beasts,' in the *Essay on Infallibility* were 'sheep,' but by the *Essay on Toleration,* were potentially rational creatures. See his *John Locke,* 64. Marshall in turn refers to H. R. Fox Bourne, *The Life of John Locke,* 1876, 176–8.

36 J. Locke, *An Essay concerning Toleration,* in D. Wootton, *John Locke: Political Writings,* 190.

37 See J. T. Moore, 'Locke on assent and toleration', *The Journal of Religion,* LVIII, no.1, 1978, 30–6.

38 J. Locke, *Essay* , IV.xvi.4. G. A. J. Rogers has shown that 'The epistemological problem of the Argument from Ignorance ... was well in the arena by the 1640s.' See his, 'Locke and the latitude-men: ignorance as a ground of toleration', in Richard Kroll, Richard Ashcraft and Perez Zagorin (eds), *Philosophy, Science, and Religion in England 1640–1700,* Cambridge: CUP, 1992, 231.

39 J. Locke, *A Letter concerning Toleration,* in *Works,* VI, 35.

40 Idem, *Two Treatises of Government,* II, in *Works,* V, 341. By focusing on the argument of *A Letter concerning Toleration,* Jeremy Waldron is able to regret that Locke's argument shows only that intolerance is irrational, not that it is morally wrong. See his 'Locke: toleration and the rationality of persecution', in Susan Mendus (ed.), *Justifying Toleration: Conceptual and Historical Perspectives,* Cambridge: CUP, 1988, ch.III, and the editor's remarks, 8–9. The implication of my observations here is that Waldron abstracts from Locke's total position. Locke was pondering a number of significant works concurrently, and we should take care lest we set aside his fundamental convictions simply because they are not everywhere mentioned. In the present case, however, as my next reference will demonstrate, there is more of a moral argument in the *Letter* than Jeremy Waldron supposes. He almost gives the game away, or at least recognizes that he begs an important question, when, on p.149, he writes, 'When stripped of its Christian premises (if indeed it can be so stripped, and I shall not here comment on that vexed question) Locke's argument proceeds as follows ...' For a more theological response to Waldron see Joshua Mitchell, 'John Locke and the theological foundation of liberal toleration: a Christian dialectic of history,' *Review of Politics,* LII, no.1, Winter 1990, 64–83, especially 77 n. 6. Elsewhere Waldron's editor argues against him to the conclusion that Locke's case is that intolerance is wrong because it is irrational. See Susan Mendus, *Toleration and the Limits of Liberalism,* London: Macmillan, 1989, 41. However, we do not attain the whole of Locke simply by turning Waldron's position upside down.

41 J. Locke, *A Letter concerning Toleration,* in *Works,* VI, 9, 17–18; my italics.

42 See further, Richard Ashcraft, 'Latitudinarianism and toleration: historical myth versus political history', in *Philosophy, Science, and Religion in England 1640–1700,* ch.VII.

43 See J. Locke, *A Letter concerning Toleration,* in *Works,* VI, 37–8.

44 See idem, *The Reasonableness of Christianity,* in *Works,* VII, 79–81 and *passim.*

45 Idem, *A Paraphrase and Notes on the Epistles of St. Paul,* II, 570.

46 See J. Locke, British Library MSS. Locke, e.7, f.35.

47 Idem, *A Letter concerning Toleration,* in *Works,* VI, 10. It would take us too far afield to consider whether Locke's (and others') restriction of religion to the private realm contributed to its increasing irrelevance in society at large. On which matter see David C. Snyder, 'John Locke and the freedom of belief'.

48 See Tertullian, *Ad Scapulam,* 2.

49 J. Locke, *A Letter concerning Toleration,* in *Works,* VI, 29.

50 Ibid., 10–11; cf. 41.

51 Ibid., 29. Cf. ibid., 54–5; idem, *A Third Letter for Toleration,* ibid., 156–8. See further, John Dunn, 'The claim to freedom of conscience: freedom of speech, freedom of thought, freedom of worship?' in Ole Peter Grell et al., *From Persecution to Toleration,* ch.VII; Mark Philp, 'Enlightenment, toleration and liberty', *Enlightenment and Dissent,* IX, 1990, 47–62. It is interesting to compare Locke's view with that of the early Luther, who recognized that belief cannot be forced or heresy driven out by violence. The combination of the antics of the Anabaptists and the Peasants' Revolt later prompted him to allow much greater powers to the authorities – this in the interests of public order. See H. Kamen, *The Rise of Toleration,* London: Weidenfeld and Nicolson, 1967, 32–41. For other harbingers of Locke see W. K. Jordan, *The Development of Religious Toleration in England,* 4 vols., London: Allen and Unwin, 1938. It is somewhat surprising that Graham Keith, who mentions these sources in his article, 'Issues in religious toleration from the Reformation to the present day', *The Evangelical Quarterly,* LXVI, 1994, 307–29, makes no reference to Locke or, for that matter, to John Owen. What Locke denied to the magistrates the latter denied to the clerics as well, on the ground that every person is required to employ reason to discern whether beliefs and practices proposed are 'agreeable or contrary to the Laws of God'. See his *Truth and Innocency Vindicated: In a Survey of a Discourse concerning Ecclesiastical Polity* (1669), in his *Works,* XIII, 343–506.

52 J. Locke, *A Letter concerning Toleration,* in *Works,* VI, 52. Cf.

Thomas Helwys, *The Mistery of Iniquity,* 1612, 69:

> Our Lord the King is but an earthly King, and he hath no aucthority as a King but in earthly causes, and if the King's people be obedient and true subjects, obeying all humane laws made by the King, our lord the King can require no more: for men's religion to God is betwixt God and themselves: the King shall not answere for it, neither may be King be judg betwene God and Man. Let them be heretikes, Turcks, Jewes, or whatsoever, it apperteynes not to the earthly power to punish them in the least measure.

Unlike Locke, but like William Popple, the translator of Locke's *A Letter concerning Toleration,* Helwys did advocate *universal* religious toleration; indeed he was the first to do so in England.

53 Susan Mendus, *Toleration and the Limits of Liberalism,* 39; cf. eadem in *John Locke: A Letter concerning Toleration in Focus,* 157: 'Locke does not think that there is a right to freedom of worship as such, but only a right not to have one's worship interfered with for religious ends.' Cf. ibid., 160.

54 In J. Locke, *Works,* VI, 156–8.

55 In his *John Locke on Toleration and the Unity of God,* Amsterdam: J. C. Gieben, 1983, 128–9 n. 25, Mario Montuori draws a sharp distinction between religious toleration and civic. He argues that Locke accords the former to Roman Catholics, but not the latter, because Locke's ban on liberty for Roman Catholics was politically motivated. He accuses Klibansky and Cranston of irrelevance in asserting that Locke did not believe in absolute liberty. But this is to play down the connection we have already noted in Locke's own words between religious belief and religious practice. For Locke full religious liberty covers the entertaining of religious convictions, the practice of religious belief, and the right not to belong to an established religion. Popple did, and Locke did not, wish to introduce such liberty immediately.

56 J. Locke, *Works,* X, 23 (Latin); ET: de Beer (ed.), *The Correspondence of John Locke,* III, 1978, 633.

57 See for example, idem, 'A Letter concerning toleration', in *Works,* VI, 34; cf. Mark Goldie, 'John Locke and Anglican royalism', 83. While great strides have subsequently been taken regarding tolerance, we find that at the end of Christianity's second millennium there is, to put it mildly, less than wild enthusiasm for disestablishment in the Church of England (not to mention continental Lutheran and Reformed churches), and even the English Nonconformists are nowadays less than strident on the matter. See further Alan P. F. Sell, *Dissenting Thought and the Life of the Churches,* ch.XXII; idem, *Commemorations,* ch.IV; idem, 'A renewed plea for "impractical" divinity,' *Studies in Christian Ethics,* VII no. 2, 1995, 68–91, especially 84–5.

58 R. Williams, *The Bloudy Tenent of Persecution for cause of conscience discussed and Mr. Cotton's Letter examined and answered,* 1644, 239–41. For Roger Williams (1604?–83) see DNB and DAB; for John Cotton (1584–1652) see DAB.

59 R. Baxter, *The Holy Commonwealth,* 1659, theses 192, 239.

60 Anon., *An Essay upon Government,* 1705, 1, 6.

61 Ibid., 31–40.

62 J. Priestley, *A General History of the Christian Church from the Fall of the Western Empire,* in J. T. Rutt (ed.), *The Theological and Miscellaneous Works of Joseph Priestley,* X, 487.

63 Idem, *Various Observations Relating to the Dissenters' Application to Parliament for Relief from Certain Penal Laws,* in ibid., XXII, 478; cf. ibid., 63.

64 Idem, *An Essay on the First Principles of Government,* (1768), in ibid., XXII, 63–5. Kippis's remarks appear in *The Monthly Review,* XXXIX, 473–4. Dissenters would probably have been equally staggered by the view of Joseph Wilks, a Benedictine monk, who opined that since Locke wrote on toleration the question had not so much been whether Catholic tenets were true as whether they were consistent with good government. See his letter to Sir J. Throckmorton of 7 October 1791, Throckmorton MSS, cited by Martin Fitzpatrick, 'Joseph Priestley and the cause of universal toleration', *The Price–Priestley Newsletter,* I, 1977, 22. They might have been slightly affronted by the use of their 'great Mr. Locke' by a Roman Catholic, and dismayed that doctrinal matters could so easily be set aside. Interestingly, the more doctrinally orthodox Presbyterian John Witherspoon was open to increased toleration for Roman Catholics. See Jack Scott (ed.), *An Annotated Edition of Lectures on Moral Philosophy by John Witherspoon,* 166.

65 J. Priestley, *Works* , XXII, 63n.

66 See further, David L. Wykes, '"A finished monster of the true Birmingham breed." Birmingham, Unitarians and the 1791 Priestley Riots', in Alan P. F. Sell (ed.), *Protestant Nonconformists and the West Midlands of England,* Keele: Keele University Press, 1996, 43–69.

67 Martin Fitzpatrick, 'Joseph Priestley and the cause of universal toleration', 20. The author of this excellent paper further notes (ibid.) that 'When the Dissenters eventually reapplied for the repeal of the Corporation and Test Acts, only the Unitarians were simultaneously and unanimously in favour of Catholic Emancipation.' Yet again, he points out (pp.14–15) that while the friends Priestley and Price were in accord in their definitions of religious liberty, Price, though in advance of Locke, would not, owing to his concern for the security of the realm, have extended toleration as far as Priestley. See, for

example, Price's letter of 7 August 1783 to Lieut.-Col. Sharman, in D. O. Thomas, *The Correspondence of Richard Price,* Durham, NC: Duke University Press and Cardiff: University of Wales Press, 1991, II, 188–92.

68 As throughout this study, I by no means deny that divines were not alone in reading Locke with approval or disapproval. In the present connection, for example, the lawyer and Christian apologist John Shute Barrington appended a defence of (unnamed) Locke to his *The Rights of Protestant Dissenters* (1704), concluding that it may be left 'to Mankind to *Judge*, which Principles look more like those of true Christianity: The Principles of Force and Constraint, which lead Men to such Heat, Rancour and Violence; or those of an Universal and Absolute Toleration, with which such Rage and Fury is altogether inconsistent' (2nd edn, 1704, 103). For Barrington (1678–1734), who was a younger contemporary of Isaac Watts at Thomas Rowe's academy in London, see DNB.

69 E. Calamy, *An Historical Account of My Own Life,* ed. J. T. Rutt., London: Henry Colburn and Richard Bentley, 1829, II, 30–1. For Calamy (1697?–1755) see DNB.

70 I. Watts, *Works,* V, 503.

71 P. Doddridge, *Works,* 1803, III, 125–6.

72 C. Chauncy, *The Only Compulsion Proper to Be Made Use of in Affairs of Conscience and Religion,* Boston, 1739, 9.

73 W. Warburton, *The Doctrine of Grace,* 1763, 259. For Warburton (1698–1779) see DNB.

74 See John Coakley, 'John Henry Livingston and the liberty of the conscience', *Reformed Review,* XLVI, no.2, Winter 1992, 119–35. For Livingston (1746–1825) see DAB.

75 Knud Haakonssen, *Thomas Reid: Practical Ethics,* Princeton: Princeton University Press, 1990, 257–8.

76 [R. Watson], *A letter to the members of the honourable House of Commons; respecting the petition for relief in the matter of subscription, by a Christian Whig,* 1772, 21–2. See further Timothy Brain, 'Richard Watson and the debate on toleration in the late eighteenth-century', *The Price–Priestley Newsletter,* II, 1978, 4–26. For Watson (1737–1816) see DNB.

77 See T. Scott, *The Force of Truth,* Edinburgh (1779), London: The Religious Tract Society, n.n., 38n. For Scott (1747–1821) see DNB.

78 P. Furneaux, *Letters to the Honourable Mr. Justice Blackstone, concerning His Exposition of the Act of Toleration,* 1770, ii.

79 Idem, *An Essay on Toleration: With a particular View to the Late Application of The Protestant Dissenting Ministers to Parliament, for Amending, and rendering Effectual, the Act of the first of William and*

Mary, commonly called the Act of Toleration, 1773, 1.

80 C. Evans, *British Constitutional Liberty. A Sermon Preached in Broadmead, Bristol, November 5, 1775,* Bristol: W. Pine, [1775], 16n. Three years later Evans preached on 5 November to mark the anniversary of the 'Gunpowder Plot'. While it could not 'be denied that the conspirators were all Papists,' some of whom

> gloried in what they had done, and only lamented that it has not succeeded. We do not, however, wish to load all the professors of Popery with the ignominy of this black transaction. It is the part of candour to acknowledge, that there were many of the Romish communion who at the time abhorred the bloody purpose, and as much rejoiced in the discovery and disappointment of it, as the most zealous Protestant. And in the present day I would willingly presume, there are none to be met with of any communion, who are not ready to join in a detestation of every transaction so inhuman and diabolical.

See his *British Freedom Realized,* Bristol: William Pine [1788], 7–8.

81 A. Kippis, *A Vindication of the Protestant Dissenting Ministers, With Regard to their late Application to Parliament,* 1773, 29–30.

82 Ibid., 46, 97.

83 Samuel Wilton, *An Apology for the Renewal of an Application to Parliament by the Protestant Dissenting Ministers. Addressed to the Thirteen Ministers who Protested against it,* 1783, 52–3n. His reference to Locke is on p. 25n. For Wilton (1744–78) see J. A. Jones, *Bunhill Memorials,* London: James Paul, 1849, 327–9.

84 *The Right of Protestant Dissenters to a Compleat Toleration, Asserted,* 1787, 76–7, citing J. Locke, *A Second Letter concerning Toleration,* in *Works,* VI, 73; cf. ibid., 342.

85 T. Belsham, *The Rights of Conscience Asserted and Defined, in Reference to the Modern Interpretation of the Toleration Act,* 1812, 9.

86 Idem, *Freedom of Enquiry,* 1800, 46. As Waldo Beach pointed out, Locke champions 'freedom for Christian consciences [we might in view of the evidence cited above insert the word 'some'], not any conscience; in this regard he belongs more to the medieval and Reformation than to the modern period'. See his 'Sectarianism and Skepticism: the strange allies of religious liberty', in Little (ed.), *Reformation Studies,* 207.

87 A. Gordon, *Heads of English Unitarian History,* London: Philip Green, 1895, 94.

88 Cf. the remark of Herbert D. Foster, 'International Calvinism through Locke and the Revolution of 1688', *American Historical Review,* XXXII, no.3, April 1927, 487: 'Through Locke there filtered to the American Revolution five points of political Calvinism held by hundreds of Calvinists, but clarified through his Civil

Government: fundamental law, natural rights, contract and consent of people, populous sovereignty, resistance to tyranny through responsible representation.'

89 See, for example, J. C. D. Clark, *English Society, 1688–1832: Ideology, Social Structure and Political Practice during the Ancien Régime*, Cambridge: CUP, 1985, 57–8; H. T. Dickinson, 'The eighteenth-century debate on the "Glorious Revolution"', *History*, LXI, 1976, 28–45. The former observes that while deference was paid to Locke as one who favoured the Revolution of 1688, almost all lay philosophers opposed his political theory, while most Anglican clerics endorsed the conservative social theory promulgated by Berkeley.

90 J. Dunn, *The Political Thought of John Locke*, 99.

91 A view endorsed, for example by Quentin Skinner, *The Foundations of Modern Political Thought*, Cambridge: CUP, 1978, II, 239; J. G. A. Pocock, 'Virtues, rights, and manners: a model for historians of political thought,' *Political Theory*, IX no. 3, August 1981, 364.

92 Richard L. Greaves, 'Radicals, rights and revolution: British Nonconformity and the roots of the American experience,' *Church History*, LXI, no.2, June 1992, 156.

93 J. Dunn, 'From applied theology to social analysis: the break between John Locke and the Scottish Enlightenment,' in Istvan Hort and Michael Ignatieff (eds.), *Wealth and Virtue*, Cambridge: CUP, 1983, 129. Accordingly, Joshua Mitchell suggests that in his *Natural Right and History*, p.205, Leo Strauss too readily construes Locke's theory as a secular one. See Joshua Mitchell, 'John Locke and the theological foundation of liberal toleration: a Christian dialectic of History', *Review of Politics*, LII, no.1, Winter 1990, 77.

94 J. Locke, *A Paraphrase and Notes on the Epistles of St. Paul*, II, 588; 586–7.

95 Shirley R. Letwin, 'John Locke: liberalism and natural law', 19.

96 J. Locke, *Two Treatises of Government*, II, in *Works*, V, 383. Locke's individual is not, therefore, a Hobbesian atom. I do not here imply that Locke's *Two Treatises* were written directly in reply to Hobbes. For his denial that this was the case see Maurice Cranston, *John Locke: A Biography*, 207–10.

97 Ibid., 396; cf. 394.

98 Ibid., 421.

99 Ibid., 339. For the way in which the American deist, Ethan Allen, utilized Locke's political philosophy in Revolutionary times see Darline Shapiro, 'Ethan Allen, philosopher-theologian to a generation of American revolutionaries', *The William and Mary Quarterly*, 3rd ser., XXI, no.2, April 1964, 237–55.

100 Ibid., 436.

101 For Filmer (*c.*1588–1653) see DNB. For his position see R. Filmer, *Patriarcha and Other Writings,* ed. J. P. Somerville, Cambridge: CUP, 1991. A considerable study might be undertaken concerning the response of eighteenth-century divines to Locke's social-contract theory of the state, but my specific concerns with the implications of his theory of government for church polity and Church–state relations precludes this.

102 J. Locke, *A Letter concerning Toleration,* in *Works,* VI, 13. Thomas Jefferson was but one of a number subsequently to echo Locke's thought and language. See Paul Leicester Ford (ed.), *The Writings of Thomas Jefferson,* 10 vols., New York: G. P. Putnam, 1892–9, II, 101.

103 Ibid.

104 In view of all Locke says concerning the divinė origin of both state and Church, I cannot agree with Sanford Kessler, who endorses the views of Kraynak and Windstrup that Locke's 'concern for safeguarding the secular realm was far greater than his concern for the sacred'. See S. Kessler, 'John Locke's legacy of religious freedom', *Polity,* XVII, no.3, Spring 1985, 493; Robert P. Kraynak, 'John Locke: from absolutism to toleration', *American Political Science Review,* LXXIV, March 1980, 55; George Windstrup, 'Freedom and authority: the ancient faith of Locke's *Letter on Toleration*', *The Review of Politics,* XLIV, April 1982, 249. For one thing, these authors appear illegitimately to read the modern distinction between sacred and secular into Locke. For him the secular/civic was not the godless. This is not at all to deny that Locke was intensely concerned for the safety of the realm, or to deny that the thought of religious toleration as a safety-valve had not bypassed him. See *A Letter concerning Toleration,* in *Works,* VI, 48.

105 Accordingly, I cannnot agree with David C. Snyder that 'Locke defended his approval of religious toleration by appealing to a dubious notion of religion as private.' See his 'John Locke and the freedom of belief', 228. Rather, the evidence suggests that because of creation and the Gospel, Locke believed that religion was personal, not private, and social – a matter of fellowship with God and with others in the Church. See further Winthrop S. Hudson, 'John Locke – preparing the way for the Revolution', *Journal of Presbyterian History,* XLII, no.1, March 1964, 21.

106 S. Letwin, 'John Locke: liberalism and natural law', 13.

107 J. Locke, *Two Treatises of Government,* in *Works,* V, 469–70.

108 Though the analysis of 'people' in Locke is problematic. See D. O. Thomas, 'Richard Ashcraft on Locke's *Two Treatises*', *Enlightenment and Dissent,* XIV, 1995, 128–54.

109 Hudson, 'John Locke – preparing the way for the Revolution', 28.

110 W. Bartlett, *ICHNOGRAPHIA, or a Model of the Primitive Congregational Way,* 1647, ch.II. For Bartlett (d. 1682), an ejected minister, see DNB.

111 T. Hooker, *A Summe of Church Discipline,* 1648, 3, 46. For Hooker (1586?–1647) see DNB.

112 In *The Savoy Declaration of Faith and Order 1658,* ed. A. G. Matthews, London: Independent Press, 1959, 121. For further examples of Dissenting ecclesiological principles see Alan P. F. Sell, *Saints: Visible, Orderly and Catholic: The Congregational Idea of the Church,* Geneva: World Alliance of Reformed Churches and Allison Park, Pa: Pickwick Publications, 1986, ch.III; idem, *Dissenting Thought and the Life of the Churches,* ch.I; Williston Walker, *The Creeds and Platforms of Congregationalism* (1893), Boston: The Pilgrim Press, 1960. For the Baptists see William L. Lumpkin, *Baptist Confessions of Faith,* Valley Forge, Pa.: Judson Press (1959), rev. edn, 1969; Charles W. Deweese, *Baptist Church Covenants,* Nashville: Broadman Press, 1990.

113 See H. F. Lovell Cocks, *Proceedings of the Seventh International Congregational Council,* London: Independent Press, 1953, 48–9, 51–2. Cf. Alan P. F. Sell, *A Reformed, Evangelical, Catholic Theology: The Contribution of the World Alliance of Reformed Churches 1875–1982,* Grand Rapids: Eerdmans, 1991, 92–3. For Lovell Cocks see idem, *Commemorations,* ch.XIII.

114 Bainton, *The Travail of Religious Liberty: Nine Biographical Studies,* Philadelphia: Westminster Press, 1959, 243.

115 See J. Angus, *The Voluntary System,* London: Jackson and Walford, 1839, 22. It is proper to add that Angus subsequently defended the theocratic nature of the Church: 'The Christian church is a theocracy, administered through the consciences and hearts of Christians. This peculiarity is an advantage in an age of democratic tendencies, when men are qualifying to exercise their rights, and are preparing to claim them.' See his *The Christian Churches: The Noblest Form of Social Life; The Representatives of Christ on Earth; The Dwelling-Place of the Holy Spirit,* London: Ward, 1862, 70. See further, John Briggs, *The English Baptists of the Nineteenth Century,* Didcot: The Baptist Historical Society, 1994, ch.II. For a further latter-day critique of Locke's definition of the Church as a voluntary society, which moves along similar lines to that of Lovell Cocks, see George Warren Richards, *History of the Theological Seminary of the Reformed Church in the United States 1825–34, Evangelical and Reformed Church 1934–1952,* Lancaster, Pa.: Theological Seminary of the Evangelical and Reformed Church, 1952, 292:

> According to this view of the Church, it is formed by men for promoting

> their own spiritual and ethical welfare. Not a word is said about the Church as the creation of God and a divine agency for the mediation of salvation and life to men. Furthermore, the Church is thought of as the local congregation without reference to its relation to the fellowship or communion of Christians in all lands, in time and eternity; it is a parochial, not an ecumenical conception of the Church.

It is not surprising that such a criticism should emanate from the heartland of the Mercersburg theology of J. W. Nevin and others, for which see J. H. Nichols, *The Mercersburg Theology,* New York: OUP, 1966; Sell, *Commemorations.* ch.XI.

116 J. Locke, *A Letter concerning Toleration,* in *Works,* VI, 10.

117 Ibid., 21.

118 Ibid., 54.

119 Ibid., 38.

120 Ibid., 28.

121 Ibid., 11.

122 Idem, *A Third Letter for Toleration,* ibid., 422–3. For Proast see further below.

123 Idem, *A Letter concerning Toleration,* ibid., 27–8.

124 Ibid., 15.

125 See ibid., *passim.* It is not difficult to hear echoes of the Huguenot divine, Du Moulin, in Locke's views on matters deemed non-essential.

126 J. Locke, *A Letter concerning Toleration,* in *Works* , VI, 14–15.

127 Idem, *A Third Letter for Toleration,* ibid., 484–5.

128 T. Tenison, *An Argument for Union,* London: Thomas Basset et al., 1683, 4. For Tenison (1636–1715) see DNB.

129 [T. Long], *The Letter for Toleration Decipher'd,* 1689, 3. For Long (1621–1707) see DNB.

130 [C. Leslie], *The Second Part of the Wolf Stript of his Shepherds Cloathing,* 1707, 3. I owe this reference to James Moore's stimulating paper, 'Theological politics: a study of the reception of Locke's *Two Treatises of Government* in England and Scotland in the early eighteenth century', in Martyn P. Thompson (ed.), *John Locke and/und Immanuel Kant,* Berlin: Duncker & Humblot, 1991, 62–82, especially 68–73. For Leslie (1650–1722) see DNB.

131 S. Johnson, 'Autobiography', in Herbert and Carol Schneider, *Samuel Johnson, His Career and Writings,* 4 vols., New York: Columbia University Press, 1929, I, 11–12.

132 B. Hoadly, *The Nature of the Kingdom, or Church, of Christ. A Sermon Preach'd before the King at the Royal Chapel at St. James's on Sunday March 31, 1717,* London: James Knapton & Timothy Childe, 1717. For Hoadly (1676–1761) see DNB.

[133] John Walsh et al. (eds.), *The Church of England c. 1689–c.1833,* 46. However this way of posing the questions must not mislead us into overlooking the fact that the Independents regarded the Church as comprising *visible* saints. In other words, 'visible' is not a High Church term only.

[134] J. Wise, *A Vindication of the Government of New-England Churches,* Boston: John Boyles, 1672, 42–3. For Wise (1652–1725) see DAB.

[135] *The Cambridge Platform,* ch.X; in Williston Walker, *The Creeds and Platforms of Congregationalism,* 217–18.

[136] See further Gaius Glenn Atkins and Frederick L. Fagley, *History of American Congregationalism,* Boston: The Pilgrim Press, 1942, 194.

[137] I. Watts, *Works,* III, 196–7.

[138] Ibid.

[139] Isaac Backus, *A History of New England,* Newton, Mass.: Backus Historical Society, 2nd edn., 1871, II, 304. Cf. idem, *A Door Opened for Religious Liberty,* Boston, 1783, in William G. McLoughlin, *Isaac Backus on Church, State, and Calvinism: Pamphlets, 1754–89,* Cambridge, Mass.: Harvard University Press, 1968, 432; idem, *Policy as Well as Honesty Forbids the Use of Secular Force in Religious Affairs,* Boston, 1779, in ibid., 376. I am here prompted by Stanley J. Grenz, 'Isaac Backus', in Timothy George and David S. Dockery (eds.), *Baptist Theologians,* Nashville, Tn: Broadman Press, 1990, 102–20. For Backus (1724–1806) see DAB.

[140] For a brief account of some of the principles and issues see Alan P. F. Sell, *Church Discipline,* London: United Reformed Church, 1983.

[141] Caleb Evans, *A Charge and Sermon, Together with an Introductiory Discourse, and Confession of Faith, Delivered at the Ordination of the Rev. Mr. Caleb Evans, August 18, 1767, in Broad-Mead, Bristol,* 1767, 13. For Evans (1737–91) see Norman Moon, *Education for Ministry: Bristol Baptist College 1679–1979,* Bristol: Bristol Baptist College, 1979, 114–15, and *passim.*

[142] Ibid., 16.

[143] T. Long, *The Letter for Toleration Decipher'd,* 1689, 3.

[144] Ibid., 4.

[145] For Proast (*c.* 1642–1710), see DNB *Missing Persons.* For reliable accounts of the historical context of the Locke–Proast correspondence see Mark Goldie, 'Locke, Proast and religious toleration', in John Walsh, Colin Haydon and Stephen Taylor (eds.), *The Church of England c. 1689–c. 1833: From Toleration to Tractarianism,* Cambridge: CUP, 1993, ch.VI; idem, 'The theory of religious intolerance in Restoration England', in Ole Peter Grell et al. (eds), *From Persecution to Toleration,* ch.XIII; John Spurr, *The Restoration Church of England,* New Haven, Conn.: Yale University Press, 1991. For the

post-Restoration political context see, for example, J. G. A. Pocock, *Virtue, Commerce, and History: Essays on Political Thought and History, Chiefly in the Eighteenth Century,* Cambridge: CUP, 1985.

146 For Charlett (1658–1722) see DNB.

147 Locke quotes Proast to this latter effect in his *Second Letter,* in *Works,* VI, 74. Since Locke immediately proceeds to say that to punish people in order to make them consider is not only impractical but *unjust* (p.75), it is difficult to see how Jeremy Waldron can maintain that Locke's 'in principle' case collapses on this pragmatic point, and with it 'the sharp functional distinction between church and state that Locke was arguing for'. See his 'Toleration and the rationality of persecution', in J. Horton and S. Mendus (eds.), *John Locke: A Letter concerning Toleration in Focus,* 119. The Locke–Proast debate is the subject of Peter Nicholson's paper, 'John Locke's later letters on toleration'. He mistakes Popple's view for Locke's in declaring (p.171) that Locke sought 'full and equal toleration'.

148 [J. Proast], *The Argument of the Letter concerning Toleration, Briefly Consider'd and Answer'd,* 1690, 10.

149 J. Locke, *A Fourth Letter for Toleration,* in *Works,* VI, 565–6.

150 Idem, *A Third Letter for Toleration,* ibid., 144.

151 [J. Proast], *A Third Letter concerning Toleration,* 1691, 20. At times Proast seems almost like a modern ecumenist, as when he argues that the conversion of Jews, Mahometans and Pagans will be more likely [a modern would say, 'the world will take more notice of the Church'] when Christians are seen to be one – for which unity Christ prayed, and Proast quotes John 17:20–1. Ibid., 4. Of course, a modern ecumenist would not advocate the use of force in this matter – though I have heard ardent souls assuring doubters in church assemblies that 'this proposed union is the will of the Holy Spirit,' which is, I suppose, a theological variety of psychological force.

152 G. A. J. Rogers, 'Locke and the latitude-men', in Richard Kroll et al. (eds.), *Philosophy, Science and Religion in England 1640–1700,* 244. With reference to the Presbyterians of the Westminster Assembly of the 1640s Robert S. Paul writes,

> Once we recognize that intolerance was regarded as a virtue rather than as a vice, and that liberty of conscience was understood as an excuse for license and immorality rather than as evidence of broadmindedness, we may have less difficulty in recognizing that the attitude of [Thomas] Edwards and [Robert] Baillie would probably have been endorsed by most people at that time.

See his *The Assembly of the Lord,* 440.

153 See *An Essay upon Government. Wherein the Republican Schemes of Mr. Locke, Dr. Blackal, etc. are Fairly Consider'd and Refuted,* 1705.

[154] See G. S. Holmes, *The Trial of Dr. Sacheverell,* London: Eyre Methuen, 1973, 107. Cf. Sell, *Dissenting Thought and the Life of the Churches,* 327–8, 448–9. For Sacheverell (1674?–1724) see DNB.

[155] E. Calamy, *Comfort and Counsel to Protestant Dissenters,* London: John Lawrence et al., 1712, 24. This was a common refrain until the early years of the twentieth century.

[156] I. Watts, *Works,* III, 211.

[157] Walter Wilson, *The History and Antiquities of Dissenting Churches and Meeting Houses in London, Westminster and Southwark,* II, 1808, 385. For a full account of Towgood's position on this and other matters see Sell, *Dissenting Thought and the Life of the Churches,* 224–9, 633–4. See also, Robert D. Cornwall, 'Advocacy of the independence of the Church from the state in eighteenth-century England', *Enlightenment and Dissent,* XII, 1993, 12–27.

[158] Henry D. Rack, *Reasonable Enthusiast: John Wesley and the Rise of Methodism,* London: Epworth Press, 1989, 308. Dr Rack cites Wesley's *Letters,* III, 251, and points out that Towgood's position was akin to that of Bishop Hoadly.

[159] Thomas Reid, *Practical Ethics,* 257. Knud Haakonssen finds some similarities between Reid's position on church establishment and that articulated in William Warburton's *The Alliance between Church and State,* 1736; see ibid., 421.

[160] See R. Price, *A Discourse on the Love of Our Country,* in D. O. Thomas (ed.), *Richard Price: Political Writings,* Cambridge: CUP, 1991, 191–3. Cf. Carl B. Cone, *Torchbearer of Freedom,* 180ff.

[161] Letter of R. Price to William Adams, 28 December 1778, in D. O. Thomas (ed.), *The Correspondence of Richard Price,* II, Cardiff: University of Wales Press, 1991, 32. Price probably refers to Tucker's *A Treatise of Civil Government,* 1781, of which Price had an earlier sight of the first part. For Josiah Tucker (1712–99) see DNB. See Joseph Towers, *A Vindication of the Political Principles of Mr. Locke in answer to the Objections of The Rev. Dr. Tucker, Dean of Gloucester,* 1782. For Towers (1737–99), printer turned Presbyterian minister, see DNB.

[162] J. Priestley, *Reflections on the Present State of Free Enquiry in this Country added to The Importance and Extent of Free Inquiry in Matters of Religion,* Birmingham, 1785, 40–1.

[163] W. Paley, *Principles of Moral and Political Philosophy,* Edinburgh: James Robertson, 1817, II, 312. For Paley (1743–1805) see DNB.

[164] R. Watson, *A Charge delivered to the Clergy of the Diocese of Llandaff, June 1791,* London: Thomas Evans et al., 1792, 10–11.

[165] De Beer (ed.), *The Correspondence of John Locke,* III, 587.

[166] Thomas Amory, Preface to *Sermons ... by the later Reverend Samuel*

Chandler, I, 1768, xii. For Chandler (1693–1766), Presbyterian divine and contemporary of Joseph Butler and Thomas Secker at Samuel Jones's Dissenting academy at Tewkesbury, see DNB.

167 J. Locke, *A Letter concerning Toleration*, in *Works*, VI, 11.

168 Ibid., 55.

Chapter 6: Christian Doctrine

1 J. Locke, *A Second Vindication of the Reasonableness of Christianity*, in *Works*, VII, 359.

2 Idem, *A Letter concerning Toleration*, in *Works*, VI, 29.

3 B. Whichcote, *Moral and Religious Aphorisms*, 1753, no.1008.

4 J. Howe, *Works*, ed. Henry Rogers, 1873, V, 232ff. For Howe (1630–1705) see DNB; Alan P. F. Sell, *Dissenting Thought and the Life of the Churches*, Lewiston, NY.: Edwin Mellen Press, 1990, ch.III.

5 R. Baxter, *The Reformed Pastor* (1656), London: SCM Press, 1956, 101. See further, Alan P. F. Sell, *Commemorations: Studies in Christian Thought and History*, Calgary: University of Calgary Press and Cardiff: University of Wales Press, 1993, ch.II.

6 For Popple see E. S. de Beer (eds.), *The Correspondence of John Locke*, Oxford: Clarendon Press, III, 1978, 623 n. 2.

7 See further Alan P. F. Sell, *The Great Debate: Calvinism, Arminianism and Salvation*, Worthing: H. E. Walter, 1982 and Grand Rapids: Baker Book House, 1983, 47–50.

8 J. Locke, *The Reasonableness of Christianity*, in *Works*, VII, 357–8.

9 Ibid., 358; cf. 387.

10 Idem, *A Letter concerning Toleration*, in *Works*, VI, 57.

11 Idem, *The Reasonableness of Christianity*, in *Works*, VII, 158. At which point one recalls James Denney's later verdict upon an earlier controversy: 'Arianism and Athanasianism both give answers to a question which multitudes of genuine Christians never ask.' See his *Jesus and the Gospel*, London: Hodder and Stoughton, 1909, 403.

12 Idem, *An Essay concerning Humane Understanding*, I.iii.21.

13 Idem, *A Letter concerning Toleration*, in *Works*, VI, 5.

14 Idem, *The Reasonableness of Christianity*, in *Works*, VII, 157; cf. idem, *Essay*, IV.xx.3.

15 Idem, *A Second Vindication of the Reasonableness of Christianity*, in *Works*, VII, 229.

16 Ibid., 228. Locke nowhere suggests that those who have not had the opportunity of assenting to this doctrine are denied eternal salvation.

17 Ibid., 194. Locke refers to J. Edwards, *Some Thoughts concerning the Several Causes and Occasions of Atheism*, 1695, 5.

18 Ibid., 352; cf. 391.

19 P. T. Forsyth, *The Principle of Authority* (1913), London: Independent Press, 1952, 261. Cf. idem, *Positive Preaching and the Modern Mind* (1907) London: Independent Press, 1964, 84.

20 J. Locke, *The Reasonableness of Christianity,* 97; cf. ibid., 100.

21 Ibid., 102.

22 Idem, *A Vindication of The Reasonableness of Christianity,* in *Works,* VII, 174. He refers to *The Reasonableness of Christianity,* ibid., 16–17.

23 Idem, *A Second Vindication,* 280. David Wootton compares Locke's *Reasonableness* with Chillingworth's *Religion of Protestants* (1638), claiming that while Locke does not insist on the Apostles' Creed, Chillingworth does. But if we cast our net wider – at least to the *Second Vindication* – we find Locke's positive affirmations concerning the necessity on the part of Christians of assent to the Creed.

24 Idem, *The Reasonableness of Christianity,* 111. It cannot be said that Michael S. Rabieh does justice to this evidence in his paper, 'The reasonableness of Locke, or the questionableness of Christianity', *Journal of Politics,* LIII, no.4, November 1991, 941, where, in insisting that Locke proposes one 'neat' article, he resembles Edwards *redivivus.* Again, Nicholas Wolterstorff's assertion that 'In his late book, *The Reasonableness of Christianity,* [Locke] was entirely silent about Christological and Trinitarian matters, arguing merely that the teaching of the Gospels is that Jesus was the Messiah' may be queried, (a) because, as I have indicated, trinitarian speech patterns are to be found in the *Reasonableness;* (b) because Wolterstorff appears not to accommodate the full connotation of 'Jesus is the Messiah' in Locke's thought; and (c) because he does not take into account Locke's motive of not giving hostages to fortune when countering the deists – his avowed purpose in the *Reasonableness,* as he makes clear in *A Second Vindication,* in *Works,* VII, 268–9. See N. Wolterstorff, 'Locke's philosophy of religion', in Vere Chappell (ed.), *The Cambridge Companion to Locke,* Cambridge: CUP, 1994, 185.

25 Idem, *A Second Vindication of The Reasonableness of Christianity,* 194.

26 See further, Dewey D. Wallace, Jr, 'Socinianism, Justification by Faith, and the sources of Locke's *The Reasonableness of Christianity*', *Journal of the History of Ideas,* XLV, January 1984, 49–66, especially 51–4; reprinted in John W. Yolton (ed.), *Philosophy, Religion and Science in the Seventeenth and Eighteenth Centuries,* Rochester, NY: University of Rochester Press, 1990.

27 J. Locke, *The Reasonableness of Christianity,* 105. In view of such a comment as this, the thesis of Michael S. Rabieh that 'The reasonableness of Christianity for Locke ... consists in the political effectiveness of a properly interpreted Christianity, and in nothing

more than this,' can be sustained only if one does not take Locke's professions of faith at face value. Rabieh accuses 'most Locke scholarship' of wrongly taking Locke's professions of faith at face value. It may be that most Locke scholars will not be persuaded by Rabieh to mend their ways, if only because they will not find it psychologically credible that Locke wrote at such inordinate length in order 'to conceal his full teaching'. See his 'The reasonableness of Locke, or the questionableness of Christianity,' 939, 938, 934. It is possible to hold both that Locke's expressions of faith are sincere, and that some of his arguments are weak or otherwise deficient, and that the seams show between his rational argumentation and his appeals to Scripture and faith. It is not necessary to conclude that he adduces ineffectual arguments in order to undermine Christianity whilst (presumably) cynically regarding it as a prop to his rational morality.

28 Ibid., 123.

29 Ibid., 28.

30 Idem, *A Second Vindication,* 352.

31 J. Edwards, *Some Thoughts concerning the several Causes and Occasions of Atheism,* London: J. Robinson and J. Wyat, 1695, 109–10.

32 J. Locke, *A Paraphrase and Notes on the Epistles of St. Paul,* ed. A. W. Wainwright, Oxford: Clarendon Press, 1987, I, 103.

33 M. Cranston, *John Locke: A Biography* (1957), Oxford: OUP, 1985, 455.

34 J. Edwards, *Some Thoughts,* 113.

35 Edwards repeats the charge in his *A Brief Vindication of the Fundamental Articles of the Christian Faith,* 1697, Epistle Dedicatory.

36 Idem, *Socinianism Unmasked,* 1696, Introduction (unpaginated), 2. The reference is to the Socinians of southern Poland who published the first Socinian Catechism at Racow in 1605.

37 Ibid., Introduction (unpaginated), 8–9.

38 Ibid. (unpaginated), 10.

39 Ibid. (unpaginated), 12.

40 Ibid., 4.

41 Ibid., 8–20; cf. *Some Thoughts,* 110.

42 Ibid., 25.

43 Ibid., 47.

44 Ibid., 50–1.

45 Ibid., 61.

46 Ibid., 65–6.

47 Ibid., 76–7.

48 Idem, *The Socinian Creed,* London: J. Robinson, 1697, 129.

49 Ibid., 120.

50 Ibid., 123.

51 Ibid., 127.

52 Idem, *The Doctrin* [*sic*] *of Faith and Justification Set in a True Light*, 1708, 139–40.

53 Ibid., 63, quoting J. Locke, *The Reasonableness of Christianity*.

54 J. Locke, *The Reasonableness of Christianity*, in *Works*, VII, 155.

55 So John C. Attig, *The Works of John Locke: A Comprehensive Bibliography from the Seventeenth Century to the Present*, Westport, Conn.: Greenwood Press, 1985.

56 [?Richard West], *Animadversions*, Oxford, 1697, 3; cf. ibid., 77.

57 Ibid., 63.

58 [R. Willis], *Occasional Paper: Number I*, 1697, 20. For Willis (1664–1734) see DNB.

59 J. Locke, *A Second Vindication*, in *Works*, VII, 420.

60 [R. Willis], *Occasional Paper: Number V*, 41.

61 Ibid., 42, quoting Locke's *Second Vindication*, in *Works*, VII, 421.

62 F.B., *A Free but Modest Censure*, 1698, 8.

63 Ibid., 15. This is presumably a reference to Edwards's jibe that Locke has much to say about 'the *Guts*, which he very feelingly and concernedly discourses of ... as if they were that part of the Body which he most minds. Which is one reason perhaps why he hates *Colledge-Commons*, and for their sake the *Universities*.' See his *A Brief Vindication of the Fundamental Articles of the Christian Faith*, 17, where the reference is to Locke's *Essay*, II.viii.18.

64 [John Milner], *An Account of Mr. Locke's Religion*, 1700, 127; cf. ibid., 49.

65 Ibid., 182–3; cf. ibid., 31.

66 [Francis Webb], *The Morality of the New Testament*, 1765, 313. Webb (1735–1815) was educated under Doddridge and Ashworth at Northampton/Daventry, and Amory at Taunton. For a time he ministered to the General Baptists at Paul's Alley, London. See DNB.

67 Ibid., 350–1.

68 Ibid., 354.

69 Ibid., 355.

70 D. Bogue, *The Great Importance of Having Right Sentiments in Religion*, 1788, 41. For Bogue (1750–1825) see DNB.

71 T. Belsham, *The Character of the Christian Teacher Delineated*, 1804, 1–2. While 'The doctrine of the superhumanity of Christ seemed to [Belsham] the one neck which supported the hydra-heads of corrupt doctrine, all of which might thus be struck off at a single blow', other Unitarians felt that

> it matters but little which link be first broken from the chain of corruption. Original Sin, Total Depravity, Vicarious Suffering, Eternal Torments,

> anyone of these will, if the inquirer persist in his course, be as sure to drag all the rest after it as the doctrine of the Godhead of Christ.

See *On the Character and Writings of the Rev. Thomas Belsham. Extracted from The Monthly Repository for February, &c., 1830,* 1830, 72.

72 T. Belsham, *The Importance of Truth, and the Duty of making an open Profession of it,* 1790, 23–4. Note, however, that Belsham's allusion is to Jesus' summary of the *Jewish* law in answer to the lawyer's question, Mark 12:28–34.

73 Idem, *Adherence to Christian Truth,* 1805, 19.

74 [S. Nye], *The Exceptions of Mr. Edwards,* 1695, iii, iv.

75 Ibid., 40.

76 Ibid., 44.

77 Ibid., 46.

78 J. Edwards, *Brief Animadversions on a late Reply of Mr. Bold* ... to what I had writ against his Defence of the One Article, appended to his *A Brief Vindication of the Fundamentals of the Christian Faith,* 1697, 97–9.

79 S. Bold, *A Short Discourse,* 1697, 1.

80 Ibid., 5–6.

81 J. Edwards, *The Socinian Creed,* 1697, 246–8.

82 Ibid., 255.

83 Ibid., 264.

84 S. Bold, *Observations on the Animadversions,* 1698, 23.

85 Ibid., 62.

86 Ibid., 91.

87 See Locke's letter to Bold in the Preface to *A Second Vindication,* in *Works,* VII, 185–9; and his defence of Bold, ibid., 388–420.

88 G. Burnet, *An Exposition of the Thirty-Nine Articles,* London: R. Roberts, 1699, 7–9.

89 For this gathering see Alan P. F. Sell, *Dissenting Thought and the Life of the Churches,* 75 and ch.V, sect. iii.

90 E. Calamy, *Thirteen Sermons concerning the Doctrine of the Trinity,* 1722 (unpaginated), 12–13.

91 [Josiah Owen], *The Difficulties and Discouragements that attend the Dissenting Ministry,* 1735, 39. For Owen (1711?–55) see DNB. However, his movements are not easy to trace; see Sell, *Dissenting Thought and the Life of the Churches,* 301–2 n. 22.

92 Catharine Cockburn, *A Vindication of Mr. Locke's Christian Principles, from the injurious Imputations of Dr. Holdsworth,* 2 parts, 1751, 188.

93 P. Doddridge, *Course of Lectures,* 1763, Part VII, Prop. CXXXVIII, Scholium 7, 430.

94 W. McGill, *A Practical Essay on the Death of Jesus Christ,* 1786, 370.

For McGill (1732–1807) see DNB.

95 See further, Alexander McNair, *Scots Theology in the Eighteenth Century,* London: James Clarke, [1928]; Henry F. Henderson, *The Religious Controversies of Scotland,* Edinburgh: T. & T. Clark, 1905, ch.V.

96 T. Belsham, *The Importance of Truth, and the Duty of making an open Profession of it,* 44–5n.

97 J. Kentish, *The Accomplished Teacher of Religion,* Birmingham, 1830, 60–1. For Kentish (1768–1853), a Unitarian divine trained under Belsham, see DNB.

98 J. Locke, *A Vindication of The Reasonableness of the Christian Religion,* in *Works,* VII, 164.

99 J. Edwards, *Socinianism Unmasked,* 1696, 43.

100 G. R. Cragg, *Reason and Authority in the Eighteenth Century,* Cambridge: CUP, 1964, 14.

101 J. Locke, *A Vindication of The Reasonableness of the Christian Religion,* in *Works,* VII, 176.

102 Locke to Limborch, 11 December 1694; see de Beer (ed.), *The Correspondence of John Locke,* V, 1979, 238.

103 On which see further Alan P. F. Sell, *The Great Debate: Calvinism, Arminianism and Salvation,* Worthing: H. E. Walter, 1982, and Grand Rapids: Baker Book House, 1983, ch.III.

104 See further, Sell, *Dissenting Thought and the Life of the Churches,* ch.II, and 118–19; John Marshall, *John Locke: Resistance, Religion and Responsibility,* Cambridge: CUP, 1994, ch.4.

105 Samuel Bourn, *Religious Education begun and carried on in Three Catechisms,* 1748, iii. For this Presbyterian divine (1689–1754) see DNB; Sell, *Dissenting Thought and the Life of the Churches,* ch.VII.

106 See further, John Marshall, 'John Locke and Latitudinarianism', in Richard Kroll, Richard Ashcraft and Perez Zagorin, *Philosophy, Science and Religion in England 1640–1700,* Cambridge: CUP, 1992, ch.XI; John Walsh, Colin Haydon and Stephen Taylor, *The Church of England c. 1689–c. 1833,* Cambridge: CUP, 1993, 36–9.

107 See further, Nicholas Jolley, 'Leibniz on Locke and Socinianism', in Yolton (ed.), *Philosophy, Religion and Science in the Seventeenth and Eighteenth Centuries,* ch.XII.

108 See Henry Halywell, preface to George Rust, *A Discourse of the Use of Reason in Matters of Religion, showing that Christianity contains nothing repugnant to Right Reason, against Enthusiasts and Deists,* 1683. For Rust (d. 1670), bishop of Dromore, see DNB. See further, Sell, *Dissenting Thought and the Life of the Churches,* ch.II.

109 S. Clarke, *Works,* II, 600–7.

110 S. C. Carpenter, *Eighteenth Century Church and People,* London: John Murray, 1959, 117.

111 I. Woodbridge Riley, *American Philosophy: The Early Schools,* New York: Russell & Russell, 1957, 16.

112 C. Colden, *The Principles of Action in Matter,* 1751, 163. For Colden (1688–1776) see DAB.

113 J. Barber, *A Sermon occasioned by the death of the Rev. Nathaniel Trotman,* 1793, 17.

114 T. Belsham, *Letters upon Arianism,* 1808, 27.

115 See further, John Orr, *English Deism, Its Roots and Fruits,* Grand Rapids: Eerdmans, 1934, 83–109. Orr concludes that 'no other man exercised a greater influence upon the deistic movement than did Locke, though he was not a deist' (p.109). I concur; however, as will shortly become clear, I think that Orr's statement that Locke 'rejected the trinitarian conception of God and the related doctrine of the deity of Christ' (p.108) is too strong. A classic discussion of deism is that of Leslie Stephen in *History of English Thought in the Eighteenth Century* (1876), New York: Harcourt, Brace & World, 1962, I. Clothing acerbic comment in elegant prose he writes, 'The deist writings are but shabby and shrivelled little octavos, generally anonymous, such as lurk in the corners of dusty shelves, and seem to be the predestined prey of moths' (ibid., 72).

116 J. Locke, *Essay,* IV.x.7.

117 Ibid., IV.x.11, 12. I do not imply that deists necessarily denied God's providence, for example; they did not.

118 See, for example, Matthew Tindal, *Christianity as Old as the Creation,* 1730, 204. For Tindal (1657–1733), Fellow of All Souls, see DNB.

119 J. Locke, *The Reasonableness of Christianity,* in *Works,* VII, 145.

120 Ibid., 5.

121 Idem, Preface to *A Second Vindication,* in *Works,* VII, 188.

122 Idem, *A Second Vindication,* in *Works,* VII, 387.

123 Ibid., 229. In view of such a declaration, it is difficult to understand how A. Campbell Fraser could say that 'The God of Locke is still one object among many, at a distance from the other objects, occasionally interposing.' See his, 'John Locke as a factor in modern thought', *Proceedings of the British Academy,* I, 1902–3, 232. Fraser made the same point in his edition of Locke's *Essay,* Oxford: Clarendon Press, 1894, I, 99, and for this he was rebuked by S. G. Hefelbower, *The Relation of John Locke to English Deism,* Chicago: University of Chicago Press, 1918, 92.

124 Ibid., 286.

125 Idem, *The Reasonableness of Christianity,* in *Works* , VII, 139; cf. ibid., 122, 138–43.

126 Idem, *Works,* X, 63–4.

127 J. Toland, *Christianity Not Mysterious* (1696), Stuttgart–Bad Cannstatt:

Friedrich Frommann Verlag, 1964, 83. For Toland (1670–1722) see DNB; Robert E. Sullivan, *John Toland and the Deist Controversy*, Cambridge, Mass.: Harvard University Press, 1982. For deism in general see P. A. Byrne, *Natural Religion and the Nature of Religion*, London: Routledge, 1989.

[128] Ibid., 146.

[129] See further John C. Biddle, 'Locke's critique of innate principles and Toland's deism', *Journal of the History of Ideas*, XXXVII, no.3, 1976, 419–20; reprinted in Yolton (ed.), *Philosophy, Religion and Science in the Seventeenth and Eighteenth Centuries*, ch.X.

[130] J. Toland, *Christianity Not Mysterious*, 82–3.

[131] See J. Locke, *Works*, X, 260–8; 270–98..

[132] Ibid., 298.

[133] Leslie Stephen, *History of English Thought in the Eighteenth Century*, I, 72.

[134] William Warburton, *Works*, 1811, I, 162–4.

[135] In this connection William Whiston was especially in Collins's sights. See James E. Force, *William Whiston: Honest Newtonian*, Cambridge: CUP, 1985.

[136] J. Locke, *Mr. Locke's Second Reply to the Bishop of Worcester*, in *Works*, IV, 482. For Stillingfleet's letters to Locke see his *Works*, ed. Richard Bentley, 6 vols., 1709.

[137] Ibid., 228. In his generally helpful study, S. G. Hefelbower may be literally correct is asserting that 'Not even Locke's severest critics classed him among the Deists', but Stillingfleet was not the only one to wonder exactly how to class him, and in view of the episcopal motivation supplied by Toland's work deism could not have been far from the bishop's mind. See S. G. Hefelbower, *The Relation of John Locke to English Deism*, 177. See further on the Stillingfleet–Locke correspondence, Robert Todd Carroll, *The Common-Sense Philosophy of Bishop Edward Stillingfleet, 1635–1699*, The Hague: Martinus Nijhoff, 1975, 90–101.

[138] For Hickes (1642–1715) see DNB.

[139] Popple to Locke, 16 January 1696; see de Beer (ed.), *The Correspondence of John Locke*, V, 1979, 519.

[140] *The Life and Character of Mr. John Locke ... Written in French, by Mr. Le Clerc. And done into English by T. F. P. Gent.*, 1706, 20–2.

[141] Anon., *The Infidel Convicted*, 1731, 40.

[142] Ibid., 56.

[143] T. Burnet, *The Judgment of Dr. Thomas Burnet, Late Master of the Charter-House, concerning the Doctrine of the Trinity*, 1732, iii.

[144] J. Conybeare, *A Defence of Revealed Religion* (1732), Dublin, 4th edn, 1788, 167, 169.

[145] J. Leland, *A View of the Principal Deistical Writers*, 1754, 37. Cf. David A. Pailin, 'Herbert of Cherbury and the deists', *The Expository Times*, XCIV, 1983, 196–200.

[146] Ibid., 379–81.

[147] J. Locke, *A Paraphrase and Notes on the Epistles of St. Paul*, ed. A. W. Wainwright, Oxford: Clarendon Press, 1987, I, 38.

[148] Idem, *A Letter to the Right Reverend Edward, Lord Bishop of Worcester*, in *Works* , IV, 4.

[149] Idem, *Essay*, II.vii.5; cf. ibid., I.i.6:

> Our Business here is not to know all things, but those which concern our Conduct. If we can find out those Measures, whereby a rational Creature put in that State, which Man is in, in this World, may, and ought to govern his Opinions, and Actions depending thereon, we need not be troubled, that some other things escape our Knowledge.

[150] Idem, *Mr. Locke's Second Reply to the Bishop of Worcester*, in *Works*, IV, 343.

[151] J. Edwards, *A Brief Vindication of the Fundamental Articles of the Christian Faith*, 1697, 39, 40, 55.

[152] J. T. Moore, 'Locke's analysis of language and the assent to Scripture', *Journal of the History of Ideas*, XXXVII, no.4, 1976, 712. Mr Moore (inaccurately) cites Locke's *Essay*, III.x.3.

[153] Quoted by F. R. Fox Bourne, *The Life of John Locke*, London: Henry S. King, 1876, 2 vols., II, 421. For a full discussion of Locke's anti-trinitarian reading in the 1690s, and his responses to it, see John Marshall, *John Locke: Resistance, Religion and Responsibility*, Cambridge: CUP, 1994, 389–398.

[154] J. C. Biddle (ed.), 'John Locke's "Essay on Infallibility": introduction, text and translation', *Journal of Church and State*, XIX, 1977, 320–3.

[155] J. Locke to W. Molyneaux, 22 February 1796/7, in *Works*, IX, 396. According to M. Montuori, Molyneaux advised Locke not to tussle with Stillingfleet, and the fact that Locke did not heed this advice shows how much he 'sincerely loathed the accusation of Socinianism'. See Mario Montuori, *John Locke on Toleration and the Unity of God*, Amsterdam: J. C. Gieben, 1983, 179. In fact, however, Molyneaux gave no such advice. While recognizing that Stillingfleet was 'a man of great name', he did not think his *Vindication* well argued. Nevertheless he thought that Locke *should* take notice of it, not in a specific response, but on some 'accidental occasion ... either in the next edition of your Essay, or some other discourse you may publish hereafter'. See J. Locke, *Works*, IX, 394.

[156] For Caffyn (1628–1714) see DNB; A.G. [Alexander Gordon], 'Matthew Caffyn and General Baptist latitude,' *The Christian Life*

and Unitarian Herald, 5 November 1892, 531–2.

157 Cf. Mario Montuori, *John Locke on Toleration and the Unity of God*, 180–1, 189, 197–8, 205; John Marshall, *John Locke*, 419n. It is thus arguable that John Orr, *English Deism*, 91, was unduly disturbed by Locke's emphasis upon the unity of God: 'In his Latin letters to Limborch, Locke put a stress on the doctrine of the unity of God that is hardly consistent with the doctrine of the Trinity.' For a recent study of the Locke–Limborch relationship see J. van den Berg, 'Creatieve vriendschap', in H. J. Adriaanse (ed.), *Voorbeeldige Vriesdschap. Vrienden en vriendinnen in theologie en cultur*, Groningen: Styx Publications, 1993.

158 See John Marshall's discussion in his *John Locke*, 341, 424–7, though beware that on p.424 Colossians is inadvertently substituted for Corinthians, and the order of the books is changed, in the title of Locke's *Paraphrase.*

159 J. Locke, *A Paraphrase*, II, 487, on Romans 1:3–4.

160 Ibid., 616 n. 10(t) 1.

161 A. Wainwright, ibid., I, 38.

162 For a careful discussion of this document, MS Locke e17, 175–223, see J. Marshall, *John Locke*, 420–4. Cf. idem, 'John Locke's religious, educational, and moral thought', *The Historical Journal*, XXXIII, no.4, 1990, 998.

163 J. Locke, *A Discourse of Miracles*, in *Works*, IX, 256.

164 Ibid., 257.

165 Ibid., 261.

166 Ibid., 264. For a recent discussion of Locke on miracles see J. J. Macintosh, 'Locke and Boyle on miracles and God's existence', in Michael Hunter (ed.), *Robert Boyle Reconsidered*, Cambridge: CUP, 1994, ch.XII.

167 Idem, *The Reasonableness of Christianity*, in *Works*, VII, 42; cf. ibid., 18.

168 Ibid., 41.

169 Ibid., 52.

170 Ibid., 93.

171 Locke to Clarke; see de Beer (ed.), *The Correspondence of John Locke*, II, 782.

172 J. Marshall, *John Locke*, 344.

173 J. Locke, *The Reasonableness of Christianity*, in *Works*, VII, 112.

174 J. Marshall, *John Locke*, xx.

175 A. Gordon, *Heads of English Unitarian History*, London: Philip Green, 1895, 31.

176 J. Locke, *A Letter to The Right Reverend Edward, Lord Bishop of Worcester*, in *Works*, IV, 66–8.

177 E. Stillingfleet, *A Discourse in Vindication of the Doctrine of the Trinity*, 1696, 235–6.

178 Idem, *The Bishop of Worcester's Answer to Mr. Locke's Second Letter*, 1698, 146.

179 J. Locke, *A Letter to the Right Reverend Edward, Lord Bishop of Worcester*, in *Works*, IV, 7.

180 E. Stillingfleet, *The Bishop of Worcester's Answer to Mr. Locke's Second Letter*, 4.

181 See, for example, J. Locke, *A Second Vindication of the Reasonableness of Christianity*, in *Works*, VII, 278.

182 Gerard Reedy, 'Socinians, John Toland, and the Anglican rationalists', *The Harvard Theological Review*, LXX, 1977, 298–9.

183 *Memoirs of the Life and Writings of Mr. William Whiston*, written by himself, London, 1749, 294.

184 J. Edwards, *Some Thoughts concerning the several causes and Occasion of Atheism*, 1695, 113.

185 Ibid., 75.

186 J. Locke, *A Vindication*, in *Works*, VII, 163, quoting J. Edwards, *Some Thoughts*, 112.

187 Idem, ibid., 163, referring to his *Reasonableness*, in *Works*, VII, 9.

188 Ibid., 164.

189 Ibid., 165.

190 J. Edwards, *Socinianism Unmask'd*, 1696, 31.

191 Ibid., 55.

192 Ibid., 57.

193 Ibid., 82.

194 J. Locke, *A Vindication*, in *Works* , VII, 166. It would not be difficult to fault Edwards's argumentation at numerous points. For example, he accuses Locke of 'winding in' the archbishop of Canterbury as if he understood trinitarian language in a Socinian sense. In fact Locke winds the archbishop in to show that since the latter is not a Socinian, and yet agrees with Locke, Locke cannot be a Socinian either. Cf. J. Edwards, *Socinianism Unmask'd*, 90–1; J. Locke, *A Vindication*, in *Works*, VII, 172.

195 [S. Nye], *The Exceptions of Mr. Edwards*, 1695, 12.

196 Ibid., 23.

197 Ibid., 31.

198 T. Burnet, *Animadversions on a late Book Entituled the Reasonableness of Christianity as delivered in the Scriptures*, Oxford, 1697, 59.

199 [J. Milner], *An Account of Mr. Locke's Religion*, 1700, 69–70.

200 Ibid., 180.

201 Ibid., 182, citing J. Locke, *A Second Vindication*, in *Works*, VII, 370–1.

[202] Ibid., 182–5.

[203] W. Carroll, *A Letter to the Reverend Dr. Benjamin Prat,* 1707, 16.

[204] W. Whiston, *Reflections on an Anonymous Pamphlet, Entituled, a Discourse of Free Thinking,* 1713, 32.

[205] Ibid., 55.

[206] Ibid. For the letter to Collins see J. Locke, *Works,* X, 298.

[207] Ibid.

[208] Letter of Locke to Molyneaux, 22 February 1696–7; in *Works,* IX, 397.

[209] W. Whiston, *Memoirs of the Life and Writings of Mr. William Whiston,* 1749, I, clxxiii. Whiston was removed from his Cambridge chair for Arianism (though he called himself a Eusebian). In view of the influence of his *The Scripture Doctrine of the Trinity* (1712) upon Anglicans and Dissenters alike, it is surprising that Samuel Clarke is omitted from Whiston's list of exemplars.

[210] Winch Holdsworth, *A Sermon Preached before the University of Oxford at St. Mary's on Easter Monday 1719, in Which the Cavils, False Reasonings, and False Interpretations of Scripture of Mr. Lock and Others, against the Resurrection of the Same Body Are Examin'd and Answered,* Oxford, 1720. For Holdsworth (matric. 1695; d. 1761) see *Alumni Oxonienses 1500–1714,* I, 729.

[211] C. Cockburn, *A Letter to Dr. Holdsworth,* in *The Works of Mrs. Catherine Cockburn, Theological, Moral, Dramatic, and Poetical,* 2 vols., 1751, 116.

[212] Ibid., 121.

[213] W. Holdsworth, *A Defence of the Doctrine of the Resurrection of the Same Body,* 1727, Preface, v.

[214] Ibid., 10–12.

[215] I. Watts, *Works,* Leeds, 1800, VII, 261–2.

[216] Ibid.

[217] Idem, *Works,* VI, 854.

[218] A. Taylor, *The Scripture Doctrine of the Trinity Vindicated,* 1728, 115.

[219] See C. Fleming, *A Letter to a Friend, Containing select Remarks upon the Rev. Dr. Isaac Watts's Treatise, entitled, The Glory of Christ, as God-Man,* 1746. See further on the theological controversies surrounding Watts, Arthur Paul Davis, *Isaac Watts,* London: Independent Press, 1943, ch.V.

[220] A. Taylor, *An Introduction to Logick, with a few Lectures, on Perception, the first part of that Science,* 1739, 44, Dr Williams's Library, London, MS 69.24.

[221] Cf. George Horne's 'put-down' of Priestley, a man 'who is defying all the world, and cannot construe a common piece of Greek or Latin'. See the *Life,* by William Jones, in Horne's *Works,* 6 vols.,

London: J. Johnson et al., 1809, I, 148.

[222] J. Conder, *A Summary of Christian Theology,* 1780–1, Part II; cited by H. McLachlan, *English Education Under the Test Acts,* Manchester: Manchester University Press, 1931, 278. For Conder (1714–81) see DNB. The notes of Conder's lectures were taken by Richard Fry (1759–1842), who subsequently became Unitarian minister at Kidderminster. Conder's text book was Johannes à Marck, *Christianae theologiae medulla didactico-elenctica,* which was used at a number of Dissenting academies, and also by John Simson at Glasgow. See J. van den Berg and G. F. Nuttall, *Philip Doddridge (1702–51) and the Netherlands,* Leiden: E. J. Brill/Leiden University Press, 1987, 6.

[223] J. Priestley, *Works* , ed. J. T. Rutt, 1818 etc., XVIII, 553n.

[224] Cameron Thompson, 'John Locke and New England transcendentalism', *The New England Quarterly,* XXXV, no.4, December 1962, 457.

[225] Carl L. Becker, *The Heavenly City of the Eighteenth-Century Philosophers,* New Haven: Yale University Press, 1932, 64–5. Becker quotes Locke's *Essay,* I.ii.1.

[226] See W. M. Spellman, *John Locke and the Problem of Depravity,* Oxford: Clarendon Press, 1988.

[227] Cf. ibid., 57. However, Spellman surely goes too far in saying that 'The nub of Reformation theology ... centred on its understanding of man's depraved nature' (p.81). It might more truly be said that its characteristic note concerned God's justifying grace. See further my review of Spellman's book in *Enlightenment and Dissent,* IX, 1990, 134–7.

[228] J. Marshall, *John Locke,* 134. Marshall regrets Spellman's oversight of Nicole's work in his 'John Locke's religious, educational, and moral thought', 995. Marshall reminds us (p.64) that in the *Two Tracts upon Government* Locke had regarded the majority of human beings as 'beasts'; in the 'Essay on Infallibility' they are 'sheep'; while in the 'Essay on Toleration' they all have minds and are potentially rational.

[229] J. Locke, *Second Treatise of Government,* in *Works,* V, 433.

[230] Idem, *Of Education,* in *Works,* IX, 93. For a fuller discussion of Locke on sin see Ian Harris, 'The politics of Christianity', in G. A. J. Rogers (ed.), *Locke's Philosophy: Content and Context,* Oxford: Clarendon Press, 1994, ch.VII.

[231] Idem, *A Paraphrase,* I, 153.

[232] For Allestree (1619–81) see DNB; W. M. Spellman, *John Locke and the Problem of Depravity,* 68–9, 122.

[233] J. Locke, *A Paraphrase,* II, 523.

234 Idem, *The Reasonableness of Christianity,* in *Works,* VII, 8.

235 Ibid., 4.

236 In the former connection Ronald Hamowy's criticism of Garry Wills is of interest. See his 'Jefferson and the Scottish Enlightenment: a critique of Garry Wills's *Inventing America: Jefferson's Declaration of Independence*', *The William and Mary Quarterly,* 3rd series, XXXVI, no.4, October 1979, 503–23.

237 J. Locke, *The Reasonableness of Christianity,* in *Works,* VII, 5.

238 Idem, *Essay* , I.i.5.

239 Ibid., II.xxi.35. See further, W. M. Spellman, 'The Christian estimate of man in Locke's *Essay*', *The Journal of Religion,* LXVII, no.4, October 1987, 474–92.

240 See, for example, the paraphrase of Romans 7:14, 17, where Paul says that his carnality forces him 'against my will to doe the drudgery of sin'. A. W. Wainwright (*Paraphrase* I, 57, citing Locke's *Essay,* II.xxi.71 and II [incorrectly cited as III].xxi.33–5) observes that this position is to be distinguished from Locke's view in the *Essay,* that unless prevented by disability people always do what they have willed, and may perform actions to their own disadvantage. But this seems to overlook Locke's admission that they do not or cannot always exercise their wills appropriately. I therefore agree with W. M. Spellman, *John Locke and the Problem of Depravity,* 3, against John Passmore, *The Perfectibility of Man,* London: Duckworth, 1970, and others noted by Spellman, who represent Locke as believing that by education and social action alone the cause of the individual's moral perfection can be advanced.

241 J. Locke, *A Paraphrase* , II, 525, note to Romans 5:15.

242 H. R. Fox Bourne, *The Life of John Locke,* London: Henry S. King, 2 vols., 1876, II, 559.

243 J. Locke, *The Reasonableness of Christianity,* in *Works,* VII, 112.

244 Idem, *A Vindication of The Reasonableness,* ibid., 175.

245 J. Edwards, *Socinianism Unmask'd,* 1696, 94 – a charge repeated in the following year in Edwards's *The Socinian Creed,* to which Locke here specifically replies.

246 J. Locke, *A Second Vindication of The Reasonableness of Christianity,* in *Works,* VII, 375. Locke here specifically replies to Edwards's *The Socinian Creed,* 1697.

247 Ibid., 418.

248 Idem, *The Reasonableness of Christianity,* 9.

249 Idem, *A Paraphrase,* II, 628–9. It would seem that Michael Jinkins's account is incomplete when he asserts that 'Locke understood Christian faith as a matter of believing certain propositions *about* Jesus.' In this, he continues, Locke resembled the federal Calvinists,

for whom see Sell, *The Great Debate: Calvinism, Arminianism and Salvation,* Worthing: H. E. Walter, 1982, and Grand Rapids: Baker Book House, 1983. ch.II, and 111–13. See M. Jinkins, 'Elements of federal theology in the thought of John Locke', *The Evangelical Quarterly,* LXVI, no.2, 1994, 137. By a slip of the pen Jinkins enlists the Anglican Samuel Bold in the Nonconformist brigade (p.225).

250 Maurice Cranston, *John Locke,* vii.

251 J. Marshall, *John Locke,* 431.

252 J. Locke, *A Paraphrase,* I, 287.

253 A. W. Wainwright, Introduction to *A Paraphrase,* I, 37.

254 [Richard West], *Animadversions On a late Book entituled the Reasonableness of Christianity As delivered in the Scriptures,* Oxford, 1697, 2–3.

255 C. Cockburn, *A Vindication of Mr. Locke's Christian Principles, from the injurious Imputations of Dr. Holdsworth,* 1751, 203.

256 Ibid., 204.

257 Ibid., 206.

258 See D. Whitby, *A Paraphrase and Commentary on the New Testament,* London: W. Boyer, 1703, on Romans 5:12.

259 [J. Milner], *An Account of Mr. Lock's Religion,* 1700, 186. James Moore does not make this qualification when discussing Milner's likening of Locke to the Socinians. See his 'Theological politics: a study of the reception of Locke's *Two Treatises of Government* in England and Scotland in the early eighteenth century', in Martyn P. Thompson (ed.), *John Locke und/and Immanuel Kant,* Berlin: Duncker & Humblot, 1991, 65.

260 J. Leland, *An Answer To a Late Book Intituled, Christianity as Old as the Creation,* 1733, 186–7.

261 J. Taylor, *The Scripture-Doctrine of Original Sin,* 1740, 244.

262 Idem, *A Scheme of Scripture Divinity,* 1762, 58, 60.

263 See further, Sell, *Dissenting Thought and the Life of the Churches,* ch.VII, especially 245–9.

264 T. Amory, Preface to *Sermons* ... by the late Reverend Samuel Chandler, 1768, I, iv–v.

265 A Rational Christian [Francis Webb], *The Morality of the New Testament,* 1765, 298–9.

266 Ibid., 302–3.

267 Ibid., 306.

268 Ibid., 309.

269 Ibid., 312.

270 W. C. Fowler, *Essays: Historical, Literary, Educational,* Hartford: The Case, Lockwood & Brainard Co., 1876, 62. For Taylor (1786–1858) see DAB; Robert C. Whittemore, *The Transformation*

of New England Theology, Bern: Peter Lang, 1987, 241–88;

271 N. W. Taylor, *Concio ad Clerum,* New Haven: Hezekiah Howe, 1828, 8. Cf. Earl A. Pope, *New England Calvinism and the Disruption of the Presbyterian Church,* New York: Garland Publishing, 1987, 72–4.

272 We recall the inspiration which considerations of this kind gave variously to the development of Kant's postulates and to John Stuart Mill's objection to the teleological argument for the existence of God.

273 J. Locke, *The Reasonableness of Christianity,* in *Works,* VII, 148–50.

274 Idem, *Essay* , I.iii.6.

275 Ibid., IV.iii.6.

276 See, for example, ibid., II.xxi.60, 70.

277 MS Locke, f7, 107.

278 Letter of Molyneaux to Locke of 2 March 1692–3, in *Works,* IX, 310. Locke says that he had acceded to this request in a letter to Molyneaux of 23 August 1693; ibid., 326.

279 See Henry E. Allison, 'Locke's theory of personal identity: a re-examination', *Journal of the History of Ideas,* XXVII, no.1, 1966, 41–3. For a concise, lucid account of 'Locke's philosophy of mind' see Jonathan Bennett in Chappell (ed.), *The Cambridge Companion to Locke,* ch.IV.

280 See A. G. N. Flew, 'Locke and the problem of personal identity', reprinted from *Philosophy* (1951) in C. B. Martin and D. M. Armstrong (eds.), *Locke and Berkeley,* London: Macmillan, n.d., 169–70.

281 J. Locke, *Essay,* II.xxvii.6.

282 Ibid., II.xxvii.9.

283 Ibid., II.xxvii.11.

284 Ibid., II.xxvii.20, 22.

285 Ibid., II.xxvii.19. As Clement Webb long ago reminded us, 'self-consciousness' as used by Locke and others played 'a considerable part in the Trinitarian controversy which agitated the learned [in England] at the end of the seventeenth and the beginning of the eighteenth century'. He cites the dean of St Paul's, William Sherlock, *A Vindication of the Doctrine of the Holy and Ever Blessed Trinity,* 1690; and Robert South, *Animadversions upon Dr. Sherlock's Book,* 1693. See C. C. J. Webb, *God and Personality,* London: Allen & Unwin, 1918, 57–8 and n. South detected tritheism in Sherlock's position.

286 J. Locke, *Essay* , II.xxvii.23.

287 Ibid., II.xxvii.26.

288 Ibid., II.xxvii.13.

289 G. Berkeley, *A Treatise concerning the Principles of Human Knowledge,*

in *Works*, eds. T. E. Jessop and A. A. Luce, London: Nelson, 1949, II, 52–3.

290 R. C. Tennant, 'The Anglican response to Locke's theory of personal identity', 198.

291 See Christopher Fox, 'Locke and the Scriblerians: the discussion of identity in early eighteenth-century England', *Eighteenth-Century Studies,* XVII, Fall 1982, 1–25.

292 See R. Bentley, *Observations upon a Sermon Intituled, A Confutation of Atheism from the Faculties of the Soul, alias, Matter and Motion cannot think: Preached April 4, 1692. By way of Refutation.* Cf. R. J. White, *Dr. Bentley: A Study in Academic Scarlet,* London: Eyre & Spottiswoode, 1965, ch.I.

293 [T. Burnet], *Remarks upon an Essay concerning Humane Understanding,* 1697, 10–12.

294 Idem, *Second Remarks upon an Essay concerning Humane Understanding,* 1697.

295 E. Stillingfleet, *Discourse in Vindication of the Doctrine of the Trinity,* 1696, 260.

296 Ibid., 261.

297 Idem, *The Bishop of Worcester's Answer to Mr. Locke's Letter,* 1697, 107.

298 J. Locke, *Mr. Locke's Second Reply to the Bishop of Worcester,* in *Works,* IV, 474–5. This only served to intensify the bishop's critique of Locke's epistemological principles, as we saw in chs.II and III above.

299 E. Stillingfleet, *The Bishop of Worcester's Answer to Mr. Locke's Second Letter,* 1698, 44.

300 Ibid., 59

301 Ibid., 175.

302 See H. Lee, *Anti-Scepticism: Or, Notes upon each Chapter of Mr. Lock's Essay concerning Humane Understanding,* 1702, 128.

303 J. Locke, *Essay* , II.xxvii.25.

304 J. Norris, *An Account of Reason and Faith, in Relation to the Mysteries of Christianity,* 1697, ch.I.

305 [J. Milner], *An Account of Mr. Lock's Religion,* 1700, 102, 108–9.

306 H. Felton, *The Resurrection of the same Numerical Body,* 1725, 7.

307 I. Watts, *Works* , VI, 599–600, quoting Locke's *Essay,* II.xxvii.9.

308 Ibid., 600.

309 Ibid., 601.

310 Ibid.

311 Ibid., 601–2.

312 Ibid., 603.

313 Ibid. Cf. Watts's argument against Locke's view that the soul does not always think. Ibid., 528, 532–4.

[314] P. Doddridge, *Works*, IV, 323.

[315] J. Butler, *Dissertation* I, para. 3. I use F. A. Malleson's edition of Butler's *The Analogy of Religion,* to which are appended *Two Dissertations,* London: Ward, Lock, n.d.

[316] Ibid., para. 5.

[317] Ibid., para. 6.

[318] A. Duncan-Jones, *Butler's Moral Philosophy,* Harmondsworth: Penguin, 1952, 38. See further, Anders Jeffner, 'Our knowledge of ourselves', in Christopher Cunliffe (ed.), *Joseph Butler's Moral and Religious Thought: Tercentenary Essays,* Oxford: Clarendon Press, 1992, ch.IX; Terence Penelhum, *Butler,* London: Routledge, 1985, ch.V, especially 132–3, where Penelhum finds that some modern philosophers have misread Butler; Jonathan Bennett, 'Locke's philosophy of mind', 109.

[319] T. Reid, *Essays on the Intellectual Powers of Man,* in his *Works,* ed. W. Hamilton, Edinburgh: MacLachlan and Stewart, 6th edn, 1863, I, 352.

[320] Ibid.

[321] V. Perronet, *A Vindication of Mr. Locke, from the Charge of giving Encouragement to Scepticism and Infidelity,* 1736, Preface.

[322] Ibid., 54, referring to P. Browne, *The Procedure, Extent and Limits of Human Understanding,* 1728, 433.

[323] Idem, *A Second Vindication of Mr. Locke,* 1738, 24.

[324] Ibid., 123.

[325] Ibid., 124.

[326] Ibid., 128–32.

[327] T. Jackson (ed.), *The Works of the Rev. John Wesley,* London: John Mason, 1829–31, XIII, 419–20.

[328] W. Law, *An Appeal to all that Doubt, or Disbelieve in the Truth of the Gospel,* 1742, 2–3, 12.

[329] Idem, *An Humble, Earnest, and Affectionate Address to the Clergy* (1761), London: G. Robinson, 1774, 39.

[330] Idem, *An Appeal to all that Doubt,* 9–10.

[331] E. Law, *A Defence of Mr. Locke's Opinion concerning Personal Identity,* Cambridge, 1769, 39.

[332] J. Hoopes, 'Calvinism and consciousness from Edwards to Beecher', in Nathan O. Hatch and Harry S. Stout (eds.), *Jonathan Edwards and the American Experience,* New York: OUP, 1988, 216.

[333] Ibid., 216–19.

[334] T. Ludlam, *Logical Tracts,* 1790, 38.

[335] J. Locke, *Essay,* IV.iii.29 and IV.xviii.7.

[336] Idem, *Mr. Locke's Second Reply to the Bishop of Worcester,* in *Works,* IV, 303.

[337] Ibid.

[338] Idem, *A Paraphrase*, II, 684.

[339] Ibid., I, 254–5. Cf. the paraphrase of verse 40 in the same chapter, ibid., 252. While John Marshall is so far correct in saying that rejection of the resurrection of the same body is a position endorsed by some Socinians, Locke's biblical glosses are important and the inference should not necessarily be drawn that Locke intends to endorse Socinianism. See J. Marshall 'John Locke's religious, educational, and moral thought', 997. In this article Marshall may be taken as implying that all Socinians opposed the doctrine of the resurrection of the same body, but in his book he states only that 'some' did this. See his *John Locke*, 399. Marshall further notes that Locke clearly denied the resurrection of the same body in the late 1690s, at a time when he was under the influence of Socinian writings. See J. Marshall, *John Locke*, 154 (though on p.400 he suggests that Locke may have reached this view as early as 1694–5, when he wrote *The Reasonableness of Christianity*). But Locke's *Paraphrase* represents his latest thoughts on the matter, and the influence upon him of New Testament, rather than Socinian, teaching is clear.

[340] Idem, *Mr. Locke's Second Reply to the Bishop of Worcester*, in *Works*, IV, 310–11.

[341] Idem, *Essays on the Law of Nature*, ed. W. von Leyden, Oxford: Clarendon Press, 1954, 173.

[342] Idem, *A Letter concerning Toleration*, in *Works*, VI, 23, 28. See also, Locke's *Essay*, II.xxi.60 and IV.xx.3.

[343] Idem, *A Letter concerning Toleration*, in *Works*, VI, 41.

[344] [J. Milner], *An Account of Mr. Lock's Religion*, 1700, 187.

[345] S. Bold, *Some Considerations on the Principal Objections* ... against Mr. Lock's Essay of Humane Understanding, 1699, 19.

[346] [C. Cockburn], *A Defence of the Essay of Human Understanding*, 1702, 25–6, 40.

[347] A. Campbell, *The Necessity of Revelation*, 1739, 174. For Campbell (1691–1756) see DNB.

[348] J. Locke, *Works*, X, 310

[349] Idem, Locke to Whitby on 17 January 1699; see de Beer (ed.), *The Correspondence of John Locke*, VI, 1981, 548.

[350] [S. Bold], *A Discourse concerning the Resurrection of the Same Body*, 1705, 89.

[351] Ibid., 90–3.

[352] W. Lupton, *The Resurrection of the Same Body*, (1711), 14.

[353] Ibid., 17–21.

[354] W. Holdsworth, *A Sermon preached before the University of Oxford at St. Mary's on Easter-Monday, 1719*, 1720.

355 [C. Cockburn], *A Letter to Dr. Holdsworth,* 1726, reprinted in her *Works,* 2 vols., 1751, I, 127.

356 Ibid., 149.

357 Ibid., 342; cf. 271.

358 H. Felton, *The Resurrection of the same Numerical Body, and its Reunion to the same Soul,* 2nd edn, 1725, 6.

359 Ibid., 12.

360 Ibid., 22.

361 R. D'Oyly, *Four Dissertations ... IV.* Of the Resurrection of the same Body, 1728, 425. D'Oyly (fl. 1710–30) was a religious writer.

362 Ibid., 427.

363 Ibid., 428.

364 Ibid., 429–32.

365 Ibid., 436.

366 Ibid., 461.

367 Ibid., 466–9.

368 Ibid., 470–3.

369 I. Watts, *Works*, VI, 555.

370 Ibid., 557.

371 Ibid., 559.

372 Ibid.

373 Ibid., 605.

374 See J. Butler, *Dissertation I,* para. 3.

375 See John Yolton's full-length study, *Thinking Matter: Materialism in Eighteenth Century Britain,* Oxford: Blackwell, 1984.

376 J. Locke, *Essay*, IV.iii.6.

377 Ibid.

378 Ibid.

379 Ibid. For a modern discussion of the subject see M. R. Ayers, 'Mechanism, superaddition, and the proof of God's existence in Locke's *Essay*', *Philosophical Review,* XC, no.2, 1981, 210–51.

380 Kenneth MacLean, *John Locke and English Literature of the Eighteenth Century* (1936), New Haven: Yale University Press, 1984, 536

381 Quoted in J. Locke, *A Letter to the Right Reverend Edward, Lord Bishop of Worcester,* in *Works*, IV, 32.

382 Ibid., 33.

383 Idem, *Mr. Locke's Second Reply to the Bishop of Worcester,* ibid., 462–7.

384 E. Stillingfleet, *The Bishop of Worcester's Answer to Mr. Locke's Letter,* 1697, 79.

385 Charles W. Eliot (ed.), *French and English Philosophers,* New York: P. F. Collier, n.d., 107.

386 Since it would be tedious to reiterate largely identical points adverse

to Locke I simply list the following examples of those in general sympathy with Stillingfleet: F.B., *A Free, but Modest Censure,* 1698, 5; Henry Lee, *Anti-Scepticism,* 1702, Preface, 246; John Broughton, *Psychologia; or, An Account of the Nature of the Rational Soul,* London: W.B. for T. Bennet et al., 1703, 26–7, 58–9; Mary Astell (of Newcastle), *The Christian Religion as Profess'd by a Daughter of the Church of England,* 1705, 253–61; [John Witty], *The First Principles of Modern Deism Confuted,* 1707 (Locke is not mentioned by name); Benjamin Hampton (of the Middle Temple), *The Existence of the Human Soul after Death,* 1711, 34–6 and 6: 'Whereas Mr. Locke was pleased to say, that we do not know but that it is in the Power of God to give Understanding to Matter, he might as properly have said, that we do not know but that it was in God's Power to have made the Moon of a Green Cheesse'; Humphrey Ditton, *A Discourse concerning the Resurrection of Jesus Christ,* 1712, appendix (no reference to Locke by name); John Edwards, *Some New Discoveries of the Uncertainty, Deficiency and Corruptions of Humane Knowledge,* 1714, 7; Samuel Clarke, *A Collection of Papers Which Passed between the Late Learned Mr. Leibnitz, and Dr. Clarke,* 1717, wherein Clarke thinks Locke may 'justly be suspected' of doubting the soul's immateriality, thereby giving comfort to materialists, 10–11; I. Watts, *Works,* VI, 12n., 507–8; Jonathan Dickinson, *The Reasonableness of Christianity in Four Sermons,* Boston, 1712, 15 where he refers to Locke's *Essay,* and to Clarke's letters to Dodwell; [Andrew Baxter], *An Enquiry into the Nature of the Human Soul; wherein the Immateriality of the Soul is evinced from the Principles of Reason and Philosophy,* 1733; John Ellis, *The Knowledge of Divine Things from Revelation, not from Reason or Nature* (1743), 1837 edn, 29; P. Doddridge, *A Course of Lectures on the Principal Subjects in Pneumatology, Ethics, and Divinity,* 1763, 204–6. For Broughton (1652?–1720) see *Alumni Cantabrigienses.*

387 [T. Burnet], *Remarks upon an Essay concerning Humane Understanding,* 1697, 7.

388 Ibid., 13–14.

389 J. Locke, *Works,* IV, 186–9.

390 [T. Burnet], *Third Remarks upon an Essay concerning Humane Understanding,* 1699, 22–3. For Locke's marginalia see his copy of this work in Yale University Library. See further, S. A. Grave, *Locke and Burnet,* Perth: Philosophy Society of W. A. and Department of Philosophy, University of Western Australia, 1981, ch.III.

391 Anon., *A Letter to a Clergy-Man in the Country Concerning the Votes of the Bishops In the last Session of Parliament, Upon the Bill against Occasional Conformity,* 1704, 16.

392 See W. Carroll, *A Dissertation Upon the Tenth Chapter of the Fourth*

Book of Mr. Locke's Essay, concerning Humane Understanding, 1706, 250–1.

393 R. Jenkin, *The Reasonableness and Certainty of the Christian Religion,* (1696–7), 5th edn, 1721, xxviii. For Jenkin (1656–1727) see DNB.

394 S. Bold, *Some Considerations on the Principal Objections* ... against Mr. Lock's 'Essay of Humane Understanding', 1699, 29.

395 C. Cockburn, *A Defence of the Essay of Human Understanding,* 1702, 47.

396 V. Perronet, *A Vindication of Mr. Locke,* 1736, 7; cf. idem, *A Second Vindication of Mr. Locke,* 1738, 106–10.

397 [M. Flemyng], *A New Critical Examination of an Important Passage in Mr. Locke's Essay on Human Understanding,* 1751, 11–12. For Flemyng (d. 1764) see DNB.

398 Ibid., 30. Though not directly within my purview in this study, I should perhaps note that by the middle of the eighteenth century Locke's speculation concerning thinking matter was receiving increasing attention in continental Europe. See, for example, Giacinto Sigismondo Gerdil, *L'immatérialité de l'âme démontrée contre M. Locke,* Turin, 1747; [Antoine Martin Roche], *Traité de la nature de l'âme et de l'origine de ses connoissances. Contre le système de M. Locke & de ses partisans,* 2 vols., Paris, 1759; and the works noted in ch.I, n.13 above.

399 J. Priestley, *Works,* III, 247. See further Yolton, *Thinking Matter,* ch.VI. Henry F. May observes that 'This curious idea of an immortal but material soul was to have an important career in America: Thomas Jefferson would pick it up from Joseph Priestley.' See his *The Enlightenment in America,* New York: OUP, 1976, 9.

400 J. Locke, *Essay,* II.xxiii.32. Cf. IV.iii.6, where it is precisely for this reason that Locke cannot deny that the omnipotent God may superadd the power of thought to matter should he choose to do so.

401 Ibid., IV.xvii.23–4; IV.xviii.7.

402 See J. Locke, *Paraphrase* I; 238; on Corinthians 13:12; *Essay,* IV.xvii.14.

403 The section on 'The Future' of Arthur W. Wainwright's Introduction to Locke's *Paraphrase* (pp.51–6) is particularly helpful.

404 Cf. J. Locke, *Paraphrase* I, 238, on I Corinthians 15:42, n. m., I; p.253.

405 Idem, *The Reasonableness of Christianity,* in *Works,* VII, 10. Cf. A. W. Wainwright's observation, 'In the *Paraphrase* Locke does not mention the possibility of eternal punishment for the wicked,' Introduction to the *Paraphrase,* 52.

406 Idem, *The Reasonableness of the Christian Religion,* 115; cf. 122.

407 Idem, *Essay,* II.xxi.60.

[408] C. Cockburn, *A Vindication of Mr. Locke's Christian Principles, from the injurious Imputations of Dr. Holdsworth,* in her *Works,* I, 1751, 207.

[409] For which see A. W. Wainwright (ed.), *Paraphrase,* Appendix VI, 679–84. It would therefore seem that H. McLachlan and D. P. Walker are correct, as against W. M. Spellman, in concluding that Locke did not believe in eternal torment. See, respectively, *The Religious Opinions of Milton, Locke and Newton,* Manchester: Manchester University Press, 1941, 94; *The Decline of Hell: Seventeenth Century Discussions of Eternal Torment,* Chicago: Chicago University Press, 1964, 93; W. M. Spellman, *John Locke and the Problem of Depravity,* 109 n. 19.

[410] J. Locke, *Paraphrase,* Appendix VI, 683. As A. W. Wainwright points out (ibid., 53 n. 7), Locke invokes the support of Tillotson on annihilation, but the latter merely said that God has the power to limit the duration of torments in hell, but did not think that he actually did this. See Tillotson's *Works,* I, 321–9.

[411] Idem, *The Reasonableness of Christianity,* in *Works,* VII, 128; cf. *Paraphrase* of Romans 4:11–13, II, 514–5.

[412] Idem, *Paraphrase,* note to Ephesians 2:8, II, 630. By comparison, his attitude towards changelings is positively liberal and humane. See *Essay,* IV.iv.14.

[413] See, for example, his remarks in *The Reasonableness of Christianity,* in *Works,* VII, 108.

[414] For the evidence on these points see A. W. Wainwright, Introduction to the *Paraphrase,* 54–6.

[415] The report of the Church of England Doctrine Commission, *The Mystery of Salvation,* London: Church Publishing House, 1995, reached me as I was writing this section. The authors acknowledge a moral protest 'against a religion of fear, and a growing sense that the picture of a God who consigned millions to eternal torment was far removed from the revelation of God's love in Christ'. They proceed to declare (albeit in ambiguous language) that 'Hell is not eternal torment, but it is the final and irrevocable choosing of that which is opposed to God so completely and so absolutely that the only end is total non-being'. However, four lines later they, more cautiously, introduce a 'might' (though I think they mean 'may'): 'Annihilation might be a truer picture of damnation than any of the traditional images of the hell of eternal torment.' See p.199.

[416] W. Whiston, *The Eternity of Hell Torments Considered,* 1740, 2. For a contemporary critique of Whiston see Matthew Horbery, fellow of Magdalen College, Oxford, *An Enquiry into the Scripture-Doctrine Concerning the Duration of Future Punishment,* 1744. For Horbery (1707?–73) see DNB.

417 C. Chauncy, *The Mystery Hid from Ages and Generations, made manifest by the Gospel-Revelation: or, the Salvation of All Men*, London: Charles Dilley, 1784, 3. Chauncy acknowledges his indebtedness to, if not his entire agreement with, John Taylor of Norwich, ibid., xi–xiv.

418 [J. Milner], *An Account of Mr. Lock's Religion*, 1700, 103.

419 Ibid., 188.

420 J. Ball, *Some Remarks upon a New Way of Preaching Propos'd in an Ordination Sermon Preach'd at Taunton*, 1736, 22. For Ball (1665?–1745) see DNB; Sell, *Dissenting Thought and the Life of the Churches*, ch.VI.

421 C. Fleming, *A Survey of the Search after Souls*, 1758, 268.

422 N. Emmons, *Works*, 1842, IV, 539.

423 J. Horsey, *Evidences of Christianity*, 77–9, Dr Williams's Library, London, MS 69.1.

424 Locke to Grenville, 6 December 1678, in de Beer (ed.), *The Correspondence of John Locke*, I, 648–9.

Chapter 7: Conclusion

1 T. Dwight, *Theology, Explained and Defended*, 5 vols., 1819, V, 610; cf. idem, *Sermons*, 2 vols., 1828, Sermon XX, p. 362.

2 T. Belsham, *Discourses, Doctrinal and Practical*, 1826, 469.

3 W. Warburton, *Works*, 3rd edn, 1809, 283.

4 H. Aarsleff, 'Locke's influence', in Vere Chappell (ed.), *The Cambridge Companion to Locke*, Cambridge: CUP, 1994, 252.

5 J. Walsh, C. Haydon and S. Taylor (eds.), *The Church of England c. 1689–c.1833*, Cambridge: CUP, 1993, 43. Cf. Jeremy Gregory's remark later in the same volume, 71.

6 B. Mitchell, 'Butler as a Christian apologist', in Christopher Cunliffe (ed.), *Joseph Butler's Moral and Religious Thought*, Oxford: Clarendon Press, 1992, 108.

7 T. Belsham, *Discourses, Doctrinal and Practical*, 478.

8 See Henry F. May's characterization of the methodology of many eighteenth-century divines in his *The Enlightenment in America*, New York: OUP, 1976, 12.

9 Cf. A. S. Pringle-Pattison, *The Philosophical Radicals*, Edinburgh: Blackwood, 1907, 217–18; Cameron Thompson, 'John Locke and New England transcendentalism', *The New England Quarterly*, XXXV, no.4, December 1962, 435–57. See further, Alan P. F. Sell, *Theology in Turmoil: The Roots, Course and Significance of the Conservative–Liberal Debate in Modern Theology*, Grand Rapids: Baker Book House, 1986, 26–37.

10 C. C. J. Webb, *Studies in the History of Natural Theology,* Oxford: Clarendon Press, 1915, 358. He here echoes Mark Pattison, 'Tendencies of religious thought in England, 1688–1750', in *Essays and Reviews,* London: Parker, 1860, 297: 'The defect of the 18th century theology was not in having too much good sense, but in having nothing besides.'

11 Elizabeth Palmer Peabody, *Reminiscences of Reverend Wm. Ellery Channing,* Boston: Roberts Brothers, 1880, 140. For Channing (1780–1842), see DAB.

12 J. H. Newman, *Apologia pro vita sua,* Harmondsworth: Penguin, 1994, 37.

13 See J. W. Nevin, 'The sect system', (1849), reprinted in Charles Yrigoyen, Jr, and George H. Bricker (eds.), *Catholic and Reformed: Selected Theological Writings of John Williamson Nevin,* Pittsburgh: The Pickwick Press, 1978, 128–73. For Nevin (1803–86) see DAB.

14 See further Alan P. F. Sell, *Commemorations: Studies in Christian Thought and History,* Calgary: University of Calgary Press, and Cardiff: University of Wales Press, 1993, ch.IV.

15 For the circumstances here alluded to see ibid., ch.V.

16 J. Locke, *Works,* III, 249.

17 Alan P. F. Sell, *Philosophical Idealism and Christian Belief,* Cardiff: University of Wales Press and New York: St Martin's Press, 1995, 235.

18 H. R. Fox Bourne, *The Life of John Locke,* 2 vols., London: Henry S. King, 1876, II, 554. Within three weeks of completing my text *The Margins of Orthodoxy: Heterodox Writing and Cultural Response,* ed. Roger D. Lund, Cambridge: CUP, 1995, came into my hands for review. It contains a balanced and lucid essay by G. A. J. Rogers on epistemological–theological relations in Locke which, I am encouraged to see, independently confirms a number of the conclusions I have reached in this book. See 'John Locke: conservative radical', op. cit., ch.IV.

Bibliography

In Part I are listed the editions of Locke's published writings used in writing this book. In Part II are listed Locke and related bibliographies. In Part III are listed biographical works of reference. Part IV comprises works prior to, and emanating from, the somewhat extended eighteenth century with which we have been concerned. Part V comprises a select list of post-eighteenth-century works referred to in writing this study. References to manuscripts in the Lovelace Collection of the University of Oxford and at the British Library are given in the Notes. Works are listed in chronological order under each author's name.

Part I: Editions of Locke's Published Writings used in Writing this Book

The Works of John Locke in Ten Volumes. The Eleventh Edition, London: W. Otridge et al., 1812.

Abrams, Philip (ed.), *Two Tracts on Government,* Cambridge: CUP, 1967.

Biddle, John C., 'John Locke's Essay on Infallibility: introduction, text and translation,' *Journal of Church and State,* XIX, 1977, 301–27.

De Beer, E. S. (ed.), *The Correspondence of John Locke,* Oxford: Clarendon Press, 8 vols., 1976–89.

Fraser, A. Campbell (ed.), *An Essay concerning Human Understanding,* Oxford: Clarendon Press, 2 vols., 1894.

Laslett, Peter (ed.), *Two Treatises of Government,* Cambridge: CUP, 1967.

Leyden, W. von (ed.), *Essays on the Law of Nature,* Oxford: Clarendon Press, 1954.

Nidditch, Peter H. (ed.), *An Essay concerning Human Understanding,* Oxford: Clarendon Press, 1975.

Pringle-Pattison, A. S. (ed.), *An Essay concerning Human Understanding,* Oxford: Clarendon Press, 1924.

Tully, James H. (ed.), *A Letter concerning Toleration,* Indianapolis: Hackett Publishing Company, 1983.

Wainwright, Arthur W. (ed.), *A Paraphrase and Notes on the Epistles of St. Paul,* Oxford: Clarendon Press, 2 vols., 1987.

Wootton, David (ed.), *Political Writings,* Harmondsworth: Penguin, 1993.

Yolton, John W. and Jean S. (eds.), *Some Thoughts concerning Education,* Oxford: Clarendon Press, 1989.

Part II: Locke and Related Bibliographies

Attig, John C., *The Works of John Locke: A Comprehensive Bibliography from the Seventeenth Century to the Present,* Westport, Conn.: Greenwood Press, 1985.

Christophersen, H. O., *A Bibliographical Introduction to the Study of John Locke,* Oslo: I Kommisjon Hos Jaccob Dybwad, 1930.

Early Nonconformity 1566–1800: A Catalogue of books in Doctor Williams's Library, London, Boston, Mass.: G. K. Hall, 8 vols., 1968.

Hall, Roland and Woolhouse, Roger, *Eighty Years of Locke Scholarship: A Bibliographical Guide,* Edinburgh: Edinburgh University Press, 1983.

A New Catalogue of Living English Authors, London, 1799, only vol. I published.

Ward, Fritz R., 'Some eighteenth-century supplements to the Yolton and Attig bibliographies,' *The Locke Newsletter,* XXIV, 1993, 107–14.

Yolton, Jean S. and John W. (eds.), *John Locke: A Reference Guide,* Boston: G. K. Hall, 1985.

Part III: Biographical Works of Reference

Alumni Cantabrigienses, compiled by John and J. A. Venn, Cambridge: CUP, 1922, etc.

Alumni Oxonienses, arranged etc. by John Foster, Oxford: Parker, 1887, etc.

Dictionary of American Biography, ed. Allen Johnson, London: OUP, 1928, etc.

Dictionary of National Biography, ed. Leslie Stephen, London: Smith, Elder, 1885, etc.

The Dictionary of Welsh Biography down to 1940, ed. John Edward Lloyd et al., London: The Honourable Society of Cymmrodorion, 1959.

Fasti Ecclesiae Scoticanae, ed. Hew Scott et al., Edinburgh, 1866, etc.

Part IV: Works from the somewhat Extended Eighteenth Century

Note: This list includes editions published during the period, together with earlier relevant works and later editions of eighteenth-century authors' works

Anon., *An account of the Dissenting Academies from the Restoration of Charles the Second,* Doctor Williams's Library, London, MS 24.59.25.

—— *The Westminster Confession of Faith,* 1647.

—— *The Savoy Declaration of Faith and Order* (1658), ed. A. G. Matthews, London: Independent Press, 1959.

—— *The Occasional Paper, no. 1. Containing an Account of the Author's Design; Together with Some Reflections on a Book, Entituled, A Letter to the Deists. In a Letter to a Friend,* London: W. Wotton, 1697.

—— *The Occasional Paper, no. 3. Being Reflexions upon Mr. Toland's Book, Called Christianity Not Mysterious. With Some Considerations about the Use of Reason in Matters of Religion. In a Letter to a Friend,* London: W. Wotton, 1697.

—— *The Occasional Paper, no. 5. Containing a Defence of the Ministry and ministers of the Gospel; against the Suggestions of Some Late Writers. In a Letter to a Friend. With a Post-Script Relating to the Author of The Reasonableness of Christianity,* London: W. Wotton, 1697.

—— *A Letter to a Clergy-Man in the Country, concerning the Votes of the Bishops in the last Session of Parliament, Upon the Bill against Occasional Conformity,* London: John Nutt, 1704.

Anon., *An Essay upon Government: Wherein the Republican Schemes Reviv'd by Mr. Lock, Dr. Blackal, &c., Are Fairly Consider'd and Refuted,* London: G. Sawbridge, 1705.

—— *A Philosophick Essay concerning Ideas, According to Dr. Sherlock's Principles. Wherein His Notion of Them is Stated, and His Reasonings Thereupon Examin'd. In a Letter to a Friend,* London: B. Bragg, 1705.

—— *A Dissertation on Deistical and Arian Corruption; or, Plain Proof That the Principles and Practices of Arians and Deists Are Founded upon Spiritual Blindness, and Resolve into Atheism ... Where Mr. Jack-n's Dissertation on Matter and Spirit, Mr. Locke's Essay, &c., Are particularly Examined, &c.*, London: G. Strahan, 1708.

—— *A Vindication of Mankind, or Free-Will Asserted. In Answer to a Philosophical Inquiry concerning Human Liberty. To Which is Added, An Examination of Mr. Locke's Scheme of Freedom,* London: S. Popping, 1717.

—— *An Authentick Account of Several Things Done and agreed upon by the Dissenting Ministers lately assembled at Salters-Hall,* London: J. Clark, 1719.

—— *The Infidel Convicted; or, A Brief Defence of the Christian Religion. In Which the Excellency of the Christian Morality Is Fully Shewn, and the Consistency of Revelation with Human Reason Proved. Corroborated by Unanswerable Arguments from Mr. Locke, on Whose Writings Many Persons Causelessly Profess to Build Their Sceptical Notions. And Address'd to the Serious Consideration of the British Youth in general; and in particular of such of the Young Gentlemen of the Inns of Court, as are tainted with Atheistical or Deistical Principles, but are not wholly given up to a Reprobate Mind. To Which is added, by Way of Postscript, A Pathetic Letter from a Father on the Degeneracy of his Son; and a Word of Advice in relation to the Universities,* London: J. Roberts, 1731.

—— *The Real Presence as it is held by the Roman Catholicks demonstrated, to be neither Contrary to Reason, nor the Evidence of the Senses upon any Principles of Knowledge, with the Notions of Mr. Locke thereon, Considered and Confuted,* Dublin, 1751.

—— Preface to J. Addison, *The Evidences of the Christian Religion,* London: J. and R. Tonson, 1763.

Anon., *An Analysis of Mr. Locke's Doctrine of Ideas, in his Essay on Human Understanding*, Cambridge: J. Bentham, 1766.

—— *A Seasonable Plea for Liberty of Conscience, Against some late Oppressive Proceedings; Particularly in the Town of Berwick, In the County of York*, Boston: Philip Freeman, 1770.

—— *Remarks on the Religious Sentiments of Learned and Eminent Laymen, viz. Sir Isaac Newton, Hon. Robert Boyle, Locke, Sir Matthew Hale, Addison, etc., With Occasional Reflections on Incredulity*, London: J. Robinson, 1790.

—— *A Discourse Concerning Faith as the Condition of the Gospel Covenant ... with an appendix containing some Remarks on Mr. Locke's Paraphrase and Notes on St. Paul's Epistles*, Georgetown: Green, English, 1796.

—— *On the Character and Writings of the Rev. Thomas Belsham. Extracted from The Monthly Repository for February, &c., 1830*, London: The Unitarian Association, 1830.

Adams, Samuel, *The Writings of Samuel Adams*, ed. Harry Alonzo Cushing, 4 vols., New York: Putnams, 1904–8.

Allen, Ethan, *Reason the only Oracle of Man, or a Compendious System of Natural Religion*, Bennington, VI, 1784.

Amory, Thomas, *Christ the Light of the World; Or, The Principal Improvements made in Religion by Christianity. Represented in a Sermon Preached at the Young Men's Lecture at Exon, Thursday, September 11, 1735. By Thomas Amory. Published at the Request of the Young Gentlemen, and of a great Number of Ministers present*, London: R. Hett, 1735.

—— *Ministers not Lords over the Faith of Christians, but Helpers of their Joy. A Sermon Preached at Lewin's Mead, Bristol, At the Ordination Of the Reverend Mr. William Richards, May the 22d. 1751*, London: J. Waugh and Bristol: T. Cadell, [1751].

—— *Twenty-Two Sermons*, London: T. Becket and P. A. De Hondt, 1766.

—— Preface to *Sermons ... by the late Reverend S[amuel] Chandler*, London: J. Buckland, 1768.

Angus, John et al., *An Introductory Discourse by Mr. John Angus, Mr. Fell's Confession of Faith; a charge by Thomas Davidson; and a Sermon by Thomas Towle, B.D., all delivered at the Ordination of the Rev. Mr. John Fell. In Thaxted, Essex, October 24th 1770*, London: E. and C. Dilly, 1770.

[Applegarth, Robert], *A Theological Survey of the Human*

Understanding: Intended as an antidote against Modern Deism, Salisbury: J. Hodson, 1776.

Ashworth, Caleb, *Reflections on the fall of a great man. A Sermon preached to a congregation of Protestant Dissenters At Daventry in Northamptonshire on Occasion of the Death of the late Reverend Isaac Watts, D.D.*, London: J. Waugh, 1749.

Astell, Mary, *The Christian Religion as Profess'd by a Daughter of the Church of England,* London: S. H. for R. Wilkin, 1705.

B., F., *A Free but Modest Censure On the Late Controversial Writings and Debates of The Lord Bishop of Worcester and Mr. Locke; Mr. Edwards and Mr. Locke; The Honble Charles Boyle, Esq; and Dr. Bently. Together with Brief Remarks on Monsieur LeClerc's Ars Critica,* London: A. Baldwin, 1698.

B., G., *The Case of Compulsion in Matters of Religion,* 1688.

B., H., *A Vindication of Robert Barclays Apology for the Principles of the People call'd Quakers; Against the Attempts of William Notcutt, In a late Pamphlet, Entituled, An Impartial Review of Robert Barclay's Pretended Apology,* London: Assigns of J. Sowle, 1732.

—— *An Examination of William Notcutt's Reply to H.B's Vindication of R. Barclay's Apology,* London: Assigns of J. Sowle, 1735.

Backus, Isaac, *The Doctrine of Sovereign Grace Opened and Vindicated: And also The Consistency and Duty of declaring Divine Sovereignty, and Mens Impotency, while yet we address their Consciences with the Warnings of Truth, and Calls of the Gospel,* Providence, RI: John Carter, 1771.

—— *Policy as Well as Honesty Forbids the Use of Secular Force in Religious Affairs,* Boston, 1779.

—— *A Door Opened for Religious Liberty,* Boston, 1783.

—— *A History of New England,* Newton, Mass.: Backus Historical Society, 2nd edn, 1871.

Bagshaw, Edward, *The Great Question concerning Things Indifferent in Religious Worship,* 1660.

—— *The Second Part of the Great Question concerning Things Indifferent in Religious Worship,* 1661.

Ball, John, *Some Remarks upon a New Way of Preaching Propos'd in an Ordination Sermon Preach'd at Taunton,* 1736.

Barber, Joseph, *Sermons on Regeneration: wherein the Nature, Necessity, and Evidences of it are considered, and practically improved,* London: J. Buckland, 1770.

Barber, Joseph, *A Sermon Occasioned By The Death of the Rev. Nathaniel Trotman, Who Departed This Life The Thirty-First Day of August, 1793, In The Forty-Third Year Of His Age, By Joseph Barber. At The Close Of The Sermon Is Annexed A Letter From Mr. Trotman, To His Church, During His Indisposition. To Which Is Added, An Address At The Interment, By Thomas Towle, B.D. Published At The Unanimous Request Of The Church and Congregation,* London: C. Dilly, 1793.

[Barrington, J. S.], *The Rights of Protestant Dissenters. In Two Parts. The First Being the Case of the Dissenters Review'd. The Second, a Vindication of Their Right to an Absolute Toleration from the Objections of Sir H. Mackworth, in his Treatise intituled Peace at Home* (1704), London, 2nd edn, corrected and enlarged, 1705.

Bartlett, William, *ICHNOGRAPHIA, or a Model of the Primitive Congregational Way,* 1647.

[Barwis, Jackson], *Three Dialogues concerning Liberty,* London: J. Dodsley, 1776.

—— *Dialogues concerning Innate Principles; Containing an Examination of Mr. Locke's Doctrine on that Subject. By the Author of Three Dialogues concerning Liberty,* London: J. Dodsley, 1779.

[Baxter, Andrew], *An Enquiry into the Nature of the Human Soul: Wherein the Immateriality of the Soul is Evinced from the Principles of Reason and Philosophy,* London: J. Betteham, 1733.

Baxter, Richard, *The Saint's Everlasting Rest: or, a Treatise of the Blessed State of the Saints in their Enjoyment of God in Glory, etc.,* London: Rob. White, 1650.

—— *The Unreasonableness of Infidelity; Manifested in Four Discourses, etc.,* London: T. Underhill and F. Tyton, 1655.

—— *The Reformed Pastor* (1656), London: SCM Press, 1956.

—— *A Holy Commonwealth, or Political Aphorisms, opening the True Principles of Government, etc.,* London: T. Underhill and F. Tyton, 1659.

—— *Additions to the Poetical Fragments, etc.,* 3rd edn, London: Tho. Parkhurst, 1699.

Beattie, James, *An Essay on the Nature and Immutability of Truth; in Opposition to Sophistry and Scepticism,* Edinburgh: A. Kincaid and J. Bell, 1770.

Beattie, James, *Dissertations Moral and Critical,* London: W. Strahan and T. Cadell, 1783.

—— *Elements of Moral Science* (1790), Edinburgh: Constable and Fairbairn, 3rd. edn, 1817.

Becconsall, Thomas, *The Grounds and Foundation of Natural Religion Discover'd, in the Principal Branches of it, in Opposition to the Prevailing Notions of the Modern Skepticks and Latitudinarians. With an Introduction concerning the Necessity of Revealed Religion,* London: W. O. for A. Roper, 1698.

Bellamy, Joseph, *The Works of the Rev. Joseph Bellamy, D.D.,* ed. Stephen Dodge, 3 vols., New York: J. Seymour, 1811-12.

—— *The Works of Joseph Bellamy, D.D.,* Boston: Doctrinal Tract and Book Society, 1853.

—— *True Religion delineated; or, Experimental Religion, As distinguished from Formality on the one Hand, and Enthusiasm on the Other, set in a Scriptural and Rational Light,* Boston: S. Kneeland, 1750.

Belsham, Thomas, *Evidences of Divine Revelation,* 1805–6. Harris Manchester College, Oxford, MS Belsham 6.

—— *Additional Lectures in Pneumatology,* Harris Manchester College, Oxford, MS Belsham 27.

—— *Lectures upon the doctrine of the prae-existence and divinity of Jesus Christ,* 4 vols., Harris Manchester College, Oxford, MS p.280X.1–4.

—— *The Importance of Truth, and the Duty of making an open Profession of it: Represented in a Discourse delivered on Wednesday the 28th of April, 1790, at the Meeting-house in the Old Jewry, London; to the Supporters of the New College at Hackney,* London: H. Goldney, 1790.

—— *Freedom of Enquiry, and Zeal in the Diffusion of Christian Truth, Asserted and Recommended in a Discourse Delivered at Bristol, July 9, 1800, before the Society of Unitarian Christians, established in the West of England, for Promoting Christian Knowledge and the Practice of Virtue, by the Distribution of books,* London: G. Woodfall, 1800.

—— *Elements of the Philosophy of the Mind, and of Moral Philosophy. To which is prefixed A Compendium of Logic,* London: J. Johnson, 1801.

—— *Letters upon Arianism and other topics in Metaphysics and Theology, in reply to the Lectures of the Rev. Benjamin Carpenter,*

London: J. Johnson, 1803.

Belsham, Thomas, *The Character of the Christian Teacher Delineated, and the Means of Forming it Represented, in a Discourse delivered at Hackney January 8, 1804, for the benefit of the Academical Institution at Exeter; and Published at the Request of the Congregation,* London: J. Johnson, 1804.

—— *Adherence to Christian Truth, Recommended in a Discourse delivered to the Unitarian Congregation at Hackney, May 5, 1805, upon the Resignation of the Pastoral Office in that Society,* London: J. Johnson, 1805.

—— *A Calm Enquiry into the Scripture Doctrine concerning the Person of Christ,* London: J. Johnson, 1811.

—— *The Rights of Conscience Asserted and Defined, in Reference to the Modern Interpretation of the Toleration Act. In a Discourse delivered at Essex Street Chapel, February 5, 1812. Being the Day appointed for a General Fast,* London: J. Johnson, 1812.

—— *Discourses, Doctrinal and Practical; delivered in Essex Street Chapel,* London: R. Hunter, 1826.

[Belsham, Thomas?], *Introduction to the lectures on the doctrine of the divinity and praeexistence of Jesus Christ,* Doctor Williams's Library, London, MS 59.22 (7).

Benson, George, *The Reasonablenesse of the Christian Religion, As delivered in the Scriptures. Being an Answer to a late Treatise, intitled Christianity not founded on Argument. In Three Parts. Part I. Containd the Arguments for the Truth of the Christian Religion. Part II. The Answers to the Difficulties and positions proposed by this Author. Part III. An Interpretation of the Texts which he hath perverted,* London: J. Noon, 1743.

—— *A Paraphrase and Notes on Six of the Epistles of St. Paul … Attempted In Imitation of Mr. Locke's Manner* (1734), London: James Waugh, 1752.

Bentley, Richard, *Matter and Motion cannot Think: or, a Confutation of Atheism from the Faculties of the Soul,* London: Tho. Parkhurst, 1692.

Berkeley, George, *The Works of George Berkeley Bishop of Cloyne,* eds. A. A. Luce and T. E. Jessop, London: Nelson, 1948 etc.

Bliss, Anthony, *Remarks on the Plea, and the Defence of the Plea, for Human Reason,* London: S. Wilmot, 1733.

—— *Observations on Mr. Chubb's Discourse concerning Reason: Wherein his Attempt to prove, That Reason either Is, or Ought to be, a Sufficient Guide in Matters of Religion, Is Consider'd; and His Arguments shown to be Frivolous and Inconclusive,* London: Samuel Wilmot, [1797].

Blount, Charles et al., *The Oracles of Reason ... In Several Letters to Mr. Hobbs and other Persons of Eminent Quality*, London, 1693.

Bogue, David, *The Great Importance of having Right Sentiments in Religion,* London: J. Buckland, 1788.

Bold, Samuel, *Some Passages in The Reasonableness of Christianity, &c., and Its Vindication,* London: A. and J. Churchill, 1697.

—— *Observations and Animadversions (Lately Printed at Oxford) on a Late Book, entituled, The Reasonableness of Christianity, As delivered in the Scriptures*, London: A. and J. Churchill, 1698.

—— *Some Considerations on the Principal Objections and Arguments Which Have Been Publish'd against Mr. Lock's Essay of Humane Understanding,* London: A. and J. Churchill, 1699.

—— *A Discourse concerning the Resurrection of the Same Body; with two Letters concerning the Necessry Immateriality of Created Thinking Substance,* London: S. Holt for A. and J. Churchill, 1705.

—— *A Collection of Tracts Publish'd in Vindication of Mr Locke's Reasonableness of Christianity ... and of His Essay concerning Humane Understanding,* London: A. and J. Churchill, 1697–1706.

Boulton, Richard, *A Full Confutation of All the Arguments That Have Ever Been produced against the Belief of Apparitions, Witches, &c. With a Judgment concerning Spirits, by the late learned Mr. John Locke.* In *The Compleat History of Magic, Sorcery and Witchcraft,* London: E. Curll and W. Taylor, vol. II, 1715.

Bourn, Samuel, *Religious Education begun and carried on in Three Catechisms,* 1748.

—— *A Vindication of the Principles and Practice of Protestant Dissenters,* London: J. Robinson, 1748.

Bradbury, Thomas, *A Confession of Faith at the Publick Ordination of Thomas Bradbury, London, July the Tenth, 1707,* London: Nath. Cliffe, 1707.

Brook, Benjamin, *Dissent from the Established Church Justified by An Appeal to Facts,* 3rd edn, London: James Black, 1815.

Broughton, John, *Psychologia; or, An Account of the Nature of the*

Rational Soul. In Two Parts. The First, An Essay concerning the Nature of the Human Soul, London: W.B. for T. Bennet, 1703.

Browne, John, *Letter to the Author of a Plea for Reason,* 1731.

Browne, Peter, *A Letter in Answer to a Book Entituled Christianity Not Mysterious; As Also to All Those Who Set up for Reason and Evidence in Opposition to Revelation and Mysteries,* London: R. Clavell, 1697.

—— *The Procedure, Extent and Limits of Human Understanding,* London: W. Innys, 1728.

Bruce, John, et al., *Discourses delivered at the Solemn Separation of the Rev. John Bruce to the Pastoral Office over The Congregational Church assembling in St. James's-Street, Newport, Isle of Wight,* 1808.

Burnet, Gilbert, *An Exposition of the Thirty-Nine Articles of the Church of England,* London: R. Chiswell, 1699.

[Burnet, Thomas], *Remarks upon An Essay concerning Human Understanding: In a Letter Address'd to the Author,* London: M. Wootton, 1697.

—— *Second Remarks upon An Essay concerning Humane Understanding, In a Letter Address'd to the Author: Being a Vindication of the First Remarks against the Answer of Mr. Lock, at the End of his Reply to the Bishop of Worcester,* London: M. Wootton, 1697.

—— *Third Remarks upon an Essay concerning Humane Understanding. In a Letter Address'd to the Author,* London: M. Wotton, 1699.

—— *The Judgment of Dr. Thomas Burnet, Late Master of the Charter-House, Concerning the Doctrine of the Trinity: and the judgment of Dr. Samuel Clarke, late Rector of St. James's, Concerning 1. The Satisfaction, 2. The Merits, 3. The Mediation and Intercession of Christ. 4. The ordinary influence and Assistance of the Holy Spirit. 5. The Two Sacraments. With a Preface concerning Mr. Locke, Sir Isaac Newton and Mr. Wollaston,* London: J. Roberts, 1732.

Burroughes, Jeremiah, *Irenicum, to the Lovers of Truth and Peace,* London: Robert Dawlman, 1646.

Burthogge, Richard, *The Philosophical Writings of Richard Burthogge,* ed. with introduction and notes by Margaret W. Landes, Chicago: The Open Court, 1921.

Butler, Joseph, *The Analogy of Religion* (1736), London: Ward, Lock, n.d.

—— *Butler's Fifteen Sermons,* ed. W. R. Matthews, (1914), London: G. Bell, 1953.

Calamy, Edmund, *Comfort and Counsel to Protestant Dissenters. With some serious Queries to such as hate and cast them out; And a Friendly Admonition to such as Desert them. In Two Sermons, Preach'd first at Westminster, on March 30. And afterwards At the Merchants Lecture at Salters-Hall, On May the 20th, and June the 3d. 1712,* London: John Lawrence et al., 1712.

—— *Thirteen Sermons concerning the Doctrine of the Trinity, Preach'd at the Merchant's-Lecture, at Salter's Hall,* London: John Clark, 1722.

—— *An Historical Account of My Own Life. With some Reflections on the Times I have lived in,* 2 vols., ed. J. T. Rutt, London: Henry Colburn and Richard Bentley, 1829.

Campbell, Archibald, *An Enquiry into the Original of Moral Virtue,* 1733.

—— *The Necessity of Revelation: or an Enquiry into the Extent of Human Powers with Respect to Matters of Religion; Especially those two fundamental Articles, The Being of God, and The Immortality of the Soul,* London: Wm. Bowyer, 1739.

Carroll, William, *Remarks upon Mr. Clarke's Sermons, Preached at St. Paul's against Hobbs, Spinoza, and other Atheists,* London: Jonathan Robinson, 1705.

—— *A Dissertation upon the Tenth Chapter of the Fourth Book of Mr. Locke's Essay ... Wherein the Author's Endeavours to Establish Spinoza's Atheistical Hypothesis ... in That Tenth Chapter Are Discover'd and Confuted. To which is subjoyn'd; A Short Account of the Sense wherein the Titles of, and the Reasonings in the following Pernicious Books, are to be understood, viz. The Reasonableness of Christianity. Christianity not Mysterious. The Rights of the Christian Church, &c. As also, how that Sense and those Reasonings are bottom'd, upon the Hypothesis establish'd in the said Essay of Humane Understanding,* London: J. Matthews, 1706.

—— *A Letter to the Reverend Dr. Benjamin Prat ... Wherein the Dangerous Errors in a late Book, Intituled An Essay concerning the Use of Reason in Propositions Are Detected, Confuted, and Gradually Deduc'd from the Very Basis of All Atheism, upon Which Alone They Are Bottom'd,* London: R. Sare, 1707.

Carroll, William, *Spinoza Reviv'd: Or, A Treatise Proving the Book Entitled, The Rights of the Christian Church, &c. (In the most Notorious Parts of it) To be the same with Spinoza's Rights of the Christian clergy, &c. And that both of them are grounded upon downright Atheism. To which is added, A Preliminary Discourse relating to the said Books, By the Reverend Dr. George Hicks,* London: J. Morphew, 1709.

—— *Spinoza Reviv'd. Part the Second. Or, A Letter to M. Le Clerc, Occasion'd by his Bibliothèque Choisie, Tom. 21,* London: J. Morphew, 1711.

Chandler, Samuel, *Sermons,* London: Samuel Chandler for the Author's Widow, 1768.

Chauncy, Charles, *The Only Compulsion Proper to Be Made Use of in Affairs of Conscience and Religion,* Boston, 1739.

—— *Enthusiasm described and caution'd against,* Boston: J. Draper, 1742.

—— *Ministers Exhorted and encouraged to take heed to themselves, and to their Doctrine,* Boston: Rogers and Fowle, 1744.

—— *The Opinion of one that has perused The Summer Morning's Conversation, concerning Original Sin, wrote by the Rev. Mr. Peter Clark,* Boston: Green & Russell, 1758.

—— *The Mystery Hid from Ages and Generations, made manifest by the Gospel-Revelation: or, the Salvation of All Men, the Grand Thing aimed at in the Scheme of God, As opened in the New-Testament Writings, and entrusted with Jesus Christ to bring into Effect,* London: Charles Dilley, 1784.

Cheyne, George, *Philosophical Principles of Religion* (1715), 4th edn corrected, London: G. Strahan, 1734.

Clap, Thomas, *An Essay on the Nature and Foundation of Moral Virtue and Obligation,* New Haven: B. Mecom, 1765.

Clark, Peter, *Man's Dignity and Duty as a reasonable Creature; And his Insufficiency as a fallen Creature: Represented in a Sermon Preached at the Anniversary Dudleian Lecture in the Chapel of Harvard-College in Cambridge, May 11. 1763,* Boston: Richard and Samuel Draper, 1763.

Clarke, Samuel, *The Works of Samuel Clarke,* London: J. and P. Knapton, 4 vols., 1738.

—— *The Scripture Doctrine of the Trinity,* London: James Knapton, 1712.

—— *A Collection of Papers Which Passed between the Late*

Learned Mr. Leibnitz, and Dr. Clarke, London: James Knapton, 1717.

[Cockburn, Catharine], *A Defence of the Essay of human Understanding, Written by Mr. Locke. Wherein its principles with Reference to Morality, Reveal'd Religion, and the Immortality of the Soul, Are Consider'd and Justify'd: In Answer to Some Remarks on That Essay, by T. Burnet,* London: W. Turner, 1702.

—— *The Works of Mrs. Catharine Cockburn, Theological, Moral, Dramatic, and Poetical,* London: J. and P. Knapton, 2 vols., 1751.

Colden, C., *An Explication of the First Causes of Action in Matter,* New York: James Parker, 1745.

—— *The Principles of Action in Matter,* London: R. Dodsley, 1751.

[Collins, Anthony], *An Essay concerning the Use of Reason in Propositions, The Evidence whereof depends upon Human Testimony,* London, 1707.

—— *A Discourse of Free-Thinking, Occasion'd by The Rise and Growth of a Sect call'd Free-Thinkers,* London, 1713.

—— *A Discourse of the Grounds and Reasons of the Christian Religion,* 1724.

Conder, John, *A Summary of Christian Theology,* 1780–1. MS (Part II, 1781, only) at John Rylands University Library of Manchester.

Congregational Magazine, various volumes.

Conybeare, John, *A Defence of Reveal'd Religion against the Exceptions of a Late Writer, in his Book, Intituled, Christianity as Old as the Creation* (1732), 4th edn, Dublin: Grierson, M'Kenzie and Moore, 1738.

[Coole, Benjamin], *Some Brief Observations on the Paraphrase and Notes Of the Judicious John Locke: Relating to the Women's Exercising Their Spiritual Gifts in the Church,* London: P. Gwillim, 1716.

—— *Reflections on a Letter to the Author of Some Brief Observations,* London, 1717.

Cooper, Anthony Ashley, third Earl of Shaftesbury, *Works,* Birmingham, 1773.

—— *Several Letters Written by a Noble Lord to a Young Man at the University,* 1716.

Coward, William, *Second thoughts concerning human soul, demonstrating the notion of human soul, as believ'd to be a spiritual and immortal substance, to be a plain heathenish invention, and not consonant to the principles of philosophy, reason, or religion* (1702), 2nd edn corrected and enlarged, 1704.

—— *The Grand Essay: or, A vindication of reason, and religion, against the impostures of philosophy*, Printed for P.G., 1704.

Cudworth, Ralph, *The True Intellectual System of the Universe* (1678), London: T. Tegg, 1845.

Daggett, David, *Sunbeams may be extracted from cucumbers, but the process is tedious. An oration pronounced on the fourth of July 1799 at the request of the citizens of New Haven*, New Haven, 1799.

Dawes, Matthew, *The Nature and Extent of Supreme Power, in a Letter to the Rev. David Williams, Showing the Ultimate End of All Human Power, and of a Free Government under God. And in Which Mr. Locke's Theory of Government Is Examined and Explained; Contrary to the General Construction of That Writer's Particular Sentiments on the Supremacy of the People*, London: J. Stockdale, 1783.

Daye, James, *The Christian's Service, compleated with Honour. A Sermon Occasioned by the Death of the Reverend Caleb Rotheram, D.D.* [1752].

Dickinson, Jonathan, *The Reasonableness of Christianity in Four Sermons*, Boston: S. Kneeland and T. Green, 1732.

—— *The True Scripture-Doctrine concerning some Important Points of Christian Faith ... In Five Discourses*, Boston: G. Rogers, 1741.

Ditton, Humphrey, *A Discourse concerning the Resurrection of Jesus Christ. Together with an appendix concerning the impossible production of thought, from matter and motion: the nature of humane souls, and of brutes*, London, 1712.

Doddridge, Philip, *A Course of Lectures On the Principal Subjects in Pneumatology, Ethics, And Divinity: With References to the most considerable Authors on each Subject*, ed. Samuel Clark, London: J. Buckland and thirteen others, 1763.

—— *The Works of the Rev. P. Doddridge, D.D.*, Leeds: Edward Baines, 10 vols., 1803.

—— *The Correspondence and Diary of Philip Doddridge, D.D.*, ed. J. D. Humphreys, London: Henry Colburn and Richard Bentley, 5 vols., 1829-31.

—— *Calendar of the Correspondence of Philip Doddridge DD (1702–51),* ed. Geoffrey F. Nuttall, London: Her Majesty's Stationery Office, 1979.

Dodwell, William, *The Eternity of Future Punishment Asserted and Vindicated,* Oxford, 1743.

D'Oyly, Robert, *Of the Resurrection of the Same Body. In Four Dissertations,* London: Robert Gosling, 1728.

Du Moulin, Louis, *The Power of the Christian Magistrate,* London, 1650.

—— *Of the Right of the Churches, and of the Magistrates Power over them, etc.,* London, 1658.

—— *Les Désmarches de l'Angleterre vers Rome,* 1679.

—— *An Appeal of all the Nonconformists in England to God, etc.,* London, 1681.

Dwight, Timothy, *Theology, Explained and Defended, in a Series of Sermons ... With a Memoir of the Life of the Author,* (1819), Glasgow: Blackie, 1835.

—— *Sermons,* 2 vols., Edinburgh, 1828.

—— *Travels in New England and New York,* New Haven (1821–2), ed. Barbara Miller Solomon with the assistance of Patricia M. King, Cambridge, Mass.: The Belknap Press of Harvard University, 1969.

Edwards, B. L., *A Sermon, Preached at Castle-hill Meeting-House, Northampton, on Sunday, the 20th of May, 1827; upon the occasion of the Death of the Rev. John Horsey,* London: Wm. Clowes, 1827.

Edwards, John, *Some Thoughts Concerning the Several Causes and Occasions of Atheism, Especially in the Present Age. With Some Brief Reflections on Socinianism: and on a Late Book Entituled, The Reasonableness of Christianity as Deliver'd in the Scriptures,* London: J. Robinson and J. Wyatt, 1695.

—— *A Demonstration of the Existence and Providence of God, from the Contemplation of the Visible Structure of the Greater and Lesser World,* London: Jonathan Robinson, 1696.

—— *Socinianism Unmask'd: A Discourse Shewing the Unreasonableness of a Late Writer's Opinion concerning the Necessity of Only One Article of Christian Faith; and of His Other Assertions in His Book Entituled, The Reasonableness of Christianity as Deliver'd in the Scriptures, and in His Vindication of It. With a Brief Reply to Another (Professed) Socinian Writer,*

London: J. Robinson and J. Wyat, 1696.

Edwards, John, *A Brief Vindication of the Fundamental Articles of the Christian Faith, as Also of the Clergy, Universities and Publick Schools, from Mr. Locke's Reflections upon Them in His Book of Education, &c., with Some Animadversions on Two Late Pamphlets, viz. of Mr. Bold and a Nameless Socinian Writer,* London: J. Robinson and J. Wyat, 1697.

—— *The Socinian Creed; or, A Brief Account Of the Professed Tenents [sic] and Doctrines of the Foreign and English Socinians. Wherein Is Shew'd the Tendency of Them To Irreligion and Atheism. With Proper Antidotes against Them,* London: J. Robinson, 1697.

—— *The Eternal and Intrinsick Reasons of Good and Evil. A Sermon preach'd at the Commencement at Cambridge, on Sunday the 2d Day of July, 1699,* Cambridge, 1699.

—— *A Free Discourse concerning Truth and Error, especially in Matters of Religion,* London: Jonathan Robinson et al., 1701.

—— *The Doctrin of Faith and Justification set in a True Light,* London: Jonathan Robinson, et al., 1708.

—— *Some Brief Observations and Reflections on Mr. Whiston's late Writings, Falsely Entitul'd Primitive Christianity Reviv'd,* London: J. Lawrence, 1712.

—— *Some New Discoveries of the Uncertainty, Deficiency, and Corruptions of Humane Knowledge,* 1714.

Edwards, Jonathan, *The Works of Jonathan Edwards, with a memoir by Sereno E. Dwight; revised and corrected by Edward Hickman* (1834), Edinburgh: The Banner of Truth Trust, 2 vols., 1974.

—— *Treatise on Grace & other posthumous writings including Observations on the Trinity,* ed. Paul Helm, Cambridge: James Clarke, 1971.

[Ellis, John], *Some Brief Considerations upon Mr. Locke's Hypothesis, That the Knowledge of God Is Attainable by Ideas of Reflexion. Wherein Is Demonstrated, upon his own Principles That the Knowledge of God Is Not Attainable by Ideas of Reflexion. Being an Addition to ... The Knowledge of Divine Things from Revelation, Not from Nature or Reason. By the Author of the Said Book,* London: J. Watts, 1743.

—— *The Knowledge of Divine Things from Revelation ... With some Additional Considerations upon Mr. Locke's Essay on the*

Human Understanding (1743), London: Thomas Tegg, 1837.

Elys, Edmund, *A Refutation of Some of the False Conceits in Mr. Locke's Essay concerning Humane Understanding, Together with a Brief Answer (in Latine) to the Argumentation of Gerardus de Vries Against the Innate Idea of God,* London: W. and J. Mashall, 1697.

Emmons, Nathanael, *The Works of Nathanael Emmons, D.D.*, ed. Jacob Ide, 7 vols., Boston: Crocker and Brewster, 1842–50.

Enfield, William, *A Funeral Sermon, occasioned by the Death of the Late Rev. John Aikin, D.D. Professor of Divinity at the Academy in Warrington,* Warrington: W. Eyres, 1781.

Evangelical Magazine, various volumes.

Evans, Caleb, 'Confession of faith,' in *A Charge and Sermon, together with an Introductory Discourse, and Confession of Faith, delivered at the Ordination of the Rev. Mr. Caleb Evans, August 18, 1767, in Broad-Mead, Bristol. Publish'd at the request of the church, and the ministers then present,* Bristol: S. Farley, 1767.

—— *Advice to Students having in view the Christian Ministry; addressed to them at the Academy in Bristol, April 12, 1770.* This is appended to T. Dunscombe, *The tribute of Affection to the Memory of the late Doctor [Hugh] Evans,* Oxford, [1770].

—— *British Constitutional Liberty. A Sermon, Preached in Broadmead, Bristol, November 5, 1775,* Bristol: W. Pine, [1775].

—— *A Letter to the Rev. Mr. John Wesley, Occasioned by his Calm Address to the American Colonies,* London: Edward and Charles Dilly, 1775.

—— *Elisha's Exclamation. A Sermon, occasioned by the Death of the Rev. Hugh Evans, M.A. Who departed this Life, March 28, 1781, in the 69th Year of his Age. Preached at Broadmead, Bristol, April 8, 1781, Published at the Request of the Congregation,* Bristol: W. Pine, [1781].

—— *British Freedom Realized. A Sermon, preached at Broadmead, Bristol, November 5, 1788, being the Hundredth Anniversary of the Glorious Revolution, under King William of immortal Memory,* Bristol: William Pine, [1788].

Felton, Henry, *The Resurrection of the Same Numerical Body and Its Reunion to the Same Soul Asserted in a Sermon ... In Which Mr. Locke's Notions of Personality and Identity are Confuted, and the Author of The Naked Gospel Is Answered. Preached before the University of Oxford, on Easter-Monday, 1725,* Oxford, 1725.

Felton, Henry, *The Christian Faith Asserted against Deists, Arians, and Socinians,* Oxford, 1731.

Ferguson, James, *A Brief Refutation of the Errors of Toleration,* 1692.

Filmer, Robert, *Patriarcha and Other Writings,* ed. J. P. Somerville, Cambridge: CUP, 1991.

Fleming, Caleb, *A Letter to a Friend, Containing select Remarks upon the Rev. Dr. Isaac Watts's Treatise, entitled, The Glory of Christ, as God-Man,* 1746.

—— *A Survey of the Search after Souls, by Dr. Coward, Dr. S. Clarke, Mr. Baxter, Mr. Sykes, Dr. Law, Mr. Peckard, and others. Wherein the principal Arguments for and against the Materialists are collected: And the Distinction between the Mechanical and moral System stated. With An Essay to Ascertain the Condition of the Christian, during the Mediatorial Kingdom of Jesus: which neither admits of a sleeping nor supposes a separate State of the Soul after Death,* London: C. Henderson, 1758.

[Flemyng, Malcolm], *A New Critical Examination of an Important Passage in Mr. Locke's Essay on Human Understanding; in a Familiar Letter to a Friend. To Which is Added, an Extract from the Fifth Book of Anti-Lucretius, by cardinal Polignac, Concerning the Same Subject, with a Translation in Prose,* London: J. Robinson, 1751.

Ford, William et al., *A Sermon Preached at the Ordination of the Reverend Mr. John Notcutt, at the Meeting-House in Green-Street, Cambridge, on July 22, 1735, by William Ford. With the Charge then given him by the Revd. Mr. Tobias Wildboar; and Mr. Notcutt's Confession of his FAITH,* London, 1735.

Foskett, Benjamin, *Pneumatology,* Bristol Baptist College, MS z.e.16 and 39.

Foster, James, *The Usefulness, Truth and Excellency of the Christian Revelation defended against the Objections contain'd in a late Book, intituled, Christianity as old as the Creation, &c.,* 2nd edn with postscript, London: J. Noon, 1731.

Fownes, Joseph, *An Enquiry into The Principles of Toleration; The Degree in which they are Admitted by our Laws; and the Reasonableness of the late Application made by the Dissenters to Parliament for an Enlargement of their Religious Liberties* (1773), Shrewsbury: J. and W. Eddowes, 3rd edn, 1790.

Fraser, James, *The Scripture Doctrine of Sanctification, Being a crit-*

ical Exposition, and Paraphrase of the sixth and seventh Chapters of the Epistle to the Romans, and the four first Verses of the eighth Chapter. Wherein the true Scope and Sense of that most important and much disputed Context is cleared and asserted, against the false Interpretation of Grotius, Hammond, Locke, Whitby, Taylor, Alexander, &c. With a large Appendix, Wherein the Apostle's Doctrine, Principles, and Reasoning, are applied to the purposes of holy Practice, and of evangelical Preaching, Edinburgh: J. Ogle, 1774.

Fuller, Andrew, *The Complete Works of the Rev. Andrew Fuller. With a Memoir of his Life by Andrew Gunton Fuller,* London: Holdsworth and Ball, 4 vols., 1831.

Furneaux, Philip, *Letters to the Honourable Mr. Justice Blackstone, concerning His Exposition of the Act of Toleration, and Some Positions relative to Religious Liberty, in his Celebrated Commentaries on the Laws of England,* London: T. Cadell, 1770.

—— *An Essay on Toleration: With a particular View to the Late Application of The Protestant Dissenting Ministers to Parliament, for Amending, and rendering Effectual, the Act of the first of William and Mary, commonly called the Act of Toleration,* London: T. Cadell, 1773.

Gerdil, Giacinto Sigismondo, *L'immatérialité de l'âme démontrée contre M. Locke,* Turin: Imprimerie Royale, 1747.

Gill, John, *Complete Body of Doctrinal and Practical Divinity: Or, A System of Evangelical Truths Deduced from the Sacred Scriptures,* (1767, 1770), reprinted from the 1839 edn, Grand Rapids: Baker Book House, 2 vols., 1978.

Greene, Robert, *The Principles of Natural Philosophy, in which is shewn the Insufficiency of the Present Systems, etc.,* Cambridge, 1712.

—— *The Principles of the Philosophy of the Expansive and Contractive Forces; or, An Enquiry into the Principles of the Modern Philosophy, that is, into the several chief Rational Sciences which are extant,* Cambridge: C. Crownfield, 1727.

Gretton, Phillips, *A Review of the Argument A Priori, in relation to the Being and Attributes of God; In Reply to Dr. Clarke's Answer to a Seventh Letter concerning that Argument ... With some Extracts from the Letters of Mr. Locke, concerning the same,* London: Bernard Lintot, 1726.

Grove, Henry, *The works of Henry Grove, Containing all the Sermons, Discourses and Tracts published in his Life Time,* ed. Thomas Amory, London, 4 vols., 1847.

—— *Sermons and Tracts; being the Posthumous Works of Henry Grove,* ed. T. Amory, London, 6 vols., 1740–1.

—— *A Sermon Preach'd at the Ordination of the Rev. Mr. Thomas Amory, and Mr. William Cornish, at Taunton, Somerset, Oct. 7, 1730 ... To which is added, a Charge Delivered on the same Occasion. By John Milner,* London: R. Hett, 1731.

Hall, Robert, *Help to Zion's Travellers, being an attempt to remove various stumbling-blocks out of the way, relating to doctrinal, experimental, and practical religion,* [1781], Halifax: Hartley and Walker, 1837.

Hallett, Joseph, Jr, *A Defense of a Discourse on the Impossibility of proving a future State by the Light of Nature. With an Answer to the Reverend Mr. Grove's Thoughts on the same Subject,* London: J. Noon, 1731.

Halyburton, Thomas, *Natural Religion Insufficient; and Revealed Necessary to Man's Happiness in his present State,* Edinburgh: Andrew Anderson's heirs and successors, 1714.

Hampton, Benjamin, *The Existence of the human Soul after Death Proved from Scripture and Philosophy. Wherein Mr. Locke's Notion That Understanding may Be Given to Matter ... and All Other Such ... Opinions, are ... Confuted, etc.,* London: S. Popping, 1711.

Helwys, Thomas, *The Mistery of Iniquity,* 1612.

[Heywood, Samuel], *The Right of Protestant Dissenters to a Compleat Toleration, Asserted, etc.,* London: J. Johnson, 1787.

Hicks, George, see under W. Carroll, *Spinoza Reviv'd,* above.

Hill, Joseph, et al., *Ordination to the Ministry, an entrusting Men with the Gospel. A Sermon Preach'd at the Ordination of Thomas Hadfield, M.D. At Peckham in the County of Surrey, October xix, MDCCXXVI. By Joseph Hill. With Dr. Hadfield's Confession of Faith, and his Answers to the Questions then propos'd to him by the Reverend Mr. John Beaumont. To which is Added The Charge given by the Reverend Mr. Thomas Reynolds,* London, 1727.

Hitchcock, G., *Natural Religion aided by Revelation and Perfected in Christianity,* 1779.

Hoadly, Benjamin, *The Works of Benjamin Hoadly, D.D.,* London, 3 vols., 1773.

—— *The Nature of the Kingdom, or Church, of Christ. A Sermon Preach'd before the King at the Royal Chapel at St. James's on Sunday March 31, 1717,* London: James Knapton & Timothy Childe, 1717.

Holdsworth, Winch, *A Sermon Preached before the University of Oxford at St. Mary's on Easter Monday 1719, in Which the Cavils, False Reasonings, and False Interpretations of Scripture of mr. Lock and Others, against the Resurrection of the Same Body Are Examin'd and Answered,* Oxford: R. Wilkin, 1720.

—— *A Defence of the Doctrine of the Resurrection of the same Body; In Two Parts. In the First of Which the Character, Writings, and Religious Principles of Mr. Lock Are Distinctly Considered: And, in the Second, the Doctrine of the Resurrection of the same Body is at large Explained and Defended, against the Notions and Principles of That Gentleman,* London: C. Rivington, 1727.

Home, Henry (Lord Kames), *Essays on the Principles of Morality and Natural Religion,* Edinburgh: R. Fleming, 1751.

Hooker, Thomas, *A Summe of Church Discipline,* 1643.

Hopkins, Samuel, *The Works of Samuel Hopkins, D.D … .With a Memoir of his Life and Character*, ed. Sewall Harding, 3 vols., Boston: Doctrinal Tract and Book Society, 1852.

Horbery, Matthew, *An Enquiry into the Scripture-Doctrine concerning the Duration of Future Punishment: In which the Texts of the New testament, relating to this Subject, are considered; and the Doctrine, drawn from them alone, is shewn to be consistent with Reason. Occasion'd by some late Writings, and particularly Mr. Whiston's Discourse of Hell-Torments,* London: James Fletcher, 1744.

Horne, George, 'Some considerations on Mr. Locke's Scheme of Deriving Government from an Original Compact,' in William Jones (ed.), *The Scholar Armed, against the Errors of the Time,* London: E. and C. Rivington, 1795.

Horsey, John, *Evidences of Christianity,* Doctor Williams's Library, London, MS 69.1.

—— *Five Lectures on Government and thirteen on the British Constitution,* Doctor Williams's Library, London, MS 69.3.

—— *Lectures to Young Persons on the Intellectual and Moral Powers of Man; the Existence, Character, and Government of God; and the Evidences of Christianity,* London: Samuel Leigh, 1828.

[Horsey, John], *Thoughts concerning the Inspiration of the*

Scriptures, Doctor Williams's Library, London, MS. 69.2.

—— *Institutes of Moral Philosophy,* Doctor Williams's Library, London, MS 69.5.

—— *Lectures Introductory to the Study of the New Testament,* Doctor Williams's Library, London, MS 69.16.

Howard, Simeon, *A Sermon Preached To the Ancient and Honourable Artillery-Company, in Boston, New-England, June 7th, 1773. Being the Anniversary of their Election of Officers,* Boston: John Boyles, 1773.

Howe, John, *The Works of John Howe,* ed. Henry Rogers, London, 6 vols., 1862–3.

Hume, David, *A Treatise of Human Nature* (1738), London: Dent, 2 vols., n.d.

Hutcheson, Francis, *An Inquiry into the Original of our Ideas of Beauty and Virtue; in Two Treatises,* (1725), London, 4th corrected edn, London: D. Midwinter et al., 1738.

—— *Illustrations on the Moral Sense,* ed. W. Bernard Peach, Cambridge, Mass.: The Belknap Press of Harvard University Press, 1971.

—— *A Short Introduction to Moral Philosophy,* Glasgow: Robert Foulis, 1747.

—— *A System of Moral Philosophy,* Glasgow: R. Foulis and London: A. Millar, T. Longman, 2 vols., 1755.

[James, Stephen], *A System of Theology,* 3 vols., The Congregational Library at Doctor Williams's Library, London, MS 1.h.1-3.

Jefferson, Thomas, *The Writings of Thomas Jefferson,* ed. Paul Leicester Ford, 10 vols., New York: G. P. Putnam, 1892–9.

Jenkin, Robert, *Remarks on Some Books Lately Published, viz. Mr. Basnage's History of the Jews, Whiston's Eight Sermons, Lock's Paraphrases and Notes on St. Paul's Epistles, Le Clerc's Bibliothèque Choisie,* London: W. B. for R. Sare, 1709.

—— *The Reasonableness and Certainty of the Christian Religion* (1698), 5th edn, London, 1721.

J[ennings], J[ohn], *Logica in usum Juventutis Academicae,* Northampton, 1721.

Jenyns, Soame, 'On rational Christianity,' in *The Works of Soame Jenyns,* London: T. Cadell, 1790, III, 245–56.

Johnson, Samuel, *Samuel Johnson President of King's College: His Career and Writings,* eds. Herbert and Carol Schneider, New

York: Columbia University Press, 4 vols., 1929.

Kentish, John, *The Accomplished Teacher of Religion: a Sermon, preached at the New Meeting House, Birmingham, November 22, 1829, on occasion of the death of the Rev. Thomas Belsham,* Birmingham: James Belcher, 1830.

Kippis, Andrew, *A Vindication of the Protestant Dissenting Ministers, with regard to their late Application to Parliament,* London: G. Robinson, 2nd edn corrected and enlarged, 1773.

—— *A Sermon Preached at the Old Jewry, on Wednesday the 26th of April, 1786, on Occasion of a New Academical Institution, among Protestant Dissenters, for the Education of their Ministers and Youth,* London: H. Goldney, 1786.

—— *An Address delivered at the Interment of the late Rev. Richard Price on the twenty-sixth of April 1791,* London, 1791.

Langdon, Samuel, *The Co-incidence of Natural with Revealed Religion,* Boston: Samuel Hall, 1776.

Lardner, Nathanael, *The Works of Nathaniel Lardner, D.D.,* London: William Ball, 10 vols., 1835-8.

Latham, Ebenezer, *Sermons on Various Subjects,* London: J. Dodsley, 2 vols., 1774.

Law, Edmund, *A Defence of Mr. Locke's opinion concerning Personal Identity; in Answer to the First Part of a Late Essay on That Subject,* Cambridge: J. Archdeacon, 1769.

Law, William, *The Case of Reason, Or Natural Religion Fully and Fairly Stated,* London: W. Innys, 1731.

—— *An Appeal to all that Doubt, or Disbelieve the Truths of the Gospel, Whether they be Deists, Arians, Socinians, or Nominal Christians, etc.,* London: W. Innys, 1742.

—— *An Humble, Earnest and Affectionate Address to the Clergy* (1761), 3rd edn, London: G. Robinson, 1774.

Layton, Henry, *Observations upon a Sermon Intituled, A Confutation of Atheism from the Faculties of the Soul, alias, Matter and Motion cannot think: Preached April 4, 1692. By way of Refutation,* 1692.

LeClerc, Jean, *The Life and Character of Mr. John Locke, Author of the Essay concerning Humane Understanding, Written in French, by Mr. LeClerc, and Done into Engish by T. F. P., Gent.,* London: J. Clark, 1706.

Lee, Henry, *Anti-Scepticism; or, Notes upon Each Chapter of ... Lock's Essay concerning Human Understanding; with an*

Explication of All the Particulars of Which He treats, and in the Same Order. In Four Books, London: R. Clavel and C. Harper, 1702.

Leland, John, *An Answer to a Late Book intituled Christianity as Old as the Creation. In Two Parts*, Dublin: S. Powell, 1733.

—— *A Second Letter containing Remarks on a Late Pamphlet, entitled, Christianity not founded on Argument*, London: R. Hett, 1744.

—— *A View of the Principal Deistical Writers that have Appeared in England in the last and present Century; with Observations upon them, and some Account of the Answers that have been published against them. In several Letters to a Friend*, London: B. Dod, 1754.

—— *The Advantage and Necessity of the Christian Revelation, shewn from the State of Religion in the Antient Heathen World: especially with respect to the Knowledge and Worship of the One True God: A Rule of Moral Duty: and A State of Future Rewards and Punishments. To which is prefixed, A Preliminary Discourse on Natural and Revealed Religion. In Two Volumes*, London: W. Richardson and S. Clark, 1764.

[Leslie, C.], *The Second Part of the Wolf Stript of his Shepherds Cloathing*, London, 1707.

Long, Thomas, *The Letter for Toleration Decipher'd, and the Absurdity and Impiety of an Absolute Toleration Demonstrated, by the Judgment of the Presbyterians, Independents, and by Mr. Calvin, Mr. Baxter, and the Parliament*, London: F. Collins, 1689.

Lowde, James, *A Discourse concerning the Nature of Man, Both in his Natural and Political Capacity: Both As He Is a Rational Creature, and Member of a Civil Society. With an Examination of Some of Mr. Hobb's Opinions relating Hereunto*, London: T. Warren for W. Kittilby, 1694.

—— *Moral Essays: Wherein Some of Mr. Lock's and Monsir. Malbranch's Opinions Are Briefly Examin'd. Together with an Answer to Some Chapters in the Oracles of Reason concerning Deism*, York: J. White for Fra. Hildyard, 1699.

Ludlam, Thomas, *Logical Tracts, Comprising Observations and Essays Illustrative of Mr. Locke's Treatise upon the Human Understanding; with Occasional Remarks on the Writings of … Reid and Stewart upon the Same Subject; and a Preface in*

Vindication of Mr. Locke, against the Mistakes and Misinterpretations of ... Milner, Dr. Horne ... Mr. Kett ... and Dr. Napleton ..., Cambridge: Watson, 1790.

Ludlam, W. and T., *Essays, Scriptural, Moral, and Logical,* London: J. G. Barnard, 2 vols. 1707.

Lupton, William, *The Resurrection of the Same Body: A Sermon Preach'd before the University of Oxford, at St. Mary's on Easter-Monday, Apr. 2, 1711,* Oxford: J. Wilmot, 1711.

McGill, William, *A Practical Essay on the Death of Jesus Christ,* Edinburgh, 1786.

Manning, James, *A Sketch of the Life and Writings of the Rev. Micaijah Towgood,* Exeter, 1792.

Martin, Josiah, *A Vindication of Women's Preaching, As Well from Holy Scripture ... as from the Paraphrase and Notes of the Judicious John Locke, on I Cor. xi. Wherein the brief observations of B. C. on the Said Paraphrase and notes, and the Arguments in His Book, intituled, Reflections, &c., Are Fully Consider'd,* London: J. Sowle, 1717.

Mason, John, *Select Remains,* reprinted as *Mason's Sayings,* Sheffield: Zoar Publications, *c.*1974.

Mather, Cotton, *Reasonable Religion: Or, the Truths of the Christian Religion Demonstrated. With Incontestable Proofs, that those who would Act Reasonably, must Live Religiously,* London, 1713.

—— *The Christian Philosopher: A Collection of the Best Discoveries in Nature, with Religious Improvements,* London, 1721.

Mather, Samuel, *An Apology for the Liberty of the Churches in New England,* Boston: T. Fleet, 1738.

Mayhew, Experience, *A Discourse shewing that God Dealeth with Men as with Reasonable Creatures,* Boston: B. Green, 1720.

Mayhew, Jonathan, *Seven Sermons ... Preached At a Lecture in the West Meeting-House In Boston, Begun the first Thursday in June, and ended the last Thursday In August, 1748,* Boston: Rogers and Fowle, 1749.

[Metternich, Wolf von], *Faith and Reason Compared: Shewing That Divine Faith and Natural Reason Proceed from Two Different and Distinct Principles in Man. Against the Notions and Errors of the Modern Rationalists, Written originally in Latin by a Person of Quality; in Answer to Certain Theses (Drawn from Lock's Principles) concerning Faith and Reason. With a new*

Preface, concerning Reason, Philosophy, Morality & Religion, London: B. Cowse, 1713.

[Milner, John], *An Account of Mr. Lock's Religion, Out of His Own Writings, and in His own Words. Together with Some Observations upon It, and a Twofold Appendix: I. A Specimen of Mr. Lock's Way of Answering Authors, out of hs Essay 1.I,c.3, where he takes upon him to Examine some of the Lord Herbert's Principles. II. A brief Enquiry whether Socinianism be justly Charged upon Mr. Lock*, London: J. Nutt, 1700.

Monthly Repository of Theology and General Literature, various volumes.

Morell, Thomas, *Notes and Annotations on Locke on the Human Understanding. Written by Order of the Queen*, London: G. Sael, 1794.

Napleton, John, *Advice to a Student in the University, Concerning the Qualifications and Duties of a Minister of the Gospel in the Church of England*, Oxford: Fletcher and Hanwell, 1795.

Norris, John, *Cursory Reflections upon a Book Call'd, an Essay concerning human understanding.* In idem, *The Christian Blessedness; or, Discourses upon the Beatitudes of our Lord and Saviour Jesus Christ*, London: S. Manship, 1690; reprinted 1692.

—— *An Account of Reason and Faith in Relation to the Mysteries of Christianity*, London: S. Manship, 1697.

—— *An Essay towards the Theory of the Ideal or Intelligible World, Part I. Design'd for Two Parts. The First Considering It Absolutely in itself, and the Second in Relation to Human Understanding*, London: S. Manship, 1701.

—— *An Essay Towards the Theory of the Ideal or Intelligible World. Part II*, London: S. Manship, 1704.

Notcutt, William, *A Reply to H.B.'s Vindication of Robert Barclay's Apology*, Ipswich, 1733.

[Nye, Stephen], *The Exceptions of Mr. Edwards, in His Causes of Atheism, against The Reasonableness of Christianity, as Deliver'd in the Scriptures, Examin'd and Found Unreasonable, Unscriptural, and Injurious.* In *A Third Collection of Tracts, Proving the God and Father of Our Lord Jesus Christ the Only True God*, 1695.

Oakes, Abraham, *The Doctrine of Hell-torments distinctly discussed*, 1740.

Ogden, Uzal, *Antidote to Deism. The Deist Unmasked*, 2 vols.,

Newark: John Woods, 1795.

Oliver, Edward, *An Analysis of Mr. Locke's Essay concerning Human Understanding,* London: B. McMillan, 1810.

[Oswald, James], *Appeal to Common Sense in Behalf of Religion,* Edinburgh: A. Kincaird and J. Bell, 1766; London: J. Hughes, 2 vols., 1768.

Owen, John, *The Works of John Owen,* ed. William Goold (1850–3), London: The Banner of Truth Trust, 16 vols., 1968.

[Owen, Josiah], *The Difficulties and Discouragements that attend the Dissenting Ministry. With the most Proper Methods to Remove Them; Impartially Consider'd, in a Sermon Preach'd to a Congregation of Protestant Dissenters,* London: R. Hett, 1735.

Paley, William, *Principles of Moral and Political Philosophy,* (1785), Edinburgh: James Robertson, 1817.

—— *The Evidences of Christianity* (1794), ed. F. A. Malleson, London: Ward, Lock, n.d.

Palmer, Elihu, *Principles of Nature; or, a Development of the Moral Causes of Happiness and Misery among the Human Species,* London, 1819.

Parker, Samuel, *Essays on Divers Weighty and Curious Subjects, Particularly on Mr. Lock's and Sir William Temple's Notions,* London: N. Cox, 1702.

—— *A letter to Mr. Bold, occasion'd by his late discourse concerning the resurrection of the same body,* 1707.

Parry, William et al., *An Introductory Discourse by Samuel Newton, an address to the minister, By Robert Stevenson, and a Sermon to the People, by William Parry; Delivered on the Solemn Separation of The Rev. Thomas Craig to the Pastoral Office In the Congregational Church at Bocking in Essex, October 12, 1802. To which is prefixed a Discourse, delivered on the preceding evening by John Pye Smith,* 1802.

[Parry, William], *Lectures on the Being and Natural Perfection of God,* New College, London, Library at Doctor Williams's Library, London, MS L.17.1.

Peirce, James, *A Paraphrase and Notes on the Epistles of St. Paul to the Colossians, Philippians, and Hebrews: After the Manner of Mr. Locke,* London: J. Noon and J. Chandler, 1727.

Perronet, Vincent, *A Vindication of Mr. Locke, from the Charge of giving Encouragement to Scepticism and Infidelity, and from several other Mistakes and Objections of the Learned Author of the Procedure, Extent, and Limits of Human Understanding. Wherein Is Likewise Enquired, Whether Mr. Locke's Opinion of the Soul's Immateriality Was Not Mistaken by ... Leibnitz*, London: James, John and Paul Knapton, 1736.

—— *A Second Vindication of Mr. Locke. Wherein his Sentiments relating to personal Identity are Clear'd up from some Mistakes of The Rev. Dr. Butler, In His Dissertation on that Subject*, London: Fletcher Gyles, 1738.

Price, Richard, *A Review of the Principal Questions of Morals*, ed. D. D. Raphael, Oxford: Clarendon Press, 1974.

—— *Political Writings*, ed. D. O. Thomas, Cambridge: CUP, 1991.

Prideaux, Humphrey, *A Letter to the Deists: shewing that the Gospel of Jesus Christ is no Imposture; but the Sacred Truth of God*, London: J. H. for W. Rogers, 1697.

Priestley, Joseph, *The Theological and Miscellaneous Works of Joseph Priestley*, ed. J. T. Rutt, 25 vols., London 1817-31.

—— *Reflections on the Present State of Free Enquiry in this Country added to The Importance and Extent of Free Enquiry in Matters of Religion*, Birmingham, 1785.

—— *Lectures on History and General Policy*, Dublin: Luke White, 1788.

—— *Memoirs of the Rev. Dr. Joseph Priestley to the year 1795*, London: Joseph Johnson, 1809.

—— et al., Preface to *A View of Revealed Religion; A Sermon preached at the Ordination of The Rev. William Field of Warwick, July 12, 1790 by Joseph Priestley LL.D., F.R.S. With a Charge Delivered at the same Time by the Rev. Thomas Belsham*, Birmingham, 1790.

[Proast, Jonas], *The Argument of the Letter concerning Toleration Briefly Consider'd and Answer'd*, Oxford: H. West and A. Clements, 1690.

—— *A Third Letter concerning Toleration: In Defence of the Argument of the Letter concerning Toleration Briefly Consider'd and Answer'd*, Oxford: H. Lichfield for G. West and H. Clements, 1691.

Rawes, William, *The Gospel Ministry of Women, under the Christian Dispensation, Defended from Scripture, and from the writings of John Locke, Josiah Martin, etc.*, London: W. Phillips, 1801.

Rees, Abraham, *The Advantages of Knowledge, Illustrated and Recommended in a Sermon, delivered on Wednesday the 30th of April, 1788. At the Meeting-House in the Old Jewry, London, to the Supporters of a new Academical Institution among Protestant Dissenters,* London: H. Goldney, 1788.

Rees, Thomas, *Address delivered at the Old Jewry Chapel in Jewin Street, on Saturday, the 19th day of June, 1825, over the body of the late Rev. Abraham Rees, D.D., F.R.S., &c., previously to his interment in Bunhill Fields,* London: Longman, 1825.

Reid, Thomas, *An Inquiry into the Human Mind, on the Principles of Common Sense* (Edinburgh, 1764), in his Works, ed. W. Hamilton, Edinburgh: MacLachlan and Stewart, 2 vols., 1863.

—— *Essays on the Intellectual Powers of Man* (Edinburgh, 1785), in ibid.

—— *Practical Ethics,* ed. Knud Kaakonssen, Princeton: Princeton University Press, 1990.

Reynolds, John, *Three Letters to a Deist,* London, 1725.

Rippon, John, *A Brief Memoir of the Life and Writings of the Late Rev. John Gill, D.D.,* London, 1738.

Robinson, Robert, *Arcana, or the Principles of the late Petitioners to Parliament for Relief in matter of Subscription,* Cambridge: Fletcher & Hodson, 1774.

[Roche, Antoine Martin], *Traité de la nature de l'âme et de l'origine de ses connoissances. Contre le système de M. Locke & de ses partisans,* Paris, 2 vols., 1759.

Rust, George, *A Discourse of the Use of Reason in Matters of Religion, showing that Christianity contains nothing repugnant to Right Reason, against Enthusiasts and Deists,* London, 1683.

[Sage, John], *The Reasonableness of a Toleration Enquired into, purely on Church-Principles,* 1705.

Scott, James, MSS, held by Messrs. Haward and Evers, Solicitors, Stourbridge.

Scott, Thomas, *The Force of Truth* (Edinburgh, 1799), London: The Religious Tract Society, n.d.

S[ergeant], J[ohn], *Solid Philosophy Asserted, Against the Fancies of the Ideists; or, The Method to Science Farther Illustrated ... With Reflexions on Mr. Locke's Essay concerning Human Understanding,* London: R. Clavil et al., 1697.

Sewall, Joseph, *Rulers must be Just, Ruling in the Fear of God,* Boston: B. Green, 1724.

Sherlock, William, *A Vindication of the Doctrine of the Holy and Ever Blessed Trinity*, London, 1690.

—— *A Discourse Concerning the Happiness of Good Men, and the Punishment of the Wicked in the Next World*, London, 1704.

Smith, Adam, *The Theory of Moral Sentiments*, eds. D. D. Raphael and A. L. Macfie, Oxford: Clarendon Press, 1976.

Smith, John Pye, *First Lines of Christian Theology, in the form of a Syllabus, for the use of the Students in the Academy at Homerton*, 1805, Doctor Williams's Library, London, MS L.18.2.

—— *A Sermon occasioned by the death of the Rev. Joseph Barber*, 1810.

South, Robert, *Twelve Sermons Preached on Several Occasions*, (1679), London, J. H. for Thomas Bennett, 1692.

—— *Animadversions upon Dr. Sherlock's Book*, London: Randal Taylor, 1693.

Stennett, Samuel, *The Mortality of Ministers contrasted with the Unchangeableness of Christ: in a Sermon occasioned by the decease of the Rev. Caleb Evans, D.D. Who departed this Life Aug. 9, 1791, in the 54th Year of his Age: Preached at Broad-Mead, Bristol, Aug. 21, 1791, by Samuel Stennett, D.D. To which is added the Address delivered at his Interment, by the Rev. John Tommas*, London: Rivington and Marshall, 1791.

Stewart, Dugald, *Philosophical Essays*, Edinburgh: W. Creech, 1810.

Stiles, Ezra, *The Literary Diary of Ezra Stiles, D.D.*, 3 vols., New York: Scribners, 1901.

Stillingfleet, Edward, *A Rational Account of the Grounds of Protestant Religion* (1665), Oxford, 2 vols., 1844.

—— *A Discourse in Vindication of the Doctrine of the Trinity. With an Answer to the Late Socinian Objections against It from Scripture, Antiquity and Reason, etc.*, (1696), London: J.H. for H. Mortlock, 2nd edn, 1697.

—— *The Bishop of Worcester's Answer to Mr. Locke's Letter, concerning Some passages Relating to His Essay of Humane Understanding*, London: J.H. for H. Mortlock, 1697.

—— *The Bishop of Worcester's Answer to Mr. Locke's Second Letter: Wherein His Notion of Ideas is Prov'd to Be inconsistent with It Self and with the Articles of the Christian Faith*, London: J.H. for H. Mortlock, 1698.

Strutt, Samuel, *A Defence of the Late learned Dr. Clarke's Notion of*

Natural Liberty: In Answer to Three Letters wrote to him by a Gentleman at the University of Cambridge, on the Side of Necessity. Together with Some Remarks on Mr. Locke's Chapter of Power, London: T. Green, 1730.

Taylor, Abraham, *The True Scripture-Doctrine of the Holy and Ever-Blessed Trinity, Stated and Defended, in opposition to the Arian Scheme,* London: John Clark and Richard Hett, 2 vols., 1727.

—— *The Scripture Doctrine of the Trinity Vindicated. In Opposition to Mr. Watts's Scheme of One Divine Person and Two Divine Powers,* London: J. Roberts, 2nd edn, 1728.

—— *Lectures on Natural and Revealed Theology; Delivered at the Academy, at Deptford,* 1739. The Congregational Library at Doctor Williams's Library, London, MS 1.d.34.

—— *An Introduction to Logick, with a few Lectures, on Perception, the first part of that Science,* 1739. Doctor Williams's Library, London, MS 69.24.

Taylor, Dan, *An Essay on the Truth and Inspiration of the Holy Scriptures,* London: T. Knott et al., 1790.

Taylor, Jeremy, *A Discourse of the Liberty of Prophesying,* London, 1647.

Taylor, John, *The Scripture-Doctrine of Original Sin,* London, 1740.

—— *A Narrative of Mr. Joseph Rawson's Case,* 2nd edn, London: M. Ferrier, 1742.

—— Dedication of *A Paraphrase, with Notes on the Epistle to the Romans,* 1745.

—— *The Scripture Account of Prayer,* London, 1761.

—— *A Scheme of Scripture Divinity,* London, 1762.

Taylor, Nathaniel W., *Concio ad Clerum,* New Haven: Hezekiah Howe, 1828.

Tenison, Thomas, *An Argument for Union, taken from the True Interest of those Dissenters in England, who Profess, and Call themselves Protestants,* London: Tho. Basset et al., 1683. This is reprinted in *A Collection of Cases and other Discussion lately written to recover Dissenters to the Communion of the Church of England. By some Divines of the City of London, etc.,* London: T. Basset and B. Tooke, 1685, vol. II.

Tennent, Gilbert, *Sermons,* Speer Library, Princeton Theological Seminary, MS T2563.

—— *Twenty-three Sermons upon the Chief End of Man, the Divine*

Authority of Scripture, the Being and Attributes of God, and the Doctrine of the Trinity, Philadelphia: William Bradford, 1744.

—— *Discourses on several Important Subjects*, Philadelphia: William Bradford, 1745.

Tertullian, *Ad Scapulam.*

Thomson, John, *The Government of the Church of Christ*, Philadelphia: A. Bradford, 1741.

Tillotson, John, *The Works of the Most Reverend Dr. John Tillotson*, ed. T. Birch, (1752), 1820.

Tindal, Matthew, *Christianity as Old as the Creation: or, the Gospel, a Republication of the Religion of Nature*, London, 1730.

[Toland, John], *Christianity Not Mysterious; or, A Treatise Shewing That There is Nothing in the Gospel Contrary to Reason Nor Above It; and that No Christian Doctrine Can Be Properly Call'd a Mystery* (1695), Stuttgart–Bad Cannstatt: Friedrich Frommann Verlag, 1964.

Tommas, John, see under Stennett, Samuel, above.

Tooke, John Horne, *Epea Pteroenta; or, The Diversions of Purley*, London: J. Johnson, 1786.

Toothill, Jonathan, *The Foundation of the dying Christian's Triumph, in the Prospect of Nature's Dissolution. A Sermon, preached, Feb. 2, 1783, at Heckmondwike in Yorkshire; on occasion of the Death of the Rev. Mr. James Scott, late Pastor of the Church, and Tutor to an Academy at that Place*, Huddersfield: J. Brook, 1783.

Toplady, A. M., *The Works of The Rev. A. M. Toplady, A.B., Late Vicar of Broad Hembury, Devon*, 6 vols., London: Ebenezer Palmer, 1828.

Towers, Joseph, *A Vindication of the Political Principles of Mr. Locke, in Answer to the Objections of The Rev. Dr. Tucker, Dean of Gloucester*, London G. Robinson, 1782.

Towle, Thomas, see Barber, Joseph, above.

Traill, Robert, *The Works of the Late Reverend Robert Traill, A.M. Minister of the Gospel in London* (1810), Edinburgh: The Banner of Truth Trust, 4 vols. in 2, 1975.

Tucker, Abraham, *The Light of Nature Pursued*, London: T. Payne, 1768.

Tucker, Josiah, *The Notions of Mr. Locke, and His Followers, That All Civil Governments Whatever, Not Founded on the Personal Choice of the Governed, Are So Many usurpations on the*

Unalienable Rights of Mankind, Considered and Examined, Gloucester, 1778.

—— *A Treatise concerning Civil Government. In Three Parts,* London: T. Cadell, 1781.

—— *Four Letters on Important National Subjects, Addressed to the Right Hon. The Earl of Shelburne,* Gloucester: R. Raikes, 1783.

Turner, Baptist Noel, *Candid Suggestions; in Eight Letters to Soame Jenyns, Esq; on the Respective Subjects of His Disquisitions, lately published; With Some Remarks on the Answerer of his Seventh Disquisition, Respecting the Principles of Mr. Locke,* London: T. Lowndes, 1783.

Warburton, William, *The Works of … William Warburton,* London, 7 vols., 1788–94; 3rd edn, 1809.

—— *The Doctrine of Grace: or, The Office and Operations of the Holy Spirit Vindicated from The Insults of Infidelity, and the Abuses of Fanaticism: concluding With some Thoughts (humbly offered to the consideration of the Established Clergy) With regard to The right method of defending Religion against the attacks of either Party,* London: A. R. Millar et al., 2 vols., 1763.

Waterland, Daniel, *The Works of the Rev. Daniel Waterland, D.D. Formerly Master of Magdalene College, Cambridge, Canon of Windsor, and Archdeacon of Middlesex; now first Collected and Arranged. To which is prefixed a Review of the Author's Life and Writings, by William Van Mildert, D.D. Lord Bishop of Llandaff,* Oxford: Clarendon Press, 1823.

Watson, Richard, *A letter to the members of the honourable House of Commons; respecting the petition for relief in the matter of subscription, by a Christian Whig,* London: J. Nichols, 1772.

—— *A Charge delivered to the Clergy of the Diocese of Llandaff, June 1791,* London: Thomas Evans, et al., 1792.

—— *An Apology for Christianity in a Series of Letters addressed to Edward Gibbon, Esq.,* Cambridge: J. Archdeacon, 1796.

—— *A Defence of Revealed Religion, in Two Sermons preached in the Cathedral Church of Llandaff; and a Charge delivered to the Clergy of that Diocese in June 1795,* London, 1795.

Watts, Isaac, *The Works of the Rev. Isaac Watts, D.D.,* Leeds: Edward Baines, 1800.

[Webb, Francis?], *The Morality of the New Testament, Digested under various Heads, Comprehending The Duties which we owe to God, to Ourselves, and to our Fellow-Creatures. With an*

Introduction addressed to Deists; in which The Character of Jesus Christ is vindicated against the Aspersions of modern Unbelievers; and also An Attempt is made to prove, that the Religion taught by Jesus Christ was the Pure Religion of Nature and of Reason. The Whole concluding with Observations on a late Treatise, intitled, The Doctrine of Grace, written by Dr. Warburton, Bishop of Gloucester; together with An Inquiry how far the Belief of any Doctrine may be Necessary to Salvation; and some Observations on the Arguments of Mr. Locke and Dr. Leland. By a Rational Christian, London: J. Johnson, 1765.

Wesley, John, *A Calm Address to Our American Colonies,* London: R. Hawes, 1755.

—— *The Works of the Rev. John Wesley, A.M.,* ed. Thomas Jackson, London: John Mason, 14 vols. 1829–31.

—— *The Letters of the Rev. John Wesley, A.M.,* ed. John Telford, London: Epworth Press, 1931.

—— *Sermons on Several Occasions,* London: Epworth Press, 1944.

—— *The Appeals to Men of Reason and Religion,* ed. Gerald R. Cragg (vol.XI of *The Works of John Wesley,* ed. Frank Baker), Oxford: Clarendon Press, 1975.

[West, Richard?], *Animadversions on a Late Book Entituled The Reasonableness of Christianity, As Delivered in the Scriptures,* Oxford: L. Lichfield for G. West and A. Piesley, 1697.

West, Samuel, *Essays on Liberty and Necessity,* Boston: Samuel Hall, 1793.

West, Stephen, *An Essay on Moral Agency: containing, Remarks on a late anonymous publication, entitled, An Examination of the late Reverend President Edwards's Enquiry on Freedom of the Will,* New Haven: Thomas and Samuel Green, [1772].

Whichcote, Benjamin, *Moral and Religious Aphorisms,* F. Burgess, Norwich, for A. J. Churchill, London, 1703.

Whiston, William, *A New Theory of the Earth,* London: R. Roberts for Benj. Tooke, 1696.

—— *Sermons and Essays upon Several Subjects,* London: Benj. Took, 1709.

—— *Reflexions on an Anonymous Pamphlet, Entituled, a Discourse of Free Thinking,* London, 1710.

—— *Primitive Christianity Reviv'd,* London, 1711-12.

—— *The Eternity of Hell Torments Considered,* London, 1740.

—— *Memoirs of the Life and Writings of Mr. William Whiston.*

Containing Memoirs of several of his Friends also (1713), London, 1749.

Whitby, Daniel, *A Paraphrase and Commentary upon the New Testament,* London: W. Boyer, 1703.

Whitefield, George, *Journals,* London: The Banner of Truth Trust, 1960.

Willard, Samuel, *A Compleat Body of Divinity in Two Hundred and Fifty Expository Lectures on the Assembly Shorter Catechism. Wherein the Doctrines of the Christian Religion are unfolded, their Truth confirm'd, their Excellence display'd their Usefulness inprov'd, Errors & Vices refuted and expos'd, Objections answer'd, Controversies settled, Cases of Conscience resolv'd; and a great light thereby reflected on the present Age,* Boston: B. Green and S. Kneeland, 1726.

[Williams, Elisha], *The Essential Rights and Liberties of Protestants, A Seasonable Plea for The Liberty of Conscience, and the Right of Private Judgment, In Matters of Religion, Without any Controul from human Authority,* Boston, 1744.

Williams, Roger, *The Bloudy Tenent of Persecution for cause of conscience discussed and Mr. Cotton's Letter examined and answered,* 1644.

[Willis, Richard], *The Occasional Papers,* London, 1697; q.v. Anon., above.

Wilson, Walter, *History and Antiquities of Dissenting Churches and Meeting-houses in London, Westminster and Southwark,* 1808.

Wilton, Samuel, *An Apology for the Renewal of an Application to Parliament by the Protestant Dissenting Ministers, Addressed to the Thirteen Ministers who Protested against it. In which the Evidence and Force of their Reasons are fairly examined, and the Application is shewn to be neither inconsistent with the Principles of Orthodoxy, or Loyalty,* London: J. Buckland, W. Harris and S. Gardner, 1773.

Winder, Henry, *Note Books* when at Whitehaven Academy, 1708–13., Harris Manchester College, Oxford, MS Winder 1.1(i).

Wise, John, *A Vindication of the Government of New-England Churches, etc.,* Boston: John Bayles, 1672.

Witherspoon, John, *An Annotated Edition of Lectures on Moral Philosophy by John Witherspoon,* ed. Jack Scott, Newark: University of Delaware Press, 1982.

[Witty, John], *The First Principles of Modern Deism Confuted. In a Demonstration of the Immateriality, Natural Eternity, and Immortality of Thinking Substances in general; and in particular of Human Souls. Even upon the Supposition that we are intirely ignorant of the Intrinsic Natures of the Essences of Things*, London, 1707.

—— *The Reasonableness of Assenting to the Mysteries of Christianity Asserted and Vindicated,* 1708.

Woolston, Thomas, *Works,* London, various edns 1705–33.

Worthington, William, *The Evidence of Christianity,* London, 2 vols., 1769.

Part V: Select Index of Post-Eighteenth-Century Works

Aaron, R. I., *John Locke,* London: OUP, 1937.

—— 'Great thinkers. (X) John Locke', *Philosophy,* XII, 1937, 19–32.

Aarsleff, H., 'Locke's influence', in Vere Chappell (ed.), *The Cambridge Companion,* q.v., ch.X.

Adams, R. M., 'Berkeley's "notion" of spiritual substance', *Archiv für Geschichte der Philosophie,* LV, 1973, 47–69.

Ahlstrom, Sydney E., 'The Scottish philosophy and American theology', *Church History,* XXIV, no.3, September 1955, 257–72.

Aldrich, P. Emory, 'John Locke and the influence of his works in America', *Proceedings of the American Antiquarian Society,* 1879.

Allison, Henry E., 'Locke's theory of personal identity: a re-examination', *Journal of the History of Ideas,* XXVII, no.1, 1966, 41–58.

Anderson, Wallace E., 'Immaterialism in Jonathan Edwards' early philosophical notes', *Journal of the History of Ideas,* XXV, no.2, 1964, 181–200.

—— 'Editor's Introduction' to *The Works of Jonathan Edwards, VI, Scientific and Philosophical Writings,* New Haven: Yale University Press, 1980.

Angus, J., *The Voluntary System,* London: Jackson and Walford, 1839.

—— *Christian Churches: The Noblest Form of Social Life; The Representatives of Christ on Earth; The Dwelling-Place of the Holy Spirit,* London: Ward, 1862.

Ardley, Gavin, *The Common Sense Philosophy of James Oswald,* Aberdeen: Aberdeen University Press, 1980.

Ashcraft, Richard, 'Faith and knowledge in Locke's philosophy', in John W. Yolton (ed.), *John Locke: Problems and Perspectives,* q.v.

—— *Revolutionary Politics and Locke's Two Treatises of Government,* Princeton: Princeton University Press, 1986.

—— *Locke's Two Treatises of Government,* London: Allen & Unwin, 1987.

—— 'Latitudinarianism and toleration: historical myth versus political history', in Richard Kroll et al. (eds), *Philosophy, Science and Religion,* q.v., ch. VII.

Atkins, Gaius Glenn and Fagley, Frederick L., *History of American Congregationalism,* Boston: The Pilgrim Press, 1942.

Axon, Francis and Nicholson, Ernest, *The Older Nonconformity of Kendal,* Kendal: Titus Wilson, 1915.

Ayers, M. R., 'Mechanism, superaddition, and the proof of God's existence in Locke's *Essay*', *Philosophical Review,* XC no. 2, 1981, 210–51.

—— *Locke,* London: Routledge, 2 vols., 1991.

—— 'The foundations of knowledge and the logic of substance: the structure of Locke's general philosophy', in G. A. J. Rogers (ed.), *Locke's Philosophy,* q.v.

Bainton, Roland H., *The Travail of Religious Liberty. Nine Biographical Studies,* Philadelphia: Westminster Press, 1951.

Baker, Frank, 'John Wesley and Bishop Joseph Butler', *Proceedings of the Wesley Historical Society,* XLII, May 1980, 3-10.

Barnes, Jonathan, 'Scepticism and relativity', *Philosophical Studies,* XXXII, 1988–90, 1–31.

Beach, Waldo, 'Sectarianism and skepticism: the strange allies of religious liberty', in F. H. Little (ed.), *Reformation,* q.v., 199-211.

Becker, Carl L., *The Heavenly City of the Eighteenth-Century Philosophers,* New Haven: Yale University Press, 1932.

Bennett, Jonathan, *Locke, Berkeley, Hume Central Themes,* Oxford: Clarendon Press, 1971.

—— 'Locke's philosophy of mind', in Vere Chappell (ed.), *The Cambridge Companion,* q.v., ch.IV.

Berg, J. van den, 'The Leiden professors of the Schultens family and their contacts with British scholars', *Durham University Journal,* LXXV, no.1, December 1982, 1–14.

—— 'Creatieve vriendschap: John Locke (1632–1704) en Philippus van Limborch (1633–1712)', in *Voorbeeldige Vriendschap. Vrienden en vriendinnen in theologie en cultur,* Groningen: Styx Publications, 1993.

—— and Geoffrey F. Nuttall, *Philip Doddridge (1702-1751) and the Netherlands,* Leiden: E. J. Brill/Leiden University Press, 1987.

Biddle, John C., 'John Locke on Christianity: His Context and Text', doctoral dissertation, Stanford University, 1972.

—— 'Locke's critique of innate principles and Toland's deism', *Journal of the History of Ideas,* XXXVII, no.3, 1976, 411-22; reprinted in John W. Yolton (ed.), *Philosophy, Religion and Science,* q.v., ch.X.

Bill, E. G. W., *Education at Christ Church, Oxford 1660-1800,* Oxford: Clarendon Press, 1988.

Blackstone, William, *Francis Hutcheson and Contemporary Ethical Theory,* Athens, Ga.: University of Georgia Press, 1965.

Bluhm, William T., Wintfeld, Neil and Teger, Stuart H., 'Locke's idea of God: rational truth or political myth?', *The Journal of Politics,* XLL, no.2, May 1980, 414–38.

Bolam, C. Gordon, Goring, Jeremy, Short, H. L. and Thomas, Roger, *The English Presbyterians: From Elizabethan Puritanism to Modern Unitarianism,* London: Allen & Unwin, 1968.

Boorstin, Daniel, *America and the Image of Europe: Reflections on American Thought,* New York: Meridian Books, 1960.

Bourne, H. R. Fox, *The Life of John Locke,* London: Henry S. King, 2 vols., 1876.

Brace, Laura, Review of D. Wootton, *John Locke: Political Writings,* in *The Locke Newsletter,* XXVI, 1995, 188–93.

Brain, Timothy, 'Richard Watson and the debate on toleration in the late eighteenth-century', *The Price–Priestley Newsletter,* II, 1978, 4–26.

Braithwaite, Joseph Bevan, *Memoirs of Joseph John Gurney with Selections from his Journal and Correspondence,* Philadelphia: Lippincott, 4th edn, 1859.

Brantley, Richard E., *Locke, Wesley and the Method of English Romanticism,* Gainesville, Fla.: University of Florida Press, 1984.

Briggs, J. H. Y., *The English Baptists of the 19th Century,* Didcot: The Baptist Historical Society, 1994.

Brinkley, Richard, 'A liberal churchman: Edmund Law,' *Enlightenment and Dissent,* VI, 1987, 3–18.

Brinton, Alan, 'The passions as subject matter in early eighteenth-century sermons,' *Rhetorica,* X, no.1, Winter 1992, 49–66.

Broadie, Alexander, 'Thomas Reid and his pre-Reformation Scottish precursors,' in Peter Jones (ed.), *Philosophy,* q.v., ch.I.

Brown, Raymond, *The English Baptists of the 18th Century,* London: The Baptist Historical Society, 1986.

Brown, Stuart (ed.), *Routledge History of Philosophy, V: British Philosophy and the Age of Enlightenment,* London: Routledge, 1996.

Byrne, James W., 'John Locke's philosophy of religious toleration,' *The Personalist,* XLVI, 1965, 245–52.

Caird, Edward, *A Critical Account of the Philosophy of Kant,* Glasgow: Maclehose, 1877.

—— *Essays on Literature and Philosophy,* Glasgow: Maclehose, 2 vols., 1892.

Cameron, James K., 'Theological controversy: a factor in the origins of the Scottish Enlightenment,' in R. H. Campbell and Andrew S. Skinner, eds., *The Origins,* q.v., ch.VII.

Campbell, R. H., and Skinner, Andrew S. (eds.), *The Origins and Nature of the Scottish Enlightenment,* Edinburgh: John Donald, 1982.

Canovan, Margaret, 'Two concepts of liberty – eighteenth-century style,' *The Price–Priestley Newsletter,* II, 1978, 27–43.

Carpenter, S. C., *Eighteenth Century Church and People,* London: John Murray, 1959.

Carroll, Robert Todd, *The Common-Sense Philosophy of Bishop Edward Stillingfleet, 1635-1699,* The Hague: Martinus Nijhoff, 1975.

Carter, Jennifer J. and Pittock, Joan H., *Aberdeen and the Enlightenment,* Aberdeen: Aberdeen University Press, 1987.

Chappell, Vere (ed.), *The Cambridge Companion to Locke,* Cambridge: CUP, 1994.

—— 'Locke on the freedom of the will', in G. A. J. Rogers (ed.), *Locke's Philosophy,* q.v.

Clark, J. C. D., *English Society, 1688–1832: Ideology, Social*

Structure and Political Practice during the Ancien Régime, Cambridge: CUP, 1985.

Cleal, Edward E., *The Story of Congregationalism in Surrey,* London: James Clarke, 1908.

Coakley, John, 'John Henry Livingston and the liberty of the conscience', *Reformed Review,* XLVI, no.2, Winter 1992, 119–35.

Cocks, H. F. Lovell, 'Congregational churchmanship: the foundation in Christ', *Proceedings of the Seventh International Congregational Council,* London: Independent Press, 1953, 45–57.

Colie, Rosalie L., *Light and Enlightenment: A Study of the Cambridge Platonists and the Dutch Arminians,* Cambridge: CUP, 1957.

Collins, V. S., *President Witherspoon: A Biography,* Princeton: Princeton University Press, 2 vols., 1925.

Colman, John, *John Locke's Moral Philosophy,* Edinburgh: Edinburgh University Press, 1983.

Cone, Carl B., *Torchbearer of Freedom: The Influence of Richard Price on Eighteenth Century Thought,* Lexington: University of Kentucky Press, 1952.

Cornwall, Robert D., 'Advocacy of the independence of the Church from the state in eighteenth-century England', *Enlightenment and Dissent,* XII, 1993, 12–27.

Cragg, Gerald R., *Reason and Authority in the Eighteenth Century,* Cambridge: CUP, 1964.

Cranston, Maurice, *John Locke. A Biography,* London: OUP, 1985.

—— 'John Locke and the case for toleration', in Horton and Mendus, q.v., 78–97.

Crimmins, James E., *Religion, Secularization and Political Thought,* London: Routledge, 1989.

Crocker, Lester G., 'Introduction' to John W. Yolton et al., (eds.), *The Blackwell Companion,* q.v.

Cunliffe, Christopher, (ed.), *Joseph Butler's Moral and Religious Thought,* Oxford: Clarendon Press, 1992.

Curti, Merle, 'The great Mr. Locke, America's philosopher, 1783–1861', *Huntington Library Bulletin,* XI, 1937, 107–51.

Dalgarno, Melvin T., 'Reid and the rights of man', *Man and Nature,* IV, 1985, 81–94.

—— and Matthews, Eric (eds), *The Philosophy of Thomas Reid,* Dordrecht: Kluwer Academic Publishers, 1989.

Davis, Arthur Paul, *Isaac Watts,* London: Independent Press, 1943.

Denney, James, *Jesus and the Gospel,* London: Hodder and Stoughton, 1909.

Deweese, Charles W., *Baptist Church Covenants,* Nashville: Broadman Press, 1990.

Diamond, Peter J., 'Reid, natural law and the science of man', in Jennifer J. Carter and Joan H. Pittock (eds.), *Aberdeen,* q.v., ch.XII.

Dickinson, H. T., 'The eighteenth-century debate on the "Glorious Revolution"', *History,* LXI, 1976, 28–45.

Duncan-Jones, Austin, *Butler's Moral Philosophy,* Harmondsworth: Penguin Books, 1952.

Dunn, John, *The Political Thought of John Locke: An Historical Account of the Argument of the Two Treatises of Government,* Cambridge: CUP, 1969.

—— 'From applied theology to social analysis: the break between John Locke and the Scottish Enlightenment', in Istvan Hort and Michael Ignatieff (eds.), *Wealth,* q.v., ch.V.

—— *John Locke,* Oxford: OUP, 1984.

—— 'The claim to freedom of conscience: freedom of speech, freedom of thought, freedom of worship?', in Ole Peter Grell, et al. (eds), *From Persecution,* q.v., ch.VII.

Duffy, E. 'A Rubb-up for Old Sores: Jesuits, Jansenists, and the English secular clergy, 1705–15', *Journal of Ecclesiastical History,* XXVIII, 1983.

Dworetz, Steven M., *The Unvarnished Doctrine: Locke, Liberalism, and the American Revolution,* Durham, NC: Duke University Press, 1990.

Eliot, Charles W., *French and English Philosophers,* New York: P. F. Collier, n.d.

English, John C., 'The Cambridge Platonists in John Wesley's "Christian Library"', *Proceedings of the Wesley Historical Society,* XXXVI, October 1968, 161–8.

—— 'John Norris and John Wesley on the "Conduct of the Understanding"', ibid., XXXVII, February 1970, 101–04.

Erdt, Terence, *Jonathan Edwards: Art and the Sense of the Heart,* Amherst: University of Massachusetts Press, 1980.

Ewing, A. C., 'Some points in the philosophy of Locke', *Philosophy,* XII, 1937, 33-46.

Ferreira, M. Jamie, 'Locke's "constructive skepticism" – a reappraisal', *Journal of the History of Philosophy,* XXIV, 1986, 211–22.

Fiering, Norman S., 'Will and intellect in the New England mind', *The William and Mary Quarterly,* 3rd series, XXIX, 1972, 513–58.

—— *Jonathan Edwards's Moral Thought and Its British Context,* Chapel Hill, NC: University of North Carolina Press, 1981.

—— 'The rationalist foundations of Edwards' metaphysics', in Nathan O. Hatch and Harry S. Stout (eds.), *Jonathan Edwards,* q.v.

Fitzpatrick, Martin, 'Joseph Priestley and the cause of universal toleration', *The Price–Priestley Newsletter,* I, 1977, 3–30.

—— 'Toleration and truth', *Enlightenment and Dissent*, I, 1982, 3–31.

—— 'Latitudinarianism at the parting of the ways: a suggestion', in J. Walsh et al. (eds.), *The Church,* q.v., ch. IX.

Flew, A. G. N., 'Locke and the problem of personal identity', in Martin and Armstrong, *Locke and Berkeley,* q.v.

Force, James E., 'Hume and Johnson on prophecy and miracles: historical context', *Journal of the History of Ideas,* XLIII, 1982; reprinted in John W. Yolton (ed.), *Philosophy, Religion,* q.v., ch. IX.

—— *William Whiston, Honest Newtonian,* Cambridge: CUP, 1985.

Forsyth, P. T., *Positive Preaching and the Modern Mind* (1907), London: Independent Press, 1964.

—— *The Principle of Authority,* (1913), London: Independent Press, 1952.

Foster, Frank Hugh, *A Genetic History of the New England Theology* (1907), New York: Garland Publishing, 1987.

Foster, Herbert D., 'International Calvinism through Locke and the Revolution of 1688', *American Historical Review*, XXXII no. 3, April 1927, 475–99.

Fowler, William Chauncy, *Essays: Historical, Literary, Educational,* Hartford: The Case, Lockwood & Brainard Co., 1876.

Fox, Christopher, 'John Locke and the Scriblerians. The discussion of identity in early eighteenth-century England', *Eighteenth-Century Studies,* XVI, 1982–3, 1–25.

Fraser, A. Campbell, 'Berkeley's idealism', *The North British Review,* XXXIV, no.LXVIII, May 1861, art. VII.

—— 'The real world of Berkeley', *Macmillan's Magazine,* 1862, 192–202.

—— *Berkeley,* Edinburgh: Blackwood, 1881.

—— *Locke,* Edinburgh: Blackwood, 1891.

—— *Thomas Reid,* Edinburgh: Oliphant Anderson & Ferrier, [1898].

—— 'John Locke as a factor in modern thought', *Proceedings of the British Academy,* I, 1903–4, 221–35.

Funkenstein, Amos, *Theology and the Scientific Imagination: From the Middle Ages to the Seventeenth Century,* Princeton: Princeton University Press, 1986.

Galbraith, Elizabeth, 'Kant and religious doctrines', *Enlightenment and Dissent,* XI, 1992, 23–45.

Gascoigne, J., *Cambridge in the Age of the Enlightenment,* Cambridge: CUP, 1989.

Gauthier, David, 'Why ought one to obey God? Reflections on Hobbes and Locke', *Canadian Journal of Philosophy,* VII, 1977, 425–46.

Gay, Peter, *The Enlightenment: An Interpretation. The Rise of Modern Paganism,* London: Weidenfeld and Nicolson, 1966.

Gibson, James, *Locke's Theory of Knowledge and its Historical Relations,* Cambridge: CUP, 1917.

Girle, Roderic A., 'The concept of revelation', *Australasian Journal of Philosophy,* LXV, no.4, December 1987, 470–82.

Goldie, Mark, 'John Locke and Anglican royalism', *Political Studies,* XXXI, 1981, 61–85.

—— 'The theory of religious intolerance in Restoration England', in Ole Peter Grell et al. (eds.), *From Persecution,* q.v., ch.XIII.

—— 'John Locke, Jonas Proast and religious toleration 1688–1692', in J. Walsh et al. (eds.), *The Church,* q.v., ch.VI.

Gordon, Alexander, 'Matthew Caffyn and General Baptist latitude', *The Christian Life and Unitarian Herald,* 5 November 1892, 531–2.

—— *Heads of English Unitarian History,* London: Philip Green, 1895.

—— *Addresses Biographical and Historical,* London: The Lindsey Press, 1922.

Gough, J. W., 'The development of Locke's belief in tolèration', in Horton and Mendus, q.v., 57–77.

Grant, Ruth W., *John Locke's Liberalism,* Chicago: University of Chicago Press, 1987.

Grave, S. A., *The Scottish Philosophy of Common Sense,* Oxford: Clarendon Press, 1960.

—— *Locke and Burnet,* Perth: Philosophy Society of WA and Department of Philosophy, University of Western Australia, (1981).

Greaves, Richard L., 'Radicals, rights, and revolution: British Nonconformity and roots of the American experience', *Church History,* LXI, no.2, June 1992, 151–68.

Green, A., *The Life of the Reverend John Witherspoon,* Princeton: Princeton University Press, 1973.

Green, T. H., *Works of Thomas Hill Green,* ed. R. L. Nettleship, London: Longmans, 3 vols., 1885.

Grell, Ole Peter, Israel, Jonathan I., and Tyacke, Nicholas (eds.), *From Persecution to Toleration: The Glorious Revolution and Religion in England,* Oxford: Clarendon Press, 1991.

Grenz, Stanley J., 'Isaac Backus', in Timothy George and David S. Dockery (eds.), *Baptist Theologians,* Nashville: Broadman Press, 1990, ch.V.

Haakonssen, Knud, 'Natural law and the Scottish Enlightenment', *Man and Nature,* IV, 1985, 47–79.

—— 'Natural law and moral realism: the Scottish synthesis', in M. A. Stewart (ed.), *Studies,* q.v., 61–85.

—— 'From natural law to the rights of man: a European perspective on American debates', in Michael J. Lacey and Knud Haakonssen (eds.), *A Culture of Rights. The Bill of Rights in Philosophy, Politics, and Law – 1791–1991,* Cambridge: Woodrow Wilson International Center for Scholars and CUP, 1991, 19–61.

—— (ed.), *Enlightenment and Religion: Rational Dissent in Eighteenth-Century Britain,* Cambridge: CUP, 1996.

Hall, G. Stanley, 'On the history of American college text-books and teaching in logic, ethics, psychology and allied subjects', *Proceedings of the American Antiquarian Society,* NS IX, 1894, 137–74.

Hall, Roland, 'The place of reason in Locke's *Essay*', *The Locke Newsletter,* XXIII, 1992, 11–23.

Hamowy, Ronald, 'Jefferson and the Scottish Enlightenment: a critique of Garry Wills's *Inventing America: Jefferson's Declaration of Independence*', *The William and Mary Quarterly*, Third series, XXXVI, no.4, October 1979, 503–23.

Hampson, N., *The Enlightenment*, Harmondsworth: Penguin Books, 1968.

Handlin, Oscar and Lilian, 'Who read John Locke? Words and acts in the American Revolution', *The American Scholar*, LVIII, 1989, 545–56.

Harris, Ian, 'The politics of Christianity', in G. A. J. Rogers (ed.), *Locke's Philosophy*, q.v.

—— *The Mind of John Locke: A Study of Political Theory in its Intellectual Setting*, Cambridge: CUP, 1994.

Harrison, Peter, *'Religion' and the Religions in the English Enlightenment*, Cambridge: CUP, 1990.

Hatch, Nathan O. and Stout, Harry S. (eds.), *Jonathan Edwards and the American Experience*, New York: OUP, 1988.

Hefelbower, S. G., *The Relation of John Locke to English Deism*, Chicago: University of Chicago Press, 1918.

Helm, Paul, 'John Locke and Jonathan Edwards: a reconsideration', *Journal of the History of Philosophy*, VII., no.1, January 1969, 51-61.

—— 'Locke on faith and knowledge', *The Philosophical Quarterly*, XXIII, January 1973, 52–67.

Henderson, Henry F., *The Religious Controversies of Scotland*, Edinburgh: T. & T. Clark, 1905.

Holmes, G. S., *The Trial of Dr. Sacheverell*, London: Eyre Methuen, 1973.

Hoopes, James, 'Jonathan Edwards's religious psychology', *The Journal of American History*, LXIX, no.4, March 1983, 849–65.

Hope, Vincent (ed.), *Philosophers of the Scottish Enlightenment*, Edinburgh: Edinburgh University Press, 1984.

Hort, Istvan and Ignatieff, Michael (eds.), *Wealth and Virtue*, Cambridge: CUP, 1983.

Horton, John and Mendus, Susan (eds.), *John Locke: A Letter Concerning Toleration in Focus*, London: Routledge, 1991.

—— 'Locke and toleration', ibid., 1–11.

Howe, Daniel Walker, *The Unitarian Conscience: Harvard Moral Philosophy, 1805–61*, Middletown, Connecticut: Wesleyan University Press, 1988.

Hoyles, John, *The Waning of the Renaissance 1640–1740: Studies in the Thought and Poetry of John Norris and Isaac Watts,* The Hague: Martinus Nijhoff, 1971.

Hudson, Winthrop S., 'John Locke – preparing the way for the Revolution', *Journal of Presbyterian History,* XLII; no.1, March 1964, 19–38.

Hutton, S. (ed.), *Henry More (1614–1687),* Dordrecht: Kluwer Academic Publishers, 1990.

James, D. G., *The Life of Reason: Hobbes, Locke, Bolingbroke,* London: Longmans, 1949.

Jeffner, Anders, 'Our knowledge of ourselves', in C. Cunliffe, ed., *Joseph Butler's Moral and Religious Thought,* q.v., ch.IX.

Jessop, T. E., 'Great thinkers (XI), Bishop Berkeley', *Philosophy,* XII, 1937, 276–90.

Jinkins, Michael, 'Elements of federal theology in the religious thought of John Locke', *Evangelical Quarterly,* LXVI, no.2, 1994, 123–41.

Johnston, Charlotte, 'Locke's examination of Malebranche and John Norris', *Journal of the History of Ideas,* XIX, no.4, 1958, 551–8.

Jolley, Nicholas, 'Leibniz on Locke and Socinianism', in John W. Yolton (ed.), *Philosophy, Religion,* q.v., ch.XII.

Jones, J. A., *Bunhill Memorials,* London: James Paul, 1849.

Jones, Peter (ed.), *Philosophy and Science in the Scottish Enlightenment,* Edinburgh: John Donald, 1988.

Jordan, W. K., *The Development of Religious Toleration in England,* London: Allen & Unwin, 4 vols., 1938.

Kamen, Henry, *The Rise of Toleration,* London: Weidenfeld and Nicolson, 1967.

Kato, Takashi, 'The *Reasonableness* in the historical light of the *Essay*', *The Locke Newsletter,* XII, 1981, 45–59.

Keith, Graham, 'Issues in religious toleration from the Reformation to the present day', *Evangelical Quarterly,* LVI no. 4, 1994, 307–29.

Kelly, Patrick, 'Perceptions of Locke in eighteenth-century Ireland', *Proceedings of the Royal Irish Academy,* LXXXIXc, 1989, 17–35.

Kelly, P. J., 'John Locke: authority, conscience and religious toleration', in Horton and Mendus, q.v., 125–46.

Kessler, Sanford, 'John Locke's legacy of religious freedom',

Polity, XVII, no.3, Spring 1985, 484–503.

King, Peter, *The Life of John Locke,* London: H. Colburn, 1829; enlarged edn, London: Henry Colburn and Richard Bentley, 2 vols., 1830.

Klocker, Harry R., 'John Locke and sense realism', in Vincent F. Daues et al. (eds.), *Wisdom in Depth: Essays in Honor of Henri Renard, S.J.,* Milwaukee: The Bruce Publishing Company, 1966.

Kloppenberg, James T., 'The virtues of liberalism: Christianity, republicanism and ethics in early American political discourse', *The Journal of American History,* LXXIV, no.1, June 1987, 9–33.

Krakowski, Édouard, *Les Sources médiévales de la philosophie de Locke,* Paris: Jouve, 1915.

Kraynak, Robert P., 'John Locke: from absolutism to toleration', *American Political Science Review,* LXXIV, 1980, 53–69.

Kroll, Richard W. F., 'The question of Locke's relation to Gassendi', *Journal of the History of Ideas,* XLV, 1984, 339–59.

—— (ed. with Richard Ashcraft and Perez Zagorin), *Philosophy, Science and Religion in England 1640–1700,* Cambridge: CUP, 1992.

Kuklick, Bruce, *Churchmen and Philosophers from Jonathan Edwards to John Dewey,* New Haven: Yale University Press, 1985.

Laboucheix, Henri, *Richard Price as Moral Philosopher and Political Theorist,* trans. Sylvia and David Raphael, Oxford: The Voltaire Foundation at the Taylor Institution, 1982.

Laird, John, *Theism and Cosmology,* London: Allen and Unwin, 1940.

Landes, Margaret W., *The Philosophical Writings of Richard Burthogge,* Chicago: The Open Court, 1921.

Lehrer, K., *Thomas Reid,* London: Routledge, 1989.

Leites, E. (ed.), *Conscience and Casuistry in Early Modern Europe,* Cambridge: CUP, 1988.

Letwin, Shirley Robin, 'John Locke: liberalism and natural law', in Knud Haakonssen (ed.), *Traditions of Liberalism,* Canberra: Center for Independent Studies, 1988, 3–29.

Levin, David (ed.), *Jonathan Edwards: A Profile,* New York: Hill and Wang, 1969.

Little, Franklin H., *Reformation Studies: Sixteen Essays in Honor of*

Roland H. Bainton, Richmond, Va.: John Knox Press, 1962.

Loeb, Louis E., *From Descartes to Hume: Continental Metaphysics and the Development of Modern Philosophy,* Ithaca, NY: Cornell University Press, 1981.

Lopston, P., 'Lockean ideas and eighteenth-century British philosophy', *Theoria,* LVI, 1990, 85-106.

—— *The Dialectic of Immaterialism: An Account of the Meaning of Berkeley's Principles,* London: Hodder and Stoughton, 1963.

Luce, A. A., *Berkeley and Malebranche,* Oxford: Clarendon Press, 1967.

Lumpkin, William L., *Baptist Confessions of Faith,* Valley Forge, PA: Judson Press, (1959), rev. edn, 1969.

Lund, Roger D., *The Margins of Orthodoxy: Heterodox Writing and Cultural Response 1660-1750,* Cambridge: CUP, 1995.

Mabbott, J. D., *John Locke,* London: Macmillan, 1973.

McCann, Edwin, 'Cartesian selves and Lockean substances', *The Monist,* 1983, no.3, 458–82.

MacCracken, John H., 'The sources of Jonathan Edwards's idealism', *The Philosophical Review,* XI, 1902, 26–42.

McGill, William, *A Practical Essay on the Death of Jesus Christ,* 1786.

MacIntosh, J. J., 'Locke and Boyle on miracles and God's existence', in Michael Hunter (ed.), *Robert Boyle Reconsidered,* Cambridge: CUP, 1994, ch. XII.

McLachlan, H., *English Education Under the Test Acts,* Manchester: Manchester University Press, 1931.

—— *The Unitarian Movement in the Religious Life of England,* London: Allen & Unwin, 1934.

—— *The Religious Opinions of Milton, Locke and Newton,* Manchester: Manchester University Press, 1941.

—— *Essays and Addresses,* Manchester: Manchester University Press, 1950.

McLachlan, H. John, *Socinianism in Seventeenth-Century England,* London: OUP, 1951.

MacLean, Kenneth, *John Locke and English Literature in the Eighteenth Century,* (1936), New Haven: Yale University Press, 1984..

McLoughlin, William G., *Isaac Backus on Church, State, and Calvinism: Pamphlets, 1754–89,* Cambridge, Mass.: Harvard University Press, 1968.

McNair, Alexander, *Scots Theology in the Eighteenth Century,* London: James Clarke (1928).

Manning, Bernard Lord, 'The eighteenth century', in *Congregationalism Through the Centuries,* London: Independent Press, 1937.

Marshall, John, 'The ecclesiology of the Latitude-Men 1660-1689: Stillingfleet, Tillotson and "Hobbism", *Journal of Ecclesiastical History,* XXXVI, 1985, 407–27.

—— 'John Locke's religious, educational, and moral thought', *The Historical Journal,* XXXIII no.4, 1990, 993–1001.

—— 'John Locke and Latitudinarianism', in Richard Kroll et al. (eds.), *Philosophy, Science and Religion,* q.v., ch.XI.

—— *John Locke: Resistance, Religion, Responsibility,* Cambridge: CUP, 1994.

Martin, C. B. and Armstrong, D. M. (eds.), *Locke and Berkeley,* London: Macmillan, n.d.

Martin, John Stephen, 'The rhetoric of grace in Jonathan Edwards' Personal Narrative', *Man and Nature,* IV, 1985, 109–27.

Martineau, James, *Types of Ethical Theory,* Oxford: Clarendon Press, 2 vols., 1885.

Maudlin, Frank Louis, 'Truth, heritage, and eighteenth-century Baptists', *The Baptist Quarterly,* XXXV no. 5, January 1994, 211-28.

May, Henry F., *The Enlightenment in America,* New York: OUP, 1976.

Mendus, Susan (ed.), *Justifying Toleration: Conceptual and Historical Perspectives,* Cambridge: CUP, 1988.

—— *Toleration and the Limits of Liberalism,* London: Macmillan, 1989.

—— 'Locke: toleration, morality and rationality', in Horton and Mendus, q.v., 147–62.

Miller, Perry, *Jonathan Edwards,* (1949), New York: Meridian Books, 1959.

—— *Errand into the Wilderness,* Cambridge, Mass.: The Belknap Press of Harvard University Press, 1956.

Milton, J. R., 'Locke's life and times', in Vere Chappell (ed.), *The Cambridge Companion to Locke,* q.v., ch.I.

Mitchell, Basil, 'Butler as a Christian apologist', in C. Cunliffe, *Joseph Butler's Moral and Religious Thought,* q.v.

Mitchell, Joshua, 'John Locke and the theological foundation of liberal toleration: a Christian dialectic of history', *Review of Politics,* LII, no.1, Winter 1990, 64–83.

Moehlman, Conrad Henry, 'The Baptists revise John Locke', *The Journal of Religion,* XVIII, 1938, 174–82.

Montuori, Mario, *John Locke on Toleration and the Unity of God,* Amsterdam: J. C. Gieben, 1983.

Moon, Norman S., 'Caleb Evans, founder of the Bristol Education Society', *The Baptist Quarterly,* NS XXIV, 1971–2, 175–90.

—— *Education for Ministry: Bristol Baptist College 1679–1979,* Bristol: Bristol Baptist College, 1979.

Moore, E. C., *An Outline of the History of Christian Thought since Kant,* London: Duckworth, 1912.

Moore, James, 'The two systems of Francis Hutcheson: on the origins of the Scottish Enlightenment', in M. A. Stewart (ed.), *Studies,* q.v., 37–59.

—— 'Theological politics: a study of the reception of Locke's *Two Treatises of Government* in England and Scotland in the early eighteenth century', in Martyn P. Thompson (ed.), *John Locke,* q.v.

—— 'Theological politics: a study of the reception of Locke's Two Treatises of Government in England and Scotland in the early eighteenth century', in Martyn P. Thompson (ed.), *John Locke und/and Immanuel Kant,* Berlin: Duncker & Humblot, 1991, 62–82.

—— 'Civic virtue and the law of nature: the eclectic "systems" of George Turnbull and Francis Hutcheson', forthcoming.

Moore, James, and Silverthorne, Michael, 'Natural sociability and natural rights in the moral philosophy of Gerschom Carmichael', in V. Hope (ed.), *Philosophers,* q.v., Ch.I.

Moore, J. T., 'Locke's analysis of language and the assent to Scripture', *Journal of the History of Ideas,* XXXVII, no.4, October-December 1976, 707–14.

—— 'Locke's concept of religious assent', *Southwestern Journal of Philosophy,* VIII, no.2, Summer 1977, 25–30.

—— 'John Locke on assent and the nature of the Church', *Andover Newton Quarterly,* XVIII, no.2, November 1977, 133–9.

—— 'Locke on assent and toleration', *The Journal of Religion,* LVIII, no.1, January 1978, 30–6.

Moore, J. T. 'Locke's development from conservative to liberal on toleration', *International Studies in Philosophy,* XI, 1979, 59–75.

—— 'Locke on the moral need for Christianity', ibid., XI, no.1, Spring 1980, 61-8.

Morris, William Sparkes, *The Young Jonathan Edwards: A Reconstruction,* New York: Carlson, 1991.

Mossner, E. C., *Bishop Butler and the Age of Reason,* New York: Macmillan, 1936.

Mouw, Richard J., 'John Locke's Christian individualism', *Faith and Philosophy,* VIII, no.4, October 1991, 448–60.

Muller, Richard A., *Post-Reformation Reformed Dogmatics,* I, Grand Rapids: Baker Book House, 1987.

The Mystery of Salvation: The Story of God's Gift: A Report by the Doctrine Commission of the General Synod of the Church of England, London: Church Publishing House, 1995.

Nevin, J. W., 'The sect system', reprinted in Charles Yrigoyen, Jr. and George H. Bricker (eds.), *Catholic and Reformed: Selected Theological Writings of John Williamson Nevin,* Pittsburgh: The Pickwick Press, 1978.

Newlin, Claude M., *Philosophy and Religion in Colonial America,* New York: Greenwood Press, 1968.

Newman, J. H., *Apologia pro vita sua,* Harmondsworth: Penguin Books, 1994.

Nichols, J. H., *The Mercersburg Theology,* New York: OUP, 1966.

Nicholson, Peter, 'John Locke's later letters on toleration', in Horton and Mendus, q.v., 163-87.

Norton, David Fate, 'Hutcheson's moral realism', *Journal of the History of Philosophy,* XXIII, 1985, 397–418.

Nuttall, Geoffrey F., *Richard Baxter,* London: Nelson, 1965.

—— *Calendar of the Correspondence of Philip Doddridge DD (1701–50),* London: HMSO, 1979.

—— (ed.), *Philip Doddridge 1702–51: His Contribution to English Religion,* London: Independent Press, 1951.

O'Brien, P., *Warrington Academy 1757–86: Its Predecessors and Successors,* Wigan: Owl Books, 1989.

O'Connor, D. J., *Locke,* Harmondsworth: Penguin Books, 1952.

O'Connor, Peg, 'Locke's challenge to innate practical principles revisited', *The Locke Newsletter, XXV,* 1994, 41–51.

O'Malley, J. Steven, 'Recovering the vision of holiness: Wesley's epistemic basis', *The Asbury Theological Journal,* XLI, no.1, Spring 1986, 3–17.

Orr, John, *English Deism: Its Roots and Its Fruits,* Grand Rapids: Eerdmans, 1934.

Pailin, David A., 'Herbert of Cherbury and the deists', *The Expository Times,* XCIV, 1983, 196–200.

—— 'The confused and confusing story of natural religion', *Religion,* XXIV, 1994, 199–212.

Pangle, Thomas L., *The Spirit of Modern Republicanism: The Moral Vision of the American Founders and the Philosophy of Locke,* Chicago: University of Chicago Press, 1988.

Passmore, J. A., 'Locke and the ethics of belief', *Proceedings of the British Academy,* LXIV, 1978, 185–208.

Pattison, Mark, 'Tendencies of religious thought in England, 1688–1750', in *Essays and Reviews* (ed.), J. Parker, London: 1860.

Paul, Robert S., *The Assembly of the Lord: Politics and Religion in the Westminster Assembly and 'The Grand Debate',* Edinburgh: T. & T. Clark, 1985.

Peabody, Elizabeth Palmer, *Reminiscences of Reverend W. Ellery Channing,* Boston: Roberts Brothers, 1880.

Pearson, Samuel C., Jr., 'The religion of John Locke and the character of his thought', *The Journal of Religion,* LVIII, July 1978, 244–62.

Peel, Albert, ed., *Essays Congregational and Catholic,* London: Congregational Union of England and Wales, (1931).

Penelhum, Terence, *Butler,* London: Routledge & Kegan Paul, 1985.

—— 'Scepticism, sentiment and common sense in Hume', *Dialogue,* XXIV, 1988, 515–21.

—— 'Butler and human ignorance', in Christopher Cunliffe, *Joseph Butler's Moral and Religious Thought,* q.v. ch. VI.

—— 'Human nature and belief: Hume and Pascal', *Lumen,* XII, 1993, 45–64.

Phillipson, Nicholas, 'The Scottish Enlightenment', in R. Porter and M. Teich, *The Enlightenment,* q.v., ch.II.

Philp, Mark, 'Enlightenment, toleration and liberty', *Enlightenment and Dissent,* IX, 1990, 47–62.

Pocock, J. G. A., 'Post-Puritan England and the problem of the Enlightenment', in P. Zagorin (ed.), *Culture and Politics,* q.v., ch.IV.

—— 'Virtues, rights, and manners: a model for historians of political thought', *Political Theory,* IX no. 3, August 1981, 353–68.

—— *Virtue, Commerce, and History: Essays on Political Thought and History, Chiefly in the Eighteenth Century,* Cambridge: CUP, 1985.

Pope, Earl A., *New England Calvinism and the Disruption of the Presbyterian Church,* New York: Garland Publishing, 1987.

Porter, Roy, 'The Enlightenment in England', in R. Porter and M. Teich (eds.),*The Enlightenment,* q.v., ch.I.

—— *The Enlightenment,* London: Macmillan, 1990.

Porter, Roy and Teich, Mikulás (eds.), *The Enlightenment in National Context,* Cambridge: CUP, 1981.

Powicke, Fred. J., *A Dissertation on John Norris of Bemerton,* London: Philip [1893–4].

Pringle-Pattison, A. S. [as A. Seth], *Scottish Philosophy,* Edinburgh: Blackwood, 2nd edn. 1890.

—— *The Philosophical Radicals,* Edinburgh: Blackwood, 1907.

—— 'Alexander Campbell Fraser 1819–1914', *Mind,* NS XXIV, 1915, 289–325.

Rabieh, Michael S., 'The reasonableness of Locke, or the questionableness of Christianity', *The Journal of Politics,* LIII, no.4, November 1991, 933–57.

Rack, Henry D., Review of R. E. Brantley, *Locke, Wesley, q.v.,* in *Proceedings of the Wesley Historical Society,* XLV, September 1985, 63–5.

—— *Reasonable Enthusiast: John Wesley and the Rise of Methodism,* London: Epworth Press, 1989.

Raphael, D. Daiches, *The Moral Sense,* London: OUP, 1947.

Redwood, John, *Reason, Ridicule and Religion,* London: Thames and Hudson, 1976.

Reedy, Gerard, 'Socinians, John Toland, and the Anglican rationalists', *The Harvard Theological Review,* LXX, 1977, 285–304.

Rich, G. E., *John Witherspoon: His Scottish Intellectual Background,* unpublished dissertation, University of Syracuse, 1964.

Richards, G. W., *History of the Theological Seminary of the [German] Reformed Church 1934–52, Evangelical and Reformed Church 1934–52,* Lancaster, Pa: Theological Seminary of the Evangelical and Reformed Church, 1952.

Riley, I. Woodbridge, *American Philosophy: The Early Schools,* New York: Russell & Russell, 1957.

Robbins, Caroline, 'Absolute liberty: the life and thought of William Popple, 1638–1708', *The William and Mary Quarterly,* 3rd series, XXIV no. 2, April 1967, 190–223.

Rogers, G. A. J., 'Boyle, Locke and reason', *Journal of the History of Ideas,* XXVII, no.2, 1966, 205–16; reprinted in John W. Yolton, ed., *Philosophy, Religion and Science,* q.v., ch.XXI.

—— 'Locke, Newton, and the Cambridge Platonists on innate ideas', *Journal of the History of Ideas,* XL, 1979, 191–205; reprinted, ibid., ch. XXII.

—— 'Locke and the latitude-men: ignorance as a ground of toleration', in Richard Kroll et al. (eds.), *Philosophy, Science and Religion,* q.v., ch. X.

—— 'More, Locke and the issue of liberty', in S. Hutton (ed.), *Henry More,* q.v.,189–99.

—— (ed.), *Locke's Philosophy. Content and Context,* Oxford: Clarendon Press, 1994.

—— 'Innate ideas and the infinite: the case of Locke and Descartes', *The Locke Newsletter,* XXVI, 1995, 49–67.

—— 'John Locke: conservative radical', in Roger D. Lund (ed.), *The Margins,* q.v., ch.IV.

Rosa, Susan, 'Religion in the English Enlightenment: a review essay', *Eighteenth-Century Studies,* XXVIII, no.1, Fall 1994, 145–9.

Rosika, Janina, 'John Locke and the Polish Enlightenment', in G. A. J. Rogers (ed.), *Locke's Philosophy,* q.v., ch.X.

Rossiter, Clinton, 'The life and mind of Jonathan Mayhew', *The William and Mary Quarterly,* 3rd series, VII, 1950, 531–58.

Rowe, William L., 'Reid's conception of human freedom', *The Monist,* LXX, October 1987, 430-41.

Ryle, Gilbert, 'John Locke on the human understanding', in C. B. Martin and D. M. Armstrong, *Locke,* q.v.

Sandler, S. Gerald, 'Lockean ideas in Thomas Jefferson's Bill for establishing religious freedom', *Journal of the History of Ideas,* XXI no. 1, 1960, 110–16.

Santayana, G., *Some Turns of Thought in Modern Philosophy,* Cambridge: CUP, 1933.

Sargent, Norman, 'John Wesley's meetings with Bishop Butler 1739', *Report of the Friends of Bristol Cathedral,* 1981, 23–7.

Schneewind, J. B., 'Locke's moral philosophy', in Vere Chappell, ed., *The Cambridge Companion,* q.v., ch.VIII.

Schouls, Peter A., *The Imposition of Method: A Study of Descartes and Locke,* Oxford: Clarendon Press, 1980.

—— 'Locke and the dogma of infallible reason', *Revue Internationale de Philosophie,* XLII, no.2, 1988, 115–132.

—— 'John Locke and the rise of Western fundamentalism: a hypothesis', *Religious Studies and Theology,* X nos.2 and 3, May/September, 1990, 9–22.

—— *Reasoned Freedom: John Locke and the Enlightenment,* Ithaca, NY: Cornell University Press, 1992.

Sell, Alan P. F., *The Great Debate: Calvinism, Arminianism and Salvation,* Worthing: H. E. Walter 1982, and Grand Rapids: Baker Book House, 1983.

—— *Church Discipline,* London: United Reformed Church, 1983.

—— 'Locke and Descartes through Victorian eyes', *Philosophical Studies,* XXX, 1984, 220–9, reprinted in idem, *Dissenting Thought,* q.v., ch.XVIII.

—— 'Samuel Clarke on the existence of God', *Enlightenment and Dissent,* IV, 1984, 65–75; reprinted in idem, *Dissenting Thought,* q.v., ch.IV.

—— 'An Englishman, an Irishman and a Scotsman ... ' *The Scottish Journal of Theology,* XXXVIII, 1985, 41-83; reprinted in idem, *Dissenting Thought,* q.v., ch. XIX (as 'An Arminian, a Calvinist and a liberal').

—— 'Dubious Establishment? A neglected ecclesiological testimony', *Mid-Stream,* XXIV, 1985, 1-28; reprinted in idem, *Dissenting Thought,* q.v., ch. XXII.

—— 'Henry Grove: a Dissenter at the parting of the ways', *Enlightenment and Dissent,* IV, 1985, 53–63; reprinted in idem, *Dissenting Thought,* q.v., ch.VI.

—— *Church Planting. A Study of Westmorland Nonconformity,* Worthing: H. E. Walter, 1986.

—— *Saints: Visible, Orderly and Catholic: The Congregational Idea of the Church,* Geneva: World Alliance of Reformed Churches, and Allison Park, Pa: Pickwick Publications, 1986.

—— *Theology in Turmoil: The Roots, Course and Significance of the Conservative-Liberal Debate in Modern Theology,* Grand Rapids: Baker Book House, 1986.

Sell, Alan P. F., 'John Locke's highland critic', *Records of the Scottish Church History Society,* XXIII pt. i, 1987, 65–76; reprinted in idem, *Dissenting Thought,* ch.VIII.

—— 'Confessing the faith in English Congregationalism', *The Journal of the United Reformed Church History Society,* IV, 1988, 170–215; reprinted in idem, *Dissenting Thought,* q.v., ch.I.

—— Review of R. E. Brantley, *Locke, Wesley,* q.v., in *Enlightenment and Dissent,* VIII, 1989, 140–4.

—— 'Through suffering to liberty: 1689 in the English and Vaudois experience', in A. de Lange (ed.), *Dall' Europa Alle Valli Valdesi,* Turin: Claudiana, 1990, 215–36; reprinted in idem, *Commemorations.* q.v., ch.V.

—— Review of W. M. Spellman, *John Locke and the Problem of Depravity,* in *Enlightenment and Dissent,* IX, 1990, 134–7.

—— 'Presbyterianism in eighteenth-century England: the doctrinal dimension', *The Journal of the United Reformed Church History Society,* IV, 1990, 352–86; reprinted in idem, *Dissenting Thought,* q.v., ch.V.

—— *A Reformed, Evangelical Catholic Theology: The Contribution of the World Alliance of Reformed Churches 1875–1982,* Grand Rapids: Eerdmans, 1991.

—— '"A little friendly light": the candour of Bourn, Taylor and Towgood', *The Journal of the United Reformed Church History Society,* IV nos. 9 and 10, 1991–2, 517–40, 580–613; reprinted in idem, *Dissenting Thought,* q.v., ch.VII.

—— *Dissenting Thought and the Life of the Churches: Studies in a Christian Tradition,* Lewiston, NY: Edwin Mellen Press, 1990.

—— 'J. H. A. Bomberger (1817-1890) versus J. W. Nevin: a centenary reappraisal', *The New Mercersburg Review,* VII, Autumn 1990, 3–24; reprinted in idem, *Commemorations,* q.v.,ch. XI.

—— 'Philosophy in the eighteenth-century Dissenting academies of England and Wales', *History of Universities,* XI, 1992, 75–122.

—— *Commemorations: Studies in Christian Thought and History,* Calgary: University of Calgary Press, and Cardiff: University of Wales Press, 1993.

—— 'Theology for all: the contribution of H. F. Lovell Cocks', in ibid., ch. XIII.

—— *Philosophical Idealism and Christian Belief,* Cardiff:

University of Wales Press, and New York: St. Martin's Press, 1995.

—— 'A renewed plea for "impractical" divinity', *Studies in Christian Ethics*, VII, no.2, 1995, 68–91.

—— (ed.), *Protestant Nonconformists and the West Midlands of England,* Keele: Keele University Press, 1996.

Sellers, Ian, 'The Old General Baptists 1811-1915', *The Baptist Quarterly*, XXIV, nos.1 and 2, 1971, 30-41, 74-88.

Seth, A., see Pringle Pattison, A. S.

Shapiro, Darline, 'Ethan Allen, philosopher-theologian to a generation of American revolutionaries', *The William and Mary Quarterly,* 3rd series, XXI, no.3, April 1964, 236–55.

Sher, R. B., *Church and University in the Scottish Enlightenment: The Moderate Literati of Edinburgh,* Edinburgh: Edinburgh University Press, 1985.

Sher, Richard B. and Smitten, Jeffrey R., *Scotland and America in the Age of the Enlightenment,* Edinburgh: Edinburgh University Press, 1990.

Short, L. Baker, *Pioneers of Scottish Unitarianism,* privately printed, [1963].

Simpson, Peter, 'The nature and origin of ideas: the controversy over innate ideas reconsidered', *International Philosophical Quarterly,* XXV, no.1, March 1985, 15–30.

Skinner, Quentin, *The Foundations of Modern Political Thought,* Cambridge: CUP, 1978.

Snyder, David C., 'Faith and reason in Locke's *Essay*', *Journal of the History of Ideas*, XLVII, 1986, 197–213.

—— 'John Locke and the freedom of belief', *Journal of Church and State,* XXX, 1988, 227–43.

Spellman, W. M., 'The Christian estimate of man in Locke's *Essay*', *The Journal of Religion,* LXVII, no.4, October 1987, 474–92.

—— *John Locke and the Problem of Depravity,* Oxford: Clarendon Press, 1988.

—— 'Locke and the latitudinarian perspective on original sin', *Revue Internationale de Philosophie,* XLII, no.2, 1988, 215–28.

—— *The Latitudinarians and the Church of England,* Athens, Ga: University Press of Georgia, 1993.

Spurr, John, '"Rational religion" in Restoration England', *Journal of the History of Ideas*, XLIX, no.4, October-December 1988, 563–85.

Squadrito, Kathleen M., *John Locke,* Boston: Twayne Publishers, 1979.

Stephen, Leslie, *History of English Thought in the Eighteenth Century,* (1876), New York: Harcourt, Brace & World, 2 vols., 1962.

Stephens, John, 'The epistemological strategy of Price's *Review of Morals*', *Enlightenment and Dissent,* V, 1986, 39–50.

Stewart, M. A. (ed.), *Studies in the Philosophy of the Scottish Enlightenment,* Oxford: Clarendon Press, 1990.

Sullivan, Robert E., *John Toland and the Deist Controversy,* Cambridge, Mass.: Harvard University Press, 1982.

Tait, G. L., 'John Witherspoon, American intellectual leader', *Journal of Religious Studies,* XII, 1986, 1–13.

Tayler, J. J., *Retrospect of Religious Life in England,* London: John Chapman, 1845.

Tennant, R. C., 'The Anglican Response to Locke's theory of personal identity', *Journal of the History of Ideas,* XLIII, 1982, 73–90; reprinted in John W. Yolton (ed.), *Philosophy, Religion and Science,* q.v., ch. XIII.

Thomas, D. O., *The Honest Mind: The Thought and Work of Richard Price,* Oxford: Clarendon Press, 1977.

—— (ed.), *The Correspondence of Richard Price,* Durham, NC: Duke University Press and Cardiff: University of Wales Press, II, 1991.

—— 'Richard Ashcraft on Locke's *Two Treatises*', *Enlightenment and Dissent,* XIV, 1995, 128–54.

Thomas, Roger, 'Philip Doddridge and liberalism in religion', in G. F. Nuttall (ed.), *Philip Doddridge,* q.v.

Thompson, Cameron, 'John Locke and New England Transcendentalism', *The New England Quarterly,* XXXV, no.4, December 1962, 435–57.

Thompson, Martyn P. (ed.), *John Locke und/and Immanuel Kant,* Berlin: Duncker & Humblot, 1991.

Tipton, I. C., *Berkeley: The Philosophy of Immaterialism,* London: Methuen, 1974.

—— *Locke: Reason and Experience,* Bletchley: The Open University Press, 1983.

Tóth, Béla, 'The influence of John Locke's philosophy in Debrecen', *Angol Filológiai Tanulmányok/Hungarian Studies in English,* XVIII, 1985, 49–57.

Tuck, Richard, *Natural Rights Theories: Their Origin and Development,* Cambridge: CUP, 1979.

Tully, James, *A Discourse on Property: John Locke and his Adversaries,* Cambridge: CUP, 1980.

—— 'Governing conduct', in E. Leites (ed.), *Conscience,* q.v., 12–71.

Veitch, John, 'Philosophy in the Scottish universities', *Mind,* II, 1877, 74-91, 207-34.

Vernon, R., 'Toleration without scepticism: John Locke, Jonas Proast and the foundations of liberalism', *Studies in Political Thought,* I, 1991, 448–60.

Waddington, John, *Surrey Congregational History,* London: Jackson, Walford and Hodder, 1866.

Waldron, Jeremy, 'Locke: toleration and the rationality of persecution', in Horton and Mendus, q.v., 98–124.

Walker, D. P., *The Decline of Hell: Seventeenth Century Discussions of Eternal Torment,* Chicago: Chicago University Press, 1964.

Walker, Williston, *The Creeds and Platforms of Congregationalism,* (1893), Boston: The Pilgrim Press, 1960.

Wallace, Dewey D., Jr., 'Socinianism, justification by faith, and the sources of John Locke's *The Reasonableness of Christianity*', *Journal of the History of Ideas,* XLV, January 1984, 49–66; reprinted in John W. Yolton (ed.), *Philosophy, Religion and Science,* q.v., ch.XI.

Walsh, John, Haydon, Colin and Taylor, Stephen (eds.), *The Church of England c.1689–c.1833: From Toleration to Tractarianism,* Cambridge: CUP, 1993.

—— and Stephen Taylor, 'Introduction: the Church and Anglicanism in the "long" eighteenth century', in ibid., 1–64.

Ward, David, 'The solution of the problem of personal identity *via* Locke, Butler and Hume', *The Locke Newsletter,* XXV, 1994, 53–63.

Ward, W. Randall, 'Divine will, natural law and the voluntarism/intellectualism debate in Locke', *History of Political Thought,* XVI no.2, Summer 1995, 208–18.

Warnock, G. J., *Berkeley,* Harmondsworth: Penguin Books, 1953.

Watts, M. R., *The Dissenters: From the Reformation to the French Revolution,* Oxford: Clarendon Press, 1978.

Webb, C. C. J., *Studies in the History of Natural Theology,* Oxford: Clarendon Press, 1915.

Webb, C. C. J., *God and Personality,* London: Allen & Unwin, 1918.

Weinsheimer, Joel C., *Eighteenth-Century Hermeneutics: Philosophy of Interpretation in England from Locke to Burke*, New Haven: Yale University Press, 1993.

White, Morton, *The Philosophy of the American Revolution*, New York: OUP, 1978.

White, R. J., *Dr. Bentley: A Study in Academic Scarlet*, London: Eyre & Spottiswoode, 1965.

Whittemore, R. C., *Makers of the American Mind*, New York: William Morrow, 1964.

—— *The Transformation of New England Theology*, New York: Peter Lang, 1987.

Wilde, C. B., 'Hutchinsonianism, natural philosophy and religious controversy in eighteenth century Britain', *History of Science*, XVIII, 1980, 2–24.

Williams, S. N., 'John Locke on the status of faith', *Scottish Journal of Theology*, XL no. 4, 1987, 591–606.

Wills, Garry, *Inventing America,* New York: Vintage Books, 1979.

Windstrup, George, 'Freedom and authority: the ancient faith of Locke's "Letter on Toleration"', *The Review of Politics*, XLIV, April 1982, 242–65.

Winkler, Kenneth P., 'Hutcheson's alleged realism', *Journal of the History of Philosophy*, XXIII, 1985, 179–94.

Winnett, Arthur Robert, *Peter Browne, Provost, Bishop, Metaphysician,* London: SPCK, 1974.

Wolterstorff, Nicholas, *Reason Within the Bounds of Reason*, Grand Rapids: Eerdmans, 1976.

—— 'The assurance of faith', *Faith and Philosophy*, VII, no.4, October 1990, 396–417.

—— 'Locke's philosophy of religion', in Vere Chappell (ed.), *The Cambridge Companion*, q.v., ch.VII.

—— 'John Locke's epistemological piety: reason is the candle of the Lord', *Faith and Philosophy*, XI, no.4, October 1994, 572–91.

—— *John Locke and the Ethics of Belief,* Cambridge: CUP, 1996.

Wood, A. Skevington, *Revelation and Reason: Wesleyan Responses to Eighteenth-Century Rationalism,* Glaston, Leics.: The Wesley Fellowship, 1992.

Wood, P. B., 'Thomas Reid's critique of Joseph Priestley: context and chronology', *Man and Nature,* IV, 1985, 29–45.

Woolhouse, R. S., *Locke,* Minneapolis: University of Minnesota Press, 1983.

Wootton, David, 'John Locke: Socinian or natural law theorist?' in James E. Crimmins, ed., *Religion,* q.v., ch. II.

Wykes, David L., '"A finished monster of the true Birmingham breed": Birmingham, Unitarians and the 1791 Priestley Riots', in Alan P. F. Sell (ed.), *Protestant Nonconformists,* q.v., ch.III.

Yolton, Jean S., and John W., 'Locke's suggestion of thinking matter and some eighteenth-century Portuguese reactions', *Journal of the History of Ideas,* XLV, 1984, 303–7.

Yolton, John W., *John Locke and the Way of Ideas,* Oxford: Clarendon Press, 1956.

—— 'Locke on the law of nature', *Philosophical Review,* LXVII, 1958, 477-98.

—— (ed.), *John Locke: Problems and Perspectives,* Cambridge: CUP, 1969.

—— *Locke and the Compass of Human Understanding: A Selective Commentary on the 'Essay',* Cambridge: CUP, 1970.

—— *Locke: An Introduction,* Oxford: Blackwell, 1985.

—— *Locke and French Materialism,* Oxford: Clarendon Press, 1991.

—— (ed.), *Philosophy, Religion and Science in the Seventeenth and Eighteenth Centuries,* Rochester, NY: University of Rochester Press, 1990.

—— *A Locke Dictionary,* Oxford: Blackwell, 1993.

—— et al. (eds.), *The Blackwell Companion to the Enlightenment,* Oxford: Blackwell, 1991.

Zagorin, P. (ed.), *Culture and Politics from Puritanism to the Enlightenment,* Berkeley: University of California Press, 1980.

Index of Persons

Aarsleff, Hans, 366
Abrams, Philip, 326–7
Adams, R. M., 293
Adams, William, 342
Addison, Joseph, 11, 211, 283
Adriaanse, H. J., 352
Ahlstrom, Sydney E., 291
Aiken, John, 70, 145, 301, 325
Ainsworth, Henry, 7, 281
Allen, Ethan, 65–7, 300, 336
Allestree, Richard, 13, 231, 283, 355
Allison, Henry E., 240, 358
Ames, William, 49, 294
Amory, Thomas, 70, 82, 101, 142–4, 184, 237, 301, 305, 311, 319, 324, 342, 346, 347
Anderson, Wallace E., 293
Angus, Joseph, 173, 338
Anne, 99
Ardley, Gavin, 286
Aristotle, 23, 27
Armstrong, D. M., 281, 284, 358
Ashcraft, Richard, 85, 142, 280, 306, 324, 327–8, 330–1, 348
Astell, Mary, 363
Ashworth, Caleb, 144, 148, 309, 325–6, 346
Atkins, Gaius Glenn, 340
Attig, John C., 346
Augustine, 153, 230
Avery, Benjamin, 313
Axon, Ernest, 296
Ayers, M. R., 288, 362
B., F., 35, 193, 290, 346, 363
B., G., 327
B., H., 312
Backus, Isaac, 138, 178, 323, 340
Bacon, Francis, 68
Bagshaw, Edward, 155, 329
Bainton, Roland H., 86, 151, 172, 307, 326–7, 338
Baker, Frank, 295–6, 299, 308
Ball, John, 266, 366
Ballou, Hosea, 300
Barber, Joseph, 14, 149, 205, 283, 325, 349
Barclay, William, 7, 281
Barnes, Jonathan, 288
Barrington, John Shute, 334
Barrow, Isaac, 13, 220, 283
Bartlett, William, 171, 338
Barwis, Jackson, 120, 131, 318, 321
Baxter, Andrew, 363
Baxter, Richard, 5, 67, 85, 88, 153, 161, 164, 167, 186, 279, 300, 306–7, 333, 343
Beach, Waldo, 327, 335
Beattie, James, 41–2, 291
Becconsall, Thomas, 8, 72–3, 123, 281, 302, 319
Becker, Carl L., 229–30, 355
Beddome, Benjamin, Dr, 323
Beddome, Benjamin, Jr., 323
Beddome, Foskett, 323
Belsham, Thomas, 37, 59, 106–7, 131–2, 145–6, 167, 195–6, 201, 206, 272, 290, 297, 314, 322,

325, 335, 346–9, 366
Bennett, Jonathan, 292, 358, 360
Benson, George, 101, 105–6, 212, 311, 313
Bentley, Richard, 220, 242–3, 350, 359
Berg, Johannes van den, 327, 352, 355
Berkeley, George, 4, 14, 39–40, 42–7, 61, 242, 247, 269, 283, 292–4, 358
Bernard of Clairvaux, 296
Biddle, John C., 309, 315, 350–1
Bill, E. G. W., 279
Bilson, Thomas, 7, 281
Blackall, Offspring, 181
Blackstone, William, 148, 165
Blackstone, William (20th cent.), 319
Bluhm, William T., 8, 280, 299
Boehme, Jakob, 65
Bogue, David, 59–60, 195–6, 297, 346
Bold, Samuel, 9, 25, 35–6, 91, 197–9, 233, 252–4, 261, 268, 282, 290, 308, 347, 357, 361, 364
Bolingbroke, Henry St John, 206, 266
Boorstin, Daniel, 279
Bourn, Samuel, 100–1, 147, 311, 325, 348
Boyle, Robert, 5, 13, 46, 68, 156, 211, 298, 329
Brace, Laura, 329
Bradbury, Thomas, 99–100, 310
Brain, Timothy, 334
Brantley, Richard E., 88–9, 295, 307
Bricker, George H., 367
Briggs, John, 338
Brine, John, 67–8, 300
Brinton, Alan, 316
Broadie, Alexander, 40, 291
Broughton, John, 245, 363
Brown, Raymond, 309, 326
Brown, Thomas, 44
Browne, Peter, 33, 36, 38, 54, 73, 83, 88–90, 92, 248, 291, 302, 306–7, 360
Bruce, John, 149
Burgersdyck, Franco, 47
Burke, Edmund, 149, 165
Burnet, Gilbert, Sr., 125–6, 153, 199–200, 211, 347
Burnet, Gilbert, Jr., 320
Burnet, Thomas, 20–1, 25, 36, 78, 116–18, 122, 128–9, 211, 223, 243, 261, 285, 304, 317–19, 321, 350, 353, 359, 363
Burns, Robert, 201
Burroughes, Jeremiah, 328
Burthogge, Richard, 18–19, 285
Butler, Joseph, 4, 6, 43, 51–4, 71, 83–4, 121–2, 205, 246–8, 258, 280, 284, 295, 306, 308, 319, 343, 360, 362
Byrne, P. A., 350

Caffyn, Matthew, 215, 351
Caird, Edward, 18, 281–2, 284, 288
Calamy, Edmund, 163, 181, 199–200, 334, 342, 347
Calvin, John, 3, 75, 97, 146, 230
Campbell, Archibald, 79, 122, 253, 304, 319, 361
Canovan, Margaret, 325
Carmichael, Gersom, 123
Carpenter, S. C., 205, 348
Carroll, Robert Todd, 350
Carroll, William, 13, 22, 33, 78, 130, 210, 224, 261–2, 283, 286, 289, 304, 321, 354, 363
Castellio, Sébastian, 86, 327
Chandler, Samuel, 107, 184, 237, 343
Channing, William Ellery, 128, 272, 321, 367
Chappell, Vere, 282, 288, 307, 315, 322, 344, 358, 366
Charles I, 327
Charles II, 155
Charlett, Arthur, 180
Chauncy, Charles, 69, 92, 138–40, 147, 164, 265, 301, 309, 323, 334, 366
Cheyne, George, 35, 274, 290
Chillingworth, William, 63, 153, 327, 344
Christie, Alexander, 102, 311
Chubb, Thomas, 212, 267
Clark, J. C. D., 336
Clark, Peter, 121, 319
Clark, Samuel, 144, 323
Clarke, Edward, 218
Clarke, Samuel, 5, 45, 47, 67, 107,

113, 124, 146–7, 199, 205, 211, 229, 279, 300, 348, 352, 354, 363
Clarkson, Samuel, 311
Cleal, Edward E., 305
Coakley, John, 334
Cockburn, Catharine, 24–5, 36, 73, 83, 111, 117, 200, 225–6, 235, 237, 252–5, 261, 268, 286, 290, 302, 306, 318–19, 347, 354, 361–2, 364–5
Cocks, H. F. Lovell, 172–3, 338
Colden, Cadwallader, 205, 349
Cole, Thomas, 151, 326
Coleridge, S. T., 65
Collier, Arthur, 47
Collins, Anthony, 25, 55, 78, 99, 130, 140, 176, 209, 212, 224, 261, 267, 286, 296, 304, 310, 350, 354
Collins, V. S., 291
Conder, John, 229, 355
Condillac, E. B. de, 45
Cone, Carl B., 127, 321, 342
Conybeare, John, 118–19, 211, 318, 350
Coole, Benjamin, 102, 311–12
Cooper, Anthony Ashley, 103, 122–3, 130–2, 138, 154–5, 267, 295, 319, 321, 329
Cornwall, Robert D., 342
Cotton, John, 161, 333
Coward, William, 244–5
Cragg, Gerald R., 54, 202–3, 296, 299, 307, 348
Craig, E. J., 292
Craig, Thomas, 101–2, 311
Cranston, Maurice, 58, 190, 234, 280, 287, 297, 308, 326–7, 329, 332, 336, 345, 357
Crimmins, James E., 316
Crisp, Tobias, 186
Crocker, Lester G., 282–3
Cromwell, Oliver, 151
Cudworth, Damaris, 27, 298, 312
Cudworth, Ralph, 42, 45, 47, 127, 225
Culverwel, Nathanael, 112, 314
Cunliffe, Christopher, 295, 319, 360, 366
Curti, Merle, 279
Dalgarno, Melvin T., 291
Davis, Arthur Paul, 293, 310, 354
Daye, James, 145, 324
de Beer, E. S., 282, 284–6, 310, 312, 328–9, 332, 342–3, 348, 350, 352, 361, 366
Denney, James, 343
Descartes, René, 7, 13, 18, 24, 39, 46, 96–7, 259
Deweese, Charles W., 338
Dickinson, H. T., 336
Dickinson, Jonathan, 363
Ditton, Humphrey, 363
Dixon, Thomas, 6, 280
Dockery, David S., 340
Doddridge, Philip, 5–6, 33, 68, 76, 103, 105–7, 136–7, 145, 163, 200–1, 246, 280, 289, 304, 309, 312–13, 323, 334, 346–7, 360, 363
Dodwell, Henry, 68–9, 301–2, 363
D'Oyly, Robert, 255–6, 362
Duffy, E., 328
Du Moulin, Louis, 151, 326, 339
Duncan-Jones, Austin, 247, 360
Dunn, John, 10, 168–9, 282, 324, 328, 331, 336
Dwight, Timothy, 66, 73, 250, 268, 300, 302, 366
Dworetz, Steven M., 282, 287, 301, 304

Edward VI, 174
Edwards, John, 6, 9, 13, 20, 35, 90–1, 104, 186, 188–93, 195–9, 202–3, 207–8, 212, 214, 219–23, 232–3, 235, 269, 273–4, 280, 283, 285, 308, 313, 343, 345–8, 351, 353, 356, 363
Edwards, Jonathan, 4, 14, 43, 47–51, 53–4, 57–8, 61, 84, 137–8, 237, 249, 269, 272, 283, 293–7, 306, 323
Elizabeth I, 174
Eliot, Charles W., 362
Eliot, Jared, 79, 304
Ellis, John, 23, 33, 72, 77, 80, 289, 302, 305, 363
Elys, Edmund, 34, 289–90
Emmons, Nathanael, 140–1, 250, 266, 323–4, 366

Enfield, William, 70, 301, 325
English, John C., 295
Erasmus, Desiderius, 86, 138, 154, 225
Erdt, Terence, 294
Evans, Caleb, 59, 133, 149, 166, 178–9, 297, 305, 334, 340

Fagley, Frederick L., 340
Farmer, Hugh, 107
Fell, John, 301
Felton, Henry, 90, 245, 255, 308, 359, 362
Ferguson, Robert, 168
Ferreira, M. Jamie, 306–7
Field, William, 148
Fiering, Norman, 8, 281, 293–4, 314, 322
Filmer, Robert, 95, 170, 230, 337
Fitzpatrick, Martin, 163, 328, 333
Fleming, Caleb, 228, 266, 354, 366
Flemyng, Malcolm, 261–2, 364
Flew, A. G. N., 358
Force, James E., 76, 303, 310, 350
Ford, Paul Leicester, 337
Forsyth, P. T., 85, 188, 306, 344
Foskett, Bernard, 80, 136, 305, 322–3
Foster, Herbert D., 7, 153, 281, 335
Fowler, William Chauncy, 239, 357
Fox, Christopher, 359
Fox Bourne, H. R., 281, 330, 351, 356, 367
Francis, Benjamin, 1
Fraser, A. Campbell, 18, 40, 44–5, 56–7, 284, 287, 291–3, 297, 312, 349
Fraser, James, 102–3, 312
Fry, Richard, 355
Fuller, Andrew, 58–60, 102, 204, 287, 311
Funkenstein, Amos, 283
Furneaux, Philip, 148–9, 165–6, 325, 334

Galileo, 44
Gassendi, Pierre, 45
Garrettson, Freeborn, 311
Gascoigne, J., 279
Gauthier, David, 115, 317
Gay, John, 37
George, Timothy, 340
Gerdil, G. S., 364
Gibbon, Edward, 102
Gibson, James, 288
Gill, John, 1, 67–8, 89, 278, 300, 308
Goldie, Mark, 327–8, 332, 340
Goodwin, John, 329
Goold, William H., 297, 307, 326
Gordon, Alexander, 3, 168, 218, 278–9, 310, 335, 351–2
Gough, J. W., 329
Grave, S. A., 286, 291, 317, 363
Greaves, Richard L., 168, 336
Green, A., 291
Green, T. H., 288, 303
Gregory, James, 41
Gregory, Jeremy, 366
Grell, Ole Peter, 324, 327, 331, 340
Grenville, Denis, 267, 366
Grenz, Stanley L., 340
Grotius, Hugo, 7, 112, 168, 225, 315
Grove, Henry, 5, 70, 82, 97, 131, 142, 266, 280, 322
Guyse, John, 105–6, 313

Haakonssen, Knud, 315, 320, 334, 342
Hadfield, Thomas, 79–80, 305
Hall, Robert, Sr., 58, 60, 297
Hall, Roland, 63, 298
Hall, Thomas, 324
Hallett, Joseph, 105–6, 313
Halyburton, Thomas, 78, 99–100, 129, 304, 311, 321
Halywell, Henry, 348
Hamilton, William, 44, 291
Hammond, 106
Hamowy, Ronald, 356
Hampton, Benjamin, 363
Harris, Howel, 204
Harris, Ian, 355
Hartley, David, 37
Hatch, Nathan O., 294, 360
Haydon, Colin, 340, 348, 366
Heereboord, Adrian, 47
Hefelbower, S. G., 298, 349–50
Helm, Paul, 49, 294, 303, 306, 323
Helwys, Thomas, 329, 331–2
Henderson, Henry F., 348
Henry VIII, 174

Herbert of Cherbury, 16, 18, 79, 81, 154, 205, 212
Hickes, George, 210, 350
Hitchcock, Gad, 82, 305
Hoadly, Benjamin, 166, 176, 339, 342
Hobbes, Thomas, 6, 18, 21, 44–5, 115, 123, 125, 190, 193, 199, 319, 336
Holdsworth, Winch, 200, 225–6, 254, 264, 354, 361
Holmes, G. S., 342
Home, Henry, 289
Hooker, Richard, 7, 63, 112, 281, 314–15
Hooker, Thomas, 49, 171–2, 294, 338
Hoopes, James, 48, 249–50, 294, 360
Hopkins, Samuel, 47, 293
Horbery, Matthew, 365
Horne, George, 26, 287, 354
Horsey, John, 82, 132, 146, 267, 305, 322, 325, 366
Hort, Istvan, 336
Horton, John, 328–9, 341
Howard, Simeon, 147, 325
Howe, D. W., 292
Howe, John, 186, 343
Hoyles, John, 89, 289, 308
Hudson, Winthrop S., 171, 337
Huetius (Huet, Pierre Daniel), 225
Hume, David, 7, 12, 14, 38–40, 42, 65, 68, 76, 126, 205–6, 267, 272, 283, 291
Humphreys, J. D., 312
Hunter, Michael, 304, 352
Hunton, Philip, 7
Hutcheson, Francis, 38, 123–8, 138, 164, 295, 319–20
Hutton, S., 322
Hyde, Edward, Earl of Clarendon, 155

Ignatieff, Michael, 336
Israel, Jonathan I., 324, 327

Jackson, Thomas, 295, 360
James I, 7, 281
James II, 154
James, D. G., 10, 281
Jefferson, Thomas, 205, 337, 364
Jeffner, Anders, 121, 319, 360
Jenkin, Robert, 104, 261, 312, 364
Jennings, John, 5, 280
Jenyns, Soame, 85, 306
Jessop, T. E., 44, 292, 358
Jinkins, Michael, 356–7
Johnson, Samuel ('Dictionary'), 2
Johnson, Samuel (1696–1772), 5, 14, 43, 46–7, 176, 279–80, 293, 339
Johnston, Charlotte, 285
Jolley, Nicholas, 348
Jollie, Timothy, 99
Jones, T. A., 335
Jones, Noah, 6, 55, 280, 296
Jones, Peter, 291
Jones, Samuel, 6, 280, 343
Jones, William, 354
Jordan, W. K., 331
Julius Caesar, 24

Kamen, H., 331
Kant, Immanuel, 206, 272, 288, 358
Keble, John, 272
Keith, Graham, 331
Kelly, P. J., 156, 279, 329
Kennicott, Benjamin, 107
Kentish, John, 201, 348
Kepler, Johann, 44
Kessler, Sanford, 337
Kett, Henry, 26, 42, 287
King, Patricia M., 300
King, Richard, 253
King, William, 18, 284
Kippis, Andrew, 128, 162, 166, 321, 333, 335
Klibansky, Raymond, 332
Kraynak, Robert P., 337
Kroll, Richard, 324, 330, 341, 348
Kuklick, Bruce, 292, 294

Laboucheix, Henri, 38, 147
Laird, John, 64, 299
Landes, Margaret W., 285
Lardner, Nathanael, 106–7, 313–14
Latham, Ebenezer, 6, 79, 280, 305
Law, Edmund, 249, 302, 360
Law, William, 11, 65–6, 249, 299–300, 360
LeClerc, Jean, 8, 22, 136, 210–11, 350

Lee, Henry, 18, 21, 25, 32–3, 71, 118, 162, 244, 284, 286, 289, 318, 359, 363
Lehrer, K., 291
Leibniz, G. W., 7
Leites, E., 324
Leland, John, 68, 79, 81, 107, 130, 212, 301, 304–5, 321, 351, 357
Leslie, Charles, 175–6, 339
Letwin, Shirley Robin, 171, 315, 336–7
Levin, David, 293
Leden, W. von, 283, 298, 314, 361
Limborch, Philip von, 8, 154, 161–2, 167–8, 183–4, 186, 208, 215, 231, 348, 352
Livingston, John Henry, 164
Locke, John
  and America, 3
  and authority, 110, 113, 132, 133, 142, 269, 271
  and deism, 6, 206–12
  and Europe, 4
  and hedonism, 113–15, 123, 128, 130–1, 269, 317
  and Puritanism, 7, 64, 113, 151, 156, 195, 230, 270
  and rationalism, 48, 112–13
  and scepticism, 9, 30, 37–8, 42
  and scholasticism, 7–8, 27, 51, 271
  and Socinianism, 6, 67–8, 212–29
  and the Bible, 9, 92–111, 123, 132, 268–9, 271, 273–4, 276, 312, 345
  as a Christian, 6–7, 10, ch. 6
  as diplomatically cryptic, 8
  his empiricism, 3, 6, 7, 28–42, 51, 113, 121, 123, 282, 285, 288, 294
  his epistemology, 8, 13, ch. 2, ch. 3, 157–8, 181, 268, 270–1, 274–5, 282, 287, 303, 308, 367
  his influence on divines, 3–8, 10–11
  on Christian doctrine, ch. 6
  on Church and state, 173–84, 270, 274, 337
  on eschatology, 262–7, 364–5
  on faith, 85–92, 218, 306, 308, 345
  on government, 132, 168–84, 341
  on humanity, 229–39, 330
  on innate ideas, 16–42, 110, 115–20, 130, 269, 284–5
  on Jesus Christ, 186–201, 212–29, 270, 273–4, 349
  on liberty, 132–51, 269, 327–8
  on miracles, 76, 216–19, 352
  on morality, 30, 109–32, 157–8, 240, 263, 269, 321, 351, 356
  on natural law, 21–2, 109–13, 129, 133, 135, 141, 158–9, 269, 315–16
  on personal identity, 239–50, 268, 270
  on resurrection, 250–8, 270, 363
  on revelation, 74–92, 233, 274, 276, 297
  on salvation, 229–39, 269, 274
  on sin, 229–39, 269, 274
  on substance, 28, 30, 37, 209–10, 213, 219–20, 239–50, 269, 289
  on the Church, 170–84, 270–1, 273–4, 337
  on the existence of God, 8, 27, 30, 63–4, 71–4, 78
  on the Holy Spirit, 85–92, 216–18
  on the indispensable minumum of belief, 186–201, 270, 273, 344, 351–2
  on the Trinity, 203, 212–29, 235, 273, 349
  on thinking matter, 258–62, 268, 270, 364
  on toleration, 9, 27–8, 151–68, 268–9, 328, 330–5, 337, 341
  on truth, 55–61, 110, 287
  and *passim*
Loeb, Louis E., 288, 292
Long, Thomas, 153, 175, 179, 339–40
Lowde, James, 19–20, 25, 72, 115–16, 118, 285, 302, 317
Lowman, Moses, 105–6, 313
Lowth, Robert, 107
Luce, A. A., 292, 358
Ludlam, Thomas, 26, 42, 140, 250, 287, 292, 323, 360
Ludlam, W., 42, 140, 292, 323
Lumpkin, William L., 338
Lund, Roger D., 367
Lupton, William, 254, 361

Luther, Martin, 138, 146, 331

Mabbott, J. D., 317, 328
McCann, Edwin, 288
Macfie, A. L., 319
McGill, William, 200–1, 347–8
MacIntosh, J. J., 304, 352
McLachlan, H., 280, 305, 310, 322, 324–5, 355, 365
MacLean, Kenneth, 362
McLoughlin, William G., 323, 340
McNair, Alexander, 348
Mahomet, 101
Mair, Mr, 40
Malebranche, Nicholas, 8, 17, 19, 28, 39, 45–7, 90, 294
Malleson, F. A., 319, 360
Mandeville, Bernard, 125, 320
Manning, Bernard Lord, 310
Manning, James, 324
Mansel, H. L., 44
Marck, Johannes à, 355
Marryatt, Zephaniah, 144, 324
Marshall, John, 103, 218, 230, 234, 312, 317, 329–30, 348, 351–2, 355, 357, 361
Martin, C. B., 281, 284, 358
Martin, John Stephen, 294
Martin, Josiah, 102, 311–12
Martineau, James, 67, 300
Marvell, Andrew, 328
Mary, 174
Masham, Lady, *see* Cudworth, Damaris
Mason, John, 64, 298
Mather, Cotton, 99, 311
Matthews, A. G., 326
Matthews, Eric, 291
Matthews, W. R., 295
Maudlin, Frank Louis, 297, 301
May, Henry F., 3, 279, 364, 366
Mayhew, Jonathan, 120–1, 147, 318–19, 325
Mendus, Susan, 160, 328–30, 332, 341
Metternich, Wolf von, 90, 308
Mill, John Stuart, 358
Miller, Perry, 294
Milner, John, 21–2, 25, 73, 86, 118, 193–4, 223–4, 252–3, 266, 285–6, 302, 306, 318, 353, 357, 359, 361, 366
Milton, J. R., 87–8, 307
Milton, John, 7, 281, 328
Mitchell, Basil, 272, 366
Mitchell, Joshua, 330, 336
Molyneaux, William, 98, 110, 141, 215, 240, 286, 314, 351, 354, 358
Monmouth, Duke of, 154
Montuori, Mario, 281, 332, 351–2
Moon, Norman S., 297, 305, 322, 340
Moore, E. C., 3, 279
Moore, J. T., 214, 303, 306–7, 330, 351
Moore, James, 320, 339, 357
More, Henry, 135
Morris, William Sparkes, 47, 57, 293–4, 297
Mossner, E. C., 65, 299, 308
Muller, Richard A., 302

Napleton, John, 26, 106, 286, 314
Nettleship, R. L., 288, 303
Nevin, J. W., 273, 339, 367
Newcome, William, 107
Newlin, Claude, 120, 318
Newman, John Henry, 272, 367
Newton, Isaac, 3, 5, 31, 44, 46, 68, 82, 97–8, 146, 211, 229, 270, 279
Newton, John, 6, 270
Nichols, J. H., 339
Nicholson, Francis, 296
Nicholson, Peter, 341
Nicole, Pierre, 230, 355
Nidditch, Peter H., 281
Norris, John, 13, 19, 28, 33–4, 42, 47, 90, 244–5, 283, 285, 289, 294, 308, 359
Norton, David Fate, 126, 320
Notcutt, John, 71, 302
Notcutt, William, 312
Nuttall, Geoffrey F., 313, 355
Nye, Stephen, 197, 223, 347, 353

O'Brien, P., 325
O'Connor, Peg, 284
Ogden, Uzal, 82, 305–6

Oldfield, Joshua, 6, 67, 280, 300
Oliver, Edward, 26, 287
O'Malley, J. Steven, 53, 295
Orr, John, 349, 352
Oswald, James, 23, 42, 69, 122, 286, 301, 318–19
Owen, John, 5, 88, 151–2, 159, 164, 168, 279, 297, 307, 326–7, 331
Owen, Josiah, 200, 347

Pailin, David A., 351
Paine, Thomas, 82, 205
Paley, William, 183, 318, 342
Palmer, Elihu, 82, 306
Palmer, Samuel, 149, 326
Pangle, Thomas L., 316
Parker, Samuel, 18, 153, 284, 327
Parry, William, 6, 280
Passmore, J. A., 324, 356
Pattison, Mark, 2, 73–4, 109, 279, 302, 314, 367
Paul, Robert S., 326–7, 341
Peabody, Elizabeth Palmer, 367
Peach, W. Bernard, 320
Pearson, John, 225
Pearson, Samuel C., 281, 303
Peel, Albert, 310
Peirce, James, 105–6, 313
Pembroke, Earl of, 43
Penelhum, Terence, 51, 295, 299, 360
Percival, John, 44, 292
Perronet, Vincent, 36–7, 248, 261, 290, 302, 360, 364
Petavius (Petau, Denis), 225
Pine, W., 305
Plato, 39, 45, 127
Pocock, J. G. A., 336, 340
Poole, Matthew, 106
Pope, Earl A., 358
Popple, William, 161, 179, 186, 210, 327, 332, 341, 343, 350
Powicke, F. J., 310
Price, Rchard, 4, 37–8, 126–8, 144, 165, 182–3, 290, 320–1, 324, 333–4, 342
Prideaux, Humphrey, 100, 311
Priestley, Joseph, 4, 14, 37, 42, 68, 77, 106, 131, 140, 144, 147–8, 162–3, 165, 183, 201, 229, 262, 270, 283, 291, 304, 314, 321–5, 333, 342, 354–5, 364
Pringle-Pattison, A. S., 30, 281, 288, 293, 366
Proast, Jonas, 60, 173, 175, 179–81, 298, 340–1
Pufendorf, Samuel, 112, 168, 177, 315

Rabieh, Michael S., 299, 344–5
Rack, Henry D., 54, 182, 278, 295–6, 342
Raphael, D. D., 127, 290, 319, 320
Raphael, Sylvia, 290
Rawes, William, Jr., 312
Reedy, Gerard, 220, 353
Rees, Abraham, 55–6, 241
Rees, Thomas, 296–7
Reid, Thomas, 14, 29, 39–42, 44–6, 164, 182, 247, 283–4, 291–3, 342, 360
Rich, G. E., 291
Richards, G. W., 3, 279, 338
Richards, William, 143
Riley, I. Woodbridge, 291, 300, 349
Rippon, John, 278
Robinson, Robert, 149, 326
Roche, A. M., 364
Rogers, G. A. J., 30, 135, 181, 279, 282, 284, 288, 298, 322, 330, 341, 355, 367
Rogers, Henry, 284, 343
Rosika, Janina, 279
Rotheram, Caleb, 145, 296
Rowe, Thomas, 5, 97, 280, 334
Rust, George, 348
Rutherford, Thomas, 66
Rutt, J. T., 323, 333–4, 355
Ryle, Gilbert, 7, 17, 281, 284

Sacheverell, Henry, 181, 342
Sanderson, Robert, 112, 314
Santayana, George, 10, 282
Sargent, Norman, 295
Schleiermacher, F. D. E., 272
Schneewind, J. B., 315, 318
Schneider, Carol, 279, 293, 339
Schneider, Herbert, 279, 293, 339
Schouls, Peter A., 298, 309
Scott, Hew, 286

Scott, Jack, 291, 320
Scott, Thomas, 165, 334
Secker, Thomas, 280, 343
Selden, John, 7, 281
Sell, Alan P. F., 84, 278–81, 284, 294–6, 300–1, 306, 309–13, 321–2, 324–5, 327, 329, 332–3, 338, 340, 342–3, 347–8, 355, 357, 366–7
Sellers, Ian, 309
Sergeant, John, 23–4, 27, 31, 39, 286–7
Servetus, Michael, 222
Seth, Andrew, *see* Pringle-Pattison, A. S.
Shaftesbury, *see* Cooper, Anthony Ashley
Shapiro, Darline, 300, 336
Sharman, Lieut-Col., 334
Shepherd, Thomas, 47
Sherlock, William, 21–2, 63, 71–2, 286, 302, 358
Short, E. Baker, 311
Simson, John, 355
Skinner, Quentin, 336
Smith, Adam, 123, 319
Snyder, David C., 156–7, 303, 307, 329, 331, 337
Socinus, Faustus, 20, 97, 203, 223, 236
Solomon, Barbara Miller, 300
South, Robert, 89–90, 220, 308, 358
Spellman, W. M., 230, 281, 321, 355–6, 365
Spenser, Edmund, 175
Spinoza, Benedict de, 7, 13, 22, 130, 261
Spurr, John, 18, 278, 284
Stennett, Samuel, 59, 297, 326
Stephen, Leslie, 349–50
Stephens, John, 290
Stewart, Dugald, 44
Stewart, M. A., 320
Stiles, Ezra, 105, 313
Stillingfleet, Edward, 13, 31, 35, 63, 77–8, 89, 153, 186, 209–14, 219–20, 226, 243–4, 251–4, 256, 259–60, 262, 269, 283, 288–9, 304, 308, 350–1, 353, 359, 362–3
Stocks, J. L., 21
Stout, Harry S., 294, 360
Strauss, Leo, 336
Strutt, Samuel, 136, 322
Stubbe, Henry, 154, 328
Sullivan, Robert E., 350

Tait, G. L., 291
Tauler, Johann, 65
Tayler, John James, 94, 309
Taylor, Abraham, 6, 66–8, 228, 280, 300, 354
Taylor, A. E., 276
Taylor, Dan, 102, 311
Taylor, Jeremy, 153, 230, 327
Taylor, John, 1–2, 14, 69, 81–2, 84–5, 101, 105–6, 127–8, 229, 236–7, 239, 278, 301, 305, 311, 319, 357, 366
Taylor, Nathaniel, 239, 357–8
Taylor, Stephen, 176, 271, 340, 348, 366
Teger, Stuart H., 8, 280, 299
Telford, John, 299, 307–8
Tenison, Thomas, 153–4, 175, 327, 339
Tennant, R. C., 242, 280, 359
Tennent, Gilbert, 14, 283
Tertullian, 99, 160, 254, 331
Thomas Aquinas, 27, 299, 303
Thomas, D. O., 290, 321, 334, 337, 342
Thomas, Samuel, 6, 55, 280
Thompson, Cameron, 292, 355, 366
Thompson, Martyn P., 320, 339, 357
Throckmorton, J., 333
Tillotson, John, 13, 153, 203, 220, 224, 230, 283, 365
Tindal, Matthew, 65, 84, 100, 118, 176, 209–10, 212, 253, 261, 304, 349
Tipton, I. C., 292
Toland, John, 13, 77, 83, 90, 208, 210, 213, 219, 283, 304, 349–50
Toplady, Augustus Montague, 139–40, 166, 323
Toth, B., 279
Towers, Joseph, 342
Towgood, Micaijah, 145, 182, 324, 342
Towle, Thomas, 324

Traill, Robert, 7, 281
Trotman, Nathaniel, 205–6
Tucker, Abraham, 119–20, 132, 318
Tucker, Josiah, 183, 342
Tucker, Judith, 318
Tully (Cicero, M. Tullus), 111
Tully, James H., 315, 324
Tyacke, Nicholas, 324, 327
Tyrrell, James, 18–19, 27, 281, 285

Vaughan, A. J., 109
Veitch, John, 320
Volkelius, Johannes, 236
Voltaire, 260

Wainwright, Arthur W., 103, 212–13, 216, 235, 287, 303, 309, 312–13, 315, 317, 345, 351–2, 356–7, 364–5
Wakefield, Gilbert, 107
Waldron, Jeremy, 330, 341
Walker, D. P., 365
Walker, Williston, 338, 340
Wallace, Dewey D., Jr., 344
Walsh, John, 176, 271, 340, 348, 366
Warburton, William, 63, 164, 209, 268–9, 334, 342, 350, 366
Ward, W. Randall, 315
Waterland, Daniel, 100, 311
Watson, George, 304
Watson, Richard, 75, 102, 165, 183, 303, 311, 334, 342
Watts, Isaac, 25–6, 37, 55, 79, 97–9, 104–5, 135–6, 148, 163–4, 177–8, 181, 226–8, 245–6, 248, 256–8, 261, 286, 290, 292–3, 304, 310, 313, 322, 334, 340, 342, 354, 359, 362–3
Watts, M. R., 3, 279
Watts, Robert, 310
Webb, C. C. J., 272, 358, 367
Webb, Francis, 92, 194–5, 197, 237–9, 270, 309, 346, 357
Weinsheimer, Joel C., 287
Wesley, John, 1, 4, 43, 49, 51–4, 61, 65–6, 68–9, 88–90, 92, 101, 133, 139, 182, 204, 237, 248–9, 269, 272, 278, 295–6, 299, 301, 307–8, 311, 322, 342
Wesley, Samuel, 326
Wesley, Susanna, 307
West, Richard, 235, 346, 357
West, Stephen, 140, 323
Whichcote, Benjamin, 13, 63, 186, 283, 298, 343
Whiston, William, 98, 104, 106, 220, 224–5, 265, 310, 313, 350, 353–4, 365
Whitby, Daniel, 106, 229, 236, 253, 357, 361
White, Morton, 111, 314, 317
White, R. J., 359
Whitefield, George, 204, 283
Whittemore, R. C., 301–2, 324, 357
Wilks, Joseph, 333
William and Mary, 2
Williams, Roger, 161, 329, 333
Williams, Stephen Nantlais, 306
Willis, Richard, 78, 193, 304, 346
Wills, Garry, 356
Wilson, Catherine, 287
Wilson, Walter, 324–5, 342
Wilton, Samuel, 166–7, 335
Winder, Henry, 280
Windstrup, George, 337
Winnett, Arthur Robert, 302
Wintfeld, Neil, 8, 280, 299
Wise, John, 79, 176–8, 340
Witherspoon, John, 42, 126, 333
Witty, John, 33, 289, 363
Wollaston, William, 25, 47, 211, 286
Wolterstorff, Nicholas, 10, 282, 298, 303, 344
Wood, A. Skevington, 300
Wood, Samuel, 106, 313
Woolston, Thomas, 211
Wootton, David, 316, 329–30, 344
Worthington, William, 119, 318
Wykes, David L., 333

Yolton, Jean S., 279, 299
Yolton, John W., 16, 25, 32, 279–81, 283–4, 286–7, 289, 299, 303, 306, 315, 344, 350, 362
Yrigoyen, Charles, Jr., 367

Zagorin, Perez, 330, 348

Select Index of Subjects

America, 3–4, 42, 66, 79, 82, 99, 120, 128, 133, 164, 205, 314, 335–6, 364
Anabaptists, 168, 175, 331
Anglicans, 63, 67, 90, 100, 103, 105–7, 139, 144, 149, 152–3, 161, 163–4, 166, 172–6, 179, 181–4, 186, 199, 201, 204, 220, 229, 271, 332, 336, 354, 365
antinomianism, 14–15, 186
apologetic method, 11–12, 57, 108, 268, 271–7
Arianism, 13–15, 67, 70, 81, 100–1, 105–6, 127, 143–5, 147, 175, 199, 203, 206, 228–9, 236–7, 310, 313, 343, 354
Arminianism, 1, 8, 13–15, 67, 70, 89, 102–3, 105, 139, 154, 168, 199, 203–4, 206, 208, 234, 270
articles of faith, 10, 91, 144, 165–6, 182, 189, 191, 199, 220, 253, 313, 344; *see also* indispensable minimum of belief
assent, 157–61, 189, 197–8
associationism, 37
atheism, 13, 20–2, 44, 46, 72, 78, 112, 141, 149, 156, 161–3, 181, 197, 202, 220, 224, 273
Attercliffe academy, 99
authority, 12, 14, 27, 81, 110, 123, 132, 142, 198, 269, 271, 273

baptism, 70
Baptist Missionary Society, 58
Baptists, 58–9, 67, 70, 102, 133, 136, 138, 149, 161, 166, 173, 178–9, 201, 215, 297, 300, 309, 329, 346
Bible, 48, 60, 92–111, 123, 132, 143, 175, 177, 181, 186, 198–9, 202–3, 205, 207, 213–15, 218, 222–3, 254, 266, 269, 271, 274, 276, 301, 312, 344
Bristol Baptist College, 59, 80

Calvinism, 1, 7, 13, 14, 35, 39, 47, 49, 59, 66–7, 69–70, 87, 89–90, 99, 101–2, 105, 107, 121, 137–40, 144, 147–8, 151, 153, 156, 166, 168, 196, 199, 201, 203–5, 208, 223, 228, 232, 234–5, 237, 239, 250, 259, 265, 300, 310, 335, 356–7
Cambridge Platform, 177
Cambridge Platonists, 13, 18, 46–7, 63
Cambridge University, 5, 66
Carmarthen academy, 6, 55
Christology, 212–29, 270, 273–4, 346–7, 349
Church, 149, 170–3, 270, 273–4, 337–9; *see also* state and Church
Clerkenwell-Deptford academy, 67
College of New Jersey, 42
common sense philosophy, 14, 23, 40–2, 69–70, 276–7
Congregationalists: *see* Independents
Coventry academy, 6, 67

Daventry academy, 144, 146, 309, 325–6, 346
deism, 6, 10, 13, 14, 25, 54, 65–6, 68, 78–9, 81–2, 92, 99–100, 149, 162, 176, 181, 203, 205–13, 224, 270, 273, 349–50
Dissenters, 2–3, 5, 11, 42, 47, 59, 66–7, 105, 107, 131, 136, 140, 142, 144–5, 149, 153, 155, 159, 161–2, 165–8, 172, 175, 181–4, 187, 199, 269–71, 326, 333, 338, 354–5
doctrine, ch. 6
donatists, 153
Duchy of Cleves, 154–6, 328
Dublin, 5

Edict of Nantes, 154
education, 299, 356
emotivism, 273
empiricism, 3, 6–7, 28–42, 51, 113, 121, 123, 282, 285, 288, 294
Enlightenment, 11, 89, 170, 271, 283
enthusiasm, 14–15, 17, 47, 54, 56, 65, 67, 83, 86, 92, 95, 117, 141, 143, 156, 296, 317
Ephrata community, 11
epistemology, 9, 13, ch. 2, ch. 3, 157–8, 268, 270, 274–6, 287, 293, 303, 308, 319, 367
eschatology, 262–7
Evangelical Revival, 14, 69
evangelicals, 70, 96, 102, 146, 195, 203–5, 229, 270, 301
Exeter academy, 145, 195
Exeter academy (3), 145

faith, 12, 14, 36, 53, 60–1, ch. 3, 139, 143, 147, 197, 210, 218, 269, 272, 303, 306, 308, 310, 345
Fall, the: *see* sin
Feathers Tavern Petition, 165
Findern academy, 6, 79, 305
France, 4, 271
freedom: *see* liberty

Germany, 4
Glasgow University, 123, 355
Glorious Revolution, 1, 14
God, existence of: *see* natural theology
government, 69, 132–3, 168–84, 341
grace, 50–1, 138–9, 172, 180, 203, 208, 232, 234
Great Awakening, 69, 120

Hackney college, 55
Happy Union, 186
Harvard University, 128, 147
hedonism, 113–15, 123, 125, 130–1, 269, 273, 317
Hegelianism, 12
Holland, 4, 16, 103, 154, 168, 204
Holy Spirit, 53, 83, 85–92, 94, 96–7, 214, 216–18, 249, 341
Homerton college, 101, 132, 146, 229
Hoxton academy, 67
Hoxton [Independent] academy, 14, 149, 325
humanity, 229–39, 274, 330
Hungary, 4

idealism, 276–7
immanentism, 12
immortality, 20, 129, 250–8; *see also* resurrection
Independents, 5–6, 14, 59, 67, 70, 79, 82, 98, 106, 136, 140, 148–9, 151–3, 165–6, 171, 176–7, 179, 186, 195, 201, 205, 228, 246, 279, 310, 326–8, 340
indispensable minimum of belief, 186–201, 270, 273
individualism, 115, 170, 271
innate ideas, 8, 13, 16–42, 110, 115–20, 124–5, 130, 269, 284–5
intuition, 34, 52, 86, 110–12, 115, 121, 127, 269

Jews, 2, 149, 160, 175, 202, 269, 341

Kendal academy, 145
Kibworth/Hinckley academy, 5
King's College, New York, 46
King's Head Society, 67

Latitudinarianism, 13, 60, 65, 103, 153, 159, 168, 176, 204, 270
liberty, 108, 132–51, 269, 273, 327–8
London, 6, 144
London Missionary Society, 59, 195

Lutherans, 156

Market Harborough academy, 5
Marischal College, 41
materialism, 18, 21, 35, 43, 54, 78, 258–62
mechanism, 13, 44
Mennonites, 168
Mercersburg theology, 273, 339
Methodists, 65–6, 312
miracles, 12, 68, 76–7, 82, 211, 216–18, 352
morality, 20, 30, 38, 57–8, 64, 71, 78–9, 81–2, 98, 108–32, 157–8, 240, 263, 269, 321, 345, 351, 356
moral sense, 123–6, 138
Moravians, 14
Muggletonians, 175
Muslims, 160, 202, 341

natural law, 21–2, 109, 111–13, 129, 133, 135, 141, 158–9, 164, 269, 315–16
natural theology, 8, 11–12, 27, 30, 33, 61, 63–4, 70–3, 79–80, 90, 270, 272, 299
neo-Platonism, 28, 33, 39, 90, 244, 270
New Brunswick Seminary, 164
New Connexion of General Baptists, 102
Newington Green academy, 5, 97
Newport Pagnell academy, 6
Nonconformist Relief Act, 325
Northampton academy (1), 6, 82, 145, 200, 309, 313, 346
Northampton academy (2), 132, 146, 267

Oxford University, 5, 151, 180, 225, 254

personal identity, 239–50, 268, 270
Plasterers' Hall academy, 144
Poland, 4, 345
postmodernists, 271, 273
prayer, 69, 128
Presbyterians, 5–6, 14, 42, 55, 67, 70, 81, 94, 100, 105–6, 127–8, 144–5, 147–9, 153, 161, 182, 186, 200–1, 228, 231, 236–7, 266, 279, 313, 319
probability, 51–2, 82, 90, 272
Protestant Dissenting Deputies, 167
Puritans, 7, 14, 47, 49, 54, 58, 61, 64, 113, 151, 156, 195, 199, 230, 270

Quakers, 14, 58, 102, 161, 168, 197, 311–12
Queen's College, 164

rationalism, 48, 67–8, 79, 89, 99, 102, 107, 109, 112, 123, 204, 220, 272–3, 296
reason, 3, 5, 12, 14, 50, 62–74, 85–92, 147, 197, 208, 211–12, 219, 236, 238, 263, 269, 271–2, 306, 310
Remonstrants, 154–5, 204
resurrection, 250–8, 270, 363
Restoration, 154
revelation, 9–10, 20, 33, 36, 53, 74–92, 122, 129, 197–8, 205, 208, 210–11, 213, 216, 233, 272, 274–5, 277, 285, 297, 303
Roman Catholics, 2, 7–8, 17, 136, 142, 146–7, 154, 156, 160–3, 165, 179, 197, 201, 225, 228, 265, 269, 328, 332–3, 335
romanticism, 272, 276, 300

Sabellianism, 223
sacraments, 48, 167, 175
St Andrews University, 78–9, 122, 129, 253
Salters' Hall, 199, 313
salvation, 229–39, 274
Savoy Declaration, 75, 151–2, 172, 326
scepticism, 9, 14, 20, 23, 30–1, 33, 37–9, 42, 45–6, 54, 71, 102, 120–1, 158, 162
scholasticism, 7–8, 27, 31, 43, 51, 74, 213, 271
sectarianism, 95, 156, 186, 173, 329
sin, 35, 47, 66, 84, 96, 98, 113, 138–9, 194, 204, 226, 229–39, 250, 269, 274, 346, 355
Socinianism, 6, 13–15, 67–8, 161, 176, 190–2, 194, 196, 201, 203,

205, 214–16, 218, 220, 223–4, 226, 228–9, 231, 235, 264, 266, 270, 273, 302, 310, 345, 353, 357, 361
Southwark academy, 67
spiritual sense, 49, 53–4, 61, 84, 269, 294–5
state and Church, 173–84, 270, 274, 337
subscription, 14, 149, 199, 313
substance, 13, 28, 30–2, 37, 43, 209–10, 213, 219–20, 239–50, 258, 289
Sweet-singers, 175

Taunton academy, 5, 70, 82, 142, 346
Tewkesbury academy, 6, 280, 343
thinking matter, 258–62, 268, 270
Thomism, 276
toleration, 5, 9, 27–8, 108, 133, 150–68, 268–9, 326–8, 330–5, 337, 341
Toleration Act, 2, 55, 155, 161, 166–7, 181, 278, 327, 329
transcendentalists, 229, 292
Trinity, 199–200, 203, 212–29, 265, 273, 313, 349, 351–2, 358
truth, 55–61, 110, 268, 287

Unitarians, 2, 14, 37, 42, 59, 102–3, 106, 195, 197, 201, 204, 206, 223, 269, 278, 309, 333, 346
Universalists, 300
utilitarianism, 115, 273

Warrington academy, 70, 101, 127, 145, 325
Westminster Confession, 75, 151–2, 201, 313, 326
Whitehaven academy, 6
Wymondley academy, 6

Yale University, 5, 46–7, 66, 105